Frank Grant

ALSO OF INTEREST

Kid Nichols: A Biography of the Hall of Fame Pitcher,
Richard Bogovich (McFarland, 2012)

The Who: A Who's Who,
Richard Bogovich with Cheryl Posner
(McFarland, 2003)

Frank Grant

The Life of a Black Baseball Pioneer

Richard Bogovich

McFarland & Company, Inc., Publishers
Jefferson, North Carolina

ISBN (print) 978-1-4766-8460-4
ISBN (ebook) 978-1-4766-4607-7

LIBRARY OF CONGRESS AND BRITISH LIBRARY
CATALOGUING DATA ARE AVAILABLE

Library of Congress Control Number 2022042846

© 2022 Richard Bogovich. All rights reserved

No part of this book may be reproduced or transmitted in any form or by any means, electronic or mechanical, including photocopying or recording, or by any information storage and retrieval system, without permission in writing from the publisher.

Illustration of Cuban Giants second baseman Frank Grant that dates back to at least September 29, 1889 (*Cleveland Gazette*)

Printed in the United States of America

McFarland & Company, Inc., Publishers
Box 611, Jefferson, North Carolina 28640
www.mcfarlandpub.com

To Don Halley of Rochester, Minnesota,
perhaps the most generous person I've ever known well.

Table of Contents

Acknowledgments ix

Preface 1

Introduction: A Superlative Career 3

1. A Family Accustomed to Freedom 7
2. Serious About Base Ball 20
3. Magic in Meriden (April to July 1886) 25
4. Buffalo and Immediate Stardom (July to October 1886) 35
5. A Bitter Pennant Battle (1887) 41
6. Winning Streak (1888) 60
7. Black Team in a White League (1889) 79
8. Ordered to Harrisburg (1890 to April 1891) 99
9. A Finale of Sorts (April–June 1891) 123
10. Barnstorming (1891–1892) 129
11. Making History from Cooperstown to Chicago (1893–1894) 146
12. A "Cuban" Rivalry (1895–1897) 157
13. Lured Away (1898–1903) 170
14. Exit from the Game (1904 and After) 189
15. From Obscurity to Enshrinement 201

Chapter Notes 209
Bibliography 257
Index 263

Acknowledgments

I enjoy research via online newspaper archives, but I am always happy to mix in a day at some public library. I only had the chance to make one trip east to Boston's main library before the COVID-19 pandemic hit us full-force. I never made it to Williamstown, which was going to be part of my second trip. At other times, I couldn't justify a trip halfway across the country when I only needed one or two articles from some newspaper that isn't accessible online. Under these circumstances, librarians became invaluable. I fervently hope I am not omitting any from this list of those who deserve my thanks and recognition: Lisa Harding of the North Adams Public Library, Massachusetts; Emily Scharf of the Carleton College Gould Library, Minnesota; Sharon Gothard of the Easton Area Public Library, Pennsylvania; Lynn Gardner of the Southington Library & Museum, Connecticut; Danielle (no last name) of the New Britain Public Library, Connecticut; an anonymous librarian in the Social Science & History Department of the Free Library of Philadelphia; and Cassidy Lent of the National Baseball Hall of Fame and Museum. In a related vein, I must also thank the Honorable Eugene G. Doherty, Appellate Chief Justice, Fourth District, State of Illinois, for providing details from Westlaw about the court case involving Frank Grant.

In February 2012, around the time I first thought of pursuing this book, I went to a presentation by Negro Leagues historian Byron Motley based on the book *Ruling Over Monarchs, Giants & Stars: True Tales of Breaking Barriers, Umpiring Baseball Legends, and Wild Adventures in the Negro Leagues*, which he helped his father write. I was very fortunate that he traveled all the way to Rochester, Minnesota. It was inspiring at just the right time, and a few months later I pitched this book idea to McFarland.

On July 23, 2016, I attended a similar presentation by Frank M. White of the Minnesota Twins RBI Program, about his book *They Played for the Love of the Game: Untold Stories of Black Baseball in Minnesota*. I had an encouraging conversation with him afterwards, and little more than a week later, I dove headlong into researching this book in earnest.

I am compelled to express gratitude for another book, *Real Influence: Persuade Without Pushing and Gain Without Giving In*, by Mark Goulston and John Ullmen. The book was published in 2013, but I didn't learn of it for a few years, around the time I started my intense work on this biography. One chapter in *Real Influence* focuses on an African American businessman in Chicago named Larry Clark, who led the integration of Prudential Insurance in that area during the second half of the 1960s. In the early 1970s, that included an all-white sales team managed by my father transferring into an office previously staffed only by African American employees, under Larry's supervision. My late father thought highly of Larry. Because of my family's personal connection, it was especially insightful to compare and contrast Larry's experiences with Frank Grant's about 80 years earlier.

In 2016, I began to write relatively short biographies of obscure African American ballplayers as a member of the Society for American Baseball Research. My editor for those has usually been Bill Nowlin. I had always considered myself a good writer, but Bill's interaction with me during the editing process has made me so much better. More recently, when I had the good fortune to team up with SABR's Rick Bush to research a particular player, he served as a reminder that I don't always have to answer every question on my own.

Other baseball writers and historians have helped with answers to very challenging questions and/or provided encouragement at key moments. McFarland's Gary Mitchem tops the list, in the "early and often" category. Others are Rod Leith, Gary Ashwill, and fellow McFarland baseball authors Jim Overmyer and the late Chris Zantow. Special mention goes out to my childhood friend Phil Arvia, who has always been my personal role model for sportswriting.

I'm very grateful for connecting with and receiving valuable feedback and input from descendants of Frank Grant and his brother Clarence, namely Theresa Atwood, Nanita Tilley, Carolyn Foote-Minich, and Emily Grant Foote.

Thanks to everyone at Rochester's Wendland Utz law firm. Allowing me to use the two-monitor setup in my office there on many work nights and weekends made me so much more productive. And the entire crew was very good about asking, "How's the book coming?" when they really should've been asking, "Aren't you done with that yet?" without their unfailing cheerfulness. The person outside of Wendland Utz who was most entitled to ask the latter question was Mitch Moore, who very graciously allowed me a four-month delay in my transition into replacing him as treasurer of the Seeds of Wisdom of South Sudan, a school that our church founded.

Naturally, I also have family members to thank oh so much. My mother let me talk her ear off during so many phone calls during my months of writing. My young-adult kids, Natasha and Joshua, also put up with that regularly, but were particularly skilled at offering encouragement and positive reinforcement. My brother's family, whom my kids and I call the Boston Bogies, were very gracious when their home served as a launching pad for visiting Boston's main public library. My sister's family, the Perreaults, have been inspirational over the past decade for their commitment to and support of athleticism at a high level, which is inspirational. In other words, their examples remind me not to just write about it, but *do* it.

Preface

Always accept a lunch invitation from Randy Johnson, whether or not he's the Hall of Famer by that name. That's the origin of this biography. It dates back about nine years, as of this writing.

I was relatively new to Rochester, Minnesota, and Randy Johnson, who headed an agency then called Workforce Development, Inc., was on the hiring team that gave me my first job in my new city. Not long afterwards, he invited me to lunch. As we were talking about our shared interest in baseball history, he told me about having bought some old postcards at an antique store or flea market. To his great surprise, upon closer inspection of one of them, it proved to be the 1887 Buffalo Bisons team photo, which featured Frank Grant in the front row.

At that point, I knew about Moses Fleetwood Walker having played in a major league during 1884, and that he was joined by his brother Weldy/Welday, but I was ignorant of Frank Grant. I did some reading about Grant online, and the more I read, the more I wanted to know—and find out, if need be.

When I wrote my previous baseball biography around 2010, about Hall of Famer Kid Nichols, I was a relatively new member of the Society for American Baseball Research (SABR). It so happened that SABR's annual convention in the summer of 2012 was in Minneapolis, so I made a point of attending. I spoke with McFarland editor Gary Mitchem, with whom I had worked on two books, and asked if his company might be interested in two new ideas I had. He expressed interest in both, but he made it very clear that a biography about Frank Grant should be a much higher priority. I didn't have time to begin researching Frank Grant's life fervently until 2016. I was thrilled to find many more details than I expected, which is the main reason I didn't actually start writing the manuscript until 2020.

Toward the end of my biography of Nichols, I devoted a page to where he ranked, according to some of the top baseball historians and statisticians, among pitchers all-time (spoiler: very high). It seemed natural to leave that until very late in the book because any fan of the game could quite easily look up his stats before cracking the cover of that book, at which point his numerous 30-win seasons would've jumped out at them, and quite possibly the fact that he had an astounding 361 career wins when he retired at the age of 36. However, when I thought about the relatively small statistical set that is readily accessible about Frank Grant, and none of it as a major leaguer, I perceived value in putting such information at the beginning of this book rather than at the end.

Part of the introduction compiles testimonials about Grant, many from anonymous sportswriters in their respective newspapers, but several strong ones from very good white ballplayers who chose to go on the record about him at length. The anonymous comments are sometimes general in nature, but some marvel in very specific detail about particular plays that he made. Interestingly, as often as such accounts described similar plays near second base, those journalists frequently noticed—and described in flowery language—nuances and subtle differences that made each of those defensive gems unique on some level. Some of these testimonials also appear in the chapters, but read in isolation, their effect is less powerful.

I came across a number of additional examples of published praise, which appeared frequently and throughout the country during Grant's career, providing some evidence of his name recognition. But I tried to be selective in sharing such material, hoping not to give the impression that the biographer takes an uncritical view of his subject, or to give the false impression that Grant's renown somehow shielded him from racism.

In the pages ahead, the reader will encounter three of my favorite baseball stories of all time—none of which I knew when I undertook this project. Two of the stories appear not to have been retold since sportswriters first reported them, well over a century ago. The other has been retold from time to time, but only from the point of view of a racist opposing manager, as an illustration, quite appropriately, of the bigotry Grant faced. But that manager stopped telling the truth halfway through his anecdote, and I don't know that any other researcher has corrected the record. The story brings to mind the saying that the best revenge is a life well lived, though in this instance it might be revised slightly to end with "a game well played." The second story brings to mind the old expression about feast or famine, but in Grant's case it was famine followed by feast. The third could be titled, accurately, "Frank Grant: Action Hero."

Introduction

A Superlative Career

In the *Politics of Glory*, baseball historian Bill James wrote thoroughly about the processes of selecting members to the National Baseball Hall of Fame. This book was published in 1994, 12 years before Frank Grant was enshrined. Though James was the first prominent champion of the mathematical approach to baseball that is now widely called analytics, he has never been an absolutist. When James reviewed arguments that arose during the 1970s about adding Negro Leagues players to the Hall, he summarized a main one as "There were no statistics to support their case, so how could you know how good they really were?" James considered such a viewpoint "interesting, but hardly a sufficient rationale for perpetuating an injustice."[1]

Elsewhere in the book, he placed some value on subjective, anecdotal assessments, at least in a sense. In response to a group of fans who championed a player named Ken Keltner for induction, he drew up a batch of questions that he has continued to call the Keltner List. The first pair of questions in that list of 15 were: "Was he ever regarded as the best player in baseball? Did anybody, while he was active, ever suggest that he was the best player in baseball?"[2] The inclusion of "while he was active" is a helpful reminder to be on guard for anyone who might attempt revisionist history, consciously or not.

It's not *required* that everyone who is already in the Hall of Fame was indeed considered the best player in baseball at some point, but by placing this pair of questions *first*, James was indicating that it sure helps a nominee's case if he was considered *the* best player at some point. Of course, sometimes a player was baseball's best one for a short time, but injuries kept him from sustaining such excellence, so it helps even more when a candidate was the very best player for at least a few years. Also, for most modern major leaguers who ever made an All-Star team, it's probably possible to find someone, somewhere who said that player was "the best player in baseball." The expertise of anyone making such a claim needs to be considered, but it helps substantially if many knowledgeable people agree on the same player.

It isn't too difficult to find experts who praised Frank Grant in this way, both in recent decades and during his career. Two modern examples should suffice. In 1983, baseball historian Jerry Malloy called Grant "the greatest black baseball player of the 19th century."[3] Malloy is so highly regarded that an annual Negro League Conference is named after him.

An equally esteemed expert is John Thorn, the Official Baseball Historian for Major League Baseball for the past decade. "The brief period in which blacks were allowed to play on the same fields as white players was best symbolized by Frank Grant," Thorn said in 2006. "He was the best African American player of the 19th century." Five years later, Thorn broadened his statement to say that Frank Grant was "by all accounts the best African American player of the 19th century yet one whose life story is barely known."[4]

Very high praise about Grant during his career spans many years and many sources. After just a half-season with Buffalo in 1886, Grant's own manager offered such an assessment that was published nationwide by *Sporting Life*. "Manager Chapman has seen many great second basemen in his time, but Grant, the colored lad, he thinks beats them all," the weekly reported. "There is nothing he can't get or fails to go after. His agility is remarkable to a double-jointed degree."[5]

Another early example was in 1890, just four years into Grant's pro career, and the compliment came from Billy Barnie, who was in his eighth year as manager of the American Association's Baltimore Orioles. "Manager Barnie, speaking of Grant, the colored short stop of [Harrisburg], said he had seen the greatest in this position, and that Grant would come near equaling any of them," the *Baltimore American* paraphrased.[6] The previous month, when the Harrisburg Ponies jumped from one league to the Atlantic Association, taking Frank Grant with them in the process, the *Harrisburg Telegraph* said that "Grant is a gentleman and the best ball player in the association." Three years later, that same newspaper called him "the greatest second baseman known."[7]

In 1891, it was a New Jersey paper's turn. "'The Gorhams' shortstop, Grant, is a jewel, whose superior as a fielder of his position cannot be found anywhere," said the *Plainfield Daily Press*. "He made some most difficult stops and catches, his recovery was extraordinarily quick, and his throwing was swift as an arrow and unerring as a shaft of light."[8]

In 1892, a major New York daily rated Grant the best in semi-professional ball, which doesn't sound so impressive until it becomes clear whom he outranked. "Grant, the third baseman of the Cuban Giants, is, without doubt, the greatest player that ever made his appearance in the semi-professional diamond," proclaimed the *New York Herald*. "But for his color he would be playing professional ball long before this."[9] This declaration came right after future Hall of Famer Willie Keeler had ended his semi-professional career in New York City to enter a top minor league, and he entered the majors just three months later.

That same summer in Kansas, the *Atchison Blade*, an African American newspaper, named men it considered the top African Americans in several fields, including Thomas Fortune among journalists, George Dixon among boxers, and Frederick Douglass among statesmen. This newspaper turned to Grant right after Douglass, but in Grant's case the paper said he was the best among "all baseball players," and thus didn't seem to be limiting that rating to African Americans alone, as with the other gentlemen.[10]

The following spring, a paper in New Jersey was explicit about its rank applying regardless of race. "Frank Grant, the ginger-colored second baseman of the Cuban Giants, has the reputation of being the best player in that position in the world, either black or white," stated the *Camden Daily Telegram*. "His renown is not the outcome of a few admiring or prejudiced friends, but the result of several years of the best work on the diamond. He is a remarkable batter."[11] That last comment was particularly important because Grant was indeed quite the hitter; he wasn't simply an excellent fielder whose offense was average, as later chapters will document.

Fast-forward a few years, and a couple of New York newspapers offered their purple prose about Grant. "Grant, the old Buffalo second baseman, was the center of attraction, and he more than proved his right to be called a born ball player and one of the best men in the business," said the *Syracuse Standard* in 1897. "His fielding at short was nothing short of marvelous. He was everywhere at once, and he got some of the hottest daisy cutters poked at him which ever flew from a bat, but he invariably ate them up as if he thought it was all a big joke and no man reached first who knocked a ball anywhere his way."[12]

"Grant, who played second base for the Buffalo team in the old International league ten years ago, played short field yesterday," the *Oswego Daily Palladium* reported the following year. "He was one of the best second basemen in the country in his day, and but for the fact that the color line was drawn would be in the game yet."[13]

In mid-1898, the *Pittsburgh Press* printed reminiscences by Deacon McGuire, who was more than 10 years into one of the longest major league careers ever. "Grant was one of the best fielding second basemen I ever gazed on, and as I witnessed his work I often thought of the hero he would have been if nature had given him a white skin," McGuire said. "He could throw himself in front of a ball and grab 'em at the right and left side. He was fast on the bases and a corking hitter."[14]

McGuire called Grant "Hughey," and so did Tom Brown, whose 17-year major league career had concluded in 1898, which suggests a previously unrecorded nickname for Grant rather than the same error in two different newspapers about 18 months apart. In early 1900, Brown said:

> One of the best second basemen the baseball game has ever seen was the colored diamond athlete, Hughey Grant, who was at his best on the Buffalo team. Grant's great forte as a fielder was his sure-thing hands. He was as near perfection in gauging swift grounders as Heine [sic] Reitz, than whom no finer hand-worker ever lived. Grant, however, had Reitz distinctly beaten as an all-around fielder, as he was faster of foot, covered larger area of ground, and was surer and quicker on double plays. He was a natural batsman, as many a twirler found to his sorrow. Grant played no favorites at the bat. High incurves, low outshoots, or slow teasers served at a shot-putting gait all looked the same to Grant. The pitchers seemed to take a fiendish delight in deliberately firing the ball at his head with the intention of driving him from the plate, but they never succeeded in taking his nerve. In the annals of the game and in the achievements of such second basemen as Burdock, Ross Barnes, Fred Pfeffer, and Yankee Robinson the name of Hugh Grant has been overlooked, though if he were a white man he would stand abreast of the others in the red-letter chapters of baseball.[15]

One month on either side of his 35th birthday, Frank Grant received praise from two newspapers that indicated he was still at the top of his game. "Grant, their second baseman, was with the original Giants, and in spite of long service and increasing years, which would have sunk most players into oblivion, is still as frisky as a kitten," a daily in Pennsylvania commented. "His superior as a baseman probably never played the national game, and except for his color he would have been the wonder of the big league."[16]

"Another player on the Cuban team that will attract attention is Frank Grant, who is the greatest second baseman in the country," said a paper in New Jersey. "Grant can field the ball quicker than any man in the business and it has only been his color that kept him from a place in the big league."[17]

After Grant stopped playing, but long before there was any inkling that he could be voted into the Hall of Fame, his name still popped up from time to time, and the emergence of many other superstars didn't dim his reputation among some knowledgeable and credible fans. For example, in 1913 a newspaper in upstate New York had reason to mention "the famous Grant, the shortstop who was considered the greatest player of his time."[18] In 1916, Edward Tranter of the *Buffalo Enquirer* said, "Grant was one of the best players in the country white or black."[19] In 1937, a minor leaguer named Joe Fern, who roomed with Cy Young on Canton, Ohio's, minor league team in 1890, still considered Grant the greatest player he had ever seen.[20] In 1962, he was similarly acknowledged by longtime columnist Fritz Pollard, who was posthumously enshrined in the Pro Football Hall of Fame as a player in 2005. Pollard wrote that "Frank Grant, second baseman of the International League [through] 1888, was considered the greatest ball player of his age."[21]

The views of Frank Grant's longtime teammate and Hall of Fame contemporary, Sol White, warrant special consideration. White was the sport's first genuine African American historian, and he continued to write at least into the 1930s. He heaped praise on Grant in early 1931. That column concluded, "When a man with the experience in the game of Jack Doyle, old first baseman of the New York Giants says there never was a player like Frank Grant, you might grasp an inkling of what we have tried to impress upon you relating to this fellow's greatness as a ball player." Doyle played in the majors for 17 years, from 1889 to 1905. About a year later, White made it crystal clear that he agreed with Doyle, and then some, when he wrapped up another column by saying, "When Frank Grant was good, there was not a ball player like him, nor has there been any ball player like him since."[22]

This focus on subjective assessments of Grant isn't to suggest a total absence of statistics about his worthiness for the Hall of Fame. There *are* five years of minor league data readily available about Frank Grant, plus the Seamheads.com website documents (as of this writing) an additional 52 games in which he played. The largest single batch among those 52 is the 14 he played in Cuba against that nation's top talent during early 1900. Most of the other 52 were championship games against the very best African American teams that didn't have him on their rosters at the time. Across those 52 games, he had a .338 batting average.

In 1990, early Grant biographer James Overmyer provided some statistical analysis covering his years at the highest level in the minor leagues, 1886 through 1888:

> Comparing Grant statistically to his International League peers, it is clear that he shone among them. His three-year batting average of .354 is 26 percent better than the league average for those three years. In his two best years, 1886 and 1888, he was 39 and 36 percent ahead of the league. For the sake of comparison, New York Yankee stars Don Mattingly and Steve Sax, current Boston Red Sox batting star Wade Boggs and ex–Red Sox great Carl Yastrzemski all played very well in their last minor league seasons before making the majors, but none of them were that far ahead of their peers.[23]

But let's circle back to the opening questions. Was Frank Grant ever regarded as the best player in baseball? Yes, he was. Did anybody, while he was active, ever suggest that he was the best player in baseball? Yes, a variety of knowledgeable people, both in the press boxes and playing on baseball teams, did say or at least suggested that he was the best player active. And finally, being a Hall of Famer implies that a person is widely known; was Grant, in his day? One of his nicknames, "The Famous Grant," provides the answer.

1

A Family Accustomed to Freedom

The front page of the local weekly paper set the scene well: The first news article noted that shortly before Abraham Lincoln's assassination less than four months earlier, he voiced opposition to hanging Confederate President Jefferson Davis as a traitor. In the next column was commentary about extending voting rights to slaves Lincoln had liberated. Sadly, below those two items were horribly racist anecdotes, both of dubious authenticity. Nearby were three additional articles on voting rights: "President Johnson's View," "The Question of Suffrage at the South," and "Negro Suffrage in Connecticut." This was what the *Pittsfield Sun* communicated in its first edition after Frank Grant was born: Resentment between North and South was bound to linger, as was racism far from the former Slave States, but their defeat was forcing the nation to grapple with equality in a way it never had before. It's no wonder that there's a widespread presumption that Grant's actual first name paid tribute to the top military hero of the recent Civil War, Union General (and soon President) U.S. Grant, because the baby's name at birth was Ulysses Franklin Grant.[1]

Frank Grant was born in Pittsfield, Berkshire County, Massachusetts, on August 1, 1865, to Franklin Grant and the former Frances Hoose, who was often called Fannie. Beyond those very basic facts, during his life and even in the decade following his election to the National Baseball Hall of Fame in 2006, almost nothing published linked Frank Grant to any of his other ancestors. Similarly, very few details had emerged about his childhood and teens.

One rare genealogical detail was revealed in 1970 by another hometown newspaper, the *Berkshire Eagle*. A first cousin to Frank Grant "was the famed Sylvanus Grant, the man who cut down the old Park Square elm" in Pittsfield during the Civil War. This ancient tree was such a well-known landmark that its need for removal was mourned in at least one New York City newspaper.[2] The Massachusetts census of 1855 and federal censuses around then, combined with other state records, confirm that Sylvanus' father, Rensselaer, was one of Franklin's siblings, making Sylvanus and Frank first cousins.

In stark contrast to the millions of slaves officially freed by President Lincoln's Emancipation Proclamation at the start of 1863, Frank Grant's grandparents knew freedom back to at least 1800, and their children were born free. His paternal grandparents were Jacob Grant and the former Lena Fields. The 1855 Massachusetts census shows Jacob as born in New York and Lena in Rhode Island (though the 1860 census said Connecticut, and her son Franklin's death record in 1865 said New Jersey; the latter called her "Lucy"). Two censuses indicate that Lena was born around 1793, while a third points

7

to 1796. Massachusetts birth records indicate that Jacob had siblings born a decade or so after him in Pittsfield.[3]

It's very fitting that Frank Grant was born in Pittsfield, the largest city and traditional county seat, in light of baseball's origins having been traced through it. "Because the old game of baseball may have originated, or at least first flourished, in the Berkshires and the Housatonic Valley, this region might not unreasonably be termed Baseball's Garden of Eden, a term that Pittsfield's civic boosters have been quick to adopt," wrote John Thorn, the Official Baseball Historian for Major League Baseball. The most concrete surviving evidence is from 1791, around the time Jacob's siblings were born in Pittsfield, when local leaders adopted a bylaw forbidding baseball and other games within 80 yards of the city's newly built meeting house.[4]

Jacob Grant passed away between the 1855 and 1860 censuses. His age in the 1855 census was recorded as 69.[5] Lena outlived her husband and Frank's maternal grandparents. She passed away in Lenox at the time of Frank's birth (though the *Pittsfield Sun*'s brief announcement didn't specify the date).[6] Birth records of their several children put Jacob and Lena in Pittsfield from 1802 to 1819. Frank Grant's father, Franklin, was born May 1, 1817.

Frank Grant's mother supplied familial connections of greater historical significance, including to an African American soldier during the Civil War and to a house added to the National Register of Historic Places in 2010. Frances Hoose Grant was the daughter of Phillip (or Philip) Hoose and the former Hannah Persip (Percip being the most common variation). "Phillip Hoose, a native of New York State, and who came to Cheshire, Mass., about the year 1800, was a slave, being owned by a man by the name of Sebron," stated a history of Berkshire County in 1885. "He, however, made his escape, but was followed by his master, who finding all efforts to recover him alive futile, was obliged to return without him."[7]

Massachusetts had been one of the first states to do away with slavery. Many sources point to rulings in 1781 and 1783 by the Commonwealth's Supreme Judicial Court as having "effectively ended slavery as a legal practice in Massachusetts," as the Massachusetts Historical Society summarized them, but the latter source also stressed that in reality slavery persisted in some forms throughout the 1790s. In neighboring New York State, slavery wasn't completely eliminated until 1827.[8] Therefore, Phillip Hoose's course of action didn't necessarily have a high chance of succeeding.

Hannah Hoose's father, John Persip, may have been the patriarch alluded to in familial lore well over a century later: "As the family story has it, two Persip brothers stowed away in Portugal—year unknown—on a ship bound for America," wrote a *Berkshire Eagle* reporter in the 1970s. "When they landed, one went South, and was never heard from again. The other made his way to Berkshire County."[9] Berkshire is the Massachusetts county that borders New York and thus stretches more than 50 miles from Vermont to Connecticut.

The maternal half of Hannah Persip Hoose's family tree was well documented back to the 1700s in a book published by the Harvard University Press in 2003, albeit without connecting "Philip" and Hannah Hoose to any of the Grants. *The Hanging of Ephraim Wheeler,* by Irene Quenzler Brown and Richard D. Brown, illuminated the execution in 1806 of "a white Yankee" who had married into the mixed-race family of Hannah's mother, the Odels (or Odells). Ephraim Wheeler's crime was sexually assaulting his 13-year-old daughter Betsy, who was Hannah's first cousin.[10]

1. A Family Accustomed to Freedom

Hannah Persip Hoose's mother, Molly, was likely the second oldest of at least six daughters of Ichabod and Elizabeth Odel, who were also known to have two sons. Ichabod was classified as "negro" in the 1800 census. Emily Grant Foote, a descendant of Clarence Grant, told this author in 2021 that Elizabeth Odel's ancestry can be traced back to a Beard family in Great Britain in the 1400s, decades prior to Christopher Columbus' voyages from Europe to the West Indies.

Molly Odel was born on April 30, 1758, at Sutton, Massachusetts (near Worcester), in the midst of the French and Indian War. During 1755, at least, her father served with a local militia company during that conflict. Twenty years later, he did likewise during the Siege of Boston, in the opening months of the Revolutionary War.[11] Molly married John Persip in 1793. In 1808, John bought a 24-acre farm from Molly's brother, Isaac. It straddled the Berkshire and Hampshire County lines to the east of Pittsfield. John paid $200 just for the four acres in the latter county. In the 1840 census, John was listed as "free colored" but the Browns said Molly was "taken to be white," partly because records listing her death in 1846 made no mention of her race.[12] When their daughter Hannah passed away in 1862, the *Pittsfield Sun* identified her as "colored," like her father.[13]

Hannah married Phillip Hoose in late 1815. Their son Amos' death record states that Hannah was born in Goshen, which is just a few miles east of her parents' farm. That same record specified Philip's birthplace as Kinderhook, New York, just like Jacob Grant's. It is thus a distinct possibility that Frank Grant's grandfathers knew one another from there. Phillip was the first of Frank Grant's grandparents to pass away. He died in April of 1845 at Dalton, about five miles northeast of Pittsfield.

Frances Hoose Grant was born around 1832 in Dalton. A single-family home there on the National Register of Historic Places is the Fitch–Hoose House, often just called the Hoose House. It was built in 1846, and there is documentation that a member of the Hoose family bought it in 1868. However, Frances' brother, Amos, must have lived there long before then, because his son Edward, who was born around 1842, grew up there. Like Sylvanus Grant, Edward Hoose was one of Frank Grant's first cousins. During the Civil War, Edward served in the all-Black 54th Regiment Massachusetts Volunteer Infantry, which was immortalized in the popular 1989 movie, *Glory*. In the years leading up to the Civil War, the Hoose House sheltered escaped slaves as part of the Underground Railroad, in the process of smuggling them from slave states to Canada. The Hoose House remained in the family until 2001.[14] It so happens that Franklin and Frances Grant lived in Dalton around 1860, with their five children.

Frances Hoose and Franklin Grant were married on October 28, 1850. In the two months leading up to that, she was listed twice in the federal census. On September 2, she was listed as part of a large household headed by William B. Cooley. He was the proprietor of the Berkshire Hotel, which stood in the center of Pittsfield.[15]

By October 11, she had switched to a similarly large household headed by Robert Melville (often spelled without the vowel at the end). He owned a mansion one mile south of Pittsfield called the Melvill House, and that year his cousin Herman bought adjacent property, which he named Arrowhead. Herman's famous novel, *Moby Dick*, was published in October of 1851. Herman of course visited the Melvill House, but other visitors of equal fame included Henry Wadsworth Longfellow, Nathaniel Hawthorne, and President John Tyler. It has been rumored that the mansion also served as a way station on the Underground Railroad. Today it serves as the clubhouse for the

Country Club of Pittsfield.[16] Frances' occupation wasn't identified at either the Berkshire Hotel or the Melvill House, but serving as a maid or something comparable seems likely.

By 1850, Frances Hoose and Franklin Grant each had a sister marry into the same household in Pittsfield, headed by William Hamilton. Franklin's sister Cornelia, who was ten years older, was William's wife. Living with the couple was their son Charles, age 20, and his 21-year-old wife, Lucretia, who was Frances Hoose's sister. In fact, Franklin Grant himself, age 33 at the time, was also part of that household in the 1850 census. That was on October 2. Like his fiancée, he was also listed in the census twice that year. On September 3, he was shown as living with his parents in Lenox (though perhaps only because he hadn't formally moved out).

In Massachusetts' 1855 census, Franklin and Frances Grant were living with his parents in Lenox. They had three children: Amelia Catherine, age 4; Charlotte, who was born in Lenox on February 28, 1853; and Willis, age 1. In the 1860 census, the family was living on its own in Dalton, except that Frances' recently widowed sister, Louisa McDonald (misspelled "McDonnell" on that census page), was living with them. Franklin was a farm laborer, and the two oldest girls were identified as schoolchildren. There were two additional children, namely Harriet (nicknamed Hattie), age 3, and Walter. He is presumably the unnamed Grant boy listed in birth records as born on November 10, 1858. Walter passed away in Dalton on August 10, 1861, meaning that Frank Grant had at least one sibling he never knew.[17]

In the 1850 census, Franklin was identified as mulatto and Frances as Black. When they were living with his parents in 1855, his parents were classified as Black, but everyone else in the household was instead categorized as mulatto. In the 1860 census, the Grant family was identified as Black, while in the Massachusetts census of 1865 they were mulattos.

In that 1865 census, which was taken during June in Pittsfield, the Grant family was living with Cornelia Hamilton, now a widow, and three teen members of her family. Two more children were part of Franklin and Frances' household: Clarence, age 4, and Lucy, age 2. Franklin was identified as a Legal Voter. Two months later, when the last of his children was born, he was listed in Pittsfield's birth registry as a farmer.

During Franklin's lifetime, an African American man in Massachusetts was generally able to vote and potentially even hold public office. Other aspects of life were a different story. It should come as no surprise that at the start of the Civil War, even in the relatively progressive Commonwealth of Massachusetts, non-whites found it much more challenging to participate in economic and social circles. As tensions over slavery were peaking in the nation's capital, first-term U.S. Senator Henry Wilson of Massachusetts went so far as to risk alienating most of his constituents by also bemoaning the fact that people of color "with the same intellectual qualities, the same moral qualities, are not in Massachusetts regarded as they would be if they were white men."[18]

This, then, was the Grant family's situation at the time Frank was born. Again, that occurred in Pittsfield on August 1, 1865. James Overmyer, the baseball historian largely responsible for getting Frank Grant into the Hall of Fame, shed some light on that infancy in 1990. "His family home was probably on land along South Street between the Housatonic River and Underhill Place, where family members for years owned what was then mostly farmland," Overmyer wrote.[19] The family's situation changed dramatically four months later when his father passed away at the age of 44. The cause of death was from inflammatory bowel disease.[20] Frances was thus left to raise seven children as a single parent.

Little is known about the Grant family's plight before Frank's fifth birthday, with the notable exception of moving halfway across the county at some point. However, there was national news in 1867 that served as the first precedent for some of the hostility he faced a few years into his professional baseball career. Various important histories of the Negros Leagues trace their origins to a decision made in 1867 at a convention of the National Association of Base Ball Players (NABBP).[21] The NABBP, the first organization that governed baseball, had been formed a decade earlier.

On December 11, NABBP president Arthur Pue Gorman, a future United States Senator for Maryland, convened a late-morning session at the New Chestnut Street Theatre in Philadelphia. "The attendance was quite large, upwards of seventy clubs being represented," reported Philadelphia's *Daily Evening Bulletin*. It listed all of those ball clubs, with about 20 based in Pennsylvania, 14 in New York State, and seven each in New Jersey and Washington, D.C. A few came from New England, and the outliers were the Union nine of St. Louis and the Pioneer team of Portland, Oregon. In sum, the NABBP was dominated by Northern clubs. The body received a report from its Committee on State Associations, which concluded by declaring "against the admission of any clubs composed of colored men, or any white clubs having any colored members. The report of the Committee was adopted," the *Bulletin* noted.[22]

The next day, a "Special Correspondent" for the *New York Tribune* began his front-page report on the NABBP action by wistfully describing, at some length, the innocence of ballgames as organized by young boys on playgrounds. He contrasted that with how the NABBP "selfishly and cowardly" approved this resolution: "No club composed of persons of color, or having in its membership persons of color, shall be admitted into the National Association." The correspondent noted that this vote elicited hearty applause from the delegates but also hisses from onlookers.[23]

On December 13, a paper in Pennsylvania expressed its condemnation of the vote with a rhetorical question: "Is not that clearly in violation of the Civil Rights Bill?" The paper also editorialized against the decision in a summarizing sentence: "The Base Ball Conventionists basely blackball colored applicants for admission."[24] (The insulting but possibly unfamiliar adverb "basely" was obviously chosen to be clever, paired in a play on words with "blackball"; a more widely understood equivalent would be "dishonorably.")

Other newspapers eventually weighed in, and one of the harshest against the NABBP was the *Evening Journal* in Jersey City, New Jersey. It condemned "the dull heads of the gentry who assume to run the baseball clubs in this country" and their "stupid action."[25] Of course, other newspapers backed the NABBP, though commentators in Southern cities who wrote more than a sentence about the topic seemed content to point out that the decision was made by Northerners.[26]

This ruling hasn't resurfaced solely in broad histories of baseball. For one, it was quoted in a biography of Willie Mays written for juveniles.[27] If that decision is significant in the context of a Hall of Fame career that began in the 1940s, it is even more relevant to a prominent player in the 1800s like Frank Grant. Even though such a policy wasn't in effect during the 1880s, when Grant began his professional baseball career, it was concrete evidence of how embedded racism was in the formal governance of the sport, which would suppress virtually all African American players from 1900 through World War II.

Was there more than a minimal chance that word of this 1867 decision reached Berkshire County, much less anyone in the Grant family? This news did get into an assortment of papers, though one example near Boston consisted of a single sentence and thus would have been easy to overlook.[28] Nevertheless, Frank's four oldest siblings presumably had ample schooling by that point, so it's conceivable that one of them read about this disappointing decision. It remains uncertain, though, what newspaper the family would have most likely accessed: It's not a given that in 1867 the Grants were still residents of Pittsfield, in the center of Berkshire County, because by the 1870 census, they had moved about 20 miles away into the County's northwest corner.

Pittsfield had been more than five percent African American dating back to 1820 and continued to have a higher percentage than Boston until 1885,[29] but that wasn't enough to keep Frances Grant there for long after her husband's death. She instead moved to Williamstown, known primarily as the site of the well-established Williams College, which remained an all-male institution for the next century. They thus moved from a community of about 11,000 to one roughly one-third that size, with 3,559 residents in 1870.[30] The Grant family was a Williamstown fixture well into the next century. In a profile of Frank Grant, baseball historian Lawrence Hogan noted that Williamstown's African American residents "were generally well-accepted members of the community."[31]

On a page of the 1870 census dated June 21, Frances was identified as a restaurant keeper, and her three oldest children were listed as waiters. Three of her children had also been enrolled in school during the prior year. A census page dated July 14 provided an additional detail, that the older of Frank's two brothers, Willis, had taken a job outside the household as a hall boy at the brand new Greylock Hall resort. It had opened at the start of June, one mile from the Williams College campus, and could accommodate about 100 visitors.[32]

Cornelia Hamilton, the sister-in-law with whom Frances and her family had been living in Pittsfield during mid–1865, was again listed as a Pittsfield resident in the 1870 census, along with her three children.[33] Thus, if Frances moved to Williamstown because some close relative had already moved there, it wasn't Cornelia. Frances' widowed sister Louisa McDonald, who lived with the Grants in 1860, is a distinct possibility, because she spent at least the last few years of her life in Williamstown. In the Massachusetts census of 1865, a widow named Louisa McDonald, about the right age, was a cook for the family of Williamstown hotel keeper Albert G. Bailey. She wasn't noted as nonwhite, but it isn't clear from that page whether the census taker was bothering to confirm anyone's race. In the 1870 census, a Black woman named Louisa McDonald, again around the right age, was a laundress at the inn where Frank's brother Willis worked. There was no trace of her in the County in the 1880 census, but in Williamstown's 1885 directory, she was entered as having a restaurant and boarding house. The directory noted that she was the widow of Duncan, and that was the name of her husband in Dalton at the time of the 1855 census (he passed away there in 1858).[34] She passed away in Williamstown in 1889.[35]

However, Frances and Louisa had at least one other sister besides Lucretia, named Lucy. She had married John Perry Duncan in 1851, and they had at least three children. In the Massachusetts census of 1865, they lived one town to the east of Williamstown, and by the 1870 census they had moved into Williamstown itself. Whichever Hoose sister moved to Williamstown first, the question that may never be answered is what motivated her to choose that town.

During the 1870s, Williamstown was visited by Edward Everett Hale, an author and historian who was famous enough to be remembered with a statue in the Boston Public Garden, and he described its "exceeding beauty." He had also visited about 25 years earlier and noticed that fences had been removed from all over the village. "Pretty footwalks have been laid out, and are carefully kept up under the beautiful trees, which are now more beautiful than ever," he wrote. "So skillfully and so thickly have these been planted and with such artful absence of art are the college buildings scattered, large and small, that college buildings and private buildings seem all to belong to the elegant arrangements of some noble estate, and for once in your life you are not annoyed by the petty arrangements of separate and peculiar properties."[36]

Based on an 1876 map of Williamstown, the four households on the same page of the 1870 census as the Grants all had property on the west side of Spring Street, which extends south from the wide corridor of its Main Street.[37] Spring may very well be the only street on which Frank Grant lived during his years in Williamstown. Into the 1860s, "Spring Street was a quiet country lane with no shops and only a dozen very simple houses," wrote one of Frank's white neighbors and childhood friends, Bliss Perry. Beginning with construction of "a big brick public school" on the east side of Spring Street in 1867, it soon became "the principal business street of the town, on which are the bank and postoffice [sic] and town school and the largest stores," he wrote in 1935.[38] Today, Spring is a one-way street for much of its length.

The Perrys were listed just before the Grants in the 1870 census. The Perrys owned a lot directly across from the school, but it extended a considerable length to the west and covered "several acres," according to Bliss. In 1872, his father had their story-and-a-half home moved to a hilltop in the lot's western half and doubled its size.[39] It thus seems very likely that the Grants also lived very close to the school, at least in 1870.

The 1870 census implied that the Grants lived in a dwelling owned by Frances, rather than a rental. Then again, she was listed as male, so that census taker's accuracy can't be trusted completely. In any case, the value of the real estate was a mere $150, while the other houses listed on that page of the census were worth at least ten times as much. She had no personal property of value, whereas three of the other households had personal estates valued from $300 to $400. The personal estate of Bliss Perry's father, Williams College professor Arthur Latham Perry, was valued at $2,500.

Also living near the Grants at the time of the 1870 census was the family of lawyer Keyes Danforth. There were only two families listed between them. On April 7, 1871, Danforth filed a probate petition extending from Franklin Grant's death, to be named the legal guardian of Catharine A., Charlotte S., Willis W., Lucy S., Harriet H., Clarence E., and Frank "B" Grant. Frances, as the surviving parent, reportedly agreed to this arrangement, though her name wasn't specified in the petition.[40] This guardianship may explain why Clarence's son George, who was born in 1903, was given the middle name Danforth. Keyes Danforth later became a judge, but he also has his own niche in baseball history: For the 1820s, an MLB.com web page cataloguing Early Baseball Milestones includes (as of this writing) an excerpt from Danforth's memoir, *Boyhood Reminiscences: Pictures of New England in the Olden Times in Williamstown*, about having played "base ball" there during his "early boyhood."[41]

On the 1876 map, the lot immediately south of the high school had a large apartment building owned by Danforth and H.B. Curtis. The two had only acquired the lot at the beginning of 1870, and, according to the *Pittsfield Sun*, they moved onto that lot "the house stood on the rear of the new church lot."[42] On the map, there does appear to be a small structure in addition to the large apartment building. Given that Danforth formally took the Grant children under his proverbial wing a few months into 1871, it's distinctly possible that this house was where the Grants lived at the time of the 1870 census. However, directly across the street on the 1876 map was a "shop" on the same lot as the home of a Mrs. E. Spooner, which was instead labeled a "cottage" on an 1889 map. Perhaps that served as the restaurant Frances Grant ran in 1870 (which could have doubled as the family's residence). That lot's backyard abutted the sprawling property of Arthur Latham Perry's family.

At some point, Frances Grant began to work for the Perry family as their "hired girl," a term which was eventually replaced by "maid." As a result, Bliss became friends with Frank and Clarence. After mentioning in his autobiography another African American who lived on Spring Street in his youth, a barber named Milo Nichols, Perry noted, "Race questions troubled us very little then." Perry also wrote about a how, "after I had seen Clarence Grant break through the ice of the New Pond—to be rescued, just as his strength was gone, by Clarence Smith—I became a timid skater." On the next page, Perry implied that this occurred no later than 1873.[43] Smith was the son of a local physician and became a judge. The anecdote in Perry's autobiography was mentioned in a tribute to Judge Smith at the time of his funeral.[44]

Another white Williamstown resident shared his memories of Frank Grant decades later. In a letter to a local newspaper during World War II, Robert A. Clark fondly recalled frequent summertime strolls with a group of boys to Torrey's dam, on Cold Spring Brook. "In our swim-group was often Frank Grant, a colored boy. Frank was a fine athlete and ball player, and I have heard that he later became a professional," Clark wrote. "I vividly recall him as he stood on the roadside rock, his black skin glistening, poised for the dive into the deep pool below. I do not recall that any of us ever wore bathing suits, and I do not think that the infrequent passers-by were annoyed for lack of them." Clark considered Williamstown "a very democratic community" because, though he was son of a carpenter, he "played with the boys of the faculty families," and named the four youngest Perry boys—Arthur, Walter, Carroll, and Lewis—among his examples, adding parenthetically that "Bliss was a few years older." The two other boys Clark named were San (Sanborn) Tenney, who served Williamstown for 25 years as a judge, and "Al Chad," presumably Albert Hopkins Chadbourne, son of the President of Williams College from 1872 to 1881. In the 1880 census, Tenney's family was listed just after the Duncans, the family of Frank's aunt and uncle. Clark identified several other "old swimmin' holes" that he and these friends enjoyed.[45] According to that same census, Clark was about two years older than Frank Grant. In the 1910 and 1920 censuses, he was a letter carrier for the U.S. Postal Service in Springfield, Massachusetts.

Around the time Frank turned 24 years old, a newspaper in Harrisburg, Pennsylvania, printed a lengthy profile of him. It lavished praise on the early years of his professional baseball career and added some biographical information. Not surprisingly, after noting that his family had moved from Pittsfield to Williamstown when he was "quite young," this profile confirmed that Frank "played his first 'scrub' game about that town and early developed a remarkable adaptability to the national game. He was quick and wiry, played an almost faultless game, and was the pride of his boy associates."[46] In 1886, the *New York Sun* provided this related insight: "His knowledge of base ball was gained on the campus of Williams College, where he was a favorite with the collegians."[47]

Knowledge of the sport would of course have been necessary, but neither newspaper shed light on his earliest teammates. Bliss Perry recalled that at the age of 12, he became the captain of a baseball team that included Clarence and Frank, "whose portrait I drew later in a novel called *The Plated City*." He was referring to mid–1873 if he was correct about his age at the time. Frank turned eight years old that summer. Their left fielder was Bob Pettit, who had a three-year major league career beginning in 1887 with Chicago's National League team. Their shortstop was Danny Collins, whose father was a janitor for the College. The team called itself the Rough and Readys, and they played together into 1875, if not later.[48] Perry was a professor at Harvard University from 1907 to 1930 and published these memories a few years afterwards.[49] His ball playing around 1875 clearly left a mark on him for the rest of his life, as noted in a 2008 profile by novelist Darryl Brock: "On one occasion in his mid-sixties he found his thoughts drifting during a Boston Symphony Orchestra concert; as the music soared in the hall, he realized that he was replaying in his mind a bunt he had muffed in a game fifty years previously!"[50]

In Perry's novel, Frank's character was called Tom Beaulieu. He wasn't quite the main character, but he was a crucial one at the center of the book's opening chapter. The character also wasn't an exact duplicate of Grant. For one, the novel's climax involved the character's long-lost and younger half-sister, but Frank Grant had no such sibling. Still, because Perry said he drew a portrait of Frank Grant in the character of Beaulieu, it seems reasonable to look at that character's attributes as generally reflecting Grant's. Though Tom Beaulieu proved to be quite heroic in the novel, Perry was probably like many writers of such fiction in not wanting to make his character perfect. On consecutive pages, Perry wrote that Beaulieu was a "simple-minded fellow" who "could scarcely read," though a letter written later by the character reflected no such issues, and the character's speech was comparable to that of the white characters. Perry was probably using himself as a measuring stick for deep thinking and literary voraciousness. He was well aware that Frank Grant didn't have the Perry family's education, and it wouldn't have been unusual if he perceived a void between himself and Grant in that regard.[51] Grant's good and longtime friend as an adult, future Hall of Famer Sol White, definitely perceived such a gap between Grant and himself. Like Perry, White had a college education. "Reared in the shadow of Williams College," White once noted about Grant, "that institution of learning had no effect, intellectually, on the mind and personality of Frank Grant."[52] On the other hand, it so happened that the profile in the *New York Sun*, at the start of his pro career, called him "intelligent, and gentlemanly."[53]

Nevertheless, two of the strongest traits Perry ascribed to Beaulieu were a "characteristic optimism" and an "almost perpetual good nature." Additionally, an overdue reunion of just two months with Tom's half-sister "had deepened wondrously her affection for him," partly because he possessed "gentleness of heart" and was chivalrous.[54] Without giving too much more away, Frank Grant never had to display the kind of heroism that Tom Beaulieu demonstrated two-thirds of the way into the novel's 21 chapters, but Bliss Perry clearly saw the potential for such fortitude in him.

For the 1875–1876 school year, Perry enrolled in a boarding school about five miles to the south, the Greylock Institute. He started there in September, but he had already visited in June with the Rough and Readys, to play the Institute's junior team. The visitors traveled to South Williamstown in the Perry family's lumber wagon after "bribing another boy to drive" the horse. He didn't specify whether both Grants and Pettit played, but he also didn't allude to any changes in the usual lineup. Perry said his nine "ravaged" their opponents, scoring 48 runs in the process.[55] If Frank Grant did play in that game, then it was a milestone of sorts in his baseball career. Alas, mid–1875 was also the first time one of the siblings with whom he grew up passed away. Lucy died in early June at the age of 13. The town's death registry listed the cause as consumption, i.e., tuberculosis.

There had already been some stress within the Grant household, starting at least two years earlier: Clarence got into trouble with the law, starting around the age of 11. That recurred periodically over the next decade, at which point he dragged Frank into one serious episode, but apparently just that once. As best as can be determined, all of Frances' other children had a clean record.

On June 14, 1873, Clarence was accused of stealing five dollars from the post office. Rumor had it that he fled all the way to South Williamstown, four miles distant, and one county paper reported that he was caught "on the base ball grounds. The money was found in his shoe."[56]

He was eventually sent to the state reform school, but during the fall of 1874, he escaped. It took until May of 1875 for authorities to determine that Frances managed to keep him hidden for more than half a year, at which point he was sent back to the reform school.[57] Lucy's death occurred less than a month later.

It's unclear how long Clarence remained at the reform school, but on August 14, 1878, he was arrested for theft at Solomon's grocery store. He was charged with taking 50 cents and a plug of tobacco. In January, he pleaded guilty and was sentenced to six months in jail.[58] He apparently kept his name out of newspapers from mid–1879 through 1882.

Clarence's first offenses might simply have been motivated largely by poverty. Bliss Perry said most residents of Williamstown were "poor or unlucky," if not both.[59] Also, three months after his first theft, the entire nation was plunged into what was often called the Great Depression, though after the stock market collapse of 1929, it was more widely called the Panic of 1873. It lasted past 1877.[60]

In the 1880 census, Frances' six children were all listed as living with her. Amelia, the oldest, worked at a bakery. She was the only family member reported to have a job on that date (June 1). Frank, though, hadn't turned 15 yet and was shown as attending school that year. He is known to have played baseball in high school, and a Williamstown House of Local History researcher believes that was at the building on Spring Street.[61]

In a document held by the local historical society, an anonymous acquaintance or friend, writing sometime after 1910, said Frank "could do more tricks with a baseball than anyone I ever saw. Kick a grounder with [his] feet to bounce [it] up into his hands. Catch a ball behind the back before Rabbit Maranville was born." Hall of Famer Walter "Rabbit" Maranville (born in 1891) was a middle infielder who burst onto the scene in 1913. This previously unknown admirer has been quoted by baseball historians with some frequency.[62] There's a good chance he was Joe Fern, Cy Young's roommate in 1890 and a ballplayer in Berkshire County before that. When Fern told the *Berkshire County Eagle* in 1937 that Grant was the greatest player he had ever seen, the second player he commented on was Maranville.[63]

One scenario in the middle of Bliss Perry's novel was also likely based on witnessing Grant demonstrate rare skills and a distinct flair during his youth. When the character based on Grant got into the major leagues under a fake name and backstory, he completed a play in such a distinct way that it was a dead giveaway to fans sitting at a distance who happened to know him.

> Just then a man hit safely, and they stopped talking. The batter following made what seemed like a safe hit too, a hot grounder almost directly over second. The crowd yelled. But Mendoza darted toward the ball, picked it up on the dead run with one hand, touched the bag in passing, and then, wheeling, threw the runner out at first as coolly as if he had the whole afternoon before him. It was a double play that sent a roar of delight all around the field: that was something like baseball as it used to be!

In that instant, the fans were absolutely certain they were watching their friend and not some nobody named Mendoza.[64]

The Grant family's page of the 1880 census didn't identify the street or any of the house numbers, but the third column was for "Dwelling houses numbered in the order of visitation." The Grants were in the 77th dwelling, but so was the next family (white), headed by widow Mary A. Hunt and her son Lyman, who ran a jewelry store on the lot. The store's address may have been 20 Spring Street. Lyman and Laura Hunt had a daughter, Emma, who was one year older than Frank, and a son, Arthur, who was four years younger. The 1876 and 1889 maps both show that the Hunts had two buildings on their property, and the latter map labeled one a "cottage." The lot was on the east side of Spring Street near its southern end.

The start of 1881 was rough for the Grants: Charlotte passed away in January, due to epilepsy and a brain affliction. Shortly before Independence Day, a national tragedy hit Williamstown particularly hard. On July 2, James A. Garfield, a Williams College alum who had been sworn in as the 20th President of the United States less than four months earlier, was preparing to return to his alma mater via train when he was shot twice at point-blank range by a crazed politician named Charles Guiteau. Garfield didn't succumb for 79 days, dying on September 19, 1881. He was one of Arthur Latham Perry's favorite pupils, and Bliss recalled then-General Garfield visiting their home shortly after the Civil War ended.[65]

The next month, Clarence Grant gave his family a reason to celebrate when he married the former Henrietta H. "Nettie" Porter on October 11. Her father was a physician.[66] According to the 1910 census, they had nine children, though three preceded them in death. They were married for more than 30 years, until her death, but it took some years before his run-ins with the law subsided.

Clarence reportedly resumed his thievery in the spring of 1883, when he was arrested for stealing both in Williamstown and nearby New York State. Oddly, the article reporting this in the local newspaper, the *North Adams Transcript*, didn't specify what he was accused of taking in either location.[67] The Grants soon experienced much greater sadness, however, when Frances passed away on September 24. The cause was listed as dropsy, which today would be called edema, i.e., excess fluid in tissues or cavities of the body. An announcement in the *North Adams Transcript* said heart disease was likely to blame. "Mrs. Grant, an old and esteemed colored lady, died very suddenly last week," that paper reported. "The funeral was largely attended on Friday [September 28], by her friends throughout the county."[68] Frances at least enjoyed more than a year as a grandmother, because Clarence's first child was born in early 1882 ("Louis" in Williamstown's birth registry, but "Lewis" on his 1942 military registration card).

It was in mid–1884 when Clarence's conduct allegedly escalated, and an even worse incident late in the year happened to involve Frank. Clarence was arrested as an accessory to an abduction, but after being arraigned he was quickly discharged, a possible sign that he didn't fully realize what was actually happening. On June 20, a sewing machine salesman named Lorenzo Griswold (presumably white, because only Clarence's race was specified in accounts) made arrangements for a horse and carriage down in Pittsfield, and hired Clarence to be his driver. The two traveled about five miles east to Dalton, where Griswold "prevailed upon" Susan E. Dell (Dill in other accounts) to ride with them. The *Boston Globe* reported that she was just 14 years old. The trio then traveled *overnight* to Great Barrington, in the southern part of Berkshire County, and arrived around dawn. Griswold then instructed Clarence to take the horse and carriage back to Pittsfield. That afternoon, authorities arrested Griswold and charged him with adultery and fornication, in addition to kidnapping. "In court the girl cried bitterly," the *Globe* reported. "She returned home this evening with her father." At least one paper in the County offered sordid details, but they were solely about Griswold. Clarence was released in less than a week.[69]

One common aspect of these several crimes and misdemeanors was that Clarence was never reported to be violent. That changed on November 17, 1884, a Monday. It so happened that his second child, Fannie, had been born eight days earlier. As the *Springfield Republican* of south-central Massachusetts reported on November 22, Clarence, Frank, and a third African American named Edward DeWitt had been drinking somewhere out of town "and were noisy on the train to Williamstown." Frank had turned 19 two months earlier. On reaching the depot, the three reportedly made "an unprovoked assault" on a railroad flagman named Samuel R. Baker, "one of them striking him with a 'billy,' felling him to the ground and injuring him very seriously." However, he was expected to recover. Baker was presumably white because his race wasn't identified. A deputy sheriff eventually caught DeWitt in Pittsfield, but the Grants were found around Williamstown. The *Republican* noted that DeWitt had been in jail for assault previously, and that Clarence had "been in the house of correction four times before." The paper also mentioned that he was Griswold's driver during the abduction in June.[70]

What the Springfield paper didn't point out—nor did any other contemporary journalists, apparently—was that the victim of the supposedly "unprovoked" attack was hardly an angel. On October 28, 1874, Samuel R. Baker of nearby Adams burglarized a store, stealing jewelry and clothing. Six days later, he and James Brolley forcibly entered the home of one Sarah A. Brolley, assaulted the residents, and may have taken $300. In January of 1875, Baker was sent to State prison for seven years.[71] With that criminal record, it's quite easy to envision Baker as the provoker who later took advantage of his skin color to assert victimhood when he received far more than he bargained for.

On January 15, 1885, the *Berkshire County Eagle* listed several cases being considered by a grand jury, including one against "Edward DeWitt and Clarence Grant, for the assault on the trackman, Samuel Baker, last November, at Williamstown." Frank was not mentioned. The *Eagle* did mention Frank in its update a week later, merely naming the parties involved as the trial continued, but when the outcome was reported in a different paper on January 28, Frank was again not mentioned. On the strength of Baker's testimony, that it was Clarence who "knocked him down and knocked out three front teeth with a billy" (a heavy wooden club), the older of the two Grant brothers received a guilty verdict and a sentence of nine months in the house of correction. DeWitt received a sentence of three months.[72]

Did Frank catch a break? Well, the American justice system of that century wasn't exactly known for that regarding African Americans. But in the context of the family's dynamic, it's certainly conceivable that Clarence's instincts were to protect his younger brother. On the other hand, Clarence didn't simply plead guilty and accept full blame. Plus, any effort to protect Frank would've required the cooperation of DeWitt, at a minimum, and Baker presumably would have challenged any mischaracterization by Clarence of Frank's involvement. Also, at age 19, Frank was less in need of shielding than, say, if he had been 12 years old. In any event, Frank Grant had a clean record prior to this trial (as best as can be determined), and it would have been admirable of Clarence to keep it spotless—which it did remain afterwards. All things considered, rather than Frank having been spared deserved consequences, for him it was more likely just a matter of wrong place, wrong time, wrong amount of alcohol.

Frank's ball playing across Berkshire County peaked during the second half of 1884, and that is documented in the next chapter. Still, there are qualities friends saw in him as an adult that had to have been rooted in his youth. For example, though he would later be known as quite the showman on ball diamonds, his longtime friend and teammate Sol White, also a Hall of Famer, considered him to be "quiet and unassuming on the ball field, never protesting a decision of an umpire, nor resenting an action of an opposing player."[73] Shortstop John Jones of the Philadelphia Giants got his start as an amateur in Harrisburg and considered Grant his mentor. That relationship presumably began in 1890, Grant's first year in Harrisburg and also when the roster of that city's Cuban Giants Juniors included center fielder J. Jones and shortstop C. Jones. If so, Grant was only 24 years old when he took Jones under his proverbial wing.[74]

In January 1885, the same month as Clarence's trial for assault, a historical "gazetteer" was published for Berkshire County that included alphabetical directories of the residents of the various towns. In the directory for Williamstown, the only entry for Grant was Willis. He was still living on Spring Street, though the house number wasn't identified, in contrast to some other residents. His job was janitor for the "Z.Z. society," the local chapter of the Zeta Psi fraternity.[75] It's possible that all of his siblings still lived with him under the same roof, and he was the only one listed because he was the oldest male. Conversely, with Clarence and Nettie having two children at that point, there's a very good chance they were living with her parents, where there wouldn't have been several adult siblings to crowd the place. Regardless, just a few months later, Frank left Williamstown to pursue an uncommon dream at that time: He was going to try making a living as an African American baseball player.

2

Serious About Base Ball

It's no surprise that as Frank Grant transitioned from the Rough and Readys and his high school's baseball team to countywide competition with and against older players, his three teammates who became major leaguers loomed large in that story. Nevertheless, it may be that two Williams College ballplayers were just as significant. The latter may have been most influential in persuading Grant to play the game in another state. Newspaper coverage providing insights into Grant's experiences as a ballplayer across Berkshire County accumulated in 1884, shortly after he turned 19, but in later years there were reports that he played in such circles prior to 1884. A challenge in documenting his ball playing prior to 1884 is the scarcity of box scores or even named players in accounts of games printed by local newspapers.

One of the future major leaguers with whom Grant played was Bob Pettit, who was four years older than Grant. Pettit's minor league career began in 1884, with the Connecticut State League team in Meriden. When Pettit passed away in 1910, the *North Adams Transcript*'s profile of him noted that he had been a member of "the Williamstown, Blackinton and Greylock teams in succession back in the early '80s at which time Frank Grant of Williamstown and Irving Curtiss of this city were also starting their careers on the diamond." Curtiss was described as one of Pettit's close friends. Pettit began playing amateur or semi-professional ball in Meriden in April 1883, so if the 1910 report was accurate, that narrows the timeframe of Grant's start with such Berkshire County teams to 1880–1882.[1] Grant turned 17 during the summer of 1882.

The mention of a Williamstown team stands out, not simply because that's where Pettit and Grant lived, but because so many communities in Berkshire County *except* Williamstown seemed to have longtime amateur teams during the first half of the 1880s. In the middle of 1883, a baseball team was "about to be organized in the village here as some of the best players of the college remain in town, and with the addition of the local players of no mean ability, will constitute quite a respectable nine." Typically, teams would have been organized many weeks earlier than that, and it's unclear whether this Williamstown team did in fact form. Whatever the case, more than 60 years later an attorney named Marc Comstock, who graduated from Williams College around 1885, reflected on Grant playing in Williamstown. "Grant was the outstanding amateur athlete in Williamstown," a *Buffalo Evening News* reporter wrote when summarizing Comstock's insights, "and when the college teams played the amateurs, Grant was on all of the local clubs opposing them."[2] As noted in a previous chapter, at the start of Grant's pro career, the *New York Sun* affirmed a strong connection between Grant and his town's famous institution: "His knowledge of base ball was gained on the campus of Williams College, where he was a favorite with the collegians."[3]

The most successful future major leaguer with whom Grant played as a teen was Frank Dwyer, who was about two and a half years younger. He had a brother named Ed who was 18 in 1880. Frank Dwyer's major league career stretched from 1888 to 1899, and he compiled a pitching record of 177–151. His best season was 1896, when he went 24–11 for the Cincinnati Reds. In 1915, the *Berkshire Evening Eagle* printed a very long article about his earliest baseball playing. Dwyer's start was traced back to 1881, in Dalton, Massachusetts, where his family lived. Dalton is about 20 miles south of Williamstown. Dalton, who was only 13, wanted a spot on a local team called the Lone Stars, but they rejected him. He formed a team called the Clippers and challenged the Lone Stars, whom his team defeated. As a result, the Lone Stars let him join after all. Frank Grant was the shortstop for the Lone Stars. The rest of the roster was Merdellon Porter, p and cf; Edward Dwyer, c; John Hardiman, 1b; William Barton, 2b; John Flynn, 3b and cf; Richard Maher, rf; and William Callahan, lf. John and Michael Mooney also played on the team.[4]

Though this article was reporting details of more than 30 years earlier, in September of 1882 that same weekly printed considerable information about the Lone Stars, and six of the players' names matched. All of the team's scores were listed from June 9 through September 9. The article noted that the roster was "considerably changed since the beginning of the season," but at that point it did include Ed Dwyer, as captain. *Not* named were his kid brother and Frank Grant.[5] That 1915 article was apparently off by at least a year, and probably two. However, Grant was reportedly already a member of the Lone Stars when Frank Dwyer joined them, and there was no indication of how long Grant had been on that roster.

The Clippers played their first game of 1883—and probably their first game *ever*—on May 12. Later that month the *Pittsfield Sun* listed the Clippers' roster, and it did include Frank Dwyer as pitcher. That item noted that the Clippers were "quite anxious to play the Lone Stars." The Clippers were a real enough team that they were "to have a uniform." At the end of that month, neither Frank Dwyer nor Frank Grant was listed on the roster of the Lone Stars, for which Ed Dwyer was still captain. On June 23, the Clippers beat the Lone Stars, 12–10; on Independence Day, they absolutely pounded the Lone Stars, 33–13, results consistent with the report in 1915 except two years later. The Clippers may not have been mentioned again in local papers later in 1883.[6]

Toward the end of July, the regulars of the Lone Stars were talking of calling themselves the Resolutes, and the expected roster included both Dwyer brothers but no Grant. That was also true when the Resolutes played a game shortly thereafter, and all of their participating players were named. Still, Grant could have been on that club on and around July 4. In mid–June, the *Pittsfield Sun* noted that the Lone Stars were "lying idle for a few weeks, on a sort of a recruiting vacation, so the next game they play they may be able to do some good work."[7] That implies a lack of rigidity about their roster, which could have resulted in Grant as a new Lone Star. It's also easy to envision Grant quitting quickly after a defeat so embarrassing that the team soon changed its name. It seems quite unlikely that his membership on the Lone Stars would have been fabricated, and he had to have been so memorable that he wasn't confused with some other player, even his own brother Clarence.

The Resolutes apparently reverted to calling themselves the Lone Stars in 1884, and on May 8 their roster included "C. Grant" as catcher. Ed Dwyer was no longer on the team, but Frank Dwyer was listed as the left fielder. A player named Grant got into at least one game, on May 31, between the Lone Stars and the Rose Hill team. "Mooney, Dwyre [sic] and Grant made some extraordinary plays," the *Pittsfield Sun* reported. The implication was that Grant played with the Lone Stars and not their opponents. By the time a revised roster was announced on July 10, there was no Grant on the Lone Stars.[8]

An amateur league had been organized for Berkshire County during May, and the first four teams to join it were Dalton's Lone Stars, the Pittsfield Eagles, the Renfrews of Adams, and the Rose Hills of Lee. The Greylocks gave the league a fifth team before the end of the month, but the Rose Hills dropped out within two months, and by the end of July, the Brunswicks had replaced the Lone Stars. At that point, the Renfrews and Greylocks were the top two teams.[9] By August, if not earlier, Frank Grant was pitching for the Greylocks.

The Greylocks existed at least as far back as 1881. The team may have originated at the Greylock Institute in South Williamstown, which Bliss Perry had attended during the 1875–1876 school year and where Grant may have played with the Rough and Readys in June of 1875. However, in September of 1882, a newspaper referred to them as the "Greylocks of North Adams."[10] It's possible two teams used that name around the same time. Because the team had existed for a few years, it's certainly conceivable that Frank Grant played for them prior to mid–1884. They simply didn't get much coverage in local papers before then.

On August 2, 1884, the Greylocks played the Brunswicks before about 300 fans. Leading off for Grant's opponents was future major leaguer Ervin Duane Curtiss, who was often called Irving but also Jim. Curtiss was three years older than Grant. His major league career consisted of 56 games in 1891, split almost evenly between Cincinnati in the National League and Washington in the American Association. Almost all of his minor league experience was in the Western League or the Western Association from 1887 to 1891. The Greylocks' lineup was Strunz, c; Grant, p; Flynn, 3b; Safford, ss; Morrisey, 1b; Bressette, lf; Mahaney, 2b; T. Crane, cf; and Basto, rf. Grant went 1-for-4 and scored a run. He gained seven of his eight assists by striking out opponents. He also had a putout. The Greylocks had a comfortable 9–0 lead after three innings and won, 13–7. Grant's only tough inning was in the eighth inning, when the Brunswicks scored all but one of their runs.[11]

The Greylocks played in Grant's birthplace on August 9, and they defeated Pittsfield's team, 11–9. The score was reported in the *Boston Sunday Globe,* yet coverage in Berkshire County newspapers was minimal. A box score for the Greylocks' game on August 16 showed that Curtiss had switched to the Greylocks. They hosted the Renfrews at Greylock, an unincorporated community between North Adams and Williamstown. Grant pitched again, but this time he had six assists other than by strikeout, plus three putouts. "In the latter part of the game the Greylocks did exceptionally fine playing, Grant, their pitcher, showing himself to much advantage," the *North Adams Transcript* reported. The Greylocks added just enough runs to take a late lead and hold on, 9–8.[12]

A week later, the Greylocks hosted the Brunswicks, but Curtiss remained with Grant's team. Grant went 4-for-5 with two doubles and three runs scored and was again the winning pitcher, 16–8. On September 11, an article previewing a rematch on September 20, "for $100 a side," listed Grant and Curtiss in the Greylocks' expected lineup, but also named Pettit as one of two substitutes.[13] There were other Pettit families in the county, but the 1870 census only showed Bob with a younger sister. Given his friendships with both Grant and Curtiss, it seems very likely that the sub was Bob or a cousin of his.

On September 27, the Greylocks hosted the Brunswicks yet again. "There was no money bet on the game, as the Brunswicks had some imported players," the *North Adams Transcript* reported. At a minimum, that probably included the Brunswicks' battery of Hubbell and Safford. Back in the springtime, the Williams College nine included pitcher J.C. Hubbell, plus captain J.H. Safford and W.B. Safford. One of those two Saffords was probably in the Greylocks' lineup with Grant in the three previous box scores, but it is unknown which one. Regardless, the visitors and their ringers won, 3–2. Grant had one of his team's three hits off Hubbell. Jim Curtiss wasn't in either lineup. He instead played with the Renfrews on the same day.[14]

At the end of 1908, the *North Adams Transcript* published a very long profile of Curtiss, seemingly based at least in part on an interview with him. A reporter for the *Berkshire Evening Eagle* interviewed him in 1944. The details presented in both articles seem fairly accurate. In the 1908 article, his early learning was traced from the Brunswicks to the Greylocks to the Renfrews. The 1944 article is less specific about that time period but indicates that Curtiss was with the Renfrews in 1885, and there are indeed at least four box scores from that year which include his surname. However, when Grant was mentioned in the 1908 article, he was identified as "a star pitcher for Renfrew," and his time with the Greylocks wasn't mentioned.[15] It's certainly possible Grant played with the Renfrews before and even briefly after his success with the Greylocks, but at present this 1908 article is the only indication of that.

It has been widely reported that the start of Frank Grant's baseball career outside of Massachusetts was in 1885 with a team named the Nameless in Plattsburgh, New York. That team's first game was on May 23,[16] but it generally didn't receive much coverage until weeks after Independence Day. As a result, it's unclear when Grant joined the team. It's possible that he played in Berkshire County before May 23 and even into August.

A lingering question has been why Grant chose to play in Plattsburgh, which is about 165 miles straight north of Williamstown. By contrast, Albany is less than 40 miles away and presumably would have presented many more options for an up-and-coming ballplayer in western Massachusetts. The answer may have been hinted at in the Nameless' box score for their loss on Wednesday, August 19 to the Witherbees of Port Henry, about 50 miles to the south. Grant had just turned 20 years old that month. The Nameless lineup against the Witherbees was: Bruley, lf; Grant, c; Safford, 3b; Hubbell, p; Weed, 2b; Squires, cf; Baker, rf; Tremblay, 1b; and Leary, ss. The score was close, 9–7, but it was a sloppy game. The Nameless made 16 errors and their opponents made 17. Grant made seven errors and had three passed balls, but the Witherbee catcher had the same total of miscues, except split five and five. As one result of the bad defense on both sides, the Nameless scored their seven runs on only two hits, one of which was by Grant.[17] The two players who batted right after him were probably why he was in Plattsburgh, because their surnames matched the Brunswicks' battery late the previous season. Barring a big coincidence, they were likely Williams College ballplayers. A Williams College box score for a game on June 8 included a Safford at third base and a Hubbell at shortstop, though J.C. Hubbell was known primarily as a pitcher.[18]

Julius Caesar Hubbell was an 1885 graduate of Williams College whose family lived about 10 miles north of Plattsburgh, in Chazy. He had a brother, George, who also attended Williams, but the latter apparently didn't play baseball there during the second half of the 1880s. "J. Safford" and "W. Safford" both appeared in Plattsburgh box scores the following summer, while Hubbell may not have, but Julius seemed to have a much stronger connection to Plattsburgh than the Saffords did.[19] Hubbell eventually moved to Washington State, where he served in the legislature from 1908 to 1926. In a fraternity's "catalogue" published in 1900, John Safford was a high school teacher in Newark, New Jersey, while his brother Walter was a lawyer in New York City.[20]

A story from around then eventually made its way to one of Grant's future teammates, Hall of Famer Sol White. As an illustration of Grant's fielding that "bordered on the impossible," White wrote that "it is said that during a game in Platsburg [sic], N.Y., while catching, he ran to a telegraph pole and climbing up about eight feet caught a foul fly. Otherwise it would have gone out of his reach over an embankment."[21] It's likely Grant was catching barehanded, as he did the following year on his first minor league team.[22] Berkshire County baseball historian James Overmyer, who helped get Grant into the Hall of Fame, traced this to a game on August 23 in which Grant was praised for his skill in catching four pop-ups. Those aren't particularly difficult plays unless they are near the stands, dugouts, or other obstructions, such as a telegraph pole. Overmyer pointed out that a few days earlier, a writer for Plattsburgh's *Morning Telegram* who usually praised Grant had already faulted him for such showmanship, which put entertaining the crowd ahead of the team's best interests (somehow). "The argument that the black participant was too flashy and undisciplined to be a truly good player was a common crutch for whites, at least until Jackie Robinson led blacks back into organized baseball," Overmyer wrote. "Although there is substantial evidence that Grant was, indeed, a flashy player, the *Telegraph*'s [sic] man may also have found it easy to rely on a not-yet-old saw to justify a touch of white superiority."[23]

Earlier in August, the Nameless played the Fort Edward Stars, and the *Plattsburgh Sentinel* called that opponent one "of the best amateur clubs in the state." Conversely, late in the month that same paper called the Nameless and the Witherbees professionals, though it was probably referring to their skills and not paychecks. Still, the regular ticket price for their next game was 25 cents, which is what Buffalo's International League team charged its fans a year later.[24] The Nameless tend to be considered semi-professional by baseball historians.

The climax of the Nameless' season was on October 1, when they played the Ogdensburg Stars on the last day of the Franklin County Fair in Malone. Originally the purse was $75, but it increased to $100. The round trip "excursion" fare from Plattsburgh for the 100-mile round trip was $1.50 "to accommodate those who may wish to visit the Malone Fair and witness the game between the Nameless and Ogdensburg nines," the *Sentinel* reported.[25] A daily in Troy, near Albany, reported that a considerable number of that city's residents also attended the fair by excursion train, to see the game that decided "the championship of northern New York."[26]

That day proved to be a very good one for Plattsburgh's nine. "The Nameless have added new laurels to their wreath of victories by their overwhelming defeat of the Ogdensburg team at the Malone fair, by a score of 24 to 1, in eight innings," a paper in Albany reported. "The only home run made was by Grant, that remarkable 'coon' of the home nine."[27] That certainly wouldn't be the last time Frank Grant was singled out for recognition but also subjected to racism in the same sentence. But the following year he would start proving again and again and again, on much bigger stages, that he wouldn't allow such primitive thinking to undercut his performance.

3

Magic in Meriden (April to July 1886)

Whenever kids have dreamed of pursuing a pro baseball career, they've surely envisioned a much prettier picture than this for themselves: In the absence of any regular media coverage of promising teenage athletes, you are a complete unknown. You recently signed your first pro contract to play with total strangers in a distant city that lacks a reputation for success in the sport. Though some of your older teammates have had some success in recent years, you might doubt early on that any of them will ever reach the major leagues (in which case time will prove you correct). Your squad seems to have been assembled hurriedly, barely had time for some practicing, and has played just two actual games. Your third opponent? A major league club! Best of luck not being humiliated or demoralized beyond belief! That sums up just the first few days of Frank Grant's career as a professional baseball player. The sequence of events leading up to this intimidating "baptism by fire" for him isn't completely clear, but it's no surprise that a key figure was his first manager.

Walter W. Burnham managed more than 20 years in the minor leagues, but 1885 was the first of those seasons, and he was only 25, or just five years older than Grant. On February 20, 1886, Burnham was named manager of a new franchise in the Eastern League, in Meriden, Connecticut.[1] He had to scramble to find players, and before the regular season, one of Meriden's daily newspapers advised readers not to be harsh about the team's performance because half of the eight teams in the league had had since the previous October to sign players for 1886.[2] Burnham had only six players under contract a week into March,[3] and on March 18, the national weekly *Sporting Life* announced that added to the Meriden roster was "Frank Grant, of Williamstown, Mass., a young colored catcher and general player, who is expected by his friends to do great work in the ball field the coming season." In the very next sentence, this article switched attention to Grant's childhood teammate, Bob Pettit, and mentioned that he lived in Meriden.[4] It makes perfect sense for experts to have theorized that Pettit set in motion his hometown pal's first professional contract.[5] In fact, Pettit began his own professional baseball career with a Meriden team in 1884, except in the Connecticut State League. In mid–1886, one Meriden daily was commenting about Frank Grant's all-round ability and mentioned that "Meriden has Bob Pettit to thank for him."[6]

It's unclear exactly when Pettit set this in motion, and how. It also seems possible that others played a role in Grant's migration to Meriden (which had a population around 20,000[7] and is roughly 100 miles south of Williamstown). One other ballplayer claimed exactly that. "Several people claim to have discovered Frank Grant, but the late

Eugene Bagley, of Long Island City, was the real discoverer of the colored wonder while playing with the Elmiras, of the New York League," claimed a Brooklyn newspaper in 1905. "Grant was a farmer's boy when Bagley first saw him and put him in a game, and he immediately made good, and a month later was signed by the Meriden Club of the Connecticut League."[8] Facts about Eugene Bagley, who played catcher and outfielder in five games for the National League's New York Giants late in the 1886 season, make this claim plausible. By April 24, 1886, Bagley had indeed joined a team in Elmira, New York, albeit in the *Pennsylvania* State Association (though by Opening Day the franchise was representing Scranton, Pennsylvania). However, a week earlier he caught for Long Island's Star Athletic Club,[9] which he played with the previous two seasons as well.[10] The Stars had started training for the 1886 season at their athletic club's gymnasium in early March, but Grant and the other Meriden players didn't begin their brief spring training in Meriden any earlier than April 9.[11]

Therefore, if Bagley did see Frank Grant in some game very early in 1886, it was most likely in or near New York City. If Grant was looking to play his 1886 home games in a city with numerous teams that likely paid players relatively well, New York was the most sensible choice as the country's most populous one. Also, Burnham was in New York on March 11 for an Eastern League meeting,[12] and he would have had every incentive for scouting for talent there, as he did less than a week later in the Boston area.[13] This isn't to say Burnham and Bagley necessarily had contact, just that if Grant played a little ball around New York City in early 1886, Burnham could have been in a position to see or hear about that. Burnham could also have made initial contact prior to any communication with Pettit. It's quite possible Grant knew that Pettit was living in Meriden, in which case Grant could have suggested to Burnham that it would be easy to get an endorsement from Pettit. If Bagley didn't flat-out fabricate this claim (and what would he stand to gain?), it's certainly possible he was unaware somebody else may have deserved more credit for having "discovered" Frank Grant.

Regardless, on April 12, 1886, Frank Grant and his new teammates had a "practice game" at their ballpark, and one local paper said all of them performed "finely, especially the (colored) catcher, who did good playing. He is a good all around player, and makes an excellent throw to the bases."[14] Meriden papers would rarely mention Grant's race again, especially once the regular season began. An immediate example of omitting that fact was the same paper's report of the team's first real game on April 14, at home against Trinity College of Hartford. Meriden devastated the collegians, 22–0. Grant was mentioned just once in the description of the game, though he was the first player named, and with good reason: "Grant's drive for a home run over the left field fence brought forth storms of applause and drove the 600 spectators wild with delight." His was the only homer that day.[15]

Two days later, he also starred in a win against a team from Springfield, Massachusetts, 14–4. "Grant, the colored player, covered himself with glory by his excellent playing and was loudly applauded many times," reported the *Daily Republican*. "His base running was especially fine. At one time when at the bat, he made a two-base hit to an ordinary man, but actually touched the third bag before the Springfields got control of the ball." This was off a pitcher named Keating, presumably the Bob Keating who pitched exactly one major league game, with Baltimore of the American Association the next year.[16] On Meriden's roster, many of the regular players had at least a little prior major league experience, though most of that was limited to 1884, when talent was spread thin by the simultaneous existence of three major leagues.[17] None of Grant's Meriden teammates ever played in a major league during 1886 or later, though the players who missed fewer than nine of the team's games were all under the age of 28.

On April 17, 1886, less than a week into his first spring training as a professional, Frank Grant and his Meriden teammates hosted none other than a National League team, the Detroit Wolverines. The visiting lineup included future Hall of Famers in Dan Brouthers and Deacon White, who, along with teammates Hardy Richardson and Jack Rowe, had been known previously as Buffalo's "Big Four" until they were acquired from that withering franchise by Detroit as that season wound down.[18] Detroit's pitcher that day was Pretzels Getzien, who went on to win 30 games that season and lose only 11. Thus, at the age of 20 and in only his third preseason game as a pro, Frank Grant already faced top-line major league pitching. It's no wonder Meriden managed only three hits in that game and lost, 11–0. Grant had played center field the first two games, but this time he was Meriden's catcher. The Detroit and Meriden papers' box scores disagreed on how many at-bats, assists, errors, and passed balls he had, though they agreed he was hitless and made six putouts. The *Daily Republican* did mention that Grant was one of only three Meriden players to reach second base during the game. More importantly, it reported that "Grant caught excellently and made good throws to bases as a rule."[19]

Starting on April 19, Meriden played on six consecutive days. The first and third games were against a team from Newburyport, Massachusetts, and Grant pitched in both. In the first, he relieved starting in the third inning of a 7–2 loss. In the other game against Newburyport, he relieved after the *first pitch*, and he was the winning pitcher when Meriden prevailed, 5–4. In between those two games, he played left field in a 10–4 loss to the New England League team in Portland, Maine (where Burnham lived).[20]

The day after Grant's pitching victory, Meriden defeated Utica of the International League by the same score, though it took 12 innings to decide. Grant pitched a complete game the next day 10 miles to the north in New Britain, as the first half of a two-city doubleheader between the same teams. Utica barely beat him and his teammates, 4–3. The later game was back in Meriden, but the home nine was shut out, 5–0. Buffalo, also of the International League, visited on April 24. Meriden batted first and scored three runs with only one out, but rain caused play to be suspended, and the game was eventually cancelled.[21]

Frank Grant wasn't even two weeks into his pro career when he received significant attention in a daily paper in New York City, *The Sun*. A long paragraph reporting about Meriden's team was almost all about him. It alluded to the game against Trinity College and to at least the first of his pitching stints. The text about him read:

> This season the interest is increased in the national game by the presence of a full-blooded African in the Eastern League team located here. His name is Frank Grant, and he comes from Williamstown, Mass. He has already proven himself to be a great ball player, especially in the pitcher's box. He hurls balls with great speed, and he stops the hottest liners with the utmost ease. He signaled his advent here by making a home run, and the ball is yet missing. Grant is black as night, intelligent, and gentlemanly. His knowledge of base ball was gained on the campus of Williams College, where he was a favorite with the collegians. Grant is only 18 [sic] years old, but he is a model athlete, and will be a great drawing card in Newark, Jersey City, and the other Eastern League towns.[22]

The *Boston Globe* printed most of this same overview three days later, so Grant was introduced early on to many sports fans in two of the country's biggest baseball cities.[23]

On April 28, the Meriden nine played one more preseason game, against Yale in New Haven. Yale put up a much better fight than did Trinity College, but Meriden won comfortably, 9–3. Grant played second base for the first time and had four hits in five at-bats, including a double. He also scored three runs. Grant presumably liked the calls by the Yale student who umpired, listed in the campus newspaper's box score as "Stagg, '88."[24] That was presumably Amos Alonzo Stagg, then a Yale pitcher, whose 71 years as a college football coach was the longest such career ever.[25]

That set the stage for the Eastern League's Opening Day on May 1. Meriden played its first game in Waterbury, Connecticut, about 15 miles to the west. Fittingly, for Frank Grant's first pro game that counted in the standings, Bob Pettit played second base for Waterbury. Grant started out at second base himself but was moved to catcher midgame. More than 2,000 fans saw Waterbury win easily, 10–2.[26] Grant was hitless in three at-bats, but his work as his nine's second catcher drew praise: "Grant came from second base, where he had been doing good work in the fifth inning, and went behind the bat," noted the *Meriden Journal*. "He did not use any gloves, and his catching was much admired."[27]

Fielding at any position without a glove had been common once upon a time, but by 1886 catchers did have means to protect their hands, and the use of masks and chest protectors was common.[28] One Meriden paper commented about catchers' mitts the month after Grant's barehanded effort: "The gloves used by catchers are now rather formidable affairs, especially in the left-hand mitten, which resembles a young boxing glove," said the *Daily Republican*. Nevertheless, there were holdouts at various positions. In fact, the last barehanded major league player, third baseman Jerry Denny, fielded that way until his retirement in 1894.[29] The dynamic between pitchers and batters also differed from today in several significant ways in 1886. That was the last season during which major leaguers could request a high or low pitch, which effectively halved the strike zone. The number of called balls by the umpire to earn a walk to first base changed between seasons several times in that era. For 1887, five were needed to get such a free pass—which was scored *as a base hit* for just that one season!—and a strikeout was the outcome after *four* strikes, not three.[30] Also, it wasn't until the 1893 season when a pitching rubber was set at the current distance of 60 feet, six inches, meaning pitchers' strides while hurling the ball during the 1880s could legally result in them ending up about four feet closer to the batter.[31]

Still, many important aspects of the game had already been locked in place, and things that sportswriters complained about wouldn't seem out of place today. As two examples, the *Meriden Journal* grumbled that the city's various pro teams had "never yet" had the pleasure of playing Opening Day at home, and when they lost their home opener by a score of just 4–3 to the same team on May 3 (with a scheduled day off in between), the paper bemoaned three blown opportunities to at least tie the game late if players had been "wide awake." The *Journal* singled out Meriden's runner on third base in the ninth inning who somehow failed to tag up and score when Frank Grant smacked a long fly to the left field power alley. Though Grant was deprived of a run batted in and went hitless for a second game, he at least scored his first official run, and he played a flawless second base with four putouts and six assists.[32]

The next day, hosting Providence, Frank Grant came alive. Though Meriden lost again, 10–5, Grant had his first two regular-season hits as a pro, both doubles, in four at-bats. Both hits apparently came off reliever Doc Landis, who had 42 starts as a major league pitcher in the American Association during 1882. Grant started out at second base but switched to catcher before the first inning was over. Later in the game, he made his official pro debut as a pitcher, and the *Meriden Journal* dubbed him "General Utility Man Grant." He relieved during or at the conclusion of the sixth inning, and didn't yield runs in the seventh or eighth frames. If he cycled through all nine Providence batters, then he had to pitch against a future Hall of Famer, Tommy McCarthy.[33] More importantly, Grant began a 14-game hitting streak only three games into his first regular season as a professional.

Rain kept the two teams from playing a rematch the next day, so it wasn't until May 5 that Meriden won its first game. Thanks in part to Grant's three hits in four at-bats, including another pair of doubles, his team beat Providence, 12–8. The next day he made his first start as a pitcher, in Hartford, and hurled a complete game in a tough defeat, 4–1. Though he gave up 10 hits and three earned runs, five errors by his teammates didn't help matters. On the other hand, Grant benefited greatly in the fifth inning when three of his fielders turned a triple play.[34]

Rain kept Meriden from playing the next four days. In the meantime, on May 10 the *Journal* reported that some baseball enthusiasts in nearby New Britain were anticipating the "disbandment" of Meriden's team and were preparing to offer a replacement.[35] Instead, it turned out that two *other* Eastern League teams, both in much larger cities, folded within a month.

Grant may have been very embarrassed in a loss on May 12 to Waterbury at home, 11–7, after he was charged with five errors.[36] However, the two teams combined to make 29! More painful for Meriden was blowing a 7–0 lead and never scoring again. Back in Hartford the next day, Meriden won its second game of the season, 4–2, and Grant reverted to errorless play. Astonishingly, Meriden turned its second triple play against that team in just under a week, and this time it came in the seventh inning when Hartford was threatening to at least tie the score after their first two men reached base. Meriden's catcher retired the batter on a foul tip, threw to Grant at second to retire one stray runner, and Grant threw to first to nail the other. Grant also made a key contribution at bat and on the bases in this close contest by scoring the first run. In the second inning, he dropped a bunt along the first-base line "not a dozen feet from the home plate," and reached safely. He stole second base and later third, which allowed him to score on a groundout.[37]

Though Grant's hitting streak continued, Meriden lost games the next two days, followed by an open date on May 16. At that point they had won only two games and lost seven. The next two days, they played the teams that soon disbanded. First, they won in Providence, 5–1. "Talk about style," commented the *Meriden Journal*. "When the Meridens arrived home from Providence this afternoon each man wore a nobby white Derby hat [and] a blue Norfolk jacket."[38] The team would later be teased for such matching outfits.

Next up was a game at home against the Long Island Athletics. Meriden won that contest as well, 4–3. In addition to a second consecutive game in which he had two hits in four at-bats, Grant helped with a key defensive gem. "Grant made a wonderful catch and received the heartiest kind of applause for it," reported the *Journal*. "It started on a dead line toward the center field fence. Like a rocket, Grant who was playing between first and second shot up in the air and grabbed the ball in his left hand. It was a remarkable catch." The game also featured an inning in which Meriden fielders threw out three runners at home plate.[39] Two days later, the Eastern League team from Bridgeport visited but Meriden was victorious again, and the three-game winning streak proved to be their longest.

The streak was snapped in Bridgeport two days later, but Grant had a very good game on offense. At least two Bridgeport sportswriters were impressed: "Grant, the colored second baseman of the Meridens, is as nimble as a jumping jack," said the *Bridgeport Standard*.[40] Another paper in that city elaborated. "Grant, the young colored boy who guards second base for the Meridens is the best player on that team," said the *Bridgeport News*. "He also led his club in batting, securing three out of their nine hits. His daring base running was greatly admired."[41] From May 25 through 29 Grant's team suffered four losses against two teams in New Jersey, but he apparently deserved no blame. "Grant, the second baseman of the Meridens, is one of the finest players in that position that has ever been seen in this city, and is a valuable player on that team," declared the *Newark Press-Register*. "In fact, in yesterday's game he was nearly the whole team."[42] He played catcher on May 28, and the *Jersey City Argus* credited his "jumping or diving to stop wide pitched balls. The fine play and good nature of Grant made for him many friends in the goodly audience, and they enthusiastically applauded his good play and encouraged him at the bat, which he handled skillfully."[43] Other papers in those two cities reportedly chimed in likewise: "Grant is the man of honors during the trip of the Meridens to New Jersey," summarized the *Meriden Journal*. "The Newark papers speak of him as a marvel, and the organs in Jersey City also give him much praise for his excellent playing."[44] As another result of the first of Meriden's games in New Jersey, Grant received positive exposure nationally in *Sporting Life* for at least the third time, and only one month into his first season as a pro: "Grant, their colored second baseman, received frequent and deserved applause for his neat playing."[45]

Speaking of New Jersey, the *Meriden Journal* boldly endorsed a rather unique team in that state to replace the Eastern League team that had just folded: "Why not try to enter the Trenton colored team in the place of the Long Islands? A colored team would draw well, particularly as they are said to be playing good ball." The *Journal* was referring to a relatively new nine of historic significance, the Cuban Giants.[46] They had formed in 1885 as the first African American professional team.

Frank Grant went hitless in the last of the four games in New Jersey, which ended his 14-game hitting streak that began back in Meriden's third game. Over that span, he had 22 hits in 57 at-bats for a .386 batting average, though he hit no higher than sixth in the batting order. His team concluded May with a doubleheader in Providence, and Grant went right back to treating opponents' pitchers mercilessly: In eight at-bats, his five hits included two doubles.[47] The Providence club disbanded less than a week later. Neither that franchise nor Long Island's was replaced.

For the first week of June, Walter Burnham slid Grant up into the fifth spot in the batting order, and on June 8 moved him into the fourth spot. That turned out to be Burnham's last game as Meriden's manager. His team won only seven Eastern League games and lost 17. For the next day's game, he was replaced by the former major league veteran Jack Remsen, a Brooklyn native who had played with Hartford's Eastern League team for most of May. In contrast to Burnham, Remsen served as a player-manager, mostly as an outfielder with a few games at first base mixed in. Remsen was the only player to continue as Frank Grant's teammate throughout 1887 and into 1888.

Remsen's first game was in Hartford, against his previous team, on June 9. He kept the second baseman batting fourth in Meriden's batting order, and Grant responded in the third inning with a triple that drove in two runs. He tried to score on a fielder's choice, but the *Daily Republican* said he "was called out at the home plate by the umpire *after turning a somersault* [emphasis added] and scoring a run fairly in the minds of many present." Nevertheless, Meriden ultimately prevailed in Remsen's debut, 8–3.[48] Around that time, a little praise of Grant was echoed in some newspapers published nowhere close to Eastern League franchises. "Grant, the colored second baseman of the Meridens, is distinguishing himself by good batting and fielding," said papers in Vermont and Maryland.[49]

By coincidence, on June 9, his team from a year earlier, Plattsburgh, had a second baseman named Grant when it hosted the University of Vermont's nine. He was in Plattsburgh's lineup again eight days later for a rematch in Burlington, except in that contest he also played catcher. He played in a few other games that month.[50] This couldn't have somehow been a case of Frank Grant moonlighting, because Meriden and Plattsburgh played far apart on the same days at least twice. Though the player's race wasn't mentioned, one possibility is that Grant's brother Clarence had been recruited by Plattsburgh. Of course, another possibility is that it was simply some local white player who happened to play Frank's main positions. There was at least one player named Grant during 1886 in that part of New York State, with Malone's Elm City club 50 miles to the west, an African American catcher on what was presumably a white team.[51] In any case, this mystery may never be solved.

Frank Grant had a historic encounter with a famous African American catcher on June 15, when former major leaguer Moses Fleetwood Walker was behind the plate for his new team, Waterbury, and Meriden visited. Walker made his major league debut on May 1, 1884, for Toledo of the American Association, and played 42 games for them that season. He started the 1885 season with Cleveland's team in the Western League, but it folded earlier in June, and the entire league did on June 15. On this occasion, Walker caught a shutout, which ended 6–0. Grant, who batted in the fourth spot, had a single in the game, to lead off the second inning. He stole second and third, but ultimately he "was put out at the home plate" by Walker. The detailed account in the *Daily Republican* was vague about that play, but the other two outs in the inning were both strikeouts, so Grant was either thrown out trying to steal home or picked off third base and retired by Walker down the baseline. For his part, Walker had two singles in three at-bats. He contributed seven putouts and two assists to offset a passed ball and an error. Grant was flawless in the field, with five putouts and three assists, one of each coming on the contest's only double play.[52]

There was a rematch the next day in Meriden, and the two African American sporting pioneers met on the field again. Waterbury had just three hits, though Walker had one of them, and he scored their only run on the way to a 3–1 loss to Grant's nine. Grant had a double to lead off the second inning but was erased on a fielder's choice. Neither Grant nor Walker was charged with an error, though the latter did have a passed ball.[53]

Meriden won three of its first five games under Jack Remsen but then lost three straight, the last two by a single run each. However, there must not have been much tension within the team, because on the following open date, they went fishing together.[54] Around that same time, the *Daily Republican* implied that Grant in particular was enjoying the camaraderie of friendly competition between teammates: "Grant is practicing all of his spare time on the checker board and is rapidly becoming an expert." This minute detail about his life was even mentioned in the *Hartford Journal*.[55]

Meriden's next game was at home on June 26 against Waterbury, one of the league's two best teams. The contest was characterized as a benefit of sorts, to save the franchise. A crowd of 1,200 turned out to support Meriden, and Frank Grant rose to the occasion. In five at-bats, he doubled and hit his first regular-season home run as a pro (and his only one for Meriden). He also scored three runs and was flawless on defense, with four putouts and five assists. Meriden won, 12–1. This was the third and final contest between Grant and Fleet Walker in 1886.[56]

Meriden's Willie Murphy had hit an impressive home run to center field in the sixth inning, and fans passed a hat throughout the stands to take up a financial reward for him. The *Meriden Journal* described Grant's at-bat in the next frame at length:

> The silver for Murphy was still remaining in the hat when Grant took up the bat in the seventh inning. The tinkle of the quarters as they fell on the "dollars of our daddies" reached the little colored baseman's ear as he swung his bat. An I-want-some-of-that smile o'erspread his face. It was changed to a set expression as an incurve came towards him about two feet from the ground. A vicious motion of the bat; a sharp crack and the ball was soaring over Mansell's head.... When Mansell got down to the fence he was tired, but he had to climb over and get the ball that had been so unmercifully pounded. The scene over Murphy's hit was repeated, as Grant came trotting home. He walked over to the players' bench, shook hands with Murphy and sat down. The hat went round again, and when at the close of the first half of the ninth inning Umpire Farrow called Murphy and Grant to the plate to receive their gifts, he handed them each a hat containing $21.35. Then the crowd cheered again. The recipients took off their caps in acknowledgement of the generosity of their admirers.[57]

The *Daily Republican*'s coverage instead focused on Grant's fielding, by describing a tactic he had perfected by that game: "Grant was up to his old tricks in making a double play. His modus operandi is to stand on the line[,] take what pick ups come along, touch the man running from 1st to 2d and then throw it quickly to 1st. He has done it many times this season."[58] In fact, he employed it once again at a crucial point in their victory on June 30.

First, though, on June 29 Grant tried to replicate his batting feat that won him some money. Before Meriden started getting clobbered at home by Jersey City that day, when he went up to bat in the first inning a fan yelled, "Home run!" The *Daily Republican* reported that this motivated Grant to swing so hard that he broke his bat (and he did make contact, but the paper didn't report the outcome so it must not have amounted to much). Over the course of the game, he only managed a single, but the day was significant because of two other ballplayers who were present. One was future Hall of Fame manager Connie Mack of the league's Hartford team, who was called upon to sub for the regular league umpire.[59] Mack made his major league debut later that season. Meanwhile, presumably watching the game from Jersey City's bench was their new African American pitcher, George Stovey, who had debuted just three days prior. Stovey ended 1886 with a sparkling 1.13 earned run average and a 16–15 record for Jersey City. All 31 were complete games, but none were against Grant's nine.[60] It so happened a few days later that Grant received a little attention in an African American newspaper of note, when the *Cleveland Gazette* reported that "Grant, the colored second baseman of the Meridens, is distinguishing himself by good batting and fielding."[61]

Meriden hosted Newark on June 30, and thanks in part to Grant's triple and two

3. Magic in Meriden (April to July 1886)

singles, the home team led, 7–1, after seven innings. However, Newark scored twice in the eighth inning and threatened in the ninth by getting runners on first and second with just one out. The next play should have been ruled a force by Grant at second base for the second out, but the umpire admitted after the game that he blew the call. "This filled the bases with Coogan, the heavy hitter, at the bat," reported the *Journal*. "It looked as if several runs would be scored, but the audience gave a sigh of relief when Coogan hit a sharp grounder to Grant, who touched Knowlton as he ran down to second and then threw to first and cut off Coogan, making a sharp double play and ending the game with a victory for Meriden." Alas, the league standings printed on that same page of the paper showed Meriden in last place, with just 12 wins to 24 losses.[62]

Even worse, that contest at the end of June proved to be the Meriden nine's final victory. They lost eight straight and played their last game on July 10, at which point their roster was scattered to the winds. Meriden survived for two full months after speculation surfaced during the second week of the regular season that its franchise was ill-fated, but those early skeptics had few reasons during that span to doubt they'd eventually be validated.

It's certainly plausible that the losing streak resulted at least in part because the players strongly sensed or even had very concrete reasons to believe the end was near. Regardless, Frank Grant did not give up the fight, and he had at least one hit in each of the seven concluding losses. In particular, during a pair of close home-and-away losses to Bridgeport on July 5, he contributed three hits in each game, with three doubles. For the last five games of June, he'd been promoted from fourth to third in the batting order, and for this two-city doubleheader he was moved up to second in the lineup.[63]

The *Bridgeport News* reported in detail about a bigot's actions during the 15-inning second game (using "kick" as slang, meaning to complain). When he first saw Grant go up to bat, the spectator "was intensely disgusted," and shared his opinion aloud:

> "I think that's a shame," said the Bridgeporter. "They've no business to put a nigger playing ball among white men. If they can't get white men to play ball they'd better give up the business." It wasn't more than five minutes before the catcher made a wild throw to second base. Little Grant jumped three feet into the air and neatly stopped the ball. The Bridgeporter who had been kicking [complaining] so vigorously was enthusiastic in praise. "Did you see that?" he demanded excitedly. "That was a beautiful catch." In a few minutes more another wild throw came in from right field, Grant bounded into the air and stopped it with one black hand. The former kicker was completely subdued by this time. "I've nothing more to say," he remarked; "that nigger can play ball. He has completely won me over. I'll never kick again about a colored man's playing ball." From that time on, during the whole game he watched Grant's playing with undisguised admiration. He was thoroughly converted.[64]

On July 8, the *Daily Republican* pointed out that "Grant played ball with a vim and freshness that relieved the spritless [sic] work of the rest of the players."[65] It was widely known for at least 48 hours before that Meriden's game in New Britain against Newark on July 10 was the nine's finale and that it would disband afterwards.[66] One of the local dailies reported that Grant exited the Eastern League with a batting average of .306, eighth best in the Eastern League. Baseball-reference.com shows it as .316, and early Grant biographer James Overmyer had a source indicating that Grant's average was .325, almost 100 points higher than the Eastern League's overall average. Grant also led all second basemen in total chances accepted with 238 in 42 games at the position (among his 44 games overall). That total was 82 more—or two per game more—than the player with the best fielding percentage at that position, Bill Greenwood of Newark. Out of 156 chances, Greenwood made only nine errors, for a fielding percentage of .942. Grant's was reportedly fifth-best, with 23 errors out of 238 chances for a .903 percentage. Greenwood, who already had two years of major league experience, added to his total by spending the next four years in the American Association.[67]

By happenstance, around this time Grant received additional nationwide exposure in *Sporting Life*, when that weekly reported that he and his hometown friend Bob Pettit were "said to be the best all-round players in the Eastern League—capable of playing any position from the pitcher's box to the outfield."[68] At this juncture, there was yet another instance of a sportswriter analyzing a very specific detail of Grant's prowess. This time it was the distinct manner in which he tagged baserunners. "Grant of the Meridens is certainly a wonderful player," reported the *Hartford Courant*. "Whenever he attempts to touch a man out he does it in such a thorough way that the umpire is seldom in doubt."[69]

Frank Grant was a free agent for only two days.

4

Buffalo and Immediate Stardom (July to October 1886)

After just two days as a free agent, Frank Grant was signed by manager Jack Chapman of the International League's Buffalo Bisons on July 12, 1886, along with Meriden first baseman-outfielder Steve Dunn and player-manager Jack Remsen. Grant and Dunn had met the Bisons in Meriden on April 24, though in a contest rained out in the first inning. When the trio's signing was announced in the *Buffalo Times*, Grant was called "a tawney colored [yellowish brown] Spaniard with a wonderful fielding record on second base."[1] This "Spaniard" charade surfaced elsewhere but didn't last for long.[2] The *Times* mentioned him again the next day, though it didn't allude to his complexion when it raved about his batting and "wonderful" fielding record. "In Grant there is no doubt but that the Buffalos have secured a prize," the *Times* proclaimed. Meanwhile, his signing by such a prominent franchise was reported back in his previous city, naturally. "His salary will be $150 a month, and he is worth every penny of it," the *Meriden Journal* asserted.[3] That was reportedly double what he was paid with the Meriden nine.[4]

Buffalo had been a member of the prestigious National League from 1879 until the end of the previous season. They had finished in third place in four of those seven seasons, most recently in 1884. Chapman had managed the Bisons in the National League for the last 88 games of the previous season, and in six other seasons before that he likewise led four other NL clubs. His best season by far as a major league manager was a little after this four-year stint with Buffalo, when he won a pennant in 1890 with the Louisville Colonels of the American Association. One Buffalo player who was a regular on the 1885 squad continued in 1886, pitcher Pete Wood, but he was cut unceremoniously as the new trio was being brought in.[5]

When Grant joined Buffalo, the team had played about as many games as Meriden had. On the morning of his debut, Buffalo was in sixth place in the eight-team circuit with a record of 18–28.[6] On July 14, 1886, Frank Grant made his debut in an International League game, when the club in first place, Toronto, visited Buffalo's Olympic Park. Chapman put Grant into the fourth spot of the batting order, followed by Dunn and Remsen. Grant's reputation must have been widely known among Bisons fans before he set foot on the field. "When Grant made his first appearance at the plate yesterday, he received a liberal round of applause, which he acknowledged by doffing his cap," one daily reported.[7]

The *Buffalo Courier* said threatening weather limited the home crowd to about 500. Grant's big contribution on offense came in the ninth inning, when he hit a triple off Toronto's ace, Daisy Davis. That drove in the final insurance run for a win in Grant's debut, 8–3. Davis, who had pitched in the majors the two previous seasons, rarely lost during 1886. He compiled a record of 16–7 and an imposing earned run average of 1.59. Grant didn't have much to do on defense, but he impressed nonetheless. "Grant had but two [chances], and picked them up in a way that aroused the enthusiasm of the spectators, and gave the impression that he is just what is wanted," the *Courier* reported. "He is quick and active as a cat, and as handy with the ball as if it were made for him."[8]

The detailed account in the *Times* differed from the *Courier*'s on a basic fact, stating that the crowd numbered only about 200. Much more significantly, it differed in tone, by blending in some casual racism with its high praise of Grant. For starters, the article's headline was "A Dusky Diamond," and the second subheadline read, "Grant, the New Second Baseman, Proves a Mascot for Buffalo." (The first subheadline simply said, "The Torontos Outplayed and Defeated Eight to Three.") Back in those days, to call a person a mascot meant someone who brought good luck, and didn't refer to the costumed characters associated with many teams of the current century. Some readers might have thought the headline's adjective was "Dusty" and referred to the playing field, but "dusky," meaning darkish, was often used in that era in reference to the skin color of African Americans. In sum, the headline seems to have been calling Buffalo's new mascot a gem, a valuable addition to the roster. Bolstering this interpretation is the fact that the first paragraph of the article was about Grant, though it swerved into bigotry. It read: "All day long yesterday Manager Chapman hummed softly 'There's a new coon in town,' and when the game between the Buffalos and Torontos was called at 4 p. m. the 'new coon' stood on second base. His name is Grant and he is evidently a ball player."[9]

Over a decade earlier, there was a popular song (or "rag") called "There's a New Coon in Town," and it was apparently still around into the 1890s.[10] Assuming the sportswriter who connected this song to Chapman didn't spend the entire day with him, the only way that journalist could've known what (if anything) the manager continuously "hummed softly" was if Chapman revealed it. It's possible the writer was trying to be playful (at Grant's expense, possibly Chapman's as well) and that this paragraph was hyperbole, not to be taken literally. Regardless, even if this humming was fiction, if might very well have captured a general discomfort Chapman had, or would have in the near future.

Buffalo also won Grant's second game the next day, against Binghamton, at the start of a road trip. The Bisons didn't score in the first eight innings but pushed across two unearned runs in the ninth and prevailed, 2–1.[11] The two

Grant made an immediate splash. "Mascot" is used to mean a provider of good luck. From July 15, 1886.

teams played again the next day, and the starting pitcher for the Bisons was Michael Firle. He gave up five runs in the first inning, and Chapman decided to switch hurlers for the second frame. He chose Grant, who proceeded to hold the home team scoreless for the next six innings. In the meantime, the Bisons quickly tied the score and led, 12–5, going into the eighth inning. Binghamton did score off Grant, but he finished the job and Buffalo won, 13–8. The next day's baseball headline in the *Times* was "The Colored Curver," and the paper's brief account gave him total credit for the victory.[12] Grant and his new teammates almost made it four in a row one day later, before about 900 fans in Utica. The Bisons trailed, 6–3, when Grant led off the ninth inning with his second hit of the game. The next two Buffalo batters reached on errors to load the bases with no outs. Grant and Remsen soon scored, but the Bisons just couldn't get a third runner home, and the game ended, 6–5.[13] Still, for Frank Grant it was so far, so good.

However, in Syracuse on July 23, the Bisons received a scare about their budding star. While running to first base, Grant sustained an unspecified injury. Box scores don't list a substitute player, but he was hampered enough to be kept out of the next day's rematch. If he'd been unable to play long-term, the *Syracuse Standard*, for one, would've considered it tragic, because that daily raved about his performance against the Stars:

> Grant, the colored player, is a dandy. He covers an acre of ground, is quicker and spryer in his movements than any other player seen at Star park [sic], and to watch him play was the interesting point of the game. If there are any more colored players lying around, be they Chinamen, Malays, or even Esquimaux, bring them to Syracuse if they can play ball like that Grant. He was the favorite with the audience and was applauded on every slight provocation.[14]

Buffalo had no game on July 25 because it was a Sunday, and the next day the Bisons returned home for an exhibition game against a local amateur team called the Travelers. Grant wasn't in the box score, so he had three consecutive days off.[15] He returned to action on July 27 when Buffalo hosted Toronto before 1,500 fans. He showed no effects of an injury, with a triple on offense and errorless fielding. In fact, a snide remark in the *Times* suggested that he would have had an inside-the-park homer if not for bad coaching at third base.[16] Buffalo led 8–7 after seven innings but ended up losing, 9–8. The *Buffalo Commercial Advertiser* blamed the loss on errors by other Bisons infielders, and added that upon his return to Buffalo, Grant had become "a general favorite."[17] Three days later, he proved again that his legs were in fine shape when he doubled and tripled in a loss to Oswego.[18]

International League statistics were published in early August, and Frank Grant's fielding percentage of .926 tied him for second among second basemen, just .001 behind the leader. Buffalo's fielding percentage as a team was .846. His batting average was .296, good enough for 15th in the circuit. As a frame of reference, Utica led all clubs with a collective average of .271.[19] At this time, the *Syracuse Standard* again sang Grant's praises, declaring that "Grant is one of the best all-around players in the country, seeming at home in every position."[20]

A few days later, Buffalo residents were again told about his prowess as a fielder, after a game against Utica. "Grant's brilliant plays for the Buffalo side were deservedly applauded by the 1,500 odd spectators," the *Sunday Truth* said. "Some of his work was truly phenomenal, of the twelve different chances offered him he made correct plays on eleven, the error being a bad throw to first of a difficult stop in the third inning."[21] Up to this point, anyone following Grant's career closely may have thought of him exclusively as a determined and serious athlete. Perhaps the frequent applause and consistent praise in newspapers prompted him to relax a little and display another facet of his personality, because after a game in nearby Hamilton, Ontario on August 10, the *Buffalo Express* mentioned that "his antics for the benefit of the grand stand were very funny."[22] He thus connected to something of a tradition among African American ballplayers: demonstrating that they weren't simply athletes, but also entertainers.[23]

Grant missed a game in Utica on August 14 due to "a strained leg," and Buffalo didn't play the next day because it was a Sunday. Monday's scheduled game against Syracuse was rained out,[24] and Grant was seemingly back to normal on Tuesday. The game was tied after five innings, 3–3, and Buffalo scored the only other run in the eighth. Therefore, every play counted, and the Bisons' second baseman contributed one: "Grant bobbed up as usual yesterday in a phenomenal play, making a running catch that looked like an impossibility," reported the *Courier*.[25] So much for the strained leg. The use of "phenomenal" by at least two Buffalo newspapers that month seems to have been the basis of compliments in the national weekly *Sporting Life*, which, in turn, were reprinted in Buffalo and cities outside New York, including in the Deep South.[26]

Around the same time, the *St. Louis Republican* noted that professional baseball now had "two very fine colored players" who both happened to be second basemen, Grant and Bud Fowler of Topeka, Kansas. The paper betrayed its bigotry in its concluding sentence (emphases added): "There is no *danger*, however, of either of them ever entering one of the prominent leagues, as base ball is *ahead* of other professions in this regard." In contrast to the widespread repeating of the *Sporting Life*'s praise, this remark might only have been quoted in a Topeka newspaper.[27] Regardless, it was evidence very far from Buffalo that Frank Grant, still in the midst of his first pro season, was already being perceived as one of the foremost challengers to any existing or expected color line.[28]

Of course, a player can compile an extraordinary record on a losing team, but that didn't apply to Grant and the Bisons. In August, they had the best record across the International League, with 14 wins and only seven losses.[29] Still, the *Times* wasn't satisfied with the team as a whole. In fact, just a few days into September, it seemed to imply that too many Bisons played it safe on defense, for fear of errors undercutting their fielding percentages. "Grant did some more of his wonderful playing at second, putting out nine men, assisting twice and making his customary error," the daily said about Buffalo's game on September 3. "If more of the other Buffalo players would play as Grant does, for the ball and not for a record, results might be greatly changed."[30]

The *Commercial Advertiser* made a similar comment later in the month: "Grant plays ball for all he is worth, regardless of errors. He is a second Dunlap."[31] Starting in April of the following year, Frank Grant was frequently called the "Colored Dunlap" or the "Black Dunlap," referring to the best fielding major league second baseman of the era, Fred Dunlap. This comment may have planted the seed for that nickname. It spread quickly among daily newspapers in just two weeks, with examples in such cities as Pittsburgh, Boston, Cleveland, and Nashville.[32] It was also used by at least two nationwide weeklies, *The Sporting News* and *Sportsman's Referee*.[33] Dunlap was an obvious choice for comparison because he led his league in assists or finished second in six years, and he was likewise first or second in double plays six times. No player was paid more than him from 1886 through 1889, his final season as a regular.[34]

During the season's final few weeks, Frank Grant continued to find new ways to

4. Buffalo and Immediate Stardom (July to October 1886)   39

remind fans of Dunlap. Early in the month, the *Times* used one play in particular to illustrate its claim that "Grant is a great ball player." On a fly ball hit near first base, Steve Dunn ran and got under it, while Grant ran to a spot behind him. "The ball bounded out of Dunn's hands and Grant caught it[,] retiring the side and saving Dunn an error," the *Times* reported. The paper credited Grant for "one of the best and neatest plays ever seen in Buffalo, which showed that it pays for one player to back another."[35]

In that same game, Grant hit his first homer in a Buffalo uniform, and it was no cheap shot: His three-run blast was to center field.[36] He added his second homer of the season on September 18, with doubles as his other two hits on the day.[37] On top of everything else he contributed to Buffalo's success, his power was starting to blossom fully.

That was the second-to-last game of the season, and when Buffalo played its last, the result was a record of 50 wins and 45 losses. In other words, the team jumped from 10 games under .500 to a winning record after Grant joined, by virtue of a 32–17 record during that span.[38] Statistics published shortly after the season concluded listed Grant with the league's third-best batting average, .347, from 67 hits in 193 at bats. Seventh on that list was teammate Jocko Fields, the 1886 Bison with the most notable major league career ahead of him. He was a year older than Grant and had just finished his second pro season. Fields played six years in the majors, from 1887 to 1892. Buffalo reportedly resigned Grant and Fields for 1887 by October 2, and it was said that Grant would "spend the winter clerking in this city."[39] Fields, however, spent all of 1887 in the National League with Pittsburgh. Despite cycling through multiple positions in most seasons and thus rarely being a regular in the majors, Fields was a .272 hitter lifetime and averaged 84 runs batted in and 24 stolen bases per 162 major league games. It's easy to envision Frank Grant entering the majors himself in 1887 or 1888 and at least matching those statistics.

On October 2, one of Grant's old teams back home, the Greylocks, had a catcher named Grant in a game against the Renfrew Reserves of Adams. The Bisons played an exhibition game on September 30 in Buffalo and parted company on October 1, so it's possible Grant sped home and played in this game.[40] Of course, other possibilities include that it was his brother Clarence, or just a player who happened to share their surname. About two weeks later, the *Buffalo Express* said that he was being employed locally by Charles W. Cushman of the Railway Car Association. Cushman was one of the directors of the Buffalo Baseball Company Limited and a member of the International League's scheduling committee.[41] (By coincidence, a Charles H. Cushman, who went by Charlie or Charley, managed Toronto's club against the Bisons in 1887 and 1888 and seemed to delight in telling a story about a racist attack on Grant in 1887.[42]) About two months later, a different Buffalo paper also reported on Grant's employment with the Railway Car Association, but just four days later, a third paper said he was working as a bellhop at the Genesee Hotel, according to an unnamed "contemporary." It's possible that he either switched jobs or added a second one, though the Genesee report could also have been erroneous.[43]

A few weeks into the offseason, Grant received high praise, and it was published nationwide by *Sporting Life*. "Manager Chapman has seen many great second basemen in his time, but Grant, the colored lad, he thinks beats them all," the weekly reported. "There is nothing he can't get or fails to go after. His agility is remarkable to a double-jointed degree."[44] The great second basemen Chapman had seen up to that point included Fred Dunlap, against whom Chapman had managed in three of the four previous seasons. Undercutting Jack Chapman's adulation somewhat was a remark he made about three months later, still in the midst of winter. "Manager Chapman perpetrates a joke at Grant's expense," revealed the *Sunday Truth*. "He says Grant is turning pale, waiting for the baseball season to open." The newspaper explained that Grant was the non-white player on the team, for those not in the know.[45] He must not have laughed much if that was the quality of humor he heard that winter.

5

A Bitter Pennant Battle (1887)

For many modern baseball fans impatiently awaiting spring training, reading up on their favorite players is one way to pass the time. Back during the offseason of 1886–1887, newspapers in Buffalo seemed to cater to that. That winter, the local fandom learned Grant's vital statistics. One daily reported Grant's weight as 150 pounds. Another reported it as 155 and added that he was 5'7" tall. In a list of 13 players, he was only taller than one, but the average was 5'9½". His teammates were all bunched from 21 to 24 years old except for Jack Remsen, who was 36. Three other players joined Grant at the low end of that age range.[1] At the end of March, the *Commercial Advertiser* provided mini-profiles of the 1887 Bisons. As part of Grant's, it mentioned that he was "sometimes called 'General.'" His marital status was stated as single, though the paper added, "but he grinned when he said so!" It didn't speculate about what that implied. Instead, it concluded with a prediction: "If all of the boys in the nine work as hard as Grant always does to win, the pennant will come to Buffalo."[2]

All eight of the International League's 1886 franchises continued in 1887, which reflected atypical stability for a minor league in that era. What's more, the circuit expanded to 10 teams by adding Newark and Jersey City from the Eastern League (in which Frank Grant had made his pro debut).[3] As a result, Fleet Walker and Frank Grant played in the same league for the second time, and Grant finally faced Walker's teammate, George Stovey, in an official game. In addition, the aforementioned Hall of Famer Bud Fowler was signed by Binghamton for 1887. Four more African American players spent time with International League teams in 1887. In addition to Fowler, Binghamton employed pitcher William James Renfroe (often spelled "Renfro") and apparently gave a tryout to an African American player named William Pointer or Pointter, though there are no known records that he played in a regular-season game. Syracuse developed a star in pitcher Robert Higgins, and Oswego had a second baseman named George Washington Randolph "Rans" Jackson, who was often called Randolph.[4] The International League's 1887 season was thus that century's high water mark for African Americans in professional baseball.[5]

For whatever reasons, very few Bisons from the 1886 team were also on the roster in 1887. The only ones were Grant, Remsen, and two career minor leaguers, pitching ace Mickey Walsh and utility man Tom Calihan. Grant, Remsen, and Walsh also played for Buffalo in 1888. Nevertheless, Jack Chapman must have been confident in his new players, because for their preseason games in April, which were all on the road, he tried to schedule as many as he could against major league teams.[6] Alas, Buffalo lost all 12 of those, plus four other preseason games, before it finally won its first of the month. On the other hand, Grant was praised all over the place during April.

On April 2, Frank Grant faced a major league team for the second time in his young career. This time it was in Pittsburgh against the National League's Alleghenys. Despite a "chilly atmosphere," 4,000 locals watched the game. The big leaguers won easily, 11–1, but that didn't obscure the day's star player, according to the *New York Sun*'s account. "The feature of the game was the brilliant work of Grant, the colored second baseman of the Buffaloes," the daily reported. "He had eleven chances, and accepted them all. His batting was also heavy." That last comment referred to the fact that he was the only Bison with two hits and had his team's only extra-base hits, both doubles. Those justified Chapman's batting him fourth.[7] Pitching for Pittsburgh was Ed Morris, who was in the middle of a seven-year major league career across which he compiled an impressive record of 171–122, for a winning percentage of .584. The *Buffalo Courier* seemed to indicate that the nickname "The Black Dunlap" originated for Buffalo's "hero" on this day because "the extent of territory covered by him in the infield earned him much applause" by the Pittsburgh fans. On defense, he also participated in both of the game's double plays.[8]

Buffalo didn't fare much better in Baltimore three days later amidst the cold and wind against that city's American Association team. In a five-inning game, the major leaguers prevailed, 10–4. Still, one Bison was again singled out for praise: "The playing of Grant, the colored second baseman of the Buffalos, was very creditable," said the *Baltimore Sun*. "He is quick in picking up and throwing the ball to bases, bats well and runs bases fearlessly." He scored a run, stole a base, and had two hits. Those both came off Matt Kilroy, whose record in the subsequent regular season was a staggering 46–19.[9] The teams played a full game the next day and though the Bisons lost again, the final score was a respectable 8–5. Grant again scored a run, stole a base, and had two hits.[10] However, it was his fielding that the *Baltimore American* focused on, calling him precise, quick, and one of the most active players ever. The paper was confident he was the top second baseman in the International League.[11]

Grant's hits in the second game at Baltimore were off Ed Knouff, a five-year major leaguer. Knouff switched midseason to the AA's eventual pennant winner, the St. Louis Browns, and five months after pitching against Grant, his new team was set to face the Cuban Giants in an exhibition. Many of the Browns signed an infamous letter refusing "to play against negroes," but Knouff was reportedly adamant about not signing it because he "had played with the Cuban giants once before last season, and … seemed to enjoy it better than a contest with white players."[12] It's certainly conceivable that Grant's success off him contributed to Knouff's stand.

On April 7, Buffalo traveled a short distance to face the Washington Nationals. The Bisons trailed, 4–1, in the ninth inning, when Grant led off. He hit a pitch over the left field fence but it was foul, and he then singled. He eventually scored, but the game ended on a close play at home and Buffalo suffered its tightest loss, 4–2. Grant's near-homer and hit came off veteran Jim Whitney, whose regular season record that year was 24–21.[13]

The teams met again the next day, and Buffalo lost yet again, this time 7–4. In his fifth game of the preseason against major league competition, Grant was held hitless for the first time, but it took future Hall of Famer Hank O'Day (inducted as an umpire, not a player) to accomplish that. Grant did get hit by a pitch and steal a base, but his seven putouts, two assists, and no errors were what won him praise again in the *Baltimore Sun*, which said he "played a brilliant fielding game and was frequently applauded."[14] By contrast, the *Washington Post* said, "Three nationalities were represented on the ball field yesterday—Irish, Dutch and darkey—and the verdict of the spectators was that it took Irishmen to play baseball." Without dignifying Grant by using his name, the *Post* suggested that Connie Mack was unfairly denied his second double of the day on a play at second base "principally because the umpire was dazzled by a one-handed catch of the darkey second baseman of the Buffalos."[15] That umpire was John McGlone, who, like Mack, had made his major league debut with Washington toward the end of the previous season. Before that promotion, McGlone had been Grant's teammate with Buffalo.

Sadly, the series finale on the third day was Buffalo's third blowout loss of the month, 16–5. The Bisons at least kept the score close through five innings, at 6–3. Grant had a single, a walk, and two stolen bases on offense. He played errorless ball at second base with four putouts and four assists.[16] Washington's pitcher for this third meeting was Dupee Shaw, who was entering his fifth and final year in a major league starting rotation.

On April 11, the Bisons were back visiting the Alleghenys, and they again lost by 10 runs, but plated seven this time instead of just one. Grant scored three runs in the lead-off spot and had two hits. They came off Bill Bishop (whose major league career lasted just seven games across three seasons). "There was a large colored delegation in the part to cheer Grant, 'the colored Dunlap,'" reported the *Pittsburgh Post*. "Grant did well and more than one dusky hill resident remarked: 'Ain't he a combusticator,' whatever that meant."[17] Following this game, one Buffalo daily declared Grant to be "the best player in the Buffalo nine, and the best second baseman in the International League."[18] At this point in the preseason road trip, his performance also earned attention in a national weekly. "The Buffalos are not doing as well as was expected," wrote a correspondent for *The Sporting News*. "Grant seems to be doing most of the playing."[19]

Meanwhile, one paper in another International League city tried to undercut Grant's burgeoning reputation. "Complaint is being made that Grant ... is being used as a star player by Manager Chapman of Buffalo," asserted the *Daily Leader* in Binghamton. "This accounts for the amount of ground he is allowed to cover ... and no attention is paid to such a thing as another man's territory."[20] It sounds like Chapman was being accused of encouraging Grant to show off, to the possible annoyance of nearby fielders who were in a better position to make a play on some batted ball. It seems doubtful that Chapman would risk undercutting team morale by imposing his will that way. Three months later, one of the Buffalo dailies described the exact opposite happening, to the team's detriment, in a play that involved right fielder Charlie Hamburg and first baseman Mike Lehane. On July 16, a Jersey City batter hit a high fly ball toward right field, which Grant and Hamburg both pursued. "Lehane called to Grant to catch it but Hamburg yelled 'I've got it,' and Grant, who could have captured it easily, stepped aside while Hamburg came thundering in from right field," the *Express* reported. "He just managed to get under, and then ingloriously made a muff." That allowed the tying run to score, though Buffalo ultimately won.[21]

The game in Pittsburgh on April 12 had a comparable result. Though Buffalo scored pairs of runs in each of the first four innings, they suffered another drubbing, 25–12. Grant contributed a double on offense. This time the home team used Jim Handiboe as its pitcher (his major league career was limited to 1886).[22] It was more of the same on April 13 as the Bisons lost, 15–6. Grant contributed a hit and a walk, this time off future Hall of Famer Pud Galvin, who had played for Buffalo's NL club from 1879 to 1885.[23]

Interestingly, after the second of these games, the periodical *Sportsman's Referee* was moved to argue on Grant's behalf:

> Grant, the colored second baseman of the Buffalos, did some more fine playing in the game on Tuesday with the Alleghenys. Several of his catches and stops were marvelous. Many persons were overheard to remark that he was playing in great luck, and that his phenomenal plays were due to Dame Fortune. It must be acknowledged that there is such a thing as luck connected with ball playing, but it generally takes phenomenal players to make phenomenal plays. All hail the "Black Dunlap."[24]

In the context of Grant's career after his stint with Buffalo, their game in Trenton, New Jersey, on April 15 was a milestone: The Bisons played the Cuban Giants. The outcome for Buffalo was little different than against the white major league teams during the first two weeks of April. Grant had four hits off Shep Trusty but Buffalo lost, 12–8.[25]

The next day, the Bisons were a short distance away for a game against Philadelphia's NL team. Buffalo lost, 18–4, but Grant did his best to contain the home team's batters, with six putouts, four assists, and no errors. On offense he contributed two hits plus a stolen base. In fact, one of those hits was a home run over the left field fence off Ed Daily, who had records of 26–23 and 16–9 for Philadelphia the two previous seasons.[26] Before the game, a newspaper familiar with Grant's work in Plattsburgh two years earlier reported that Daily "made fun of Grant" before the game by singing "There's a New Coon in Town" and telling teammates that he would toy with "that nigger." After Grant's home run and other at-bats that day, the *Glens Falls Times* wrote that Daily's opinion of Grant changed "and it is said he is ready to fight when anyone whistles 'There's a new coon in town.'"[27]

The Bisons were next scheduled to play a few games in Connecticut. Weather apparently allowed only two of them to take place, and both were losses, to Bridgeport's Eastern League team and to Yale collegians. On April 22, Grant played his first game as a professional back in his home state, against Boston's NL team. This time the home team's margin of victory wasn't 10 or more runs; the final score was 15–9. In the leadoff spot, Grant had three hits in five at-bats, including a double, and scored twice. That output all came against Bill Stemmyer, who was fresh off a 22–18 season in 1886. One Boston daily drew attention to Grant's "remarkable" fielding: "Such quick and accurate work is rarely seen in Boston, and if it was a specimen of his usual performance, he need not play second fiddle to any baseman," said the *Globe*.[28]

The margin was about the same in the next day's rematch, with Boston prevailing, 17–12.

BASE BALL!
—EAST STATE STREET GROUNDS.—

FRIEAY, APRIL 15.

CUBAN GIANTS

vs.

BUFFALO.

OF THE INTERNATIONAL LEAGUE.

Game called at 3.30.
Admission—25 cents. Grand Stand Chairs, 15 cents. Grand Stand, 10 cents. Ladies admitted free. Chairs, seat and stand, 15 cents.

A historic game was advertised in the *Trenton Times* on April 17, 1887.

Grant scored a run but was 0-for-5 with a walk (scored as a hit for just 1887) so he was shown as 1-for-6 in the box score. This time it took another future Hall of Fame pitcher, Old Hoss Radbourn, to keep Grant hitless.[29] At this point, Buffalo had played its 12th game against major league teams in five different cities, and the *Rochester Democrat and Chronicle*, which had some of the most comprehensive International League coverage among its member cities, summed up the tour by noting that Grant "is praised wherever he goes."[30]

During the final few days of the month, just before Opening Day on April 30, the Bisons played minor league teams in Maine, Massachusetts, and Connecticut. Buffalo finally broke its losing streak on April 27 by trouncing the New England League team in Lynn, Massachusetts by a score of 16–7.[31]

In sum, across Frank Grant's 12 games against major league teams during April of 1887, he compiled 17 hits (minus the three walks presumably scored *as hits* in 1887), including four doubles and a homer. If he had five at-bats per game, then he hit for an average of .283 (again, ignoring walks). He achieved that against eight imposing pitchers: three future Hall of Famers, two others who surpassed 40 victories in a campaign, and three more who had seasons exceeding 20 wins. This consistently good performance against major league talent may be why *Sporting Life* again gave him some attention around this time. The weekly paper noted that some unnamed Buffalo reporter declared not only that Grant was the game's best second baseman, but also that he was the best player any Buffalo team ever had.[32]

Amazingly, Buffalo's spring training futility didn't carry over for long into the regular season, which began on April 30 with two more weeks on the road. The Bisons did, however, get clobbered on Opening Day at Newark, 12–3, and lost the rematch two days later, 4–3. Frank Grant and Fleet Walker played both days, but the latter game was particularly significant because it was Grant's first against George Stovey. Buffalo trailed by three runs after the first inning, but in the fourth inning Grant started a rally that tied it. Newark scored the decisive run in the next frame. In addition to scoring, Grant had one of Buffalo's nine hits off Stovey (unless he was the recipient of his team's only base on balls, which would've been scored as a hit).[33]

Buffalo finally won its first game by a whisker on May 4, its second of two contests in Jersey City. The final score was 7–6, and Grant helped keep it close when the home team was threatening late, with what one Jersey City daily called "a notable catch and a fine throw in the eighth." On offense he contributed a single, a sacrifice, and a run scored.[34] Buffalo evened its record at 3–3 by winning both games in Utica. A newspaper in that city raved about him after the second game, during which his output on offense included a double and a triple. "The great player of the afternoon was Grant, the colored second baseman of the visitors," said the *Utica Herald*. "He seemed to hit everything, steal everything (no reflection) and catch and stop everything within a radius of a hundred feet around his position. He retired the Uticas in the ninth inning by making a remarkable catch of a fly hit by Griffin over into Remsen's territory," that is, center field.[35]

On the next day, May 7, Buffalo played in Binghamton, and there was another historic meeting. According to one account, the main attraction for the 1,400 fans who turned out was comparing "the two colored second basemen, Grant of the Buffalos and Fowler of the Binghamtons." Each was productive on offense, and Bud Fowler played an errorless game, with a putout and four assists. Grant made an error but logged seven putouts and six assists, plus he helped turn the game's only double play. Fowler's team held off a late Buffalo rally to prevail, 8–7.[36] The rematch was two days later, and the home team blew out the Bisons early on the way to a 16–9 final. Fowler and Grant each matched their first-game performances at bat, except Grant contributed a double. The biggest difference on defense was that Grant was charged with three errors. A noteworthy difference in the home team's lineup in this game was that Eugene Bagley, who claimed to have "discovered" Frank Grant, batted ninth and played catcher.[37] Even if Bagley's contention wasn't accurate, at least it's certain the two did meet little more than a year into Grant's professional career.

The Bisons won their next four games to conclude the road trip with a record of 7–5. That must have helped to counteract their very long losing streak during spring training. The second of those four games was in Syracuse, and in the sixth inning, Grant singled home the game's only run.[38]

The Buffalo nine thus had momentum when it played its first home game against Toronto on May 14, before 3,500 customers, including the famous heavyweight boxing champion John L. Sullivan. "Grant, as usual, was the favorite with the on-lookers," said the *Buffalo Express*. In response to the cheers when he first went to bat in the second inning (in the Bisons' fifth slot, his usual place around then), he walloped a pitch onto Richmond Avenue but it was foul. He then lifted a catchable fly to left field, but the 1,000 kids in the left field seats made such a roar that the fielder dropped it, and Grant reached second base. He soon scored the game's first run, and his tiebreaking single in the sixth inning gave them a lead they kept in a 7–3 win. In between those innings, he helped extinguish Toronto's only rally, in the process of playing errorless defense on the day. The visitors took a temporary lead when they scored three times in the fourth inning with only one out and Pit Gilman on first base. Pitcher Mickey Walsh tried to pick Gilman off, and Gilman ended up in a rundown between first and second, which ended when he collided with Grant. "The sprightly second baseman rolled over in the dust a few times, but held on to the ball and Gilman was declared out," the *Express* reported. Walsh beaned the next Toronto batter, but he was then thrown out trying to steal, so Grant made a second putout to end the threat.[39]

The Bisons extended their winning streak two days later by pushing the tying and winning runs across in the bottom of the ninth inning to prevail over Toronto, 6–5. They won again the next day, hosting Hamilton, 3–2. Grant drove in Buffalo's final run.[40] Their streak maxed out at eight with a 6–4 victory against Hamilton the next day.

The two teams met for a third consecutive day on May 19 in Hamilton. The home team chose to bat first, and thanks partly to single runs in the eighth and ninth innings, they defeated Buffalo, 7–4. However, manager Jack Chapman penned a lengthy diatribe (to whom was unclear) about how the outcome reflected one of the sport's greatest robberies ever. He condemned two Hamilton baserunners in particular, Chub Collins and Rasty Wright:

> There was plenty of dirty work on the part of some of the Hamilton players, and had it not been for that we would have won the game. If ever a player ought to have been fined it was Collins. [John] Reidy had the ball waiting for him and he jumped on Reidy at third base, tearing his breeches, cutting his leg, and kicking the ball out of his hands. The umpire, McDonald, decided him not out where he ought to have been decided out and fined for his dirty work.... In the fourth inning when they made three runs the side ought to have been decided out without runs. There was a man on first (Wright) when a ball was hit to Grant. He put

Wright out at second, and when Grant was about to throw the ball to first, to make an easy double play, Wright with cap in hand, hit Grant's arm to prevent the play. They also jumped on Grant, ripping his breeches to pieces. Our boys played hard to win, but could not get there on account of the dirty work of Hamilton. If Hamilton is to continue this sort of thing the League ought to drop them or Buffalo will go into one of the big associations where such dirty work is not allowed.[41]

None of this was even hinted at in the wire service account of the game published in the *Rochester Democrat and Chronicle*. In fact, its "special dispatch" concluded by asserting that "McDonald's umpiring was very satisfactory."[42] At least the Bisons got some revenge in the rematch at Hamilton the next day, by scoring twice in the bottom of the ninth inning to tie the game and winning it in the next frame, 6–5, on a leadoff homer by Charlie Hamburg.[43]

Speaking of umpires, if Chapman and his Bisons caught wind of a news item about International League umpire Billy Hoover, they would've had a second umpire to hate. "It is said that Hover [sic], the umpire, stated in Binghamton that he would always decide against a team employing a colored player on a close point," the *Oswego Palladium* reported. "Why not dispense with Mr. Hover's services if this be true? It would be a good thing for Oswego if we had a few players like Fowler and Grant." The first sentence was reprinted a few days later in a Rochester paper.[44]

Buffalo continued to play winning baseball for the remainder of May, including its first four games of the season against Rochester. After one of those games, in which Grant handled 11 chances without an error, the *Rochester Herald* said his work was "wonderful" and may have implied that mental sharpness was yet another aspect of his success. "He seemed to be all over at once, and was usually in the right place at the right time," the paper observed. "It is doubtful if any other second baseman in the league covers as much ground as Grant."[45] But his most impressive performance as the month wound down was during the first game of a doubleheader on May 30 at home, hosting Toronto again, when he hit for the "cycle." In that day's lineup, he batted fifth, and his triple led off the second inning. His home run was hit in the next frame with a teammate on base. His double came in the fourth inning. One Buffalo paper specified that he singled in his fourth plate appearance and drew a walk the fifth time up.[46] Buffalo ended the month of May with a record of 18–8, good enough for second place in the 10-team International League.[47]

The Bisons began June by hosting first-place Newark, which had an astonishing record of 24–2. More than 2,500 locals braved threatening weather to see the League's top two teams battle. George Stovey and Fleet Walker both played for the visitors, though Stovey patrolled center field instead of pitching. Newark led 2–0 after five innings, but after that it was all Buffalo. The Bisons scored twice in the sixth inning, and Grant led off for them in the seventh. He broke the tie with a home run over the left field fence. "The scene on the grand stand at that moment beggars description," the *Buffalo Times* commented. "Ladies waved their handkerchiefs, men stamped and yelled and the [grand] stand seemed as though it might collapse. The spectators could not be and were not quieted throughout the inning," during which the Bisons added an insurance run.[48] The next day Stovey was in the pitcher's box for Newark (and Walker had the day off). Buffalo scored once in the first inning and not again. The Bisons had a good chance to add to their lead in the fourth when Grant got on base to lead off and his keystone partner, Henry Easterday, did likewise, but Stovey escaped that jam. The score remained

1–0 through the first seven frames, but a light rain helped Newark score in the final two innings and prevail, 3–1. Buffalo had a good chance to at least tie the game in its half of the eighth when an error by Stovey helped put runners on second and third with one out. Stovey regained his composure to strike out Remsen on "four wide balls" and then retired Grant on a foul tip. At least Grand did manage to hit a double earlier in the contest.[49]

Over in Canada, the *Hamilton Spectator* claimed that the Bisons had "refused to have their photographs taken in a group last season, and as Grant is with the team the players will now doubt object to doing so this year." One Buffalo paper quoted this, with a rebuttal: "You're wrong, neighbor; two excellent groups have been taken this spring," the *Sunday News* replied. "Grant is very popular with his associates." One of these group shots has been circulated widely over the years, and it remains one of the very few photos of Grant. It's intriguing to think that a second group shot may still exist. Regardless, this exchange foreshadowed a widely reported controversy of Buffalo's 1888 season.[50]

When Buffalo hosted Utica on June 6, Grant produced a double and four singles in five at-bats. Buffalo was trailing by a run when it had its last chances at the plate. Grant's fourth single advance Remsen to second base, and one hit later he scored the tying run. Two batters later, Grant scored the game-winner.[51] The *Buffalo Express* quipped that the reason for the Bisons' luck was that local attorney Moses Shire's dog, named Punch, was allowed into the box seats of the team's other directors before the start of the inning. The

The famous 1887 Buffalo Bisons team photograph. In front, from left to right, are Walsh, Fanning, Grant, and O'Neill. In the middle row are Lehane, Hamburg, Reidy, Purvis, and Calihan. Standing are Chapman, Remsen, Roschi (crouching), Easterday, Zell, and Galligan.

Times chided the other paper for "trying to steal Grant's honor" as the real basis of the team's good fortune.[52]

At the start of June, Buffalo had a record of 18–8 and trailed only Newark, which had an astonishing record of 24–2. However, the franchise in Oswego disbanded at the end of May, and when Scranton was admitted as its replacement on June 3, all games involving Oswego were removed from the standings. Newark had played more games against Oswego than Buffalo had, so after the games of June 6, Buffalo's record was 20–9 but Newark's was 18–5. Newark retained first place because it still had a better winning percentage, but Buffalo was much closer than it had been a week earlier.[53] The continuing imbalance of games meant that International League standings tended to emphasize winning percentages going forward.

On June 8, Frank Grant and the other Bisons faced Robert Higgins for the first time when they hosted Syracuse. "Higgins, the Stars' left-handed colored pitcher, did excellent work," the *Buffalo Times* reported, but that daily jumped to the defense of the entire visiting team, which was disadvantaged by the umpiring. "McDonald's decisions yesterday were very rank and manifestly unfair and several times given against the Stars, when the just decision was of vital importance and would have brought them in runs," the *Times* declared. This was the same McDonald (first name possibly lost to history) who allowed Hamilton players to abuse John Reidy and Frank Grant on May 19. Before June was over, the International League released him. In any case, the Bisons beat Syracuse with the umpire's help, 6–2. Against Higgins' hurling, Grant had a double in three at-bats (plus a walk not scored as a hit by the *Times*).[54]

On Friday, June 10, Buffalo reached the top of the International League standings momentarily by beating first-place Newark. Mickey Walsh shut out the visitors on just five singles (and no walks), while the Buffalo nine scored just enough against the battery of Stovey and Walker to send almost 5,000 fans home after a totally satisfying 5–0 outcome. Grant went 1-for-4, fielded eight of nine chances cleanly, and helped turn a double play, but the star on offense was John Reidy, whose two-run homer in the eighth inning helped considerably.[55]

One immediate result of the team's achievement was that the Globe Clothing Company gave the Bisons nice new walking sticks, and manager Jack Chapman's cane was a gold-headed model.[56] The players also received $5 each from the team's directors. The *Buffalo Commercial Advertiser* blamed this decision by the directors, as much as any other reason, for losses the next three games, two to "the little Scrantons" and a 21–3 demolition by Binghamton. But the *Express* was inclined to focus blame on the Sunday between the games against Scranton, when at least three of the Bisons were accused of getting drunk on "the seductive weiss beer at the Parade House," a large hall in a city park. *The Sun* in New York City reported that the players' time together ended in some sort of disturbance "in which a knife is said to have been used." The directors suspended one player, James Purvis, and fined him $50, or 10 times the handout. Fines of $25 were charged to Frank Grant and outfielder John Galligan, but neither was suspended. The *Express* said the directors "let other players off with lesser punishment for their part in Sunday's racket."[57] Purvis, a utility player and career minor leaguer from Canada, was two years older than Grant. Galligan, who was Grant's age, later played 31 games in the major leagues for Louisville of the American Association in 1889.

The Bisons ended their short losing streak by eking out a win in the second game against Bud Fowler and Binghamton, 8–7. Though they had won 17 of their previous 19 home games to reach first place, that success seemed quickly obscured by the three-game skid and the scandal in the midst of it. Still, when their home stand ended on June 18, they were back in first place. Their record was 26–12; they had five more wins than Newark but only one more loss.[58] Around this time, *Sporting Life* pointed out that Buffalo had built the best attendance total among International League cities.[59]

Buffalo played road games from June 20 through July 12, except for a doubleheader at home on Independence Day. A few days into the initial road trip, one Buffalo paper reported that Bud Fowler had unveiled a plan to lead a team of African American ballplayers on a tour of the country that autumn, all the way to San Francisco, and during the winter months they would play in the South. He was hoping to take Grant, Stovey, Walker, and five members of the Cuban Giants. During Buffalo's disastrous preseason road trip, *The Sporting News* had announced a similar plan, except with several different players: "Grant, of Buffalo; Frey [sic], of the Cuban Giants; Walker and Stovey, of the Newarks; Selden, of the Resolutes, of Boston; Malone, of the Keystones, and Mayfield, of the Falls Citys, are forming a representative colored team to go to California next winter. They have been offered dates by Jim Hart's California club and the Pioneers."[60]

June ended on a good note for Grant and his fellow Bisons in Toronto, before 5,000 fans. The home team rallied late but Buffalo hung on to win, 7–6. Grant batted fourth in the lineup and had three singles in four at-bats, plus he scored a run. A Buffalo daily said his performance "aroused the enthusiasm of the crowd."[61] Alas, Toronto fans treated him horribly in the near future.

International League fielding statistics through June were released in early July. For second basemen, Frank Grant was sixth in fielding percentage, with a mark of .896. Bud Fowler was eighth, at .863. In first place, with a figure of .940, was Hamilton's Chub Collins, who had been John Reidy's nemesis on May 19.[62]

According to research by James Overmyer for his seminal 12-page biography of Frank Grant in a 1991 book, Grant had quite a slump at the plate during the first two weeks of July, and an even worse one over the first three weeks of August. From July 1–13, he batted .214 (9-for-42), and from August 1–20, his average was just .164 (12-for-73). In between, at least, he managed a healthy slugging percentage of .421 over 13 games.[63] As illustrations, on July 22 he had a triple, the next day he smacked two doubles, while on July 27 he had two triples (plus a walk and at least one single), and a day later he had a double and two singles in five-at bats. Lastly, on August 1, he had a double and a home run despite an arm "in bad condition," according to the *Courier*. By that time, he had slid from fifth or fourth in the batting order to seventh.[64]

Hot and cold streaks on offense can be identified in the careers of all Hall of Famers, but at times during July, even Grant's fielding was noticeably shaky. After the doubleheader on July 4, the *Buffalo Express* wrote that Grant had "fallen off badly in his hitting and fielding," though it didn't elaborate.[65] He did have a very rough day in a doubleheader at Toronto on July 1, committing five errors with just a lone single at the plate.[66] In the doubleheader at home three days later, he again had five errors, while going 2-for-9 at bat.[67]

By the time Buffalo finally got to start an extended home stand in mid–July, the team again trailed Newark in the standings. Though Grant's first batting slump ended then, things only got worse in other regards. For one, a Rochester paper asserted that on July 14, Grant was fined $5 and Remsen $10, though the reasons weren't specified. Each of them had three hits and a walk, plus Grant stole two bases, in a win at home against Rochester, so it presumably wasn't their manager who fined them. Interestingly, the umpire, Ted Sullivan, was released after the game.[68] (Either these fines weren't of much importance to Buffalo sportswriters on the whole, or they somehow escaped their attention.) But of far more lasting significance was a decision made by the International League's directors on July 14, by coincidence in Buffalo.

At a special meeting (or "secret" one, as a widely circulated dispatch called it), presumably called to address the imminent transfer of Utica's franchise to Wilkes-Barre, Pennsylvania, several other matters were discussed. "Several representatives declared that many of the best players in the League were anxious to leave on account of the colored element, and the Board finally directed Secretary White to approve of no more contracts with colored men," said the dispatch printed in at least a few International League cities the next day.[69] A Rochester paper printed a somewhat different summary, as told to a reporter by Rochester's manager, John Humphries. He had heard that a petition seeking to exclude African American players was presented during the meeting, with the outcome being the instructions given to Secretary C.D. White,[70] who was from the Utica club. Curiously, though at least four Buffalo dailies reported about the meeting that same day or the day after,[71] within four days of it, they said almost nothing about the supposed decision potentially affecting their star second baseman. Embodying their collective quietness was the terse report in the *Express* on July 17: "According to report Secretary White of the International League has been instructed to promulgate no more contracts with colored players."[72]

One possibility is that the Buffalo sportswriters didn't take the report seriously. Buffalo was represented at the meeting by Frank T. Gilbert, the League's President, and Charles W. Cushman. If the supposed decision applied to Frank Grant, the local sportswriters might have assumed—or were even told—that Gilbert and Cushman would have objected strongly. Whatever, the case, word of this action spread gradually and widely by the end of the month. For example, on July 22, a newspaper in Virginia noted that "Grant, Stovey, Renfroe, and Higgins are the leading colored players now in the International League who will have to seek work elsewhere next season." The *St. Louis Globe-Democrat* printed the same sentence but tacked on editorial remarks: "It is really a pity that the League should draw the color-line, for it is a treat to see Grant play second base. He is quite a ball player. Jack Chapman values him at $5000." In 2006, a Hall of Fame press release considered this "quite a compliment when Chicago had recently sold superstar Mike Kelly to Boston for $1,000."[73] A paper in New Jersey echoed the *Globe-Democrat*'s sentiment the next day, but on July 26 the *Rochester Democrat and Chronicle* quoted the *Globe-Democrat* explicitly and replied, "Chapman would like to give Grant away. He is what ball players call a 'yellow' second baseman."[74] Grant and Chapman both remained with Buffalo through the 1888 season, so this paper may have been fabricating that. In any event, by the end of the month, a Rhode Island newspaper, for one, replaced Renfroe (who was out of the International League by then, like teammate Bud Fowler) with Walker in that same sentence, and expressed an opinion on a par with the St. Louis paper's. "All are good players and behave like gentlemen, and it is a pity that the line should have been drawn against them," said the *Sunday Telegram* in Providence.[75]

Whether or not such comments interpreted the decision accurately, it certainly didn't bode well, partly in the wake of Bud Fowler's recent release by Binghamton around Independence Day. That occurred at Fowler's request, but it stemmed from nine racist teammates having threatened to quit if he remained on the roster.[76] Also, on the same day as the International League meeting, future Hall of Famer Cap Anson, the manager of the NL's Chicago White Stockings, refused to play an exhibition game in Newark if George Stovey pitched. This wasn't widely reported at the time but has ballooned in infamy over the years.[77]

Though Frank Grant had a run of decent batting spanning the second half of July, starting with the game on the day of the League's meeting, less than a week later, he had some problems fielding. On July 19, he had trouble all game. "Grant played wretchedly at second as well as at the bat," said the *Buffalo Commercial Advertiser*. "He couldn't hit a balloon!" A day later day it simply asked, "What's the matter with Grant?" It must not have asked the player himself, or his manager. The *Express* similarly weighed in about what it perceived as a trend, writing that Grant, "who started out in Buffalo with such brilliant prospects, is fast losing the confidence of his friends. His work both at the bat and in the field is by far not what ought justly to be expected of him."[78]

The next day, one of these harsh dailies suggested that Grant made a commitment to turn things around. "Grant braced up and covered an unusual amount of territory around second base with credit to himself," said the *Commercial Advertiser*.[79] Still, around that time at least one paper in another International League city chose to go negative about him. "Grant, the once famous second baseman of the Buffalos, is losing his reputation," declared the *Rochester Herald*. "Even the home grand-stand spectators have soured on him." On July 24, the *Buffalo Courier* rebutted that Rochester paper directly: "Not so bad as that. Grant has dropped off a little in his playing, but he is striking his gait again," the *Courier* countered. "He played a great game yesterday."[80]

Over the next few weeks, evidence piled up indicating that the *Courier* was correct. For one, though the entire team played errorless ball on July 25, the *Commercial Advertiser* singled Grant out for having "played splendidly at second."[81] He played without making an error the next two games as well. On August 1, Grant was suffering from a bad arm injury, but the *Courier* said he managed to play "in his old-time form."[82] He was again playing well enough on defense that he resumed receiving praise in big, distant cities. "A Buffalo newspaper man of many years standing says that he never saw a second baseman who could cover as much ground as Grant, the colored player," noted one Washington paper.[83] The *Boston Globe* provided these details on August 5:

> Grant, Buffalo's colored second baseman, is playing a wonderful game. This is the way his record runs in the last five games: Five put-outs, 6 assists, no errors; 5 put-outs, 3 assists, 2 errors; 2 put-outs, 3 assists and no errors; 4 put-outs, 4 assists and no errors; 4 put-outs, 6 assists and no errors. In other words, he accepted 42 out of 44 chances in five games.[84]

But as mentioned before, Grant mostly struggled at the plate from August 2 through 20. One bright spot at bat during that stretch was on August 8 in Wilkes-Barre. His childhood teammate Bob Pettit hit a double and a triple for the home team, but Grant homered. "Grant, the colored second baseman of the visitors, is a good ball player," that city's *Evening Leader* noted. "He made some remarkably fine plays, a running catch of a fly to right field being especially brilliant."[85] Less than a month later, on September 2, Pettit made his major league debut with Cap Anson's team.

Toward the end of Grant's batting slump, his defense was vital in a battle for first place in Syracuse on August 19. The Bisons had climbed back atop the International League standings by then, but both Newark and Syracuse were breathing down their necks. Four other Bisons were hitless that day, but errorless defense by the nine kept

5. A Bitter Pennant Battle (1887)

the game scoreless through ten innings. Grant's five assists were more than any of his teammates,' and his eight putouts gave him as many chances as his first baseman, Mike Lehane (all putouts), with whom he turned Buffalo's only double play. Lehane drove in the only run of the game in the bottom of the 11th inning with a sacrifice fly. As a result, the League's top three teams were Buffalo (53–31, .631), Newark (46–28, .622), and Syracuse (45–28, .616).[86] Grant tried to help his team's cause when he reached first base after two outs in the 10th inning and stole second. For some reason, this prompted at least one newspaper in New York to highlight the fact that bigotry wasn't limited to men back in 1887: "I would like to slap that darkey," a young "lady" reportedly said when Grant put himself in scoring position.[87]

As the pennant race was entering its final weeks, Frank Grant proved his stardom. On August 22, Buffalo had again slipped out of first place, and in that day's contest in Scranton, there was no score after four innings. His "terrific" homer over the center field fence gave Buffalo a brief lead, and it ultimately won, but by a score of just 2–1. The standings were thus topped by Buffalo, at .628; Newark, at .627, and Syracuse, at .621.[88]

Unfortunately, not all of the Bisons handled the pressure of a very tight pennant battle well. Toronto was also in the race, and the game at Olympic Park on August 27 drew 3,500 fans (including many Canadians). After eight innings, Toronto led, 16–13. Both teams piled on many more runs in the ninth, and Toronto left town with an important win, 26–19. The *Buffalo Express* said, "Grant was the hero of the day." And how! He hit two homers and a triple, which netted him eight runs batted in and four runs scored. He was also hit by a pitch. That particular plate appearance might have been connected to quarrels in the fourth inning between two of his teammates and two Canucks. The *Express* was a little vague when it described the sequence of events, but Gus Alberts, the first batter in Toronto's lineup, reached first base and soon collided with Grant at second base to prevent a double play. Buffalo pitcher Jack Fanning gave "Alberts a piece of his mind for running into Grant," said the *Express*. Perhaps it was no coincidence that Fanning sat on one side of Grant in that year's team photo. In any event, Toronto pitcher Ed Crane batted fifth in his team's lineup that day and also got on base that inning. On a subsequent play at second base, he likewise collided with Grant, who had the ball but dropped it. Umpire William McLean still declared Crane out. Fanning's next time up to bat was apparently in the bottom half of that inning, and Buffalo third baseman John Reidy (possibly coaching third base) overheard Alberts, the shortstop, tell Crane to hit Fanning with a pitch. Reidy got into a shouting match with Alberts. Toronto led by nine runs in the top of the seventh inning when one of their other players protested a call by the umpire so wildly that some "roughs in the crowd" yelled threats at the visiting ballplayer. The game's starting time was earlier than scheduled because Toronto wanted to catch a particular train that evening, but nobody expected all that time-consuming scoring. "Suffice it to say that they didn't catch the train," the *Express* noted. "They caught a carload of rocks in their 'bus' [sic] after the game." The Leagues' top four teams, in order, were Newark (50–28, .641), Buffalo (56–34, .622), Syracuse (48–30, .615), and Toronto (46–32, .590).[89]

In 1891, manager Charlie Cushman looked back on an 1887 game between his Canucks and Buffalo, and virtually all signs point to this August 27 slugfest. Between the 1889 and 1890 seasons, Cushman had switched from managing Toronto to leading Milwaukee's team in the Western League, and leading up to the 1891 season, he addressed a rumor that he might sign an African American second baseman. *Sporting Life* shared his Canucks' version of the story with its nationwide readership:

> They were at Buffalo one day, and the latter team had an African named Grant playing second base. Early in the game Gus Alberts started out by hitting safely for first, and then shot down to second with the pitcher's arm. Grant squared away as the ball came down to him, and swinging about caught Gus in the pit of the stomach with his arm. Alberts was badly doubled up, but came in and said nothing. Ed. Crane was looking at the play and said:
>
> "Well, boys, what'll we do to him?"
>
> "Put him out of the game," in a chorus.
>
> This was agreed, and when Crane went down to steal second Grant got fairly in front of him. Crane was going like the wind. He ducked his head after measuring the distance and caught Grant fairly in the pit of the stomach with his shoulder. The son of Ham went up in the air and when he came down he looked as if he had been in a threshing machine. They took him home on a stretcher, and he didn't recover for three weeks.
>
> "The crowd came near mobbing us," said "Cush," "but there were no more darkies in the League after that."[90]

The first half of this is either true or at least plausible, but most of what Cushman said at the end was wrong, very far from undeniable facts. The location matched, and the sequence of events—Alberts, and then Crane—does align closely with what the *Buffalo Express* reported, even if minor details differ (trying to break up a double play versus a steal attempt). Also, in the preface to this passage, Cushman had said that the game took place in 1887, Crane's only season with Toronto. Alberts was only on Toronto in 1886 and 1887. Interestingly, while the *Express* had reason to consider Alberts a villain, it was Cushman who made his own player seem like a weakling, in light of the fact that Alberts' playing weight is commonly listed as 25 pounds more than Frank Grant's 155. In fact, Crane outweighed Grant by 50 pounds.

How hard Crane hit Grant is certainly open to interpretation, but as Cushman was wrapping up his tale, only one of these four facts was true:

- Frank Grant was taken "home on a stretcher" (immediately, Cushman seemed to imply).
- "He didn't recover for three weeks."
- "The crowd came near mobbing us."
- There were no more African American players "in that league after that."

The only truthful statement reflects *well* on Grant, that Toronto infuriated local fans. It is easy to prove, beyond any doubt whatsoever, that the other three were false, and Cushman knew better.

In reverse order, Grant not only completed that season, but he played in the league once again in 1888, from start to finish. Sure, there were fewer African American players in the International League/Association after 1887, but Fleet Walker played in the league during 1888 *and* 1889. In those two years, Cushman continued to manage Toronto.

Frank Grant didn't miss a single game as a result of Crane's malice, much less three whole weeks. August 27 was a Saturday, so there was no league game the next day. On August 29, Buffalo played in Rochester, but it was an exhibition game and thus didn't count in the standings. The same was true about the next day's rematch in Buffalo. If Grant had been hurting, those would have been perfect opportunities to rest him. He didn't just play both days, he *excelled*. "The most remarkable play of the day and probably of the season, was the running pick up of Lewis' grounder by Grant," the *Rochester Democrat and Chronicle* reported about the first game. "Grant ran for the ball and leaning forward for it until it seemed to every one that he must fall on his face he picked it up with both hands and threw Lewis out at first when everybody thought he had made a safe hit." Grant made three other assists and three putouts, without an error, and went 3-for-4 at bat with a double and a run scored. In Buffalo, Grant hit two triples, and the *Buffalo Times* called his overall performance "excellent." On August 31, the Bisons played a third consecutive exhibition game, against a local amateur team. Grant homered in that contest.[91]

Even if Cushman was unaware that Grant played in his nine's next three games, there is absolutely no doubt Cushman knew full well that Grant was in the lineup when the Bisons visited Toronto on September 1, *just five days*—not even a full week, much less three—after Crane targeted him. Grant was Buffalo's star on offense that day, but there was also an infamous reason for Cushman to remember the proximity of the two games. But that's getting ahead of the story. In 1887, Grant wasn't out of action for consecutive games, much less a week or more. He did miss about three weeks midway through the 1888 season, but that started after a game against Hamilton and there were no reports of any collisions being a factor; he simply had arm problems all season. Also, both Alberts and Crane weren't on Toronto in 1888.

But the facts that Cushman most conveniently omitted were Frank Grant's plate appearances immediately following Crane's attempt to injure him. In the fifth inning, Grant hit a two-run homer off Crane. In the seventh inning, he faced Crane with two Bisons on base. He cracked a triple, after which Crane uncorked a wild pitch on which Grant scored again. In the ninth inning, Grant faced Crane with the bases full, and he walloped a grand slam. *All eight of Grant's runs batted in during that game came after Crane tried to injure him.* It's inconceivable that Cushman forgot all these facts to the contrary, in which case his yarn amounts to little more than revisionist history, expect for documenting his players' overt bigotry. As James Overmyer commented (after noting that Grant played almost every game in 1887), "Cushman's tale gets right to the heart of the way prejudice translated into violence and intimidation against blacks, even on the field of fair play that the baseball diamond is thought to represent."[92] In hindsight, it's no surprise that *Sporting Life* reported on a race-based ploy attributed to Cushman shortly before the summer of 1888: "Manager Cushman, of the Torontos, is said to be engineering a scheme to have colored players ousted from the International Association," that national weekly stated. "There are only three colored men in the Association—Grant, of Buffalo, and Higgins and Walker, of Syracuse—and they behave themselves very nicely."[93]

Baseball's intolerance was also in the news at the end of August when commentary about the International League's recent race-based policy made the rounds again. "Buffalo will very reluctantly release Grant, their colored second baseman," reported one paper in New Jersey. "He is a modest fellow and a heavy batter." This short item reported his slugging against Toronto on August 27. The exact wording may have originated with the *Cincinnati Times-Star*. At least one paper in Connecticut ran this in early September, and even the *Buffalo Evening News* printed it.[94] Meanwhile, another Buffalo daily praised Grant on August 31 after an exhibition game at home. "Grant was the only man that made an effort to play ball. He always does and that is the reason he is so popular," said the *Commercial Advertiser*. "If the rest of the nine would try to win as hard as Grant, the Bisons could beat any club in the International League."[95]

It may have helped maintain Grant's spirits if such praise got back to him, because he was treated horribly by fans in Toronto during Buffalo's loss there on September 1. He batted fourth in the lineup and was his nine's star at bat that day with three hits, including a triple, though the home team won easily, 12–4. The Toronto fans had reportedly prepared to seek revenge for their nine's "ruffianly treatment" in Buffalo on August 27, but because the Canucks won easily on their home turf, a dispatch from Toronto said "the audience confined itself to blowing their horns and yelling out 'kill the nigger,' when Grant was at bat."[96] The *Buffalo Express* quoted from this dispatch but added its own comment (echoed in Connecticut paper): "Nice people, those Torontonians." Buffalo's *Sunday Truth* quoted a Toronto newspaper directly about this game, albeit without obscenities, and confirmed that "Grant was vilely insulted."[97] *Sporting Times* quoted from the same dispatch and condemned it with a mixture of anger and sarcasm: "So the 'audience confined itself to blowing their horns and yelling 'kill the nigger.' That was indeed considerate. No doubt Grant appreciated it." To this publication, which was quoted in Boston and St. Louis dailies, this incident proved that Toronto was "undoubtedly the worst city in the international league for visitors to play ball."[98]

Frank Grant maintained his determination, as he demonstrated the next two days in Hamilton. In the first game, he homered, albeit in a 10-inning, 5–3 loss. He helped keep the score close with four putouts and six assists, a double play turned, and no errors. In the rematch, a 6–4 loss, he had three hits and played flawless defense, which included another double play.[99] On September 6, he found an uncommon way to contribute on offense during a win over Scranton before 1,000 Buffalo fans. He had a double, single, and walk on the day. At one point, "Little Grant made a dash for home from third base when Pitcher [Kid] Gleason had the ball in his hand and succeeded in scoring all right," reported one Buffalo daily. "This nearly crazed the spectators with mirth and the greatest excitement prevailed."[100] In fact, one source implied that stealing home happened just five times during 1887 across the majors and high minor leagues, when it listed only "Robinson of the St. Louis Browns, April 12; Reeder of the Nashville club, April 28; Sunday of Chicago, June 28; Powell of New Orleans, Sept. 1; and Grant of Buffalo, Sept. 5 [sic]."[101]

Papers in several big cities across the country gave Grant a little attention for his 12 total bases against Toronto back on August 27. "Colored Second Baseman Grant of Buffalo recently made a total of 12 bases in a game," noted the *Boston Herald* on September 8, as one example. This one-liner was even printed a week later down South, in Memphis.[102]

Alas, as the middle of the month approached, Grant was mentioned in various newspapers for a very different reason. The St. Louis Browns of the American Association were scheduled to play the Cuban Giants on September 11 in an exhibition game, but many of the Browns signed an infamous letter refusing "to play against negroes." A dispatch printed in one St. Louis paper called *this* decision "the first time in the history of base-ball the color line has been drawn," though it concluded by mentioning the International League's recent "resolution prohibiting the employment of colored players by its clubs." Grant and George Stovey were singled out as the players to whom white counterparts objected. The *New York Times* was among other newspapers that also used this dispatch.[103] It so happened that on September 14, Grant had a very good day in front of more than 3,000 Buffalo fans in an important win against Newark's battery of Stovey and Walker. Grant had two singles, two walks, a stolen base, and a run scored in the 11–3 win, and he helped contain Newark's offense with ten chances, no errors, and a double play turned with Lehane.[104]

Grant had a defining moment at home against Wilkes-Barre on September 17. In the eighth inning, Buffalo had the tying run in scoring position with one out and their two best hitters coming up. The *Buffalo Courier* reported vividly what happened next:

> Great things were expected of Lehane, but he knocked up a fly to short and retired ingloriously. In Grant lay the Bisons' only hope, and Manager Chapman promised him the town if he would save the game. Grantie kept the fielders busy and his arm in practice knocking fouls for a while, and then he proceeded to business. The grand stand went fairly wild when they realized that the ball that left Grant's bat was going over the left fielder's head, and when the sphere sailed over the fence to boot, language fails to picture the scene of frenzied delight. Old men jumped for job [sic], wives embraced their husbands, small boys gave themselves a headache by shouting, and several business men in their enthusiasm tore up promissory notes for large amounts. Grant had saved the game, the score stood four to three in Buffalo's favor, and Manager Chapman smiled proudly as he patted the colored brother on the back and slid a greenback into his hand.[105]

If only that had happened in the ninth inning instead. Sadly, two of his teammates' errors in the final frame helped the visitors score three times and steal the game. Instead of being in second place, with a winning percentage of .626, one Buffalo paper reported the International League's top three teams at that point as: Toronto (56–32, .636), Newark (57–35, .620), and Buffalo (61–38, .616).[106]

Grant had three singles and two runs scored during an easy 12–5 win in the rematch on Monday, September 19. On defense he also demonstrated again that he was willing and able to do something that teammates wouldn't attempt or didn't think to do. With Wilkes-Barre down to its final out, their leadoff man sent a deep fly toward left field, and while a Bison gave chase, he "was well backed up by little Grant, who made a beautiful throw from away out in the left field to the home plate." It wasn't in time to prevent an inside-the-park home run, but no explanation was given about why the shortstop or third baseman wasn't out there in Grant's place. Regardless, as a result of the victory, Buffalo climbed back into second place but Toronto continued an amazing double-digit winning streak to maintain its lead.[107]

Buffalo next hosted Syracuse for two games. The Stars scored a run in the first inning, and Grant countered to lead off the second by swatting a triple. He soon scored to tie the game, but the Bisons managed just four singles after Grant's blow and only reached third base twice more, while the Stars gradually scored five unanswered runs to win comfortably. Grant and a Syracuse player, Mox McQuery, were involved in two incidents during the game that brought the wrath of Buffalo papers down on the visitor. Syracuse broke the 1–1 tie with a run in the third inning. "At a critical point" in that inning, the *Buffalo Times* reported that McQuery yelled to Buffalo catcher Dan "Dugdale as though he were one of the home team 'hold the ball don't throw it,' thus preventing Dugdale from throwing to Grant and putting a man out at second." The umpire fined McQuery $5 for that trick. "Another dirty act was to run purposely into Grant and knock the ball from his hands to prevent a double play," the *Times* added. "He plays what is known as dirty ball," said the *Buffalo Express* about the two plays. The *Commercial Advertiser* called McQuery "the most ungentlemanly base ball player in the International League."[108] Nevertheless, there must not have been bad blood between the two nines overall, because that night they went together to Buffalo's Academy of Music to watch a farcical play called "Little Puck."[109]

The next day's rematch was rained out after two innings, and on September 22 Buffalo ended its season against Newark by being shut out for the only time at home in 1887. Fleet Walker caught for the visitors, who won 6–0, but Stovey didn't crack Newark's lineup. "Grant played ball all the time, but it availed nothing," the *Express* wrote.[110] The International League season ended with Toronto winning the pennant and Buffalo in second place. There were just 16 men who played for Toronto during that season, and all but two made it to the major leagues at some point. By contrast, Jack Chapman used 24 players in his Buffalo lineups, and 10 besides Frank Grant never made it to the majors.

If Grant's reputation had suffered some at midseason, by the conclusion he was again held in high esteem. For one, the *Times* singled Grant out for "playing splendid ball" during the season's final week. "A cheer always goes up for little Grant when he goes to bat," the *Commercial Advertiser* said around the same time. "He is one of the best men in the nine." Neither statement was unprecedented, but it had been some weeks since Buffalo sports fans had read them. "The whole nine except Grant have fallen off terribly in batting," the *Express* commented about the team's final games.[111]

Official 1887 statistics for the International League showed Buffalo having the fourth-best batting average as a team, at .335. This presumably reflected the scoring rule unique to that season, which counted walks as base hits. Frank Grant was listed with the 29th-highest batting average, at .366, resulting from 459 at-bats, but if players who had fewer than 300 at-bats are excluded (such as his childhood friend Bob Pettit, who was listed third with an average of .443 but in only 79 at-bats), Grant ranked 16th. He had 40 stolen bases and scored 81 runs, which put him 25th and 23rd, respectively, in those categories. He led all second basemen in three fielding categories: games played, 105; putouts, 366; and assists, 395. He tied for most errors, with 74, and his fielding percentage of .911 was ninth out of 16 second basemen listed. However, only four other second basemen played in more than 60 games, and three of them had lower fielding percentages than Grant.[112]

Additional details weren't circulated until later in the offseason, and those showed what a powerhouse Frank Grant was during 1887. He hit 11 home runs, and that led the International League. That was as many as future Hall of Famer Dan Brouthers smacked to lead the National League; Bug Holliday (who began a 10-year major league career in 1889) reportedly led all of organized ball with 17 homers.[113] Grant also led the International League in extra-base hits with 49 (28 doubles and 10 triples). His teammate Mike Lehane was second, with 47 "long hits."[114] Research published in 2003 credited Lehane with the most runs batted in, 118, but listed Grant second with 114.[115] These were his achievements in only his second professional season, and he had just turned 22 on August 1.

Around the end of the season, the national weekly *Sporting Life* asked a question that must have been on the minds of Buffalo's baseball fans: "Where will the colored Dunlap, Grant, of Buffalo, play next season, considering that everywhere the colored player is being shut off by the white leagues!"[116] This was settled soon enough. The club's board of directors met on September 29, rehired Jack Chapman as manager, and reserved nine players for 1888, including Frank Grant.[117] Shortly thereafter, Newark reserved Fleet Walker for 1888, but George Stovey was one of two players who were "permanently released, to do as they please."[118] In actuality, Walker instead played for Syracuse in 1888 (and 1889 as well).

Grant was seemingly confident about continuing with the Bisons, because that very same day at least two dailies in the city announced that he had opened a restaurant or saloon. "His next move will be to get married," one of them added. The other expressed some concern. "The lovers of baseball about town are all sorry that Grant has gone into the saloon business," the *Express* said. "Of course they wish him the best of luck in his venture, but the wisest shake their heads and say that a winter behind the bar is not the best of training for the diamond of 1888."[119] About a week later, even the city's Catholic newspaper weighed in similarly: "'Twill be a wonder if next season does not see a falling off in his base ball record."[120] (Happily, that didn't occur.) Another paper later noted that his saloon was on Vine Street, which was near the intersection of Michigan Avenue and William Street. According to a master's thesis about Buffalo's lower east side, by the 1850s the 600 to 700 African Americans in Buffalo lived in an area centered on Vine Street.[121] Naturally, he was a celebrity in that part of town. "The colored population of Buffalo are very proud of Grant ... and very jealous of any criticism of their favorite," the *Courier* had reported that season. "The hotel waiters, to a man, swear by Grant," the paper added, and asserted that diners had learned "to tell their waiter that he resembles the colored ball player and thereby tickle him" to ensure topnotch service.[122]

Though Grant was reserved, he didn't sign his contract until most of the others on the list did. One Buffalo paper reported on October 22 that Lehane, Mickey Walsh, and John Reidy had signed by that point.[123] In the meantime, there was some intrigue about whether Grant might have a more appealing offer to play elsewhere. Most notably, a Philadelphia paper reported on October 16 that manager Billy Barnie of Baltimore's American Association club had been looking for talent to add to the roster, and the first two players mentioned as candidates were Bisons, namely utility man Joe Kappel and Frank Grant. Barnie surely remembered Grant's excellent displays during the two games Buffalo played in Baltimore back in April. Barnie had recently "stopped a while in Buffalo and watched the playing" of the pair, and he immediately addressed the question of race. "Barnie says he will never draw the color line; that the Baltimore Club will play with colored clubs of recognized ability, as it did in New Jersey the other day, and that if he could improve the nine by the addition of a first-class player he would do so," said the *Philadelphia Times*.[124]

Speaking of color lines, an interesting development in the context of the International League was announced about ten days after Barnie brought up Frank Grant. "Syracuse will join Buffalo in the effort to have the rule prohibiting International clubs from signing colored players rescinded," the *Commercial Advertiser* reported. "Syracuse wants the services of Higgins and Buffalo wants Grant."[125] In fact, that paper reported on November 21 that Syracuse had tried to sign Grant as well the previous week.[126] Nevertheless, the *Evening News* announced on its front page two days later that he had signed again with Buffalo.[127] As a result, he became the only African American of the 1800s to play three years on the same largely-white team.

6

Winning Streak (1888)

During the 1888 season, some of Frank Grant's teammates reportedly expressed discomfort about playing with him. There were even reports or unnamed sources claiming *all* of them opposed him at some point or another, and that such tension supposedly dated back to at least his first preseason with the club. Conversely, following the 1887 season there were some signs of which teammates he liked, and vice versa, based on time they spent together, presumably by choice, away from their summertime jobs. For starters, on the evening of October 7, pitchers Jack Fanning and Mickey Walsh left the city on a train for New York (Fanning only for a few weeks), and one Buffalo paper reported that a "large number of friends escorted the boys to the depot." "Young Paddy Grant" was the only teammate specified by that paper "to wish them a fine trip."[1] Fanning was the teammate who chewed out Toronto's Gus Alberts for running into Grant on the basepaths in August. Back in mid–May, after a different Toronto runner similarly collided with Grant at second base, Walsh was the Buffalo pitcher who hit the next batter with a pitch. Perhaps Grant thought (or was told shortly thereafter) that Walsh's immediate beanball was no coincidence and was actually retaliation on behalf of his teammate.

There were several indications during the offseason that John Reidy was the Bison with whom Grant was the closest. If they didn't have any particular rapport quickly when Reidy first played with the club, one could have developed after they had both suffered great physical abuse by Hamilton players back on May 19, with no intervention by the umpire. Throughout that October, Reidy and Grant were scheduled to have some fun playing on local amateur or semipro teams, beginning with a newly formed team called the Hayseeds. For that game, to be played in nearby Tonawanda, Bisons pitcher Charles Miller was going to pitch to Reidy, and Grant would occupy his usual spot near the middle of the diamond. The game was cancelled due to cold weather.[2] It was announced that on October 23, Reidy would rejoin his old local team, the Travelers, and Grant would help their big rivals, the Clippers, "for $50 a side on the East side grounds." It was rained out but rescheduled for October 30. Then it was postponed due to frigid weather, and apparently the two teams gave up on 1887 after that.[3]

In mid–December, at least a few newspapers around the country listed Grant first among nine African American ballplayers who'd been organized to play in California. Similar announcements had been made in June and April. This lineup was to be "Grant of the Buffalos, Fowler of the Binghamtons, Thomas of the Cuban Giants, Chambers, Rob Jackson and Trusty, Nelson, Dave Jackson, A. Davis of the Gorhams of Boston."[4] If that trip was even begun, and if Grant took part, he was back in Buffalo by February 11.

Instead, he was again in the news just four days into the new year for a very different reason: "Frank Grant, the popular second baseman of the Bisons, will lead to the altar Miss Hattie East of Washington, next March," one Buffalo paper reported. "Grant says, no more single-blessedness for him." This was also reported back in Meriden a few days later.[5] Grant made a statement to the contrary by midmonth: "Grant asks THE EXPRESS to deny that he has been married to a Washington colored lady," that paper said. "He is looking for the man who started the rumor." This news item shifted focus in a strange direction: "The great second baseman has found a dog which he believes to be a mascot, and he proposes to bring the dog out to Olympic Park next season to aid in winning games." Despite this denial—which, to be technical, only said he hadn't been married *yet*—at least one Buffalo paper printed a similar item toward the end of March: "Frank Grant, the celebrated second baseman for the Bisons, says he will marry Miss West, the colored belle of the First ward, Washington, D.C., upon the arrival of the Bisons in that city in April," the *Commercial Adviser* asserted. "John Reidy of this city will be best man."[6] Yes, her surname had shifted geographically between January and March, from East to West. Regardless, if there was minimal or no truth to this, it seems a little strange that it became more specific in its retelling. But if this reported role for Reidy was anywhere close to reflecting accurately his relationship with Grant, then best *friend*, at least, may have been true at the time.

Frank Grant received far less attention from another announcement early in 1888, but it suggested he had friends in Buffalo besides his teammates: A local amateur team called the Queen Citys named him their manager for the upcoming season. Buffalo's 1889 city directory had listings for a Francis E. Grant and for a machinist named Frank Grant, and this announcement wasn't explicit that the Queen Citys' manager was the famous ballplayer. However, when the Bisons had an off-day on Sunday, May 20, between home games against Rochester, "Grant, Buffalos 2d baseman" accompanied the Queen Citys to a game and that club asked its opponent if he could play for them that day. Predictably, local rules wouldn't allow a professional to play.[7] Grant presumably wasn't actually their manager at that point, because a Dr. M. Retel was identified in that roll shortly before the Bisons began their preseason tour, but it's no surprise that Grant maintained some sort of connection to that amateur club.[8]

On February 11, Frank Grant and John Reidy joined players from a few other clubs at a Buffalo hotel in which the league had a meeting for the 1888 season. Jack Chapman was also in town.[9] About five weeks later, Grant and Reidy started working out together at the city's arsenal, located on Broadway. During their first week, they were joined by two other infielders, Edward Allen of Toledo's minor league club and Jim Dee of Albany's new entry in the renamed International *Association*, which reverted to an eight-team league for 1888.[10] Allen, Dee, and Reidy were all involved in the Clippers-Travelers rivalry during 1886. Allen played six games for the Bisons right before Grant, Remsen, and Dunn were signed. Dee had played for Scranton in 1887.[11]

On March 31, Grant and Reidy left on a 5:00 train for Washington, D.C. to meet their teammates for their first preseason game. By that point, Grant had reportedly added a little weight compared to the previous season. (A brief preview of the team's roster in February listed his height as 5'7½", a half-inch more than a year earlier, but his weight still as 155.) More importantly, as the duo began their trip, Grant was suffering from "a very sore finger," according to one Buffalo paper.[12]

The Bisons played their first preseason game of 1888 on Monday, April 2. As had happened a year earlier, future Hall of Famer Hank O'Day held Frank Grant hitless, but Grant played errorless ball at second base. Washington won, 13–4.[13] In light of the previous year's spring training futility, the Bisons who had made that 1887 road trip were probably stunned and thrilled the next day when they managed to play Washington to a 6–6 tie in 10 innings. Buffalo trailed 5–1 after three innings but produced almost all of the offense after that. Grant again had seven chances on defense without an error and hit a triple off Frank Gilmore, whose three-year National League career consisted of 49 games for Washington.[14] The teams played a third consecutive day, and the Nationals clobbered the Bisons, 20–3. Grant hit a double off Ed Daily, whom he had homered off of memorably about a year earlier.[15]

Buffalo was supposed to play in Baltimore on April 5, but that contest was rained out. Next up was a visit to Pittsburgh's NL team for three games over four days (skipping Sunday). Grant and the Bisons faced future Hall of Famer Pud Galvin, against whom he had singled and walked a year earlier. Of comparable significance was the fact that none other than Fred Dunlap was now a member of the Pittsburgh nine. Grant batted third in Buffalo's lineup, and Dunlap batted sixth for the home team. The latter went hitless but fielded five chances cleanly. Grant had eight chances but made an error. At bat, Grant scored a run and had three hits off Galvin, including a triple. Buffalo rallied in the eighth and ninth innings, but Pittsburgh countered and hung on for a 9–8 victory. The *Pittsburgh Press* admitted that the result "was due more to good luck than good management. On its merits in every way Buffalo should have been the winner." That daily singled out one of the Bisons for high praise but also some sympathy: "Should King Dunlap ever be called upon to abdicate his throne, a worthy successor, so far as ability goes, might be found in Grant, the colored second baseman of the Buffalos, who, but for his color, might have found his way into the [National] league before this. Grant is very handy with the stick."[16]

Unfortunately, Grant sat out the second game two days later because he "had a lame arm," and Pittsburgh pummeled Buffalo, 12–2. The third game in the series was rained out.[17] The Bisons then played two games in Wheeling, West Virginia, against that city's Ohio State League club, and Grant was in the lineup for both. In the first game, he had two hits, handled nine chances without an error, and helped turn a double play in a 5–4, 12-inning win for Buffalo. In the rematch, the Bisons suffered a one-hit shutout.[18]

At this time, a newspaper in Berkshire County, Massachusetts chose to provide a mini-profile of Frank Grant and brag about his Pittsfield roots. The *Pittsfield Sun* connected the dots of his short career up to that point by confirming that the pitcher for the Greylocks in 1884 was the same ballplayer who caught for Plattsburgh in 1885 and moved on to Meriden in 1886. The paper then piled on the praise: "He is a great all-round player…. He is a very accurate thrower, and withal swift. He is exceedingly hard to fool at the bat … and his shots are generally long." The paper proudly related his total extra-base hits for 1887.[19] There's a good chance a few cousins and other relatives in that area happened upon this long paragraph or had it brought to their attention.

On Saturday, April 13, the Bisons played Cincinnati's American Association nine. The Reds built an early lead and held on to win, 8–5. Grant managed a single in five-at bats off Billy Serad, whose first two years in the majors had been with Buffalo. But the second paragraph of the *Cincinnati Enquirer*'s account focused on Grant's fielding:

> Grant, the colored second basemen [sic] of the team, was the favorite with the crowd. He is very active on his feet, and covered a great deal of territory. He chased a number of difficult flies away out into right field, and after hard runs captured them. He also made a beautiful double-play. The crowd seemed well pleased with his work, and he was applauded repeatedly.[20]

In the second game—a rare Sunday contest for Buffalo—Grant went hitless in four at-bats against Billy Hart, who soon joined Buffalo's nine. Hart had already played two years in the majors and played six more after his stint with the Bisons. As for Grant, despite not wowing the locals at bat in the first two games, following the rematch, the *Enquirer* declared him to be "the greatest colored player in the United States" and asserted that he had "again put up a strong game. He made several remarkable stops, and was loudly applauded." In this game, fielding was crucial, because the Reds led by a score of just 3–2 at the end of four innings, and there was no more scoring the rest of the way.[21]

Things fell apart for Grant and the Bisons in the third game. He had a walk but went 0-for-3, kept hitless this time by rookie Lee Viau, who went 27–14 that season. But the *Enquirer* said his "very bad off day" was evident when he "fumbled" three balls in play, plus "his throwing was very bad." The Reds didn't experience much of a challenge from the other Bisons and strolled to a 15–2 win.[22]

Buffalo played Louisville's American Association club the next day, April 16. It was a cold day, so attendance was estimated at only 500. "Most of the people in the twenty-five cent seats were colored, and their interest and enthusiasm was awakened by the appearance of Grant, a colored ball player of some reputation," the local *Courier-Journal* reported. "During the game if Grant lifted his hand or moved a foot he was loudly cheered by the colored contingent of the bleaching boards." After five innings, he was the only Bison who had a hit off Guy Hecker, whose nine-year major league career had peaked with a 52–20 record for Louisville in 1884. Grant also drew a walk in five plate appearances. The home team led 5–0 after seven innings, but Buffalo suddenly came alive against a relief pitcher in the final two frames and pulled off an upset, 6–5! They had finally defeated a major league club! The *Courier-Journal* said three Bisons played particularly well in the field, especially Grant, whom the paper called "the colored wonder."[23]

The two teams played again the next day, and Louisville topped Buffalo, 8–3. Grant scored two of those three runs. In four at-bats, he got one of Buffalo's five hits off rookie Scott Stratton, whose eight-year major league career peaked in 1890 for Louisville with a 34–14 record. Grant's hit drove in at least one run. He also earned a steal after he "ran to second like a deer," which the *Courier-Journal* actually depicted with a drawing of two stick figures. Grant made three errors, but that daily still called him "the Black Diamond" and blamed his poor fielding on "a strained arm."[24] That was at least the second such explanation of the month.

Buffalo visited a major league team for the final time on its 1888 spring training trip when it played against Indianapolis' National League nine on April 18. One Indy paper's preview called Grant "the best colored ball-player in the country," as the *Cincinnati Enquirer* had similarly declared three days earlier.[25] The Bisons were shut out, 8–0, by young Lev Shreve (who concluded 1888 by leading the NL with the most earned runs and homers allowed). Grant did manage a single in the game. Cold weather the next day caused the cancellation of a scheduled rematch.[26]

In sum, the Bisons played five different major league teams (plus games in Wheeling) from April 2 through 18. Frank Grant played in 10 of the 11 games against National League or American Association opponents. Though he started by going hitless against one future Hall of Famer, just before the Pittsburgh game in which he didn't play, he'd had three hits off a different future Hall of Famer, and that was in his third consecutive game with a triple or double. In the six games after the game he missed, he went hitless twice and swatted only lone singles in the other four contests. Neither batch of games represents a big sample size, but the before-and-after difference is consistent with some sort of new or worsened arm injury just before the second game in Pittsburgh.

Following the game in Indianapolis, Buffalo played five consecutive days against minor league teams in Ohio before returning home for a pair of games against a local team. Around that time, several newspapers, including one in Colorado, borrowed from a long *Louisville Post* commentary about Grant. The longest version was reprinted in a Meriden paper:

> Grant, the colored second baseman of the Buffalos, is the only negro player professionally with any club in the different associations [inaccurate]. He is a fine ball tosser, all the same, and hasn't many superiors among players either white or black. I think he gets $600 a year for his services, while, if he had a white skin, he could easily demand $2,000. Grant is very popular in Buffalo, and for that reason the management is forced to hold him, although the players of the club are said to feel keenly having to play with a colored man. In the East, Grant goes with the other members of the club, stops at the same hotels, eats at the same table and possibly occupies the same room. While in this city he registered at the Galt House, but is roomed with the colored help and takes his meals with them.[27]

Racial tensions within his team were certainly an issue for Grant in 1888, but as Opening Day approached, he had a more immediate concern: On April 25, the *Buffalo Times* reported a slightly different impairment for him, that he was "suffering from a lame shoulder." Happily, the next day's *Evening News* said he had "nearly recovered."[28]

The Bisons opened the regular season back on the road on April 28, against one of the International Association's new franchises, Troy, a former National League city. The teams played to a 6–6 tie. Grant batted third and went 1-for-5 with a stolen base. He didn't make an error, but he also didn't record an assist. His five putouts included two that concluded double plays.[29] Buffalo beat Troy the next day, 8–5, and Grant showed more life on offense, with a triple and single in five at-bats, two runs scored, and two steals.[30]

On May 4 and 5, Buffalo played its first two games against Syracuse, in that city, and lost both. Fleet Walker caught in both, including a 5–0 shutout in the second contest. Thus, Buffalo fans had a quick reminder that the sympathetic article in the *Louisville Post* was wrong to say that Frank Grant was the only African American left in the minor leagues. Syracuse also still employed Robert Higgins, though its second baseman with that surname was a white player whose first name was Bill. In fact, after the shutout, the *Buffalo Sunday Morning News* pointed that out and added that Bud Fowler was still playing in minor league ball, in Indiana. But the Buffalo paper first challenged the claim that, as they paraphrased it, Grant was "not liked by the players in the club. The statement is absurd. Grant is liked by everybody in Buffalo including the players."[31]

GRANT STOLE SECOND.

At least he didn't attempt a riskier headfirst slide. From the *Louisville Courier-Journal*, April 18, 1888.

Buffalo's home opener was on May 10, and 3,000 fans helped them host the nine from London, Ontario, the third new International Association team. Frank Grant was the leadoff hitter, and he responded by going 3-for-5 with a double and a run scored. He also played errorless ball and finished a double play, but London led 7–0 after four frames and prevailed, 8–6. In the rematch, he performed similarly, going 3-for-4 with a walk and two runs scored. He again played errorless ball and helped turn another double play. More importantly, his two-run homer helped give the Bisons a 5–1 lead after two innings, and they held on to win at home for the first time in the young season, 9–5.[32] He had another errorless, 3-for-4 game including a walk and a homer against Rochester on May 19, but that 13–5 win only improved Buffalo's record to 6–7, which put the team in fifth place in the eight-team circuit.[33] The next day was a Sunday, and thus the two teams met again on May 21. The score was tied, 1–1, after two innings. The *Buffalo Evening News* reported the game's early turning point:

> When Grant went to the bat in the third there was fire in his eye. He looked savage and hit the ball viciously. "Home run, Grant!" a spectator yelled. Grant smiled benevolently and grasped the bat firmly. The next ball that came along he sent flying over the fence, amid tremendous applause.[34]

By contrast, the *Times* might have earned some chuckles with its understatement: "Grant as usual got in his home run and won deserved applause." It was his only hit of the game, but the Bisons never trailed afterwards and hung on for a 4–2 win.[35]

Grant had an even bigger game the next day, when the Bisons destroyed Albany with a 12-run third inning, on their way to an 18–1 laugher. In that devastating inning, Grant had a double and a triple. On the whole, he went 4-for-6 with a stolen base. That apparently came after he led off Buffalo's first time at bat, on a play that might have been much more significant than fans realized at the time. Important details were printed in the *Buffalo Evening News*, but that paper was vague about the beginning of the sequence of events:

> Grant started the ball rolling in the first innings [sic]. He hit a single, then started for second. The catcher threw the sphere to the second baseman. The baseman started to head off Grant. He never thought that a colored player had a hard head. It was Dee, an old Buffalo boy. Grant simply tried to run through him, and both men rolled in the dust. Dee dropped the ball, picked it up, and Grant started for third. The third baseman muffed the ball and Grant scored. Tremendous applause![36]

So it sounds like after Grant singled, he didn't try to stretch it into a double but rather "started for second" on a subsequent *pitch*, because it's unlikely any Albany fielder would've thrown to the catcher after a single. Regardless, the Dee with whom he collided was the same Jim Dee with whom he worked out back in March at the arsenal. "He never thought that a colored player had a hard head" may have meant that none of the African American ballplayers in the league around that time were known for aggressive base running. In this case, though, Grant may have had ample reason to believe that if there was any white opponent he could risk a collision with and not fear violent revenge, it was Dee (or Bob Pettit previously). It's certainly possible that Dee and Grant were expecting to have a friendly rivalry that season.

Whatever the case, despite the fact that Grant played the remaining eight innings, he missed the next day's game. The *Express* simply alluded to "lameness," while other papers in town limited their comments to the inadequacy of his replacement during that loss.³⁷ Even worse, the next day the Bisons had a doubleheader in London, and he didn't play in either contest—both of which his club lost. A paper in Rochester implied that he hadn't even made the trip.³⁸ After their two wins versus Rochester, Buffalo newspapers fully expected wins against lesser opponents in those three subsequent games. The *Commercial Advertiser* went so far as to ask, "If the Buffalo management pay big salaries, why don't they get first class men? A nine like little Frank Grant, the best player in the Bisons, could beat the world."³⁹ Another local paper mentioned a few days later that Grant had the league's fifth-highest batting average, near .400, through the day in London.⁴⁰

The Bisons returned home after just that one day in Canada, and Grant returned to the top of their batting order in a game against Troy. He went 3-for-5, scored three runs, made five putouts, had five assists without an error, and completed a double play in an easy victory, 16–7. It was about this game that the *Evening News* said a few days later: "Grant has many dusky admirers in the ladies' stand. Four of them applauded him there during the game last Friday."⁴¹ The next day, he scored twice and again played errorless ball in an 8–6 win. One of his two hits was a double.⁴² He seemed no worse for wear, but the team was stuck with a record of 10–10.

Of course there was no game on Sunday, May 27, but readers of that day's *Express* were treated to an array of Bisons portraits sketched "from recent and first-class photographs taken by Potter." The ballplayers were all dressed very fancily. Fittingly, near the center of the display were Grant and Reidy, among the few pairs of players whose portraits were placed so that they were looking toward one another.⁴³ A later sketch of Frank Grant with the Cuban Giants has been printed often in recent years in articles or on web pages about him and his African American contemporaries, but this distinctly different 1888 sketch might only have been used by the Hall of Fame prior to 2020.

This sketch was based on a photograph which has never been found. From the *Buffalo Express*, May 27, 1888.

Grant had a bad game on defense during a 10-inning loss in Hamilton on May 29. He committed four errors, at least two of which were costly,⁴⁴ but it didn't represent the start of any downward spiral. The next day, Buffalo hosted Toronto for a doubleheader, and he played errorless ball in the first game. On offense, he had two of his team's four hits, but his triple drove in Buffalo's only run of the morning, and 1,500 fans thus saw the visitors pull off a 3–1 win.⁴⁵

The second game was witnessed by a whopping 7,000 fans. "Grant was presented with a handsome basket of flowers as he stepped up to the plate at Olympic Park yesterday afternoon," one Buffalo paper noted. "He tipped his hat coquettishly and grinned all over!"[46] The Bisons led 2–1 after four innings, but Toronto scored once in the top of the seventh to tie it. The visitors then took a 4–2 lead after their half of the eighth. The thousands of hometown fans were surely in agony at the thought of losing such a game so late and thus losing a doubleheader at home. Two local papers disagreed about some important details about the sequence of events in the bottom half of that inning, but Grant went up to bat with Hart on second base and none out. He reached base himself, and Hart advanced to third. Grant then stole second, and he moved to third when Hart scored on the next play. If Grant hadn't risked that stolen base, he might not have tied the game and set up the eventual winning run.[47]

On June 1, they met Toronto again, except as the visitors. Grant led off the game with a single, and that proved to be the team's only hit of the entire game. Buffalo was stifled by former major leaguer Al Atkinson, who went 25–17 for Philadelphia's American Association team in 1886. Grant also coaxed a walk from him and scored twice, but Toronto won easily, 8–3.[48] The next day's game in Toronto was rained out, and many of the Bisons may have considered that a merciful happenstance.

In any case, knowledgeable Bisons fans who read the *Buffalo Evening News* around then—when it quoted a Toronto newspaper about Grant—surely rolled their eyes: "Grant, the Buffalo second baseman, always receives a warm welcome in Toronto," claimed the *Toronto Mail*. Toward the end of the 1887 season, at least two Buffalo papers had reported the horrific verbal abuse he suffered from fans in Toronto. The *Mail*, by the way, added that he had "a sore arm," so he was "not fielding nor batting in his old-time form."[49] It wasn't clear whether that was old news that had only come to their attention, or whether he was managing to play through that potential limitation. Though he had that embarrassing game against Hamilton on May 29, his three games against Toronto didn't extend any kind of defensive or offensive slump. As if to rebut the *Mail's* conclusion, when Toronto promptly visited Buffalo again on June 4 and 5, Grant was dominant on offense. In an intense slugfest on June 4 that the Bisons won, 15–14, in 10 innings, Grant went 2-for-5 with a double, a walk, and two runs scored. He also drove in at least one run, on a sacrifice fly. The next day, he went 3-for-3 and walked twice, though Toronto had an easy 14–5 victory.[50]

Arm issues for Grant were mentioned often enough by this point in the season that many Bison fans may have been on edge any time something along those lines was mentioned. Therefore, some readers of four Buffalo dailies may have panicked on June 8 when they read about the previous day's loss in Rochester, when "Grant threw his arm out of joint in the eleventh inning," during which the home team (having chosen to bat first that day) scored twice and won, 4–2. Grant had played errorless ball, with two putouts and seven assists.[51] Nevertheless, he returned to the lineup the next day in Syracuse with a lone error in eight chances on defense, and another good day on offense. He went 2-for-4 with two runs scored, and his double in the eighth inning helped pull the Bisons within a run of the Stars, but the home team held on, 10–9. He did make two errors in the next day's rematch but also went 2-for-4 again, albeit in a 9–0 shutout by Syracuse. About one of these games, the *Syracuse Standard* wrote that "Grant, in spite of his lame shoulder, played a pretty game."[52]

On June 13, the *Evening News* reported that Grant was the leading hitter of the

Bisons with a .381 batting average. That paper couldn't help but add that few of his teammates had "decent averages." In the very next paragraph, it quoted the *Syracuse Standard* about Buffalo having occupied every spot in the International Association standings between first and last, and said that the Bisons were dangerously close to the cellar.[53] If fans were thinking that Grant was carrying the team, there was more evidence that same day, in a 3–2 win at Albany: Grant had two of the team's four hits, scored twice (including the run that either tied it or was the game-winner in a two-run eighth inning), and his double was Buffalo's only extra-base hit.[54] He had yet another similar game at home two days later, hosting London, with 2-for-4, a double, walk, and two runs scored on offense, plus five putouts, five assists, and no errors on defense. This time, though, the whole nine played well and the Bisons treated 2,500 fans to a slugfest, which ended 11–4.[55]

About two weeks prior to that year's preseason trip to face various major league teams, Jack Chapman announced that he'd scheduled additional games against four major league teams for some of his club's days off during the regular season. The two games hosting Detroit's National League team on June 18 and 19 were apparently the only ones that occurred.[56] How far Frank Grant had progressed since he faced that same team on April 17, 1886, in Meriden, in only his third game as a professional! Meanwhile, Detroit was the defending world champions after winning the 1887 NL pennant and beating St. Louis of the American Association in a postseason series. Grant—and the entire team—did better in the second game. In the first contest, before more than 4,000 fans, it became grim for the Bisons when they let Detroit score five times in the third inning. Grant misplayed an easy ball hit to him, and the home team made two other miscues that inning. In the end, Buffalo came part of the way back but still lost, 9–6. Grant went 0-for-5 against second-year pitcher Ed Beatin (who went 20–15 the next year for Cleveland), but he did steal a base and score a run. On defense, he committed a second error in addition to his four putouts and three assists.[57]

Pitching for the Wolverines in the second game was second-year pitcher Henry Gruber, who was in the midst of an 11–14 season but with an impressive earned run average of 2.29. Jack Fanning and John Reidy were the battery for the Bisons. Future Hall of Famer Dan Brouthers wasn't in Detroit's lineup that day, but future Hall of Famer Deacon White was, along with Hardy Richardson and Jack Rowe, who, as mentioned previously, had been known once upon a time as Buffalo's "Big Four." Future Hall of Famer Ned Hanlon (inducted as a manager, not for his playing) also sat out, but future Hall of Famer Sam Thompson did play. It was still a powerhouse lineup.

This time, about 3,000 fans turned out. Frank Grant led off for the Bisons in their half of the first inning and drew a walk. He soon reached third base, but was stranded there. In the third inning, he singled and stole second base, but the Bisons again couldn't drive him home. Reidy drove in the first run of the game in the fourth inning. The next frame was huge for the hometown nine. Grant reached on a fielder's choice with two outs and soon scored Buffalo's second run. Before the inning ended, three teammates followed him across home plate on Lehane's blast over the left field fence. "The yelling lasted for several minutes," the *Buffalo Courier* reported. Grant's one bad play on defense was in the sixth inning, and it gave the Wolverines only their second runner of the game. The next batter singled, and just like that, the visitors had two men on with no outs. The next batter was retired on a third strike that Reidy dropped, and Grant's friend saw the lead runner stray too far toward third base, so his throw to Grant completed a

6. Winning Streak (1888)   69

double play. The *Courier* said the runner on first had also strayed and that Grant missed an opportunity to turn a *triple* play and thus totally extinguish the threat. In the seventh inning, Grant more than made up for his error by smashing a triple deep to right field, after which he was promptly singled home. Detroit managed to avoid a shutout by scoring just once in the ninth inning, but the Wolverines were outhit on the day, 10—5, and the Bisons had a sweet victory, 6–1. In sum, Frank Grant went 2-for-4 including a triple and a walk, two runs scored, a steal, six putouts, five assists, that one error, and that double play.[58]

Unfortunately, this achievement didn't sustain the Bisons for long at all. They lost, 10–2, in Hamilton the next day. Hamilton's batters might very well have benefited from the fact that Fanning pitched for the second consecutive day. As for the offense and fielding behind him, "Grant made two inexcusable errors, but he was the only one that had any real success with the stick," the *Times* said. He had two of the Bisons' five hits, in four at-bats, and his double was their only hit for extra bases. He also scored one of the two runs.[59] Three days later, he had an even bigger game at the plate in an easy 10–2 victory against Albany. He went 3-for-5, including a homer and a steal, scored three times, and provided errorless defense. "Grant gets a bouquet about once a week," the *Express* observed.[60] No wonder.

Around this time, the *Rochester Democrat and Chronicle* reported briefly about a "scheme" to have Grant, Walker, and Higgins "ousted from the International Association." The Rochester correspondent for *Sporting Life*, who may or may not have reported for the *Democrat and Chronicle*, said Buffalo and Syracuse had "disregarded" the promise made almost 12 months earlier "that 1887 would be the last year that colored players would be allowed to play." That correspondent singled out Grant for an additional jab: "I think that much of the trouble in the Buffalo Club is due indirectly to the playing of their 'dusky star.'" The *Buffalo Sunday Morning News* rebutted that directly, saying, "Without Grant, the Buffalo's [sic] are like a ship without a rudder."[61] Everyone involved would find out one way or the other from mid–July to late August.

For the end of June, however, Grant remained pretty hot, at least every other game. On June 25, he scored half of his team's runs in a 6–1 win at home over Rochester. He went 3-for-5, including a double and a homer. Two days later, Troy couldn't keep him off first base and had trouble keeping him from reaching home, when he had a single, double, three walks, and three runs again. Against Syracuse and Fleet Walker two days later, he went 2-for-4 with a run scored, and on defense had two double plays (one unassisted). The league standings for the end of the month showed Buffalo in fifth place with a record of 19–24, ahead of only the three new teams, namely London, Troy, and Albany.[62]

Sadly, the Bisons didn't win a game during the first week of July, and that included a doubleheader in Toronto on July 2, the Canadian Dominion Day holiday, plus another hosting London on Independence Day. In the first game of the latter pair, Grant injured himself trying to steal second base, but he bounced back in the second game by going 3-for 5 with a single, double, triple, and two runs scored, while playing errorless at his usual second base post.[63]

Buffalo's game on Thursday, July 5 ended with its seventh straight loss. "Several men who played a conspicuous part in the loss of yesterday's game were very properly fined for the wretched performances," the *Courier* reported. Grant was fined the most, $25. The other two players named were shortstop James Flynn, $15, and Remsen, $10. The latter went 0-for-5 and made an error. Grant and Flynn each went 2-for-5 with a run scored, but Grant made two errors and Flynn three. However, it might have been incorrect to include Grant in that list, at least at that high amount, because two days later the *Express* didn't mention a fine for Grant but instead reported that "Remsen, Flynn, and Hart were fined $10 each after Thursday's game for their chump ball-playing." Hart had gone 0-for-3 at bat and made a lethal error in right field.[64]

The latter newspaper also seemed to absolve Grant of any blame for the losing streak generally, asserting that he'd "had hard luck, nursing a lame arm and leg."[65] Fortunately, the Bisons halted the losing streak at nine on July 9 by beating Rochester on the road, 4–2. The *Express* called the team's fielding "very good" but singled out Grant for "being as certain as usual of everything that came anywhere in his way." He had four putouts and seven assists without an error, and was half of a double play. "Grant played remarkably," the *Evening News* said, but quickly switched to frustration: "If he would only play that way every day!"[66]

Buffalo's newspapers had reported consistently about his arm problem(s), but rarely did they get as specific as the *Courier* did on July 11: ""Grant's arm has not been right all season, and he needs a rest. It is only with difficulty that he throws a ball to first base, while a double play is almost impossible." In other words, his problem was getting the ball to teammates, especially if they were 90 or more feet away, and not catching the ball.[67] As if to illustrate this distinction, in that same day's edition of the *Rochester Democrat and Chronicle*, Grant was praised when one Rochester batter bashed "a hard ball which ought to have been good for a two-bagger, but which was captured by a phenomenal catch of Grant's, who was playing in good form, though indulging, as usual, in unnecessary contortions for the benefit of the grand stand." Not surprisingly, this rival city's paper couldn't resist undercutting its praise with a snide remark. In fact, two columns over, the *Democrat and Chronicle* also commented that "Remsen probably played his last game yesterday, and Grant must go." That was correct about Remsen, Grant's longest-lasting teammate to that point, but the *Express* rebuffed the comment about Grant explicitly a few days later: "Yes, he will go wherever the Buffalos go."[68] Alas, late that month Grant's only other teammate from 1886, Mickey Walsh, was also released.[69] Walsh, it will be remembered, was one of the players Grant made a point of saying goodbye to at the end of the previous season. Manager Jack Chapman was thus the one constant during Grant's three years with Buffalo.

After a hitless game in Hamilton on July 12, Chapman dropped Grant from first to fifth in the batting order. Grant responded by going 4-for-5 with a run scored and a stolen base. He had a good game the following day as well. "Grant fielded and batted finely and was rewarded with copious applause," the *Courier* reported. "His daring steal of third base in the fifth was a great play."[70] It is anyone's guess whether Grant paid attention to comments in the local newspapers, but whenever a player is struggling, it's surely appreciated when the fans have their back.

Grant experienced an unusual game on July 16 when the Bisons hosted Hamilton. First, the good news: In the cleanup (fourth) spot in the lineup, his two hits in five at-bats were a double and a homer, and in the eighth inning he recorded the final out after Flynn threw to Reidy to begin a triple play. "The applause was deafening," the *Express* noted. But there was just too much badness earlier in the game, in the form of his *five* errors. The *Express* blamed him alone for the outcome, a 12–7 loss, and in the next column noted that "Grant will be laid off a couple of weeks."[71] The reality was more than three weeks.

This bottoming out brought forth some harsh statements, but also at least one that was merely unusual. "He claims his arm is still in poor shape, but this is no excuse for three passed grounders and a muffed thrown ball," the *Courier* said. The *Express* said he "fumbled" three balls hit to him, and even the *Courier* called two of his errors "fumbles," yet this summation by the *Courier* seemed to imply that three batted balls got past him that he failed to stop at all. Regardless, Grant was fined $25, or a fiver for each error. Elsewhere on the same page, the *Courier* commented that "Grant never plays well after a Sunday or a holiday." This may have been their way of suggesting that he partied too hard when there was a day off. The somewhat odd comment that day was in the *Express*. "Will somebody please present Grant with a water-melon? It is his favorite fruit," that daily wrote.[72] Perhaps they zoomed in on something trivial as a form of denial, or they were suggesting an easy way fans could cheer him up, while also boosting his health. Of course, it's possible that simply wasn't true about Grant, and the *Express* was perpetuating a stereotype, unwittingly or otherwise.

On Tuesday, July 17, Grant was inactive for the first of 19 consecutive games, not counting an exhibition on July 25 when the American Association's Louisville club visited Buffalo to inflict a pounding upon them. Some Buffalo newspapers may have been unaware that he was expected to remain idled for more than a game or two. For example, the *Times* said, "Grant had a chance to sit on the bench and meditate on his misdeeds the day before." In fact, they didn't even agree on where within the ballpark he sat. "Grant looked forlorn after his suspension on Monday," said the *Sunday Truth*. "Tuesday he watched the brilliant play of Hamburg at second, and left the grand stand feeling like the last rose of summer."[73]

Grant's primary replacement was a career minor leaguer, journeyman Henry Bittman. The known start of Bittman's career was in 1885 with Atlanta in the Southern League, and he finished it with three teams in 1890. He had been with Syracuse for part of 1886 and apparently all of 1887. Before July was over, he was being contrasted with Grant in print. For example, "Bittman cannot guard second as well as Grant," one paper complained.[74]

Though the *Commercial Advertiser* joined the *Express* in blaming Grant entirely for that loss to Hamilton, it focused its fury on the person it considered the bigger, longer-term problem: the manager. "The trouble is the boys will not play together. They all dislike Manager Chapman," that daily claimed. "He has not a genuine friend in the nine." Chapman was blasted more in a few additional sentences, and the daily pointed out that the most populous city in the league had "next to the poorest club." The next day, another paper in town disagreed directly with the *Commercial Advertiser*: "This is untrue as the best of harmony prevails," the *Courier* replied. "Discontent has not been an element in the loss of Buffalo's games."[75]

A week later, the *Express* decided to take a turn stirring the proverbial pot. "'Tis said 'Patsy' Grant wants his release from the Buffalos," that paper stated. (Buffalo papers periodically called Grant "Paddy" or "Patsy," which may have been a nickname for him limited to that city or mainly that newspaper.) It was Chapman's turn to be the rebutter, and the *Express* acknowledged the next day that he had denied that rumor.[76] A week later, though, the *Express* was blunt about spreading a "rumor," that Grant's salary had been reduced to $200 a month. At least when the *Commercial Advertiser* found another reason to mention Grant in print, it was for a neutral reason. On July 28, that daily said he was scheduled to umpire a game the next day between the Manhattans and the Queen Citys.[77]

After Grant's first day out of uniform, local papers didn't seem to report whether he continued to watch or even travel with the club. Therefore, it is anyone's guess what he did on a typical day during his extended leave of absence, but one would like to think he'd have some ability to page through his press clippings, at least the local ones. Grant had recently been invoked in newspapers for some atypical or unusual reasons. On May 28, the *Buffalo Evening News* decided to emblazon on their front page an image of a local African American ballplayer named Walter Dallas, a 15-year-old whose "vim and abandon" at second base for that paper's Newsboys team were of course compared to Frank Grant's. As the "smallest lad" on the team, he was being called its mascot (a bringer of good luck). He was "hereby introduced to the public" by virtue of this eye-catching decision, though he'd already been called "a second Grant" by another local paper. In fact, the *Evening News* speculated that there wasn't any other kid "known so widely as he" across the city.[78] Still, the large sketch was clearly intended to cement his status as a local celebrity, and it seems unlikely that this would ever have happened if Frank Grant's popularity among local fans hadn't paved the way.

Shortly thereafter, a newspaper in Pittsburgh printed a very long comedic dialogue (made available to other papers via wire service) between a Washington politician and a local baseball fan. The politician mentioned several famous people—by last name only—but the baseball fan thought he was talking about ballplayers who shared those surnames. Toward the end was the following exchange, which started with the politician bringing up Frederick Dent Grant, the oldest son of General and President Ulysses S. Grant, an unsuccessful political candidate in New York in 1887:

> "I'm sorry the New Yorkers didn't take to young Grant."
> "He seems to be popular in Buffalo."
> "Yes."
> "I suppose his color was against him in New York."
> "His color?"
> "Yes; he's a coon, you know."
> "Get out. He's white all around."
> "What! Grant of the Buffalos?"
> "I don't know about his being in Buffalo. He's been living in New York since the old man died."
> "What old man?"
> "Why Grant, you ass. Gen. Grant, U.S. Grant. Did you never hear of him?"
> "Well I swear. You mean Col. Fred Grant.... Well, I'm blessed! I thought you were talking about men—real men who can hit a ball."[79]

The full dialogue was printed from Maine to Kansas, if not farther west, and provides a different indication of the extent to which Frank Grant was a celebrity nationwide. But perhaps the more significant use of his name was in a product endorsement early that summer, under the headline Groves Is a Mascot:

> Frank Grant, who used to be the Buffalo's mascot, says that mascotterie is played out; that the only mascots worth depending on are good playing and good shoes. He thinks that G.W. Groves makes the best shoes worn by any players. They are sensible, everyday shoes, easily worn, light and durable. Tennis players, campers out, bicyclists, and even dudes wear them to advantage. Price 60 cents to $2 a pair. Don't miss the store, 41 & 43 Seneca street, first store below Main.[80]

6. Winning Streak (1888)

After Grant's recuperation entered its third week, something of a conspiracy against him seemed to surface in some major league cities' newspapers. "There is an organized effort in the Buffalo team to freeze out Grant, the colored second baseman," the *Cincinnati Enquirer* claimed on August 5. "The members recently refused to sit for a group photograph [if] Grant was included." The same day, a paper in New York City printed something similar yet didn't simply parrot from some common source it may have shared with the *Enquirer*. "It transpires that Grant, the colored player, was laid off by Buffalo principally because the rest of the team refused to play with him," the *Sun* asserted. A third paper localized the crisis: "Manager Chapman, of the Buffalo club, wired the manager of the Keystones last night asking what he would pay for Grant, the colored second baseman's release," the *Pittsburgh Daily Post* reported about that city's prominent African American team. "Grant is broken down and nothing was offered for him." The *Buffalo Express*, at least, fended off a comment similar to this last one with some sarcasm. "The *New York Press* says: 'Grant, the celebrated colored second baseman, is said to have broken down completely.' Well, well! It's funny how the news reaches Gotham before creeping out in Bisonville. Send for the ambulance."[81]

None other than the famous *Sporting News* helped offset such negativity with the nationwide reach of its August 11 edition. That weekly noted that Grant was leading the league in batting average. Its next paragraph was a one-liner about a Toronto pitcher, and then it mentioned Grant's leadership again, specifying that his average was .408. This fact was picked up by newspapers from Pennsylvania to Kansas.[82] It would have been more impressive to add that the batter in second place wasn't even close, with an average of .380, according to a chart of the top 20 in the *Syracuse Courier*.[83]

So how did the Bisons fare without Frank Grant in the lineup for 19 games from July 17 into August? They lost their first two without him, but split the first dozen games. During those 12 games, Buffalo never won or lost more than two in a row. That changed on August 3, when the Bisons began a seven-game losing streak. Local papers bemoaned this streak. After the sixth straight loss, in which Buffalo couldn't exploit seven Syracuse errors, one daily wrote, "The whole herd of Bisons played like amateurs."[84] If any of his teammates were happier with him out of the lineup, their performance certainly didn't reflect that. The club thus concluded Grant's furlough with an awful .316 winning percentage.

As a matter of fact, overwhelming evidence to the contrary piled up over his first two weeks back in the lineup: In Frank Grant's first 13 games back in the Bisons' lineup, their record was 13–0. That streak immediately followed their 0–7 skid without him. It should come as no surprise that he made many contributions to that dramatic turnaround.

With minimal advance notice, he returned to active duty with the Buffalo nine on Saturday, August 11, at home versus Troy. Instead of his usual second base, he was assigned to right field. "It was a source of delight to the 1,500 spectators to see Grant back on the field," the *Courier* reported. He hit fourth in the batting order and responded with a double in two at-bats, plus two walks, a stolen base, and two runs scored. As for fielding, his official chances were limited to catching a lone fly ball, but the *Courier* opined, "judging from the manner in which he sprinted about, and captured flies before the game it is safe to assume that he will fill the place acceptably." It was a satisfying return, and, more importantly, Buffalo earned a comfortable 6–1 victory.[85] In case local fans were unsure why he had been out of the lineup, the *Sunday Truth* reminded them (or supplemented sketchy reports in July) that he had "a rest of three weeks to nurse a lame arm."[86]

The two teams met again on Monday, and the Bisons chose to bat first. With a run in and Lehane on third, Grant drove him in with a sacrifice. Every run counted that day, because Troy pushed across a run to tie the score at 5–5 in the bottom of the ninth. Grant saved his best for the tenth frame. With one out and Hamburg on first, Grant contributed his only hit of the game, a single over the first baseman's head which the right fielder overran. Hamburg ran all the way home on the play, to give Buffalo the lead, and Grant reached third. Up next was Flynn, against young pitcher George Keefe (who had a 2.84 ERA in 13 starts for Washington in the National League that year). Keefe got three strikes past Flynn, but Troy's catcher couldn't control the last one. "The ball rolled back about ten feet," the *Courier* noted. "Grant saw his opportunity and by a desperate dive succeeded in evading Keefe's touch at the plate." That may have seemed a great risk by Grant in his second game back, but an insurance run was obviously important to him. Buffalo ultimately didn't need it, and the game soon ended, 7–5, with a second consecutive victory.[87]

Grant homered in his third game back, at home hosting Albany, but one Buffalo daily chose to focus on his defense. "Grant romped all around the outfield, and was very ubiquitous and useful," the *Express* said. "He made two good catches and an equal number of marvelous throws, one from the furthermost fence to second base being especially fine." He thus logged an assist in addition to the two putouts, and made no errors.[88]

Grant was particularly hot at bat during the fifth, sixth, and seventh games of the winning streak. All told, he went 7-for-15, including a triple and a double, scored six runs, and drove in at least three. In that seventh game, he played the first of four consecutive games in left field instead of right.[89]

The 11th game of the winning streak was at Syracuse on Saturday, August 25, and knocked the home team into a first-place tie with Toronto. The Stars led, 5–2, after three innings, but the Bisons took control after that to eke out a 6–5 victory. "Grant played a marvelous game in fielding," said the *Courier*, singling him out on defense (in right field). At bat he was 1-for-3 with a walk. Fleet Walker was the catcher for the Stars, and that was the final time the two African American pioneers competed against one another in any official minor league game.[90]

The rematch was two days later, and the final score was the same. However, it took 10 innings for the Bisons to beat Billy Serad (who had played with Buffalo's NL team) and the rest of the Stars. That inning began with Grant grounding to the shortstop but reaching second base after a bad throw. The next two Bisons made outs but Grant scored the winning run three batters later when Flynn smacked a long hit.[91]

The streak reached 13 at Rochester the next day, August 28, with another 10-inning nail-biter, but Rochester beat Buffalo the following day. The Bisons quickly rebounded to win their next two contests, back home against London, to conclude August with 15 wins in Grant's first 16 games back. During the 13-game winning streak, Grant went 14-for-51 for a batting average of .275. That's not bad, considering that he was returning from a serious injury, but it was far below his .408 average from before his extended absence. More likely to impress moderns fans was his .412 slugging percentage during those 13 games. Also, he had at least eight walks during the streak and more likely 10 (box scores sometimes being vague about those counts), which would have meant an on-base percentage of .373 to .393. For comparison, only nine National League batters had a slugging percentage above .400 in 1888, and the League's five best on-base percentages ranged from .374 to .400.[92]

Speaking of statistics, during Buffalo's home game on August 30, one fan decided to count just about everything he could. For starters, he had apparently noticed prior to that game that some of Buffalo's hitters had a habit of tapping home plate with their bats. Reidy was the only Bison who didn't do that at all during that day's game, while Grant led his nine with 17 taps. Three of his teammates did that at least a dozen times. Buffalo batters hit 25 foul balls that day, and Grant was the Bison with the most, five. Grant and Flynn tied for the most pitches seen during the game, with 21 each. London's pitcher threw to batters 134 times, while Buffalo's made 122 pitches. The latter, by the way, was Charles Gibbs, whose nickname was "Lady," at least according to the *Courier*. Grant must have liked him, because Gibbs homered that day and Grant amused his teammates with an enthusiastic outburst. "Manager Chapman laughed as loud as anybody," the *Courier* noted.[93]

September turned out to be Frank Grant's final month with the Bisons. Early in the month, he was moved up to the third spot in the batting order and played three straight games in center field. "Of course he played well in that position. He could manage the team if necessary," said the *Express*. "He is the most versatile and ubiquitous darkey on earth, so tis said." This use of a derogatory term was just three sentences after that paper referred to Grant as a "colored gentleman."[94] Such casual slurs weren't unusual even in otherwise well-meaning newspapers, and the *Express* generally seemed supportive of him. A year earlier, it was the *Express* that had documented the two Toronto baserunners' intentional collisions with Grant, and made a point to report that Jack Fanning and John Reidy blasted the duo. It was also the *Express* that made a snide remark aimed at all Toronto fans a few days later after they had shouted "kill the nigger" when he batted there.[95]

Frank Grant actually played a fourth consecutive game in center field, but it was in an exhibition on September 6. That contest was a final appearance with Buffalo against a National League team, Washington. The starting pitcher for Washington was their regular shortstop, George Shoch. Shoch had minimal pitching experience as a pro but did hurl three innings in a regular-season game for Washington that year and logged six innings for Milwaukee's Western Association team in 1889, all with no runs allowed. After two innings, Shoch switched positions with Washington's regular first baseman, Billy O'Brien, who had much more experience as a professional pitcher. From 1884 through 1892 he pitched in 38 games and had an ERA of just 1.08.[96]

Grant doubled off Shoch in the first inning and was listed in the *Courier*'s box score as 1-for-5, though he had a sacrifice that was presumably counted as one of those at-bats (a scoring rule discontinued a few years later). Grant played errorless defense and made one putout. Though that box score showed "0" for him in the assists column, the *Courier* noted that he helped undercut a Washington rally in the eighth inning by throwing Shoch out at second base trying to stretch a single into a double. That was vital, because the Bisons hung on to beat the NL visitors, 7–5.[97]

Buffalo didn't have a game scheduled the next day, so Chapman's plan for the day was to take his team to the local fair after a morning practice. "A special watch will be kept on the poultry when Grant comes around," the *Courier* remarked.[98] Just three days after the *Express*' casual use of "darkey," a different Buffalo daily appeared to make a joke based on a stereotype, yet the *Courier* also had a track record of commenting quite warmly about Grant. In fact, just a few days later that paper singled him out for praise during a doubleheader sweep hosting Troy. "The feature of the game was a beautiful catch by Grant in the sixth inning [on a] low fly to short right field," the *Courier* said. "Grant was playing back but he made a quick forward run, barely got up to the ball, and although he turned a somersault in the act he held on to it."[99]

On September 13, Frank Grant performed what the *Express* called "a terror" as well as "the banner record on the home grounds this season" by any Bison batter when he went 5-for-6 with two homers and four runs scored in a win against Albany. He swatted his home runs in the seventh and ninth innings, and both came after blasts umpire Wesley Curry declared to be foul but which the *Courier* said were "questionable" calls.[100] That same newspaper gave Curry some negative publicity after the Bisons hosted the Hamilton Hams on September 17: "Some of the spectators yesterday took offense at Umpire Curry for calling two strikes on Grant. When Curry came back to the stand he heard somebody say that Buffalo couldn't play nine men and the umpire," the *Courier* reported. "Curry singled out the man, and calling a policeman, had the offender ejected from the grand stand." However, the critic was allowed to sit in the bleachers, and he soon returned to his original seat without further incident.[101]

By the time Hamilton arrived for this game, it was guaranteed that the Bisons would end the season with a losing record, but the latter still had strong motivation that day because the Hams had beaten them 12 games in a row. Grant went hitless that day but contributed in other ways. For one, in the first inning, he walked and scored Buffalo's second run. After five frames the Hams led, 5–4, but the Bisons tied it in their half of the sixth. That brought up Grant with a teammate on third base and one out. His sacrifice broke the tie, and the hometown fans "hugged each other and wept for joy." The Bisons kept the lead after that inning and ended up winning, 7–6.[102]

In the rematch the next day, Charlie Hamburg had a second consecutive rough game early on at shortstop, and after committing errors in the first two innings, he swapped positions with outfielder Joe Kappel. Kappel likewise committed errors in his two innings there and was replaced by one of the other outfielders. "There was great applause in the fifth inning when Grant ambled out to short," the *Express* reported. He didn't have any grounders hit to him there, but a Hamilton hitter did fly out to him to end the eighth inning and thus ended a minor threat. The game lasted an extra inning but darkness caused it to end as a 6–6 tie. Though Grant "had little to do" at shortstop in that particular game, the *Express* stated that he was "the man for that position and should be kept there."[103] An anonymous Buffalo sportswriter for *Sporting Life* endorsed the idea during the subsequent offseason.[104] Instead, Grant was back in the outfield for the club's few remaining games.

On September 21–22, Frank Grant played his last two home games for Buffalo, both against Hamilton. He went out with a proverbial bang by going 4-for-8 with a double, a walk, two stolen bases, and three runs scored.[105] The Bisons' last game of that regular season was a blowout loss in London on September 25. Grant batted cleanup and had a single in five at-bats. Two days later, he was one of a dozen players reserved by Buffalo for the 1889 season.[106] The Bisons ended up in sixth place in the eight-team International Association with a record of 48–60,[107] but the club enjoyed a record of 21–10 (with two ties) when Grant returned from his 19-game break.

On September 28, the Bisons played a seven-inning exhibition game against the Cuban Giants, who had played one another in April of 1887. Buffalo led 6–0 after two innings and won, 8–2. Grant went 1-for-4 at bat against William Whyte.[108] The two teams met again the next day, but in the second inning the contest was called off when snow started falling. The Bisons were scheduled to play Baltimore of the American Association on October 1, but rain kept that from happening.

International Association statistics were released by the beginning of October, and Grant ranked sixth in fielding percentage among 12 second basemen. In 53 games, he made 161 putouts, had 191 assists, and committed 46 errors for a fielding percentage of .884. Chub Collins again had the top fielding percentage at that position, and he was the only regular second baseman who came close to averaging as many assists per game as Grant. Among all outfielders, Grant had the fourth-best fielding percentage, .939, in 31 games. He committed three errors, was credited by the league with one assist, and had 44 putouts. Though his batting average was just .258 after his 19-game hiatus, by the season's end his average only slid to .346, which was tied for sixth-best in the league. Slightly revised statistics and rankings later in the month instead credited him as tied for the fifth-best batting average, the third-best fielding percentage among outfielders, and the seventh-best fielding percentage among second basemen. He also had the third-best slugging percentage, .530, and trailed only Hank Simon's .560 for Rochester and Len Sowders' .549 for London. No other regular batter reached the .500 mark.[109]

In 1990, James Overmyer provided statistical analysis covering 1886 through 1888:

> Comparing Grant statistically to his International League peers, it is clear that he shone among them. His three-year batting average of .354 is 26 percent better than the league average for those three years. In his two best years, 1886 and 1888, he was 39 and 36 percent ahead of the league. For the sake of comparison, New York Yankee stars Don Mattingly and Steve Sax, current Boston Red Sox batting star Wade Boggs and ex-Red Sox great Carl Yastrzemski all played very well in their last minor league seasons before making the majors, but none of them were that far ahead of their peers.[110]

On October 4, the *Courier* reported on where Jack Chapman and his Bisons would be spending the offseason, and noted that "Grant will join the Cuban Giants for the winter." In fact, two days later the *New York Sun* announced that they had recruited him for their remaining games that fall. "He will play his first game to-morrow at the Long Island grounds against the Norwalks," that daily noted.[111] But there was a rainstorm in that region the day before the game, and the *Sun* made no mention of it on its sports page the day after, though that page did include a challenge by the Cuban Giants to the Newarks "to play a series of five games for the professional championship of the State of New Jersey." The Cuban Giants beat that team in Newark on October 8, 5–4. The *Sun* reported that the winning nine received $2 each as a result.[112] The next day, the Cuban Giants played at a fair in Wilmington, Delaware, against an ad hoc local nine named the Quicksteps. The home team won, 8–7. Grant, who batted fourth and played second base, doubled for his team's only extra-base hit.[113] It's unclear whether the Cuban Giants returned to the Newark area for additional games that month, but on October 15 a Buffalo newspaper reported that Grant was "in town," along with Jack Fanning and John Reidy.[114]

Toward the end of October, several reports of turmoil within the Buffalo franchise circulated in newspapers elsewhere. For example, the *Courier-Journal* in Louisville wrote that Frank Grant had been released and a likely replacement for him had been identified. The rumors were such that a board member, Cassius C. Candee, rebutted them all publicly, except word that President Charles W. Cushman had communicated an intention to resign.[115]

The Cuban Giants weren't quite done playing ball that autumn, and on November 6 a paper in New York City announced that they would play that day against the New York Giants, winners of the National League pennant, at Elysian Fields in Hoboken. Coverage afterwards was almost nonexistent, and the result was a 2–1 win for the National Leaguers.[116] At the Long Island Grounds five days later, the Cuban Giants played a team that reportedly included three of the champs who were still in town, including a battery of Ledell Titcomb and Pat Murphy versus George Stovey and Arthur Thomas for the Cubans. Reports about this game were minimal, and there was disagreement about whether 200 or 500 was the estimated attendance, but cold weather caused play to end after four innings with the Cuban Giants leading, 13–9.[117] Frank Grant presumably played in at least the second game, if not both, because one newspaper named only him on its sports page on November 12. However, that wasn't because of anything he did on the field. "Grant, the great colored second baseman of the Buffalo Club, appeared at the Long Island grounds yesterday wearing a high silk hat, purple plush coat, light-colored kid gloves, very loud pantaloons, and patent-leather pumps," reported the *Sun*.[118]

On November 19, the Cuban Giants became a charter member of the newly formed Middle States League, representing Trenton, New Jersey. The other seven founding franchises would have all-white rosters. Shortly thereafter, a resolution was adopted by the International Association allowing Buffalo to keep Grant on its roster and Syracuse Fleet Walker on its, but no other African American players could be signed. By coincidence, in the *Buffalo Express* this news was near an announcement that Grant would likely tour Southern states with the Cuban Giants soon.[119]

In mid–December, there was a major announcement that had to affect whatever planning Grant may have been doing for the 1889 season: Two stars of Buffalo's old National League team, Jack Rowe and future Hall of Famer Deacon White, bought a majority of the Bisons' stock and became Vice-President and President, respectively. Grant had played against them back on April 17, 1886, when they were with Detroit and he had just started with Meriden. One immediate consequence was the dismissal of Jack Chapman as manager. "The Buffalo club has fallen into good hands," Chapman wrote immediately in a telegram to the *Courier*. "I wish Rowe and White every success with the Bisons." Rowe said he expected to play shortstop for Buffalo and White third base. "I don't know much about the other men you had last year," Rowe said. "We really haven't given much thought to the matter of players next year but from what I hear, Hamburg, Carroll and Grant make a very strong outfield and I suppose we will keep them."[120] Rowe should have at least been familiar with center fielder Cliff Carroll, who had been a regular in the National League from 1884 through 1887 (and who was good enough to return to the National League for four more seasons as a starter from 1890 through 1893). The year ended with uncertainty about Grant's future.

7

Black Team in a White League (1889)

By early 1889, the *Buffalo Courier*, for one, was referring to Jack Rowe as Buffalo's manager and summarized communication by him that was less equivocal about Frank Grant. "Rowe says he will keep Grant," the *Courier* conveyed. "The talk about Grant being released is all bosh, he says."[1] The roster was almost a blank slate at that point. The *Sun* reported that only one player had been signed, Wyman Andrus, who had been Hamilton's second baseman in 1888. (That New York City daily decided to tack on this odd detail: "Grant of the Buffalos is becoming an expert left-handed thrower.")[2] As a frame of reference, a *Sporting Life* reporter wrote later in January that Andrus would be paid $175 per month.[3] In April, Frank Grant would insist on being paid more than that, and who could blame him?

Other pronouncements by Rowe throughout January communicated consistent interest in and optimism about signing Frank Grant again. Late that month, one Buffalo daily confirmed that he had indeed traveled south for the winter and was in St. Augustine, Florida. "He is touring with the Cuban Giants, and the Giants are not above earning their board by acting as waiters at the Florida hotels," the *Express* said. "In a recent game between the Giants and a picked nine Grant covered second base for the picked team, and the Giants were defeated 16 to 2. Grant made four runs, two hits, one put-out, and no assists or errors."[4] Two weeks later, Grant's challengers were being called the Standards, captained by Arthur Thomas. However, they were no longer providing much competition. "Grant is doing the biggest share of the hitting and fielding for his nine," the *Express* reported.[5]

By February 10, among Buffalo's priority players, only Lehane, Carroll, and Grant remained unsigned. Rowe spoke to his dilemma about the latter two:

> I know that a lame arm interferes with a player's work in every branch of the game. I hurt my arm when I was with the Buffalo club in 1882, and ever since then I have not been able to make a natural throw. I have got so now that I can throw almost as far as even [sic] and as accurately, but it is with much less ease. I fear Grant's arm will bother him. If the salary limit had only been put up to a respectable sum like $15,000 instead of $13,500 you see we could easily sign both men. We may make arrangements yet to keep both of them.[6]

On or just before February 21, Rowe signed Lehane to play first base again. "This fills every position except right field and I will sign either Grant or Carroll for that place probably," Rowe said. "You see, just now I don't know exactly where Grant is, and cannot tell whether or not his arm is in good condition."[7]

Rowe doubled down two days later by invoking a future Hall of Famer and alluded to testing Grant's arm strength for throwing:

I admire Grant's work as much as anybody, but nobody can tell me that a man with a bad arm is any help to a club. Take Sam Thompson of the Detroits, for instance. It cannot be disputed that he is one of the best fielders and hitters in the country—Grant's superior without any doubt—and yet with a lame arm he was a positive drawback to the Detroit club. I can assure you though that if Grant is in condition, we will not let him go.[8]

At least one Buffalo paper seemed to take Grant's side in this quandary. "Manager Rowe might go further and get worse men than Grant," the *Evening News* said, and then offered a clear understatement. "If he can't throw, he knows a little about hitting."[9] Rowe ended the month saying he still hadn't signed Carroll, either, but he shifted from his earlier fear about having to choose between them. "It is quite likely we will sign both of them," he said.[10] Toward the end of March, however, Carroll hadn't replied to written communication from Rowe, and the manager seemed uncertain he could reach Grant with the Cuban Giants.[11] Rowe didn't have much to say about this over the next few weeks, except to mention in early April that the Cuban Giants had requested that the Bisons play them in Trenton toward the end of that month. Buffalo declined because Rowe and White decided not to play any preseason exhibition games. It wasn't revealed whether Rowe or White tried to relay an inquiry to Grant via whoever requested that exhibition game.[12] Whatever Grant's inclinations were when the request was made, it's difficult to envision the request being made if he had been openly hostile to the idea of rejoining the Bisons.

Opening Day for Buffalo was on April 30, and its first home game was scheduled for May 4. Across the month of April and into early May, Buffalo's newspapers grappled in different ways with the distinct possibility, if not probability, that Frank Grant wouldn't be returning for a fourth season as a Bison. Some of their sportswriters simply claimed to speak on behalf of the fan base—and could do so credibly, given how widely and frequently reported his popularity was from 1886 through 1888. The *Evening News* said, "Buffalonians want to see Grant in the nine, and if Manager Rowe can find him he had better get his signature to a contract immediately." This echoed a comment by the *Commercial Advertiser* in early March that "everybody wants to see him prominent in the nine."[13]

The *Express* may have written more about Grant from the beginning of April to the beginning of May than the other Buffalo papers combined. On April 1, that newspaper reacted to the *Sun*'s prediction over in New York City that "Grant will play with the Cuban Giants during April, after which he will join the Buffalos." The *Express* wasn't convinced. "If Grant wants to join the Buffalos at all it behooves him to apprise Messrs. Rowe and White of his present whereabouts," that daily advised. Its tone was similar on April 7, in a preview of the season (accompanied by individual photos of the regulars who had been signed by then). "Grant cannot be found," the *Express* maintained. "If Grant will only come out of his hiding-place and show himself to be in good condition, a place will be made for him on the team."[14] The *Express* didn't appear to question Rowe's sincerity about wanting to sign Grant or whether Buffalo had actually made much of an effort to reach him. The *Express* was aware that the Cuban Giants had played a game in Washington, D.C., on April 12, and Buffalo's new owners had to have known that as well. The day before that game, the *Express* said that "Grant seems to be wedded to the Cuban Giants," and two days after that game, all that paper could say was, "There is no news from either Grant or Carroll."[15] The *Express* aligned itself a little more closely with the Bisons' management on April 18 by commenting that "Grant will have to sever his connection with the Cuban Giants before April 30th. It is a question, indeed, if he has any right to play with them now." Finally, on May 2 that daily may have tried to convince itself he might not be worth it. "A Buffalo man who saw Grant play in Florida last winter says that Grant's arm is completely gone," the *Express* conveyed. "Perhaps that's why he isn't anxious to show up."[16]

Frank Grant had two stronger reasons for not wanting to rejoin Buffalo. In fact, the *Express* had already commented on both, but other local papers had scooped them, separately, on April 14. For one, the *Courier* reported on the Bisons' internal turmoil of a racist nature:

> It is very doubtful if the present members of the Buffalo baseball team would play ball if the colored player, Grant, of last year's team was to sign. Said one of the members of last year's team, "The only reason why we didn't have our pictures taken last year was on account of that nigger. Chapman wanted us to come around and be photographed, but one of the boys said: 'Not if the nig is in the picture,' and we all backed him up."
>
> The feeling is pretty general among professional ball players that colored men should not play with white men. "He's where he belongs now, with the Cuban Giants," said one of the players, "and I hope he stays there, for I won't play with Buffalo if he does." This is rather hard on Grant. The boys acknowledge that he is a good player, but don't like to travel with him.[17]

Perhaps not coincidentally, a reporter named Hamilton, in a "special to the Sunday News," told about crucial communication with Frank Grant in Washington on April 13:

> Grant, late second baseman of the Buffalo base ball team, when asked this evening whether he would return to the Buffalo nine, said he was perfectly willing if his price, $250 per month, is given, but he would not otherwise. He has spent the winter at St. Augustine, Fla., endeavoring by rest to effect a cure of his right shoulder, which was badly strained last winter. He is now much better and feels able to do good work again.[18]

Both of these newsflashes appeared in summarized form in other newspapers, though not always combined. The next day, the *Cleveland Plain Dealer* said, "The Buffalo players threaten to strike if Grant, the colored player, returns to the team. He is now with the Cuban Giants. This will hurt the Deacon's feelings and not please Jack Rowe." Back in Buffalo, the *Commercial Advertiser* reprinted this without comment and thus gave credence to rumors of internal dissension.[19] On April 17, the *Chicago Tribune* said, "The Buffalo team objects to playing with 'Mascot' Grant, the colored second baseman, at the same time admitting that he is gentlemanly and a good player." The *Trib* likely summarized a seven-sentence "special dispatch" connecting Grant's $250 monthly demand and the threat by teammates, which was printed by newspapers in such cities as Boston, Washington, D.C., Pittsburgh, Cincinnati, and Omaha on April 15.[20] The *Express* took notice when the *Syracuse Herald* reported similarly. "This talk of a rebellion if Grant returns is all bosh," the *Express* replied. Grant might have appreciated that assessment, but certainly not that daily's other comment: "The Buffalo management will not pay Grant $250 a month. He will have to come down in his terms or be locked out."[21]

The *Sunday Morning News* had a similar assessment when it followed up a week later on its salary scoop, but it chose to add a dig about Grant's ego:

> Nothing more has been heard from Grant. The dusky heavy-hitter telegraphed THE NEWS that he wouldn't sign for a cent less than $250 a month. He will have to sign for less money than that or not play ball at all this season. Grant evidently has recently bought a hat several sizes too large for his head.[22]

On April 28, the *Evening News* echoed the point about Grant not being able to play ball professionally during 1889 except with Buffalo. "The managers can insist upon the Cuban Giants dropping Grant," that paper asserted. "If Grant refuses to sign at the terms of Buffalo he will have to lay idle for a season." Apparently no newspaper in town realized why White and Rowe might not be inclined to make such a demand: They had spent more than half a year arguing with the National League after its defunct Detroit franchise sold their contracts to Pittsburgh, to which they refused to report.[23] They might simply have disliked the appearance of hypocrisy, or they could have feared that if they were stern with Grant, Pittsburgh and the NL might have tried to use that against the duo.

However true the *Courier*'s report on April 14 was, it's certainly possible Frank Grant had grown very tired of the bigotry he experienced from players on other teams, at a minimum. Even if he had some solid allies among the Bisons, he didn't have a single teammate with whom he could genuinely commiserate. About two weeks earlier, *The Sporting News* had given voice to his plight at length:

> There are only four or five colored professional baseball players who have gained any prominence on the diamond. What fame they have won has been made in the face of very disheartening circumstances. Race prejudice exists in professional baseball ranks to a marked degree, and the unfortunate son of Africa who makes his living as a member of a team of white professionals has a rocky road to travel.
>
> The rest of the players not only cut him in a social way, but most of them endeavor to "job him" out of the business. He gets the wrong instructions in coaching, and when a field play comes up in which he is interested, an effort is always made to have an error scored against him.
>
> An International League player, talking to the writer the other day, said, "While I myself am prejudiced against playing in a team with a colored player, still I could not help pitying some of the poor black fellows that played in the International League. Fowler used to play second base with the lower part of his legs encased in wooden guards. He knew that about every player that came down to second base on a steal had it in for him and would, if possible, throw the spikes into him. He was a good player, but left the base every time there was a close play in order to get away from the spikes."
>
> "I have seen him muff balls intentionally, so that he would not have to try to touch runners, fearing that they might injure him. Grant was the same way. Why, the runners chased him off second base. They went down so often trying to break his legs or injure them that he gave up his infield position the latter part of last season and played right field. That is not all."
>
> "About half the pitchers try their best to hit these colored players when at bat. I know of a great many pitchers that tried to soak Grant…. One of the International League pitchers pitched for Grant's head all the time. He never put a ball over the plate but sent them in straight and true right at Grant. Do what he would he could not hit the Buffalo man, and he trotted down to first on called balls every time."[24]

The mention of wooden shin guards was repeated in a long *Sporting Life* article shortly after the 1891 season by Edward "Ned" Williamson, a longtime infielder for the Chicago White Stockings, except Williamson attributed them to Grant. Williamson spent almost no time in the minor leagues, and none of that was around Grant's three years in Buffalo, so Williamson obviously was passing along reports from other players. Williamson didn't name Grant but that is clearly whom he described, a second baseman for Buffalo who "was one of the best players in the old Eastern League," which matched Grant's time with Meriden. "The haughty Caucasians of the [International] association were willing to permit darkies to carry water to them or gaurd [sic] the bat bag, but it made them sore to have the name of one in the batting list," Williamson said, maybe with a little sarcasm. Williamson claimed that a widespread desire to spike Grant "gave rise to the 'feet first slide'" and thus "introduced a new feature into the game." Baseball historians have pointed to earlier and different origins of this slide, but it's possible that Williamson was correct about the origin of any such conspiracy across professional baseball. Regardless, Williamson's report definitely unraveled towards the end. "The poor man played in two games out of five perhaps; the rest of the time he was on crutches," Williamson said. Even after this second baseman started wearing "wooden armor" below his knees, opposing baserunners would simply sharpen their spikes and try to split those strips taken from kegs, he continued. "The colored man seldom lasted beyond the fifth inning, as the base-runners became more expert," he added. "The practice survived long after the second baseman made his last trip to the hospital."[25] As previously stressed, except for a three-week break to rehabilitate his right arm or shoulder, Frank Grant barely missed a game during his three seasons with Buffalo, and he wasn't known to be removed after any collisions. Nevertheless, overall this does dovetail with the very sympathetic commentary in *The Sporting News* shortly before the 1889 season.

All that being said, Frank Grant had at least one firm white ally on another team during the 1888–1889 offseason, though it is anyone's guess whether he ever caught wind of that. In early March, at least three Buffalo dailies repeated a claim in his defense made anonymously by a "Pittsburg boy who was in that league" to the *Pittsburg Chronicle Telegraph*: "That colored man Grant really led the International League in batting," the man stated. "They cheated him out of it, for he had an average over .400 before he was laid off, and he hit well after resuming play." Two of the three Buffalo papers that chose to print this added their own brief comments but didn't question the allegation (though it's possible they simply considered it too ludicrous to warrant a rebuttal).[26] In any case, despite the league's final statistics for 1888 seeming to be reasonably accurate, this anonymous source—presumably a player, though that wasn't explicitly stated—may have mostly been taking aim at the integrity of official scorers. *The Sporting News* did so around the same time, except in the context of assigning errors to Grant and Fowler as fielders. It's just as plausible that base hits by them were sometimes scored as errors if a minimal deflection or the slightest bobble was involved.

However legitimate this charge was, baseball fans in Pittsburgh may not have had a likeliest suspect because they didn't live in an International League city where the eight franchises' rosters would have been familiar. Still, the number of credible candidates for the identity of this "Pittsburgh boy" may be in the single digits. There weren't any Pittsburghers on Buffalo itself, at least among the core players who ended the season with the Bisons.[27] There were other teams in the league that also didn't have players from Pittsburgh, at least among their regulars, as best as can be determined. The prime suspect might be the aforementioned Bill Bishop, who pitched for London and Syracuse in 1888. Bishop had two brief stints of major league experience with Pittsburgh in 1886 and 1887, and he had wintered in that city after the 1888 season. By virtue of pitching for Syracuse, he had Fleet Walker as a teammate, and a respect for Walker could have made anyone on the club more likely to sympathize with Grant. Bishop was the only obvious "Pittsburgh boy" on Syracuse. In fact, that term was even used to describe him in a Pittsburgh paper as he was reengaging with Syracuse for the 1889 season.[28]

So, while Buffalo's newspapers and Jack Rowe were dwelling on Frank Grant's status in March and April of 1889, what were he and the Cuban Giants actually doing? For one, on March 20 the team won a game in St. Augustine that was witnessed by ex-President Grover Cleveland, who had just left office early that month (but who would become President again in 1893). Cleveland's party spent a night at the Hotel Ponce de Leon, with which the Cuban Giants had a strong association in their early years. "The local club had refused to play them, but after witnessing this game they arranged for one," an African American newspaper added.[29]

The Cuban Giants were still in Florida on April 4, while owner John M. Bright[30] was in Philadelphia to help finalize a schedule for their membership as Trenton's representative in the new Middle States League. The Philadelphia Giants (not the later Black team) also joined, and the other Pennsylvania cities with franchises were Harrisburg, York, Lancaster, and Reading.[31] The Cuban Giants then left Florida for a few exhibition games as the club progressed northward along the Eastern Seaboard. The most noteworthy games by far were scheduled against Washington's National League nine on April 12 and 13. The arrival of the Cuban Giants was planned for well in advance. According to the *Washington Bee*, an African American weekly paper, a "grand testimonial" celebrating the Cuban Giants was scheduled for the evening of April 11 at Congressional Globe Hall on Pennsylvania Avenue. Music would be provided by an orchestra, and dancing would begin at 8:30. Admission was set at 50 cents. The *Bee* named 15 people who helped plan the event.[32] The *Washington Post* reported on this celebration the day after, though that article began by quoting a young attendee and a doorman who both supposedly spoke in broken English. The *Post* called the Cuban Giants "the only colored ball team in the country" and concluded by naming the same 15 planners. Most valuably, the *Post*'s account also offered these evocative details after the Cuban Giants arrived:

> A large number of their admirers determined to make their visit a memorable one, and when they entered the hall they were enthusiastically greeted. They were introduced to the large crowd present, and at the conclusion of the reception dancing was indulged in until a late hour. During the evening a number of the Washington players, who had been invited, called and enjoyed the scene.[33]

On April 12, Frank Grant faced George Keefe for the second time in less than a year. However, for the final two innings (of eight, a ninth not being played due to diminishing sunlight), Keefe was replaced by rookie Alex Ferson, who had a record of 25–7 in the New England League during 1888. Grant batted fourth and played right field. "The several hundred people who visited Capitol Park yesterday with an idea that the Cuban Giants would be easy victims for the home team were sadly disappointed, for the crack colored nine from Trenton played the hardest kind of ball, and had it not been for the evident partiality" of the umpire, would have won, said the *Post* the next day. "There are folks who say and believe that the umpire's aid was a powerful factor in the Senators' victory," added the *Evening Star*. But there were apparently several hundred additional people who were rooting for the visitors, because the *Post* reported that "a large majority" of the fans in attendance were African American. George Stovey pitched for the Cuban Giants, and Washington scored all three of its runs off him by the end of the third inning. In the visitors' half of the fourth inning, a double play almost extinguished a rally, and it was especially disheartening because the batter beat the throw to first base, according to the *Post*. However, Grant came up next and drove in the remaining baserunner with a triple. In the sixth inning, his double off Keefe drove in the only other run scored by the Cuban Giants that afternoon. The other Cuban Giants combined for just two singles, but the Senators only managed three singles plus a homer, and the *Evening Star* said, "there were many spectators who said that yesterday's game was one of the finest ever played here."[34]

The next day's game was rained out, so the only remaining game for the Cuban Giants before their exhibitions in Trenton was against New York City's independent Metropolitan nine across the Hudson River in Weehawken, New Jersey. The Cuban Giants lost, 12–7, but they had to be enthused that the attendance exceeded 3,000. Grant received praise in the *New York Age*, an African American weekly, which was just 18 months into more than 13 decades of continuous publication. "The new acquisition, Grant of the Buffalo's, is an excellent player and though on second base he plays almost the whole infield," that newspaper observed. "He is a sure catcher and a reliable batter."[35]

For their first exhibition games in Trenton, the Cuban Giants hosted Syracuse's International League team, the Stars, on April 15 and 16. The new manager for the visitors was none other than Jack Chapman, the only manager for whom Frank Grant had played in Buffalo. The Cuban Giants beat Syracuse in the first game, 7–3, but lost the next day, 6–5. Bishop and Walker served as Chapman's battery for both games. They held Grant hitless in the first game, but he showed Chapman his old form at second base with six putouts and six assists to offset an error. Oddly, Syracuse's pitching ace of 1888 and 1889, Con Murphy, pitched for the Cuban Giants, caught by one of the Williamses, presumably Clarence and not George.[36]

A game against Princeton College scheduled for April 17 was rained out, and the next day's game against Detroit's new International League club was cancelled because the grounds remained too wet.[37] That meant the remaining exhibition games the Cuban Giants played in April were against independent teams or minor league nines in smaller cities. Two of those games were of historical significance, because they were Frank Grant's first times facing the Gorhams, one of the country's other leading African American ballclubs. At the Long Island Grounds on April 21, 1,700 fans saw the Cuban Giants prevail, 19–16. In Stamford, Connecticut on April 24, "The Gorhams and Cuban Giants played a draw game, 10 to 10, but it was given to the Gorhams on a dispute," according to the *Hartford Courant*. Alas, box scores for games between the Cuban Giants and the Gorhams tended to be scarce that year.[38]

Newspapers in major league cities had made it clear that they were paying attention to Frank Grant's fate, and for some odd reason, as the month of May approached, sports fans all over Kansas also read about this intrigue. From April 22 to 27, the same seven-sentence article that had appeared in a few major league cities on April 15, about Grant's requirement of $250 per month and the supposed rebellion threatened by teammates, was printed in at least 55 newspapers across the state of Kansas.[39] In addition, from April 25 into early May, papers in a few states east of the Mississippi in which there weren't major league teams, including the Carolinas and Alabama, printed a statement that "Grant, the colored player, late of Buffalo, will play with the Cuban Giants this year."[40]

After Buffalo's home opener in early May, that city's newspapers barely mentioned Frank Grant the rest of that month. They seemed to collectively give up; there was no anger or whining, simply silence. The *Express* was an exception to this general rule on May 16. The Bisons had won only three of their first 10 games before a surprise win over third-place Toronto slid Buffalo up to sixth place in the eight-team league. Meanwhile,

Jack Chapman's Syracuse Stars were in first place with a record of 11–2. The first of the random comments and brief announcements under "Sporting Notes" that day read, "Please add Grant and Carroll." The *Express* reprinted that two of the next three days.[41] One of the few other mentions was on May 26. "The spectators attending the games at Olympic park greatly miss Grant, and as for playing second base he is Andrus' superior," said the *Sunday Truth*.[42]

On May 1, 1889, Frank Grant and the Trenton Cuban Giants played their first game of the regular season of the Middle States League (MSL) in Lancaster. A drizzle limited the crowd to about 500 fans. The lineup for the Cuban Giants was: Whyte, rf; C. Williams, c; Grant, 2b; Harrison, ss; Frye, 1b; Boyd, cf; Selden, lf; Malone, 3b; and Stovey, p. The opposing pitcher was Mike Kilroy, who had pitched a major league game in 1888 and played in three more in 1891. Though Trenton lost, 7–3, Grant had a double and two singles. (Frustratingly, many printed MSL box scores lacked a column for at-bats.) In the field, he had three putouts and three assists but was charged with two errors.[43]

The Cuban Giants bounced back in the next day's rematch and won, 6–0. Though Grant was hitless, he walked, stole two bases, and scored a run. More importantly, he provided errorless defense and touched the ball often, with five putouts and seven assists. "Grant, the colored Dunlap, played a remarkable game at second base, some of his stops and fly catches being remarkable," said Lancaster's *Daily New Era*, so impressed that they did in fact use the adjective "remarkable" twice. "A double play in the ninth inning, in which he was the chief actor, cut off all hope of the Lancaster [sic] scoring." The *Lancaster Intelligencer* similarly enthused: "The greatest feature of the game was the second base play of Grant, who accepted twelve chances, capturing balls that seemed impossible."[44]

On the evening of May 2, the Cuban Giants arrived at Harrisburg's Washington Hotel from Lancaster. That was probably Frank Grant's first visit to Pennsylvania's capital city, in which case it was the first time he set foot in his son's birthplace. But the detective work uncovering that is best left for the 1891 preseason. Trenton already had an open date on May 3, so they reportedly practiced in Harrisburg, where they played their third game of the season the next day. "The colored population of this city have declared a half holiday to-day and have turned out in large numbers to the game between the locals and the Cuban Giants this afternoon," reported the *Harrisburg Telegraph* in a brief preview on May 4. "The colored players are, to them, a greater attraction than Barnum's circus." The paper also pointed out that Clarence Williams was from Harrisburg.[45] That may have been one reason why Grant might have initially spent more time in that city than he otherwise would have.

According to the *Telegraph*, the crowd that Saturday numbered "about 3,000 enthusiasts, 900 of whom were colored people." Frank Grant singled in five at-bats, scored a run, and stole a base. At second base he had six putouts, two assists, no errors, and a double play turned. "The game was exciting from start to finish, and as each club forged ahead of the other it was loudly applauded," said the *Patriot*. The home team led, 5–4, after five innings but the Cuban Giants tied it in their half of the seventh. There was no more scoring until the tenth inning, when Harrisburg came out on top, 6–5. Out of the blue, on May 13 the *Telegraph* declared, "The greatest second base player in the country is Grant, of the Cuban Giants."[46]

The MSL had a policy of not playing on Sundays, so Trenton's game in Harrisburg was a one-shot. Strangely, Trenton's next scheduled MSL game was on Friday, May

10. They thus played exhibition games on five consecutive days. The first was on that Sunday, against the Gorhams somewhere in or near New York City. The game went 13 innings, and the Cubans came out on top, 12–10.[47]

However, by far Trenton's most significant exhibition game that week was at home, hosting Boston's National League team on May 7. Pitching for Boston was Bill Sowders, brother of the aforementioned Len. Sowders had a record of 19–15 and an impressive ERA of 2.07 as a rookie for Boston in 1888. In the second inning, Abe Harrison led off by reaching on an error but then "was most unfairly called out" when trying to steal, according to the *Boston Herald*. Harrison complained so long and indiscriminately that captain Arthur Thomas removed him from the game and manager S.K. Govern suspended him, though very briefly. Sowders held the Cuban Giants hitless through the first four innings and limited them to three hits after that, singles by Ben Boyd and Thomas and a double by Clarence Williams. Williams scored both of Trenton's runs, but Boston scored five runs. Williams' second run was in the ninth inning, on a sacrifice fly to center field by Frank Grant, but terror must have swept over the Trenton bench as Williams scored. "At the home plate, [Jerry] Hurley, who was stooping for a low-thrown ball, raised up just in time to collide with C. Williams, giving him a heavy fall," the *Trenton Times* reported. "It was thought at first that he had broken his leg, but Dr. Steen, who is always in attendance at the Giants' games, pronounced it only a serious sprain."[48]

For the week starting on May 10, Grant and Trenton as a whole experienced something of a comedy of errors in the context of the Middle States League. They started playing Reading's MSL team in that city on that date, but the game was halted after three innings due to rain. Grant wasn't even there, reportedly because he missed a train at Philadelphia. The Cuban Giants defeated Reading easily the next day, but without Grant, who instead umpired an amateur game back in Trenton between the Young Cuban Giants and a team called the Trappers.[49]

Grant also wasn't with his teammates when they played an exhibition game at the Long Island Grounds on Sunday, May 12. That side trip apparently delayed the Cubans' arrival in Trenton for their MSL home opener the next day, hosting Reading. Accounts of what happened that afternoon differ somewhat. The game was to begin at 4:00, and one local paper said that when there was no sign of the home team a few minutes before the top of the hour, Reading's manager decided that his nine should leave. Another local paper said the Reading players didn't even go to the ballpark because the weather was threatening. In either case, the Giants arrived just before 4:00, and the

BASE BALL.   BASE BALL.
ON THE
New Grounds, Hetzel's Grove.
THE GREAT BOSTONS
(National League,)
vs.
CUBAN GIANTS,
— ON —
Tuesday Afternoon, May 7th, 1889.

GENERAL ADMISSION, 25 cents; Grand Stand, 25 cents; Boys' Admission, 15 cents.
GAME CALLED AT 3:45.

A game between the Cuban Giants and Boston's National League club was advertised in the *Trenton Times*, May 3, 1889.

umpire awarded them a forfeit. Grant was finally back in the lineup the next two days, in victories over the MSL's Philadelphia Giants, but the day after the second contest, the League ruled that the games wouldn't count because the home team didn't use the League's approved Mason ball. Conveniently, sporting goods manufacturer Charles E. Mason, a former major league player and manager, was then manager of the Philadelphia Giants and the MSL's President. A more serious topic discussed during the "special meeting" of the League was whether Trenton was employing players who hadn't been signed to regular contracts.[50] On or shortly before May 29, the Middle States League announced the approval of seven contracts across five teams, and three were Trenton players: William F. Whyte, Arthur Thomas, and Frank Grant. It's possible that the MSL's independent existence, outside the National Agreement that governed most of professional baseball, facilitated the signing of Grant, or at least made it difficult for Buffalo to interfere if it wanted to.[51] At least one Buffalo daily noted that Grant had signed with the Cuban Giants.[52]

On May 17, the Cuban Giants played their first MSL game in York. Pitching for the home team was 21-year-old Happy Jack Stivetts. As a major leaguer during the 1890s, Stivetts won 20 or more games in six seasons, including five in a row. In fact, he went 33–22 and 1891 and 35–16 in 1892. Grant singled off him in that game and scored twice, but York prevailed, 7–6. When Grant faced him again on June 3, the slugger logged a double and two singles. However, Stivetts got the best of him on June 18, holding Grant to an 0-for-4. Eight days later, Stivetts made his major league debut.

On May 23, the Cuban Giants had an easy win in Reading, 8–1, though the box score didn't show anything special about Grant's performance. On offense he was hitless, though he did score a run. He made no putouts, had just three assists, and was charged with an error for not handling one ball hit to him. Nevertheless, the *Reading Times* just raved about him. "There is but one second baseman in the Middle States League. His name is Grant and he was here yesterday," that daily stated. "The scores of games cannot convey any idea of the game he plays. He can give pointers to League and Association basemen."[53] A day after that glowing review, he also received praise in the *New York Age* for the second time in five weeks, as that paper reported on a recent exhibition loss in Weehawken. "Grant, the second baseman, from Buffalo, is a clever player and worked hard to win," the *Age* observed. "He is a sure batter, a nice slider and a sprinter."[54] The season wasn't even a month old and yet Grant was piling up praise as often as he had at other times, such as during his 12 games against major league teams during April of 1887.

From May 28 through May 30, the Cuban Giants played four games in Harrisburg. Box scores that included at-bats are available, so this provides a rare instance of easily assessing Grant's batting accurately over a few consecutive MSL games. Alas, he fared poorly at bat, going only 2-for-14, and both hits were singles, but he did field well, with only one error out of 25 chances, plus he turned an unassisted double play. He impressed at least one Harrisburg paper in the process. "Grant, second baseman of the Cubans, is called the colored Dunlap," noted the *Telegraph*. "The great second baseman is no better than Grant."[55]

On May 31, Frank Grant played his 30th game against a major league team, when Cincinnati's American Association club visited Trenton. It was presumably threatening weather that limited the turnout to about 100 fans, because the game was ended after five innings on account of rain. The Red Stockings won, 1–0. Pitching against the

Cuban Giants was Mike Smith, who went 34–17 for them in 1887, with an ERA of 2.94 that led the AA, and in 1888 he won 22 games with a slightly better ERA. From the cleanup spot in the batting order, Grant was probably 0-for-2, unless he drew one or both of his team's walks. On defense, he made four of his team's 15 putouts, and Trenton played errorless ball.[56]

The Cuban Giants collectively did a very good deed in Trenton on June 7, when they played a local team for charity. On May 31, the city of Johnstown, Pennsylvania—about 65 miles east of Pittsburgh—was devastated by an infamous flood, the worst in the United States during the 1800s and still one of the deadliest disasters in American history. More than 2,200 people died, and the number of victims who were never identified exceeded 750. Many businesses and organizations quickly rallied to raise funds for the relief effort, and $12,000 was collected in Trenton through the date of this game.

> BASE BALL!
> Friday, June 8th.
> FOR THE
> —:BENEFIT:—
> OF THE
> JOHNSTOWN SUFFERERS.
>
> CUBAN GIANTS
> vs.
> MADDOCK'S ★ POTTERY ★ TEAM.
>
> TICKETS, - 25 CENTS.
> GRAND STAND, 10 CENTS.
> Game called at 4 o'clock.

The Cuban Giants helped raise money for victims of the famous Johnstown Flood (though the ad should have read Friday, June 7, not June 8). From the *Trenton Times*, June 6, 1889.

One newspaper said the exhibition game raised roughly $100, but the *New York Tribune* reported the total as "several hundred dollars." "The Giants changed the positions of their men so that the game would not be too one-sided," the *Trenton Times* noted.[57]

By June 10, rumors were swirling that there would be an attempt to expel the Cuban Giants from the MSL. "When the League was formed there was much complaint about admitting the Cuban Giants, principally on account of their color, and now that they are proving their superior strength against all the other clubs in the League, the complaints have become more general and bitter," wrote the *New York Sun*. That daily's source(s) apparently conceded that the Cubans "have been a great drawing attraction in the towns of this League, and it is explained that for that reason they were taken into the League, but it is thought that finally a close contest for the championship will increase patronage in all the towns better than the novelty of a game with colored players, and for these reasons the Giants will be forced out." Trenton would be accused at an upcoming meeting of paying some individual players more than the $75 limit. In fact, it was believed some of the Cubans were paid as much as $175 per month. "It is said that Grant, Frye, Seldon [sic] and the Williams brothers, of the Cuban Giants, all receive more than the salary limit," the *Harrisburg Telegraph* specified (though George and Clarence Williams weren't siblings). "And they all play good ball, too." An overview of the club the next month in the *Cleveland Gazette*, an African American newspaper, reported that the "salary list for the club for one season is twelve thousand dollars," though that could have included the team's many exhibition games, and it's unclear how that total might translate to a monthly amount.[58]

The MSL held a special meeting in Philadelphia on June 12, and S.K. Govern represented Trenton. "All the delegates denied the story that there was trouble in the league, and that the Cuban Giants were to be forced out on account of their color." The main order of business reported from the meeting was the addition of two more franchises, in Norristown, Pennsylvania and Norwalk, Connecticut, to increase the circuit to eight. Of course, this required the delegates to spend considerable time revising the MSL schedule accordingly. Through June 11, the pennant race had been crystalizing around three of the MSL's six original clubs: Trenton at 15–4, York at 18–6, and Harrisburg at 17–6.[59] The league didn't stay at eight teams for long, as the three original teams with losing records soon folded.

Another MSL meeting was called later in June, but that time it was York in the crosshairs. Harrisburg had filed a complaint about mistreatment during games in York. This prompted Govern to validate Harrisburg's characterization by reporting that a "crowd at York threatened to mob him and his players during a recent visit and used very insulting language." One neutral party said that "rigid rules should be enforced against the York management to prevent a repetition." A decision on any such rules may have been deferred. "During all the time this question was being discussed the York representatives appeared to be ashamed to make an attempt at defense," reported one Harrisburg daily.[60]

For two weeks starting on June 13, the Cuban Giants played all of their games away from Trenton. They beat the new Norwalk team on June 25 and 26, and that made it convenient to play the Resolutes in Meriden, 50 miles to the northeast, on June 27. The two teams were scheduled to play on May 20, but weather apparently kept that from happening. Not surprisingly, African Americans in that community were looking forward to Grant's return as that May date approached. "The colored men about town are talking up a testimonial to be given Grant, the former Meriden player," the *Meriden Daily Journal* had announced on May 18. On the evening of May 19, the Cuban Giants reportedly traveled by boat from New York City to New Haven and waited there "for the weather to clear so that they could come to Meriden to play." With that timeline, there may have been little opportunity to hold the testimonial, if he and the Cuban Giants even made it to Meriden.[61]

Similarly, their travel plans for the June 27 game sound like there also wasn't time for a special pre-game event (though who knows about afterwards): "The Cuban Giant ball team, bag and baggage, arrived at 12:53, and are quartered at the Meriden house," the *Meriden Daily Republican* announced on the day of the game. "They are playing the Resolutes, beginning at 4 o'clock this afternoon." However, a preview of the game in the *Journal* suggested, quite amusingly, that the game should be of great interest to all local fans, regardless of race: "It will be the game of the year," that paper declared. "Do not miss it or you will regret it during the whole course of your life."

The visitors won, 4–2, "in a very interesting, close and exciting game," according to the *Republican*. "Nearly every man on the Cuban Giant team could play in one of the big leagues, but for his color, and Grant, the bright particular star, formerly of Meriden, is a jewel of the finest water," that paper added. "His fine playing was cheered to the echo." On defense, the *Republican* singled out "Grant's one-hand stops," and he did not disappoint on offense, either. At bat, he went 3-for-4 with a single, double, and triple.[62]

The *Journal*, meanwhile, drew particular attention to the very funny coaching by Grant and Harrison. These were the duo's "witty, good-natured" utterances that stood out, in the *Journal*'s view:

> "Tick-tick-tick-tick-tick-Bang!"
> "Meet it and kill it."
> "Eat 'em, eat 'em, socks and all!"
> "Down de alley now, ole man!"
> "What's dat? Three strikes? You must have a glass eye, Mr. Umpire."
> "Oh me, oh my, oh me, oh my, oh mum."
> "Move de fence in so he can knock de ball over it."[63]

Because the *Daily Republican* named a lodging establishment, the Cuban Giants may have spent the night in Meriden, so perhaps Grant was honored with a testimonial after the game. In either case, the team did play a game the next day, back in Trenton. The visiting team was an atypical one, consisting entirely of Native Americans. They were from a charitable institution in Philadelphia called the Educational Home. Chief Bender, the future Hall of Fame pitcher, took up residence there about two years later. A preview in the *Trenton Times* identified the players' English and Native American surnames. Afterwards, the paper reported almost nothing besides the final score, 10–2 in favor of the home team, plus "good attendance." However, another local paper printed a box score which showed that Grant led his nine with four hits, one of which was a triple.[64]

Starting on Independence Day, the Cuban Giants won five straight MSL games on consecutive days, and the big one for Grant was in the middle of that streak, at Trenton on July 6. The Cuban Giants beat Harrisburg easily, 11–3, thanks mostly to Grant smacking two doubles and a triple. The next day, Trenton defeated Norristown in 10 innings, 7–6, and Grant made a crucial play in the ninth inning. The *Times* reported that a Norristown batter "sent a high-liner towards right which looked good for two bases, but Grant jumped into the air and pulled it down with one hand. For a few seconds the spectators were spellbound, and when they realized what he had done Grant was cheered to the echo." That was how the *Times* illustrated its declaration that the Cuban Giants had "in Grant one of the best second basemen in the country."[65]

Grant wasn't in Trenton's lineup on July 12 when they played a game against Norristown in Reading. However, on July 14 he played shortstop in Albany for a team called the Colored All-Americans. It was that team's second game there in as many days, though he didn't play in the first one, a 7–0 loss. With Grant's help, the All-Americans won the rematch, 17–12. One Albany daily estimated the attendance as 3,500. Homering for the other team was a player named Davis, who was very likely future Hall of Famer George Davis.[66] Grant and Davis played against each other at least three more times, on August 4 and September 15 and 29.

About a week later, the *New York Sun* explained why Grant and a few teammates might not play with the Cuban Giants from time to time. "Owing to the fact that the Cuban Giants and the Gorhams are unable to accept many dates offered them by out-of-town clubs, President Bright of the Cuban Giants and President Davis of the Gorham[s] have formed a combination team, to be known as the Colored All-Americans," the *Sun* revealed. "Red, white, and blue uniforms have been secured." Grant was this team's captain. The Gorhams had replaced the Philadelphia Giants in the MSL, so the two teams were traveling in the same circles. This combined team made its debut with those two games in Albany. At a minimum, it had a mini-tour scheduled for July 27 through August 3, mostly in New York State.[67] For Grant in particular, the appeal of this secondary team might have been as a way to supplement his income and sidestep the MSL's salary cap. Another possibility is that he was looking for a different kind of challenge. Trenton was winning many of its MSL games comfortably, which may have given the team confidence about doing without a star of Frank Grant's caliber from time to time.

That decision promptly backfired on July 15, against one of their two very good rivals in the MSL, York. Without Grant in the lineup, the Cuban Giants lost their first game of the season in Trenton, and it wasn't even close: 12–4. He was also absent the next day, when the Cubans traveled 100 miles to the northwest for the first game of the MSL's new team in Hazleton, Pennsylvania. At least Grant's team was able to win that one without him, 8–6.[68]

Starting on July 17, Grant was back in the Cubans' lineup for all of their MSL games over a ten-day period. In the midst of that was a 3–1 win in Harrisburg before 2,500 fans, and a 6–0 loss there two days later for which one paper printed a batter-by-batter account (uncommon for MSL games). On July 25, the *Trenton Times* reported a close race for the top spot in the MSL with the Cuban Giants having a record of 33–10 for a .765 winning percentage, while Harrisburg was 38–14 for a .731 winning percentage.[69]

On July 29, Trenton played the Resolutes up in Meriden again, but neither Frank Grant nor Arthur Thomas was in the lineup. The *Meriden Daily Republican* was told that they were playing with the All-Americans. As a result, Meriden clobbered the Cubans, 14–6. Meanwhile, the *Journal* made it sound like Grant was away without permission and even said he had "been suspended,"[70] which seems unlikely given the team's described origin.

The *Sun*'s report on the All-Americans mentioned that the team was scheduled to play in Hudson, New York, on July 29, the day Frank Grant was missing from Meriden. On that date, a team called the "Cuban Giants" by the *Hudson Daily Evening Register* lost a game there, 4–2, but it was surely the All-Americans. The *Register* didn't print a box score but named four of the visiting players: Grant, Stovey, Fisher, and Evans. On July 30, the All-Americans played in Canajoharie, New York (a day earlier than the *Sun*'s schedule). They beat a local team called the Clippers, 19–14.[71]

On the morning of July 31, the All-Americans played a game limited to seven innings about 20 miles to the northeast, in Gloversville, so that they could make an afternoon game 13 miles away in Amsterdam. Gloversville's Annexes prevailed, 9–8. "The special features of the game were the fine work of Grant as shortstop and batting," said a local paper. The All-Americans returned to Gloversville from Amsterdam for a rematch the next day, August 1. A crowd of 1,000 fans watched two scoreless innings and then a rout, as the visitors left with a 30–6 victory. The game lasted five minutes shy of three hours.[72] It was Frank Grant's 24th birthday.

On August 2 they played in Kingston, New York, and beat the West Shore team, 13–12. The next day they played in Albany again, where the visitors lost, 11–6. A preview of the latter game named five of the visiting players, specifically "Nat Collins, the famous coacher," Stovey, Selden, Holmes, and "Grant, 'the colored Dunlap,' of last year's Buffalos," then added that the other players were from the Gorhams.[73] Grant batted third and played shortstop. One of his two hits was a double.[74]

Meanwhile, the rest of the Cuban Giants and Gorhams faced one another in Easton,

Pennsylvania (the city the latter nine was representing in the MSL) on August 1 and 2. The Gorhams won both by identical scores, 4–3. This pair of games has been called an early instance of a "Colored Championship" Series, as noted by the Center for Negro League Baseball Research.[75] At the time, though, this meeting was much bigger news to Pennsylvania newspapers, in MSL cities and a few others, because of what happened away from the ballpark: Both teams "were refused lodging at Easton hotels," according to the *York Gazette*, for one. "Easton hotel-keepers, although the statement is not true, claim that all their rooms are occupied." The Gorhams crowded into the two-story home of a local African American family. "The Giants were accommodated last night at Patrick Doyle's hotel in South Easton, two miles from the ball grounds," and the Irishman was "praised for his hospitality." The *Hazleton Sentinel* clarified that three or four of the Cubans received rooms at the Central Hotel before the rest ended up in South Easton. That daily also quoted a dispatch naming the Swan Hotel as the first place to turn the Gorhams away. The latter newspaper framed this news with some commentary: "The hotel keepers of Easton stand a good chance of getting into trouble under the civil rights law," the *Sentinel* said before quoting the dispatch. "No complaint against the conduct of the men is made," that paper added. "They behave admirably."[76] Even though this didn't affect Frank Grant directly, it foreshadowed episodes in an adjoining state the following season.

After playing the Gorhams in Easton, the Cubans' next MSL game was on August 7, hosting the Gorhams. The Gorhams forfeited the first game of a doubleheader and lost the second, 7–1. Frank Grant was absent again. He and some friends were in the central Connecticut town of Southington for a ballgame. With about 1,200 fans in the stands, his nine lost, 14–11. A weekly paper there published a rare box score of an All-Americans game, though it called them the "Giants" (no "Cuban" distinguisher). It must have been the All-Americans, partly because the visitors "wore several different styles of uniform, no two being alike." Their batting order was Grant, 3b and ss; Malone, ss and p; Frye, 2b; Johnson, 1b and c; Catto, lf; Barton, c and 1b; Holland, p and cf; "Schruck" (presumably Schenk), cf and 3b; and Peterson, rf. Grant scored three runs and contributed three hits, including a double.[77]

Grant returned to the lineup of the Cuban Giants on August 8 and played with them on nine consecutive days (including two exhibitions). They began that stretch against their main rivals, the Harrisburg nine, in that city. He contributed two hits and accepted eight chances without an error in the first game, but the Cuban Giants were victims of a no-hitter by William Stecher in the next day's rematch, which was shortened to five innings by rain. One of the Harrisburg papers noted that George Williams and Frank Grant left for Philadelphia the night of the no-hitter—without mentioning why the two of them had separate travel plans—but both played in a doubleheader in York the next day (the first game was terminated as a tie, 6–6, after 10 innings).[78]

On Sunday, August 11, the Cuban Giants and the Gorhams played in Gloucester, New Jersey, and this was likely the only time Frank Grant played against the Gorhams while they were in the MSL. Leading off for the Gorhams was another future Hall of Famer, second baseman Sol White. Each played errorless ball, scored a run, and had a double, though White had three hits to Grant's two. The much bigger difference that day was the Cubans scored early and often, on their way to an easy 9–2 triumph. The game didn't count in the standings; there were no actual bases, "and the grounds were improperly marked out," noted the *Philadelphia Inquirer*. Around the same time, the

All-Americans were trounced by the Metropolitans at the Long Island Grounds, 26–4, in front of 1,200 fans.[79] The next day, the West End Base Ball Club of Somerville, New Jersey, similarly embarrassed the "All Americans (colored) of Trenton," 22–0. Frank Grant was in the Cubans' lineup that day in York as the visitors lost, 6–3.[80]

On August 16, he was also in the Cubans' lineup for their first game against the MSL's relatively new franchise in Lebanon, Pennsylvania. "Grant's work pleased everyone, he seemed to play the whole infield," said the *Lebanon Daily News*. After 10 innings, the score was tied at 4–4 when Grant batted with one out. "Grant got first on four bad ones, stole second by a wonderful head-first slide and came home" with the winning run after an error, the *Daily News* reported. The Cuban Giants also won the next day's rematch, and that contest is described in detail on a Society for American Baseball Research web page.[81]

Grant was absent from the Cubans' home win against Hazleton on August 17, and from a doubleheader they split with Norristown in Gloucester. The latter were unusual because they were MSL games on a Sunday. His absence against Hazleton, at least, can be explained by the Colored All-Americans' game at the Long Island Grounds against a team called the Stars (apparently Eugene Bagley's old club). A brief account in a Brooklyn daily indicated that Stovey and Fisher were the battery for the visitors, and a player named Grant hit a double. The Stars had no player named Grant in a box score earlier that month.[82]

Grant's absence was brief, and he played in all 10 of the Cubans' MSL games from August 19 through the end of the month. They went 8–2 in that span, though the first of those contests was a tough loss at home to Hazleton, 12–11. Trenton's *Daily True American* said one of the defensive highlights was "a runaway fly" catch by Grant, but surpassing that was a triple play, "Williams to Thomas, to Grant, to Williams."[83]

On August 27, the Cuban Giants defeated a team in Cape May, New Jersey, at the state's southern tip. The final score was 5–2. The local team used lefty Dave Anderson as its pitcher, three days after his major league debut with the NL's Phillies. One sportswriter said that "Grant's second base playing was equal to that of any League or Association player."[84] In other words, his defense was on a par with any major leaguer at that position. That certainly wasn't the first time such an assessment was made of him, but it's especially meaningful in the wake of his injury-plagued 1888 season.

The next day, the Cuban Giants played an exhibition game against a team in Burlington, New Jersey, about 15 miles southwest of Trenton. The visitors scored twice in the ninth inning to achieve a narrow win, 3–2. The *Trenton Times* seemed to take at face value a quote the *Burlington Enterprise* attributed to Frank Grant. Prior to the game, he supposedly told one of his opponents, "We is goin' to wipe you people clean off de earth to-day," though even if he did say something like this (and possibly just kidding), it's important to keep in mind the distinct possibility that any improper grammar or diction was fabricated. Regardless, this is one of the few instances of any newspaper ever claiming to quote him directly.[85]

The Cuban Giants finished August with four games against the MSL's new Wilmington Peach Growers, two at home and two away. Wilmington won the first, 9–4, but the Trenton nine won the other three by scoring more than a dozen runs in each. Grant was particularly productive, with seven runs scored and eight hits. Across the four games, he also amassed 15 putouts and 17 assists, offset by only one error. In the first victory, he played shortstop and homered, both of which were rarities for him during his

MSL season. In the third win, he smacked a double and a triple. The *New York Age*, the African American weekly, reported that both of the games in Wilmington "were largely attended by both races."[86]

On September 9 and 10, the Cubans played in Lebanon. In the first game, the score was tied at 11–11 after 10 innings, and Grant scored the winning run in the 11th for the second time in less than a month. Trenton piled up runs again in the rematch but with a minimal challenge, as they won, 16–7. Grant had three hits in each game.[87]

The latter game turned out to be the Cubans' MSL finale. Therefore, Grant ended that season very strongly. Trenton's leadership decided it wasn't worth playing the few remaining games scheduled, partly because York had folded near the end of the season despite a healthy winning percentage. The MSL was limping to a conclusion, after which is became mired in a heated argument about whether Trenton or Harrisburg won the league's pennant. The official standings credited Harrisburg with a record of 64–19, for a winning percentage of .771. The record shown for the Cuban Giants was 55–17, which translates to a winning percentage of .764.[88]

Researcher Paul Browne did an exceptional job of explaining and analyzing this convoluted controversy in his 2013 book, *The Coal Barons Played Cuban Giants: A History of Early Professional Baseball in Pennsylvania, 1889–1896*.[89] Trenton president J.M. Bright stated his case in a letter to the *Philadelphia Inquirer* dated October 6. Here is most of it:

> Harrisburg was scheduled to play the Gorhams two games in Hoboken, N.J. The first game the Gorhams failed to put in an appearance, and the umpire awarded the game to Harrisburg, 9 to 0. This is all right, but now comes the game I protest. That very night Harrisburg, finding that there was no prospect of playing the next day, started for home instead of remaining and going to the ground again and have the umpire award them the second game as the first one was, but on the contrary they go home and claim both games, which were very wrongly allowed by the president of the League. This is the first game that does not belong to them, and they are to blame for not putting in an appearance the second day.
>
> Next comes two games they claim in the latter part of September, when Harrisburg was scheduled to play Wilmington, 13 and 14. They claim both those games and they never were awarded to them by the umpire at Wilmington for the simple reason that the Wilmington Club was disbanded for the season and they did not go to Wilmington. That cuts them off of two more victories, bringing their record to 61 instead of 64 games won. September 6 and 7 Harrisburg was scheduled to play at Lebanon, but for some reason or other they only played on the 7th and Lebanon won the game, and then Harrisburg turns it in as an exhibition game. These are the little schemes that were practices to deprive us out of our just rights.
>
> Now then in regards to the Cuban Giants' record. The Cubans defeated the Philadelphia Giants two games in Trenton, N.J., but on account of not using the right ball the games did not count. The very same thing occurred in Easton, Pa., later on, with the Gorhams and Cuban Giants, the Gorhams winning both games, but using the wrong ball both games should have been thrown out, but much to our amazement only one game was not counted. These are all little points that count in the long run.
>
> Next comes two games in Hoboken with the Hazletons, two regular schedule games and two postponed ones, which were won by the Cuban Giants. At the last two (postponed games) there was no official umpire or scorer on the ground, but the secretary was duly notified by telegraph the night [they] played. When they were played the scores by innings appeared in the official organ of the League the next morning, but we only got credit for two games after winning four. So, any fair-minded person can see at a glance that the Cuban Giants are the real champions of the Middle States League for 1889.

As a result of Bright's analysis, he insisted that the records of the teams should be fixed as Cuban Giants, 57–16, with a winning percentage of .780, and Harrisburg, 61–20 with a winning percentage of .753. He added a postscript to his letter: "The New York papers conceded the championship to the Cuban Giants."[90] The annual *Spalding Guide* published that offseason printed a table of the League's "official" records of all 13 teams head-to-head, but also summarized Bright's claims and typed up his counts in a smaller chart, seeming to take his side in the process. It wouldn't have been surprising if that famous publication had simply chosen to be silent about the dispute. The table showing the head-to-head totals is formatted in a logical way, by listing Harrisburg and the Cuban Giants first in each row and column, while the two worst teams by far, the Philadelphia Giants and Shenandoah, were relegated to the last rows and columns. It is thus readily apparent, for example, that neither Harrisburg nor the Cuban Giants lost to those cellar dwellers. But this format also communicated a few other facts quickly that further undermine Harrisburg's claim to the pennant. Most notably, Harrisburg managed to win only four out of 14 games against the Cuban Giants. What's more, Harrisburg played the Philadelphia Giants and Shenandoah 11 times combined, while the Cuban Giants faced those two clubs just five times total.[91]

There are 10 MSL games played by Trenton for which box scores might no longer exist, plus Grant was out of the lineup several times. As best as can be determined, the League never published year-end statistics. One of the Harrisburg dailies promised them more than once, and then a week into November simply announced the "averages are being temporarily withheld for speculative purposes."[92] Nevertheless, Frank Grant had 70 hits in 55 MSL games for which box scores are readily available—though as mentioned, at-bats were rarely reported in them. It so happens that a frame of reference is provided by the 2020 season shortened by the pandemic. Trea Turner led the NL with 78 hits in 59 games, and José Abreu led the AL with 76 hits in 60 games. Frank Grant's rate of hits per game falls between the rates of those two league leaders.

Whatever Grant's full statistical package, toward the end of the regular season his overall performance inspired one Harrisburg journalist to sing his praises at length and provide a profile of him. This tribute began:

> There is no position on the base ball field that demands greater agility, endurance and sound judgment than that of second basemen. He must of necessity be as wiry as a cat, possess the endurance of a race horse and command unerring discrimination. In the history of the diamond probably no player more fully met these requirements than does Frank Ulysses Grant, the famed second baseman who now does such fine work for the Cuban Giants, of Trenton, New Jersey. Wherever he has played he has quickly become a favorite, alike with the audience and the trained managers of the great teams. When it is remembered that his experience in the professional field only covers four short seasons, his success appears almost phenomenal. Were it not for the fact that he is a colored man, he would without a doubt be at the top notch of the records among the finest teams in the country.

After mentioning his Pittsfield and Williamstown roots, the profile naturally reported about his professional start in Meriden, and wound down by noting that his injured right arm in 1888 meant he "could not throw five yards." His weight was specified as 160 pounds. All of this was accompanied by a pencil sketch of him, presumably drawn from a recent photograph.[93]

After the MSL season fizzled, the Cuban Giants played a number of games in New York State, for at least a week into October. On September 14 they won in Albany, 4–3, and on September 23 they led a "picked nine" in Gloversville, 28–2, after five innings (at which point the game might have been ended, mercifully, but a local paper's report didn't make that clear).[94] They generally didn't stray too far from the state's eastern border, but the Cubans also had at least one destination in mind toward the western end of the state, the city in that region Frank Grant knew best.

On September 16, the *Buffalo Commercial Advertiser* was delighted to announce that the Cuban Giants would play the Bisons on consecutive days that month. That daily seemed to imply September 19 and 20, and maybe that was the original plan, but other local papers announced the games for a week later, on September 26 and 27. The Bisons ended the 1889 season in seventh place out of eight teams. Their record of 41–65 represented a decline from Grant's final season with them, when they went 48–60. Jack Chapman's and Fleet Walker's Syracuse Stars finished in second place, with a record of 63–44. By the end of the 1889 season, Buffalo was being managed by Deacon White's brother, Will. When the *Commercial Advertiser* first announced the pair of games, it couldn't resist twisting the proverbial knife: "Grant, the great second baseman who wasn't good enough for Buffalo(?) will teach some of Will White's kids a new trick or two on the diamond," that paper proclaimed, with that extra parenthetical question mark seemingly serving as an extra dig. "Won't it be fun to see the Giants wallop the white caps?" Another local paper's brief preview on September 22 took a gentler tone. The *Sunday Truth* asserted that there would "no doubt be a large attendance at both games as Frank Grant, formerly with the Buffalos, will play at second for the Giants. He has been playing great ball and his many friends in this city will give him a warm reception." Alas, the games were cancelled because the Cubans were somehow "stranded" almost 250 miles to the east, in Fonda, New York.[95]

SECOND BASEMAN GRANT

A well-known sketch which dates back at least to the *Cleveland Gazette*, September 29, 1889.

On September 27, an African American team in Albany, called the Capital Citys, had the uncommon experience of having its lineup bolstered for a game by Frank Grant and three of the other Cuban Giants, namely Whyte, Thomas, and either George or Clarence Williams (probably the latter, because he was the starting catcher that day). Conversely, the local Walshes' team was supplemented by three ringers from Albany's main team. Williams and Thomas both had pitches from Whyte hit them in the head while playing catcher, so Frank Grant played catcher as well, for the first time in a long while. Grant led off the game with a double, stole third, and scored on a passed ball, and he drove in their final run with a single. The Capital Citys held that early 1–0 lead after three innings, but they ultimately lost, 12–3. However, in single games the next two days, the full lineup of Cuban Giants beat the full Albany nine.[96]

During the first week of October, they played at least twice at the Polo Grounds and split games on consecutive days in Port Jervis, about 75 miles northwest of Manhattan.[97] Around mid–October, the club disbanded for the season. In late November, J.M. Bright sent a letter to at least one newspaper in which he reported that the Cuban Giants had played 148 games in 1889 and had a record of 114–31, with three ties. As for the 1890 season, he also announced that S.K. Govern would not continue with the club in any capacity. Bright also named a number of players he had already "engaged" for the next year, and Frank Grant was in that list.[98]

8

Ordered to Harrisburg (1890 to April 1891)

In January of 1890, at least, Frank Grant was reportedly in Washington, but that was apparently the extent of any knowledge among sportswriters about where he spent that winter or what he did to keep busy.[1] Maybe the rumors two years earlier about his engagement to a woman in Washington didn't name that city at random. Of course, another plausible possibility is that he spent at least part of that offseason back home in Williamstown. He was definitely in Williamstown in early May of 1890, though only briefly.

Just before the new year, J.M. Bright sent a letter to at least one newspaper in Trenton with more news about the 1890 season. For one, Grant had been named assistant captain, to George Williams. Also, Bright claimed that Fleet Walker would be added to the roster. Bright confirmed that the team had "parted company" with S.K. Govern, and he reportedly explained that this was because his players no longer considered him acceptable.[2]

Speaking of Walker, he and Grant were associated together in a "Pacific Slope" tour announced in the *New York Age* as winter was winding down. Though no timeframe was identified, the organizers had "already arranged to play the major if [not] the best white clubs throughout the principal cities of the West." Others named to this team were "Nelson, pitcher," George Stovey, Oscar Jackson, "Collins, 1st base," Sol White, Andy Jackson, and "Bell, centre field. Mr. William White will be the official scorer on the tour." This plan had "Prof." Ambrose Davis' Gorhams at its core, and there was an incredibly ambitious second phase: "The management will take a team of 22 to Australia for exhibition games."[3]

Long before there was even a remote chance of something like this happening, Frank Grant had to choose a nine for April and May of 1890. For about two months starting in early March, there were frequently conflicting reports about that. Bright faced persistent challenges from two other white men for Grant's services. One was very familiar: James Farrington, who had managed the MSL's Harrisburg club. The other was named J. Monroe Kreiter. The latter was the overt contender during March.

Harrisburg and four other Pennsylvania cities that had teams in the MSL in 1889 also had teams in the new Eastern Inter-State League (EISL) in 1890. Those other cities were York, Lebanon, Lancaster, and Easton (the latter having been represented by the Gorhams in the MSL). The sixth city in the EISL was Altoona. However, Farrington and Kreiter were rivals *with each other* early on because Farrington had been hired by a new ownership group in Harrisburg that got its franchise into the EISL. The old franchise recruited Kreiter in an attempt to get a second Harrisburg club into the same league. Kreiter's nine ultimately represented York instead, about 25 miles away. Kreiter's coup by early March was to assert that he had recruited many of the Cuban Giants to be his team's regulars. Farrington, for his part, reported that he had signed Clarence Williams to his new Harrisburg squad.[4] On March 9 or 10, Kreiter specified that he had signed these nine men to his "Harrisburg" club: "Thomas, catcher; Whyte, Selden and Malone, pitchers; Frye, first base; Grant, second base; George Williams, third base; Harrison, short stop; Boyd, center field." On the morning of March 10, Kreiter went out of his way to address reports that Walker, Stovey, and Grant were preparing to play with the Gorhams. "Now, I don't pretend to know anything about the actions of the first-named pair, but I do know that I have a signed contract with Grant now reposing in my inside pocket, and here it is," he said, as he handed a document to at least one local sportswriter.[5] That same week, Kreiter reportedly ridiculed Bright for challenging him about Frank Grant. In fact, Kreiter showed contracts for all nine players to at least two Harrisburg reporters.[6]

This news reached Trenton soon enough, because during the second half of March there were reports that baseball fans there suddenly worried about whether they would have a team representing them in any league during the upcoming regular season. According to one report, in anticipation of the Cuban Giants losing so much talent, there was disappointment among fans in Trenton that local entrepreneurs weren't scurrying to get a franchise into the Atlantic Association.[7] This handwringing was such that it motivated Bright to write a lengthy letter about the situation in Trenton. To begin, he had "positively engaged M.E. Fitzgerald, of Trenton to look after" his interests in that city, and he "engaged Mr. H. Johnson to manage the team." In late March, Johnson was in Washington to finalize contracts with four pitchers and three catchers of that city's longstanding Douglass club. This could be related to the report in January that Frank Grant was in that city. In any case, Bright had "positively signed" Grant to captain the team, Harrison to return as shortstop, and Stovey to "pitch all the big games." Bright also mentioned a catcher named Clark and "Miller, the Pittsburg pitcher." That was surely Frank Miller, who remained Grant's close friend 40 years later. Bright's plan for the subsequent few weeks was to have the entire team report to New York City on March 30 for an initial game at Monitor Park in Weehawken, followed by training and exhibition games in several cities, including against Boston's National League club. Upon arriving in Trenton on April 15, he hoped Kreiter's Harrisburg team would accept a challenge "to a series of games to be played in Trenton for the colored championship" of the entire sport.[8]

Just before Bright's letter, Frank Grant was apparently at New York City's Polo Grounds. On March 26, a team of white semipro players from two Upper Manhattan neighborhoods accepted a challenge from a team that mixed players from the Cuban Giants and Gorhams. Stovey and Grant represented the former club. The teams battled to a 13–13 tie.[9]

Over in Harrisburg at the end of the month, the *Daily Patriot* looked into the near future and asked openly, "Where will Grant play?" The *Patriot* noted that Kreiter's club was now associated with York, but it seemed to presume that this relocation would have no effect on the contract with Grant in that team's possession. At the same time, Bright wasn't inclined to talk about the situation with Harrisburg journalists as openly as he had in Trenton. Still, the *Patriot* revealed that "in a personal letter to a friend in this city

Mr. Bright, owner of the Cuban Giants last year, declares that both Grant and Harrison will remain with him, and his reason for not publishing the fact in the newspapers is a good one for his own benefit." In this letter, he conceded that the other seven players Kreiter signed had indeed left Bright's employment, but the *Patriot*'s article concluded with this cryptic statement: "Mr. Bright says he is aware that Grant signed a Harrisburg contract, but he did it for a purpose, and will not remain with the new club."[10]

On April 1, the *Patriot* and the *Telegraph* reported that Kreiter's Cuban Giants were gathering together to start practicing, though those two papers didn't concur on which players had already arrived. Grant was expected to join them that evening or the day after. The *Patriot* took a jab at Bright the next day: "The presence of Harrison and the promise of Grant to report to-morrow does not speak much for the veracity of Mr. Bright, who, in a letter to Manager Farrington, said: 'Harrison and Grant have not signed with Harrisburg and both men will be with me this year.'"[11] Across the month of April, evidence would accumulate proving that Bright was more than half accurate.

To begin with, on Sunday, March 30, the *New York Sun* mentioned that a game would be played that day between a local club called the Allertons and a "colored team, at Monitor Park." The day before, it said that Bright would be using that park regularly on Sundays, so the unnamed team was probably the Cuban Giants. Therefore, the earliest date on Bright's timeline of a few days earlier bore out.[12] On April 5, the Cuban Giants played what the *Brooklyn Daily Eagle* called "their first regular game" against the Stars of Long Island City, Eugene Bagley's old club. More than half of the names in the lineup of the Cuban Giants were familiar. Batting third and playing second base was Frank Grant, as Bright maintained over the entire month of March. The first two men in the batting order were Jackson at third base and White at shortstop. These were almost certainly Andy Jackson and Sol White, who had both been named on that Pacific Slope tour team in mid–March, as had Grant. Stovey batted fourth but played right field before becoming the relief pitcher at some point. Batting fifth was the left fielder, Holmes, presumably the Ben Holmes who was among the earliest Cuban Giants of 1885–1886. A Holmes had also been on the roster of Grant's All-Americans the previous summer. Rounding out the batting order were Johnson, 1b; Freeman, cf; Nelson, p and rf; and Brown, c. Johnson may have been the manager Bright mentioned in his letter to the editor toward the end of March, and another early Cuban Giant was named Harry Johnson. Nelson was likely John Nelson, a pitcher for the Gorhams in 1889 and probably the "Nelson, pitcher" on the Pacific Slope roster. The Stars won that opener, 16–10.[13] Far more important than the outcome is the distinct possibility that this box score was the first to confirm that the two future Hall of Famers, Sol White and Frank Grant, were in the same lineup.

The teams met again the next day, and Grant's charges had a somewhat different lineup. White played second base instead of shortstop, and Grant caught, which opened up the shortstop position for Ross Garrison, who had played that position for the Gorhams in the MSL. Nelson switched to center field to make room for Miller to pitch. That was presumably the Pittsburgh hurler Bright mentioned about one week earlier. Out of the lineup were Freeman and Brown. Miller did a very nice job containing the Stars, but the Cubans suffered a one-hitter and lost, 4–3.[14]

Across five more box scores from April 9 through 16, the quartet of Jackson, White, Grant, and Garrison were fixtures in the lineup. Stovey, Holmes, Johnson, and Miller were each absent once. Nelson played in two more games, and Freeman played a second time. Nat Collins, formerly of the All-Americans, played in one game, as did a man named Clark, probably the player named by Bright toward the end of March. The least-known player who appeared once was named Rothwell. There was a B. Jackson at catcher in one box score, followed by R. Jackson at that position two days later. They were probably the same man, because Andy Jackson had a catching brother named Robert, who sometimes went by Bob, and he was also formerly with the Gorhams. The Cuban Giants lost four of those five games.[15] At least in the fifth contest, a 20–17 loss in Hartford, Grant was able to enjoy a very good game on offense. He scored four runs, stole a base, walked twice, and had four hits, including a double and a homer. The *Buffalo Commercial Advertiser* reported on his "great record" in that game to its readers later that week.[16]

One of the losses was against the Washington Senators of the minor league Atlantic Association, before about 700 fans. "The Cuban Giants are by no means the team they used to be, Grant being about the only player of any skill on it," said Washington's *Evening Star*. "Grant made the play of the day, a high one-hand catch of a badly thrown ball at second, putting out the runner." That paper was also struck by the personality he displayed. "He was the life of the game, and his loud voice and unique methods of coaching made things quite lively, even when the home team had a lead of a dozen runs or so," the *Star* commented. In separate "Notes" about the game, this paper added:

> Grant talks all the time in a game. Here are some of his expressions in coaching: "Don't you dare to run back; keep away from the base." "Put the ball out of sight, hit it in the eye, old man, take all the stitches out of it."[17]

At least one other paper in town mentioned a similar impression. "Grant's coaching caught the crowd in the early part of the game," the *Washington Post* reported. That daily perceived his favorite encouragement to the teammate batting to be, "Cut wood; now is your chance."[18]

On April 7, the *Harrisburg Telegraph* acknowledged its awareness of Grant's second game against the Stars, at a minimum, and its edition the next day included this statement: "Manager Kreiter declares that Grant will play with his York team this year notwithstanding all rumors to the contrary."[19] The Cuban Giants played in Worcester, Massachusetts on April 8 but must have returned to New York City by the next day, because the *Sun* reported that on April 9, Kreiter was there "trying to induce White, Jackson, Garrison, Stovey and Grant to jump the Cuban Giants and join his team. Capt. Grant, however, gave him to understand that he would stay with the Cuban Giants." At least one Harrisburg sportswriter met up with Kreiter when he returned home on the evening of April 10. "When asked concerning Grant, he said that he would be playing second base for the York team when the League season opened," the *Daily Independent* reported. Kreiter did soon succeed in signing Sol White, though that didn't take effect prior to the Hartford game on April 15.[20]

In Bright's letter to the editor toward the end of March, he identified April 15 as the date he hoped to begin playing in Trenton. He also alluded to a game against Boston's National League team. Either he didn't issue a formal challenge to Kreiter to begin a series of games on that date, or Kreiter declined. In either case, Bright arranged to host the Boston team that day, but later cancelled.[21] Perhaps the drubbings the Cuban Giants received in three of their first four outings, through April 11, quickly convinced him that playing an NL club would only be demoralizing. On April 15, the Cuban Giants ended up playing in Hartford on a second consecutive day. They reportedly missed a scheduled game in Lebanon on April 17, and suddenly there was speculation that they had disbanded.[22] Fuel was added to that fire on April 17, when Farrington announced that games the next two days between Bright's team and his were cancelled.[23]

Suddenly, on April 18 the *Harrisburg Telegraph* announced that "Grant, the famous second baseman of the old Cuban Giants, is likely to be signed by the Harrisburg club." Sure enough, in its next edition that daily announced that Farrington had signed Grant on April 18. The *Daily Independent* confirmed that Farrington had telegraphed that news from New York to a director of the Harrisburg Athletic Association. From the *Telegraph*'s account, Farrington and Kreiter may have met with Grant around the same time:

> Manager Kreiter, of the York club, returned from New York this morning. He has signed Ross Garrison, who played short for the Gorhams last year, but failed to get Grant, who is alleged to have signed with Manager Farrington. Last night Manager Kreiter saw President Voltz, of the Inter-State League, and that official stated that the contract made with Grant by Manager Kreiter some time ago could not be broken with impunity, especially as advance money had been paid and the terms stipulated. Grant told Mr. Kreiter that he had been offered more than the salary limit by an Inter-State League club, presumably the Harrisburg.[24]

Even though Grant had signed with a new team, his Cuban Giants rose from the ashes to play a game in Easton on April 21, and on April 26 they began a two-week road trip with a game in Albany.[25] A few days before that trip, the *York Gazette* said Grant wouldn't report to Harrisburg until Opening Day of the EISL season, which was May 1. He presumably did this with permission from both Bright and Farrington. It seems quite possible that Farrington, in expectation of an aggressive challenge by Kreiter, figured it was best for Grant to play a few more games with his old team away from tension in the vicinity of Harrisburg and York. On the day of the Easton game, the *York Dispatch* reported that "Kreiter says he will not give up Grant without a fight for him. Farrington's actions in signing that player was [sic] anything but creditable."[26]

Less than a week after Farrington swooped in to sign Grant, the *Telegraph* bemoaned the swift accumulation of misinformation. "There have been so many gross misstatements of facts with the Grant matter that patrons of the game will no doubt appreciate an authentic version of the case," that daily said on April 23. The *Telegraph* began by noting that Kreiter's initial contracts expressly applied to a franchise located in Harrisburg, so "it became necessary for those players who had signed the first contract with Manager Kreiter to re-sign regular Inter-State League contracts." All did so except Frank Grant, who "considered himself a free agent in the matter. Manager Farrington signed the colored Dunlap in a perfectly legitimate manner," the *Telegraph* continued. "The fact that Grant did not sign a York club contract is proven by President Voltz's official bulletin, in none of which, up to the present time, can Grant's name be found." In its lengthy effort to set the record straight, the *Telegraph* didn't happen to mention Bright at all.[27]

Kreiter immediately challenged the *Telegraph* on a key point, in a letter the next day. He took issue with an early assertion by the *Telegraph* about the original contract, that Grant signed it "with the express understanding that the club was to be located in this city." Kreiter denied that, flatly: "There was no understanding of that kind, nor is there anything in the contract signed by Grant which would suggest such language."

Kreiter also noted that Grant accepted advance money, and he alluded to Farrington without naming him, saying, "if overtures has not been made to him, the 'colored Dunlap' would have reported to me, and signed a York Inter-State League contract, just as the other players did."[28] All of this was playing out on this daily's front pages.

On April 25, at least two Harrisburg dailies reported that none other than Nick Young, president of the National League, responded to a letter about the Grant situation. Young reportedly wrote to the management of Farrington's club that "if Grant signed a contract to play ball in Harrisburg, he cannot be held to play in York."[29] Beyond that, coverage of the controversy died down for the last few days of the month. On April 30, the *Telegraph* did report that Grant was expected to arrive that afternoon, but he hadn't arrived by 3:00. His teammates soon left without him for their opener in Altoona the next day, May 1. The *Daily Independent* reported on May 2 that he would make his debut in the home opener, scheduled for May 5.[30]

What was Frank Grant up to in the meantime? To begin with, around April 23 it was announced that the Cuban Giants had signed his brother Clarence. A newspaper in the Grant brothers' home county specified that Clarence would receive a salary of $25 plus expenses.[31]

It was a minor miracle that Clarence Grant, who was 30 years old at the time, was physically able to play baseball with his kid brother. On August 7, 1889, Clarence was shot by another African American man named Elijah Williams, and a doctor initially thought one of the two bullet wounds would be fatal. Accounts in different newspapers conflicted somewhat (e.g., a Buffalo daily incorrectly said Williams was white), and none seemed to provide a complete picture, but the shooting happened at a dance, and drunkenness was assumed to be a cause. When only a few people were still present, two white men and Grant attacked Williams for some unstated reason. As he was being beaten severely, he drew a pistol and shot only at Grant. One bullet missed but two hit him.[32] On August 22, Williams and Grant appeared before the latter's former guardian, Judge Keyes Danforth. Williams, who had been claiming self-defense, was discharged, and though Grant was held for an appearance before the grand jury, the lack of subsequent coverage suggests he suffered no serious legal consequences.[33] The two white men weren't identified, but there's a good chance one of them was James McMahon, with whom Clarence Grant apparently tried to extract some payback later that year or in very early 1890. In January, McMahon and Grant only had to pay costs after the latter was charged with assaulting Williams again, while McMahon was charged with the same offense but also an assault on the man's wife, Blanch.[34] That was presumably the same James McMahon with whom Frank Grant played ice polo about seven years later.

It's difficult to be certain when Clarence Grant's first game with the Cuban Giants was, because reports on the team's games weren't always accompanied by box scores, but it was apparently no later than April 28, against Albany's New York State League (NYSL) team. At least three daily newspapers in that city printed box scores for that game, in which the Cuban Giants had two players named Grant, although first initials weren't used to distinguish one from the other. The one who batted third was certainly Frank Grant. The other Grant batted eighth and split his time on defense between left field and third base.[35] Albany is less than 40 miles from Williamstown, so Clarence Grant wouldn't even have had to travel with the team to take part. There had also been a game between the same two teams on April 26 (with a rainout in between), but none of those three Albany dailies printed a box score for it.[36]

The Cuban Giants next split a pair of games in Troy on April 29 and 30. That Troy team was also a member of the NYSL. There wasn't a second Grant in either box score, but playing left field for the home nine in both games was Grant's old Meriden and Buffalo teammate, Jack Remsen.[37] George Stovey joined this Troy club that summer.[38] On May 2, the Cuban Giants did have a pair of Grants in its lineup against a team in Hudson, New York. Frank Grant batted third and hit a double and a homer. Batting seventh was "E. Grant," the team's catcher in that box score. (It's easy to envision how a C could be misinterpreted as an E.) He contributed a single in their 14–3 romp over the home nine.[39]

On May 3, the Cuban Giants played a very special game for the Grant family and its many friends. It was against Williams College, in Frank and Clarence's longtime home city, Williamstown. The collegians won, 8–2. Though Frank went hitless in three at-bats, he did draw a walk, steal a base, and score one of his team's two runs. The other Grant in the Cubans' lineup, who caught and played right field, scored their other run, and went 1-for-4 at bat. "The most noticeable feature of the game was the coaching of the visitors," according to the *Boston Sunday Globe*.[40] Grant likely put on a very good show for his many acquaintances, friends, and loved ones in the crowd. At least one paper in the county made it clear they knew he was in town: "Baseball lovers turned out in force last Saturday to witness the game between the Cuban Giants and Williams," the *Pittsfield Sun* reported. "Much interest was exhibited in the former team from the fact that its captain is Frank Grant, a boy born [not quite] and brought up in Williamstown and who has a national reputation as a baseball player."[41] Frank and Clarence's first baseball captain as youths, Bliss Perry, was on the college's faculty at that time, and if he didn't attend the game, he almost certainly knew about it. Evidence of that was in Perry's autobiography in 1935, when he mentioned several of the players on the "Rough and Readys" and specified that Clarence later played catcher for the Cuban Giants.[42] Clarence presumably played at least a fourth game with the Cuban Giants. The Cubans had a Grant in their lineup on May 5 against Utica's NYSL nine, but it *couldn't* have been Frank because he was in Harrisburg that same afternoon.[43]

It is anyone's guess whether Frank Grant avoid playing in Harrisburg's first few EISL games because of the contractual controversy, or if he had used that as an excuse to miss those games in early May because he was very eager to play in Williamstown *and* especially with his brother there. Though the *Telegraph* had been optimistic that Grant would play in Harrisburg's first game on May 1, the *Daily Independent* reported on May 3 that the League would need to settle the matter and that "in the meantime Grant will not play ball."[44] Anyway, despite having spent little more than a month captaining this new version of the Cuban Giants, he established some relationships that would be important in 1891 and the rest of that decade. That was particularly true regarding Andy Jackson and John Nelson, plus he seemingly cemented a rapport with George Stovey.

Harrisburg's EISL opener in Altoona on May 1 was almost cancelled due to persistent rain. The teams did complete a game but it was decided at the onset that it would be considered an exhibition and thus not count in the standings.[45] Altoona won on May 2, and Harrisburg won on May 3. That was a Saturday, so there was an open date prior to Harrisburg's first home game, hosting Altoona.

On May 5, Frank Grant did play with James Farrington's Harrisburg Ponies in the team's home opener. About 2,000 fans were in attendance. The umpire didn't show up by the scheduled starting time, and the teams waited about half an hour, until 3:55, to start playing ball, with a player from each team subbing for the EISL appointee. The *Patriot* described Frank Grant's arrival most vividly:

> The long wait for the umpire was not without its advantages. Long before it was time for the game to begin, it was whispered around the crowd that Grant would arrive on the 3.20 train and play third base. Everybody was anxious to see him come and there was a general stretch of necks toward the new bridge, all being eager to get a sight at the most famous colored ball player in the business. At 3.45 o'clock an open carriage was seen coming over the bridge with two men in it. Jim Russ' famous trotter was drawing it at a 2.20 speed and as it approached nearer, the face of Grant was recognized as being one of the men. "There he comes," went through the crowd like magnetism and three cheers went up. Grant was soon in the players' dressing room and in five minuets [sic] he appeared on the diamond in a Harrisburg uniform. A great shout went up from the immense crowd to receive him, in recognition of which he politely raised his cap. Grant's splendid work at the bat and on the bag pleased the "fans," and he was greeted with applause each time he came to the bat.[46]

The account in the *Philadelphia Inquirer* asserted that the "vociferous applause" upon Frank's arrival "was heard in the city a mile away."[47] The *Telegraph* decided to play up a comparison to a Union General's morale-saving appearance that turned the tide of the Civil War's Battle of Cedar Creek, shortly before President Lincoln's reelection in 1864: "Grant's arrival at Island Park yesterday afternoon has been likened to Sheridan's [f]amous ride" from Winchester, about 100 miles from Harrisburg.[48]

Grant was put in the second slot of the Ponies' batting order and assigned to third base on defense. One column over, the *Patriot* provided comfort to any astute fans who were worried that Grant had never fully recovered from the injury to his throwing arm in mid–1888: "Grant throws with spirit to first base. A large number of whiskers dropped off the ball on its way over to McCormick yesterday."[49] First baseman Jerry McCormick, a former major leaguer who had been with Harrisburg's club the previous season as well, had played regularly with Grant for Meriden in 1886.

Grant made quite an impression on offense in the second half of the game. He got on base for the first time with a walk in the fourth inning, but his first hit was a single in the sixth. In the seventh and ninth innings, he hit doubles. He went 3-for-5 and scored three times. His new team beat Altoona easily, 14–1. However, undercutting this good news for Harrisburg was an announcement the same day that "the York Club has decided to make application to the Dauphin County Court for an injunction to restrain Grant, late of the Cuban Giants, from playing with the Harrisburg Club, on the ground that the colored player had signed a contract with Manager Kreiter, of the York Club, before attaching his signature to a Harrisburg contract."[50]

The rematch the next day was rained out, so Harrisburg and Altoona played a doubleheader on May 7. The first game ended around 3:45.[51] About 45 minutes earlier, E.K. Meyers, the president of the York franchise, applied to Judge John Simonton for an injunction to prevent Grant from playing until the contractual controversy was resolved. Meyers reportedly recruited some very important local officials to advance his cause: District Attorney George Kunkel and County Solicitor Albert Millar "were engaged as counsel by the York club and they hustled themselves on the petition for an injunction this afternoon," the *Telegraph* revealed. "Sheriff Sheesley was requested to be on hand, so that the writ might be served the moment it was granted by the court and prevent Grant taking part in the second game to-day." The *Daily Independent* identified a third member of York's legal team, Benjamin M. Nead. He had been editor-in-chief of the *Daily Patriot* in 1887 and was in charge of the *Harrisburg Morning Call* in 1888 and 1889.[52]

The trio of lawyers' plan didn't work, and Frank Grant played in both games. Harrisburg thus swept the three-game series. Clarence Williams hadn't played in Grant's debut, but he did play in both games of the doubleheader, as catcher in the first and at shortstop in the second. In each game that day, Grant scored two runs and had three hits. Three of his six hits on the day were doubles, which put him at 9-for-14 with five doubles and seven runs scored in the series. He was also particularly productive on defense in the earlier of the two games, with three putouts, three assists, and no errors. "His playing at third was as brilliant as any third base playing seen here in two seasons," the *Daily Patriot* said. "He and Eagan made two double plays, in both of which Grant displayed great skill and activity."[53] Bill Eagan was the second baseman and leadoff hitter for the Ponies.

The judge didn't approve an injunction immediately, but as Grant and the Ponies were preparing to travel about 40 miles to Lancaster on the morning of May 8 for a game that afternoon, Deputy Sheriff Harry Roat served Frank Grant "with a notice from counsel that the matter would be presented to court on Monday," May 12. According to the *Telegraph*, Grant merely asked what was probably a rhetorical question, "What are they going to do about it?" It was a fitting response, because the local bigwigs didn't succeed in obtaining an injunction prior to the 12th. That Harrisburg daily said Judge Simonton had decided against that the day before because he "preferred to hear both sides before interfering in the matter in any way." Nevertheless, the "bill in equity" that had been filed with the court included more details than had previously been circulated by newspapers. The original contract he signed with Kreiter stated that he could be assigned to any position on defense, and that he would "receive $64 per month, boarding and lodging and all traveling expenses," the *Telegraph* reported. "It is alleged further that $20 advance money was paid Grant at the time of the signing of the contract."[54]

Grant was able to play in all three games against last-place Lancaster, and the Ponies enjoyed another sweep. Thus they were undefeated in his first six games. In the first game, he went 2-for-5, and in the second he went 2-for-4 with a triple, which meant he was 13-for-23 in his first five games. The third game was a shellacking in which the Ponies scored more than 20 runs to Lancaster's two, but box scores disagreed on whether Grant contributed two or three hits. They did agree that he swatted his second triple of the young season.[55]

While that series was being played, an angry letter written by Grant's new manager, James Farrington, leaked out to newspapers. It was reportedly dated May 4 but might not have been reported on prior to May 9. The most complete version may be the one in the *Patriot*, which indicates that Farrington was replying to a letter written by EISL President Voltz. Farrington expressed disappointment that no official league bulletin had confirmed that only the Ponies had signed Grant to a *league* contract. He alluded to having received backing from NL president Nick Young, "the highest authority in base ball in the country," toward the end of April. Toward the end he wrote:

> You must not think we are all blockheads. Remember you are only the servant of the league and not the dictator. Please return contract and affidavit of Grant to me as it is my property. I have always tried to act a man's part by and to you and got nothing but the dirty end of the stick in return. So now pitch in and you will find me right with you.[56]

A response from Voltz was published in at least one Philadelphia newspaper on May 11, the day prior to the scheduled hearing before Judge Simonton. Voltz noted that the EISL was similar to other leagues on such a controversy, by empowering only its board of directors to resolve them. He also pointed out that the York club had filed a protest about the situation seven days before Farrington's club even filed its contract with Grant. This letter by Voltz apparently didn't address why the EISL board of directors hadn't acted in all that time, nor did he indicate when it might get around to doing so.[57]

By 10:00 on the morning of May 12, a local courtroom was packed with many observers, including some ballplayers. One Harrisburg paper said there were "several hundred base ball enthusiasts" present. According to the *Daily Independent*, "Grant himself was in the Prothonotary's office, where he attracted consideracle [sic] attention while he made an affidavit." When B.M. Nead finally arrived at the courtroom, the reporters present learned that there had been a change in plans that would necessitate a delay, and later Kunkel and Millar made a motion to add the Harrisburg Athletic Association, the parent of the Ponies' team, as a co-respondent with Frank Grant. The parties expected to reconvene four days later.[58] At least for a few more days, Grant was free to play with the Ponies.

Fittingly, Harrisburg played at home that day against York's ex–Cuban Giants, who were now being called the Monarchs. A crowd of about 2,500 fans turned out to see Frank Grant against his former teammates. The *Daily Independent* set the scene, which included an unusual first two innings:

> The game was liberally advertised, numerous devices being employed early in the afternoon to attract a crowd, one being a team in which was nine small colored boys, a sort of miniature representation of the "Monarchs" and the other two small boys carrying a large banner on which was printed, "Grant will play with Harrisburg to-day." The game was postponed for some time because Umpire Dean had not arrived, but was finally commenced with Clarence Williams and White officiating as umpires. Dean arrived after two innings had been played and took his position.[59]

Sol White also played in the game, but Clarence Williams didn't. William Selden became the first EISL pitcher to limit Grant to just one hit, as York handed him his first loss in that league, 10–5. As a result, there was a three-way tie for first place, with Harrisburg, York, and Lebanon all having records of 7–2. In the next day's rematch, it was William Malone's turn to hold Grant to just a single. Clarence Williams was in the Ponies' lineup and also managed a lone single. York won again, 6–2.[60]

On May 15, the board of directors of the EISL had a meeting in Lebanon to address the Grant controversy. Only Lebanon's director was present, but proxies subbed for the Easton and Altoona directors. That left only Lancaster unrepresented among the four uninvolved franchises. Farrington urged an immediate decision, but the small group adjourned without making one. Still, it was expected the board would render a decision within a few days.[61]

Lebanon's team happened to be visiting Harrisburg for a pair of games, but the one on May 14 was terminated by rain after two innings. On the day of the EISL board's meeting, the Ponies broke their two-game losing skid with a 9–1 win, and Grant produced another 3-for-5 outing, with a double.[62] Friday, May 16, happened to be an open date for the Ponies, which allowed all attention to focus on Judge Simonton's courtroom.

Perhaps for the first time, the attorney for Frank Grant and the Harrisburg Athletic

8. Ordered to Harrisburg (1890 to April 1891)

Association was identified: S.J.M. McCarrell. Samuel John Milton McCarrell had served two terms as Dauphin County's District Attorney from 1880 through 1887. In 1892 he was elected to Pennsylvania's legislature, the General Assembly, where he would serve eight years as a Senator.[63] Frank Grant and James Farrington were both present. Millar spoke first and laid out the basics. Grant then received his first legal defense, reported at some length by the *Telegraph*:

> Mr. McCarrell, for the Athletic association, presented the affidavits for the defense and argued that the court had no jurisdiction on its equity side because the old policy of the law was against interfering with contracts of this kind, mainly because the injunction, if granted, would prevent Grant from making a livelihood. He also claimed that there was a prior contract between Bright (manager of the Cuban Giants) and Grant, and that the latter's release had been purchased by the Athletic association. He also took the position that the complainant was not a member of the Inter-State League at the time Grant was signed; but is a York club and owns a franchise in that city. Letter heads were shown to substantiate the assertion that the complainant was not the "Harrisburg base ball club," but is the "York club."

District Attorney Kunkel spoke next. He argued that the court did have jurisdiction and that the contract was binding. He also said that the change of cities by the club he represented was less important than the fact that it was a member of the EISL. Lastly, he contended that by signing Grant, the Harrisburg Athletic Association had violated the National Agreement governing much of professional baseball. Nead was the fourth and final speaker. Judge Simonton had made an incidental remark which the *Telegraph* summarized as, "the organization of professional base ball clubs to go into business was a perversion of the act of the Assembly, which intended that such associations should be for the mutual benefit of its members and not for money-making purposes." Nead may have spent half his speech respectfully challenging that comment. In the end, Simonton said he would not issue an immediate decision.[64] It wasn't clear how long that could take, but it didn't happen during May.

This controversy had been reported on by major newspapers outside of Pennsylvania,[65] but some were alarmed by Simonton's aside about baseball contracts, such as the *New York World* and the *Boston Daily Globe*. Both said that based on his opinion, "it is doubtful if most contracts of players are binding." Both papers were so struck by this possibility that they each put the article on the front page of at least one edition.[66]

The day before Judge Simonton's hearing, EISL President W.H. Voltz sent a letter to his board of directors, though its contents might not have been made public prior to Saturday, May 17. He had immediately followed up on the EISL board meeting of May 15 by sending a letter to board members in which he requested a vote by mail. Voltz wrote:

> I have just laid the case of York's protest against the signing of Grant before John I. Rogers, the leading attorney on base ball law, and he says, according to Section 33, of our constitution, the Harrisburg club is entitled to Grant's services, because of the contract being made prior to the York club's admission to the league. He thinks as far as the league is concerned, the Harrisburg club, having accepted Grant's terms and forwarded a contract, in his (Rogers) opinion, the York's protest is overruled.
>
> I enclose you a copy of section 33. On receipt of this tell me one of the following:
>
> 1. York's protest sustained,
> 2. York's protest overruled, Grant goes to Harrisburg.[67]

On the afternoon of Monday, May 19, Harrisburg Ponies manager James Farrington received a telegram from Voltz which read, "The Board of Directors, after due deliberation and consultation with highest legal authority, declares that York's protest is overruled, and that Grant must play with Harrisburg. Will mail full decision."[68] That provided Farrington and Grant some peace of mind for a time, though there remained the potential that Judge Simonton would rule otherwise.

Over the second half of May and into the first week of June, the Ponies continued to do well, as did Grant. Against Lancaster on May 23 the Ponies scored 10 runs in the first inning and ultimately won, 24–0. Grant went 3-for-7 with a homer and three runs scored. The teams met again the next day, and it was a much closer contest. In fact, it was tied, 5–5, when Grant led off the Ponies' half of the sixth inning with his second homer in as many days. He also had a double among his three hits.[69] One Harrisburg newspaper chose this occasion to rave about several aspects of Frank Grant's capabilities. "Grant played at short stop on Saturday and his work was simply great," the *Daily Patriot* said. After just one game at that position, the *Patriot* said he should remain there. The paper also complimented his tendency to back up other fielders. "Grant is always behind the catcher when a ball is thrown from the [out]field to catch a runner going home," it noted. *Twice* in the same column of comments about the Ponies, the *Patriot* mentioned that Grant's tie-breaking homer was the longest at Harrisburg's ballpark, and they didn't qualify it by specifying *that season*.[70]

The Ponies were supposed to play games in York on May 26–27, but the first was rained out. On the second day, the York nine drew its largest home crowd, 1,400 strong. A group of 125 fans had traveled from Harrisburg. York led 1–0 after four innings, but Grant tied it with a hit in the Ponies' half of the fifth inning, and later scored. The Ponies hung on for a 5–4 victory, their first over the former Cuban Giants. Grant went 2-for-4 with a walk off Selden.[71] The two teams met again for a single game on May 29 in Harrisburg, and the Ponies won again, 8–5. Grant went 2-for-4 with three stolen bases and two runs scored, and he played errorless ball at third base with four putouts and four assists. Clarence Williams didn't play in the first win versus York, but he was catcher for the second. As a result of the two triumphs over York that week, the race for first place narrowed. York had a record of 16–4 and Harrisburg 14–5. The teams in third and fourth place were each just two wins over .500, so the pennant race had narrowed quickly.[72]

On June 2, the *Daily Patriot* published a chart of the team's batting averages, and in 20 games, Frank Grant had 38 hits in 88 at-bats for a robust .432 batting average. The next-best average among Harrisburg's regulars was .337. Above the chart, the *Patriot* noted that Grant also had "the largest number of long drives," i.e., extra base hits. However, someone's arithmetic was off, because it said a homer, four triples, and seven doubles added up to 32 bases but actually those equate to 30. The miscalculation may have been related to the fact that he'd homered *twice*. Whatever the explanation, it was sad to see that Clarence Williams had struggled, with a batting average of .149 in 11 games.[73]

On June 5, Williams took advantage of a chance to begin turning that around when he filled in at third base for Frank Grant, who was out of the lineup due to some unspecified illness. Clarence had a triple, double, and single in an easy win over Easton. The Ponies didn't play on June 6, but Grant was right back in the lineup the next day for another struggle with York, in that city. Though Grant was hitless against William Whyte, the Ponies prevailed, 6–3. That resulted in York, Harrisburg, and Altoona all having 18 wins, but with six, 10, and 13 losses, respectively.[74]

Harrisburg happened to defeat York in a very different competition that morning, because back in Dauphin County, Judge Simonton issued a ruling against York. The *Daily Independent* said it covered about a dozen pages. The *Telegraph* quoted from Simonton's opinion at length on its front page, and editorialized about it on its second page. "This controversy over Grant has excited universal interest in the base ball world and the opinion of the Dauphin county court will be widely quoted," the *Telegraph* predicted. "On the hearing Judge Simonton expressed some decided views on the subject of professional base ball, and his conclusions have been anxiously awaited. It is evident that he regards the whole matter as of too trifling a nature to occupy the attention of the court." Nevertheless, the *Telegraph* noted that the opinion cited "many authorities in support of the position taken by the court."[75]

The first sentence quoted by the *Telegraph* suggested that newspapers may not have understood exactly what kind of remedy York had been seeking. "It is to be noted that the court is not asked to make an affirmative decree compelling defendant Grant to play ball for the plaintiff, and it was conceded on the argument that such a decree could not be enforced, and therefore ought not to be made," Simonton wrote. "The injury complained of here is distinctly stated … to be the loss of receipts to the club by the absence of a player of such exceptional skill as the defendant Grant," the Judge continued, and then he quoted similar language from a brief submitted by York's lawyers. "Grant being a player of great skill and reputation[,] his absence and refusal to play with [York] lessens its drawing powers," those attorneys wrote. "Such damage cannot be estimated in dollars and cents. The absence of so great and skillful a player involves loss at every game played." Simonton noted that York's attorneys didn't claim any "distinct" harm from Grant playing specifically for the Ponies. In essence, Simonton took the position that because he couldn't force Grant to play for York, no judge should try to do that "indirectly" by preventing him from playing for the Ponies. The *Telegraph* quoted two paragraphs from Simonton's opinion elaborating on that point. But the final point the *Telegraph* focused on may not have been reported on previously—assuming that McCarrell made it to begin with, and Simonton didn't just speak to it on his own. Simonton wrote that Kreiter's contract from late winter wasn't "mutual," and he implied that it was patently unfair to Frank Grant because it was one-sided in an important aspect. Simonton quoted this language from that contract: "It is further agreed between the parties hereto that the party of the second part (the plaintiff) reserves the right to abrogate this agreement at any time when it appears that the said party of the first part is not fulfilling his agreement to the best of his ability."[76] In other words, there should have been corresponding language allowing Frank Grant to also abrogate (invalidate or nullify) the contract. Regardless, as far as is known, Kreiter's legal team did not appeal Simonton's decision.

The ruling didn't seem to get much attention outside of Pennsylvania, though the *Washington Post* and the *Boston Herald* did report it, as did at least one newspaper in Buffalo.[77] The EISL's determination against York in May might have led many sportswriters to view Simonton's ruling as little more than a formality. In any event, it might have undercut York's morale, because they lost to the Ponies on June 9 and 10 as well, giving Grant's team five straight wins against its top rival. In the first of these two games, Grant went 3-for-4 off Selden, stole a base, and scored twice in a 9–5 win at home. Off two pitchers the next day, he went 2-for-5, stole another base, and again scored twice. The Ponies broke a 7–7 tie with a run in the fifth inning, and there was no scoring in the next three frames. "In fielding Grant saved the day for Harrisburg in the last inning after Williams had reached first safely," the *Daily Patriot* reported. Thomas batted next, and "made a solid hit between third base and short stop. Like a cat, Grant sprung toward the fast flying leather and by a most dexterous turn stopped its flight," that newspaper continued. He then threw to Eagan to begin a crucial double play. Selden doubled, and the *Patriot* concluded its account by reporting that "Boyd sent a stinging hard line fly ball in the direction of Grant which he caught and thus ended the game."[78]

With the two teams having small streaks in opposite directions, on June 13 the Ponies moved into first place with a record of 21–10. York was second at 18–10.[79] One week later, Frank Grant took part in what the *Daily Patriot* called the greatest game ever seen in Harrisburg, when Ponies pitcher Frank Baxter, a career minor leaguer, no-hit Lebanon's nine, 13–0. Grant went 3-for-6 with three runs scored. By that point, however, York was back atop the EISL standings after a five-game winning streak. Its record of 23–10 equaled a winning percentage of .697. The Ponies' record of 25–12 corresponded to a winning percentage of .676.[80]

On June 23, at least two Harrisburg dailies reported updated EISL statistics for the Ponies and selected opponents. The two newspapers identified Harrisburg catcher Harry Koons as the league's top batter with an average of .446, but that was accomplished in only 13 games. Among regular players, George Williams of York ranked first with an average of either .436 or .430 (depending on which paper one believes), and Frank Grant was third, with an average of .385. Based on a chart in the *Daily Patriot*, the league's batting average was .251 across about 6,600 at-bats. Grant was tied for 12th place in stolen bases with 15. Among regular third basemen, he had the second-best fielding percentage, though the *Patriot* pointed out that he had more chances in fewer games and only two more errors than the leader.[81]

On June 28, the Ponies played a close game against Allentown, which had joined the EISL about two weeks earlier as Lancaster's replacement. Frank Grant was the key to turning a "triple play which retired the visitors at a most critical juncture," as one hometown paper put it. Alas, two dailies disagreed somewhat on the sequence of throws, and neither identified the inning. "It was made possible by the capture of a ball by Grant that was apparently far beyond his reach," the *Telegraph* reported. "He jumped high in the air and caught it with one hand. Then he fired it to Eagan and the latter passed it on to McCormick. The applause was tremendous." The two box scores agreed that the four fielders involved were Koons at home, then Grant, and ultimately Eagan at second and Jerry McCormick at first.[82] The *Patriot* elaborated as follows:

> Probably the finest play yet made on the ground was executed by Koons, Grant, Eagan and McCormick, by which the entire visiting side was put out. In this play Grant deserves great credit for he saved Koons from an error by putting the first man out between third base and the home plate. He did it by jumping high in the air and catching with one hand a high thrown ball. After the first man had been put out, however, Koons used good judgement in getting the other two men out, one at second and the other between first and second.[83]

This was at least the fourth triple play Frank Grant helped turn in five minor league regular seasons. His first was with Meridian in May 1886, his very first month as a pro. He was also involved in one with Buffalo in July 1888 and one in the MSL during August 1889.

The Ponies and their top rivals, the York Monarchs, began a series in Harrisburg on Saturday, July 5, before a crowd of 3,000. The Ponies held a 3–2 lead after six innings but

8. Ordered to Harrisburg (1890 to April 1891)

an eight-run ninth inning gave York a win, and that dropped the Ponies to third place, behind Altoona. York also won Monday's rematch, 4–1. That set the stage for what may have been Frank Grant's best pair of games to that point. On July 8, the Ponies recovered for an easy win against York, 18–6. Grant went 4-for-5 against Winslow Terrill, including a double and a walk. He also stole a base and scored three runs. He played errorless ball at third base, with three putouts and four assists. Sadly, only 500 fans saw that outburst.[84]

In York on July 9, in a 20–8 romp against William Selden, Grant had four more hits (or five, according to the *Daily Independent* and *Patriot* box scores), including a home run, and scored four runs. His homer came with two teammates on base in the fourth inning, when the game was tied, 4–4.[85] He homered again in York the next day, one of his two hits against William Whyte in a 13–5 loss. He scored three of the Ponies' runs. It was York's first win at home against the Ponies.[86]

As strong as this rivalry was, about a week into July the EISL's bottom two teams, Allentown and Easton, disbanded.[87] That left the league with four franchises, in York, Harrisburg, Altoona, and Lebanon. There didn't seem to be much talk of adding teams to restore the EISL to a six-club circuit.

On July 16, the Ponies were in Altoona for a battle for second place. Grant had another four-hit, three-run game. He also experienced quite a rarity when he was awarded first base after being hit by a pitch. Much more importantly, his four hits included two for extra bases. One was either a double or triple (at least two newspapers said he had a triple but the box scores showed a double). There was absolutely no doubt about the other long hit. "In the eighth inning Grant knocked the ball over [the] centre field fence, a feat heretofore supposed to be impossible," an Altoona paper reported, and added that with one exception, "Grant's hit yesterday was the longest ever made on the Fourth street grounds." The blast came with a teammate on base. "He seemed to have superhuman strength and he met the ball squarely on the nose and the way it sailed westward and skyward astonished everybody on the grounds," according to the special dispatch printed by the *Daily Patriot*. As a result of the Ponies' win, their record of 36–23 translated to a winning percentage of .610. Altoona's record of 34–22 gave them a winning percentage of .607.[88]

Around that time, word surfaced that the Ponies were considering a jump to the Atlantic Association, to replace Jersey City.[89] This league included teams in Baltimore and Washington, which had both been major league cities in 1889. However, one immediate sticking point was an Atlantic Association resolution reportedly adopted on Thursday, July 17. As the *Telegraph* understood it, if "the Harrisburg club is admitted they will not be allowed to play with the two colored men now employed by the team." The Ponies' management was expected to object, "especially in the case of Grant, who has time and time again proven his worth to the home team in whatever position placed." The *Telegraph* was of the view that baseball fans in Harrisburg generally wouldn't accept the Association's resolution. "Down goes the club in the people's estimation and patronage if the silly colored line is drawn, and the club may as well understand that," the daily stated. The *Washington Post* reported on July 20 that Harrisburg would be willing to release Clarence Williams if needed, but the club would reject membership in defense of Frank Grant. Atlantic Association President James Braden was thus in Harrisburg to conduct negotiations, but he feared that most of managers of the Association's franchises wouldn't agree to having Grant in their league.[90]

On July 21, the *Telegraph* reported that only two clubs of the Atlantic Association, namely New Haven and Newark, had voted to admit Harrisburg with Frank Grant on the roster, but that paper was confident a special meeting of the Atlantic Association in New York City that evening would result in the Ponies joining with him on board. The *Telegraph* was correct. After the lengthy meeting, Farrington sent a concise telegram to at least the sports editor of the *Patriot*, which read, "Grant all right. We play Washington on Tuesday and Wednesday, at 4 p. m."[91] Not surprisingly, the *Telegraph* was delighted that the objections to Grant were indeed overcome. It said:

> Harrisburg is a pretty good ball town. Its gate money is not to be sneezed at. It will be a mint for a number of needy Atlantic Association clubs. They saw the point. They came down gracefully. Grant, the colored player, will play with Harrisburg. The Harrisburg club was right in standing by Grant. If he were a poor player and were discharged for inefficiency nobody would say a word, but when the color line is drawn on him it is a fight for principle and the Harrisburg club could not take any other stand than it did. Grant is a gentleman and the best ball player in the association. His color has nothing to do with the case.[92]

Though Washington and Baltimore were reportedly the teams that objected most strongly to Frank Grant, the *Washington Post* chose to counter that indirectly on July 22 by quoting an anonymous "old baseball patron" on the subject, perhaps to prevent a future insurrection:

> I cannot understand why any of the ball clubs of the Atlantic Association should object to admitting Harrisburg because it has a couple of colored men among its players. The leading ball clubs of the East have played games with nines composed entirely of colored men. The Cuban Giants and the Gorhams have played with the Washingtons and other Eastern nines repeatedly. If the Harrisburg players themselves do not object to Grant and his colored associate, I see no reason why the other clubs should. The time when the color line could be drawn in baseball passed away some time ago, at least in the North.[93]

If only that had been true. But in a relatively short amount of time, Harrisburg transitioned from the EISL to the eight-team Atlantic Association. In addition to the four franchises already mentioned, the Atlantic had teams in Hartford, Wilmington, and Worcester. However, the latter was replaced by the EISL's Lebanon club.[94]

The Ponies played one more game in the EISL on Monday, July 21, hosting their top rivals, the first-place York Monarchs. Grant batted fourth against Whyte and went 2-for-5 with a run scored. Clarence Williams batted right after him and went 2-for-4 with a double and two runs scored. The Ponies prevailed, 12–5. York thus had a record of 40–17, and the Ponies finished second with a record of 39–24. The Ponies beat the Monarchs eight times and lost to them five times.[95] The *Telegraph* bemoaned the fact that Clarence would not continue with the Ponies in the Atlantic Association. "Must Clarence Williams walk the plank? Well, good bye, Clarence," the daily wrote. "You were a whole team."[96]

On July 22, the Ponies played their first game in the Atlantic Association by hosting the Washington Senators. The visiting pitcher was lefty Pete Daniels, who had made his major league debut on April 19 with Pittsburgh.[97] There were 1,800 fans in attendance, and for eight innings they were disappointed in the home team's batting. Daniels gave up a two-out hit in the top of the first inning, after which Frank Grant, batting cleanup, lined out to end the frame. From the second through seventh innings, Daniels retired the Ponies in order. After eight innings, the Senators led, 3–0. "The score man was taking down the row of goose eggs for Harrisburg, and many in the crowd were leaving," according to the *Patriot*. In the home team's half of the ninth, Eagan tripled on the first pitch he saw, and he scored on Daniels' wild pitch. Daniels struck out the next batter but then gave up a single. That brought Grant to the plate as the potential tying run. He had been 0-for-3 before that, but he also singled to extend the inning. Koons then tripled to tie the game, though the Ponies couldn't get him in from third. The bottom of the Ponies' lineup won the game in the extra inning, 5–3. In addition to a timely hit, Grant was a major contributor near third base to keeping the score close with six putouts, five assists, and no errors. As the *Telegraph* commented, "Grant was very much in that game yesterday."[98]

About 1,500 fans turned out the next day for the rematch. The Ponies led, 1–0, after three innings but the Senators were handed a potential rally in the fourth when their first two batters reached base on walks. Grant then made his biggest contribution of the day by beginning a double play that released the pressure and allowed his team to escape the inning with their foes still scoreless. The Ponies later led 4–3 after seven innings, and that also proved to be the final score. Rain prevented a third game.[99]

A few days later, the *Washington Post* commented on Harrisburg's first two games in the Atlantic Association. The Ponies made a very good impression, both in terms of their skill and the size of their crowds, which the *Post* called "good." That daily was inclined to believe that Harrisburg would be an asset to Atlantic Association franchises that were struggling financially, and asked about Frank Grant, "What are the personal prejudices of a few players worth when an entire Association wants a club to complete its circuit?" Nevertheless, the *Post* also reported that Harrisburg had signed third baseman Frank Foulkrod, a career minor leaguer who'd been playing in the International Association, "to take Grant's place in cities where there is objection to the colored player."[100]

Baltimore manager Billy Barnie, for one, had reportedly said as much about Baltimore. By contrast, after the 1887 season he had expressed interest in *signing* Frank Grant to a *major* league contract. It's not a given that Barnie changed his attitude; he may simply have been communicating the hostility of his players. In fact, a Baltimore daily implied as much. "Many of the Baltimore players are strongly opposed to taking part in games with Grant, the colored third baseman of the Harrisburg Club, although they realize that it is a matter for the Atlantic Association managers to settle among themselves," the *Sun* reported. "The most decided objections are naturally made by [Pop] Tate and [Mike] O'Rourke, who live in Richmond, and [Reddy] Mack, who is a son of Kentucky." Both Tate and Mack had five years of major league experience at that point. In a twist, these players said the real unfairness to Grant would be "to persist in keeping him as a regular member of the Harrisburg team in the face of the prejudice which is sure to be shown against him." Regardless, Harrisburg's *Daily Telegraph* challenged Barnie and two days later rebutted those players.[101] In fact, Atlantic Association statistics for Harrisburg show that four players led the team in games played, with 47, and Frank Grant was in that quartet. Foulkrod played 43 games at third base, but that's because Grant played only four games at that position before becoming the Ponies' shortstop for the duration.

The Ponies lost two close games at home to Wilmington on July 25 and 26, and thus split its first four games in the Atlantic Association. However, Harrisburg had inherited Jersey City's record of 27–46, so its official record was 29–48 after the second loss to Wilmington. The first loss was 3–2 in 11 innings, but the *Daily Patriot* considered the turning point to have been in the seventh inning when Grant threw a ball ten feet over the first baseman's head and allowed a Wilmington base runner to score his team's second run. Wilmington won the next day, 1–0. Each team only had four hits. Grant's double was the only hit for extra bases, but the Ponies squandered it.[102]

On a much happier note for Grant's many fans, the renowned historian and statistician eventually elected to baseball's Hall of Fame, Henry Chadwick, weighed in on his behalf in the new issue of *Sporting Life*. After quoting from the *New York Sun* and the *Philadelphia Times* about all the controversy in the Atlantic Association, the man often called the "Father of Baseball" offered his concluding thoughts. "The glorious inconsistency of objecting to a gentlemanly colored man in a team, while making not objection to the presence of so many white 'toughs,' 'roughs' and drunkards, who have been allowed for years to bring disgrace on the fraternity, is one of the absurdities of the existing condition of things in the base ball world," Chadwick wrote. "I hope to see the Atlantic Association show some common sense in this matter."[103]

The Ponies played their first Atlantic Association road game on July 28, against Wilmington again. Grant batted fourth and made his switch to shortstop. He didn't see much action at that position. He made just one putout and had one assist, with no errors. Grant led all batters with three hits, and his single in the sixth inning advanced a teammate who soon scored the Ponies' first run, which tied the score. However, the game remained knotted at 1–1 after nine innings. The home team didn't score in the top half of the next frame. In the bottom half, Joseph Jones led off with a walk. A Wilmington newspaper's otherwise detailed account got vague at this point. Grant batted next and hit a ball that was scored as a single. Jones apparently tried to score on the play but Wilmington's pitcher threw him out there, presumably after a relay of some sort. While that was unfolding, Grant raced to third base. He scored the winning run easily when the next batter, Whitey Gibson, singled. The rematch scheduled for the next day was postponed, so the Ponies traveled to Newark for two games.[104]

The Ponies lost the first game, 3–1. The next day, a Philadelphia paper reported that their major league Athletics, of the American Association, had made an offer to Harrisburg for second baseman Bill Eagan.[105] He hit well for the Ponies in the EISL as well as in the Atlantic Association, but Frank Grant exceeded him. Eagan didn't leave the Ponies, but he did become a major leaguer the next season, as regular second baseman for the American Association's St. Louis Browns.

The Ponies also lost a second close game in Newark, a 10—9 slugfest. Grant led all batters with four hits, including a double.[106] The Ponies returned home to host Hartford, and poor field conditions necessitated a doubleheader on August 2. The teams split them, reportedly before 2,500 fans.[107] The Ponies also split games on August 4 and 5 with the talented New Haven nine, who were managed by Walter Burnham, Grant's first manager with Meriden. After that, the Ponies made their second trip to Wilmington. Unlike Harrisburg's first visit, this one began on a very bad note. The hotel in which they stayed in late July turned the team away on the evening of August 5. "When the club was last here, all of its members, including Grant, stopped at the Clayton House, the regular headquarters of visiting clubs, and were treated as other guests," read a dispatch from Wilmington printed in the *Telegraph*. "To-day, however, Proprietor Pyle refused to receive the Harrisburg men and they went to Boer's Hotel."[108] The Ponies won their game there on August 6, 4–2, and Frank Grant scored two of those runs. The attendance was 500 or so, which "was much higher than for several days, and the spectators showed their appreciation of the good playing on both sides by frequent loud applause,"

8. Ordered to Harrisburg (1890 to April 1891)

Wilmington's *Evening Journal* said, singling out one player: "Grant, the dusky visitor, was compelled to lift his cap twice."[109] Unfortunately, the home team won the next day, 7–5, though Grant's hit was a double. The turnout among fans was even higher, around 800.[110]

Around this time in Washington, there was trouble of a very different sort for an Atlantic Association team. Its franchise had folded, but manager Ted Sullivan was scrambling to organize a replacement with himself higher in the hierarchy. He ultimately failed, and Washington played its final games on August 2, against Lebanon.[111] In the end, the franchise wasn't replaced.

Across the month of August and into early September, weekly African American newspapers in Great Lakes states demonstrated a keen interest in Frank Grant's persistence as a pro ballplayer. This was particularly true of the *Cleveland Gazette*. He was mentioned in at least four of its weekly editions over little more than a month. The first was the longest, on August 2. The first third of the article adapted reports about a few franchises having opposed Harrisburg's admission to the Atlantic Association if Clarence Williams and Frank Grant remained on the roster. In the middle of the article, the *Gazette* focused on Farrington's firmness about keeping Grant in the lineup. The bottom third quoted the *Harrisburg Telegram* (distinct from the *Telegraph*) without rebuttal or other commentary, which may mean the *Gazette* considered this to be an accurate assessment:

> The view taken by Baltimore and Wilmington, as to Grant, is a mistake. Composed as these places are with a colored population of considerable magnitude, no harm could possibly result from his playing and the attendance would be increased instead of diminished as claimed. There is no class that caters more to amusements than the colored folks and every effort is made by them to do so. This has been demonstrated in this and other cities and would be the case in the places mentioned. If a man is a good mechanic, whether colored or white, he does not lack for patronage in any place. Grant is a good ball player and it is not his color, but his "style" of handling the ball and bat that causes the trouble.[112]

On August 9, the *Gazette* utilized the dispatch naming Tate, O'Rourke, and Mack as the Orioles who most strongly objected to Grant, but concluded with a solid insult: "The funny part of it is, Grant is a better player than any of the objectors." On August 15, Detroit's *Plaindealer* also reported on how "stoutly" Farrington stood with Grant. Interestingly, the *Gazette* had used "colored" and "Afro-American" interchangeably, but the *Plaindealer* used only the latter. On August 23, Indianapolis' *Freeman* printed a brief item about Grant being denied lodging in Wilmington, which ended, "The entire club left with him." Further down that same column, the *Freeman* reprinted the Gazette's very long article from three weeks earlier.[113] Needless to say, African American journalists in the nation's northeastern quadrant would be monitoring teams like Baltimore carefully.

On Saturday, August 9, the Ponies played the Baltimore Orioles for the first time, in Harrisburg. This was particularly significant because roughly two weeks later, the Orioles made the very unusual jump from a minor league to a major league, when it rejoined the American Association. The Ponies managed just three hits off pitcher Norm Baker, who had a 13–12 record in 1885 for Louisville in the American Association in an otherwise short major league career. He had a record of 29–10 for Baltimore in the Atlantic Association. In this game against the Ponies, Baltimore had just five hits to its own credit, but the visitors prevailed before about 2,500 fans, 2–0.[114]

The Orioles moved on to Lebanon after just that one game, and Washington was scheduled to play in Harrisburg on August 11, so the Ponies were reportedly awarded a 9–0 forfeit. The Ponies filled that void with an exhibition against the York Monarchs, who now had Clarence Williams as their catcher.[115] The two teams followed that contest with doubleheaders the next two days, although the second game on August 13 was cancelled in the fifth inning due to rain.

Around that time, it was reported that Frank Grant was receiving the highest salary among the Ponies, at $175 a month. Probably by coincidence, the *Telegraph* made it painfully clear what the ownership *wasn't* spending money on: matching uniforms. In fact, this daily said the team's "dirty, old, faded, ragged, stained and tattered clothes" shouldn't actually be "called uniforms, because not two are alike." The *Telegraph* offered a few examples: "Grant wears a black and orange jersey; Vallee a white suit (it was once white), Gittinger [sic] and Foulkrod brown caps, and the other players any kind of togs they can pick out of the rag heap in the grand stand dressing rooms."[116] Perhaps a sportswriter had become self-conscious about his local team after seeing the quality of attire Atlantic Association teams could afford.

On the eve of the Ponies' first trip to Baltimore, Billy Barnie offered an assessment of Frank Grant that was very much in line with what he'd said three years earlier. "Manager Barnie, speaking of Grant, the colored short stop of [Harrisburg], said he had seen the greatest in this position, and that Grant would come near equaling any of them," the *Baltimore American* paraphrased. "He is a quiet sort of chap and exceedingly polite."[117]

On the morning of August 15, the Ponies left for Baltimore, about 75 miles to the south, for a game there that afternoon. On the front page of that day's *Baltimore Sun*, just a few inches down the first column, a brief blurb of sorts promoted the game with this tagline: "First Appearance of GRANT, the Wonder." However, the *Baltimore American* said there was widespread doubt that Grant would actually play.[118]

The *Sun* reported a crowd of 1,700 for the game, and Grant had "attracted to the grounds a considerable number of colored onlookers." That certainly could have factored into why the *American* said he "was well received." The *American* added that the Orioles themselves showed some negativity toward him, but it was mostly in the form of extra hustle whenever he was involved, such as running at full speed on groundballs hit to him. Still, the *Harrisburg Daily Independent* said the more overt hostility toward him that some predicted "did not materialize."[119]

The Ponies managed just six hits and three runs in the game, and couldn't overcome a four-run first inning by the Orioles. The home nine ultimately won, 8–3. Grant contributed a single and a sacrifice on offense, but his errorless defense, including four putouts and five assists, made a strong impression. "Everybody was looking to see Grant, the famous colored short-stop, play, and those who had expected a great exhibition were not disappointed," Baltimore's *Morning Herald* reported. "Grant is certainly a remarkable player. He has a natural aptitude for hot

A thin ad touting "GRANT, the Wonder" on the front page of the *Baltimore Sun*, August 16, 1890.

grounders, covers a large territory and is quick with the ball." "He is of medium height, heavy set, but active as a cat, and his quick stops, followed by lightning throws, were cheered frequently," the *Sun* said. "He is a great player, however, and strengthens the Harrisburg team greatly."[120]

Alas, the Ponies were even less effective in the next day's rematch, which they lost, 8–1. Grant was hitless, and on defense had one putout and one assist. "Grant, the colored short-stop, did not have much opportunity to distinguish himself, but whatever he was called on to do he did well," the *Morning Herald* reported.[121]

Between the two games in Baltimore, there was some very disheartening news reported, with some inaccuracy presumably mixed in, by a reporter jumping to a conclusion. "Grant, the colored short-stop, only associates with his fellow-players on the field," said the *Sun*. "The headquarters of the Harrisburg team in Baltimore are at Kelly's Hotel, but Grant lodges and takes his meals at the house of Roy, the head waiter of the hotel, on Pear alley."[122] The latter fact is the obvious disappointment, because it contrasts with the very recent Wilmington report of the Ponies refusing lodging when Grant wouldn't be accommodated. In this instance, it's certainly conceivable the team was prepared to take the same stance, but Grant talked them out of it. Whatever happened, the *Sun*'s journalist made a hasty generalization about his teammates only associating with him at ballparks.

The Ponies had other disappointing developments to worry about during that visit, when it was reported that the Atlantic Association's franchise in Hartford was folding. At the same time, the effort to reorganize a team in Washington officially fizzled out after two weeks of trying. That left the Atlantic Association as a six-club circuit.[123] Frustratingly, that was true for less than two weeks.

Harrisburg next traveled to Newark for two games. The Ponies' offense continued to slump there, but Grant saved the first game on defense by preserving a shutout. The game was scoreless until the Ponies scored once in the seventh inning, the only run that nine managed in the game. "Grant made a wonderful one-handed stop of [Leo] Smith's apparently safe hit in the ninth inning, which prevented the Newarks from tying the score, if not winning the game," according to the *New York Tribune*. Oddly, several other newspapers that printed brief descriptions emphasizing Grant's crucial role instead echoed the *Philadelphia Inquirer*'s account, that "Grant's great stop and throw in the seventh inning won the game for Harrisburg."[124] It's certainly possible he made impressive plays in both innings.

That evening, Baltimore announced that it would become a major league franchise again, though not immediately, by leaving the Atlantic Association to rejoin the American Association. The Orioles committed to playing its Atlantic Association games through August 26. The *Harrisburg Telegraph*, for one, printed a very long paragraph expressing fury about this decision, aiming venom first at Barnie and then Atlantic Association President Braden.[125]

The Ponies had no choice but to continue their road trip, and Newark won the next day's rematch, 4–2. The Ponies traveled up to New Haven for two more games, and in the first one they were shut out, 2–0. They squandered the game's only extra-base hit, a double by Grant. He also stole a base and walked, but no teammate could drive him home. Harrisburg's batters finally showed some life in the second game, on August 21, led by Grant's 3-for-4 performance, which included another double and a walk. Sadly, New Haven's batters were even more productive, and the Ponies lost, 10–6.[126] Harrisburg finished its tour on a positive note by taking two games in Wilmington without much difficulty.

After an open date on Sunday, August 24, the same two teams played two more games to start a home stand for Harrisburg. The Ponies won both, 8–5 and 16–2. In the first contest, Grant went 2-for-5, both doubles. In the second game, he went 3-for-3 and scored four runs. One of those hits was another double.[127] That loss was Wilmington's final game in the Atlantic Association, because that night it was expelled during a special meeting for not having paid dues. Kreiter attended to apply for membership on behalf of the York Monarchs, but the delegates decided to continue as a four-team league.[128] Baltimore did indeed play its final Atlantic Association game that same day. The remaining quartet of teams—Harrisburg, Lebanon, New Haven, and Newark—did complete the regular season, at the end of September.

New Haven shut the Ponies out in Harrisburg on August 27, 1–0, and the visitors won the next day as well, 2–1. Newark then arrived for two games, and the first provided a clear indication that Frank Grant continued to play the infield *without a conventional fielder's glove*. The Ponies had a comfortable lead going into the ninth inning, 9–3, but Newark scored a run and continued to threaten with runners on second and third. "Grant ended the game by making the greatest catch yet seen on the grounds," the *Patriot* enthused. Journeyman Dan Murphy "got a full swing at the ball and it darted through the air like out of a cannon. Quick as lightning Grant leaped out and with his left hand snatched the ball, to the great surprise of all on the grounds." Grant had already contributed well on offense by going 3-for-5 with a stolen base and a run scored.[129] In 1924, a Buffalo fan named Bill Young told a newspaper there that Grant never wore a glove while covering second base for the Bisons.[130]

The Ponies defeated Newark again, 3–1, in their last game of the month, then had a day off. On September 1, they hosted Lebanon for a doubleheader, and the second game drew more than 1,500 fans. Each team won a game, but it was quite the day for Frank Grant. All told, he went 5-for-9 with a triple, a stolen base, and two runs scored.[131] The Ponies spent the rest of the week losing four games to Lebanon, with two open dates.

On Monday, September 8, Frank Grant had a new teammate who was just 13 pro games into a Hall of Fame career: Hughie Jennings. He had played with Allentown's EISL team, but when they folded around Independence Day, he resumed playing semipro ball in Lehighton, Pennsylvania. Jennings' debut with the Ponies was at home, hosting Newark. A late rally by the Ponies fell short and they lost, 10–9. Jennings had a double in four at-bats plus a run scored, while Grant went 3-for-5, including a double, with three runs scored. Grant played errorless ball, with four putouts and four assists. Jennings was a shortstop in his prime but played catcher for the Ponies. He made two errors but wasn't charged with a passed ball.[132] Jennings played in eight more games for Harrisburg that month. According to Negro Leagues expert Ted Knorr, this is the earliest instance in baseball history of two future Hall of Famers, one African American and the other white, playing on the same team.[133]

Newark won by just one run again the next day, 2–1. The two teams met on September 10 for a third consecutive game, and that time the 2–1 outcome was in favor of Harrisburg. Grant was the only Pony with more than one hit. In fact, he went 4-for-4 with a double and scored Harrisburg's first run. He had only one putout but made seven assists without an error.[134]

The Ponies were scheduled to play three games in New Haven starting on

September 11, but the entire series was rained out, as were games back home on September 15 and 16. The next day, the Ponies finally got a game in, a win hosting Newark, 7–2. Grant went 2-for-5 with two runs scored, and both of his hits were doubles.[135] The Ponies then won two games at home from New Haven. The second, on September 19, was tied at 4—4 after five innings, but the Ponies score the game's remaining two runs. Grant had three hits, one a double. According to the *Patriot*, one of the day's highlights occurred during a break in the action. "Grant was presented with a five dollar bill during the progress of the game, and that was one of the features," the daily said. "Everybody is of the opinion that he deserves all he gets in addition to his small salary, if merit and skill are to be rewarded."[136]

The Ponies beat New Haven a third time in a row, 1–0, and after a day off, extended its winning streak to five on September 22 by beating Lebanon, 7–1. The visitors ended Harrisburg's streak the next day with a 7–0 whitewashing. On September 24, Harrisburg and New Haven played the first of two games in Reading, Pennsylvania. The Ponies won, 10–7, but Grant had a very rough day on defense with four errors. He misplayed two grounders and made two wild throws. The *Reading Times* mentioned those throws but also noted that he "made two or three brilliant stops," and the box score showed three assists plus a putout.[137] Though he had a very quiet day in the following day's rematch, with just an assist and an error while going hitless, the *Times* still noted that he was one "of the greatest stars seen in Reading this season."[138]

Around that time, one of the Harrisburg dailies looked back on the Ponies' previous 16 games and noted that they went 8–8. Among the other four remaining Atlantic Association clubs, only their former EISL rivals, Lebanon, had a winning record over the same span, a very impressive 14–5. New Haven had gone 7–9 and Newark 6–14.[139] As fans of the Ponies would or should have expected, the club didn't enjoy the easy success it experienced in the EISL, but it was holding its own in the Atlantic Association and proved that it had indeed deserved admission.

In the wake of that recent five-game winning streak, the final few days of September, and the Atlantic Association season, ended with a whimper for the Ponies. Two games against Newark scheduled were rained out, and on Monday, September 29, the Ponies were trounced at Lebanon, 18–11. Grant had just a modest personal highlight on the eve of the season's end: His hit in that game was a double, and he scored twice. The same two teams played their season finale in Harrisburg on September 30, and it ended on a very sour note for Grant. The game was scoreless through seven innings, but his overthrow to first base in the eighth inning allowed the only run of the game to score. He also went hitless in four at-bats, though his putout, four assists, and initiation of a double play had constituted "some very fine work," according to the *Daily Independent*.[140]

Nevertheless, Frank Grant could have taken plenty of comfort in the fact that he had the third highest batting average among Atlantic Association players who appeared in as many games as he did, 47. A chart in *Sporting Life* showed that he had 62 hits in 187 at-bats, for an average of .332. Also, despite his defensive lapses toward the end of September, during his 43 games at shortstop he had the third-best fielding percentage at that position, with a mark of .901.[141] Also, according to his EISL statistics published by baseball-reference.com (as of this writing), his .333 average when Harrisburg left was barely exceeded only by Jerry McCormick among regular Ponies, who hit .336. York had four regulars near or above Grant in the EISL rankings: George Williams at .386, Sol

White at .350, Arthur Thomas at .333, and William Selden at .330. The only other regular to rank higher than Grant in batting average was Altoona's Whitey Gibson, who had an average of .335 in 44 games. Also, the five home runs credited to Frank Grant were enough to lead the EISL, but, as already noted, he homered on consecutive days in May, plus he hit *four* more in July, on the 2nd, 9th, 10th, and 16th.[142]

Speaking of the Monarchs, all signs indicate that they were the only opponent the Ponies faced in an exhibition game after Harrisburg's last Atlantic Association game. A "Picked Nine" from among the Ponies was defeated by York on October 1 by a score of 14–7. York was supposed to play Lebanon, but the *Daily Independent* said the latter hadn't officially disbanded, so an exhibition game would have violated the National Agreement. The Ponies *had* already formally disbanded, so nine of their players stepped in, albeit without calling themselves the Ponies. Their lineup included Frank Grant and Hughie Jennings. Each of those future Hall of Famers doubled, but the Monarchs jumped out to a 7–2 lead after just two innings and were up, 11–3, after five frames.[143]

On October 10, the Atlantic Association issued the 1891 reserve lists for each of its four remaining franchises, and Harrisburg's had 12 names on it. Included were Frank Grant and Hughie Jennings. President James N. Braden declined to predict which and how many clubs would constitute the Atlantic Association in 1891, except to predict that Jersey City would rejoin.[144]

It wasn't immediately clear what Frank Grant did with his free time after that exhibition game on October 1. The *Daily Independent* reported that the players "were paid off" on the afternoon of October 3, and most were expected to leave for their respective home cities the next day.[145] If Grant remained in Harrisburg for more than a week, he surely would have been invited to "the grand benefit ball" held in honor of the "Colored Monarchs of the Diamond" at Harrisburg's Shakespeare Hall on the evening of Thursday, October 9. "Ladies, attired in fashionable garments, were there in profusion and were attended by chivalric men," the *Independent* reported. York Captain and master of ceremonies George Williams joined Miss Georgia Sanders to lead a grand march at midnight, in which about 100 other couples participated. "Vogt's brass orchestra furnished the music," the *Independent* noted, and dancing continued until early the following morning.[146]

On November 21, the *Daily Patriot* reported that "Frank Grant, the king of second basemen, is wintering in Harrisburg." By contrast, on December 4, the *Telegraph* wrote that "Grant, our colored Dunlap, is in the city for a few days." However, on January 24, the national weekly *Sporting Life* affirmed that Grant was wintering in Harrisburg.[147]

9

A Finale of Sorts (April–June 1891)

On February 20, 1891, the *Harrisburg Telegraph* noted that "Frank Grant is said to be getting restless over the inactivity of the club here." His frustration might have really been in response to news reported that day, which the *Telegraph* said "startled" fans in Harrisburg, that Bill Eagan had been signed by the American Association's St. Louis Browns. Whether or not the failure to retain Eagan disappointed Grant, the *Daily Patriot* similarly characterized him the same day as "becoming impatient" but added that a few days earlier, he stated "that he might sign with a new club of colored players forming in New York city." Grant presumably said that before the Browns signed Eagan, but Grant might have known about that distinct possibility days before it was announced, despite the *Telegraph*'s total surprise.[1]

More than three weeks passed until there was any significant news about the Harrisburg club. On March 16, the Atlantic Association held a meeting to reorganize for 1891. That night, Frank Grant became the first Pony to sign a contract for the 1891 season. Farrington planned to move him back to second base, because he also signed shortstop William Zecher, who had hit .241 for Altoona in the EISL. Zecher would reportedly captain the nine. The Ponies planned to play some home exhibition games starting in mid-April. It was unclear which franchises would be members, but others at least alluded to included Lebanon, Wilmington, Trenton, and Altoona. The latter was seeking to be represented by the Cuban Giants/Monarchs, and the *Telegraph* expected that to occur. "The salary limit was fixed at $1,200, no one player to receive more than $125 per month," a York newspaper reported.[2]

Alas, the reorganized Atlantic Association faced immediate turmoil within 48 hours when Lebanon instead joined the International League (which ultimately played under the name of the Eastern Association). As a result, the *Harrisburg Daily Independent* immediately expressed doubt that the Atlantic Association would be revived for 1891. A second Atlantic Association meeting was held in Harrisburg on March 23, at which Wilmington, Lancaster, Reading, and Harrisburg clubs were represented. Trenton's club communicated that its membership would depend on Harrisburg's. Altoona's participation required an ordinance change there. Teams in three other cities also expressed interest in membership. The *Independent*'s report of this meeting was inconsistent. Early on, it said Harrisburg was committed to the Atlantic Association, but toward the end it was iffy about a club actually being organized. It also included this cryptic comment: "Harrisburg can not join the International League unless Grant is released."[3]

The next day, the *Telegraph* gave the pot of uncertainty a few more stirs. It noted that the Cuban Giants were to be based in Portland, Maine and play in the New England League. "Already George Williams, Thomas, Malone, Harrison and Clarence Williams have signed," that daily said. "It is reported that George Williams is working on Frank Grant to induce him to jump his contract with Harrisburg and sign with Portland." The *Telegraph* pointed out that Grant had already accepted advance money from the Ponies and thus couldn't jump that contract. The previous year's high-profile lawsuit about Grant's supposed contract with Kreiter should've made the *Telegraph* less certain about the significance of advance money.[4]

There was another Atlantic Association meeting in Harrisburg on March 30. The most important announcement coming out of that meeting was that Portland, Maine would no longer have the "Colored Monarchs" there; instead they would play for Altoona in the Atlantic Association.[5] That put an end to speculation that Frank Grant would be based in northernmost New England, though in early April it was announced that the Connecticut State League would include two African American teams: the Gorhams representing Norwalk, and the Cuban Giants representing Ansonia.[6]

The leaders of the Atlantic Association met again in Harrisburg on April 6. Both Trenton and Wilmington remained noncommittal based on rumors that the Ponies were still a candidate to switch to the International League/Eastern Association. The Harrisburg club's leadership were expected to issue a statement on April 7 about not joining the International League.[7]

While Frank Grant was waiting for spring training to start for him *somewhere, sometime*, the national weekly *Sporting Life* published the aforementioned recollection by former Toronto manager Charlie Cushman about the August 27, 1887, game between his Canucks and Buffalo, which contained some major fabrications. Cushman's long and wrong anecdote was published in the April 11 edition. The *Patriot*, *Telegraph*, and *Independent* all ignored his attempt to rewrite history.[8]

On April 14, the *Telegraph* announced the demise of the Atlantic Association. Reading and Lancaster were suddenly silent, while both Trenton and Wilmington said to count them out, and that left only Harrisburg and Altoona firmly on board. The day before, the *Telegraph* also reported that a Providence team had entered the Eastern Association, "thus destroying whatever hope Harrisburg might ever have had of entering this league." Nevertheless, the *Patriot* reported that on April 14, Farrington left "for Albany, N.Y., to confer with leading men of the Eastern base ball association, formerly the International league, with a view of having Harrisburg admitted to that association." The Ponies' odds weren't good. "The only chance Harrisburg will have for admission is to induce the Eastern to add two more clubs, of which this city shall be one, and Utica, N.Y., the other, to its membership, making it a ten [team] association," the *Patriot* noted. That daily didn't discuss the potential fate of Frank Grant in this context.[9] Ultimately, the Eastern Association played its 1891 season as an eight-team circuit. Grant's near future was murkier than it had ever been.

On April 18, the *Daily Patriot* brought up the possibility that the "Colored Monarchs" would instead be based in Harrisburg for the upcoming summer, with Farrington as manager and Grant joining them. "Abe Harrison is carrying bricks just now," the *Patriot* added, tangentially.[10] That happened to connect directly to Frank Grant, because by May at the latest, he and Abe had become housemates. It's entirely possible they had lived at the same place since October, if not even earlier.

Harrisburg's 1891 city directory, which included a street map dated May 1891 and

9. A Finale of Sorts (April–June 1891)

was copyrighted the following month, contained entries for nine men whose occupation was specified as "ball player." Among them were Clarence Williams, William Selden, Abraham L. Harrison, and Frank Grant. The latter two had the same address, 602 South. The home's other resident was Mrs. Mary E. Wilson, and in all likelihood, she was the mother of Grant's son. Mary's first husband, James, had lived at 602 South at least dating back to 1884, and Mary's father or stepfather, William J. Adore, lived there as far back as 1882.[11] In fact, although Abe Harrison was living elsewhere when the 1892 directory was compiled (no earlier than March and no later than May), Frank Grant, the now-widowed Mary Wilson, and widower William Adore all lived at 602 South.

To understand the obscured birth of Grant's son, it makes most sense to start a few years ago and work backwards. Grant was enshrined in the Hall of Fame in 2006, but it was after that when researchers learned that he had a son. Between 2006 and the fall of 2013, the existence of Grant's son was discovered through the Negro Leagues Baseball Grave Marker Project. Shortly after Grant had passed away, the funeral home that arranged for his burial received authorization from a son, "Frank W. Grant (aka William Francis Grant) of West Philadelphia, Pa.," as reported in 2013 by historian Rod Leith of the Meadowlands Museum in Rutherford, New Jersey.[12] This major discovery received almost no publicity, and apparently no researcher pieced together his son's life, until now.

It certainly wasn't a given that this man also lived in Philadelphia at the time of the 1930 census—and even if he did, there was a chance he was omitted from it. There were more than 800 people named Grant in Philadelphia in that census, but only about 15 were African American men named William or some variation of that. Almost all of them were born in states to the south of Maryland, where Grant spent almost no time, so they seemed unlikely candidates. However, among African American men named Francis or the like, one stands out: Frank Grant, age 42, born in Pennsylvania (around 1888), who had a wife named Hattie.[13] In the 1920 census, they had a daughter named Dorothy, who was born around 1914. The family's address was 3335 Wallace Street.

In 1934, an African American man named Frank William Grant filed a Veteran's Compensation Application with the Commonwealth of Pennsylvania for military service at the end of the First World War. He listed his address at the time of his military service as 3335 Wallace Street. His wife was Hattie May Grant, and he had a daughter named Dorothy. His mother, Mary Elizabeth "Grant" was deceased, but his father, Frank U. Grant, was still living in 1934 (which was true).

He was born in Harrisburg and listed his date of birth as March 6, 1885. On his 1942 military registration card, Frank William Grant instead listed his date of birth as March 6, 1887. There may be no surviving record of his birth from the 1800s, and he apparently wasn't listed in the 1900 census. The document closest to the time of his birth that points to the year is the 1910 census. On April 19 of that year, 75-year-old William J. Adore was living on Baltic Avenue in Atlantic City with grandson Frank Grant, who was just 19. City directories around then even specified Frank's middle initial, W. Grandfather and grandson lived there together from 1907 until the elder man's death in 1913. If age 19 was correct in that census, then he was born in 1891 and conceived no earlier than June of 1890, when Frank Grant was starring for the Harrisburg Ponies. Mary Elizabeth Adore Wilson's husband James, who passed away in March of 1892, wasn't even listed in the 1891 directory. It's possible the two endured a marital separation in 1890, though if he had been sickly for some time, another reason for not listing him in 1891 could have been that he was confined to a long-term medical facility, such as a sanatorium. In that era, city directories typically didn't list wives, only husbands, and never children living with them unless they were adults. Women tended to be listed only if they were widows or otherwise single.

If Frank Grant's son was indeed born on March 6, 1891, that may be why he seemed committed to playing ball in Harrisburg in mid–April of that year, despite the fact that the Ponies suddenly had no league in which to compete. It had to have helped considerably that by April 17, the roster included two former Cuban Giants, Arthur Thomas and William Malone. Besides Grant, the only returning Ponies from the end of the 1890 season were pitcher John Cox and outfielder Tom Gettinger. Zecher was gone already.[14] Harrisburg scheduled its first few games against Lebanon's Eastern Association team, the very one that had left the Atlantic Association little more than a month earlier. Farrington may have been preparing for the distinct possibility that at least one minor league team in the region would fold and need replacing within two months, but it's possible the Harrisburg players themselves felt they were auditioning for a last-minute addition to the Eastern Association.

If so, the first game, on April 20, didn't help Harrisburg's case, because they were shut out, 4–0, and managed just five hits, three of which were by Thomas. At least 800 fans turned out for the game. The *Daily Independent* didn't even consider the Harrisburg squad to be an organized team, and instead referred to them as "a picked nine of this city, including several members of the Colored Monarchs." That hinted at a pleasant surprise: Clarence Williams played center field for the locals.[15] He must not have been too bitter about his release when the Ponies quit the EISL in July of 1890.

The two clubs met again the next day, and about 600 people attended. William Malone hadn't played the previous day, but he pitched the second game, and thus Harrisburg had four former Cuban Giants in its lineup. Lebanon went down to defeat, 7–5, in the wake of a bases-loaded double by Grant in the eighth inning. This time the *Daily Independent* called the winners "Farrington's picked nine."[16] Harrisburg notched a 9–3 victory the next day. On April 23, the teams played a fourth time, and it was a seesaw battle in the final three innings. Lebanon batted last and broke a 3–3 tie with two outs in the bottom of the ninth inning. Grant played all four games at second base.[17] All told, Harrisburg played respectable baseball.

The next two days, a Friday and Saturday, the Harrisburg team hosted the "Maryland club of Baltimore." The left side of the infield for the visitors featured former major league brothers, Lou and Jimmy Say. The local team won both games handily, 15–7 and 14–7. The second day, April 25, was Opening Day for the Eastern Association. On the morning of Monday, April 27, Frank Grant left for New York to join Bright's Cuban Giants. The *Daily Independent* announced that in two different columns on the same page. Clarence Williams also agreed to join the Cubans. Grant's departure might very well have been known during the second game with the Maryland club, because he "was presented with a basket of flowers during the game on Saturday by Manager Farrington," the *Independent* noted. "The presentation was made by Miss Lottie, Mr. Farrington's daughter."[18]

Less than a week later, Frank Grant began his sixth professional season by returning to the Cuban Giants, which did indeed represent Ansonia in the Connecticut State League (CSL). Ansonia is just over 100 miles south of Williamstown. Nine other cities had teams in the league, one of which was Meriden. "The team comprises Grant, the two Jacksons, Clarence and George Williams, Stovey, Garrison, Ball, Boyd, Sol White, Malone, Thomas, Nelson and others," the *Waterbury Evening Democrat* announced two days prior to Opening Day.[19]

Waterbury hosted Ansonia on May 2, with about 700 fans in attendance. Waterbury apparently batted first. The batting order for the visitors was Williams, c; White, 3b; Grant, 2b; Bell, ss; Frye, 1b; Boyd, cf; B. Jackson, lf; Stovey, rf; and Nelson, p. It was a low-scoring game, and the future Hall of Famers, White and Grant, each had just a single. Ansonia scored once in the second inning, and there was no additional scoring until Waterbury got two runs in the seventh frame. Each team scored once in the ninth inning, and the home team captured a 3–2 win.[20] The Cuban Giants simultaneously played in the New York (City) Semi-Professional League, and on Monday, May 4, Frank Grant played for them in a 7–5 against the Manhattan Athletic Club.[21]

The Cuban Giants played their first game in Ansonia, and only their second league game overall, on May 5, hosting Waterbury. The Cuban Giants had an easy time of it and won, 11–2. Grant had three singles and scored once.[22]

The next two days, Ansonia beat Norwich in both games, and on May 9 they added a fourth consecutive CSL win, against Bristol-Plainville. The next day was a Sunday, and the Cuban Giants handed a 15–3 drubbing to New York's Metropolitans. Grant's hits were a double and a homer. This performance inspired the *Buffalo Enquirer* to inform its readers of their former player's current success. The *Harrisburg Telegraph* likewise reported on how productive Grant, Clarence Williams, and Sol White were that day.[23]

Ansonia's next CSL game was apparently on May 13, against Hartford. The Cuban Giants won for the fifth time, 11–10. Waterbury broke Ansonia's winning streak the next day, though Frank Grant didn't play.[24] Ansonia's next CSL game was a full nine days later. Ansonia was supposed to play Hartford on May 19 and in Meriden on May 20, but neither game happened. Hartford was initially awarded two forfeits, one for the Ansonia game and another by Waterbury, but those were later reversed because Ansonia and Waterbury each had "a misunderstanding about the schedule."[25]

The Cuban Giants kept themselves busy during that CSL gap of more than a week, first with a three-game series against the Gorhams starting on Sunday, May 17 at the Long Island Grounds. The Gorhams' lineup in the first game included George Williams, Oscar and Andy Jackson, William Selden, Henry Gant (not Grant), and William Malone. The Cuban Giants had little difficulty winning, 17–2. Sol White and Frank Grant each went 3-for-6.[26]

The rival teams switched to the Polo Grounds for the other two games. The Cubans won again, but they needed a late rally to take the contest, 15–10. Between those two games, George Stovey jumped from the Cubans to the Gorhams, and Arthur Thomas turned up in the latter's lineup as well. This time, the final score was even closer, 10–8, yet the Cubans still prevailed.[27]

On Wednesday, May 20, the Cuban Giants played a collegiate team, Princeton, but rain ended play in the fifth inning. However, Frank Grant wasn't in the Cubans' lineup. He also wasn't in the lineup of the "Gorhams (Cuban Giants)" in Reading that day, where the home team won a 15-inning marathon, but suddenly the visitors had both George and Clarence Williams atop their batting order.[28]

Ansonia resumed CSL play on May 23, before 800 fans in Southington. Frank Grant was in the lineup, but Sol White was not, nor were George Stovey or Clarence Williams. Three days earlier, the *New York Sun* explained why there was movement of players from the Cuban Giants to the Gorhams, and mentioned Sol among players expected to make the switch soon.[29] But Frank Grant remained. He had a single and scored twice, but his real contribution was his play at second base, with nine putouts and four assists. He also may have concluded a triple play. The box score in the *Southington Weekly Phoenix* listed "double and triple plays, Frye and Grant, Terrill, Frye and Grant, Lambert, Kintry and Gaynor." The last three named were home team players. If that trio—pitcher, second baseman, and first baseman—didn't turn a triple play, then one of those two Ansonia combinations did, both of which included Frank Grant. Though the box score was accompanied by a long paragraph, it didn't mention any triple play. "A few costly errors were made by the home boys" was the only comment about the locals' fielding, which suggests it was indeed the visitors who accomplished that rarest of fielding feats.[30] A paper in nearby Meriden also reported about the game, without simply reprinting the Southington paper's account, though without a box score. The *Meriden Journal*'s account was actually longer, but it also didn't mention a triple play. It barely mentioned the Cuban Giants, though it did squeeze in a remark about them complaining constantly. It would have been consistent with the article's bias for it to exclude any acknowledgment that the Cuban Giants completed a triple play.[31] As mentioned previously, Grant's first triple play was with Meridian in May 1886, and he was involved in one each season from 1888 through 1890.

The next day, which was a Sunday, found Grant and the Cuban Giants winning a Semi-Professional League game at the Long Island Grounds against the Monroes, 9–6. One of Grant's two hits was a homer.[32] The Southington game on the day before proved to be Frank Grant's final appearance in the Connecticut State League, and thus his final one in an otherwise-white minor league. He had come full circle, in a way, because his professional career in white minor leagues ended where it began in 1886, that is, with a Connecticut team.

Until Major League Baseball was integrated after World War II, there were just a few more instances of African American players defying the color line. One notable example occurred in 1892, when Bud Fowler and a few other African Americans played in the Nebraska State League. In 1895, the Adrian team in the Michigan State League included Fowler and four other African American players, including pitcher George Wilson, who garnered a sparking record of 29–4. That same year, Sol White played on the Western State League's team in Fort Wayne, Indiana. MLB Historian John Thorn has compiled all such instances, and researchers are always on the lookout for others that have been obscured by the passage of time.[33]

The remaining Cuban Giants continued to represent Ansonia in the CSL without him, but for fewer than 10 more games. The league folded by June 15. On the front page of its next edition, *Sporting Life* noted how rare it was for a minor league to collapse before the Fourth of July. That weekly was a bit surprised that a low-salary league couldn't survive, though the CSL had "been in a disorganized condition almost from the start, owing to a lack of discipline among players, the neglect of the league officials and the disregard for schedule obligations and the rules evinced by a majority of the clubs."[34]

Regardless of the Gorhams' raids on Ansonia's roster, Frank Grant had to have sensed early on that the Connecticut State League was a shaky circuit. Still, he stuck it out longer than the team's other stars. He only left when he was presented the opportunity to play for a bigtime Harrisburg club after all.

10

Barnstorming (1891–1892)

Frank Grant could continue to play ball on a high-level team when he returned to Harrisburg toward the end of May 1891 because James Farrington was persistent. About a week after his daughter presented Grant with flowers as the star player was preparing to join the Cuban Giants, the *Telegraph* announced that Farrington was trying to convince Lebanon to play a number of its Eastern Association games in Harrisburg. Another week later, he informed a *Daily Independent* reporter that he was working hard to provide the city with a strong baseball team.[1]

Just one more week after that, Farrington announced that he had united with Gorhams owner Ambrose Davis to locate that team in Harrisburg. "George and Clarence Williams, William Selden, Frank Grant, Sol. White and a young player, a resident of Harrisburg, named Borten [sic], have already been engaged," reported the *Harrisburg Call*.[2] On that same day, a paper in Lancaster announced that "Farrington, of the Cuban Giants of Harrisburg" and representatives of several other clubs in Pennsylvania would meet that week to discuss the formation of a Pennsylvania state league.[3]

On May 21, the "Gorhams (Cuban Giants)" played a 15-inning game in Reading before 1,235 fans. They lost, 6–4. The visitors' lineup didn't include Grant or White, but the other four players named on May 18 did play. Rounding out the Gorhams' lineup were Thomas, Oscar and Andy Jackson, Miller, and Malone.[4] According to the *Daily Patriot*, the team had arrived in Harrisburg the next day before the Reading game. The *Patriot* added that Frank Grant "is in New York at present but will be here in a few days." On May 26, that paper said the team was "now complete" and named 11 players, including Sol White and Frank Grant.[5] Word of Grant's arrival must have gone out over a wire service. "Grant, the wonderful colored second baseman, who made such a sensation a few years ago, is playing a great game still," read the *Courier-Journal* in Louisville on May 28. "He is with the Gorham team." Over the month of June, this same item appeared in a scattering of newspapers, such as in North Carolina, and of course elsewhere in Pennsylvania.[6]

On May 27, the Gorhams hosted some Philadelphia amateurs, the Athletic Club of the Schuylkill Navy (ACSN), but only about 200 people attended, and Harrisburg papers could barely be bothered to write about it, beyond the 20–2 final score and the fact that George Stovey allowed only three hits.[7] Grant played his first road game for Harrisburg's new club the next day, against the Demorests of Williamsport. The visitors won handily, 14–4, before that city's largest crowd of the spring. On June 1 the "Gorham's Cuban Giants" were in Reading, where about 1,000 fans saw the visitors dominate, 10–1.[8] On June 4, a paper in Connecticut reported that Grant was receiving $200 a month to play with Harrisburg's new nine.[9]

The Gorhams and *New York* Cuban Giants began a series of five contests on June 11. The first game drew only about 300 fans to Harrisburg's Island Park. The Cuban Giants won, 6–3. "The coaching of Grant, of the Gorhams, and Gant, of the Cuban Giants, is worthy of special mention," said the *Patriot*. The two teams met at the same place again the next day, again to a small crowd. The Gorhams won, 7–2. "The work of Grant at short stop could not have been excelled," the *Patriot* noted. The third game drew 700 people. It was relatively close until the ninth inning, but it ended 15–6 in favor of the Gorhams.[10] The two teams then met in Lebanon on June 15. The Gorhams were shut out, 4–0. In the same city the next day, the Gorhams lost again, 7–5. That gave the Cuban Giants bragging rights, three games to two. Though attendance for the fifth game was below 200, there was an atypical fan in the stands, a longtime local Catholic priest named Adam Christ. He told the *Lebanon Daily News* that he had witnessed good ball playing. According to a Harrisburg paper, he and the rest of the crowd spent almost two hours at a temperature of 100 degrees.[11]

The lineup for the Cuban Giants in the second Lebanon game included Gant, Barton, and Miller. When the Gorhams played a team in Norristown, Pennsylvania the next day, those three players comprised the bottom of the *Gorhams'* batting order—except at least one box score listed a second "Grant" in the lineup, at first base. This was almost certainly Henry Gant. That would also explain away a confusing announcement in the *Daily Independent* later that week: "Grant [sic], late of the Cuban Giants, has been signed by the Gorhams. He is playing first-base."[12]

In fact, Gant, Barton, and Miller had already played in the Gorhams' Sunday lineups in New York City's Semi-Professional League, for example on May 24, which was Frank Grant's last game with the *Cuban Giants* in that league. They also played for the Gorhams a week later.[13] Though the two Gorhams teams had some overlap, at times they seemed almost like separate clubs. The New York version gave lesser-known Cuban Giants a chance to see some action. Semi-Professional League officials were aware that the Gorhams and Cuban Giants often weren't

An unusually wordy ad for such a game, in the *Lebanon Daily News*, June 15, 1891.

fielding their top players, and on June 18 a special meeting was held to discuss the resulting mediocrity, but nothing decisive occurred. After the games of June 21, the Cuban Giants had a record of 3–2 and occupied fourth place in the eight-team league. The Gorhams were tied for last, at 1–5. A few days later, the Gorhams were expelled from the league, but instead of the Cuban Giants joining them, the league expelled the third-place Metropolitans instead. The Gorhams and Metropolitans were charged with unspecified violations of the league's bylaws dating back to the start of the season.[14] Nevertheless, a team called the Gorhams continued to play in and around New York City on subsequent Sundays, and Frank Grant resumed playing there eventually. The league folded rather quietly in the middle of July.[15]

Gant, Barton, and Miller weren't in the Gorhams' Pennsylvania lineup for very long, and when the Gorhams and Cuban Giants played in Reading on June 25, that trio was back in the latter's lineup. The game drew a crowd of 1,300 fans. The Gorhams won, 9–0.[16] They finished June with two games against a local team in Wilkes-Barre, and their second win there was against a pitcher name Joe Gormley, who had played his only major league game two weeks earlier, a complete-game loss for the NL's Phillies.[17]

The Gorhams began July with a game against a semi-pro team in Scranton, before about 1,000 fans. "There are old familiar faces in the Gorham team," the *Scranton Republican* reported. "Big Thomas is still doing magnificent back stop work and Grant, the 'colored Dunlap,' is putting up a wonderful game at short." This comment was in an article that stretched a full column. The Gorhams fell behind early but chipped away at Scranton's lead and won the game with two outs in the 10th inning.[18]

The Gorhams had played before at least 1,000 fans three times in a month, and this was at least the second city in which the attendance was at that level. To put this in perspective, good attendance data exists from 1892 for the home games of Chicago's National League club. The total of 91,892 for 75 games equaled an average of 1,225 fans.[19]

On July 6, there was a major announcement affecting the Gorhams: James Farrington had agreed to take over as manager of Lebanon's team in the Eastern Association. Two of the players he immediately expressed interest in adding to his new team were Frank Grant's teammates a year earlier, John Cox and Bill Eagan. Farrington signed neither. There was a little coverage in Harrisburg newspapers about his departure, but possible effects on the Gorhams apparently weren't at the forefront of those journalists' minds.[20] After Farrington's departure, coverage of the team in Harrisburg newspapers seemed to drop, although it hadn't exactly been voluminous in June. Still, subsequent reports about the team were often limited to a single sentence. That could've been a result of Farrington leaving, but it may simply have reflected the fact that the Gorhams were much more of a traveling team and not one that played half of its games in Harrisburg, as a team in a minor league would typically do.

Over at New York's Polo Grounds on July 8, "Manager McGovern, of the colored Gorhams" (presumably S.K. Govern) and several other baseball enthusiasts got into an argument about the strength of the Gorhams compared to former members of the Metropolitans, six of whom were recent major leaguers of multiple seasons. Five of them were members of the Metropolitans in 1884 when that club won the American Association pennant, namely Candy Nelson, Dasher Troy, Chief Roseman, Eddie Kennedy, and Charlie Reipschlager. The sixth was Sam Crane, who finished a seven-year major league career in 1890. Five of them were around 35 years old, past their primes. A game at the Polo Grounds was arranged, and the stakes were all the gate receipts plus $200. A crowd of about 700 fans turned out for the contest, on July 10. Grant made three errors, but Stovey hurled a four-hitter for the Gorhams and had a shutout through eight innings. The Metropolitans scored a run to tie the game at 1–1 in the ninth, but the Gorhams won the game and all the money with a run in the 10th inning.[21]

Over the following nine days, the Gorhams had at least five more games in or around New York City, and they continued to play there on Sundays for a spell. At least two of those were against the Cuban Giants. The easy win for the Gorhams at the Polo Grounds on July 13, 21–1, featured Frank Grant's 1891 housemate, Abe Harrison, at shortstop for the Cuban Giants. Harrison hadn't played against the Gorhams in the two mid–June games, nor in Reading on June 25. He likewise didn't play on July 27, when the Gorhams similarly romped to a 22–7 victory.[22] Around that time, the Gorhams also mixed in two games at Cape May, New Jersey. On August 6, the *Harrisburg Daily Independent* reported that their victory the prior day against a Poughkeepsie team was their 29th win in a row.[23]

On Sunday, August 9, the Gorhams played the regular Metropolitans nine, instead of their alums, though atop their batting order was Candy Nelson, and batting second was Shorty Howe, who played 19 of his 20 National League games a year earlier. The Metropolitans were actually just a seven instead of a nine that day, so Clarence Williams and Winslow Terrill rounded out the Metropolitans' batting order. Those two went a combined 5-for-7 against Stovey, but the Gorhams built a big lead early and won, 20–5.[24]

By mid–August, the Eastern Association's New Haven and Providence teams had folded, and the *Harrisburg Daily Independent* reported that two of the remaining six franchises were shaky. Meanwhile, on August 15, the Gorhams were back in Cape May. The two teams had met for the third time the day before, and the Gorhams won, 7–2.[25] But their fourth meeting was a truly historic one, due to a certain gentleman who happened to be in town: U.S. President Benjamin Harrison. The lineup for the Gorhams was George Williams, rf; Sol White, 2b; Clarence Williams, c; Arthur Thomas, 1b; Frank Grant, ss; William Selden, p; Oscar Jackson, cf; Andy Jackson, 3b; and William Malone, lf. Pitching for Cape May was Jack Leiper, about three weeks prior to his major league debut with Columbus' American Association team. The start of the game was delayed because Harrison was known to be on his way, and it started as soon as he was seated in the grandstand. "The President had an exceedingly busy day, receiving callers and attending to official business," read the report in the *Brooklyn Daily Eagle* and other papers. "The President appeared much interested in the game and applauded all the good plays." As busy as his day supposedly was, he only left after the eighth inning. The Gorhams had added a run in the seventh inning to increase their lead to 5–0, and that was the final score. The contest lasted one hour, 45 minutes. "The Gorhams played an errorless game and their best playing was done by Grant, A. Jackson and White," according to the account in the *Philadelphia Inquirer*. Grant had two putouts and five assists. His one hit was a triple, and Sol White's two hits included a double. Harrison's attendance was reported from Boston to Savannah, Georgia, and of course in Washington, D.C.[26]

It's unclear how large the crowd was in Cape May, but the next day near New York City, at Monitor Park in Weehawken, the Gorhams drew almost 1,500 fans. They faced the Allertons, one of the top two teams in the recently folded Semi-Professional League. Grant went 3-for-4, including another triple, and the Gorhams piled on runs late in a 15–7 victory.[27]

The Gorhams traveled to the University of Vermont, in Burlington, for a game on August 19. It may have been Grant's first game against collegians since he and his brother Clarence played against their hometown Williams College more than a year earlier. Playing against collegiate teams in the springtime became a staple of the Cuban Giants later in the decade. The Gorhams jumped out to an early lead against the varsity squad and were never threatened. The final score was 12–1. "The Gorhams ran bases in a manner entirely new to the home team," a local paper reported, but it didn't elaborate on that intriguing remark, unfortunately. All six stolen bases in the game were accomplished by the Gorhams, including two by Grant.[28] The pitcher for the home team was Frank O'Connor, who pitched in three games for Philadelphia in the National League in 1893.[29]

One of the more famous people to watch Frank Grant in a game: Benjamin Harrison, the 23rd President of the United States, who served from 1889 to 1893 (Library of Congress).

Over the next few days, the Gorhams added another win against the Allertons, as well as in Reading, but the game later in August that might have been as memorable for the Gorhams as playing in front of the President occurred on August 28, in Trenton. The former Cuban Giants were returning to the city they represented in the Middle States League two years earlier. According to one Philadelphia daily, 1,500 fans watched the fireworks.[30]

The umpire for the game was Charles McGurk, President of the city's Trades League. Pitching for the locals was 22-year-old Charles Randow, who made a living as a potter, and in early 1892 became McGurk's Vice President. Though there's no sign that Randow ever played in any minor leagues, he had the Trade League's best batting average that season.[31]

The most detailed account of the game, in Trenton's *Daily True American*, called it the best of the season there. It began at 4:00 and lasted just 90 minutes. The game was scoreless until the Gorhams put two runs on the board in their half of the fourth inning. Grant drove in the second run with a single. A four-run seventh inning gave the visitors a lead of 8–2, and the game ended 8–4.[32]

At least five different accounts were published about the scuffling at the game's conclusion, in New Jersey, Philadelphia, and New York newspapers. Four versions were two paragraphs long, give or take. The longest of those five, published in the *Jersey City News*, seems to have been the basis for a paragraph in newspapers far to the west, in cities like St. Louis, Lincoln, Nebraska, and Carroll, Iowa.

Here's what these accounts tended to agree on—though not completely: A dispute arose about one of the baseballs brought to the ballpark, though the full *Jersey City News* version implied there were two baseballs argued over. Most, but not all, reported that the home team was angry because a ball belonging to them was *cut* by Thomas. Clarence Williams and Randow exchanged punches. The *Jersey City News* version seems to imply that Randow started it, but the version in at least two New York City dailies said Williams threw the first punch. The *Jersey City News* version said Randow won the fistfight, but the New York version said Williams gave Randow a severe beating. Of course, such one-on-one fights often break wide open and involve other combatants, and in this case, the papers named Selden, Thomas, and Clarence Williams as the "ringleaders" of a near-riot, though Philadelphia's *Times* added George Williams as a fourth instigator. However, the credibility of the account in the *Times* is weakened by the fact that they got Randow's and Selden's first names wrong. What's more, most accounts agreed that Clarence Williams had pocketed a baseball, but the *Times* said Randow did, and Selden demanded that he produce it. In the end, most or all of the Gorhams were arrested, but released after a short while because nobody appeared before the police to press charges. Nevertheless, warrants were reportedly later issued for Selden, Thomas, and at least one of the Williamses. The New York version specified that it was Randow who secured those warrants. It also claimed that baseball bats were used as weapons, guns were drawn, "and a few of the followers of the Gorhams displayed razors."[33]

Oddly, one of the shortest accounts was in the *Trenton Times*, but in its four sentences, it undercut some of the supposed facts printed in those outlying newspapers. Most significant is how it concluded: "Arrests were threatened, but none were made to-day." That is, there were no arrests on the day of the game nor by press time on the next day.[34]

Another Trenton newspaper, the *Daily True American*, provided a very detailed—and even more stirring—account of what occurred after the game, under the headline, "Almost a Riot." Before they got to a couple of astonishing plot twists, they introduced a crucial figure not mentioned in those other accounts: Frank Grant. The *True American* didn't cast some of the Gorhams in the best light, but that was more than offset by the end, and this balance would seem to suggest that the writer was striving to be objective. After an introductory sentence, that journalist wrote:

> In the early stage of the game one of the balls was missing, and Frank Grant, one of the Gorhams, threw a ball to the umpire to be played with. The missing one was discovered in the pocket of C. Williams. Williams denied having it at first, but after being ordered by Umpire McGurk to hand it over, did so. By the time, however, that it reached the umpire, it was found to have been cut. This fact became generally known and, in conjunction with Williams trying to take the ball, it engendered a bad feeling against the visitors.
> At the close of the game, the ball of Grant's was thrown back to him, and the cut one was offered to the Gorhams, who refused it and tried to get the other one, they claiming that it was with the latter they won the game and that they were entitled to it. Hot words ensued and in a few moments the crowd gathered en masse about the teams. They sided with the home team, and it looked as if the visitors would be subjected to rough handling. While the crowd, which had become an enraged mob, closed in about the players, Seldon [sic] endeavored to take the ball from the pocket of Umpire McGurk. Randow took exception. An insulting name by Seldon followed and Randow struck Seldon full in the face. The crowd were about Seldon and he could not return the blow. Whereupon C. Williams, finding that his brother player

was in trouble, rushed and struck Randow a single blow on the left side of the head. The scene that followed was awful. The mob surged to and fro, threats were heard and it had the appearance of becoming a general fight.

At this point a pistol was pulled by a young white man living in the Eighth ward. He flourished the deadly weapon about threateningly. Grant seeing it, started for him, to take it away. Down they went towards centre field, the young man first, followed by Grant, Clarence Williams and Thomas, with the motly [sic] crowd at their heels. Grant reaching the pistol-waver, struck him, knocking him down, and took the pistol from him and handed it to Thomas. C. Williams protected the fallen man.

George D. Voorhees, the North Broad street hardware merchant, seeing the man struck and the pistol in the hands of Thomas, drove to town at a breakneck speed, got Officer Fay and took him to the scene of disturbance. Detectives Clancy and Lane were on the grounds. Mr. Voorhees thought that Thomas had pulled the revolver, and in consequence the two detectives took charge of the Gorhams on his complaint and drove with them to the station house.

R. Henri Herbert secured Justice Matheson, and had him on hand when the ball-players were brought into the station house. Mr. Herbert was prepared to [post] their bail. As the fight occurred in Wilbur borough, the Justice could not give them a hearing, and as Mr. Voorhees failed to appear to enter a complaint, the men were released from custody.

It is stated that Randow had a warrant issued for the arrest of C. Williams, and that it was placed in the hands of an officer, but no arrest could be learned of last night.[35]

The man who was prepared to provide bail for the Gorhams, R. Henri Herbert, was a prominent African American journalist and businessman in Trenton. From 1880 to 1883, he had published one of the first African American newspapers in New Jersey. In 1890 he became a cigar manufacturer. By July of 1891, he had succeeded in persuading the U.S. Postal Service to hire its first African American letter carrier in Trenton. Herbert's reputation might very well have helped defuse the situation, and he undoubtedly acted wisely by making sure that Justice of the Peace John Matheson was present when the Gorhams reached the police station.[36]

But the day's awfulness wasn't limited to the ballfield and the police building. The Gorhams apparently returned to the site of the brawl, perhaps to pick up belongings. They left the ballpark in a wagon, and it collided with the buggy of a local Civil War veteran, Captain Charles H. Seaman. He was ejected from his seat, and his buggy landed on top of him. The *Trenton Times* thought he probably would have been killed if his horse hadn't remained calm. Fortunately, Captain Seaman began feeling better within 24 hours. (It so happened that in mid–1863, Seaman's Company had helped defend Harrisburg when that city seemed at risk of capture by Confederate soldiers.[37]) Still, who could blame the Gorhams if they never wanted to return to Trenton?

On September 18, the Gorhams were back in Trenton to play the same team. In the interim, they played games scattered across Pennsylvania, New York, and New Jersey. One of the more noteworthy was a fifth win against Cape May on August 31, despite four errors by Grant. He more than made up for that against the Allertons in Weehawken on September 13 when he went 4-for-6 in a 19–2 win. Batting fourth for the Allertons was future Hall of Famer Willie Keeler. "Wee Willie" went 2-for-4 with a run scored.[38]

In front of a "good-sized crowd," as the *True American* put it, the Gorhams encountered the same umpire and the same local pitcher on September 18. For the visitors, Stovey pitched instead of Selden. Leading up to the game, local papers didn't seem to play up the astounding aftermath of the game three weeks earlier, and the *True American* didn't report anything at all that hinted at lingering anger. After two innings, the

Gorhams had a lead of 8–0, and they ultimately triumphed, 15–2. Randow didn't hit any of the Gorhams with a pitch. Stovey did bean batters twice, but neither was Randow.[39]

As mentioned, Harrisburg's newspapers occasionally printed brief reports about the Gorhams late that summer. The *Patriot*'s single-sentence status report on September 21 alluded to the team's unusual governance at the time: "The colored Gorham club is being run by the players on the co-operative plan."[40] In other words, the players didn't have a boss, exactly. It's possible that relates to why Frank Grant and Sol White may not have appeared in a Gorhams box score after their game at Long Island's Recreation Park on Sunday, September 27. On that occasion, they defeated a former Semi-Professional League rival called the Senators, 8–2.[41]

It's unlikely that Frank Grant decided to leave the Gorhams' lineup due to any lingering injury, based on the skill he demonstrated in a win the day before that one on Long Island. On September 26, the Gorhams played in Plainfield, New Jersey, against a team of all-stars from that city's Crescent League. Grant was clearly at the top of his game, according to the local newspaper. "The Gorhams' shortstop, Grant, is a jewel, whose superior as a fielder of his position cannot be found anywhere," said the *Plainfield Daily Press*. "He made some most difficult stops and catches, his recovery was extraordinarily quick, and his throwing was swift as an arrow and unerring as a shaft of light." The Gorhams won, 9–2.[42]

The departure of Grant and White might have been connected to an article published in a New York newspaper on September 29. By that point, J.M. Bright had already recruited George Williams to captain the Cuban Giants in 1892. Bright had also secured a new ballpark in Hoboken, New Jersey. "Abe Harrison has been signed to play short stop and Henry Grant [sic] will cover center field," the *Elmira Gazette* reported. "Barton, Nelson and Terrill will be signed in a few days and four others whom Captain Williams is after."[43] The Gorhams lost in Camden, New Jersey, on October 2, 10–6, and one difference was that they were called "Bright's great colored Gorhams" in the *Philadelphia Inquirer*'s account. Seven of their players were the same as against the Senators on September 27; instead of Grant and White, there were Barton and Terrill.[44] Conversely, it was "Manager Bright's Cuban Giants" who played against the Gorhams at Recreation Park on October 4. Grant and White weren't in either lineup, but Barton and Nelson were back with the Cuban Giants. The two teams met again a week later at the same park. Again, neither Grant nor White played that day.[45] Regardless, White considered that roster to be "the best" among the African American teams of the 1800s.[46]

Frank Grant had a low profile during the 1891–1892 offseason, but he presumably wintered in Harrisburg, given that he appeared in both the 1891 and 1892 city directories—and at the

BASE BALL,
TRADES LEAGUE GROUNDS,
EAST STATE STREET,
Trenton vs. Gormans
(Formerly Cuban Giants).
FRIDAY, SEPT. 18th, 1891.
Game called at 4 P. M. Admission, 25c.
Cars run to and from the grounds.

An ad promoting the rematch following the game in which Frank Grant had to disarm a fan. From Trenton's *Daily True American*, September 17, 1891.

same address. No later than March, however, Abe Harrison was living elsewhere in the city. On January 19, Bright confirmed that Harrison was among 12 players his Cuban Giants had signed for the 1892 season. Alas, trouble was brewing at that early date because Ambrose Davis, as manager of the Gorhams, asserted that he had already signed five of that dozen, namely George and Clarence Williams, William Selden, George Barton, and Henry Gant. Frank Grant and Sol White weren't mentioned in the context of this squabble. In mid–February, the names of Frank Grant and Sol White were on Ambrose Davis' roster for the Gorhams.[47] How valid those listings were remained to be seen.

Toward the end of March, a new rival for the services of both Grant and White emerged: the Keystones, Pittsburgh's African American nine, with which Henry Gant was associated. The appeal of the Keystones to Sol White was strong, because his first seven games as a professional were with that team when it was a member of the very short-lived National Colored Baseball League early in the 1887 season.[48] Even though the *Pittsburgh Daily Post* called Frank "Fred Grant," it was clear who that paper meant when it added that the signee was "known throughout the country as the 'Colored Dunlap.'" In mid–April, the *Cleveland Gazette* affirmed those signings and named Clarence Williams among 12 additional players on the Keystones' roster.[49]

It was around this time that Harrisburg's directory for 1892 was published. That occurred no earlier than March and no later than May. In addition to Grant, the now-widowed Mrs. Mary Wilson, and her father or stepfather, William J. Adore, living at 602 South was a Lizzie Barber. There was also a Mrs. Maria Werner at the same address, but that pairing of names is close enough to "Mary Wilson" to raise suspicion that this was a duplicative entry based on a compiler's sloppy penmanship.

Assuming that Grant spent his free time in Harrisburg when winter turned to spring, he didn't remain idle at 602 South for very long as the weather warmed up. On the evening of April 5, Frank Grant and Clarence Williams left Harrisburg for New York City, to play with the Gorhams. Or at least that was the plan, but more on that momentarily. A reporter for the *Daily Patriot* noticed him at the Union train depot, "looking sleek and in good condition," and decided to conduct an interview. The result was rare quotations by Grant outside the context of a particular baseball game:

> "Where do you think you'll play this season?" asked the reporter.
> "Baseball is a very uncertain thing, and there's no telling where I'll wind up at," said he.
> "Would you play in Harrisburg if there was a team here?"
> "Yes, indeed," said he. "When I played in Buffalo some years ago I thought there was no place like it. Since my coming to the capital city, however, I have changed my mind, and would sooner play here than any other place."

The unnamed *Patriot* reporter concluded the article by noting that both Grant and Williams would probably play with Pittsburgh's Keystones "after they close their engagement with the Gorhams."[50]

Their immediate reason for seeking to meet up with the Gorhams was to help them in their game on April 6, against none other than the National League's New York Giants. But there was some sort of complication regarding the Pennsylvania Railroad, and the two ballplayers didn't make the game. In eight innings, the National Leaguers won, 36–1. Mercifully, the *Brooklyn Daily Eagle* noted that only five regulars were in the Gorhams' lineup.[51]

Ambrose Davis was furious at the Pennsylvania Railroad for depriving him of two star players in Grant and Williams. Within a week, he reportedly filed a lawsuit against the railroad. A report in the *New York Press* was a little vague, but Davis claimed that he had a contractual arrangement with the railroad's agent in Harrisburg to provide the two players with train tickets. It was unclear whether Davis had already paid for them or was simply committed to do so in a timely manner. "Mr. Davis also claims that such a disgraceful defeat would not have happened if Williams and Grant [had] been on hand, and that such an inglorious beating has injured his chances of arranging other games and occasioned consequential financial loss," concluded the report.[52]

A couple of snide remarks made during the first half of May were consistent with Davis' anxiety. Through May 4, the Baltimore Orioles had lost 15 of their first 16 National League games, and that prompted the *Boston Herald* to sneer that the Orioles "would find it hard work to beat the Cuban Giants." About a week later, those very same New York Giants were on the receiving end of an insult by future Hall of Famer Mike "King" Kelly of Boston when they were playing almost as poorly as Baltimore: "He says the New Yorks are not the real article," said the account printed in at least a few major league cities. "He believes them to be the Cuban Giants whitewashed." This may have first been printed in the *New York World*, and it eventually made it into newspapers in such cities as Wheeling, West Virginia, St. Paul, Minnesota, and Lincoln, Nebraska.[53]

It's unclear what Grant did during the week following that missed game, but the Keystones penciled Sol White, Frank Grant, Clarence Williams, and Henry Gant into their lineup for a game on April 15. Wet grounds caused the game to be delayed one day.[54] On April 16, Grant and Williams were instead in the Gorhams' lineup in Albany, where they suffered through a 19–8 loss before 1,000 fans who were undeterred by unpleasant weather. Grant and Williams played with the Gorhams for a few more days, most notably in lopsided losses at New Haven on April 19 and 20. The first of those games drew also drew about 1,000 fans. The Gorhams lost the second game, 14–5, despite Grant going 4-for-4 with a double and Williams hitting the day's only homer.[55]

Obviously this stretch of games was so very different from the incredible win-loss record the Gorhams had maintained throughout the previous season, but Sol White said 1891 actually "marked the decline of colored base ball in the East for several years." Success during games hadn't equaled success pulling in dollars. "The season of '91 was so disastrous financially that the Big Gorhams did not re-organize in '92," he wrote. That's not strictly true, though because he was in Pittsburgh at the time, he may have been unaware that Davis fielded a professional team for a short time in 1892. In fact, the Gorhams existed in some form through at least August, but with precious few players who were even somewhat familiar to fans. "During this season of 1892 there was only one colored team in the East, the Cuban Giants under the management of J.M. Bright," White reported.[56] By April 24, Grant and Williams jumped to the Cubans. The subsequent half-year was crucial in determining whether the multiyear decline White observed would end in complete disaster or instead set the stage for prosperity. Would the Cuban Giants prove to be sustainable for the long haul and serve as a model for other professional African American teams?

On April 24, Grant and Williams experienced a very nice change of pace from all that losing with the Gorhams, when they walloped the Monroes, one of the Semi-Professional League teams in 1891, 21–3. The game was played at the Long Island Grounds, and the price of admission was 15 cents. One of the better hitters for the losing team was Frank Bowes, who played with Brooklyn's American Association team in 1890. Grant committed four errors but went 4-for-7 at bat with a double and five runs scored. The Harrisburg duo's new teammates were Boyd, cf; Harrison, ss; Nelson, rf; Dan Penno, 3b; Gifford, 1b; Bell, lf; and Whyte, p.[57]

Disappointingly, the very next day Grant had to experience a drubbing all over again. This time, Clarence Williams wasn't in the lineup, which was also true most or all of the following month. On April 25, the Cuban Giants played in Elmira, New York, and managed just two hits in a 16–0 humiliation. The next day's result was about the same, 19–1.[58] The Cubans then lost two games in Binghamton. The first had a respectable final score, 7–2, but the second ended 22–4. Right after that it was back to Elmira for a third crushing defeat, 25–8. The Cuban Giants finished April with a collegiate team, Cornell, in Ithaca, New York. Grant went 3-for-5, including a double, but he had half his team's hits. The Cuban Giants led early, 3–2, but trailed 9–3 after three innings and lost, 12–4.[59]

At least the month of May began on a positive note for the Cuban Giants. Clarence Williams again wasn't in the lineup, but George Stovey suddenly was, and he pitched his nine to an 11–5 victory over the Flushing team at the Long Island Grounds. The attendance was reported as above 1,000.[60] For whatever reason, the Cuban Giants fared better during those early weeks of the season in and around New York. On May 7, they trailed the Passaic Athletic Club after eight innings, 6–4, then suddenly exploded for a 10-run ninth. The next day they played a team called the Leontines at the Long Island Grounds before 1,438 fans, and they breezed to a 16–5 victory. Neither Stovey nor Clarence Williams helped out in those two games.[61]

For the first three weeks of May, final scores of Cubans' games on weekdays are hard to come by, much less box scores. It's possible that Ambrose Davis' worries became reality to an extent for his main Black rivals, and they simply had fewer games day to day. Still, they remained active on weekends and maintained a high profile. Those games certainly seemed to turn the tide of their April slump.

At the Long Island Grounds on May 15, the Cuban Giants began play in a three-team tournament to determine New York City's semi-professional champions. The other two teams were the Allertons and the local Senators. The Cubans played the Senators in this initial contest. George Williams was pressed into service by the Cuban Giants at second base, which shifted Grant to third. About 2,000 fans attended and saw a nail-biter for the first five innings. The Cubans scored in each of the final four frames and won, 7–0. John Nelson pitched the complete-game shutout.[62]

At the same location a week later, the Cuban Giants hosted a team from Port Jervis, roughly 85 miles away. About 700 people braved rain to see the two teams manage a five-inning game. In the lineup for Port Jervis was Chief Roseman, the former major leaguer of seven seasons (whose career had ended less than two years earlier). The Cubans won, 6–3.[63]

Over the next four days, the Cuban Giants split games against a team in Norristown, beat a team in Pottstown, and lost to a team at Camden. Though the Cubans weren't putting together impressive winning streaks, at least they had put a stop to getting blown out by such teams multiple times in a short span. The Cuban Giants added one more Sunday victory for the month at the Long Island Grounds on May 29, before close to 1,000 fans. Their victims were again the Senators, this time by a score of 7–3.[64]

On June 5, the Cuban Giants and the Allertons played their first game for the semi-professional championship. Willie Keeler played shortstop for the Allertons and batted fifth. Frank Grant batted second and played third base. His hit in four at-bats was a double, the only extra-base hit of the day. But Keeler was his nine's hitting star with a 3-for-4 performance. The Allertons handed the Cuban Giants their first loss of the season at the Long Island Grounds, 7–4. The next day, Keeler made his debut in the Eastern League with Binghamton, and on September 30 he played his first major league game with the New York Giants.[65]

Speaking of first defeats, on June 6, the Cuban Giants played in Walden, New York, and handed the local nine its first loss of 1892, 9–5. Two days later, they played the first of three games against the University of Vermont. In the first contest, the home team led 8–0 after six innings, and single runs in the seventh and eighth frames by the visitors didn't seem to help enough. But the Cubans exploded for a six-run ninth and sent the game into extra innings. Grant's only hit of the game was a double in the top of the 11th inning, and Harrison sacrificed him to third. Grant scored on an error, and that proved to be the winning run. In the rematch on June 9, the collegians prevailed, 4–3. Grant went 2-for-4, including a double, off Bert Abbey, who hurled his last game as a student and promptly left to join the National League's Washington Senators. He made his major league debut on June 14 and was in the majors for five years.[66]

The decisive third game was played in Rutland, about 65 miles to the south. About 800 fans stood for almost three hours to watch. The Cuban Giants faced the pitching of Arlie Pond, who went on to impressive seasons with the National League's Baltimore Orioles in 1896 and 1897, with records of 16–8 and 18–9, respectively.[67] The local *Daily Herald* described the game at length, across two pages. Pond walked Grant in the first inning, but the hurler "caught him napping at first" and Grant was picked off. After that, he went 1-for-3 off Pond. The Vermont nine led, 5–0, after five innings, but the Cubans quickly threatened in the bottom of the sixth. Albert Douglass walked to lead off, and Benjamin Boyd followed with a double. Douglass stopped at third but scored to end the shutout when Frank Grant singled him home. The Cubans still had two men on base with nobody out, but Pond struck out Abe Harrison. Up next was Clarence Williams, who had become a regular in the Cubans' lineup by that week. Pond got Williams to ground out to first, and when Dan Penno followed with another ground ball, Pond escaped with just that one run allowed. John Nelson, who pitched a complete game for the Cuban Giants, gave up a homer in the top of the seventh, but the Cubans scored four times off Pond in the bottom half of that inning to pull within one run. In the eighth inning, John Frye of the Cubans "made a long hit over the fence for a home run, tying the score," the *Daily Herald* reported. "There was a big kick over this, the U.V.M.'s claiming that according to ground rules he was only entitled to two bases, but the kick did not work." Pond followed by striking out the next four Cuban Giants, but the one who reached on a dropped third strike was Nelson, who stole second and third before scoring on a passed ball. That proved to be the winning run, and the Cubans triumphed, 7–6.[68]

By this point, the lineup of the Cuban Giants hadn't changed all that much since Frank Grant jumped from the Gorhams around April 24. Other regulars were Clarence Williams, Boyd, Harrison, Penno, Frye, Nelson, Douglass, William Jackson (usually at catcher), and sometimes William Whyte. However, after this series Douglass was replaced by George Stovey. It is to Frank Grant's great credit that he remained patient over those seven weeks as this Cuban Giants lineup grew from a frequent laughingstock to a constant threat. About half of these men were his most frequent teammates of the 1890s.

On Sunday, June 12, the Cuban Giants were back at the Long Island Grounds to continue the semi-professional championship series. One hopes that Grant was made aware of effusive praise he received in the *New York Herald* that day: "Grant, the third baseman of the Cuban Giants, is, without doubt, the greatest player that ever made his appearance in the semi-professional diamond," asserted the *New York Herald*. "But for his color he would be playing professional ball long before this." This was high praise indeed, given that Willie Keeler had just completed his tenure in that circuit. Grant lived up to that hype before 2,000 fans, the largest at that ballpark so far that season. He went 3-for-5 with a home run and triple in an 18-5 drubbing of the Allertons. At that point, the Allertons and Senators hadn't played one another in the tournament, so the Cubans led it, three wins to one loss.[69]

Two days later, the Cuban Giants returned to Trenton and again faced the pitching of Charles Randow. He didn't complete the game, but it's unclear when he exited. In any case, the visitors jumped out to a 4-0 lead in the second inning and added a 10-run fourth on their way to an easy 19-9 win. One of Grant's two hits was a triple. He started out at third base but later became one of his nine's four pitchers, and played catcher as well. Randow was relieved by third baseman Barney Uplander, who had played against the Cuban Giants with Hazleton in the Middle States League during 1889 and with Hartford in the Connecticut State League during 1891. Uplander pitched at least one inning, because he struck out three of the Cuban Giants (in contrast to Randow, who only fanned one).[70]

Beginning with the game in Rutland on June 10, the Cuban Giants started piling up wins, often lopsided ones. The blowouts against the Allertons and in Trenton are obviously examples. Others include easy wins in Camden on June 16, against the Houston nine in Chester, Pennsylvania on June 18, and against Newark's Star Athletics before 1,200 at the Long Island Grounds on June 19. For the latter team, batting fourth was 34-year-old Jack Farrell, whose 11-year major league career had concluded in 1889.[71]

The Cuban Giants also outscored their opponents with ease on June 21, in Great Barrington, Massachusetts, about 20 miles south of Pittsfield, Frank Grant's birthplace. The score was 17–7.[72] Over the

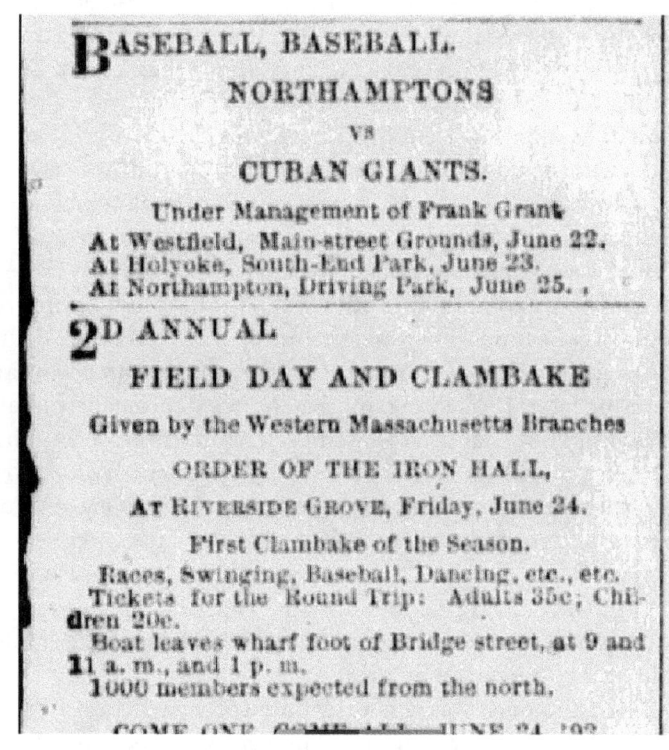

"Under the Management of Frank Grant." From the *Springfield* (Massachusetts) *Republican*, June 22, 1892.

next four days, they played not far to the east, in and around Springfield, Massachusetts. The opposing team would be the same at each park, the nine from Northampton, one of the sites. Ads promoting those games named one ballplayer, thusly: "Under Management of Frank Grant." The Cuban Giants won the first game, 9–4, but the next day's game was apparently rained out. The Northamptons then cooled the Cubans' winning ways by defeating them on June 24 and 25. The *Boston Globe* printed box scores for those two games. In the second, Grant went 3-for-4, including a double and a triple, but the Cuban Giants were held to just two runs for the second consecutive contest.[73]

While the Cuban Giants were in Massachusetts, the *Buffalo Courier* printed an article about Grant's old manager with Buffalo, Jack Chapman, who had been fired that week by Louisville's National League club. "He managed the local International team in 1887 and 1888, and in the latter year would have won the pennant had it not been for dissensions among the players caused by the presence of Grant, the colored second baseman," the *Courier* claimed.[74] This was some sloppy journalism on the daily's part. For one, Chapman also managed Buffalo's International League team for all of 1886, but the *Courier* also somehow failed to note that he managed their *National League* team for 87 games in 1885. Secondly, the Bisons were out of the pennant race by midseason in 1888, and that was just four years earlier. More importantly, that was also the season when the supposed dissenters went 6–13 when Grant missed a stretch due to an injury, followed immediately by a 13-game winning streak that began the instant he returned to the lineup.

The Cuban Giants enjoyed some success during the first few days of July. On July 2, Frank Grant returned to Meriden. He batted leadoff and went 2-for-5, including a double. That hit tied the game at 5–5 in the sixth inning. In the eighth, he singled and eventually scored the tie-breaking run. The Cubans won, 7–5. On Independence Day, they won a 10:00 game in New Brunswick, New Jersey, and beat a different team before 1,000 fans at Manhattan Field that afternoon.[75]

Another significant game for Frank Grant was two weeks later, on July 18, before 500 fans in Waterbury, Connecticut, against a team called the Acmes. The two teams had met at the Long Island Grounds the day before, and the Cubans won, 4–3. But the rematch was more significant because the pitcher for the Acmes that day was 21-year-old Waterbury native Fred Klobedanz. He compiled an impressive record of 53–25 for the National League's Bostons, including a record of 26–7 in 1897, his second season. His catcher that day was Candy LaChance, who began a 12-year major league career about 13 months later. Klobedanz and LaChance had recently been with Portland's team in the New England League. The Acmes' leadoff hitter, second baseman W. Fox, was probably future major leaguer Bill Fox, who played with Waterbury's Connecticut State League team beginning in 1894. Fox reached base on an error or on a walk by John Nelson, and eventually scored the game's first run. The Cubans collected only six hits off Klobedanz, one by Grant, but the Cubans managed to score twice in the fourth inning and a third run in the next frame. Meanwhile, Nelson experienced some smooth sailing, and the Acmes only scored once more, in the eighth inning. All told, Nelson limited them to two hits and two men left on base.[76]

Of course, it was generally noteworthy whenever Frank Grant batted against pitchers who were either soon to be, presently, or recently major leaguers, especially if those hurlers had some significant success at that top level. But it spoke to the quality of the Cuban Giants as a whole when their pitching combined with their defense to contain major league hitters. Such an instance occurred on July 24 at the Long Island Grounds, when a team called the Ridgewoods benefited from a current National Leaguer in their lineup. Batting third for them and playing second base was George Frederick Miller, who was in the prime of a 13-year major league career. Perhaps to distinguish him from an earlier major leaguer who was also named George Miller, this one had no shortage of nicknames: Doggie, Foghorn, Calliope, and Midget. George Stovey easily contained Miller's squad, and the Cubans feasted on the Ridgewood nine's pitcher in a 12–2 win. The *New York Herald*'s box score showed Miller as 0-for-2 with two walks, and "although he failed to distinguish himself in any way, he was cheered to the echo by the fifteen hundred spectators that were present every time he stepped to the plate."[77]

Because the Cuban Giants had been so dominant at the Long Island Grounds, it wasn't surprising if regular opponents tried to augment their lineups with players who had at least a little major league experience. The Flushing team was just such an example for the Cubans' final game of July. The Flushing lineup that faced the Cubans on May 1 already included at least one recent major leaguer, Herman Pitz, but for this rematch it included at least one more, Grant's old Meriden teammate, "Gentle Willie" Murphy. The two had shared a memorable experience in 1886 when fans there lavished them with coins after they homered in consecutive innings. Also among the Flushing nine this time was a first baseman named Bowes, probably the aforementioned Frank Bowes, which would mean the Cubans faced at least three former major leaguers that day. It ultimately didn't matter, as the Cuban Giants won, 6–1.[78]

On August 5, Grant displayed the slugging power for which he became known, starting with his earliest games for Meriden. The Cuban Giants lost a close game to the Jeanesville club in or near Hazleton before 700 fans, but Grant became the first player at that ballpark during 1892 to homer to deep center field. He thus won prizes of $5 and a silk hat.[79] Two days later, the Cubans defeated the Senators again at the Long Island Grounds, before almost 2,000 fans. The Cubans held off a late rally to prevail, 9–7. Three dailies that covered the game didn't put it in the context of New York City's semi-professional championship, so perhaps the Senators and Allertons had already conceded that title to the Cuban Giants.[80]

On August 20, Grant may have felt quite nostalgic when the Cuban Giants played in the city where his career outside of Massachusetts began: Plattsburgh, New York, on Lake Champlain. The Cubans defeated an African American team there, from the local Hotel Champlain. That game didn't receive much coverage in the area,[81] but the two teams met again about five weeks later at the Long Island Grounds under notable circumstances. Meanwhile, the Cuban Giants were scheduled to play in Grant's birthplace of Pittsfield one week later, and, in contrast to Plattsburgh's newspapers, papers in western Massachusetts played up his local connection, including his formative time with the county's Greylocks nine. Alas, a rainstorm soaked Pittsfield's Wahconah Park two days before the game, and the day prior to it, there was an announcement that the Cuban Giants would not play there after all.[82]

Frank Grant and his charges played a game of historic significance when they began a series of three games in Washington, D.C., on Wednesday, August 31. The occasion was momentous because of a particular man who was among the nearly 900 spectators: Frederick Douglass, the famous African American abolitionist, orator, author, and statesman. The Cuban Giants played games on three consecutive days against an African American team called the All-Washingtons at the city's National Park. The Cubans' lineup was: Grant, 3b; Frye, 1b; Williams, c; Harrison, ss; Boyd, cf; Jackson, lf; Nelson, p; Penno, 2b; and "White" (almost certainly Whyte), rf. Grant smacked his team's only triple, and Penno swatted the game's only homer. The home team batted first and promptly scored three times, but Nelson kept them from scoring in the following six innings. In the meantime, the Cubans plated a run or two often enough to prevail, 8–5. The *Washington Post* said most of the crowd was African American, but a famous white person in attendance was attorney Campbell Carrington, "and one-half of the crowd knew him at once."[83]

The *Post* didn't note the presence of any celebrities at the second game, which drew about 500 fans. "Grant's third base play was as fine as ever seen on the local grounds," the *Post* asserted. "He also carried off the batting honors, making four hits out of five times at bat." One of those hits was a triple, and he scored three runs. The Cubans put the game out of reach with a seven-run fourth inning and won, 15–5. On the third day, the Cubans swept the series with an 11–6 win. Apparently attending all three games were 15 members of an African American organization called the Blaine Invincible Republican Club. It was a long-lasting organization, based on the fact that it marched in the inaugural parade for President Theodore Roosevelt in 1905.[84]

Starting on September 19, the Cuban Giants played a series of three games in Scranton, Pennsylvania, that reunited Frank Grant with an old Meriden and Harrisburg teammate, Jerry McCormick. In the second half of July, Scranton replaced James Farrington's Harrisburg Ponies in the Pennsylvania State League. Scranton had an awful record of 2–22 during its month in that minor league, but they swept the Cubans comfortably by scores of 11–7, 15–6, and 12–6. The winning pitcher in the first two games was Jack Fee, who went 2–2 in seven games for Indianapolis' National League team in 1889. The Cubans were disadvantaged somewhat by the fact that Abe Harrison had returned to his residence back in Harrisburg, though before leaving he made a commitment to rejoin the team in 1893. In addition to the two former major leaguers, Scranton's lineups included Charlie Gelbert, a future member of the College Football Hall of Famer and father of a longtime major league shortstop of the same name. Gelbert was deemed the hitting star for Scranton in the third game, in which he went 5-for-5 off Nelson, with a homer (offsetting Grant's).[85] Though the home team looked very good in the series, the *Scranton Times* made the team's manager look like a weasel, if not a crook. The Cubans were guaranteed

The famous abolitionist and statesman Frederick Douglass, who watched Frank Grant play on August 31, 1892 (Library of Congress).

$50 after each game, but when "Manager Frank" visited Scranton manager Larry Ketrick after the first game, Ketrick handed over only $20. He promised to pay the remainder the next day. After the second game, Ketrick handed over only $16 more and said a business partner would pay the balance with a check. That partner never turned up. "Manager Frank is still in the city waiting for Ketrick's return from Wilkes-Barre, where he is on business," the article concluded. The *Times* didn't subsequently report whether the Cuban Giants ever received even a dollar more.[86]

Despite the failures in Scranton, the Cuban Giants ended up with a pretty good season, especially in the wake of their very shaky beginning. Of course, after any rough patch they could always be optimistic about returning to the Long Island Grounds. When they did so shortly after the Scranton series, on September 25, they were greeted by a whopping 2,500 fans. The occasion was a rematch against the Lake/Hotel Champlain nine, whose lineup included such old friends as Andy Jackson, Sol White, William Malone, and Winslow Terrill. Despite such talent, the Cuban Giants led 6–0 after four innings and piled on a 10-run fifth on their way to an 18–1 trouncing. Grant went 2-for-5 off Malone's pitching and hit the game's only homer.[87]

The Cuban Giants continued to play until mid–October, but weekday box scores were suddenly hard to come by. Grant wasn't in the lineup on October 2, and J.M. Bright simply decided not to play a scheduled game a week later. The snubbed team was the Murray Hills, who called "themselves the amateur champions of this city" according to the *New York Herald*. Nevertheless, that club was kind enough to play a benefit game on October 16 for the Cubans. In other words, the Cuban Giants were allowed to keep the proceeds of the ticket sales. Unfortunately, cold winds suppressed attendance. The Cubans had four new names in their lineup, but Frank Grant played shortstop in the six-inning game, which his nine won, 15–2. This game was the finale at the Long Island Grounds for 1892, and, as far as is known, the Cuban Giants didn't play elsewhere later in the month.[88]

11

Making History from Cooperstown to Chicago (1893–1894)

Shortly before Christmas of 1892, there was some exciting news for the Cuban Giants, when they were listed among 12 teams to be included in a new Middle States League covering Pennsylvania, New Jersey, New York, and Connecticut. "The Cuban Giants will represent Hoboken, and will play at the St. George cricket grounds on Saturdays," a New York daily reported. "The colored team will also play championship games on Sundays at either the Long Island grounds or at Mt. Vernon." Unfortunately, the plan was scuttled within two months, after the Cubans and three other franchises withdrew.[1]

Towards the end of January, J.M. Bright announced that he had six players lined up for the 1893 season: Frank Grant for shortstop, Abe Harrison for left field, and four unnamed players from the integrated Nebraska State League. A version of this announcement published a few days later specified this quartet's positions as first and third bases, pitcher, and catcher, but also didn't name them.[2] On March 22, at least two dailies in New York City reported Bright's announcement about the Long Island Grounds. A new grandstand was expected to be completed by the first game, which was scheduled for April 23. The players weren't expected to report until the day prior. At that point, additional games had been booked for April 30 and May 14, and the club's roster was Clarence Williams, c; Stovey, p; W. Jackson, 1b; "Paterson, of last season's Nebraska League," 2b; Frank Grant, 3b "and captain"; Harrison, ss; Catto, lf; Barton, cf; Nelson, rf, "and Whyte and Penn[o] extras."[3]

On Sunday, April 16, Frank Grant was one of the "Colored Giants" who played against the semi-pro Senators at the Long Island Grounds. One New York paper characterized this nine as a blend of the Cubans and the Gorhams, but another said they were "virtually the Cuban Giants." In any event, the Colored Giants broke a 5–5 tie with a three-run seventh inning, but their second pitcher, George Stovey, walked multiple Senators in the eighth inning and that resulted in a 9–8 loss. Stovey was so wild that he was apparently relieved by Grant, who added two walks himself.[4]

The Cuban Giants played their actual first game on April 22 in Orange, New Jersey. The visitors jumped out to a 4–0 lead after the first inning and ultimately won, 9–4. The lineup for the Cubans was A. Jackson, 3b; O. Jackson, cf; Grant, 2b; Williams, c; Harrison, ss; Stovey, rf; W. Jackson, 1b; Nelson, p; and Catto, lf. All nine played the next day as well, except Penno was a tenth man, and they won their opening game at the Long Island Grounds by beating a Paterson club, 18–11.[5]

The Cubans faced a big early-season test on the last day of April at the Long Island

Grounds when they hosted Easton's club of the Pennsylvania State League. Half of the Easton lineup consisted of future major leaguers, including second baseman Ace Stewart, center fielder Joe Wright, and third baseman Bobby Rothermel. Their starting pitcher was named Keener, very likely future Phillie Harry Keener, who was born in and is buried at Easton. He was relieved at some point by Chauncey Fisher, a five-year National Leaguer. "Frank Grant, the colored 'phenom,' made a great record, accepting seven fighting chances without an error, besides making two home runs and a double," the *Press* reported. The Cubans won easily, 10–2.[6] Grant's captaincy for 1893 got off to a much better start than in 1892.

Two days later, Frank Grant and his teammates played another game where his family lived, in Williamstown, Massachusetts. The Cubans made an astonishing 14 errors, including two by Grant, while the entire Williams College nine only made two, so it's no surprise the home team won, 9–4. At least Grant rose to the occasion at bat, by going 2-for-4 with a walk. Also, his hits were a double and a triple.[7]

On Sunday, May 7, the Cuban Giants experienced a major complication of their weekend routine. Seemingly without warning, local authorities stopped ballgames at three parks on Long Island, including one between the Cubans and the Xavier Athletic Club. "The friends of Sunday baseball propose to make a vigorous protest and declare that it is a peculiar law which allows dance halls of low repute and liquor stores to remain open and which stops baseball," the *New York Tribune* reported. Leaders of the teams that were affected made threats of legal action, but in the short term, more than "5,000 people went out to the parks and returned disappointed."[8]

Beginning on May 9, the Cubans played games on four days in Vermont, splitting them. They began by defeating beat Middlebury College, 16–8, and then lost two games to the University of Vermont, 10–6 and 21–13. A Burlington paper noted that only one of the nine collegians who started the first game hadn't been a member a year earlier. That included Arlie Pond, who started the third game. Pond's teammates committed 12 errors, but a local paper also pointed a finger at him for wildness in the first inning that led to six runs for the visitors.[9] But after the disheartening shock of Sunday's legal action, Frank Grant was probably more pleased than ever that on May 13, the Cuban Giants returned to the Williamstown area. They played about five miles to the east, in North Adams. Their opposition was the local Blackinton team, which fielded at least two Williams College players, brothers named Lynch. It was a seesaw game, but the Cubans held on for a 9–8 win. Though Grant made three errors, he was also impressive at bat again. He went 3-for-4, including a double a walk.[10]

If the Cuban Giants played in or around New York City on Sunday, May 14—or anywhere else, for that matter—then the game was played in relative secrecy. On Monday, May 15, the Cubans were about 120 miles to the west, in Reading, Pennsylvania. The home nine mostly remained with that team when it joined the Pennsylvania State League for the second half of the 1893 season. A local paper described the size of the crowd as "fair" and not as good as a year earlier, when the attendance was specified as 1,235. But what the *Reading Times* said next is intriguing to baseball historians today: "During the game a photographer took some snap shots at the base runners." Too bad the paper didn't name that person. Grant wasn't in the Cubans' lineup that day, though he certainly could have been present and coaching. Regardless, the visitors won, 22–14.[11]

Grant was back in the lineup on May 17 when his team beat the home nine in

Royersford, Pennsylvania, 11–7. After a game two days later in Camden, he received some of his greatest praise since his years in Buffalo. The day after the Cubans' second dominant win over the Camden Athletics, the *Daily Telegram* began its front-page coverage thusly:

> Frank Grant, the ginger-colored second baseman of the Cuban Giants, has the reputation of being the best player in that position in the world, either black or white. His renown is not the outcome of a few admiring or prejudiced friends, but the result of several years of the best work on the diamond. He is a remarkable batter, and yesterday drove two home runs over the fence and up the street in the vicinity of the shipyards. Grant was in the game with an emphasis, with his two homers, two singles, three runs, five put-outs and four assists.[12]

Sunday, May 21, was a triumphant day for the Cuban Giants in more ways than one. Yes, they defeated the Emeralds of the New York Catholic Protectory, 19–12, but the setting was much more important: They resumed Sunday ball in New York (ironically, given the religious nature of their competition), in the Van Nest neighborhood of the Bronx, and the attendance was a staggering 3,500 fans. It turned out that the moralizing authorities on Long Island had actually done the Cubans a favor. And Frank Grant responded at the plate in a big way with three doubles and a single, plus two stolen bases.[13]

The next day, the Cuban Giants began a series of games against various teams in Washington, D.C.,[14] but, true to their plans dating back to December, on Saturday they returned to Hoboken for weekly games on the St. George's Cricket Grounds. They defeated the Murray Hills, their late-1892 opposition, 14–3. On Sunday, May 28, they played at Olympic Park in Paterson, New Jersey, instead of in New York, but they drew 1,500 fans anyway. A late four-run rally by the Olympics gave them a come-from-behind victory over the Cubans, 5–3.[15]

The Cuban Giants began the month of June where Grant's pro career began, in Meriden. Two local papers eagerly reported the arrival time of the Cubans' train. In their half of the first inning, Grant drove in the game's first run with a single, and he scored as well moments later. The home team fared well after that but couldn't generate much offense, losing 4–1. "For the visitors, Grant was as limber as ever," reported one local daily. At this point, the lineup of the Cuban Giants was: A. Jackson, 3b; O. Jackson, lf; Williams, 1b; Grant, 2b; Harrison, ss; Catto, p; Nelson, cf; Penno, rf; and W. Jackson, c.[16]

Grant was in the Cubans' lineup in Newark on Sunday, June 4, for their lopsided win over a team called the Ironsides, but when they played in Reading the next day, he again didn't play in that city. Was it just a coincidence that about 55 miles farther to the west was Harrisburg, his home away from home? Whatever the case, he was back in the batting order the next day, in nearby Pottsville. The visitors won a slugfest, 15–11, but in the ninth inning M.J. Salmon of the home team suffered a horrible injury. He was on third base and tried to score on a ground ball, but when he slid, he "came in collision with Catcher [William] Jackson who fell on top of him," the *Pottsville Daily Republican* reported. Another local paper, the *Daily Miners' Journal*, made a point not to fault Jackson. "It was purely unavoidable, one of those distressing accidents that are often the result of a noisy coacher's misdirected advice to a runner," the *Journal* said. A doctor in the crowd promptly determined that Salmon's arm was broken just above the elbow. The *Republican* questioned whether he'd ever play baseball again. The teams quickly decided to play a benefit game for him three days later.[17]

On the day before the benefit game, the Cuban Giants won in Shenandoah, 4–3.

An unnamed Giant sold 30 tickets for the benefit. "These darkies are as good natured and generous as they are humorous," observed the local *Evening Herald*. Joining those 30 residents at the benefit was the home team's leadoff hitter, catcher Chris Fulmer. He had a five-year major league career which ended in 1889. Fulmer took over Salmon's spot atop Pottsville's batting order in the benefit game. The Cuban Giants won easily, 14–4, but it's likely very few people cared much about the outcome. What really mattered was that the game raised an impressive $207.25 to facilitate Salmon's recovery. Fortunately, he was able to return to baseball with his hometown team by mid–1894.[18]

The Cuban Giants had been doing quite well of late, but in Brattleboro, Vermont on June 12, they were humbled by the Yale Law School's baseball team. Though the final score, 4–2, wasn't embarrassing, the Cubans were no-hit by Herbert Bowers. For whatever it may be worth, a number of fans attended from nearby Bellows Falls, and they weren't too impressed by Bowers' feat. "The general sentiment seemed to be that the Giants were roasted unmercifully by the umpire," the *Bellows Falls Times* reported. With a career in law ahead of him, it's no surprise that Bowers' pro career may have been limited to two losses in the Connecticut State League in 1895, though there are some players in that era for whom baseball-reference.com doesn't have first names.[19]

Frank Grant's game on June 16 was a historic one, as the Cuban Giants played the Oneonta Normals, a collegiate nine. The significance was due to the location: Cooperstown, New York, where the National Baseball Hall of Fame and Museum opened in 1939. At the time of Grant's induction in 2006, former Hall Librarian Tom Heitz suggested that this game was the earliest in that town involving a future Hall of Famer. In the Giants' easy 21–4 victory, Grant scored three runs, hit a double, and offset one error at second base with nine putouts, four assists, and two double plays turned.[20] Three days later, Grant had a truly impressive day on offense during a 12–6 win in Middletown, New York, against the Asylum team. He amassed a double, two triples, and a homer. The home team hadn't lost a game prior to that day.[21]

On Sunday, June 25, the Cuban Giants had a rematch against the Emeralds at the same ballpark in the Bronx. They didn't draw anywhere near as many fans as previously, but the attendance of about 1,500 was as good as they drew at the Long Island Grounds. The Cubans won handily, 16–7. By this point, John Patterson had reappeared on the Cubans' roster at shortstop, and Frank Miller became one of the team's few pitchers. Before Independence Day, a pitcher named "Caston" also turned up in Cubans' box scores, and that was presumably George William Castone.[22]

The big news from the Cuban Giants during the first week of July was that they would no longer play regularly in Hoboken. Perhaps with some exaggeration, the *Jersey City News* said that each of the Giants "registered a solemn vow never to play there again." However, it was simply a financial decision. "The reason for leaving is that there is not enough patronage to pay the expenses," the *News* reported.[23] The other noteworthy change for the Cubans around this time was that Sol White rejoined them. His first game back may have been on July 7 in a 17–7 win against the Asylums.[24]

A few days later, the Cuban Giants dealt the first home loss of the season to the club in Watertown, New York, 9–2. The *Cleveland Gazette*, the noteworthy African American weekly, occasionally reported on the Cubans' roster or overall accomplishments, and this particular game drew their attention. The attendance for that game was just 350, but on July 16 their game in Paterson drew 1,669 fans. The Cubans also won that game, 5–2, thanks to a three-run eighth inning, but the real excitement came earlier, due to a dispute that was only described vaguely by the *Paterson Daily Press*. At some point, one of the three Jacksons in the visitors' lineup, called only "Captain" by the *Press*, displayed such anger after a disputed foul ball call that the umpire, named Hopkins, quit. "Manager Wright [sic], of the colored club, was appealed to, but it was no use," the *Press* noted. A replacement ump eventually stepped in, but many fans left "in disgust" with the original. The account in the *Paterson Evening News* specified that it was Andy Jackson who challenged Hopkins' authority, but that daily aimed its anger solely at the home team for agreeing to continue the game with a substitute ump.[25]

On July 31, the Cuban Giants played the Asylum nine again in Middletown, New York, where they had ended that team's home winning streak on June 19. In turn, the Asylums ended a 16-game winning streak by the Cubans, 8–6, before 1,200 fans.[26] Verifying any such streak for the Cuban Giants around that time is complicated, for a few reasons. For one, there were other teams called the Cuban Giants in the same part of the country, such as in Paterson (at least in April of that year), Harrisburg, and Jessup, Pennsylvania (near Scranton).[27] As a result, the unavailability of box scores can make it difficult to be certain whether a particular game featured *Bright's* Cuban Giants. But this particular "streak" required that at least three games not be counted.[28]

One was on July 21, back in Meriden (a game in which Grant didn't play). The Cuban Giants rallied late, with big eighth and ninth innings, and insisted that they had tied the score, 14–14, with two outs in the ninth and Miller at third base. At that point, the Cubans' third base coach pretended to attempt a steal of home, and the umpire surprised many fans by declaring Miller out, thus ending the game. The ump had made another unusual decision during the previous inning. "Williams put a ball over the fence, but was held at third," the *Journal* reported, though he apparently scored soon anyway. The debate about the score focused on just how many runs the Cubans scored in that inning, and it didn't help the home team's case that two newspapers' line scores didn't agree. One credited the visitors with five and six runs in the final two innings, while the other showed them with four and seven. Meanwhile, a paper over in New Haven reported the final score as a tie.[29]

However annoyed or frustrated the Cuban Giants may have been after this outcome in Meriden, it likely bothered them much less than games in Poughkeepsie on July 17 and 18, right after the unpleasantness in Paterson. In the first game, the visitors led, 7–0, after five innings and 8–4 after seven. The only other scoring that day was the home team's 10-run eighth inning. The *Pokeepsie Evening Enterprise* editorialized about the umpire on two separate pages the next day, but vaguely. "The Pokeepsies [sic] with the umpire's assistance defeated the Cuban Giants on Monday afternoon, 14 to 8," said one page. On a later page, an anonymous columnist called the Tourist offered longer commentary in response to "a number of comments on the game of ball by the Pokeepsies and the Cuban Giants on Monday, all condemning the umpire for his decision that gave the game to the home club." Unfortunately, this writer continued without detail. "Nothing can be more satisfactory to spectators than victory for the home team but, at the same time, they want to see victory fairly won, and the umpire that thinks he favors his club or helps the management by an unfair decision at a critical moment, makes a great mistake," the Tourist added. "The game of Monday did not help the Pokeepsie team nor did it help the hard working manager." Meanwhile, though the *Poughkeepsie Daily Eagle* printed a long paragraph about the game, it made no mention of any umpiring controversy. The two teams had a rematch the next day, but the Cuban Giants quit the scoreless game after the third inning because "several decisions given by the umpire were considered by the visiting team as very 'rocky,'" in the *Eagle*'s words.[30]

Therefore, to have claimed a 16-game winning streak spanning at least the second half of July, the Cuban Giants must have decided those three games didn't count. In any case, they did pile up many wins that month. In the wake of the anger the team experienced in Paterson and Poughkeepsie from July 16 to 18, it may seem a little ironic that one of their subsequent wins was in Trenton on July 24, versus their old nemesis Charles Randow again. The Cubans won, 16–3, though they didn't blow the game open until the seventh inning.[31] It was at least the third time they returned to Trenton after the infamous 1891 game that involved local law enforcement, and there were no reports of any lingering tensions during those three subsequent meetings. The Giants obviously possessed an ability to put old grievances behind them, at least to an extent. They soon demonstrated that on Sunday, August 6, when they visited Paterson for a rematch after just three weeks, with Hopkins again as umpire and Andy Jackson continuing to lead off the Cubans' lineup. This time the crowd was even larger, about 1,800 fans. The game took place without any bad blood reported. As a matter of fact, a local paper reported that the visitors "worked in a number of double plays which were loudly applauded and finally won by a score of 14 to 6."[32] The Cuban Giants also returned to Poughkeepsie in 1893, though not until the end of September. The visitors won easily, 11–1.[33]

What had been the Cubans' final win during their July streak? That was in Shenandoah on July 30, before a truly massive crowd for a city of that size, about 2,500 fans. The home team led, 5–0, after five innings but one frame later the game was tied, 6–6. A three-run seventh for the visitors was the only additional scoring.[34]

As the calendar turned from July to August, there was some intrigue in Pennsylvania regarding Frank Grant. As mentioned previously, Reading had a team in the Pennsylvania State League during the second half of the 1893 season, called the Reds.[35] Its manager was a local celebrity, William Abbott Witman (often misspelled Whitman), who later served as President of the upstart United States Baseball League, an attempt to form a third major league in 1912.[36] On July 29, the *Reading Eagle* and the *Reading Times* both announced that Witman had signed Grant, along with a second baseman named George Finke, who played with New Orleans' team in the Southern Association the previous season. Both players were expected to join the Reds for their game that day, against Easton, and the *Easton Free Press* also said as much.[37] That was apparently the only time the *Times* mentioned Grant in this context, but this announcement was printed in other State League cities.[38]

Finke did play for Reading on July 29, but there was no Grant in the lineup. The same was true the next day. "Grant, of the Cuban Giants, played second base at Shenandoah on Saturday," the *Reading World* acknowledged. "Manager Whitman [sic] still has hopes that he can be secured for Reading."[39] Reading's newspapers very quickly dropped such wishful thinking.[40]

The most noteworthy game for the Cuban Giants during August was probably the one scheduled for Sunday the 13th. The plan was to face St. Louis College, and a Brooklyn paper said a celebrity had been lined up to umpire: Canadian boxer George Dixon, who the previous year became the first athlete of African descent to win a world title in any sport. There was only one problem: The venue was on Long Island. "The game between the Cuban Giants and St. Louis College team, which was to have been played yesterday at Leo Park, was stopped by the police at the instance [sic] of Judge

Montiverde," the *Sun* reported. It then had to add a snide remark. "The picnic grounds and saloons in the immediate vicinity, however, were in full blast." There was no word on whether Dixon was on site to ump.[41]

Otherwise, August was primarily notable from the Giants' perspective simply for accumulating additional wins.[42] They reportedly didn't lose a game that entire month. Their winning streak reached 31 until a loss at Hempstead, Long Island, on September 4.[43]

On Labor Day, September 2, the Cuban Giants played in the coal-mining town of Lykens, less than 40 miles northeast of Harrisburg. The game received good publicity in advance from Harrisburg papers, and that included praise for Grant. For example, on the day before the game, the *Telegraph* noted foremost that "Frank Grant, of Boston, the greatest second baseman known, will be among the number." That also included the "celebrated Clarence Williams." Labor Day was a Saturday, but the mines closed at 1:00, and the game started at 3:30. The Giants won, 10–1. "The Giants spent Saturday night in the city," noted the *Patriot*, presumably referring to Harrisburg and not the much smaller community of Lykens.[44]

On Sunday, September 10, the Cuban Giants played Paterson before a crowd of 2,600 fans. For this occasion, Paterson had recruited 28-year-old pitcher George Meakim, a four-year major leaguer whose best year was as a rookie in 1890 with Louisville's American Association team, for which he had a record of 12–7, three shutouts, and an ERA of 2.91. For the first five innings, he held Grant and his teammates to no runs and no hits. After seven innings, the Cubans trailed, 4–1, but they kept themselves in the game by committing just one error. Frank Grant went 1-for-4 off Meakim, a single in the middle of the five-run eighth inning that decided the game, in which Grant scored the tying run.[45]

By the time Paterson played the Cuban Giants yet again on September 24, they had added at least one former major leaguer to support Meakim, and probably a second. The former was Leo Smith, who had a 35-game major leaguer career with Rochester's American Association team in 1890. The leadoff hitter for Paterson was likely Ted Scheffler, who was a major leaguer in 1888 and 1890. This time Grant went 2-for-3 against Meakim, and the Cubans held on to win, 11–9.[46]

Frank Grant saved his best against Meakim for one of the Cubans' last games of 1893. He went 3-for-4 and scored twice in his team's 5–1 victory. He hit a triple, but his other extra-base hit was unusual. "The only feature of the game was a home run by Grant," the *Paterson Daily News* declared. "Batting left handed he hit the right field fence on the fly."[47]

During the second half of September, various newspapers published a column by well-known sportswriter O.P. Caylor under the headline, "The Color Line Again." A subheadline shared by many of these papers read, in part, that "Many Stars of the Diamond Never Shine Because They Have No Opportunity to Do So." If Caylor did intend to challenge racial discrimination in baseball, his approach was questionable. He noted that African American jockeys had "attained prominence" in horseracing, but the Cuban Giants and Gorhams hadn't had any "player who would be able to hold a place on a National league nine even if there were no prejudice against them." Even if Caylor was implying that there was ample and superior African American baseball talent yet to be discovered, on October 11 the *Harrisburg Telegraph* printed a rebuttal on its front page by an anonymous "old base ball player," who said:

There is one colored base ball player now before the public who is the equal of any player on the diamond. Any judge of ball play who has ever seen Grant, the colored second baseman, will say that in the field and at the bat he stands in the front rank. The only thing that keeps him out of a league club is his color.... He subsequently played in Harrisburg, but it was not a league team, and Grant was ahead of the class of players in the club. A team of nine ball players like Grant would be simply invincible. Give the colored ball player his due.[48]

In late October, the *Boston Herald* reported that the Cuban Giants had compiled a record of 121–16, plus two ties. "The club will make a California trip, visit the Southwest, and return to New York Feb. 1," that daily added.[49] If there actually was any such trip, sportswriters largely ignored it. In early December, J.M. Bright announced that he signed William Selden and James Robinson, creating a pitching staff of five with holdovers Nelson, Stovey, and Miller, but there was no mention of any western trip in progress.[50]

At Christmas, Bright made a major addition to his offense by signing Grant "Home Run" Johnson. According to baseball historian Gary Ashwill, Johnson was eventually the captain of "at least five teams that claimed the colored world's championship, and played for at least three more."[51] In early 1894, Bright reportedly lost Frank Grant and Frank Miller to a team in Ogdensburg, New York. Apparently, both were wintering in Pittsburgh. They were supposed to report to their new team in mid–March, but nothing ever came of that, at least regarding Grant.[52]

Grant was back home toward the end of March, at least briefly, according to a preview of a game on March 24 between Williams College and a North Adams team. "Spaulding and Mackey are the North Adams battery and Grant and Cary of the Cuban Giants are expected to win much favor," said the *Springfield Republican*.[53] The latter player could have been John Cary of the Boston Monarchs.[54] Regardless, it's unknown whether conditions allowed the game to be played. It apparently wasn't reported on afterwards in two county papers.[55]

J.M. Bright instructed all Cubans players to report in New York City on April 21 (and that included Sol White, penciled in at first base). The team's first two games were scheduled for April 24 and 25 in Harrisburg.[56] Before the first game, the President of the home team, E.K. Meyers, criticized several of the city's hotels for refusing to accommodate the Cuban Giants because of their race. The Park Hotel on Walnut Street finally provided that lodging. "I can't fathom the action of these hotel people," Meyers said. "I had the Cuban Giants for two seasons and I know that they are more gentlemanly and cleanly than many of the white teams now traveling about the country."[57]

In actuality, just before the two games at Harrisburg, the Cuban Giants squeezed in a game at Easton against that city's Pennsylvania State League team. They faced pitcher Zeke Wilson, exactly 365 days before the start of a five-year major league career in which he went 52–44. The game went 10 innings, and Easton prevailed, 3–1. Grant had one of the Giants' four hits off Wilson. The Cubans' lineup was: A. Jackson, 3b; O. Jackson, cf; Williams, c; Grant, 2b; Patterson, lf; Johnson, 1b; Nelson, p; W. Jackson, rf; Terrill, ss; and Selden, p.[58]

Harrisburg's team was in the same minor league as Easton's, and the next day they clobbered the Cubans, 13–4. Grant went 2-for-4, including a double, and scored twice. Four of Harrisburg's first five batters had or would have major league experience, including Grant's former Buffalo teammate, Charlie Hamburg. The Cuban Giants didn't let that drubbing discourage them, and they won the rematch, 6–4. Grant again went 2-for-4.[59]

By early May, Sol White was in their lineup. On May 2, his first name was specified in a box score against the University of Rochester in New York. The game was limited to eight innings because the Cubans had a train to catch, but the outcome was certain after four. The visitors won, 20–1, before about 700 fans. "The Giants swooped down on this city at 2:15 P.M., hastily devoured their prey, and departed at 6:25 P.M. taking with them the $60, which was guaranteed them," noted a local paper.[60] As mentioned previously, Bright developed a habit of scheduling games against collegiate teams in the spring, and 1894 provided ample examples.

On May 5, the Giants defeated Williams College, 14–5, and the score was even reported in the *Washington Post*. Grant was in his birthplace two days later, as more than 800 spectators watched his Giants win, 12–5. Their opponents were Pittsfield's first minor league team, though it was a member of the New York State League (the border being less than 10 miles away). Pittsfield's lineup included three players who later had very brief National League careers. "Many of Grant's friends throughout the county were present and he was applauded when he came to bat," noted one local paper.[61]

On May 18, the Cuban Giants defeated a team in Lock Haven, Pennsylvania, by a score of 19–6. The home team's relief pitcher beginning in the third inning was likely Davey Dunkle, who had a five-year major league career starting in 1897. The game's proceeds, after expenses, were given to a Lock Haven player named Jahns who had broken his arm that week.[62]

On May 23, the Cubans clobbered an amateur team in New Bedford, Massachusetts, 25–3. Rain helped limit the game to six innings, though the visitors led, 11–1, after the first. New Bedford's pitcher for the remaining innings was the famous Harry Stovey, whose 14-year major league career had ended the previous season.[63] The next day, a paper in Grant Johnson's hometown of Findlay, Ohio, said he was "tired of his engagement with the Cuban Giants," and he reportedly left when Bright was late in paying him.[64] The Giants ended the month by winning a slugfest versus Harrisburg's minor league team, 13–9. Grant again had two hits against that club.[65] The *Washington Post* soon announced that if a Pennsylvania State League franchise folded, the Cuban Giants were expected to replace it.[66]

A notable game for the Cuban Giants in June was in New Haven on the 20th, when they defeated another minor league team, 8–6. New Haven's club belonged to the Connecticut State League. Grant went 2-for-5 with a double and a triple, and White hit the Giants' only homer.[67]

On Independence Day, the Giants played a doubleheader in Camden, New Jersey, and won both games. The scores were 19–8 and 11–6. The Giants hit six homers in the first game, including one by White and two by Grant. Kid Gleason, the manager of the infamous Chicago "Black Sox" in 1919, hit one for Camden, and he added two more in the second game. At that point, Gleason was six seasons into a 22-year career as a major league player.[68]

Grant and White faced a future Hall of Fame pitcher on August 6, 20-year-old Jack Chesbro. He was with the Asylum club of Middletown, New York. Grant and White each had two hits off Chesbro, who shut out the visitors for the first five innings. Grant's triple was the key blow in the Cubans' three-run seventh inning, and he doubled in the ninth inning, as they came close to tying the score. The game ended 8–7 in favor of Chesbro's side, shortly after Andy Jackson was called out trying to steal third on a "doubtful decision," as a local paper conceded.[69] That would not be Grant's only encounter with Chesbro.

Four days later, the Cuban Giants easily defeated a team in Salem, New Jersey, 19–6. Most of that team's lineup played for Salem the following season when it had a minor league franchise in the South Jersey League.[70] On August 19, the Cubans beat the Ironsides at Newark, 5–1, to claim the semi-professional championship of New York City.[71] Late in that month, the Cubans added a victory in Atlantic City before 2,000 fans.[72]

The Cuban Giants had a monumental triumph at Newark's Koehler Park on Sunday, September 2. They played the National League's St. Louis Browns, though baseball historian Tony Kissel found that no box score exists. The batteries were Dad Clarkson and Art Twineham for the Browns versus Nelson and Williams for the Giants. Clarkson was reportedly hissed for lobbing easy pitches to the Giants in the early going. The Giants led, 5–0, after two innings but the score was 6–4 after four. A five-run seventh put the Browns on top, 9–8, but the Giants took the lead back with three runs in the bottom half, then added two insurance runs in the eighth. The final score was 13–9. Dailies in St. Louis largely ignored the game, though a week afterwards, one of them noted that outfielder Tommy Dowd of the Browns had his hand stepped on by a Giant and had been out of the lineup since. Kissel noted that the Giants didn't face any National League team later that decade.[73]

On September 11, the Cubans defeated another minor league team in Fall River, Massachusetts, before about 1,400 fans. Fall River won the New England League's championship, and its first four batters that day were former or future major leaguers. Their pitcher was Ezra Lincoln, who had started 18 major league games in 1890. Despite 13 errors by the Cubans, including three each by Grant and White, the visitors rallied late to take it, 17–11. The Cubans also won the next day's rematch, 13–6.[74]

From September 25–28, games involving the Cuban Giants were a featured attraction at a fair in Mansfield, Pennsylvania, near Corning and Elmira, New York. A local paper was creative in advertising them, and early. Reporting afterwards, conversely, was minimal.[75]

The Cuban Giants' final two games of the month were in Buffalo. Frank Grant received at least a little recognition in advance. "Our old favorite, Grant, is with them and is playing in fine form and is sure to amuse the crowd," said one daily there the day before the first game. That season, the Bisons belonged to the Eastern League. The Cubans were trounced in the first game, 18–6, but won the rematch, 5–4. The home team's pitcher both days was Tom Vickery, who had spent the previous four years in the National League. His best work was as a rookie when he went 24–21 for the Phillies, and overall he had a record of 42–41. Grant went 1-for-4 off him both days, with a double in the first game. Also playing for the Bisons was future Hall of Famer Jimmy Collins, who began his 14-year career in the majors the following April.[76]

The Cubans continued westward in October and won games in Findlay, Ohio, on the first two days of the month. The visitors won the first game easily, 12–3, against future major leaguer Bill Reidy. He began a six-year major league career in 1896. The home team's two stolen bases were both by Bud Fowler. One homer in the game was hit by a player named Johnson, presumably the Cubans' former teammate, Grant "Home Run" Johnson. White also homered in the game, and Grant homered twice. Grant also homered in the rematch, which the Giants won, 8–6.[77]

The Cuban Giants played in Chicago on October 6 and 7. They won the first game

> **MANSFIELD FAIR**
> Sept. 25-28, 1894.
> 26 Reasons Why You Should Attend.
>
> **XIX**
> The Cuban Giants
> the greatest Colored aggregation of ball players on the globe, have been secured for three games this year....
>
> **XX**
> Frank Grant
> the wonderful Short-stop.............
> Clarence Williams
> the celebrated Coacher, are among the Colored Champions of the World.

Someone promoting the Mansfield Fair in Pennsylvania really got carried away, and about three weeks in advance. From the *Mansfield Advertiser*, September 5, 1894.

easily, 14–7, at the South Side City League Park against another African American team, the Unions. "Frank Grant had an off day and did not play his usual game," said one daily there, presumably referring only to his three errors because he had two hits and scored four times. The next day, the Cubans also defeated a team called the Edgars, 6–3.[78]

There was widespread speculation that the Cubans would continue to California, but they were back in New Jersey for a game on October 14. They lost in Paterson, 17–4. At that time, the *Brooklyn Daily Eagle* reported that "Ed Bowen of Chicago and Sol White, second baseman of the Cuban Giants, have signed articles agreeing to take seven men from the Cuban Giants to play base ball in Chicago next season."[79]

Whatever that foreshadowed regarding their future, the Cuban Giants had another fantastic season in 1894. Their record was reported as 124–22, with three ties.[80] According to Tony Kissel, their record against minor league clubs was 14–6.[81]

Clarence Williams and Frank Grant wintered in Harrisburg. In November, one of the city's newspapers noted that Grant was in town as "the guest of Edward Foley, State and Spruce streets." In the city's 1894 directory, an E. Foley had a hotel at 451 State Street, and in early 1895, Grant was a bartender for Foley.[82] Mary Adore Wilson had remarried in December 1892. Her new husband was named Milton Ricketts.[83] Amazingly, in October 1893 Ricketts reported her to local law enforcement for "keeping a bawdy house [and] selling liquor on Sunday and without license." A grand jury dropped the charges in January.[84] It would come as no surprise if they divorced, and signs of that were in the 1894 and 1895 city directories, where she was listed as "Wilson, Mary E., seamstress," living with her father at 407 N. 5th Street. Frank W. Grant was presumably living there as well. Alas, Mary passed away on January 14, 1896. She was buried at Lincoln Cemetery, as was her mother, Elizabeth.

12

A "Cuban" Rivalry (1895–1897)

An early test for Frank Grant and the Cuban Giants in 1895 was a series of three games in Fall River, against the New England League champions they defeated twice the previous September. On April 18, Fall River won the first game easily, 16–4. The Giants' lineup was Patterson, 2b; C. Williams, c; Grant, ss; A. Jackson, 3b; O. Jackson, lf; W. Jackson, rf; Harrison, cf; Selden, p; Stovey, p; Robinson, p; and Nelson, 1b. With a similar lineup the next day, they won a tense slugfest, 11–10. The crowd for the second game was the largest ever at that ballpark to that point, with a paid admission of 5,417 and a total above 6,000. The Cuban Giants led, 8–2, after two innings, but the score was 9–6 after three. The visitors hung on for an 11–10 win. They won the third game as well, 10–6. Fall River used more than one pitcher in each game, and Fred Klobedanz hurled in all three.[1]

On April 23, the Cuban Giants split a doubleheader against Reading's team in the Pennsylvania State League, and the next two days they won and lost blowout slugfests against Pottsville's club in the same league. Pottsville's lineup included three position players who had major league experience at some point, and one of their two pitchers in the first game was Mark Baldwin, whose seven-year major league career concluded in 1893. He started at least 30 games in each of those seasons and peaked in 1890 with a record of 33–24 for Chicago's team in the Players' League.[2]

In the first game at Pottsville, there was a fight on the field. "The beginning of the afternoon's sport was marked by a row between Jack Tighe and Jackson," the *Pottsville Daily Republican* reported. "The colored first baseman called Jack a low name and they were at it hammer and tongs in a minute. Officer George Cooper prevented any serious damage and got the men apart." Tighe was Pottsville's' second baseman, and it was Oscar Jackson who played first for the Giants that day. Another paper placed the blame squarely on Tighe. "Shenandoah people who witnessed the game at Pottsville yesterday say that Tighe's conduct on the diamond was disgraceful and that the blows struck were brought on by his use of foul language," reported Pottsville's *Evening Herald*. "The Pottsville management should reprimand Tighe and nip such conduct in the bud."[3]

The novel by Frank Grant's childhood friend Bliss Perry, *The Plated City*, was announced during the first half of May. It's possible that no publication connected it to Grant that year. For example, one thoughtful review about four months later didn't report that the heroic ballplayer in the novel was based on any real person. That Wisconsin journalist called it "a story that illustrates the sorrow and injustice which are caused by a close drawing of the color line."[4]

Two noteworthy games for the Cuban Giants in May were against the College of the Holy Cross in Worcester, Massachusetts. Patrolling left field for the home team in both games was the famous Native American, Louis Sockalexis, who played for the National

League's Cleveland Spiders from 1897 to 1899. Sockalexis was enjoying the first of his two seasons on that school's team. The Giants won the game on May 18, 9–1. Grant led the Giants on offense by going 3-for-5 with two steals and three runs scored. Holy Cross won the rematch ten days later, 12–5. Grant again led his team at bat by going 3-for-4. Sockalexis was 1-for-3 in the first game with a walk, a stolen base, and a run scored. He also turned a double play with his second baseman. In the second game, he was 2-for-4 including a double and a walk.[5]

In between those two games, the Cuban Giants had some reason to believe their troubles with authorities on Long Island were a thing of the past. At Recreation Park on May 19, they defeated the Long Island Stars, 11–4. The game drew 2,500 fans. On June 9, they drew 1,500 fans for a game at the same diamond.[6]

On June 5, the Cuban Giants defeated Hazleton's team in the Pennsylvania State League, 10–3, in only 80 minutes. Within a month, the Cubans added wins against two clubs of the three-team South Jersey League. On June 24, they beat Bridgeton, 9–5, without Grant in the lineup. On July 2, the Giants pounded Salem's team, 20–7.[7] The Giants were faring well against minor league teams despite the absence of Sol White.

In August, if not the previous month, Frank Grant was associated with a team called the Capital Colored All-Americans, of Lansing, Michigan. In July, Bud Fowler had announced this team as a spinoff of his Page Fence Giants in Adrian, Michigan, which he and Grant Johnson had launched during April. Fowler said he would captain this new team on trips to California, England, and Australia after the regular season. Fowler said Grant would be his shortstop and that he had signed four other Cuban Giants: Clarence Williams, pitchers Selden and Robinson, and one of the Jacksons to play center field (presumably Oscar). Vasco Graham, George Wilson, and other Page Fence Giants would round out the roster.[8]

Just as visionary was a letter to the editor published by the *Philadelphia Inquirer* later in August. Someone with the initials H.T.J. wrote, "Why should the managers of the Phillies not employ the service of Grant, of the Cuban Giants base ball team, and thus strengthen their one weak place, namely, short stop? This player would draw enough of the colored citizens to more than pay for his salary, to say nothing of the vast service he would be toward landing the championship for '95." The Phillies finished in third place that season. Around that same time, the *Washington Post* reported that some unnamed sportswriter in New York "suggests that the Cuban Giants be transferred to New York to take the place of their Giants in the League race."[9] The New York Giants finished ninth in the 12-team National League that season. Three years earlier, a similar comment by "King" Kelly mocked both teams, but the Cuban Giants had rehabilitated their image by mid–1895, and thus the journalist's recommendation could have been at least half-serious.

Grant continued to play with the Cuban Giants, such as in another win against a minor league team on August 7. The Giants held off Hartford's Connecticut State League team, 8–6. The home team's starting pitcher was John Henry, who had four years of major league experience. Grant's double was the Giants' only extra-base hit.[10] The Cubans edged the same team again on September 10, 16–15. Grant's three hits, which included a double and a homer, were off Bill Gannon, who converted to the outfield long before his 15 games in the National League with Chicago in 1901.[11]

The Cuban Giants were back at Grant's birthplace the next day, for the last day of the fair in Pittsfield, and their game drew the largest crowd ever in that city to that point (although the *Berkshire Evening Eagle* didn't quantify that). They defeated the Stanleys, 13–6. Grant's hit in the game came in an 11-run fifth inning. He played errorless ball at second base, with eight putouts, an assist, and a double play from second base to third base to home plate.[12]

For about two weeks starting on September 9, the Cuban Giants played New England League teams in Fall River and New Bedford, plus a team in Newport, Rhode Island.[13] The four teams were even called the "quadrangular league" by newspapers in at least four cities.[14] The Giants were scheduled to play in each of the cities from September 26 through 28, but the series ended a few days early. The final records were Fall River, 9–2; New Bedford, 5–4; Cuban Giants, 2–5, and Newport, 3–8.[15] The Cubans' victories came against Newport on September 16 and 17. In the first win, 10–4, Grant went 2-for-4 plus a walk and scored twice.[16] Though the Cuban Giants lost their games against the two New England League teams, Tony Kissel reported that their record against minor league teams in 1895 was 9–10.[17]

The Cuban Giants did enjoy a bright spot late that month. On September 28, they played the Orange Athletic Club in Orange, New Jersey, before 5,000 fans. The visitors trailed after two innings, 2–1, but scored enough single runs to take the game, 4–2. The Orange pitcher was presumably 25-year-old Huyler Westervelt, who went 7–10 in 23 games for the New York Giants a year earlier.[18]

The Cubans played some games during the first half of October, primarily in Pennsylvania, but none were particularly noteworthy. In contrast to the previous year, there wasn't widespread reporting of their win–loss record during and after the season. On September 11, one paper said that the Cuban Giants had "won 96 out of the 118 games played" to that point,[19] and if that included no ties, their record was 96–22. However, that was just before the first of their "quadrangular league" games.

It's unclear where Frank Grant spent the winter, but he did go home by early November. "Frank Grant, the star Cuban Giant baseball player, is visiting at the home of his sisters on Spring street," said a paper in neighboring North Adams.[20] There was no subsequent word of any trips to California, England, and Australia.

In early 1896, confusion was brewing—and maybe some trouble—in the world of the Cuban Giants. Though the name "Cuban Giants" was used by many other teams during the first half of the 1890s, they were low-profile and didn't have the talent to get much attention outside of their home cities. That changed in 1896, when some former Cuban Giants sought to match the fame of Bright's club and had success assembling the talent to do so. Bright sought to prevent that in mid-February. "The team which was incorporated in 1886 publishes the notice that any manager booking any club claiming to be Cuban Giants, ex-Cuban Giants, or formerly Cuban Giants, without consent of John M. Bright, the manager of the above original team, is liable to a suit for damages." Thus concluded one such announcement, which named Frank Grant as captain of Bright's "original Cuban Giants."[21] Though this rival team's name was rendered inconsistently in newspapers during 1896, often simply as the "Cuban Giants" without distinction, historians generally call it the Cuban X-Giants. It was managed by E.B. Lamar, Jr. out of New York City.[22]

By late February, Bright announced that the Cuban Giants had already booked more than 100 games for the upcoming season. At that point he had signed Grant, Sol White, Robinson, Miller, Patterson, and Job Trusty. Players were to report for duty on April 14.[23]

In the meantime, Lamar wrote a letter to the *New York Sun* in which he claimed to have signed eight players: "Clarence Williams, O. Jackson, A. Jackson, B. Jackson, Selden, Nelson, Sol White and Terrill."[24] Bright revealed his own roster at that point: "Catchers, William Jackson, J. Trusty, Robert Gordon [sic; Jordan], William Cole, and probably C. Williams; pitchers, James Robinson, Frank Miller, Frank Hinson, and Higgins, of Pittsburg; first base, John Frye; second base, Sol. White; third base, J. Trusty; left field, John Patterson; centre field, Jim Taylor; right field, W. Jackson, and Frank Grant, short stop and captain."[25] White was the only player claimed by both clubs. Late that month, Bright announced that he had secured the Grand Street athletic grounds in Brooklyn for periodic games, the first of which was scheduled for April 26.[26]

As projected, the Cuban Giants did play on April 14. They faced York's team in the Pennsylvania State League. It was a pitcher's duel which the Giants won, 2–0. York's pitcher was Jimmy Sheckard, who began a 17-year career in the major leagues the following season. The batting order for the visitors was: Patterson, lf; White, 2b; Jackson, c; Grant, ss; Taylor, rf; Cole, cf; Robinson, p; Frye, 1b; and Trusty, 3b. By contrast, the next day's rematch was a slugfest, won by the home team, 15–9.[27]

The Cubans also lost high-scoring games the next two days against another team in the same minor league, at Carbondale. A local paper's subheadline noted that "Mr. Grant, Formerly of Buffalo," had a dispute with the first umpire—whose replacement, Pete Anderson of the home team, went unquestioned. The quirky exchange offered rare quotes by Grant in print:

> There was life in the game at only two points. First, when captain Grant objected to umpire Sontag. It was on a line ball over third base and this Cuban, not U.S. Grant, felt called upon to go into history to prove that he knew more about baseball than the umpire.
> "Why, I used to play with Buffalo!" he shouted.
> "Used you?"
> "I used!"
> "I thought you used," answered Jolie.
> There were outfielders too who know more about balls and strikes than the man who stood behind the bat and sighted through a mask at the risk of having a broken wire driven into his cranium. So Jolie quietly threw up his hands and resigned.[28]

On April 19, the Cubans played their fifth consecutive day against a minor league team, Rochester of the Eastern League. The home team had six players in its lineup with major league experience at some point, including pitcher Dan McFarlan. The Giants lost, 5–1. They also lost the next day's rematch, 9–2. Pitching for Rochester was Bill Day, who had National League experience in 1889–1890.[29]

The next day the Cuban Giants were in Hartford to face that city's team in the Atlantic League. The home team's leadoff hitter was Grant's childhood teammate, Bob Pettit. Each of them hit a double but Pettit had four hits to Grant's two, and that reflected the overall contrast between the teams that day. The Cubans were clobbered, 20–6.[30]

The Cuban Giants may have been rained out on April 21; their game scheduled for the next day in Portland, Maine was cancelled due to wet grounds. They then played a New England League team, up in Lewiston, Maine. The Cubans were shut out for eight innings and lost, 9–1.[31]

On April 24, the Giants couldn't hold off a late scoring by Portland's New England League team and lost a heartbreaker in the 10th inning, 9–8. Portland's lineup included four position players who had major league experience at some point, and the first of

Portland's pitchers was John Buckley, who started four games for Buffalo's team in the Players' League in 1890. The home team also won the next day's rematch, 14–5. Both of Portland's pitchers that day, Walt Woods and Sandy McDougal, were National Leaguers at different points. Grant went 2-for-5 and played errorless ball. He also received praise from the *Portland Daily Press*:

> Captain Grant is an excellent all around player, and his efforts have a great deal to do in inspiring his men. The old Buffalonian is as agile as ever. He was brilliant in the extreme yesterday and enthusiasm over his playing was at a topnotch.[32]

Grant's teammates were inspired enough to win two of their final four games in April. On April 27, they beat Scranton's club in the Eastern League, 12–7. Leading off for that Pennsylvania team was Piggy Ward, who had six years of major league experience, and pitching was Archie Stimmel, who was with the Cincinnati Reds from 1900 to 1902. Grant went 2-for-4 off him, including a double. Scranton won the next day's rematch, 13–6.[33]

On April 29, Frank Grant was opposite his manager with Buffalo, Jack Chapman, who was leading Wilkes-Barre's team in the Eastern League. The first four position players in Chapman's lineup had major league experience at some point. It was a high-scoring game, but the Cuban Giants won, 13–9. Grant went 3-for-5, including a triple, scored a run, and played errorless ball. The loss was the home team's first of its preseason.[34]

The Giants' final loss of the month was to the Pennsylvania State League team in Easton.[35] The visitors were trounced, 18–6. This rough start to the Giants' season was reminiscent of Grant's time with the Gorhams and the Cuban Giants during April and May of 1892, the previous time that there was a divisive rivalry among the top African American players along the East Coast. A big difference in 1896 was that the Cuban Giants were losing to more talented professional teams.

May 1 was Opening Day for the Eastern, New England, and Pennsylvania State Leagues, so the Cuban Giants' schedule shifted toward collegiate teams in the short term. As a noteworthy example, on May 5 they defeated Holy Cross and Louis Sockalexis, 7–6. Grant went 2-for-3, including a triple and a walk, stole a base, and scored twice. At second base, he had seven putouts, five assists, no errors, and started a double play. Sockalexis also batted well, with 3-for-5 and a run.[36]

On May 23, a paper in Washington, D.C., printed a statement from John M. Bright. He began, "Owing to the fact that there is a club (colored) calling themselves the Cuban (X) Giants, and getting most terribly defeated everywhere, and when defeated they send in their scores, calling themselves the Cuban Giants, thereby injuring the Genuine Cuban Giants' great reputation and fooling the public at large, I am therefore compelled to take this means to notify the various managers and public as well." He named his players at that point: John Frye, Sol White, John Patterson, William Jackson, Frank Grant, Robert Jordan, John [sic] Trusty, Frank Miller, James Robinson, and Doc Howard. "We have won seventeen out of the last twenty-three games played," Bright concluded.[37]

Another noteworthy collegiate game late in the month was back in Grant's hometown, Williamstown. On May 27, the Cuban Giants defeated Williams College, 16–8.[38] Three days later, the Giants were in Meriden briefly. A local paper paid attention to their presence:

Frank Grant was with the team. During their half hour's wait at the New England depot Grant looked around the West side ball grounds where ten years ago he played his first professional ball. On it instead of base lines he saw nearly a score of fine dwelling houses and was greatly surprised at the change.[39]

The Cuban Giants started June with three wins in four games against minor league teams. The first was 6–2 over Bridgeton of the four-team South Jersey League. Batting third for the home team was Grant's old Buffalo teammate, Joe Kappel, a former major leaguer. One of Grant's two hits that day was a homer, and his errorless defense included four putouts and four assists. The next day, they defeated the Hagerstown, Maryland club of the four-team Cumberland Valley League in 12 innings, 12–11. The following day's rematch lasted 10 more innings, but the home team won that time, 8–7.[40]

On June 4, the Cuban Giants played another team in the Cumberland Valley League, in Hanover, Maryland. In the lineup for the home team was Tommy Leach, who began a 19-year major league career two seasons later. The Giants had an easy time of it, 8–1.[41]

Grant had a particularly impressive game on June 25, in Newark, New York. The Cubans beat a local team thanks in part to his triple, double, walk, and three runs scored. In fact, a box score showed that he did the impossible by going 5-for-4.[42]

Two days later, the Cubans played the Orange Athletic Club and their pitcher, Huyler Westervelt. Besides a line score, most details are sketchy. The home team led, 6–3, after four innings and 8–6 after seven. The game went 11 innings, and the Giants won, 9–8. Two days later, the *Philadelphia Inquirer* reported that the shortstop for the Giants "was hit on the head by a pitched ball from Huyler Westervelt and seriously injured." Bizarrely, the *Inquirer* said the injured batter was named Crappy.[43] Sol White often played shortstop for the Cubans around that time, but Grant certainly could have played there that day. Whatever the case, if it was either Grant or White who was injured that way, no effects showed two days later when they each had two hits in a 5–4 win against a team comprised mostly of collegians, about 50 miles away in Asbury Park. In fact, Westervelt also pitched that game. In a rematch to close the month of June, the Cuban Giants trailed, 10–9, going into the top of the ninth inning. Grant scored the tying run, and his teammates added one more, then held the home team scoreless in the bottom half to win it.[44]

A rarity for the Cuban Giants in July was a trip up to Canada. On the 7th, Montreal's *Gazette* promoted games there scheduled for July 11 and 12. "This wonderful and extremely funny colored championship team of the world, under the captaincy of Frank Grant, will play our local team," the Nationals or Le National. That daily didn't publish on Sunday, and its Monday edition didn't appear to cover either game. However, at least one American paper reported a score for the first game, and the visitors won, 15–5.[45]

Otherwise, during July the Cuban Giants played mostly in New Jersey, and a noteworthy game there toward the end of the month drew before more than 5,000 fans. That was on July 25, for a rematch against the Orange Athletic Club, and Westervelt apparently pitched in relief. The home team won it in 11 innings, 8–6. The Giants managed only five hits, and Grant had two of them.[46]

The Cuban Giants had a historic game on August 18, in Cooperstown. Pitching for the local Athletics was future Hall of Famer Jack Chesbro. Batting second and third for the Giants were Sol White and Frank Grant. In the first inning, Grant and Jackson scored the game's first runs, both unearned, after two outs. Grant had one of the

Giants' eight hits off Chesbro. A seven-run third inning by the home team was all Chesbro needed for a 16–2 win. The two teams met again the next day, and the result was almost identical, 13–2. The local *Freeman's Journal* devoted just three sentences to the rematch and didn't name a single player or even print a line score.[47]

On September 9, the three future Hall of Famers met again back in Berkshire County, Massachusetts, where both Grant and Chesbro were born. The game was played in Grant's birthplace, Pittsfield, and drew the largest crowd of the year. Chesbro played for the local Stanleys and switched to first base for the last two innings. He held Grant hitless and limited White to a single, but the Stanleys committed seven errors to the Cubans' two. That partly explains why the Stanleys gave up 10 runs during Chesbro's seven innings of hurling. The Giants won, 11–2.[48]

On September 24, the Cuban Giants played Williams College at the end of a three-day local fair, and the Cubans won, 10–4. Attendance was close to 1,000. Robinson and Jordan were the battery for Grant's team, but otherwise details were minimal in the local paper.[49] On September 26, a Cuban Giants nine lost a game to the Orange Athletic Club, but neither Grant nor White played. In fact, the batting order looked like a merger of the original Cuban Giants and the X-Giants. White had left by September 25 to play with the Cuban X-Giants in a 15-game championship series to the west, against the Page Fence Giants.[50] Grant was reported in Williamstown on October 2, though he may have simply stayed there the entire week after the game against Williams College.[51]

It's unclear when the Cuban Giants disbanded for the offseason. Their record during 1896 was reportedly 102–37–1.[52] As was true during the autumn of 1895, this results total wasn't widely reported.

Frank Grant spent the offseason in Williamstown and remained physically active into the winter. In fact, on October 9 he was associated with Chesbro yet again, except as a teammate. Their county's Blackinton team was scheduled to play the next day against a team from nearby Pownal, Vermont, and the Massachusetts lineup was to be augmented by Chesbro, Grant, and infielder Art Madison of the 1895 Phillies, another county native. Chesbro did pitch part of the game, which was won by Blackinton, 10–4, but in the absence of a box score, it's unknown whether Grant and Madison also played.[53] On Halloween, Chesbro, Grant, and Madison were again projected to play for the Blackintons, against the local Renfrews. If the game was played, there may not have been any coverage afterwards.[54]

In mid–January, teams of students and "town boys," as the *North Adams Transcript* called them, put on ice skates and met on the Williamstown Manufacturing company's pond to play ice polo, a competition similar to hockey. By the first week of February, the "town boys," who were really adults, challenged all teams in the county. They were under the management of a James McMahon, likely the friend of Clarence Grant from seven years earlier. Frank Grant was one of the six other players. High winds had prevented a rematch with the students on February 6.[55] Less than a year later, several of this ice polo club's members would discuss forming a hockey club.

By that point, John M. Bright was already signing players for the 1897 baseball season. By early February, he had signed Grant anew and added Henry Gant of Pittsburgh plus George Williams. The team would be based in the twin cities of Johnstown and Gloversville, New York, 45 miles northwest of Albany. About two weeks later, Bright also resecured Robert Jordan as a catcher and added "Jacob Jamison of the Indian school, Carlisle, Pa., the great half-back foot ball player and a star pitcher." *The Sporting*

News printed a letter by Bright in which he announced two efforts: to line up games against National League teams and to launch "a colored base ball tournament for the genuine colored championship, and a suitable trophy emblematic of the colored championship." He invited six other teams to play such a tourney at Johnstown and Gloversville: The Page Fence Giants of Adrian, Michigan; the Unions of Chicago; the Keystones of Pittsburgh; the Pinchbacks of New Orleans; the Red Sox of Norfolk, Virginia; and the Gorhams of New York.[56] Noticeably absent from this list was Lamar's Cuban X-Giants. That could've been due to lingering bitterness on Bright's part, though he could also have argued that they'd already been eliminated by having lost 10 of 15 games in September's series to the Page Fence Giants.[57] If Bright did continue to harbor hostility toward Lamar's club, that softened in the following month.

In early March, Bright announced this roster: George L. Williams, 1b and captain, George Jones lf, Robert Jordan c, Frank Grant 2b, Sol White 3b, Ross Garrison ss, Henry Gant lf, Abe Harrison cf, and Frank Miller, John Mackey, Eddie Day, William Malone, John Nelson, and James Robinson, all pitchers. Bright had arranged for games against nine teams across the Atlantic, Eastern, and New England Leagues. However, when the *North Adams Transcript* reported that Grant left Williamstown on April 10 to report to the team, it said he was the captain.[58]

Toward the end of March, *The Sporting News* printed another letter from Bright, in response to dialogue with the Chicago Unions. The latter club declined to play at Johnstown and Gloversville despite Bright's willingness to travel west for return games. Bright was told their schedule was already full. "If they wanted to convince the world by playing that they have such a world beating club they would soon make a few open dates so as to be in the tournament," Bright replied. "The Page Fence Giants have written that they want to be in, also the Cuban X Giants of New York."[59] The latter team, the Unions, and Bright's Giants would play one another at least 10 times in 1897.

In early April, Bright instructed his players to report to Lancaster, Pennsylvania on April 12, for the first game of a two-week preseason. The team's "regular season" was to begin at Newport, Rhode Island, on April 26, and their first game in Johnstown was scheduled for May 14.[60] Though the Giants weren't in a league and thus distinguishing between a preseason and "regular season" seems like a meaningless distinction, he may have made it in case his team again had a poor record against minor league teams in April, in which case he could omit those games from its final win-loss record.

By April 12, 13 members of the Cuban Giants were staying in Lancaster's Maennerchor Hotel. The skies were clear, but a chill limited the turnout to about 500 fans. The starting pitcher for Lancaster's Atlantic League club that day was Joe Yeager, who began a 10-year major league career the following season. His best mark in the majors was 12–11 for the Detroit Tigers in 1901. There were five other players in the home team's lineup who played in the majors at some point, including Art Madison of Berkshire County and Piggy Ward. It also included Socks Seybold, who began a nine-year career in the majors during 1899 and whose 16 homers in 1902 stood as the American League record until 1919, when Babe Ruth broke it. On the day, Grant went 1-for-5. One local paper said his single in the bottom of the third inning drove in his team's first run, but a more detailed account in another local daily, the *Intelligencer*—which confirmed that he was "Captain Grant"—said his hit merely put a teammate in scoring position, and he scored on a subsequent error. Regardless, Lancaster's eight-run outburst in the fifth inning put the game out of reach, and the final score was 13–4. The Cubans' batting order was: Grant, 2b; Garrison, ss; Jordan, c; Moulton, 1b; Malone, 3b; Galley, lf; Day, rf; Miller, cf and p; and Robinson, p and cf.[61]

Moulton, Galley, and Day were newcomers, and Grant hadn't played much, if at all, with Garrison or Malone since early in the decade. Fresh faces in a lineup sometimes inject new energy, but often a batch doesn't bode well. Still, Bright's team may have taken a little comfort in the fact that Lamar's X-Giants played Lancaster the next two days and the outcomes were similar, 17–6 and 10–2.[62]

On April 13 and 14, the genuine Cuban Giants played another Atlantic League club, Reading. Though the visitors lost slugfests, the final scores were both closer than against Lancaster, 15–11 and 14–9. Reading's second reliever in the first game was Doc Amole, who made his National League debut later that season with Baltimore and led their pitchers with a 2.57 Earned Run Average while going 4–4 in 11 games.[63]

The Giants' game scheduled for April 15 against Scranton's Eastern League team was rained out, but the two nines were able to play the next day. The Cubans managed just five hits and lost, 8–2. Atop the batting order again, Grant went 1-for-2 with a double and a hit by pitch, and he scored one of those two runs. He played errorless ball at second base with six putouts, three assists, and a double play turned.[64]

The Cubans played the next two days against the Atlantic League team in Paterson, New Jersey. They suffered drubbings in both games. The first game ended 13–3, and the next day both teams doubled their offensive outputs.[65]

On April 19, the Cuban Giants played their first collegiate game of the season, in Carlisle, Pennsylvania, against Dickinson College. The Cubans also picked up their first win, 17–13. Grant helped stifle a rally by the home team in the second inning when they attempted a delayed double steal and he threw the lead runner out at the plate. Grant's two hits were doubles, at least one of which drove in a run.[66]

The Cubans may have had an open date the next day, but on April 21 they came close to their first win against a minor league team of that preseason. They played the Rochester Brownies of the Eastern League in a 10-inning contest. Four of Rochester's position players had major league experience at some point, and their pitcher was Dan McFarlan. Grant went 3-for-5 against him, validating Bright's statement to a local paper that the ex-Bison was playing better than ever. The Giants tied the game at 3–3 with a run in the bottom of the eighth, but Rochester scored three runs in their half of the next inning. The Giants threatened to retie the game in the bottom half. They loaded the bases on two hits and a walk, but with two outs. Grant stood on second base and Garrison was on first. McFarlan threw a poor pitch that escaped his catcher. The ball was loose so long by the stands that Grant reached home plate safely, and Garrison tried to score a third run on the same wild pitch. However, according to the report in the *Rochester Democrat and Chronicle*, Grant stopped on the plate in front of "McFarland"[sic], to interfere with him and to help Garrison, who was doing some tall hustling toward the plate. So although Grant had scored, umpire O'Loughlin called him out for interference and his run didn't count. That retired the side, and the Giants hustled to a streetcar. At the beginning of their account of the game, that local daily said Grant had been "a little too foxy" on the play.[67]

Grant's team played an equally competitive game the next day against the Syracuse Stars of the same league. The account in the *Syracuse Standard* began as follows:

> The Cuban Giants claim they were roasted out of yesterday's game with the Stars, and to an unprejudiced lover of fair play it looked a good deal that way. The record of the game shows

that the African champions greatly outbatted the home team. They outfielded them, too, for that matter, and deserved the game on the merits of their playing. Pitcher Lampe acted as umpire and his decisions were a good deal off color in more than one instance where bases meant runs.

The visitors led, 5–3, after five innings, but the Stars scored twice in the seventh and once in the ninth to win it, 6–5. Grant, now at shortstop but still atop the batting order, went 2-for-5 with a double and a run scored. That came off future Hall of Famer Vic Willis, who began a 25–13 rookie season with Boston one year later. But the *Standard* focused on his defense:

> Grant, the old Buffalo second baseman, was the center of attraction, and he more than proved his right to be called a born ball player and one of the best men in the business. His fielding at short was nothing short of marvelous. He accepted 14 chances without an error, having four put outs and 10 assists. He was everywhere at once, and he got some of the hottest daisy cutters poked at him which ever flew from a bat, but he invariably ate them up as if he thought it was all a big joke and no man reached first who knocked a ball anywhere his way.[68]

The Cuban Giants were supposed to play the next day all the way over in Hartford, Connecticut, but they missed a train connection and instead played that city's Atlantic League team one day later, on April 24. The visitors were contained by Cy Bowen, who lost his only National League start for the Giants a year earlier. Grant's double was one of six hits off Bowen, and at shortstop he accepted seven more chances without an error. Still, Hartford won easily, 10–1.[69]

The Giants were hung up at Hartford long enough that they were late for their game on April 26 in Newport, Rhode Island, against that city's New England League team. Pitching for Newport was Marvin Hawley, who lost his only National League game with Boston in 1894. The visitors took a 5–0 lead in the fourth inning, but after the following frame they were only ahead, 7–5. Newport tied it with two runs in the seventh inning, but the Giants scored the game's final run in the eighth to win against a minor league nine at last, 8–7. Grant went 2-for-5 and scored a run.[70] The two teams met again the next day, and the final score was the same, except the home team won. Grant went 2-for-4 and scored twice.[71]

The Opening Days for the Atlantic, Eastern, and New England Leagues were around this time, so naturally the Giants started playing more collegiate teams. On April 28, they defeated Wesleyan in Middletown, Connecticut, 7–0.[72] The next day, the Giants easily defeated Bristol's minor league team in the Connecticut State League, 10–2, though coverage was minimal. Pitching for the Cubans was Charles "Kid" Carter, who was recruited during their visit to Middletown.[73]

On May 8, the Cuban Giants played in Grant's hometown versus Williams College yet again. The students rallied late but fell short, 8–7. One of Grant's two hits was a triple.[74]

The Cuban Giants were scheduled to open their season at Johnstown on May 14, against Union College of Schenectady, New York. Wet grounds caused that game to be cancelled, so the Cubans' debut in Johnstown was the next day against a team from the villages of Bainbridge and Sidney. The Cubans won easily, 19–10.[75]

On May 20, they played another minor league team, the Auburn Maroons of the New York State League. Alas, Auburn led 8–0 after four innings. Pitching for them was Ed Murphy, who began a four-year National League career the following season. His best record was 10–6 with St. Louis in 1902. Grant went 1-for-5 off him, and his hit was a homer. One paper said it was the longest ever made at that ballpark.[76]

On May 22, the Giants played their second home game in Johnstown, hosting Albany's Roche team. The Cubans won easily, 17–8. The game was notable for two reasons. The obvious one was that the Giants sported new uniforms. A local paper described them as "of gray material with maroon trimmings and black and yellow stockings." The other reason only became apparent a few days later, when it became known that Bright was ending his experiment in Johnstown after less than a month. The *Amsterdam Sentinel* mocked Bright for his "egregious blunder" in choosing Johnstown, but also mocked that community in the process. In response, the *Johnstown Daily Republican* came nowhere close to the high road when it called the *Sentinel*'s editor "an egotistical nincompoop" and defended "the people of Johnstown [who] would not flock to see some uninteresting games of ball put up by a lot of niggers."[77]

On May 29, the Cuban Giants were back in North Adams, coincidentally a day after the Cuban X-Giants played there. The home team won, 9–8, thanks to five late runs. The Cubans played there again on June 19 and 26, and the visitors lost by comparable scores, 8–7 and 11–8. Both of the games in June drew about 1,800 fans, and box scores were published in at least one Boston paper. Though the Cubans were jinxed in Grant's backyard, at least he homered in the third contest. Grant's team didn't fare any better in his birthplace on June 30, when they lost to the Stanleys, 6–4.[78]

The Giants had passed a much tougher test earlier in June, on the 6th, at North Hudson, New Jersey. They faced Kid Carsey, who wasn't even 25 years old but had already pitched six major league seasons, which peaked at 24–16 for the Phillies in 1895. That team and St. Louis were fighting over his services, so he bided his time with the West New York Field Club. The game was scoreless through five innings, but a four-run seventh helped the Giants win, 6–1.[79] On June 20, Louis Sockalexis and the Cleveland "Indians" only managed to beat Carsey's team by a score of 8–6.[80] The Cubans played against Carsey's team again on June 27, but the Kid didn't pitch. The Giants trailed, 3–1, after eight innings but triumphed with a three-run ninth.[81]

On June 16, the Cubans apparently defeated another minor league team, Cortland of the New York State League. Disappointingly, two local papers only printed a single sentence about the game, so it's not certain the team was Grant's.[82] But it wasn't the Cuban X-Giants, who were in Illinois at that time.[83]

Frank Grant took his team to his career's out-of-state roots on July 15, for a game in Plattsburgh, New York. He went hitless, but he offset an error at shortstop with five putouts and four assists. The home team won, 10–6. Grant was again hitless in the next day's rematch, but played errorless ball while accepting seven chances at third base. This time, his nine contained a late rally to win, 7–4. The teams played a third game, in which they exchanged batches of runs in the ninth inning, and when the dust settled, the Cubans won again, 8–7.[84]

The Cuban Giants traveled about 60 miles for a game in Canada on July 18. They faced their foes of the prior summer, the Nationals. The home team's pitcher, Belcourt, was quite likely the same hurler who appeared in four games during 1897 for Montreal's team in the Eastern League, which it took over from Rochester. Grant went 1-for-4, scored three runs, and played errorless ball on the way to a 15–0 cakewalk.[85]

On July 24, the Cuban Giants finally won a game back in the county of Grant's birth. They beat the Dalton team in a six-inning game, 11–2. Grant had a double, stole a base, and scored three times.[86]

The Giants began August with another win against Kid Carsey's team, and Carsey pitched. Though Grant went hitless—on his 32nd birthday—the score was the same against the Kid as on June 6, 6–1.[87] On August 9, the Cubans returned to Plattsburgh and won, 6–3. The played again the following day, but the home team had it easy and won, 12–2.[88]

The Cuban Giants took part in a historic game on August 28, as they began a three-game series in Chicago against the Unions, "for the colored championship and a purse of $100 a game," as the *Chicago Tribune* had set the stage. The Cubans' starting lineup for the first game was: Malone, p; Jordan, rf; Jackson (presumably William), c; Garrison, 2b; Grant, ss; Harrison, 3b; C. Smith, lf; Howard, rf; Galley, cf. Total hits for the two teams told most of the tale. The home team had 22, while the visitors had eight. Frank Grant had three of his team's, including a double, and provided errorless defense. The Cubans only trailed, 3–2, after the first inning but 11–2 after four frames. Howard took over as pitcher but fared no better, and the Giants lost, 21–12. The teams concluded with a doubleheader the next day, and the morning match was tied at 9–9 after seven innings. The Unions scored twice more in the eighth, and that was the end of the scoring. Grant had a hit and scored twice. He really went all-out in the afternoon game, with two runs and four hits, including a double and triple, but the Unions led, 7–0, after three innings and 9–3 after six. The Giants' two late rallies were bigger than the Unions', but they weren't quite enough, and the visitors were swept, 14–12.[89]

Over the next week or so, the Cuban Giants played some games in Michigan, such as on September 2, when they split a doubleheader in Traverse City with a team called the Hustlers. The Cubans subsequently swept a three-game series in Muskegon. "They had to pay $40 to get the steamer Maxwell to bring them here from Ludington but they had more than $40 worth of fun," reported a local paper.[90]

While the Cubans were in Michigan, Kid Carsey announced that he would try to arrange a championship series at Weehawken between those "Genuine" Cuban Giants and the Cuban X-Giants. This was even news in the Deep South.[91] Carsey ultimately succeeded, shortly before Grant's club beat his team yet again on September 26, though not against Carsey himself again.[92]

The series was announced as a best-of-three format, and the winner would get 75 percent of the net receipts. The "Genuine" lineup printed on September 30 differed considerably from the first game in Chicago little more than a month earlier: Jordan, c; Grant, 2b; Harrison, ss; William Jackson, cf; Smith, lf; Howard, 3b; Perrin, rf; De Mond, 1b; plus pitchers Jupiter and Mickey. Their opponents included Sol White, Clarence Williams, Selden, Nelson, and Garrison, the latter apparently a relatively recent defector.[93] Perhaps Bright's team picked up some new talent in Illinois or Michigan.

The series was well-promoted, but coverage after each game was generally lacking. For the first game, at Weehawken on October 3, one paper simply printed a line score with the batteries, which showed Grant's Giants as the winner, 11–9. However, that line score only showed eight innings, and a different paper noted a few days later that it actually ended in a tie after nine, due to dimming light.[94]

The teams met again in Stamford Depot, Connecticut, three days later. The X-Giants led, 8–0, after two innings, and that was all they needed. The final score was 19–4. The two rivals were supposed to play in New Haven the next day, but that didn't occur. The only reason provided, according to a local paper, "was the reported arrest of several of the players in Stamford Wednesday."[95]

The next two games in the series were on October 9 and 10. In Jersey City on the 9th, no more than 250 fans turned up, but a newspaper printed a box score nonetheless. The X-Giants had another big lead after two innings, 6–0, and won 10–1. Grant was hitless. His team did much better at Weehawken the next day, leading 9–1 after three innings. The final score was 13–4.[96]

> A Great Game. Colored World's Championship. Cuban Giants vs. Ex-Cuban Giants. Williams, Grant, "The Jacksons," Sol Whyte, Harrison, all the colored stars. Elm City Park. Today, 3 p. m.
>
> **The Wonderful Gramer Piano**
> Is made by the Emerson Piano Co. Sold only by C. M. Loomis Sons', 833 Chapel street. Sold on easy terms.

Two future Hall of Famers were mentioned in an ad, of sorts, from New Haven's *Morning Journal*, October 7, 1897.

The final game of 1897 for Bright's Cuban Giants may have been on October 17, reported in the *Brooklyn Daily Eagle*. They lost to a team called the Nationals, 15–13. Grant wasn't in the lineup. One of the Jacksons led off, and the only other familiar names were Robinson and Mickey.[97]

Grant spent his second consecutive winter back in Williamstown, based on news about a week into December. "Frank Grant, the well known baseball player," was among eight local men who considered transformed the previous year's ice polo team into an ice hockey team. The list of those men was a little different than back in February. One new name was Arthur Hunt. In the 1880 census, the Grants shared a house with a Hunt family, including jeweler Lyman and his son Arthur, who was a few years younger than Frank. In 1892, Frank's brother Willis purchased a lot on Spring Street from Lyman Hunt.[98] Therefore, it's quite possible that Hunt was a longtime friend of Grant. Whatever the case, that winter and the following spring might have constituted the final time Frank Grant actually resided in Williamstown.

13

Lured Away (1898–1903)

At the beginning of 1898, an unnamed man in or near North Adams reported written communication from the Cuban X-Giants about their interest in representing that city during the upcoming season. According to one local paper, the club's interest emerged after having played "several" good games there in 1897.[1] About two weeks later, J.M. Bright named left-handed catcher William Jackson the captain of his Genuine Cuban Giants for 1898. No other players were named. Bright said their first game would be on April 4, and about two weeks later he would head to Detroit, Chicago, and Piqua, Ohio "to return with the strongest colored players in the west," as one account put it.[2]

On January 26, E.B. Lamar was in North Adams to explore the possibility of basing his team there. None of the reports that month happened to mention that Grant lived just five miles to the west. However, about four weeks later, Lamar announced that his roster included these players: "Selden, Nelson and Howard, pitchers; Williams and Jordan, catchers; [Ray] Wilson, first base; R. [sic; Sol] White, second base; Grant, short stop; A. Jackson, left field; centre and right field will be taken care of by the extra pitchers, who are also hard hitters."[3]

There may not have been an explanation anywhere about why Grant didn't sign with Bright yet again. One possibility is that the two had a private falling-out over something. Another is that Grant perceived the X-Giants to have a better future, or he simply enjoyed the company of men on that team more. One more is that Bright simply couldn't afford Grant any longer.

But in mid–March, Lamar announced that his team would in fact be based in New Adams. The plan was to play many more home games than Bright's team since the Trenton days. Specifically, starting on May 14, the Cuban X-Giants would schedule games in North Adams for Tuesdays, Wednesdays, Thursdays, Saturdays, and holidays. They would host Holy Cross College on that first date. Lamar also released a partial schedule from April 2 through 29, identifying 13 locations from Virginia to Massachusetts, with some games against Eastern, Atlantic, and New England League clubs. Finally, he listed a longer roster, including pitcher James Robinson and left fielder Ross Garrison. Andy Jackson, at third base instead of in left field, was specified as the team captain.[4]

Grant presumably enjoyed playing ball in and around North Adams, given how often he had games there with Bright's team. Also, Grant had spent at least the past two winters back home, after sampling residency in a few cities to the west and south. Therefore, the main reason he may have switched to Lamar's team was the prospect of going home even more regularly during warmer months.

The Cuban X-Giants played their first game on April 1, in New York City against

13. Lured Away (1898–1903)

Manhattan College. Beyond the four players listed in the X-Giants' battery by the *North Adams Transcript*, it's unknown who was in their lineup. The professionals won, 16–12.[5]

On April 2, the X-Giants visited the Atlantic League team in Newark, New Jersey. The home team batted first and scored twice. In the bottom half, Clarence Williams drew a walk and advanced to second after a poor pickoff throw. Grant followed with what a local paper called "a terrific drive" toward the third baseman, who stopped it, "although it was a base hit." That fielder tried a throw across the diamond anyway but it was wide of the first baseman, and Williams scored the X-Giants' first run. They tied the game in the fourth inning, but Newark led 5–2 after seven innings, when rain started pouring heavily and ended the contest early. The visitors' starting lineup was: White, 2b; Jackson, 3b; Williams, c; Grant, ss; Wilson, 1b; Garrison, cf; Jordan, rf; Howard, p; and Selden, lf. A rematch was scheduled for the next day, but the conditions may not have allowed it to be played.[6]

On April 4, the X-Giants were at Hampton, Virginia, playing in "the series for the colored championship of the South" against a team called the Chamberlans. On that date the visitors prevailed, 10–9.[7] They won the next two days, but on April 8 they lost to the Hygeia Hotel's team, 11–7, in their second game against them.[8]

They played four more games in Virginia against African American teams.[9] On April 9, they defeated the Chamberlans again. The Northerners only led, 4–2, after five innings, but something prompted their opponents to forfeit the game at that point. On April 12, they were in Petersburgh, Virginia, where they trounced a team called the Centrals, 27–5. The next day they beat the Hygeia club again, 18–8, and one more day later did likewise to the Chamberlans, 9–4.[10]

The X-Giants' first game back in their usual territory was apparently in Allentown, Pennsylvania, against that city's Atlantic League team. The home team scored four times in the first inning and added a five-run fifth on their way to an easy win, 13–2. Grant went hitless, and Allentown hitters kept the ball away from him; he had two assists and no putouts or errors.[11]

Two days later, the X-Giants played the Eastern League team in Springfield, Massachusetts. All eight of the home team's position players had major league experience at some point, and their average was above five years. Springfield quite possibly had the most talented batch of batters Grant faced since his time with Buffalo. Nevertheless, the visitors battled them to a 7–7 tie after nine innings, and Springfield only won it in the bottom of the 11th due to an error with two outs. Grant had two hits, scored a run, and played errorless ball at shortstop.[12]

On April 19 and 20, the X-Giants played in New Bedford, Massachusetts, against that city's New England League team. The game was tied at 8–8 after eight innings, but the home team scored twice in the top of the ninth to win it. In the rematch, Grant homered off of one of New Bedford's three hurlers and his team won, 11–9. He went 2-for-4 with a walk and three runs scored.[13]

On the next day, the X-Giants played Fall River's team in the same minor league. The home team won a relatively low-scoring game, 6–2. Grant went 0-for-3 with a walk and had two errors among his eight chances. The second pitcher for Fall River was 16-year-old Tom Walker, who went 5–6 for Fall River during the regular season and whose short major league career peaked with the Reds in 1904, when he went 15–8.[14]

On April 22, the X-Giants played a team in Brockton, about 30 miles to the north. Reporting about the game was minimal. The home team's pitchers were identified as

Monahan and Hatcher, but if those were actually Moynihan and Thatcher, then the home team was indeed that city's entry in the New England League. And in that case its manager was Walter Burnham, who was Grant's first manager with Meridian. In any event, the X-Giants won, 5–4, via a two-run ninth inning.[15] The X-Giants won again the next day, 15 miles away, against Taunton's team in the New England League. The scored was even at 6–6 through eighth innings and the visitors won it, 8–7.[16]

On April 25, the X-Giants returned to Fall River. They were supposed to play a three-game series, but bad weather negated the second and third games. The visitors batted against two hurlers that day, Jack Cronin and Jack Katoll. Cronin had already pitched briefly in the majors but had six more years at that level ahead of him. Katoll made his major league debut late in the 1898 season and pitched at that level three more years. Cronin and Katoll limited the visitors to two runs, while their side scored 10. Grant went 0-for-4. At shortstop, he had five putouts, three assists, and an error.[17] On April 27, the *North Adams Transcript* reported that the X-Giants had gone 11–8 in their first 19 games.[18]

The X-Giants' schedule started mixing in more collegiate competition, and an early example was a game against Holy Cross on May 4. The Giants visited their campus in Worcester, and all the scoring was limited to the first two innings. The visitors took the game, 3–2.[19]

On May 5 and 6, the X-Giants played their first home games at North Adams, against a club from nearby Albany, New York. They won both, and Grant helped considerably. Poor weather limited attendance the first day to 125 fans. "The Cubans have the happy faculty, missing in many professional teams of playing baseball as if they enjoyed it, and the whole game was filled with fun and jokes," reported the *North Adams Transcript*. The home team did all of its scoring off the second Albany pitcher, John Pappalau, a former Holy Cross pitcher who pitched two games for Cleveland in the National League 11 months earlier. Grant's hits were both doubles. He also stole a base and scored once. The weather was nice for the second game, but attendance might not have reached 100. The home team won easily, 19–5. Grant had a walk and three hits, one of which was a triple, and he scored three times. Meanwhile, Sol White homered twice. The next day, the X-Giants made the very short trip west to Grant's hometown to embarrass Williams College, 17–0.[20]

On May 9, the X-Giants beat another minor league team, Oswego of the New York State League. Grant's counterpart at shortstop was Jimmy Barrett, who made his major league debut the following year and was a lifetime .291 hitter in 10 major league seasons. The visitors won, 9–6. Grant had a double in four at-bats and scored twice. He had four putouts and four assists but also two errors. A local paper's subheadline called his crew "an Exceptionally Strong Team," and its reporter knew full well who the visitors' cleanup hitter was:

> Grant, who played second base for the Buffalo team in the old International league ten years ago, played short field yesterday. He was one of the best second basemen in the country in his day, and but for the fact that the color line was drawn would be in the game yet. There is no rule to that effect, but there is an unwritten law which debars colored players.[21]

The X-Giants were back home to host Holy Cross on May 14. Happily, the turnout was much larger, estimated from 1,200 to 1,500. The collegians' seven-run inning in the middle of the game decided it in their favor, 12–5.[22]

After a string of games up in Vermont, the X-Giants played in North Adams again on May 21. They hosted the Worcester Lyceum nine and won, 14–7. Attendance was about 800.[23] During the week following, a personal highlight for Grant came in Poughkeepsie on May 27. "In the second inning Grant gave the ball a punt and sent it screeching over the center field fence, making a home run and bringing in three men," reported a local paper. From that description, it's unclear if his blast was a grand slam. Regardless, the visitors won, 17–2.[24]

The X-Giants were back at home the next day. They beat the Greenfield team, 9–3. Memorial Day was two days later, and they hosted the Stanleys for a doubleheader, which they swept. The morning game was a tight slugfest, 15–14, but the afternoon game was a laugher, 23–1.[25] Alas, on the morning of Wednesday, June 1, Lamar announced that the Cuban X-Giants would discontinue playing in North Adams. He had made the decision a few days earlier, and made sure the team's bills were paid in full. "Saturday night he told one of his acquaintances in this city that the cause of his leaving was poor support, combined with the expense of bringing his team to this city from New York every week," the *North Adams Transcript* reported. "He said that he could do better, financially, by playing near New York Saturdays."[26]

A high point for Grant came on June 13 in Bristol, Connecticut. "The feature of the game was the hitting of Grant for the Cuban Giants, he making three hits with a total of eleven bases in four times at bat," wrote the *Hartford Courant*. That means he hit a triple and two home runs. That was about all the offense his team needed as they defeated a local team, 9–3.[27]

The most talented team the Cuban X-Giants played during June was likely Meriden's minor league team, whom they visited on June 20. At that time, Meriden occupied first place in the Connecticut State League with a record of 20–11. As usual, local papers promoted the game by mentioning Grant's connection to the city, and one even did so over two weeks in advance. None of them, however, seemed aware that the home team's manager, Jack Chapman, was Grant's manager at Buffalo. Whatever the case, Grant went 1-for-4 with a double, a stolen base, and four runs scored. At shortstop, he offset an error with four putouts and three assists. "Grant, the old Meriden player, showed that he has lost none of his sprightliness," said one local daily. "Grant, the old Meriden player, was loudly applauded when he went to the bat," reported another paper. "Howard in left made some remarkable catches, as did Grant at short."[28]

In early July, the *Pittsburgh Press* printed reminiscences by Deacon McGuire, who was more than 10 years into one of the longest major league careers ever. "Grant was one of the best fielding second basemen I ever gazed on, and as I witnessed his work I often thought of the hero he would have been if nature had given him a white skin," McGuire said. "He could throw himself in front of a ball and grab 'em at the right and left side. He was fast on the bases and a corking hitter."[29]

On July 11, the Cuban X-Giants played against a team that would be its primary opposition for the remainder of 1898, the Atlantic City Collegians. The two played together 15 more times. Atlantic City had a 15-game winning streak when it started a five-day series with the X-Giants on that date. It added two more before the visitors won, 4–3, on July 13. Through early September, the X-Giants had a record of 4–12 against them. As a sign of what the X-Giants were up against, Atlantic City played the National League's Cleveland Spiders on consecutive days. Cleveland won the first game, 2–1, but lost the next day 7–0. The only shutout Atlantic City suffered was at the hands of the Cuban X-Giants on August 24, 2–0.[30]

On Sunday, July 31, the X-Giants started playing regularly at the St. George Cricket Grounds in Hoboken. In that initial game, they stifled Hoboken's own team, 8–0. Prior to that week, the X-Giants reportedly hadn't played in or near New York City since mid-June.[31]

A noteworthy game in August took place on the 11th. For one, it was in Gloversville, near the bad Johnstown experiment Grant experienced the previous season. But for the other X-Giants who didn't experience that, it was significant due to its length, 16 innings. Grant Thatcher went the distance for the home team but lost, 10–7.[32]

Starting on Sunday, September 11, the Cuban X-Giants played a series of historical significance against the Chicago Unions. First, though, the X-Giants went to a western suburb to play a warmup game of sorts. On September 10, they played a local team in Oak Park, Illinois, and lost, 17–11.[33]

The X-Giants' first lineup against the Unions themselves was White, ss; Jackson, 3b; Williams, 1b; Grant, 2b; Jordan, c; Garrison, cf; Nelson, rf; Robinson, p; and Howard, lf. The *Chicago Tribune* said the teams were playing "for the colored baseball championship." On that first day, they played a doubleheader, but the first contest was terminated at 3–3 after 12 innings. Grant's hit was a double, and he scored once. On defense, he had seven putouts, three assists, an error, and a double play turned. In the second game, he had two hits. At second base, he had five putouts, an assist, and an error. The X-Giants won, 6–2.[34]

On September 14, the X-Giants went just across Illinois' northern border to play the Featherstone team in Sharon, Wisconsin. The game went 12 innings and the visitors lost, 6–5.[35] Two days later, the X-Giants played the Unions again in Elkhorn, Wisconsin. The X-Giants led, 10–0, after just two innings and won, 11–4.[36]

The X-Giants were supposed to play a team in Fond du Lac, Wisconsin on Saturday, September 17. Instead, the X-Giants faced the Unions in Oak Park. The Unions won, 5–3. Grant had a hit, a putout, two assists, and an error.[37]

On Sunday, September 18, the Unions hosted the X-Giants for a doubleheader. The *Tribune* mentioned only a final score for the morning game, but the *Inter Ocean* merely said the Unions won. The *Tribune* reported the score as 8–4, though a list Lamar compiled showed it as 18–4. In the afternoon game, Grant had two hits, scored twice, and provided errorless defense at second base, with seven putouts and an assist. Every little bit helped greatly, because the X-Giants barely won a slugfest, 11–10. Both papers indicated that the series would continue on September 20 in Sheldon, Illinois, about 80 miles to the south.[38]

However, on September 19, the two teams also played in Michigan City, Indiana. That game was apparently won by Chicago, 5–3. The X-Giants won the next day in Sheldon, 6–2, and the *Tribune* said they could "claim the colored championship of the world, having won four, lost one, and tied one of series of seven games with the Unions." That paper overlooked or excluded either the Unions' win in Oak Park or their win the next morning, and the game in Michigan City presumably didn't count.[39]

The X-Giants were apparently back in or near New York City by September 24, announcing the victory in the Chicago series. They didn't relax for long. On September 25, they played another minor league team, Newark of the Atlantic League, in West New York, New Jersey. They faced pitcher Frank McPartlin, who had a four-inning National League career with the Giants about 11 months later. Newark scored four runs in the first inning, but the X-Giants scored three single runs from the second through sixth innings. The latter team added just enough in the ninth inning to defeat Newark, 5–4.[40]

On October 2, the X-Giants and the Genuine Cuban Giants met for the first of three games. That first contest was at the St. George Cricket Grounds in Hoboken. Grant went hitless and made a costly error, but the X-Giants still won, 9–7. The first rematch was at the same place a week later, but Grant wasn't in the lineup. The X-Giants held off a late rally to win again, 7–6. "This places the winners in the position of champions of the colored teams in this country," the *Jersey City News* declared. The teams played one more time that month, on the 16th, in Newark. The X-Giants won a slugfest, 17–10, but coverage may have been almost nonexistent.[41]

A few days prior to that third game, there was a brief report that the X-Giants planned a trip to California, but got no farther than Chicago before giving up. Doc Howard, at a minimum, was back home on October 11 (East Liverpool, Ohio).[42] In 136 games played, Lamar reported the team's record as 101–31–4. "Next season this team will be much stronger, as several new men from the West will be included in the same," he wrote.[43]

Frank Grant's whereabouts during the offseason are unknown, and there was very little talk of the X-Giants that winter. Rather suddenly, on March 29 they played a 10-inning game against Fordham College in New York City and won, 12–11. On April 8–9, the X-Giants played tie games in Paterson, New Jersey against that city's team in the Atlantic League.[44] On April 15, the X-Giants visited Manhattan College and won, 11–8.[45] It's unknown whether Grant played in those four games.

At the St. George Cricket Grounds on April 23, the X-Giants beat Hoboken's team, 9–6. The batting order for the winners (from a box score that omitted positions for three players) was: W. Jackson; Grant, ss; A. Jackson, 3b; Wilson, 2b; Jordan, c; Smith, 1b; O. Jackson, lf; Nelson; and Selden. Over the next few days, the X-Giants played rematches against Fordham and Manhattan Colleges but lost both.[46] The month was a stark contrast to the previous few Aprils for Grant, in light of almost no minor league teams on the schedule.

On May 13, the X-Giants visited Meriden's minor league team in the Connecticut League. "Frank Grant, the humorist of the diamond, is with the Giants and will keep the spectators convulsed with laughter," one local daily said in advance. The game lasted only five innings, but there was plenty of scoring. The home team won, 9–6. Grant batted second and went 2-for-3 with a run scored.[47]

The X-Giants played in Meriden again nine days later, and their two runs in the ninth inning resulted in a 5–5 tie, after which the game was called. Grant did not have a good game. At shortstop, he had six assists but two errors. At bat he was 0-for-5, though he did steal a base and score a run.[48] The X-Giants followed that moral victory with collegiate games. They split a pair with Dartmouth in Hanover, New Hampshire, then won two against the University of Vermont.[49]

The X-Giants' most significant games in June established the dominant theme of the season. Starting on June 11, they played a series of at least 15 games against the Union Giants across Illinois, Indiana, and Wisconsin.[50] Naturally, the first game was played in Chicago, and the Unions won easily, 16–6. The visitors' lineup was: W. Jackson, lf; White, 2b; Grant, ss; A. Jackson, 3b; Jordan, c; Williams cf; Nelson, rf; Wilson, 1b; and Robinson, p. On defense, Grant played errorless ball. One of his two hits was a triple, and he scored twice.[51]

The X-Giants picked up their first win the next day 60 miles to the west, in DeKalb. It was an easy shutout, though sources disagreed on whether the X-Giants scored nine runs or 10. The Unions won a game in Dixon, Illinois, on June 15, 11–6. Though Grant made two errors at shortstop, he had another good day at the bat: Two of his three hits were doubles, and he scored two runs.[52]

On June 16, the Unions held off a late rally by the X-Giants to win again, 12–11, in Sharon, Wisconsin. Two days later, the teams played their second game back in Chicago, and the home team won it with one out in the bottom of the 10th inning, 7–6. Grant had one hit, and his errorless play at shortstop included a Grant-White-Wilson double play. The next day, the Unions came from behind in the ninth inning to win, 8–7, in nearby Hobart, Indiana.[53]

The series proved to be quite popular in at least some of the communities where games were played, and it wasn't unusual for newspapers to mention—and even name—groups of people who made trips from outlying communities to attend games. In particular, a game in Evansville, Wisconsin, drew about 2,500 people despite its population only being 2,000. "The gate receipts amounted to something over $500," a nearby paper added. The crowd in Rochester, Indiana on June 22, where the X-Giants won, 10–4, was reported as 2,000. In Fort Wayne, about 60 miles away, a newspaper was enthused for a much simpler reason, a brush with celebrities: "The Cuban Giants, a base ball club of twenty-three members, passed through the city last night, and took supper at the Harmon house."[54]

On June 25, the two teams met for the third and final time in Chicago. The Unions started a rally in the eighth inning that fell short, and the X-Giants won, 7–5. Grant was hitless but accepted five chances at second base without an error. The series didn't end with that game. At least three games were played in Wisconsin over the next few days, the last of which may have been in Sturgeon Bay on the 30th, which the X-Giants won, 12–5. Contrary to the impression the above sampling of games may have created, the X-Giants won the series. Some sources say their record was 10–5, but the Unions won more games than the five examples noted here. Of course, it's always possible that certain games didn't count, for whatever reason. Regardless, a source that credited the X-Giants with a record of 11–7 seems more accurate.[55]

On July 2, the X-Giants played at least one more game near Chicago, in Joliet, against a team called the Standards, and defeated them, 9–6. On Independence Day, the X-Giants were back in New Jersey for the first of many games against Atlantic City, their great rivals of the previous summer. The home team hosted a three-team doubleheader for 3,000 fans. The Cubans played the second game. Grant wasn't in the lineup, nor for about two weeks afterwards. He finally reemerged, seemingly no worse for wear, in a win on July 19 against a team in Mount Holly, New Jersey. He was back in the cleanup spot of the batting order and on defense at second base. One of his two hits was a double, and he scored a run. He played errorless defense, with two putouts and two assists.[56]

In mid–August, the Cuban X-Giants faced an uncommon opponent, a team from Havana called the All Cubans. They had arrived in the vicinity of New York City toward the end of July. On Sunday, August 13, the two teams met at the St. George Cricket Grounds in Hoboken. The X-Giants won, 7–3. One of Grant's two hits was a triple, and he scored once. There was a rematch a week later, and the X-Giants won again, 11–6. Grant had a hit, a run, and no errors at second base.[57]

On September 10, the X-Giants were back in Chicago for another historic series, against the *Columbia* Giants. Their leadoff hitter was often second baseman Charlie Grant, with whom Frank was frequently confused. The Cubans won the initial game,

7–4. Frank's hit was a double, and he played errorless ball at second base, with two putouts, five assists, and a double play. After that, the two teams toured Michigan.[58]

The X-Giants earned a few more wins before concluding their first week by squeezing in a game against the Detroit Tigers of the Western League (the same franchise in today's American League). The game drew about 1,000 fans. The visitors faced Jack Katoll, who had made his major league debut in 1898. The X-Giants held off a late rally to win, 10–8. Grant went 3-for-5, scored twice, and played errorless ball at second base.[59]

The X-Giants continued to play against the Columbia Giants. They split games in Oxford, Michigan, on September 20 and 21. The Columbians were scheduled to host a three-team doubleheader back in Chicago on September 24, with the X-Giants slated for the afternoon game, but that half of the event was rained out. The X-Giants won seven of the 11 games played.[60]

The X-Giants were back in Pennsylvania by September 28, for a game in Chester before 1,500 fans, but Grant wasn't in the lineup. However, he did play no later than September 30.[61] The biggest news about the X-Giants in October is that they had sailed for Cuba on October 7 and would be gone until December 1.[62] That wasn't reported widely, and it's a good thing, because it was quite inaccurate. They *did* go to Cuba, but not for a few more months. In the meantime, it's unknown where Grant spent the remainder of 1899.

In February, Frank Grant received considerable praise in print from Tom Brown, whose 17-year major league career had concluded in 1898. It was somewhat similar to the praise by Deacon McGuire in mid–1898, but much more detailed. Like McGuire, Brown knew Grant as "Hughey." Regardless, Brown said:

> One of the best second basemen the baseball game has ever seen was the colored diamond athlete, Hughey Grant, who was at his best on the Buffalo team. Grant's great forte as a fielder was his sure-thing hands. He was as near perfection in gauging swift grounders as Heine [sic] Reitz, than whom no finer hand-worker ever lived. Grant, however, had Reitz distinctly beaten as an all-around fielder, as he was faster of foot, covered larger area of ground, and was surer and quicker on double plays. He was a natural batsman, as many a twirler found to his sorrow. Grant played no favorites at the bat. High incurves, low outshoots, or slow teasers served at a shot-putting gait all looked the same to Grant. The pitchers seemed to take a fiendish delight in deliberately firing the ball at his head with the intention of driving him from the plate, but they never succeeded in taking his nerve. In the annals of the game and in the achievements of such second basemen as Burdock, Ross Barnes, Fred Pfeffer, and Yankee Robinson the name of Hugh Grant has been overlooked, though if he were a white man he would stand abreast of the others in the red-letter chapters of baseball.[63]

There's a good chance Frank Grant didn't see this at the time of publication, because he was on his way to Cuba. The X-Giants left on February 10 "by the Munson line steamer," reported one daily in New York City. "They will play a series of games with the teams of the Cuban National League at Havana, Matanzas and other cities and will end their trip April 1." Lamar reportedly took 10 players: Clarence Williams, Robinson ("the black Rusie"), John Nelson, Ray Wilson, Frank Grant, Andrew Jackson, "Chesty" Carter, "Delehanty" Stewart, Bob Parker, and Nat McClennan.[64]

Their first game was on Friday, February 23, before 3,000 fans in Havana. The X-Giants won, 7–5. Grant played second base, had two hits, and scored once. Two days later, the visitors won again, 6–5, and the crowd numbered 4,500. The X-Giants were down two runs after eight innings but scored twice in the ninth by bunching three hits and a walk. Grant played errorless ball at second base, with three putouts and three assists. On offense he had a hit, a sacrifice, and a run scored. His nine's lineup was: Jordan, ss (not named among the original 10 on the trip); Wilson, 1b; Grant, 2b; Williams, c; Jackson, 3b; Nelson, p; Robinson, cf; Parker, lf; and McClennan, rf.[65]

The club from the United States won again on March 2, 7–3. They again played in Havana, but their opposition was the San Francisco team. Grant's eight chances included two errors, but on offense he contributed two hits. On March 7, the X-Giants lost their first game on the big island, to the Criollos in Havana, 6–4. Grant played errorless ball at second base, with six putouts, and had two hits.[66]

In the middle of this trip, J.M. Bright of the Genuine Cuban Giants announced that he had reengaged Frank Grant to serve as his team captain and second baseman. Bright planned a 10-week western trip starting on May 28, and it would include 15 games against the Columbia Giants in Chicago. Bright specified Wisconsin and Kansas City as potential destinations, and the club would return through Indiana and Ohio. He also reported that both teams would attempt to play at the Exposition Universelle, that is, the world's fair in Paris, France. If arrangements could be made, they would depart on August 1.[67]

On April 1, the Criollos beat the X-Giants again, 6–4. That reportedly gave the visitors a record of 13–2.[68] As of this writing, the database at seamheads.com has detailed statistics compiled from 14 of 16 games, and Frank Grant tied three teammates for the most runs batted in, with 10. His batting average was a solid .279. On the night of April 15, the X-Giants arrived at New York via the Munson Line's steamer *Curityba*. The very next day, the Cuban X-Giants played a game in Weehawken. Grant wasn't in that lineup, but eight of the nine men who did play had just returned from Cuba with him.[69]

It's unclear whether Grant's genuine Giants played games in the second half of April, and box scores for them were scarce in May. On May 13, they lost in Jersey City to a team called the Jerseys, 5–3. The Giants' lineup was: Hill (probably Pete), lf; Brown, cf; Grant, 2b; Parker, rf; Butts, ss; Bailey, c; J. Hill, 3b; Watkins, 1b; and Bell, p.[70]

The Genuine Cuban Giants made newspapers nationwide later in May, but only by association. World heavyweight champion James J. Jeffries had taken up umpiring in his spare time, and 1,920 people were in attendance on May 20 when he called a game between the Giants and a local team in Paterson, New Jersey. In one account, Grant only showed up beneath the line score for having stolen a base. The Giants lost,

The Cuban X-Giants in Cuba, early 1900. Frank Grant was with the team at this time and may be pictured, though no one has definitively identified him in this photograph.

13. Lured Away (1898–1903)

9–7. By the time the *St. Louis Post-Dispatch* and other papers covered this a few days afterwards, the crowd had somehow grown to 6,000. Fittingly, that particular report was under the headline, "Gossip of the Game."[71]

But Grant's Giants didn't escape Jeffries' shadow after that one game. Starting on May 25, papers from coast to coast, and even into Canada, made a big deal about another game to be umpired by Jeffries. He was scheduled to call a game in Trenton between the Genuine Cuban Giants and another African American team, the Princeton Giants. However, the field to be used for the game belonged to the local Y.M.C.A., and its leadership had no tolerance for giving a prizefighter such a showcase. Two Trenton papers there made no reference to the Jeffries controversy in their accounts, though both reported the full name of the umpire, Harry Catto (Grant's old teammate). The *Times* said the game was "to decide the colored baseball championship of the State." Alas, chilliness and a threat of rain limited attendance to about 200 paying customers. The Cuban Giants won, 17–11.[72]

Scorecard from Cuba, early 1900. Frank Grant is the third batter in the bottom half.

On June 10, the Genuine Cuban Giants lost to Niagara University, 5–4, before 2,000 fans, and from June 12–16, they played in and around Ashtabula, Ohio. This is important to note because the Cuban X-Giants barnstormed with the Chicago Unions across southern Wisconsin from June 11 to 15 and then played in Sycamore, Illinois, on June 16, yet newspapers rarely printed the "X'" to distinguish them from Grant's Genuine team that week.[73] Of course, the scarcity of box scores or even line scores identifying batteries didn't help. The possibility for confusion was amplified on June 17, when Grant's Genuine Cuban Giants played in Chicago against the Columbia Giants. The latter team still included Charlie Grant as well as Grant "Home Run" Johnson, but in 1900 it also included Sol White. Previews in at least three Chicago dailies singled out Frank Grant among the players and noted that the umpire would be Tony Mullane, a well-known retired major leaguer who is a member of the Cincinnati Reds Hall of Fame.[74]

The Cuban Giants were held to three hits. The Columbians didn't generate much more offense, but they beat the visitors, 3–1. Frank Grant got on base at least once, after being hit by a pitch. He made an error but had five putouts and five assists. Each of the second basemen named Grant turned a double play. "Frank Grant's work at second base was the feature of the game," said the *Daily Inter Ocean*.[75]

Over the next few days, the Unions apparently played across northern Illinois with the X-Giants, while activity by Grant's Giants is uncertain. Papers did at least provide a few clues to the identity of the Unions' opposition, such as identifying their battery or even calling them the X-Giants. On the other hand, it's possible the Union Giants mixed in games with the Genuine Cuban Giants. Whatever the case, at least one paper mixed up the two traveling teams from the East Coast. In a preview of the Unions' game played on June 19 in Belvidere, Illinois, a local paper mentioned that "the short-stop of the Cuban Giants is said to draw one of the largest salaries paid any man in the business." The X-Giants didn't have a middle infielder with any particular star power, so that comment was almost certainly about Frank Grant.[76]

On either side of June 22, the Chicago Unions played near and in Sterling, Illinois, against a team of Cuban Giants. Meanwhile, on June 22, the Columbia Giants played a team of Cuban Giants more than 200 miles away, in Cassopolis, Michigan. The latter team was presumably Frank Grant's. The Columbia Giants won that game, 9–4.[77]

On Sunday, June 24, there was no question that Grant's Cuban Giants played the Columbia Giants. They met at the latter's ballpark, and Mullane again served as the umpire. The Cubans jumped out to a 3–0 lead in the first inning, but by the end of the third inning, the game was knotted, 4–4. The home team added five runs, but the Cubans countered with three in their half of the seventh. The teams both scored in the ninth inning, but the visitors fell short and lost, 10–9. Frank Grant's hit was a double, and he scored twice. His errorless defense at second base included a double play.[78]

On July 1, the Genuine Cuban Giants faced a local team in Erie, Pennsylvania. The visitors won, 7–3. "Grant, their second baseman, was with the original Giants, and in spite of long service and increasing years, which would have sunk most players into oblivion, is still as frisky as a kitten," the *Erie Daily Times* commented. "His superior as a baseman probably never played the national game, and except for his color he would have been the wonder of the big league."[79]

Less than three weeks later,

World heavyweight champion James J. Jeffries was going to umpire this game, but the local Y.M.C.A. wouldn't allow him to set foot on their grounds. From the *Trenton Times*, May 24, 1900.

John M. Bright announced that he had released Frank Grant.[80] Sure enough, he wasn't in their lineup during the first few days of August. At the same time, he wasn't in the much more frequently printed box scores of the X-Giants, either, from July 20 into mid–August. However, he did rejoin Bright's team by the time of a game in Hoboken on August 26, and was in that lineup again for a game in Rutherford, New Jersey.[81]

Within a week, Frank Grant changed teams abruptly. On September 14, he played with the Columbia Giants in Detroit, against the D.A.C. nine. The Giants' lineup was Charlie Grant, 2b; White, 1b; Patterson, lf; Buckner, p; Frank Grant, ss; Johnson, c; Binga, 3b; P. Bell, cf; and P. Ward, rf. The Giants won easily, 19–3. Frank went 2-for-6 with four runs scored and played errorless ball. A box score showed him with two putouts and no assists, but the game's only double play was C. Grant to F. Grant to White.[82]

On September 24, the Columbia Giants played the first of two games against Connie Mack's Milwaukee Brewers of the American League (the season before the AL became a major league). Though the game was only about 50 miles to the southwest of Milwaukee, in Delavan, it apparently received minimal or no coverage in Milwaukee's daily papers. The game went 10 innings and was called after that, a 1–1 tie. The crucial hit for Milwaukee was by Pete Dowling, who may have pitched for them, though he did play in the outfield once for them during the regular season. In his four major league seasons, he was a pitcher exclusively. "Grant in the ninth batted the ball over the fence for a home run, which tied the score," read what might be the only account of the game. Trouble is, there was probably more than one Grant in the Giants' lineup that day.[83]

The two teams met in Joliet, Illinois, for their rematch, and Dowling definitely pitched for Milwaukee. The teams played extra innings again, 11 total this time, and the Brewers won, 4–3. Frank Grant went hitless. He played first base and made 18 putouts plus an error.[84]

On September 29, the Giants played a local team in Racine, Wisconsin, for which the home team brought in a 20-year-old pitcher from Toledo's minor league team. That was future Hall of Famer Addie Joss, who made his American League debut in 1902. Frank Grant went 1-for-4 off Joss, with a double. The Giants won, 9–3.[85]

They ended the month playing a team that included four members of the American League champion Chicago White Stockings. Pitching for the opposition was Chauncey Fisher, a five-year National Leaguer. Frank Grant had a hit and a run. He also played errorless ball at first base, with 10 putouts. The Giants won, 5–3.[86]

On the morning of October 7, the Giants hosted the Chicago Unions. They game was scoreless after nine innings, after which the teams agreed that they had had enough. Frank Grant went hitless. At first base, he had 14 putouts. That same day, the Giants played the "White Stockings" again, though they faced a pitcher named Wiggs. That was probably Jimmy Wiggs, who played parts of three major league seasons starting in 1903. The Giants lost a five-inning game, 8–4.[87]

A few days later, it was announced that two games between the Giants and Unions on the upcoming Saturday and Sunday would be played at Chicago's National League ballpark "for the colored championship of the world," according to the *Chicago Daily News*. "This is the first time in years that President Hart has allowed the grounds to be used for other than league games." In another preview, the *Chicago Tribune* noted that the umpire would be Bobby Caruthers, presumably the retired pitcher who went 218-99 in a nine-year major league career.[88]

On Saturday, October 13, the two teams each scored twice in the fourth inning, then not again through the ninth. The Unions won it in the extra frame, 3–2. Frank Grant went hitless but also played errorless ball at first base. That game did take place at the West Side National League Park, but the *Tribune* noted that Sunday's game would be at the Unions' home field. It's possible that no Chicago papers even reported a score of Sunday's game, but a paper in Michigan reported a few days later that the Giants won it, and the *Tribune* did imply on October 21 that the series was tied. That was in a preview of an additional game at the Giants' ballpark that very day. According to the *Detroit Free Press*, that game "was declared no contest because only eight innings were played before darkness set in."[89]

Players from the Unions and Giants united to face some white major leaguers on October 28 and November 4, and for the rematch, either Charlie or Frank Grant was expected to play second base. However, coverage of the games wasn't very detailed. Still, the white teams lost both times.[90]

It's unclear where Frank Grant spent the winter, but his name came up in March, even though the Grant in question wasn't him, but Charlie. Famously, starting at the end of February, Baltimore owner/manager John McGraw decided to bring a plot element of Bliss Perry's novel to life by trying to pass Charlie Grant off as a Native American under a fake name, in which case the major leagues' unofficial color line wouldn't apply. When the ruse was uncovered, some media outlets reported that it was *Frank* Grant who McGraw had recruited under false pretenses.[91]

Instead, by the end of March, Frank Grant had reportedly signed anew with the Genuine Cuban Giants, and as captain. John M. Bright's plan was to base the team in Newark. The team's first game was scheduled for April 14.[92] The team did play on that date, against the Brooklyn Field Club. The Giants were clobbered, 11–2, though Grant did swat a triple for his side. Their lineup was: Penno, 3b; Bell, ss; Grant, 2b; Watkins, 1b; Jones, p; Green, lf; Buck, cf; Garcia, c; and Dumont, rf.[93]

Shortly after this game, a team in Pittsburgh called the Barnes Colored Americans, under the management of Bud Fowler, claimed that it had signed Grant. Box scores of Barnes games might not exist during their season's first two months, but that also applied to the Genuine Cuban Giants during May, so it's possible he moonlighted with that other team for up to six weeks. Minimal coverage of the Giants could've been a sign of a team in some disarray in the absence of its captain and star. Whatever the case, on June 2 he was in the lineup of the Cuban Giants (if he hadn't been with them in all of May). They lost to the Hollywood Inn team in or near Yonkers, New York, 2–1. Grant then appeared in Cuban Giants box scores with regularity, such as one detailing a loss on July 6 against the Harrisburg Athletic Club, 7–2.[94]

Enthusiasm for a visit by Grant's Giant's probably peaked a few days later in Potsdam, New York. Potsdam had a minor league team that season in the Northern New York League. In promoting their games on July 12 and 13, someone printed up a special handout of some sort, and two days in advance, a local paper mentioned the Cuban Giants at least eight times on a single page. "See the funny antics of Frank Grant, Wm. Kelly and Johnny Watkins with the Cuban Giants at Potsdam Friday," the paper said in one of those spots.[95]

The home team won the first game in front of 400 fans, 12–5, but Grant's club won the rematch, 6–2. The visitors' lineup for the first game varied considerably from the lineup in mid–April: Kelly, cf; Grant, 2b; Wilson, p; Day, 1b; Watkins, c; Miller, 2b;

Garcia, rf; Samson (or Sampson), ss; and Green, lf. Samson pitched for the Giants in the second game. Potsdam's pitcher for the final three innings was Dike Varney, who went 1–1 in three American League games for Cleveland a year later. The Giants scored two insurance runs off him in the ninth inning. A Potsdam resident named Finnegan (or Finnigan, as a second paper spelled it) played short for the Cubans. The basketball team of the Potsdam Normal School (today the State University of New York at Potsdam) did have a forward by that name. It's likely that the Cuban Giants included a white college player on July 13.[96]

As additional examples of games the Genuine Cuban Giants played that summer, with Grant in the lineup, they won a game in Penn Yan, New York on August 13, they eked out a victory on September 8 before 2,000 fans in Brooklyn, and they added another victory there on September 22.[97] All told, 1901 was easily the least noteworthy season of his career to that point. Happily, it was not a major drop-off, or even the start of a downward trend.

In 1902, the first team that claimed Frank Grant as one of its own may have been the Philadelphia Giants, founded by Sol White and *Philadelphia Evening Item* sportswriter Walter Schlichter. Toward the end of February, he was among a dozen players listed on Philadelphia's roster. Grant did join them about two months later. However, in a game toward the end of March, a player named Grant was at third base for the Genuine Cuban Giants.[98] The Philadelphia Giants didn't play their first game until April 23, so Frank Grant may have played for his old club simply to get some real-game action; the Genuine Cuban Giants had at least two more games scheduled prior to April 23.[99]

Frank Grant definitely played in the Philadelphia Giants' first game, on April 23, though four days later the Genuine Cuban Giants had a second baseman named Grant in a game on Long Island, before more than 3,000 fans.[100] If it was Frank, it's possible that he switched back to his old team briefly because he sensed the game would be important to his old teammates, as the size of the crowd at Long Island indicated. Another possibility is that the Genuine Cuban Giants borrowed

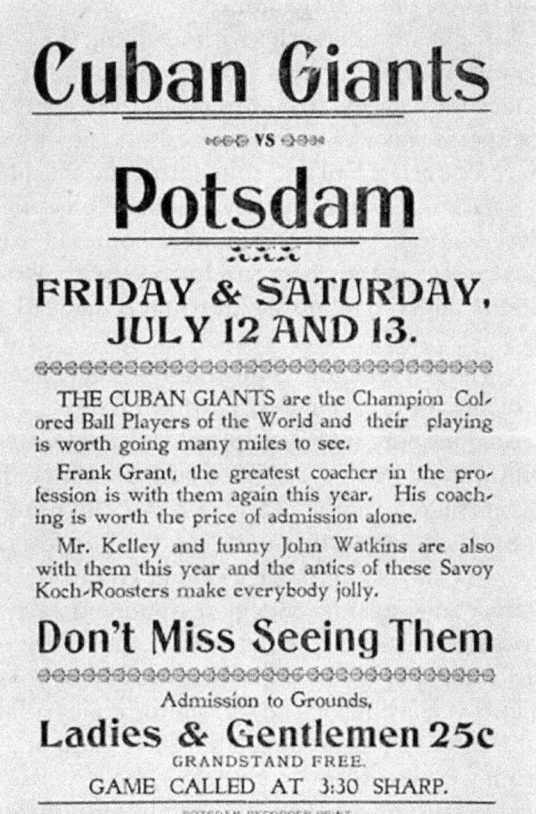

A leaflet promoting mid–1901 games. In the second, a white college student may have played shortstop for the Cuban Giants.

Charlie Grant for the game; he was on the Cuban X-Giants at that time. Whatever the case, no Grant was in the Genuine Cuban Giants' lineup on May 7 or in later box scores.[101]

On April 23, 1902, the starting lineup of the Philadelphia Giants was: Smith, 1b; White, ss; Grant, 2b; Williams, c; Hill, 3b; Payne, lf; Bell, rf; Bolen, cf; and Carter, p. Bell took over the pitching at some point, and Trusty went into right field. They defeated a team from Camden, 12–4. Grant had three hits, including a double. He didn't see much action on defense, but he did turn a triple play with White and Smith. The next two days, the Giants played the All-Virginia team, the "colored Champions of the South," as Schlichter's newspaper called them.[102]

On April 28, Grant played in the first of three games between the Philadelphia Giants and Reading's minor league team in the Pennsylvania State League. The home team won easily, 15–5, but Grant had a decent game. His hit was a double, he scored twice, and he contributed a sacrifice hit. He played errorless ball at second base with six putouts. After a gap of two days, the Philadelphia Giants won the other two games at Reading, on consecutive days, by scores of 8–7 and 3–1. Grant went either 2-for-4 or 1-for-4 in the middle game (depending on which Reading paper's box score was correct), and 1-for-4 in the third game.[103]

Right after the series with Reading, the Giants won at least four consecutive games against another African American team, the West Jersey Giants. At least three of the games were played in Atlantic City. The game on May 5 drew 1,000 fans. Grant's hit in that game was a double, and he stole the only base that afternoon. At second base, he played errorless ball and concluded a double play begun by White.[104]

Grant was particularly valuable to his new team a month into their season, in a close slugfest against Altoona. He homered over the left field fence in the third inning, and he scored the tying run in the eighth shortly after his triple drove in White. The Giants added one more run to take the lead, but lost the game in the ninth inning, 11–9.[105]

The Philadelphia Giants had two games of some historical significance during the first week of June. On the 3rd, they played in a rare night game against a team called the Cosmopolitans at Philadelphia's Columbia Park. The novelty only drew about 400 fans, who watched a slugfest filled with 15 errors. The Giants won, 15–13.[106] On June 6, the Giants played another African American nine, the Orient Giants, at the same ballpark. The Giants won easily, 20–1. Grant scored five runs and had five hits.[107]

In contrast to Bright's Cuban Giants, in 1902 White and Schlichter didn't mix in many games against collegiate opponents. An exception was the Bloomsburg Literary Institute and State Normal School, the baseball team of which, according to a Pennsylvania newspaper some distance away, was ranked "well up with the larger colleges." The Giants won a doubleheader from the collegians on May 27 and split games with them on June 23 and 24. Eight days later, Dave Williams of the home team made his major league debut with the Boston Americans.[108]

White and Schlichter tended to limit their travels to Pennsylvania, New Jersey, and Delaware. The Giants were sustained by games against Camden and the Wilmington Athletic Association sprinkled frequently throughout their schedule. The farthest the team may have traveled was into western New York for some games in the middle of August. They played few games in or near New York City, and may never have gone into New England.[109] Therefore, Grant probably didn't play at all back in Berkshire County

13. Lured Away (1898–1903)

or up in Meriden, as he did in so many other years, though he did play in Harrisburg a few times.[110]

Grant had huge games offensively on three consecutive Mondays beginning August 18. On that first date, he and the Giants defeated the Haverling club at Bath, New York, 22–10. Grant went 5-for-6 with three doubles and three runs scored. On August 25, the Giants beat "Jackson's" nine in Mahanoy City, Pennsylvania, 13–2. Grant again scored three times, while his four hits included a double and two triples.[111] On September 1, the Giants swept a doubleheader in Easton, Pennsylvania, from "the Ingersoll team, champions of the Lehigh Valley," as the *Philadelphia Inquirer* called them. In the first game, Grant had a single and a sacrifice hit. In the afternoon, during a nine-inning slugfest, he had six hits, including a double.[112] While the opposing pitchers in those two games may not have been particularly good, none of the other Giants came close to matching Grant's slugging.

The Philadelphia Giants played two very significant games toward the end of their season. They faced none other than the American League's pennant winners, the Philadelphia Athletics. The first game was on October 2 and drew 800 fans to Columbia Park. The starting pitcher for the Athletics was Bert Husting, who had gone 14–5 for the Athletics that season. He was relieved by Highball Wilson, who had gone 7–4. Grant had a hit and scored once. He also contributed errorless defense at second base, with three putouts, seven assists, and a double play turned. The Giants actually led after four innings, 1–0, but lost, 8–3.[113]

The two teams also met at the same ballpark on October 6. The lineup for the Giants was: White, ss; Grant, 2b; Smith, 1b; Payne, cf; Day, lf; Nelson, 3b; Farrell, c; Bell, p; and Griffin, rf. The Athletics led, 9–1, after five innings, but the Giants had late rallies that got them close. The Athletics won, 13–9. In addition to Wilson, the Athletics' pitchers were Fred Mitchell, a five-year major leaguer, and outfielder Socks Seybold, who pitched in the minor leagues during 1895 and 1896. Grant had three hits, including a double, plus a run scored. His fielding was as impressive as in the other game. He had seven putouts, three assists, and no errors, and had a hand in two double plays.[114]

In early 1903, the Philadelphia Giants' leadership helped form the National Association of Independent Base Ball Clubs, for the mutual protection of members' rosters. Therefore, when Frank Grant was reported on that club's roster to this new organization toward the end of March, it was more official than any such grouping of teams since he was in Organized Baseball.[115] Decades later, Sol White recalled that the players in 1903 were put on salaries ranging from $60 to $90 a month.[116]

The first game of 1903 for the Giants may have been at Wallace's Grounds in Brooklyn on April 19, against the Ridgewoods. The batting order for the Giants was: Monroe, ss; Binga, 3b; Patterson, lf; Buckner, cf; White, 1b; Grant, 2b; Footes, c; Bell, rf; and Carter, p. Attendance was reported at a staggering 10,000. Grant went hitless but scored twice, and the Giants won, 16–12.[117]

One change for the 1903 Philadelphia Giants that pleased Sol White was that they were able to play lucrative games against the Atlantic City Collegians. For Frank Grant, this would have been pleasing if his son had moved there by then, with his maternal grandfather. One of Grant's better games in Atlantic City that year was on May 26, though not against the Collegians. He had two hits and scored twice in a 17–2 win against a team called Dale's Athletics.[118]

Grant had a couple of really good games not long after Independence Day. On July

The 1902 Philadelphia Giants. Frank Grant is seated, second from left (National Baseball Hall of Fame and Museum, Cooperstown, NY).

9, he scored three runs and had three hits, including a homer, to help the Giants win in Chester, Pennsylvania, 10–8. He batted second in the batting order instead of sixth. One week later, the Giants won their third game of the season in Harrisburg, and Grant went 4-for-5 with two doubles and a triple. If his son was still living in Harrisburg then, one hopes he attended that game. The final score was 10–3.[119]

On August 17, the Philadelphia Giants took part in a three-team doubleheader in Wilmington. The home team played the Cuban X-Giants in the second game. The first game was umpired by the famous former boxing champion, John L. Sullivan. That contest was scoreless until the sixth inning. Grant drove a runner in from first base with a double, though Sullivan called Grant out when he tried to stretch his hit into a triple. The Giants eventually won, 2–1.[120] At this point, the Giants had reportedly played 99 games. Their record was 76–23, and all were considered road games.[121]

A few days into September, the Philadelphia Giants and the Cuban X-Giants agreed to play up to eight games in four states to decide "the colored championship of the world," as the *Philadelphia Inquirer* called the series. The two teams hadn't played one another previously. The winner of the series was to be awarded 60 percent of the receipts. Including a doubleheader on the second day, the games were originally scheduled for September 12 through18 (although rain interfered twice).[122]

This series has been well-documented, including by the database at seamheads. com. Seven games were played, but the Philadelphia Giants won just two of them. Future Hall of Famer Rube Foster won all four of his games for the X-Giants and had an astonishing Earned Run Average of 0.75. Grant's batting average was a modest .250, though

The 1903 Philadelphia Giants. Frank Grant is in the front, on the right (National Baseball Hall of Fame and Museum, Cooperstown, NY).

only White at .360 and Monroe (who played in just three games) at .273 hit for higher average in the Philadelphia lineup.[123]

In the first game, at Philadelphia, the home team's batting order was: Patterson, lf; Binga, 3b; Grant, 2b; Monroe, ss; White, 1b; Buckner, rf; Footes, c; Nelson, cf; and Bell, p. Foster pitched for the X-Giants, and their leadoff hitter was Charlie Grant, also playing second base. Frank Grant went hitless, and the X-Giants won, 4–2.[124]

The teams played a doubleheader at Wallace's Grounds in Brooklyn the next day. The first game drew 3,000 fans and the second 7,000. The X-Giants won in the morning, 8–1, but Philadelphia won in the afternoon, 5–3. Frank Grant had a hit in each game, and he scored in the second game. However, he also committed three errors at second base in that victory. One Brooklyn daily's

Caricature of Frank Grant by cartoonist A.F. Thomas from Brooklyn's *Daily Standard Union*, September 15, 1903.

coverage of the twin bill was beneath five cartoons by an artist named A.F. Thomas, and one of them showed "Grant as a coacher." It was probably Frank and not Charlie, because the artist used an "X" belt buckle to denote one of the Cuban X-Giants in the sketch right next to Grant's.[125] All things considered, from a modern viewpoint it's the least offensive of the five.

On September 14, Foster hurled a three-hitter at Trenton to beat Philadelphia, 3–1. Grant had one of his team's two singles. Philadelphia won its second and final game in Camden the next day, 3–0. In the seventh inning, Grant's lone hit in that game moved White into scoring position, and both soon scored important insurance runs.[126] The same teams were to compete again in Wilmington the following two days, but rain cancelled the first game and terminated the second one after two innings.

Frank Grant had his best game of the series in Harrisburg on September 18, though on the wrong end of a 12–3 drubbing. He went 2-for-4. The rivals met one extra time on September 25, in Camden, where Foster hurled another three-hitter, which he won, 2–0. Grant went hitless. His lone error in the game cost Philadelphia a run, as did Sol White's in the same inning.[127]

Grant's last game with the Philadelphia Giants may have been on October 7, in Harrisburg. He went 2-for-5 in a 7–1 win. Surprisingly, Sol White didn't play for the Giants that day.[128] Frank Grant would not be a Philadelphia Giant in 1904, though Charlie Grant would.

14

Exit from the Game (1904 and After)

As the familiar saying goes, it's nice to be wanted. Prior to 1904, it wasn't unusual for more than one team to announce, around the same time, that it had Frank Grant on its roster. However, after his days in Organized Ball, such overlapping claims tended to be limited to the preseason. Even after his long stint with the (Genuine) Cuban Giants, when he switched to the Cuban X-Giants for two years, and continuing with his two years as a Philadelphia Giant, he was largely a one-team player within the context of regular seasons. But starting in 1904, it was often difficult to keep track of which team Frank Grant was on. That may have been due, at least in part, to those teams tending to have lower profiles than the Philadelphia Giants. Some of those new teams may have lacked stability and consistent leadership. Grant had provided the latter for Bright's Cuban Giants, but his new teams probably had leaders already, at least nominally. Because his remaining teams were generally less accomplished and lacked multiple stars like the Philadelphia Giants, confirming that teams which claimed him *actually got him into games* (or at least had somebody named Grant in their lineups) is often difficult. Also, it's likely that some of his new teams didn't actually announce his acquisition; he simply started playing for them, without fanfare. The fact that Charlie Grant was a second baseman in the same part of the country during this time had the potential to be confusing, though from 1904 through 1907 his playing may have been limited to the Philadelphia Giants (after which he joined Sol White's Philadelphia Quaker Giants).

The first team to claim 38-year-old Frank Grant in 1904 may have been a team in Pittsburgh, starting in February. The team's name was uncertain early on, but its backers were John A. Brown and John Bates. "Among the players already secured are James Robinson, of the X-Cuban Giants, and Frank Grant, the colored Dunlap, who played with the Philadelphia Giants," said the *Pittsburgh Daily Post*. "Frank Miller, the crack local pitcher and all around player, will coach the team, which will be open to meet all the strong teams in this section." Around the middle of March, this team was called the Smoky City Colored Giants and was to be under the management of Jimmy McKeever, a local ballplayer and umpire. Among the players mentioned then was "Henry Grant" of the Cuban Giants, presumably referring to Henry *Gant*. In April, another *Post* overview of these Colored Giants alluded to how "one of them gained a National reputation as a member of the Buffalo team." A few days later, a different Pennsylvania paper specified that Frank Grant would play second base while Gant, presumably Henry, would split time between first base and the outfield. Gant did show up as right fielder in a few of this team's box scores in May and June, but there was never any Grant as well. The *Post* mentioned Frank Grant one more time, in mid–June, as having just been signed at that point, but the subsequent reality remained that he didn't appear in box scores.[1]

On April 3, the Royal Giants, "the champion-colored professionals of New York," opened their season against a New York team called the Marquettes. It's possible no newspaper printed a box score, but later that month the manager of the Marquettes happened to mention that "Grant of the Cuban X Giants played third base for them" in a letter to a New Jersey newspaper.[2] Charlie Grant was a Cuban X-Giant much more recently than Frank Grant was, but plenty of sportswriters back then mixed up those two ballplayers, as well as confusing the X-Giants with the Genuine Cuban Giants. In fact, Charlie Grant had signed with the Philadelphia Giants by then, and his new team happened to play on April 3 (albeit also in or near New York City).[3]

In April 1904, the Genuine Cuban Giants were led by a former teammate, "Pop" Watkins. On the 18th, the *Morning Call* in Paterson, New Jersey previewed a Giants game scheduled for six days later and noted that Frank Grant and Clarence Williams were expected to play. A few days closer to game day, the same paper made it crystal clear it wasn't confusing Grant with someone else by alluding to his time with Buffalo: "Even at that time Frank Grant was acknowledged to be one of the best infielders in the country, and only the fact that the color line was drawn pretty close kept him out of the major league."[4]

The Cuban Giants did play on April 24, and their lineup was: Grant, 2b; Lavelle, lf; Nelson, ss; Watkins, 1b; Wallace, 3b; Abbott, cf; Williams, rf; Garcia, c; and Lyons, p. Paterson's pitcher for the first seven innings was George Merritt, who had played briefly with the Pittsburgh Pirates each of the previous three years. Though he played mostly in the outfield for the Pirates, he did retire with a 3–0 record as a pitcher. The home team won, 5–3, but Grant went 3-for-5, stole a base, and scored once. He played errorless defense, with three putouts and three assists.[5]

Grant was also in that team's lineup when they won a game out toward Lake Ontario on May 1. Though he was dropped to sixth in the batting order, he had two hits, a steal, and a run scored as the Giants won, 6–4.[6] The Cuban Giants apparently didn't receive much newspaper coverage over the following two weeks, but Grant wasn't in their lineup in box scores printed by the *Philadelphia Inquirer* on May 17 and May 22. Grant also didn't play for the Cuban Giants on May 28, when they were near his birthplace in Berkshire County, Massachusetts.[7]

In April and May, there was a player named Grant on the roster of the Princeton X-Giants, whom Frank Grant had played against in 1900 when they were simply the Princeton Giants. In his first appearances that season, he played outfield but was soon a middle infielder. In May, a paper in New Brunswick, New Jersey wrote that "Williams and Grant, former Cuban Giants, who are well known here, are on the team." The Princeton Giants had a shortstop named Grant the previous season, but that was when Frank Grant was a fixture on the Philadelphia Giants. The latter team even played at least one game on the same afternoon as the Princeton Giants: On June 27, 1903, the Princeton Giants and that third Grant played in Asbury Park, New Jersey, while Frank Grant and the Philadelphia Giants played 75 miles away in Camden.[8]

In late May, Frank Grant was probably with a team called by two names. The "Colored Opequon Giants, of Savannah, Ga.," or sometimes the *Orpheum* Giants, included "Grant, Auster, Abbott and King Kelly, all of [the] Cuban Giants, and Schenck, Simmons and Dudley, of [the] Philadelphia Giants." Only two of those players were mentioned in another preview of a game about two weeks later, when these Giants were said to include "such well-known players as Grant, Reno [presumably Penno], Abbott, Nelson and Devoe, formerly of the Cuban Giants."[9] On Sunday, June 13, the Opequon team was trounced by the Brightons, 16–8, before 1,320 fans. The visitors' lineup was: L. Buck, lf; King Kelly, 3b; Grant, 2b; Penno, ss; Abbott, p; Love, cf; M. Kelly, rf; Demont, 1b; and Tucker, c. Grant went 2-for-4 with a double and three runs scored. An "Orpheum Giants" box score was printed on June 23, but it included no Grant.[10]

Within a few days of June 13, some of the Opequon Giants appear to have broken away to form a team simply called the Colored Giants. On June 19, a shortstop named Grant played for them against the Ontario Field Club of Harlem. The game drew 2,500 fans. The score was knotted at 2–2 after seven innings, but three runs in the next frame by the Ontario team produced the final score. The lineup for the Colored Giants was: Smith, 1b; Kelly, 3b; Grant, ss; Butler, 2b; Devoe, c; Richardson, cf; Matthews, lf; Marley, rf; and Valentine, p.[11] Frank Grant was specifically named as a member of the New York Colored Giants in a New Jersey newspaper around this time, and on July 9 another confirmed that the New York Colored Giants included "Pop" Grant, "one of the best known negroes playing baseball," at shortstop.[12]

Of course, it's possible that Grant played on more than one team during the same period of time, especially if neither of them played as frequently as his teams of yesteryear did. That may have been true for him in September, though in July and August, Grant seems to have played only with the New York Colored Giants. As examples of their short traveling radius centered on New York City, they played in Plainfield, New Jersey on July 16, in Stamford, Connecticut, on August 14, and in Asbury Park, New Jersey, on September 8. The game at Stamford went 14 innings, and Grant scored the decisive run. Among his three hits were a triple and double.[13]

In mid–October, the New York Colored Giants made a short trip to Hackensack to play a minor league team, the Paterson club of the Hudson River League. Paterson's lineup included one former National League player, Dick Cogan, who had spent a little time with three different teams from 1897 to 1900. Paterson won, 11–6. Grant went 1-for-3 with a double plus a stolen base. Box scores in two newspapers differed considerably, even with regard to the Giants' batting order and names of players, but the eight players named in both box scores were W. Jackson, lf; Nelson, ss; Grant, 1b; Kelly, 3b; Butts, 2b; Carrillo, c; Booker, cf; and Penno, p.[14]

In 1905, Frank Grant lived in New York City, and he appeared in that year's State census. He had a wife, listed as "Rellia," though her full first name was likely Aurelia. Her ages in that census and 1910's don't align. Her municipal death record, which showed her name as Aurelia Moore Grant, indicated she was about three years older than her husband. That record named her parents as Harry Feat and Mary Hasel. In 1905, Aurelia had a job as a laundress, while Frank was identified as a ball player, no great surprise. Living with them at 6 Minetta Street in Manhattan were his adopted children, 22-year-old Frank Moore, who was working as a porter, and 8-year-old Irene Harris, a student. She and Frank Moore are mysteries. In the 1910 census, Aurelia was listed as having only one child (still living at that time). It's possible that Frank Moore was her nephew or a much younger brother-in-law and not her son.

On April 2, the New York Colored Giants had a rematch against the minor league team they played the previous October, in Paterson. About 1,200 fans braved chilliness to watch a close game which the Giants lost, 5–2. Their batting order was: Grant, 1b;

Nelson, 3b; Devoe, c; Carrillo, ss; Smith, cf; Butler, 2b; Booker, rf; Penno, lf; and Dawson, p. Grant's hit was a double, and he scored once. The Giants ended April with a loss to the Paramount Field Club, 9–6, before a crowd of 2,400. Grant led his team with three hits and two runs scored.[15]

On May 13, the Colored Giants defeated a pitcher named Red Waller in Westfield, New Jersey. He's presumably the minor league pitcher who had a one-inning National League career with the New York Giants four years later. One newspaper blamed his 8–4 loss on a sore pitching arm. Nevertheless, Frank Grant went 4-for-4 off him, with two doubles.[16]

The Colored Giants didn't seem to get much coverage of their games in June and July. An exception was on June 24, when they played their second game of the season in Yonkers, New York, against that city's Hollywood team. The visitors rallied for three runs in the top of the ninth inning, only to lose the game in the bottom half, 8–7. Grant had a good game on offense. He went 3-for-5 with a double and three runs scored.[17]

On August 20, the Colored Giants played a 12-inning tie against New York City's Bay Ridge team. About 4,000 fans attended. The game ended 4–4 thanks to a four-run ninth inning by the Giants. Grant had three hits, all doubles.[18]

A week later, Grant was at second base for the Genuine Cuban Giants for a game against the Loughlin Lyceum team. The size of the crowd broke a record, with nearly 7,300 turning out. Grant went hitless and the Giants lost, 4–1. The Cubans' lineup was: Satterfield, ss; Grant, 2b; Gordon, 3b; Williams, rf; Gallaway, lf; Kelly, cf; Bradley, c; Best, p; and Watkins, 1b.[19]

It appears that Frank Grant spent the remaining weeks of the 1905 season mostly back with the Genuine Cuban Giants. On September 3, he had three hits and scored twice in a victory over the Marquettes, 8–5. That game was played before 3,200 onlookers. On September 26, the Cubans played the Berwick team in Bloomsburg, Pennsylvania. Though Grant was hitless, he handled seven chances at second base without an error as the Giants won, 2–1.[20]

In between those games, Frank Grant visited his home of Williamstown "for the first time in nine years and saw his family," a paper in Pittsfield reported. That couldn't have been quite accurate, because he wintered there in early 1898, and the Cuban X-Giants called nearby North Adams their home city later that year. Still, even if seven years was much more accurate than nine, someone felt it necessary to inform a newspaper that he hadn't visited in a long time.[21]

On September 29, Grant rejoined the Cuban X-Giants for an Asylum baseball club reunion game, pitting him against Jack Chesbro one more time. Art Madison was also in the Asylum lineup. This was about a year after Chesbro's staggering 41–12 season in the American League. Grant went 0-for-3 against Chesbro that day, and the X-Giants lost, 4–0. This game was the subject of a very long article by SABR member Bob Mayer.[22]

On October 1, Frank Grant may have played for two different teams, both at second base. The Cuban X-Giants played a doubleheader that day at New York City's Ridgewood diamond. In fact, there was apparently a tripleheader there, which would explain why the X-Giants' morning game was limited to seven innings. Grant played second base as they clobbered the New York Colored Giants, 8–0. There wasn't anyone named Grant in the X-Giants' lineup in their afternoon game. Frank Grant spent that afternoon contributing errorless fielding at second base to help the Genuine Cuban Giants beat the Marquette team, 5–3. That game drew a crowd of 5,000.[23]

14. Exit from the Game (1904 and After)

The Cuban X-Giants, from the Asylum reunion game against future Hall of Fame pitcher Jack Chesbro on September 29, 1905. Grant is kneeling on the far left.

A week later, Grant played in two games on the same day for the Genuine Cuban Giants at two different ballparks and against two different opponents. In the morning at Brighton Oval, they took a 2–1 lead against the Philadelphia Giants into the ninth inning, only to lose, 5–2. In the afternoon game, Grant helped the Genuine Cuban Giants win, 8–3, against the Loughlin Lyceum team at the Loughlin Oval.[24] Grant played at least one more game that month with the Genuine Cuban Giants, a loss on October 22 to the Paramount Field Club.[25]

Frank Grant was now 40 years old, and he had played 20 seasons of baseball for a living. Though he had a few more seasons left in him, by 1906 he was in a period of time when the occasional sportswriter would look back on his early days nostalgically, and often wistfully as well. Of course, memories can be tricky, and sometimes exaggeration creeps in on purpose, for the sake of a good story. One very long example was printed in the *Buffalo Evening News* in early 1906. That daily reported on some barbershop banter, when one customer noted that he, his wife, and daughter lived directly across the street from Buffalo's ballpark when Grant was on the team. But before he told his story, he sang the praises of not only Grant but also Higgins, Walker, and Stovey. "Each one of that colored quartet was a good ball player, and were of material aid to their teams," he stressed. He elaborated about his experience with Buffalo's star. "Grant, who was a mighty hitter, seemed to hold some sort of grudge against my domicile as it frequently suffered bombardment from his hands," the customer continued. "He had the left field fence down pat and would often poke the sphere over it and straight for my house." His household got in the habit of closing their shutters during ballgames to protect their windows, but one day his wife and daughter were doing extensive cleaning while he was detained at work, and they had the windows open to air out their home. Shortly after he arrived home, there was a noisy commotion in several rooms before his family had a chance to enjoy their late dinner, and in the yard he spied a neighbor's dog running away with the roast that his wife had set out. He doubted that the dog could've gotten into their house, so he was bewildered—until he noticed a baseball, presumably another Grant souvenir. "The sphere had been driven over the ball ground fence, had struck in the middle of the street, hand rebounded into our parlor, demolished a motto on the wall, banged into the sitting room and broke a vase then traveled into the dining room and knocked the roast through the window," he concluded. "I tell you that ball had terrific power behind it."[26]

On April 1, it was announced that Grant's old teammate, George L. Williams, was negotiating with him to join a new ball club, the Wilmington Giants.[27] Williams didn't succeed in signing Grant, but his new team quickly became prominent that season.

On April 6, a Brooklyn paper said, "Home Run Johnson and Grant, of the Philadelphia Giants," had joined the Royal Giants in time for their game against the Brightons two days later. That could've been referring to Charlie Grant, though he had already been appearing atop Philadelphia Giants batting orders by then and continued to do so throughout April. It ultimately didn't matter which Grant the paper had in mind, because there was no Grant in the Royal Giants' lineup that day, nor was there a Grant in that team's box score printed on April 21.[28]

On May 19, a preview of a Genuine Cuban Giants game the next day listed Grant at second base, though he hadn't appeared in their box scores printed on April 2 and 23.[29] Grant didn't play for the Genuine Cuban Giants on May 20 because he played for the New York Colored Giants instead, in Yonkers. A crowd of 2,000 watched the visitors stifle the Yonkers Field Club, 5–0. The Giants' lineup was: Nelson, cf; Grant, 2b; Butts, ss; Parker, 1b; Land, 3b; Penno, lf; Devoe, c; Abbott, rf; and Dawson, p. Grant had two hits, a stolen base, and a run scored.[30]

In contrast to the Wilmington Giants, the Royal Giants, and the Genuine Cuban Giants, there was minimal coverage of the New York Colored Giants to that point. One possibility is that they were very late in reorganizing, for whatever reason, and didn't play any actual games in April. As for Grant, there's always the possibility that he didn't play in April for any team, perhaps due to an injury.

A preview of a New York Colored Giants game about a month later made a comparison that, with the passage of time, is unsettling. "Grant, the Anson of the colored teams, will hold down second, and is going as well to-day as he did many years ago," a Brooklyn daily said.[31] Yes, Anson was known for having had the longest career, 27 years in the majors, but he is also strongly associated with Organized Baseball's unofficial but rigid color line.

During the second half of July, the New York Colored Giants played a few games against one of the best African American teams in the country that season, the Brooklyn Royal Giants. On July 19, the two teams met at New York City's Saratoga Grounds. The Royals won, 6–0, though Grant had two hits, both doubles. He only had four chances at second base and handled them without an error. The teams had a rematch at the same diamond the next day, but they only played six innings. That was long enough for the Royals to win again, 13–2. Grant had a putout, an assist, one of his team's two hits, a run, and at least one of his team's two walks. Alas, both games only drew about 500 fans each.[32]

On July 27, a game between the New York Colored Giants and the Brooklyn Royal Giants was a special attraction during "old home week" in Greenfield, Massachusetts.

That contest drew a crowd of about 750. The Royals won again, but they only led 5–3 after four innings, and the final score was 7–3. At second base, Grant had two putouts, five assists, and an error. At bat, he went 3-for-4, including a double. He scored once and drove in a run.[33]

On August 11, Grant played for the Colored Giants in a win against a local team in New Brunswick, New Jersey, and that might have been his final game with that team. He wasn't in their lineup on September 2, for instance. On that day, he instead played with the Baltimore (Colored) Giants against a local team in Orange Valley, New Jersey. The game drew a crowd of 5,000 fans, and the home team won, 8–4. One of his two hits was a double, and he scored once. He played an errorless game at second base, with three putouts and four assists. Baltimore's lineup was: Hayes, ss; Ramsley, lf; Jackson, cf; Grant, 2b; Nelson, rf; Washington, c; Murphy, 3b; Meanor, 1b; and Brokaw, p.[34]

About ten days earlier, one paper said this club had "recently been strengthened by half of the Philadelphia Quaker Giants, who disbanded," but didn't name any of them. An article on September 5 said the Baltimore Giants included "several of the strongest players on the Philadelphia Giants of last year, including Washingon, Grant, Bell, Lancey, Smith and Manning."[35] It seems that Frank was once again being confused with Charlie Grant, though the latter was continuing to appear regularly in the Philadelphia Giants' box scores. The most extensive coverage the Baltimore Giants received in September was for a three-game series in Fitchburg, Massachusetts, that started a few days after the game in Greenfield.[36]

If Frank Grant played baseball with one or more of his previous teams during the first half of 1907, any such games went largely unreported. In fact, a newspaper in the county of his birth reported on July 26 that he had "given up baseball playing."[37] Up to that point, there wasn't much evidence to the contrary. He did eventually reemerge on a team led by Pop Watkins (the name of which was reported differently from week to week), but he wasn't on the roster of Watkins' Cuban Giants on March 1. A daily in Brooklyn also reported the initial rosters of the Royal Giants, Philadelphia Giants, and Cuban X-Giants. The only Grant listed was Philadelphia's second baseman, and that was surely Charlie.[38]

Late that same month, there was no Grant on the roster of Watkins' All-Professionals, nor in late June when they were called the Cuban Giants again.[39] The New York Colored Giants received little publicity in 1907, and the Baltimore Giants were practically unheard-of. A roster of the former team was printed on April 19, and the closest name on it to Grant was a first baseman named Goad. In mid–May, a player named Grant did get mentioned in a preview of a Colored Giants game, and it was probably him, but there was no Grant in the box score.[40] On July 13, a center fielder named Grant was listed as a member of the Iona Colored Giants, and that team could've been sufficiently appealing to Frank Grant based on its new battery of Lefty Buckner and Williams, "both late of the Royal Giants," according to one New Jersey newspaper. Unfortunately, that team's box scores were almost as scarce as the Baltimore Giants' that season.[41]

Frank Grant played for Watkins' Colored Stars against the Loughlin Lyceum team on August 11. The game had a tense ninth inning, but the Stars lost, 9–8. Grant was hitless but did score twice. The lineup for the Stars was: Andrews, p; Kelly, 3b; Johnson, c; Hawke, cf; Grant, 2b; Delaney, ss; Henry, lf; Foote[s], 1b; and E. Williams, rf. Grant didn't make any errors but he only had three chances, which may have indicated that he didn't have anywhere near the range of his prime years.[42] That may have been why a week later he was at first base against the Utica Athletic Club. His team was called Pop Watkins' Colored Professionals that time. It won, 7–6. Grant had three hits and scored two runs.[43]

On August 24, Pop Watkins' Colored Giants swept a twin bill from a new team called the Brooklyn X-Giants. Watkins played first base in both games, so Grant shifted back to second.[44] The two teams were reportedly battling for "the colored championship of Greater New York."[45]

Grant temporarily shifted to another team in early September. On the 4th, he played with the Royal Giants against the Cuban Stars. The game took place in Atlantic City, where his son lived that year with his maternal grandfather, William J. Adore, at 1111 Baltic Avenue. Grant batted last and started out in right field, but in the first inning the Giants' catcher, Phil Bradley, had a finger split by a foul tip and needed to shift to right field. Grant moved to second base, and Gus James moved from that assignment to behind home plate. Grant's fielding statistic for the game was one assist. He batted ninth and went 0-for-2 but was hit by a pitch and scored a run. He may have considered it an indignity when Billy Holland pinch-hit for him in the top of the ninth inning. The Cuban Stars won, 6–2.[46]

This game was particularly noteworthy because both teams were members of a little-known but historically significant league, the National Association of Colored Baseball Clubs of the United States and Cuba. This league's name was shortened inconsistently in the press, often as either the National Association of Colored Professional Clubs or with "Colored" and "Professional" reversed (if the latter was even used at all). The other two members were the Philadelphia Giants and the Genuine Cuban Giants. The Royal Giants played the most games against the other three teams, 25, with a record of 10–14–1. The Cuban Stars played the fewest, six, and only had one other win besides this one.[47] Therefore, though Frank Grant apparently only played one game in that league, it was a meaningful one for his opposition that day.[48]

Grant wasn't in the Royal Giants' lineup the next day, and he was back with Watkins' club no later than September 14.[49] He was also listed in a box score on September 23, for which Watkins' team was called the Brooklyn Giants. They played a six-inning game against Paterson's minor league team, which won, 2–0. Grant went 1-for-3, and played without an error at second base. He had four putouts and two assists in five innings of defense, which might be evidence that his range hadn't narrowed too much after all.[50]

Perhaps to make up for lost time, Grant not only continued playing into the second half of October, but into November as well. In both months, Watkins' team faced all-stars organized by Joe Wall, who had a brief National League career in 1901 and 1902. On October 19, Watkins' players faced a pitcher named Girard. There's a good chance that was Brooklyn native Charlie Girard, who pitched seven games in the National League as a Phillie in 1910. Wall played left field. His right fielder was possibly Ed Poole, who had a five-year career in the National League as a pitcher and outfielder, which concluded in 1904 with Brooklyn. Wall's team won, 8–2. Grant's hit was a double, and he scored once.[51]

In the game on November 5, Wall played first base, and his right fielder may have been Mal Eason, who concluded a six-year career in the majors at Brooklyn in 1906 as a pitcher and outfielder. Wall's pitcher was likely Pembroke Finlayson, who pitched one game for Brooklyn's National League team in 1908 and again in 1909. This time the game went an extra inning, though Wall's nine ultimately won again, 5–4. Grant again had a hit and a run, but he shifted to first base for this game, where he had 12 putouts without an error.[52]

In 1908, Grant played on Pop Watkins' Colored Giants for the first time no later than April 18, so there isn't much mystery about his whereabouts that spring.[53] It's unlikely the team was active for more than two weeks before then, because Watkins had only returned to New York from the South, with new players, on April 3.[54] However, when Watkins' team played a doubleheader on May 3, there was no Grant in either of his lineups. By May 13, Grant had been signed by manager James E. Boone of the Brooklyn X-Giants. One Brooklyn daily provided an overview of Boone's recruits:

> After many drawbacks and disappointments Manager Boone has at last successfully signed for his team Billy Holland, late of the Royal Giants; Grant, of the Cuban Giants; and Murphy, of the New York Colored Giants. Associated with these men will be the well-known Hawk, of the Royals, and Reeves, of the Philadelphia Giants; Franklin and Hudson, of the old Cuban X Giants, ably assisted by the following all-star artists and coaches: L. Myers, Wright, E. Myers and the old war horse, Barney Green.[55]

On May 24, Grant played for the Brooklyn X-Giants against a local team in Nyack, New York. The only positive was that he played errorless ball. He went hitless as his new team was trounced, 12–0. The Brooklyn lineup was: Delaney, 2b; Myers, ss; Grant, 1b; Reeves, cf; "Ox," 3b; Emory, rf; Footes, c; E. Myers, lf; and Franklin, p. A similar lineup lost at the end of June to the Marquette team, 9–8, except the box score called them the Georgia Giants. Grant had two hits, including a double, and scored once.[56]

On August 15, Grant played with four of the same players though a newspaper article called them the Brooklyn Colored Giants. The defeated a local team in Glen Cove, Long Island, 9–5. Grant had two hits. A week later they were properly called the Brooklyn X-Giants again in coverage of a game against the Woodhaven team. The home team pulled out a win, 6–5, by scoring twice in the bottom of the ninth inning. On August 30, the X-Giants beat the Baltimore Giants, 10–4. "The only feature of the struggle was the fielding and batting of Frank Grant," wrote a *Brooklyn Daily Eagle* reporter who made reference to his stardom with Buffalo and later the Cuban Giants. Grant had three hits, including a double, and scored two runs.[57] If Grant and some of these teammates played in September and October, the press largely ignored them.

In December, *Sporting Life* printed a lengthy appeal from sportswriter F.D. Ellis of the *New York Press* and the *Brooklyn Daily Eagle*. It was directed particularly to Frank Grant and other baseball friends of "Budd" Fowler, about the latter player's illness and need for assistance. Ellis was undoubtedly the reporter who had written so knowledgeably about Grant at the end of August. Ellis hoped to arrange a benefit game to raise money for Fowler.[58] On March 25, 1909, the *New York Age* announced that a benefit game for Fowler was scheduled for one month later. Ellis had teamed with Sol White to promote the game, and old-timers expected to play included Grant, George Williams, Ben Holmes, Bob Jordan, Pop Watkins, Clarence Williams, and Nat Clarke, plus White. Happily, Fowler's health had reportedly improved by then. A few days later, the *Eagle* added Nat Collins, Bob Jackson, and Oscar Jackson to the list. On April 22, the *Age* reported that too few of the players would be available three days later, so the game was postponed indefinitely.[59] Fowler passed away in 1913.

As was true in 1907, any playing by Grant during the first half of 1909 tended to go unreported. He reportedly emerged in August as a member of Booker's Giants, in Paterson, New Jersey. When Grant played Paterson's minor league club in 1904 and 1905, Booker was one of his teammates. Billy Booker had played with the New Jersey Cuban Giants on August 15 but left them to quickly form his own team. His first lineup against Paterson's Totowa team was announced as: Frank Grant, 1b; former Cuban Giant Johnny Nelson, 2b; Booker, rf; Mathews, lf; Corrilo, 3b; Fuller, ss; Smith, cf; Devoe, c; Henerey or Dawson, p. The two teams played three games, but three different dailies in Paterson didn't print any box scores, and none happened to mention Grant in their brief accounts. In previews of the second and third games, Grant was listed as a coach instead of a player.[60]

On September 26, Grant was likely the second baseman for the New York Colored Giants in a seven-inning game against Joe Wall's All-Leaguers. The attendance was 1,500. Pitching for Wall's was Lafayette "Lave" Winham, who had short stints in the National League during 1902 and 1903 and ended that service with a record of 3–1. Winham threw a one-hitter and was victorious, 7–1. At least Grant played errorless ball at second base, with two putouts and two assists. The lineup for the Giants was: Dorow, 1b; Grant, 2b; Nealson (possibly Nelson), 3b; Satterfield, ss; Johnson, cf; Smith, c; Kelly, lf; Dawson, rf; and Thompson, p.[61]

Wall's team was scheduled to face Watkins' Giants or Stars for three games, followed by "Frank Grant's Colored Stars" on October 1.[62] Based on subsequent coverage in Brooklyn papers, the teams didn't meet until the 3rd. A crowd of 800 watched at the Marquette Oval. Wall's right fielder that day was probably Brooklyn native Bugs Reisigl, who pitched two games for Cleveland's American League team in 1911. Grant's Colored Stars were stifled, 7–0, though Grant got two hits and stole a base. He also played errorless defense. His lineup was: Wilson, 3b; Grant, 1b; Reese, p; Mowke, c; Ferrell, ss; Holland, 2b; Johnson, lf; Kelly, rf; and Jones, cf.[63]

Grant apparently got in one more game that month, and at second base, when he, Reese, and Kelly joined Pop Watkins' Giants for a game against a team called the Woodhills. Watkins' lineup won, 5–3, and Grant had two hits. His other six teammates were Addison, ss; Parks, c; Robinson, 1b; Bragg, 3b; Fisher, lf; and Mathews, cf.[64]

On February 27, 1910, a paragraph in the *New York Press* announced that several "old-timers" would play as the reorganized Gorhams, namely "Bob Jordan, Frank Grant, John Nelson, John Hill, Kid Carter, Bell, King, Kelly, Fuller, Mathews and Wallace Devoe." Devoe was the person to contact for scheduling games.[65] A few of these names would show up in box scores together later that year, but possibly never as the Gorhams. This might be the last time Grant's first name appeared in a newspaper in the context of being an active player.

Whatever team names Devoe, Grant, and Nelson would play under, this announcement may help explain why Frank Grant was listed as a baseball player in the 1910 census. The page on which his family was listed is dated April 19, and he indicated that he was employed on April 15. He and "Relia" had been married five years, and Grant's stepson, Frank Moore, was still living with them, as was a 55-year-old female boarder whose name appeared to be Nelles Morris.[66] Mrs. Grant was in her second marriage and had only given birth once, and that child was still living. Therefore, if Frank's adopted daughter in the 1905 census, Irene Harris, was his wife's daughter from her first marriage, then Irene was still alive. Between 1905 and 1910 the household had moved a very short distance, from 6 Minetta Street to number 17 on the same Manhattan street. Many of their neighbors were natives of Italy.

In July of 1910, "Grant, 2b" started showing up frequently in box scores of the New York Black Sox. Most baseball historians have believed this to be Charlie Grant, but award-winning SABR historian Gary Ashwill has raised the possibility that it was a much younger player at the start of his very long career, Leroy Grant.[67] Regardless, it was probably Frank Grant who was in box scores not quite a week apart in August, both of which also included Devoe and Nelson.

On August 14, it was quite possibly Frank Grant who played for the New York Colored Giants in a game against a Paterson team at Olympic Field. At least two dailies printed box scores, and four of the Giants had their surnames spelled differently. That batting order was: Pole or Poole (possibly Spottswood Poles), cf; Frances or Franas (possibly Bill Francis), 3b; Bashra or Basbra, lf; Addison, ss; Devoe, c; Rigler, rf; Grant, 2b; Nelson, 1b; and McDonald or McConnell, p. On September 4, the first three batters for the Philadelphia Giants in a game against the Black Sox were Poles (presumably Spottswood), rf; Francis (presumably Bill), 3b; and Barber, lf. The Giants also had a shortstop named Addison.[68]

At the same ballpark six days later, Grant, Nelson, and Devoe played for the Colored Stars against Joe Wall's Professionals. The lineup for the Colored Stars was: Gordon, ss; Good, lf; Nelson, p; Nott, rf; Grant, 2b; Robinson, 3b; Fuller, c; Devoe, 1b; and Johnson, cf. Grant had a double and a sacrifice hit.[69]

As springtime was approaching in 1911, the Savannah Colored Giants proposed games with the Pittsburgh Giants and the New York Colored Giants at Olympic Field, "for the colored championship of Greater New York." Their roster reportedly included a right fielder named Grant.[70] However, in at least two subsequent box scores and two previews of their games, the right fielder's name was Gant. In both of the box scores he batted eighth. In the latter of the two previews, Gant "had lots of experience with the Manhattan Giants," while three teammates and not Gant were instead described as former members of the "famous Cuban Giants."[71] There was indeed a Gant in Manhattan (Colored) Giants box scores in 1910.

Gant may also have been the "Grant, 2b" who led off for the New York Colored Giants in a game on June 19. They played a team called the In-Er-Seals before 800 fans at Olympic Field. The rest of the Giants' lineup was: Chase, 1b; Hargrove, ss; Womsley, lf; Dawson, p; Simonds, c; Terrell, 3b; Fiall, cf; and Butler, rf. Frank Grant did play for the New York Colored Giants in several seasons previously, and often with a pitcher named Dawson, so it's possible this player was him. On the other hand, Gant and the next five batters in this lineup, except Dawson, all played for the Savannah Giants on July 2. Whoever that leadoff hitter was, he scored his team's only run in a 7–1 loss by hitting a home run.[72]

It would have been natural if Frank Grant had spent much time thinking about a future without baseball, at least as an active player at a high level. Sadly, in September of 1911 he had to dwell on his future living alone. The 6th may have been a bittersweet day when he and Aurelia made their relationship official with the local government, because she passed away just 12 days later. The timing could have been a coincidence, but it is quite plausible that on the 6th, they knew she didn't have long to live and that inspired them to have a formal marriage ceremony. Aurelia Moore Grant was 49. She was buried in Cypress Hill Cemetery, on the border between Brooklyn and Queens, on September

21.[73] Eight days later, a newspaper in Hackensack previewed a visit from the Manhattan Colored Giants for a game the next day, on September 30. The Giants' lineup was to include "Grant and Williams, of the old Cuban Giants; Pop Green, the southpaw from the Pittsburg [sic] Giants, and Gardner, the comical shortstop." The Giants used two extra players in that game. Their batting order was: Grant, 3b; Gardner and Fuller, ss; Harvey, lf; Gross and Jackson, cf; Powell, rf; Goode, 1b; Mallete, 2b; Williams, c; and Greene, p. The Giants managed just two hits but only lost, 3–2. Grant went 1-for-3, probably drew a walk, and had at least one stolen base. He scored his team's first run, and his defense consisted of an assist.[74] The fact that the aforementioned Gant had played for the Manhattan Giants calls into question whether this "Grant" actually was the old Cuban Giant. Conversely, the fact that Grant was replaced on the Philadelphia Giants by Charlie Grant serves as a reminder that coincidences did happen in their careers. But if it really was Frank Grant in that Manhattan lineup, then it could have been the last time he ever appeared in a box score.

15

From Obscurity to Enshrinement

While Frank Grant may not have played baseball at a high enough level after 1911 to get into any newspapers, he could of course have continued to play on some amateur teams. In addition, whenever it was that he played his last game ever, he obviously could have maintained some involvement in the sport as a coach, manager, or even umpire, and not have limited himself to being a fan. There just weren't many signs or reports of such involvement.

Not too surprisingly, on occasion he would still get confused with other ballplayers named Grant, especially Charlie, as usual. In 1913, Sol White was managing one of at least two teams calling themselves the Pittsburgh (Colored) Giants, and Charlie Grant was atop at least one of White's batting orders.[1] When Charlie was reportedly managing that team in April 1914, he was described "as having played with Harrisburg, in the old State league," which clearly applied to Frank only. Such comments were repeated in previews of Giants' games, including in Harrisburg's *Daily Patriot* on May 14 and the *Harrisburg Telegraph* on May 18. However, two days later the latter newspaper changed to saying the Giants were "managed by Frank Grant, the first colored baseball player who ever made good," though the *Telegraph* didn't characterize this as a correction.[2]

What's perplexing about this is that there exists ample evidence that Charlie Grant was back in his hometown as player-manager of a team called the Cincinnati Stars. That was announced there in late March. In August he even bragged about his team in a letter or the like to at least one leading African American newspaper.[3] On the other hand, toward the end of May, a paper in Cincinnati noticed that the Stars had been limiting themselves to the occasional road game. Charlie pointed to their ballpark needing work, plus potential opponents not offering enough of a financial guarantee. "Every leading club in Cincinnati is wondering when Manager Charley Grant is going to get his park in condition," that same newspaper stressed more than a month later.[4] It could be that Charlie had been secretly moonlighting with the Pittsburgh Giants, which appear to have fizzled out by early June. Another possibility was that it was Frank Grant who actually piloted the Pittsburgh Giants in April and May of 1914, though the frequency of Charlie's first name being used argues against this, the misidentifications about his Harrisburg experience notwithstanding. Still, it may be significant that in five Giants box scores during May, there wasn't actually a player named Grant in their lineup, whereas Charlie Grant did play for his Cincinnati Stars. The final mention of this team may have been in a Pennsylvania newspaper on June 2, when the club was suddenly referred to, perhaps quite tellingly, as "Jim Bright's Pittsburg[sic] Colored Giants."[5] If "Jim" was supposed to read J.M., then it would have referred to the magnate of the Cuban Giants with whom Frank Grant had a very long association, but Charlie Grant didn't. Pittsburgh

Giants box scores in 1915, which include a player named Gant, raise the possibility that Henry Gant or some relative was actually the manager in 1914, though almost all known newspaper accounts in 1914 specified Charlie Grant as the manager.

A very different mystery involving Frank Grant centered on 1916. At its core was coverage in the *Philadelphia Tribune*, the nation's oldest continuously published African American newspaper. On April 7, the Manhattan A.A. baseball team elected a Frank Grant as its business manager, along with several other officers. The former Cuban Giant's son, Frank W. Grant, moved to Philadelphia from Atlantic City no later than 1917, and records indicate that his only child, Dorothy, was born in Philadelphia prior to 1916. In Philadelphia around that time, there was at least one other African American named Frank Grant of roughly the same age as Frank W. Grant, but obviously there's a good chance the latter was this Manhattan baseball team's business manager. Whoever he was, this business manager was presumably the team's second baseman in their game on May 13. Conveniently, the box score listed him as "F. Grant" despite no other player in either lineup sharing that surname. The Manhattan team was trounced, 11–2, but at least Grant had one of his team's four hits and scored once.[6] Thus, in that decade Frank Grant became a grandfather and gained a daughter-in-law called Hattie (the former Harriet Crocker), though it's unknown whether he knew about either happy event in advance.

Other than the fact that Frank W. Grant approved his father's funeral arrangements about two decades later, there's currently no way of assessing the extent to which father and son had contact during the 20th century. At the same time, there were indications in the 1920s that the elder Frank Grant had minimal contact with his siblings, if any. As noted in a previous chapter, when Frank Grant visited Williamstown in September 1905, a paper reported that it he hadn't seen his family for nine years, though in actuality it was more likely seven. Still, for whatever reason, someone felt it necessary to inform a newspaper that he hadn't visited in a long time.[7] That may have been the last time he ever visited Williamstown, and by 1920, his siblings either lost track of him and weren't sure he was even still alive, or they simply agreed to no longer acknowledge him.

A horrific dispute may have been the cause, as it is for so many families when adult siblings make no effort to communicate. In 1909, something flared up publicly between two of his sisters, when the following announcement was printed in the *North Adams Transcript*: "I hereby warn all people not to trust or

A widely used photograph of Frank Grant, and possibly the only close-up of its kind (National Baseball Hall of Fame and Museum, Cooperstown, NY).

have any business dealings with Amelia Grant of Spring street, Williamstown, on my account as I will be responsible for no bills contracted or any deals consummated by her after this date. HARRIET GRANT, Williamstown, Mass. February 27, 1909."[8] Fortunately, the situation improved enough in a few years that when Amelia Catherine died in 1916, Hattie (Harriet) cosigned with their brother Willis a "Card of Thanks" to all the mourners who helped them grieve their "dearly beloved sister, Amelia Catherine Grant." Clarence and Frank were not also signers of this "card," but they were named in the announcement of her death.[9]

That changed after Hattie died in mid–1920. The *Transcript*'s announcement said she was only "survived by two brothers, Willis Grant of Williamstown and Clarence Grant of North Adams." After Clarence's death in 1926, the *Transcript*'s announcement of course noted that he was survived by six children, but his only surviving sibling named was Willis. In turn, when that newspaper reported Willis' death in 1929, a niece and three nephews were named, but otherwise he left "no near relatives."[10] Did Frank know about some or all of these deaths? Did they know about his first marriage, or that he remarried around the end of the First World War? Those questions may never be answered, but one of Clarence's descendants, Emily Grant Foote, told this author during a long telephone conversation in 2021 that she is convinced the family had no idea Frank Grant had a son.

By Septemberf 1918, when the elder Frank Grant filled out a military registration card, he had moved from Minetta Street to 250 West 17th Street. That move may have been necessitated by an urban improvement plan announced about two years earlier to "wipe out" Minetta Street because it was "Tough, Crooked and Dilapidated," as one headline put it.[11] A month after completing that registration, Frank Grant took a wife for the second time. He married the former Malvania Holden Morris, whose previous spouse was also deceased. It's unknown whether she was related to the Grant household's boarder in 1910, Nelles Morris. The new Mrs. Grant's first name was spelled quite differently in several sources, including "Malomia," "Malvina," and "Melvino." In a government document, her parents were identified as Joseph Holden and Louisa Brown. The ceremony occurred at the Municipal Building on October 17, and it was apparently performed by Deputy City Clerk Michael J. Cruise.

The employer on Grant's military registration cards was "L. Bachman" of 22 West 22nd Street. Based on a 1918 city directory, this was a woolens business, L. Bachmann & Co., owned by Louis and Norbert H. Bachmann, in some kind or arrangement with a David Haas and a Sol Livingston. Grant's job was entered as a porter. On the back of the card, it was noted that his eyes were blue. In the 1920 census, Grant was still a porter for the same kind of business, if not that exact one.

Very sadly, Grant's wife passed away less than three years after they were married, on March 21, 1921. Her age at the time of her death was entered as 53, or two years younger than her husband. As far as is known, Frank Grant never married again.

In the 1920 census, Frank Grant's address was 250 West 17 Street. In 1925, 1930, and at the time of his death, he was just up the street, at 136. He was identified as a truck driver in 1925. In the 1930 census, he was a porter in the Loft Building at 376 Lafayette Street, a landmark built in 1888. It was designed by Henry J. Hardenbergh, who was also the architect of the Plaza Hotel and the equally famous Dakota Apartments.

Current baseball historians who have written about Frank Grant's final decades tend to sum them up as a time of obscurity, and while that may generally be accurate, there were at least two occurrences in the final years of his life that suggest he wasn't as lonely as assumed, nor was he forgotten by all but the occasional sportswriter. The first was a modest occasion, but it showed the durability of two of his professional friendships. In November 1930, the *Pittsburgh Courier* reported that Mr. and Mrs. Louis McTurner of the Bronx, N.Y., had recently celebrated the first anniversary of their wedding. Ida McTurner was a daughter of Frank Miller, Grant's longtime teammate on the Cuban Giants. "Their guests were Mr. and Mrs. Sol White, Mr. and Mrs. Green, Frank Grant, Miss Willia Williams, formerly of Pittsburgh, Mr. and Mrs. Wayland Bryant, of Pittsburgh, and Master Wayland Bryant and Frank E. Bryant, also of Pittsburgh." Mrs. Bryant was his daughter Geraldine. It was implied that Frank Miller (then a widower) and his son, Frank, Jr., were also present for the festivities.[12] The depth of Miller's friendship with both Grant and White was demonstrated by their invitation to and attendance at this very personal event.

In early 1932, the New York Black Yankees initiated a plan to unite "old-time" African American ballplayers and have them meet present-day counterparts. The idea was reportedly inspired by an event held at the beginning of that year by an athletic club called the Old-Timers Association, Boys of Ten and Twenty Years Ago. Chairing a planning committee was M.E. Goodson of the Black Yankees, and its membership included Frank Grant and Sol White. Others serving included "Fats" Jenkins, George Scales, Joe Williams, Bill Holland, Connie Rector, R. Hudspeth, Larry Brown, Red Ryan, Dick Seay, Tex Burnett, Willie "Knucks" James, Jules Thomas, Jock Waters, Spottswood Poles, Louis Santop, Sam Mongin, and G. McDonald.[13]

W. Rollo Wilson of the *Pittsburgh Courier* provided the agenda this committee drew up. The event was to be held at Goodson's own "café" at 67 West 135th Street on Thursday, February 4. The starting time would be 2:00 in the afternoon, and the gathering was expected to last 12 hours.[14]

Though coverage after the fact was minimal, at least Wilson's paper did confirm that the reunion happened. It had a headline spanning all but two columns at the top of a page that read, "Old-Time and Present Ball Stars Meet," though the actual article was printed a few inches below that, under a different headline. It wasn't very long, and a third of it focused on the Black Yankees' plan for the upcoming season. It concluded with a suggestion by Gus Greenlee of the Pittsburgh Crawfords to plan a similar reunion in his city. The report indicated that the event was held a day later instead, but it was called "a tremendous success." The account listed some of the "notables" present, including Goodson, Greenlee, Frank Grant, Sol White, and Frank Miller. Others named were "Bob Jackson of

New York City's historic Loft Building, the landmark where Frank Grant worked in 1930.

Jamaica, the oldest catcher of the Cuban Giants club," Oscar Charleston, Josh Devoe of the 1919 Chicago Giants, and a C. Egan, as well as Smokey Joe Williams, George Scales, Larry Brown, Red Ryan, "Fats" Jenkins, and Tex Burnett, but there were "many others" in attendance.[15] Thus, the turnout included at least four future Hall of Famers in Grant, White, Williams, and Charleston.

Frank Grant passed away on May 26, 1937, at the age of 71. His death occurred at Bellevue Hospital in Manhattan, and the primary causes were cerebral arteriosclerosis and senility. His occupation was identified as waiter for a caterer, and he had last worked that job in December of the prior year. He was supposedly in that occupation for 36 years, which would have dated back to the beginning of the century, when his baseball career was still thriving. He was said to have lived in New York for 45 years, or starting in 1892. He clearly wintered in other places later in the 1890s, but he might have lived in New York during the baseball season, on those occasions when his team wasn't on a tour in some other state. The Certificate of Death indicated that the information on it, including correct details about his parents, was supplied by Grant himself.

According to the announcement in the *New York Age*, the funeral was early on the afternoon of June 2 at the chapel of local undertaker Mamie Anderson-Pratt. Future Hall of Famer Cum Posey, at the start of his regular column in the *Pittsburgh Courier*, noted that the pallbearers included Sol White, Smokey Joe Williams, and "Knucks" James, all of whom had been at the reunion five years earlier.[16] Because Frank's son Frank W. signed the paperwork for his funeral, one hopes he actually attended it and met those baseball legends.

Frank Grant was buried at East Ridgelawn Cemetery in Clifton, New Jersey.

Frank Grant's gravestone.

Baseball historians have attempted to determine why that location was chosen but can only speculate. The grave was unmarked until 2011, five years after his enshrinement in the Hall of Fame. That was the result of Jeremy Krock's non-profit Negro Leagues Baseball Grave Marker Project.

Frank W. Grant passed away less than a decade later, on July 16, 1946. He is buried in New Jersey's Beverly National Cemetery. His gravestone notes that he was a Private in the Army during the First World War.

For more than two decades prior to Frank Grant's death, he had already become obscure and was mostly forgotten. That would continue for another half-century, until the chapter by Jim Overmyer was published in 1991. Not long before that, it is to the credit of the Buffalo Baseball Hall of Fame that it inducted Grant, as part of only its fourth annual class in 1988. That happened to occur a full century after his final game for the Buffalo Bisons.[17] But what really built momentum for getting Grant into the National Baseball Hall of Fame was Overmyer's appointment to a 12-member committee of the National Hall that was directed to review the careers of the more accomplished African American players and executives who hadn't already been voted in.

Various sportswriters from the 1920s through the 1980s made a point of bringing up Frank Grant and thus kept his memory alive (though a few presented very inaccurate information). Along the way, there was one tremendous lost opportunity, in 1945. Bob Stedler, the Sports Editor of the *Buffalo Evening News*, had already shown an interest in educating readers about Frank Grant when he reported on tragic timing. "Only last week we attempted to get in contact with John J. 'Sandy' Reidy to obtain his recollections of Frank Grant, Negro ball player, with whom he played as a member of the Buffalo Baseball Club," Stedler reported. "Late Monday we learned of his death Sunday, following an operation." What was intended as a follow-up column by Stedler about Frank Grant instead became a tribute to the longtime Buffalo resident who was perhaps Grant's best friend on the Bisons.[18]

On February 28, 2006, media outlets across the nation announced that Frank Grant had been voted into the National Baseball Hall of Fame. The induction ceremony in Cooperstown was on July 31. According to Marion Grant Royston, a descendant of Clarence Grant, about 15 family members attended the big event. Alas, nobody connected with the Hall knew that Frank Grant had a son, and especially that he had living descendants.

In August of that same year, Frank Grant was honored in Williamstown with a plaque on Spring Street. It was the idea of Williamstown resident and former Commissioner of Major League

The plaque honoring Frank Grant in Williamstown.

The location of the plaque honoring Frank Grant in Williamstown.

Baseball Fay Vincent. "Imagine what this guy went through," Vincent said. "He couldn't play in the established leagues, he was discriminated against, he ended up working as a waiter in New York, dying and buried in a pauper's grave."[19]

Assessments like Vincent's from other current baseball experts are quite common, and rightly so, but Frank Grant also seemed to consistently make the best of a bad situation. "He was a courageous man," Grant's grandniece, Emily Grant Foote of Enfield, Connecticut, had said on the day of his enshrinement. "It was his dream, and he knew he was going to play baseball no matter what."[20] He also seemed to strike balances well, at least as a player. He aimed high at a young age, yet he wasn't naïve or rash. Though Sol White considered him quiet and unassuming on the ball diamond, during their time as teammates on the Cuban Giants and later, that didn't also mean Grant was inhibited during his years integrating white teams.

It reflected so well on him that white players went out of their way to issue testimonials about him. Even if they didn't always speak to the injustice of Grant being blocked from the major leagues—though they might have, and such comments were simply omitted by newspapers—it's easy to read that into their comments that did get printed, and it's not wishful thinking to do so.

He performed at a high level for such a long time. Granted (no pun intended), as he approached the age of 40 he started playing with teams that were at a lower level, but that probably means he wasn't deluding himself—as many of the very best athletes in all sports have done for decades—about the status of his skill set from year to year, and chose new teams astutely.

As interest in and knowledge of the Negro Leagues surges across the country these days, it is fitting that Frank Grant's descendants are connecting with his brother Clarence's. As relatives of the greatest African American player of the 19th century, they should have plenty to talk about.

Chapter Notes

Introduction

1. Bill James, *The Politics of Glory* (New York: Macmillan, 1994): 186–187.
2. *Ibid.*, 274.
3. Jerry Malloy, "Out at Home: Baseball Draws the Color Line, 1887," *The National Pastime* (Society for American Baseball Research), Fall 1983: 14–28.
4. Dom Amore, "For Baseball Pioneer, Meriden a Key Stop," *Hartford* (Connecticut) *Courant*, July 30, 2006: A1, A11; John Thorn, "Safe at Home," June 18, 2011, available at https://ourgame.mlblogs.com/safe-at-home-97756ecc6861.
5. *Sporting Life*'s paraphrasing of Chapman's assessment was quoted in "Sporting Notes," *Sunday Truth*, November 14, 1886: 2.
6. The *Baltimore American* was quoted in "Grand Stand Chat," *Harrisburg* (Pennsylvania) *Telegraph*, August 14, 1890: 1.
7. "Grant Will Play," *Harrisburg Telegraph*, July 22, 1890: 1; "Bunted Balls," *Harrisburg Telegraph*, September 1, 1893: 1.
8. "Great Game for the Gorhams," *Plainfield* (New Jersey) *Daily Press*, September 28, 1891: 4.
9. "Amateur Baseball Stars," *New York Herald*, June 12, 1892: 29.
10. "Stage People Talked About," *Atchison* (Kansas) *Blade*, August 27, 1892: 1.
11. "Cubans Again Victorious," *Camden Daily Telegram*, May 20, 1893: 1.
12. "Cubans Downed," *Syracuse* (New York) *Standard*, April 23, 1897: 2.
13. "Lost by the Outfielders," *Oswego* (New York) *Daily Palladium*, May 10, 1898: 6.
14. *Pittsburg Press*, July 5, 1898: 5. There was no headline per se.
15. "Hughey Grant," *Buffalo Commercial*, February 8, 1900: 5. The original source for this tribute may have been the *Washington Post* two days earlier, but it's nice to know at least one Buffalo daily printed it.
16. "Cuban Giants Won," *Erie* (Pennsylvania) *Daily Times*, July 2, 1900: 5.
17. "The World of Sports," *Jersey Journal* (Jersey City, New Jersey), September 7, 1900: 8.
18. "Cuban Giants, Old Favorites, Are Here for Three Games," *Gloversville* (New York) *Morning Herald*, May 27, 1913: 2.
19. Edward Tranter, "Sport Comments," *Buffalo Enquirer*, August 14, 1916: 8.
20. John M. Flynn, "The Referee's Sporting Chat," *Berkshire County Eagle* (Pittsfield, Massachusetts), June 23, 1937: 17.
21. Fritz Pollard, "The Story of Negro Baseball," *New York Amsterdam News*, May 26, 1962: 35.
22. Sol White, "Sol White Recalls," *New York Age*, January 17, 1931: 6; Alvin Moses and Sol White, "Fleet Walker Was Catcher on Toledo Mudhen's Nine," *Afro-American* (Baltimore), February 6, 1932: 15.
23. James E. Overmyer, "The Unhappy Odyssey of a Great Ballplayer," *Berkshire Eagle* (Pittsfield, Massachusetts), February 5, 1990: A1, B6.

Chapter 1

1. "Lincoln and Davis," *Pittsfield* (Massachusetts) *Sun*, August 3, 1865: 1. The adjacent commentary about voting rights (which drew from a *Chicago Times* editorial) had no headline. Pittsfield's handwritten birth registry at the time listed the future Hall of Famer's name as Ulysses F. Grant.
2. Roger O'Gara, "Fair or Foul," *Berkshire Eagle* (Pittsfield, Massachusetts), August 11, 1970: 16. O'Gara's source was "84-year-old John Persip, a patriarch in our city among colored baseball enthusiasts." He was born around the time Frank Grant began playing professionally on otherwise all-white teams. Sylvanus Grant was the paternal grandfather of John Persip's wife, Estella. See also "Correspondence of the N.Y. Commercial Adv.," *Pittsfield Sun*, August 25, 1864: 2
3. This author had a lengthy telephone conversation on March 24, 2021, with Emily Grant Foote, a descendant of Clarence Grant. Jacob's father was apparently named Titus, though she cautioned that there was at least one other Titus Grant in the county around the same time (including a father and son). A Titus Grant passed away in Pittsfield on December 1, 1822, around the age of 70.
4. John Thorn, "The Pittsfield 'Baseball' Bylaw of 1791: What It Means," August 3, 2011, available at https://ourgame.mlblogs.com/the-pittsfield-baseball-bylaw-of-1791-what-it-means-940a3ccf08db.

5. A Jacob Grant, possibly Frank Grant's grandfather, died on October 27, 1859, in Lenox, just south of Pittsfield. One of two registries of death listed his parents as Titus and Katy (Catherine in other records) and indicated he was born around 1783 in Kinderhook, New York, less than 30 miles from Pittsfield. One Ancestry.com search result shows the name of Jacob's mother as Ann and not Katy, but that appears to be a misreading of the same registry.

6. "Died," *Pittsfield Sun*, December 5, 1822: 3; "Died," *Berkshire County Eagle*, November 3, 1859: 3; "Deaths," *Pittsfield Sun*, August 10, 1865: 3. Lena's maiden name was specified on the Massachusetts death certificate of their daughter Caroline E. Michael in 1914. Massachusetts death records appear to show Lena's date of death (due to consumption) as August 31, i.e., three weeks *after* the newspaper's announcement. August 31 could be the date on which the town clerk was notified. In any case, she and Jacob are buried in Church on the Hill Cemetery, Lenox.

7. Hamilton Child, *Gazetteer of Berkshire County, Mass., 1725–1885* (Syracuse, NY: Syracuse Journal, 1885), 178. Cheshire is just north of Pittsfield. It was also reported that Phillip and Hannah had 12 children, nine of whom were still alive in 1885.

8. Massachusetts Historical Society, "The Legal End of Slavery in Massachusetts," https://www.masshist.org/endofslavery/index.php?id=54. The end of slavery in New York State unfolded differently, and over a later span of time, according to the New York Historical Society: "In 1799, New York passed a Gradual Emancipation act that freed slave children born after July 4, 1799, but indentured them until they were young adults. In 1817 a new law passed that would free slaves born before 1799 but not until 1827." See https://www.nyhistory.org/community/slavery-end-new-york-state.

9. Steve Turner, "Berkshire Blacks: The Struggle for Equality Began Two Centuries Ago," *Berkshire Eagle*, August 28, 1976: 18.

10. Irene Quenzler Brown and Richard D. Brown, *The Hanging of Ephraim Wheeler: A Story of Rape, Incest, and Justice in Early America* (Cambridge, MA: The Belknap Press of Harvard University Press, 2003), 268–269, 358n34. Betsy Wheeler's mother was the former Hannah Odel, and it's a distinct possibility that Hannah Persip was named after this aunt.

11. Ibid., 136. See also *Vital Records of Hinsdale, Massachusetts: To the Year 1850* (Boston: New-England Historic Genealogical Society, 1902), 89. Molly is a nickname or informal variation of Mary, and various Massachusetts records accessible online render her first name as the latter.

12. Ibid., 139, 268–269, 358n31, 358n34.

13. "Died," *Pittsfield Sun*, March 13, 1862: 3.

14. See https://nationalregisterofhistoricplaces.com/ma/berkshire/state.html and resources offered by the federal Upper Housatonic Valley National Heritage Area, particularly http://www.africanamericantrail.org/imagesN/MA54Map.pdf. See also Phil Demers, "Dalton House Tied to Underground Railroad to See Renovation, Excavation," *Berkshire Eagle*, April 20, 2015, at https://www.berkshireeagle.com/stories/dalton-house-tied-to-underground-railroad-to-see-renovation-excavation,328258.

15. See Allen H. Bagg, "Historical Paper," September 16, 1937, at https://berkshirehistory.org/wp-content/uploads/2014/10/Historical-Paper-about-Pittsfield-by-Mayor-Allen-Bagg-1937.pdf. The Berkshire Hotel was replaced by the Berkshire Life Insurance Company Building.

16. J.E.A. Smith, *The History of Pittsfield, Massachusetts, from the Year 1800 to the Year 1876* (Springfield, MA: C.W. Bryan, 1876), 7; Tony Dobrowolski, "$700K Makeover to Wrap by May," *Berkshire Eagle*, March 22, 2008: A1. See also https://www.pittsfieldlibrary.org/explore/herman-melville-memorial-room. In 1949, at least, Robert Melvill ran ads in the *Pittsfield Sun*, such as on page 3 of the August 30 edition. "The rooms are very large, with many conveniences not usually found in ordinary boarding houses," the ads asserted.

17. Because recordkeeping could be spotty during that century, censuses are often the best way to confirm a young person's siblings. Children who are born and die *between* censuses are often at risk of going undiscovered.

18. Leon F. Litwack, *North of Slavery: The Negro in the Free States, 1790–1860* (Chicago: University of Chicago Press, 1960), 104. Henry Wilson became President Grant's second Vice President in 1873.

19. James E. Overmyer, "The Unhappy Odyssey of a Great Ballplayer," *Berkshire Eagle*, February 5, 1990: A1, B6.

20. A local death registry listed the date of his death as December 1, though it was identified as December 2 in "Deaths," *Pittsfield Sun*, December 7, 1865: 3. The latter listed his middle initial as "B."

21. Examples include the seminal work by Robert Peterson, *Only the Ball Was White* (Englewood Cliffs, NJ: Prentice-Hall, 1970), 16 and Leslie A. Heaphy, *The Negro Leagues, 1869–1960* (Jefferson, NC: McFarland, 2003), 10.

22. "City Bulletin," *Daily Evening Bulletin* (Philadelphia), December 11, 1867: 3.

23. "The Base-Ball Players' National Convention," *New York Tribune*, December 12, 1867: 1.

24. *Intelligencer Journal* (Lancaster, Pennsylvania), December 13, 1867: 2; "Facts and Fancies," *Daily Evening Bulletin*, December 13, 1867: 1.

25. "Prejudice among the Small Potatoes," *Evening Journal* (Jersey City, New Jersey), December 16, 1867: 2.

26. For example, see "Another Reproof for Negroes," *Richmond* (Virginia) *Daily Dispatch*, December 14, 1867: 3.

27. Shaun McCormack, *Willie Mays* (New York: Rosen Publishing Group, 2003), 29.

28. "Colorphobia," *Fall River* (Massachusetts) *Daily Evening News*, December 16, 1867: 2.

A similarly terse example halfway across the continent was "Base Ball," *Atchison* (Kansas) *Daily Free Press*, December 30, 1867: 4.

29. Steve Turner, "Berkshire Blacks: The Struggle for Equality Began Two Centuries Ago," *Berkshire Eagle*, August 28, 1976: 18.

30. *Twenty-Ninth Report to the Legislature of Massachusetts Relating to the Registry and Return of Births, Marriages and Deaths in the Commonwealth, for the Year ending December 31, 1870* (Boston: Wright & Potter, 1872), iv.

31. Lawrence D. Hogan, *Shades of Glory: The Negro Leagues and the Story of African American Baseball* (Washington, D.C.: National Geographic Society, 2006), 60.

32. "Greylock Hall" (advertisement), *Pittsfield Sun*, April 21, 1870: 3. The Grant family's listing in the 1870 census includes a teen girl whose name Ancestry.com and FamilySearch.org read as "Nellie," but there's no such person in any of the family's other records. If that wasn't some cousin living with them temporarily, the most likely explanation is that this was actually Willis, who wasn't elsewhere in the list of family members. Nellie was identified as female, but Frances has been identified as male, so the census taker certainly could have made more than one such mistake in haste.

33. There was a Pittsfield directory published for 1868, and the aforementioned Sylvanus Grant was listed in it, but Frances Grant wasn't. However, neither was Cornelia Hamilton, who lived in Pittsfield at the time of both the 1865 and 1870 censuses.

34. Hamilton Child, *Gazetteer of Berkshire County, Mass., 1725-1885* (Syracuse, NY: Syracuse Journal, 1885), 455. Her first name was entered as "Louise," but all the other details dovetail with various other records. Interestingly, at the start of 1870 a Mrs. McDonald bought "the Cole place on Spring street" to use as a boarding house, according to "Williamstown," *Pittsfield Sun*, January 13, 1870: 2.

35. A corrected death registry entry for Louisa in 1889, accessible via Ancestry.com, changed the place of her death from Pittsfield to Williamstown, added her maiden name as Hoose, and though it showed her mother's name as "Honora" rather than Hannah, it correctly specified her father's name and her parents' birthplaces as Kinderhook and Goshen, respectively. By coincidence, at the time of the 1900 census a Duncan and *Louise* McDonald lived in Williamstown, though they were whites from Scotland.

36. "Berkshire Scenery," *Berkshire County Eagle*, May 31, 1877: 2. This newspaper quoted excerpts from a letter Hale had written for the *Boston Advertiser*, a daily newspaper his father had founded and published.

37. See the Williamstown and Williams College Map Collection at https://unbound.williams.edu/williamsarchives/collections, which also includes an informative map from 1889 showing the home owned by Frank's cousin Evelina (nee Duncan) and her husband, Richard H. Lansing, on the west side of Spring Street near its north end, across from a post office.

38. Bliss Perry, *And Gladly Teach* (Boston: Houghton Mifflin, 1935), 8, 194.

39. *Ibid.*, 8-9.

40. Around the same time, Danforth served as legal guardian for two minors named Walker, and they were presumably part of a local white family by that name in the 1870 census. See the legal ad in the *Pittsfield Sun*, December 21, 1871: 4. There were also such ads on February 22, 29 and March 7, 1872.

41. See http://mlb.mlb.com/memorylab/chronology/index.jsp?start=1801&end=1825.

42. "Williamstown," *Pittsfield Sun*, January 13, 1870: 2.

43. Perry, 11, 22. It was on page 15 where Perry explained what "hired girl" meant. On page 22, Perry agonized that his subsequent timidity as an ice skater was just one example of a growing fear that he was a "born coward," but on the next page he described how a local butcher named Hancock helped him start to counter that feeling by teaching him a nifty wrestling move. Perry said that lesson occurred in 1873. On page 21, Perry also implied the time frame centered on 1873.

44. "Judge Clarence M. Smith Eulogized At Bar Service," *North Adams* (Massachusetts) *Transcript*, January 20, 1938: 11.

45. Robert A. Clark, "Communication," *North Adams Transcript*, March 22, 1944: 9. All those decades later, Clark was able to identify the five Perry brothers in order correctly, from oldest to youngest. For a profile of Judge Tenney, see Williams College, *Alumni Obituary Record*, April 1914: 226.

46. The *Harrisburg Telegram* (distinct from the *Telegraph* published in the same city) was quoted in full in "Second Baseman Grant," *Cleveland Gazette*, September 21, 1889: 1.

47. "Base Ball Gossip," *The Sun* (New York City), April 25, 1886: 6.

48. Perry, 22, 24, 29-30. Danny Collins became a police officer in Indianapolis. Perry said Clarence Grant was a catcher *and captain* for the Cuban Giants, and though he played very briefly for that team, Perry was confusing Clarence with Frank with regard to the team's captaincy.

49. For more about Perry, see https://www.britannica.com/biography/Bliss-Perry.

50. Darryl Brock, introduction to Bliss Perry, *The Plated City* (Westport, CT: Rvive Books, 2008), xi.

51. Perry, *The Plated City*, 88, 89, 173-174.

52. Sol White, "Sol White Recalls," *New York Age*, January 17, 1931: 6. White had gotten together with Grant about two months earlier.

53. See Note 43.

54. Perry, *The Plated City*, 49, 89. The Cuban Giants are even mentioned on pages 157 and 172.

55. Perry, *And Gladly Teach*, 29-30.

56. "Williamstown," *Berkshire County Eagle*, June 19, 1873: 3.

57. "Williamstown," *Berkshire County Eagle*, May 20, 1875: 2.

58. "Williamstown," *Troy* (New York) *Weekly Times*, August 15, 1878: 3; "The January Term," *Berkshire County Eagle* (Pittsfield, Massachusetts), January 23, 1879: 2. Neither article mentioned his race.

59. Perry, *And Gladly Teach*, 12.

60. See Nancy Lovas, "The Panic of 1873," Library of Congress, August 2017, at https://www.loc.gov/rr/business/businesshistory/September/Panic1873.html.

61. Brian McKenna, "Frank Grant," https://sabr.org/bioproj/person/2f633c50. McKenna credited Sarah Harding of the Williamstown House of Local History for "answering several questions about the area—particularly Grant's probable high school."

62. This anonymous profile has been quoted in a few books, such as in the 12-page chapter on Grant by one of the foremost researchers into his baseball career. See James E. Overmyer, "Frank Grant," *Baseball History No. 4: An Annual of Original Baseball Research* (Westport, CT: Meckler, 1991), 25.

63. John M. Flynn, "The Referee's Sporting Chat," *Berkshire County Eagle*, June 23, 1937: 17.

64. Perry, *The Plated City*, 165–166.

65. Perry, *And Gladly Teach*, 14. Garfield's sons, Harry and James, were at the train station and preparing to accompany the President to his Williams class reunion. "The brothers entered Williams on Sept. 5, 1881, just two weeks before their father died." See https://specialcollections.williams.edu/williams-history/presidents/garfield-harry-augustus/.

66. Henry Porter had been listed simply as a "laborer" in the 1880 census (and the only others listed as part of the household were Henrietta, age 15, and her mother, Nancy). However, by 1885 he was identified as a doctor by Hamilton Child, *Gazetteer of Berkshire County, Mass., 1725–1885* (Syracuse, NY: Syracuse Journal, 1885), 458. See also "Death of Mrs. Grant," *North Adams Transcript*, May 9, 1913: 9. His own death record in 1900 identified him as a physician.

67. "Williamstown," *North Adams Transcript*, March 29, 1883: 2. North Adams lies about six miles east of Williamstown, which didn't have its own newspaper.

68. "Williamstown," *North Adams Transcript*, October 4, 1883: 2.

69. "Seventy Miles in a Hot Day," *Boston Daily Globe*, June 22, 1884: 6; "Abduction or Worse," *Berkshire County Eagle*, June 26, 1884: 2.

70. "Berkshire County," *Springfield* (Massachusetts) *Republican*, November 22, 1884: 6. Baker's middle initial was identified in "Superior Court," *Berkshire County Eagle*, January 22, 1885: 2.

71. "Superior Court," *Pittsfield Sun*, January 20, 1875: 2; *Pittsfield Sun*, January 27, 1875: 2. The latter article had no headline; it was in the sixth column on that page.

72. "Superior Court," *Berkshire County Eagle*, January 15, 1885: 2; "Superior Court," *Berkshire County Eagle*, January 22, 1885: 2; "Superior Court," *Valley Gleaner* (Lee, Massachusetts), January 28, 1885: 3.

73. *Sol White's History of Colored Base Ball with Other Documents on the Early Black Game, 1886–1936* (Lincoln: University of Nebraska Press, 1995), 110–111. The adjectives "quiet" and "unassuming" were again the first applied to Grant in Sol White, "Our Baseball Leagues," *New York Amsterdam News*, February 20, 1929: 6.

74. "John Jones Dead; Popular in the South," *Harrisburg* (Pennsylvania) *Telegraph*, March 10, 1914: 10; James E. Brunson III, *Black Baseball, 1858–1900: A Comprehensive Record of the Teams, Players, Managers, Owners and Umpires* (Jefferson, NC: McFarland, 2019), 349.

75. Hamilton Child, *Gazetteer of Berkshire County, Mass., 1725–1885* (Syracuse, NY: Syracuse Journal, 1885), 451. See also https://en.wikipedia.org/wiki/Zeta_Psi, which notes that the chapter at Williamstown was just the second in its history.

Chapter 2

1. "'Bob' Pettit Dies at Home in Derby," *North Adams* (Massachusetts) *Transcript*, November 3, 1910: 3. "Ball Game at the Park," *Meriden* (Connecticut) *Daily Republican*, April 19, 1883: 2.

2. "Williamstown," *North Adams Transcript*, July 12, 1883: 2. Bob Stedler, "Sport Comment," *Buffalo Evening News*, October 25, 1945: 29. As a result of Grant's familiarity to Williams College students, he may have had the chance to meet future Hall of Famer Tim Keefe, who was to coach the school's nine during the winter of 1883–1884, starting around November 1, according to "Williamstown," *North Adams Transcript*, October 25, 1883: 2.

3. "Base Ball Gossip," *The Sun* (New York City), April 25, 1886: 6.

4. "How Dwyer Broke into Baseball," *Berkshire Evening Eagle* (Pittsfield, MA), December 3, 1915: 24. This article spelled Porter's first name as "Medallian"; other variations included Merdelen and Merdellen. Sometimes he was simply called M.D. Porter. By the time of that article, he, Barton, Flynn, and John Mooney were deceased.

5. "Dalton," *Berkshire County Eagle*, September 14, 1882: 2. In addition to Edward Dwyer, the roster included John Mooney, Richard Maher, "Merdelon" Porter, and William Callahan. Also, "John Fenn" was correctly identified about a month earlier as John Flynn in "Dalton," *Pittsfield* (Massachusetts) *Sun*, August 17, 1882: 2. At that point, the club's record was reportedly 5–4, whereas their detailed record about a month earlier was presented as 9–2.

6. "Dalton," *Pittsfield Sun*, May 17, 1883: 2; "Dalton," *Pittsfield Sun*, May 24, 1883: 2; "Dalton," *Berkshire County Eagle*, May 31, 1883: 2; "Dalton," *Berkshire County Eagle*, July 12, 1883: 2.

7. "Dalton," *Pittsfield Sun*, July 26, 1883: 2; "Base Ball," *Pittsfield Sun*, August 2, 1883: 2; "Dalton," *Pittsfield Sun*, June 14, 1883: 2.

8. "Dalton," *Pittsfield Sun*, May 8, 1884: 2; "Dalton," *Pittsfield Sun*, June 5, 1884: 2; "Dalton," *Pittsfield Sun*, July 10, 1884: 2. The announcement on May 8 read: "The Lone Star base ball club will consist of these players: Captain and 1 b., John Hardiman; C. Grant, c.; M.D. Porter, p.; W. Barton, 2 b.; John Flynn, 3b; John Mooney, s. s.; Frank Dwyre, l. f.; W. Callahan, c. f.; M. Kane, r. f.; F. Murry, substitute; scorer, B.C. Rockwood; umpire, Matt Stockbridge. The opening game will be Saturday May 24. They play the Russells at Pittsfield."

9. "Local Intelligence," *Berkshire County Eagle*, May 22, 1884: 2; "Berkshire County," *Springfield* (Massachusetts); *Daily Republican*, July 21, 1884: 6. "North Adams," *Springfield Daily Republican*, July 23, 1884: 6; "The Local News," *Pittsfield Sun*, July 31, 1884: 2.

10. "South Williamstown," *Pittsfield Sun*, June 29, 1881: 1; "Sporting Matters," *Springfield Daily Republican*, September 12, 1882: 5.

11. "Base Ball," *North Adams Transcript*, August 7, 1884: 2. Confirmation that it was Frank Grant who played with the Greylocks, at least in 1884, was provided occasionally in later years, such as in a long paragraph without a headline in the *Pittsfield Sun*, April 12, 1888: 4. See also "The Cuban Giants Saturday," *Berkshire Eagle*, August 23, 1892: 3.

12. "Other Games," *Boston Sunday Globe*, August 10, 1884: 3; "Base Ball," *North Adams Transcript*, August 21, 1884: 2.

13. "Base Ball," *North Adams Transcript*, August 28, 1884: 2; "Base Ball," *North Adams Transcript*, September 11, 1884: 2.

14. "Base Ball," *North Adams Transcript*, October 11, 1884: 2; "Williams College Notes," *Boston Daily Globe*, April 19, 1884: 4. It was easy to obtain these four box scores thanks to James E. Overmyer, "Frank Grant," *Baseball History No. 4: An Annual of Original Baseball Research* (Westport, CT: Meckler, 1991), 25.

15. "Curtiss Big Leaguer in Arlie Latham's Time," *North Adams Transcript*, December 26, 1908: 2; John M. Flynn, "Saw Latham Call His Shot to President Harrison and Then Hit Home Run," *Berkshire Evening Eagle* (Pittsfield, Massachusetts), May 12, 1944: 12.

16. "Paragrams," *Plattsburgh* (New York) *Sentinel*, May 29, 1885: 1.

17. "Base Ball," *Plattsburgh* (New York) *Republican*, August 22, 1885: 4.

18. "Williams vs. Springfields," *North Adams Transcript*, June 11, 1885: 2. Williams College and governmental records around that time, including the 1880 census, help identify John Henry Safford as a student there, with his brother Walter Bradbury Safford. By very odd coincidence, the latter overlapped with a second Walter B. Safford, whose middle name was Bramhall.

19. George Hubbell was identified as a Williams College student from the Plattsburgh area in "Chazy," *Plattsburgh Republican*, April 10, 1886: 1. A few months later, Julius Hubbell was in town to attend their sister Mary's wedding, according to "Chazy," *Plattsburgh Republican*, August 28, 1886: 1. "J. Safford" and "W. Safford" both appeared in box scores in July and August 1886 printed by the *Plattsburgh Telegram*. Their team was simply called the Plattsburghs.

20. "Julius Hubbell Taken by Death," *Spokesman-Review* (Spokane, Washington), October 18, 1949: 1; "John H. Safford; Former Teacher," *North Adams Transcript*, August 15, 1938: 9; "Walter B. Safford, '85, Dies in New York City," *North Adams Transcript*, April 29, 1943: 12.

21. *Sol White's History of Colored Base Ball with Other Documents on the Early Black Game, 1886–1936* (Lincoln: University of Nebraska Press, 1995), 110.

22. "Quinn's Magnificent Pitching," *Meriden Journal*, May 3, 1886: 2.

23. James E. Overmyer, "Frank Grant," *Baseball History No. 4: An Annual of Original Baseball Research* (Westport, CT: Meckler Publishing, 1991), 26. Overmyer drew on the *Morning Telegraph* (Plattsburgh, New York) editions of August 24 and 20, 1885, respectively.

24. "Paragrams," *Plattsburgh Sentinel*, August 14, 1885: 1; "Base Ball," *Plattsburgh Sentinel*, August 28, 1885: 1; "Sporting Matters," *Buffalo* (New York) *Times*, August 17, 1886: 5; The Plattsburgh Athletic Association charged ladies and children only 15 cents, and seating in the grand stand was free.

25. "Paragrams," *Plattsburgh Sentinel*, September 11, 1885: 1; "Paragrams," *Plattsburgh Sentinel*, October 2, 1885: 1; "Paragrams," *Plattsburgh Sentinel*, September 25, 1885: 1.

26. "Notes from out of Town," *Troy* (New York) *Daily Times*, October 2, 1885: 3.

27. "Plattsburgh," *Argus* (Albany, New York), October 5, 1885: 2. On, September 25, the Nameless had won their 10th game of 1885, according to "Local Sporting Items," *Plattsburgh Sentinel*, October 2, 1885: 1. However, their number of losses wasn't mentioned.

Chapter 3

1. "Pointers," *Boston Herald*, February 21, 1886: 7.

2. "The National Game," *Meriden* (Connecticut) *Journal*, April 27, 1886: 2.

3. "New England Baseball," *New York Herald*, March 8, 1886: 6.

4. Short Stop, "More Players for Meriden," *Sporting Life*, March 24, 1886: 2. "Short Stop" is an example of *Sporting Life*'s comfort with identifying reporters only by nickname or pseudonym.

5. Derek Gentile, "A Place in Baseball History," *Berkshire Eagle* (Pittsfield, Massachusetts), July 31, 2006: A1. See especially the continuation of this article on page A3 (though it incorrectly conflated Grant's Meriden team with the Resolutes, a team discussed herein at the end of Grant's time in Meriden; see Note 56).

6. "Base Ball Notes," *Meriden Journal*, July 6, 1886: 2.

7. Meriden's population was surging, according to https://portal.ct.gov/SOTS/Register-Manual/Section-VII/Population-1830-1890, and increased from 18,340 in the 1880 census to over 25,000 in 1990.

8. "Notes of the Local Base Ball Players," *Greenpoint Daily Star* (Brooklyn, New York), May 13, 1905: 4.

9. "Base Ball," *Daily Star* (Long Island City, New York), April 24, 1886: 4; "In and about the Diamond," *Evening Leader* (Wilkes-Barre, Pennsylvania), May 7, 1886: 1. Other newspapers around then suggested that Bagley's team represented both Elmira and Scranton simultaneously, at least early on, though as of this writing, Bagley's 1886 Pennsylvania State Association statistics at baseball-reference.com only identify his team as Scranton.

10. "Batted Balls," *Boston Daily Globe*, August 2, 1886: 8. Though Bagley signed his National League contract on July 31, 1886, he didn't make his debut with the Giants until September 11.

11. "The Meridens will all report for duty April 9," according to "Base Ball Notes," *Meriden* (Connecticut) *Daily Republican*, March 29, 1886: 4. However, one day prior to that scheduled arrival, the same paper reported that most players weren't expected to arrive until April 12 or 13. See "National Sports," *Meriden Daily Republican*, April 8, 1886: 4.

12. "Base Ball Notes," *Meriden Daily Republican*, March 11, 1886: 4.

13. "Base Ball Gossip," *Boston Post*, March 17, 1886: 4. "Manager Burnham of the Meriden team is at the Sherman House. His intention is to secure several more strong players around Boston."

14. "Meriden and Vicinity News," *Meriden Daily Republican*, April 13, 1886: 4.

15. "Meriden Defeats Trinity," *Meriden Daily Republican*, April 15, 1886: 4.

16. "Meriden and Vicinity News," *Meriden Daily Republican* April 17, 1886: 4. Bob Keating was born in Springfield, and also died there.

17. The National League, which exists to this day, and the long-lived American Association were joined for just one year by an unstable circuit called the Union Association, which typically had eight franchises at any given point.

18. For more on Buffalo's Big Four, see White's biography by Joe Williams at https://sabr.org/bioproj/person/99417cd4.

19. "Sporting Matters," *Detroit Free Press*, April 19, 1886: 5; "Meriden and Vicinity News," *Meriden Daily Republican* April 19, 1886: 4.

20. "Lost Through Errors," *Meriden* (Connecticut) *Journal*, April 20, 1886: 3; "National Sports," *Meriden Daily Republican*, April 21, 1884: 4; "Shannon's Men Beaten," *Meriden Journal*, April 22, 1886: 3.

21. "Three Base Ball Games," *Meriden Journal*, April 24, 1886: 2; "Meriden and Vicinity News," *Meriden Daily Republican* April 26, 1886: 4.

22. "Base Ball Gossip," *The Sun* (New York City), April 25, 1886: 6.

23. "Drives and Grounders," *Boston Daily Globe*, April 28, 1886: 2. As was common practice, the *Globe* didn't credit the original source, whether that was *The Sun* or some third periodical. Back in his home county, this was also shared by the *Adams Freeman*, according to "He Knocked the Ball Sky High," *Berkshire County Eagle*, May 6, 1886: 1. The latter, at least, prefaced the reprinting by noting that he had played locally with the Greylocks.

24. "Yale Vs. Meridens, April 28," *Yale News*, April 29, 1886: 1.

25. See https://www.britannica.com/biography/Amos-Alonzo-Stagg.

26. "Meriden and Vicinity News," *Meriden Daily Republican*, May 3, 1886: 4. See also "Base Hits and Errors," *Meriden Journal*, May 3, 1886: 2. The only real drama during the game occurred just beyond the field. About 100 boys were watching the game atop a large shed that reportedly peaked close to 30 feet above the ground, located not far from third base. The roof collapsed, and adult spectators rushed to lend assistance. Miraculously, just six boys needed medical attention, and only three of those were hurt seriously.

27. "Quinn's Magnificent Pitching," *Meriden Journal*, May 3, 1886: 2. Except where noted, all subsequent scores of Meriden's games and Frank Grant's statistics in them are from either this daily or the *Meriden Daily Republican*, typically the next day—or two days later in the case of Saturday games, because neither paper published on Sundays. Both papers tended to publish box scores with seven columns, for at-bats, runs, hits, total bases, putouts, assists, and errors. However, those numbers didn't always agree with one another.

28. "Meriden and Vicinity News," *Meriden Daily Republican*, May 11, 1886: 4. "Umpire Farrow always wears a chest protector and mask same as the catcher," the paper mentioned under the subheading "Base Ball Notes," implying that protective gear worn by umpires wasn't a given.

29. "General Base Ball Notes," *Meriden Daily Republican*, June 8, 1886: 4. (A bias against catchers who threw left-handed had apparently taken hold already.) See also Jerry Denny's biography by Chris Rainey at https://sabr.org/bioproj/person/221e2aee.

30. Dennis Thiessen, "Radical Changes to the Playing Rules: The 1886 Winter Meetings," *Base Ball's 19th Century "Winter" Meetings* (Phoenix, AZ: Society for American Baseball Research, 2018), 252.

31. John Thorn, "A Brief History of the Pitching Distance," February 27, 2015, https://our

game.mlblogs.com/a-brief-history-of-the-pitching-distance-3210e7874d5c.

32. "Concerning the Diamond," *Meriden Journal*, May 1, 1886: 2; "Stupid Ball Playing," *Meriden Journal*, May 4, 1886: 2.

33. "Three Straight," *Meriden Journal*, May 5, 1886: 2; "Meriden and Vicinity News," *Meriden Daily Republican*, May 5, 1886: 4.

34. "Base Ball," *Meriden Daily Republican*, May 8, 1886: 4.

35. "Base Ball Matters," *Meriden Journal*, May 10, 1886: 2.

36. His errors were primarily wild throws. The *Republican* defended him and blamed his use at so many different positions on the diamond during the young season, insisting that "any man must have a certain amount of steady practice to enable him to judge all his throws to a nicety." See "Meriden and Vicinity News," *Meriden Daily Republican*, May 13, 1886: 4. It so happened that this game was the first of eight straight in which he played at second base exclusively.

37. "Meriden's Second Victory," *Meriden Journal*, May 14, 1886: 2.

38. "Mere Mention," *Meriden Journal*, May 18, 1886: 2.

39. "Doyle and Reardon," *Meriden Journal*, May 19, 1886: 2. The teams were to meet again the next day, but in its May 20 edition, the *Journal* reported that rain had left the grounds too wet.

40. The *Bridgeport Standard* was quoted in "The Long Islands Disband," *Meriden Journal*, May 25, 1886: 2.

41. The *Bridgeport News* was quoted in "Base Ball Notes," *Meriden Journal*, May 24, 1886: 2.

42. The *Newark Press-Register* was quoted in "Diamond Dots," *Meriden Journal*, May 26, 1886: 2.

43. The *Jersey City Argus* was quoted in "Victims of the Newarks," *Meriden Journal*, May 31, 1886: 3. Two days earlier. the *Journal* had printed its own assessment of Grant's full game as catcher on May 28: "Quinn was very wild in his delivery, and, under the circumstances, the catching of Grant was marvelous. He was continually jumping from one side of the home plate to the other, and his gymnastic antics caused the spectators to applaud quite frequently. It was only when the ball sent several yards outside of his reach, that he did not succeed in grasping it." See the next endnote for the full citation.

44. "One More Defeat," *Meriden Journal*, May 29, 1886: 2.

45. Vet, "Base Ball," *Sporting Life*, June 2, 1886: 8.

46. "Diamond Dots," *Meriden Journal*, May 26, 1886: 2. In fact, the *Newark Journal* reported that the Cuban Giants were one of three teams under consideration to replace the Long Island franchise, according to an item quoted in "Meriden and Vicinity News," *Meriden Daily Republican*, May 27, 1886: 4. When the Eastern League shrank to a five-team circuit in July, the Cuban Giants reportedly applied for membership "but were refused," according to "The Eastern League," *Philadelphia Inquirer*, July 20, 1886: 1.

47. "Morning Games To-Day," *Evening Telegram* (Providence), May 31, 1886: 2; "Game to Game," *Evening Telegram*, June 1, 1886: 6. By this time, coverage of Eastern League games was becoming quite elaborate. For example, an inning-by-inning, batter-by-batter account of the game that ended Grant's 14-game hitting streak was provided in "Meriden and Vicinity News," *Meriden Daily Republican*, May 31, 1886: 4. Such reports subsequently became more frequent in that paper. Far less common in that era was the set of detailed pitch counts that began a lengthy description of the penultimate game of Grant's streak, in "Sporting Notes," *Jersey Journal* (Jersey City, New Jersey), May 28, 1886: 3.

48. "Meriden and Vicinity News," *Meriden Daily Republican*, June 10, 1886: 4.

49. For example, see "The National Game," *Burlington* (Vermont) *Clipper*, June 10, 1886: 4. The exact same sentence appeared in "Base Ball," *Frostburg* (Maryland) *Mining Journal*, June 12, 1886: 3.

50. "The U.V.M.'s at Plattsburgh," *Burlington* (Vermont) *Free Press and Times*, June 10, 1886: 8; "Yesterday's Ball Game," *Burlington Free Press and Times*, June 19, 1886: 8. Meriden played daily from June 14 through June 19, and Plattsburgh played on at least two of those days. For example, see "Glens Falls Wins," *Morning Telegram* (Plattsburgh, New York), June 17, 1886: 4.

51. "Brasher Falls, Aug. 31," *Ogdensburg (New York) Advance and St. Lawrence Weekly Democrat*, September 2, 1886: 1.

52. "Meriden and Vicinity News," *Meriden Daily Republican*, June 16, 1886: 4. This account describes every plate appearance in every inning (except one Waterbury batter in the eighth). Hurling the shutout was Jack Quinn, Grant's former teammate, who pitched in just three games for Waterbury. The two teams were supposed to play the day prior but rain prevented that. For insights about Walker's 1886 season, see his biography by John R. Husman at https://sabr.org/bioproj/person/fleet-walker/.

53. "Meriden and Vicinity News," *Meriden Daily Republican*, June 17, 1886: 4. The paper again provided a batter-by-batter account. Grant had a putout and five assists, while Walker had two of each. Grant participated in a 6–4–3 double play.

54. "Meriden and Vicinity News," *Meriden Daily Republican*, June 24, 1886: 4.

55. "Meriden and Vicinity News," *Meriden Daily Republican*, June 26, 1886: 4. The *Hartford Journal*'s mention of Grant's expertise playing checkers was noted in "Base Ball Talk," *Meriden Journal*, June 28, 1886: 2.

56. "Meriden and Vicinity News," *Meriden Daily Republican*, June 28, 1886: 4. The paper again provided a batter-by-batter account. Meriden and Waterbury played a final time on July 3, but Fleet Walker wasn't in his team's lineup that day. For the box score, see "Won in Fifteen Innings," *Meriden Journal*, July 6, 1886: 2.

57. "Timely and Terrific," *Meriden Journal*, June 28, 1886: 2.

58. "Meriden Base Ball Notes," *Meriden Daily Republican*, June 28, 1886: 4.

59. "Meriden Base Ball Notes," *Meriden Daily Republican*, June 30, 1886: 4; "Base Ball Notes," *Meriden Journal*, June 30, 1886: 2. The latter reported that Mack traveled to the game with three teammates. The former said some of his calls "on balls and strikes were perhaps a little doubtful, but on the whole he was impartial." The *Republican* also quipped that if Grant and Murphy could repeat their home runs hosting Bridgeport, their great rival, instead of silver coins "the audience would hand out bank accounts and deeds of land."

60. For a description of Stovey's debut in Organized Baseball on June 26, 1886, see his biography by Brian McKenna at https://sabr.org/bioproj/person/george-stovey/.

61. "Doings of the Race," *Cleveland Gazette*, July 3, 1886: 1.

62. "The Little Giants Beaten," *Meriden Journal*, July 1, 1886: 2. It was mentioned previously that Grant had tripled on June 9, meaning that on June 30 he'd hit his second of the month. However, his baseball-reference.com statistics show him with one triple for Meriden all season.

63. Meriden and Vicinity News," *Meriden Daily Republican*, July 6, 1886: 4.

64. The *Bridgeport News* was quoted at length in "Meriden's Second Baseman," *New Haven* (Connecticut) *Evening Register*, July 13, 1886: 4.

65. "Meriden Base Ball Notes," *Meriden Daily Republican*, July 8, 1886: 4.

66. "Meriden and Vicinity News," *Meriden Daily Republican*, July 9, 1886: 4. Actually, the franchise lingered in the Eastern League for two more games but with an entirely new roster consisting of a local amateur team called the Resolutes. See "Miscellaneous," *Boston Journal*, July 13, 1886: 3; "They Show Up Finely," *Meriden Journal*, July 13, 1886: 2; "Fare Thee Well, $666," *Meriden Journal*, July 14, 1886: 2.

67. "Base Ball Notes," *Meriden Journal*, July 12, 1886: 2; James E. Overmyer, "The Unhappy Odyssey of a Great Ballplayer," *Berkshire Eagle*, February 5, 1990: A1, B6. Grant played in all 44 of Meriden's games, but had one entirely behind the plate and one complete game as pitcher.

68. "Notes and Comments," *Sporting Life*, July 14, 1886: 5. This item called him "Fred" instead of Frank, and was printed in at least one Buffalo newspaper the day before, adding a note that their team had just signed him. See "Sporting Notes," *Buffalo Courier*, July 13, 1886: 4.

69. This *Hartford Courant* item was quoted in "Sporting Notes," *Buffalo Times*, July 15, 1886: 5.

Chapter 4

1. "New Players for Buffalo," *Buffalo Times*, July 13, 1886: 5. This paper appeared to use "the Spaniard" as a nickname for him two days later. See "Sporting Notes," *Buffalo Times*, July 15, 1886: 5.

2. If "Spaniard" was sometimes intended to obscure his race, that was undercut in "Grand Stand Echoes," *Rochester* (New York) *Democrat and Chronicle*, August 1, 1886: 7. "'The Spaniard' is what Grant, the colored player, is called in Buffalo," that paper reported.

3. "Base Ball Notes," *Meriden Journal*, July 13, 1886: 2.

4. "Base Ball," *Hartford* (Connecticut) *Daily Courant*, July 21, 1886: 2.

5. "Queen City Sports," *Buffalo Commercial Advertiser*, July 16, 1886: 3. Two other players were on Buffalo in both 1885 and 1886, Pete Wood's brother Fred and longtime major leaguer Dave Eggler, but both played minimally in those two seasons.

6. International League standings weren't necessarily published regularly back then, but one Buffalo paper reported the Bisons' record as 18–26 through Sunday, July 11, and they lost on each of the next two days to Hamilton. See "Dusty Diamonds," *Buffalo Commercial Advertiser*, July 12, 1886: 3.

7. "Sporting Notes," *Buffalo Times*, July 15, 1886: 5.

8. "The Sporting Record," *Buffalo Courier*, July 15, 1886: 4.

9. "A Dusky Diamond," *Buffalo Times*, July 15, 1886: 5. A few months later, Chapman's line was used in a neighboring state about the formation of the short-lived National Colored Baseball League. See "A New Coon in Town," *The Post* (Pittsburgh), November 24, 1886: 1.

10. James E. Brunson III, *Black Baseball, 1858–1900: A Comprehensive Record of the Teams, Players, Managers, Owners and Umpires* (Jefferson, NC: McFarland, 2019), 28–29. See also "Crooked Racing," *San Francisco Call*, May 14, 1893: 7.

11. "Outdoor Pastimes," *Buffalo Courier*, July 16, 1886: 4. The box score shows that the two runs were scored by the batters who were just ahead of Grant in the lineup, and he did have one of his team's for singles on the day, but Buffalo's dailies otherwise skimped on details.

12. "The Colored Curver," *Buffalo Times*, July 17, 1886: 5. Buffalo's dailies often omitted box scores of road games around this time, including for Grant's pitching debut, but papers in other International League cities sometimes printed multiple IL box scores on the same day. In this instance, see "Base Ball News," *Rochester Democrat and Chronicle*, July 17, 1886: 6.

13. "The Sporting World," *Buffalo Courier*, July 18, 1886: 6. This account included a box score.

14. "Badly Beaten by Buffalo," *Syracuse* (New York) *Standard*, July 24, 1886: 2.

15. "The Sporting World," *Buffalo Times*, July 27, 1886: 5. The lineup for the Travelers included infielders James and John Reidy. The latter became Grant's good friend and teammate in 1887–1888.

16. "Sporting Notes," *Buffalo Times*, July 28, 1886: 5.

17. "Hours of Pleasure," *Buffalo Commercial Advertiser*, July 28, 1886: 3.

Notes—Chapter 5

18. "Weir Retired," *Buffalo Times*, July 31, 1886: 5.
19. "The Base Ball Averages," *Buffalo Times*, August 3, 1886: 5.
20. "The Stars Do It Again," *Syracuse Standard*, August 3, 1886: 4.
21. "Some of the Sports," *Sunday Truth* (Buffalo, New York), August 8, 1886: 2.
22. "The Buffalos Beaten," *Buffalo Express*, August 11, 1886: 8.
23. Brunson, 25.
24. "At Last Utica Wins a Game," *Syracuse* (New York) *Herald*, August 15, 1886: 7; "Sporting Matters," *Buffalo Times*, August 17, 1886: 5. The *Times* noted that ticket prices were 25 cents.
25. "Sporting Notes," *Buffalo Courier*, August 18, 1886: 4.
26. For an example of *Sporting Life* being quoted in Buffalo, see "Notes," *Sunday Truth*, August 29, 1886: 2. However, several other papers printed this high praise without attributing it to any source, such as in "Gloves and Masks," *Rochester Democrat and Chronicle*, August 26, 1886: 6. Examples during September appeared in such papers as the *Rogersville* (Tennessee) *Herald*, *The Mercury* (Sandersville, Georgia), the *Abbeville* (South Carolina) *Press and Banner*, and a few each in Alabama and Vermont.
27. "Base Ball Briefs," *Daily Commonwealth* (Topeka, Kansas), August 31, 1886: 4.
28. When Jackie Robinson began the process of integrating the National League in April 1947, it's often been said that he crossed or broke the "color line," referring to the unwritten rule that kept African Americans out of the major leagues and almost every affiliated minor league since before 1900. The aforementioned policy adopted in late 1867 at a convention of the National Association of Base Ball Players was one example of a formal "drawing" of a color line. For a very concise overview of color lines in the 1800s, see https://www.loc.gov/collections/jackie-robinson-baseball/articles-and-essays/baseball-the-color-line-and-jackie-robinson/1860s-to-1890s/.
29. "Sporting News," *Buffalo Evening News*, September 2, 1886: 1.
30. "A Hard Fought Game," *Buffalo Times*, September 4, 1886: 5.
31. "Games and Pastimes, "*Buffalo Commercial Advertiser*, September 14, 1886: 3. Cuban Giants second baseman Harry A. Johnson had been called "a second Dunlap" a few months earlier, but that apparently didn't become an ongoing nickname for him. See "Base Ball," *Trenton* (New Jersey) *Evening Times*, May 9, 1886: 8.
32. "Bishop's Good Work," *The Post* (Pittsburgh), April 12, 1887: 6; "Diamond Points," *Boston Daily Globe*, April 15, 1887: 2; "The World of Sport," *Cleveland Leader*, April 17, 1887: 11; "Diamond Dust," *Nashville Banner*, April 26, 1887: 3. See also "The Season Begun," *Buffalo Courier*, April 3, 1887: 5.
33. Mac, "The Smoky City Boys," *The Sporting News*, April 23, 1887: 1. *Sportsman's Referee* was quoted in an African American newspaper (an item without a headline): see the *Cleveland Gazette*, April 30, 1887: 4.
34. See "MLB Forgotten Greats: Remembering Fred Dunlap, June 30, 2017, at https://www.foxsports.com/stories/mlb/mlb-forgotten-greats-remembering-fred-dunlap. See also Michael Haupert, "MLB's annual salary leaders since 1874" at https://sabr.org/research/article/mlbs-annual-salary-leaders-since-1874/.
35. "Caught on the Fly," *Buffalo Times*, September 2, 1886: 5.
36. "The Bisons Win Again," *Buffalo Times*, September 2, 1886: 5. Speaking of Buffalo uniforms, the team reportedly wore new ones beginning on September 3, according to "Sporting News," *Buffalo Commercial Advertiser*, September 3, 1886: 3. On that occasion this daily asked, rhetorically, "Won't 'Gen' Grant look nobby?" Nobby was an old compliment equivalent to "stylish."
37. "Autumn Athletics," *Sunday Truth*, September 19, 1886: 7.
38. Baseball-reference.com shows Grant as having played 49 games for Buffalo, but he missed two during the team's 32–17 finish. Buffalo was supposed to play four games after the one in which Grant accumulated eight total bases, but it only played one more. See Note 33.
39. "The Baseball Season," *Buffalo Express*, October 3, 1886: 14.
40. "Reserves 7, Greylocks 5," *Springfield* (Massachusetts) *Republican*, October 3, 1886: 1; "The Baseball Season," *Buffalo Express*, October 3, 1886: 14.
41. "In General," *Buffalo Express*, October 17, 1886: 8; "The Baseball Company Incorporated," *Buffalo Express*, March 21, 1886: 10; "Athletic Affairs," *Sunday Truth*, November 21, 1886: 2. The Railway Car Association (called the "Car Tracers' Association" in the October item) was headquartered in the historic Dun Building, which still stands at the intersection of Pearl and Swan Streets.
42. See "Color Line in Baseball," *Buffalo Enquirer*, April 15, 1891: 3. The *Enquirer* reprinted a racist anecdote from *Sporting Life* without comment.
43. "Christmas Sports," *Sunday Truth*, December 19, 1886: 8; "Sporting News," *Buffalo Evening News*, December 23, 1886: 1. The Genesee Hotel employed enough African American men in 1884–1885 to field a baseball team. See also Brunson (Note 78) at pages 159, 314, 319.
44. *Sporting Life*'s paraphrasing of Chapman's assessment was quoted in "Sporting Notes," *Sunday Truth*, November 14, 1886: 2.
45. "Science and Skill," *Sunday Truth*, February 20, 1887: 8.

Chapter 5

1. "Mid-Winter Sporting," *Buffalo Commercial Advertiser*, January 17, 1887: 3; "The Buffalo B.B.C.,"

Buffalo Times, January 31, 1887: 4. Both papers listed Grant's age as 20, but he was actually 21.

2. "The Happy Bisons," *Buffalo Commercial Advertiser*, March 30, 1887: 3. Grant's birthplace was mistakenly called "Pittsford, Mass."

3. Various sources in recent years change the name of the International League to the International Association for 1887, but newspapers in that year generally continued to call it the International League. This circuit did become the "International Association" the next year. See "Baseball in 1888," *Buffalo Express*, January 20, 1888: 6.

4. Jeffrey Clarke Rowell, "Moses Fleetwood Walker and the Establishment of a Color Line in Major League Baseball, 1884–1887," *The Atlanta Review of Journalism History* 12, (Spring 2015): 98, accessible at https://cime.gsu.edu/files/2014/04/ARJHVolume12.pdf. See also Brunson (Note 78) at pages 333, 337, 798, 834, 1079. Higgins played in Memphis with Renfroe on a team called the Eclipse and with Pointer on a team called the Eurekas. The Eclipse also included infielders named Matt and Sam Pointer. Jackson joined Oswego a few days after Frank Grant faced that club on May 12 and 13, and his stint with that club was brief. See "Base Ball Notes," *Oswego* (New York) *Palladium*, May 17, 1887: 4; "Base Ball," *Oswego Palladium*, May 27, 1887: 4.

5. Lawrence D. Hogan, *Shades of Glory: The Negro Leagues and the Story of African American Baseball* (Washington, D.C.: National Geographic Society, 2006), 53.

6. Chapman's original schedule for April didn't match the eventual reality, but it was close. See "Our Buffalo Boys," *Buffalo Times*, February 24, 1887: 1.

7. "The Pittsburghs Win," *The Sun* (New York City), April 3, 1887: 3. This account was also printed in the *Buffalo Express*, the *Brooklyn Daily Eagle*, and the *New York Times*.

8. "The Season Begun," *Buffalo Courier*, April 3, 1887: 5. There was supposed to be a rematch on April 4 but it was cancelled due to rain, according to "The World of Sport," *Buffalo Commercial Advertiser*, April 5, 1887: 3.

9. "Base Ball," *The Sun* (Baltimore), April 6, 1887: 1 (of Supplement).

10. "Base-Ball," *The Sun* (Baltimore), April 7, 1887: 4. The game's "two very pretty double plays" were both turned by Grant throwing to his catcher.

11. The *Baltimore American* was quoted long after these two games in "The National Game," *Abbeville* (South Carolina) *Press and Banner*, May 18, 1887: 2. It was unclear whether the Abbeville paper was quoting or merely paraphrasing the *American* about Grant being "one of the most active men ever seen, and [that[his plays are quick and precise."

12. "The Browns Refuse to Play," *St. Louis Globe-Democrat*, September 12, 1887: 8.

13. "Good Ball Playing," *Washington Post*, April 8, 1887: 2.

14. "Buffalo Beaten Again," *National Republican* (Washington, D.C.), April 9, 1887: 1; "Another Victory for Washington," *The Sun* (Baltimore), April 9, 1887: 6.

15. "Plenty of Base Hits," *Washington Post*, April 9, 1887: 2.

16. "A Victory Every Day," *Washington Post*, April 10, 1887: 2. The box score shows him with two hits but also specifies that he walked once, and under the rules in place for just 1887, walks were counted as base hits. The box score only listed stolen base totals for each team, but details beneath at least one line score elsewhere specified that Grant had two for Buffalo. See "The Sporting World," *Plain Dealer* (Cleveland), April 10, 1887: 6.

17. "Bishop's Good Work," *The Post* (Pittsburgh), April 12, 1887: 6.

18. "Sporting News," *Buffalo Commercial Advertiser*, April 12, 1887: 3.

19. T.M. Coyden, "The Binghamton Club," *The Sporting News*, April 23, 1887: 5. Coyden's "special correspondence" had a dateline of April 13.

20. James Delaney Jr., "The 1887 Binghamton Bingos," https://sabr.org/journal/article/the-1887-binghamton-bingos/.

21. "The World of Sport," *Buffalo Express*, July 17, 1887: 8. Late in the season, Grant did get faulted for his range by a hometown paper thusly: "Not an error was made by either nine except the one charged to Grant. That was a piece of hard luck, too, as Grant was trying to cover too much territory. The result was that he got away out and tried to get a fly ball that in reality belonged to [right fielder Joe] Kappel and which the latter could have captured. Grant muffed it, but it did not affect the score in the least."—"In Second Place," *Buffalo Courier*, September 11, 1887: 3. However, Grant apparently yielded to Kappel later, because the paper then reported that Kappel "grabbed another fly after running almost into the diamond for it."

22. "Slaughtered Then Again," *The Post* (Pittsburgh), April 13, 1887: 6.

23. "'Twas Something Great," *The Post* (Pittsburgh), April 14, 1887: 6. The box score shows him with two hits but also specifies that he walked once, and under the rules in place for just 1887, walks were to be counted as base hits.

24. *Sportsman's Referee* was quoted in "Monday Sporting," *Buffalo Commercial Advertiser*, April 18, 1887: 3. A prominent African American weekly reprinted just the first, second, and final sentences of this praise. See *Cleveland Gazette*, April 30, 1887: 3.

25. "The Giants on Top," *Trenton* (New Jersey) *Times*, April 16, 1887: 1. The other Cuban Giants in the box score were Clarence Williams rf; Boyd cf; G. Williams 2b; Fry[e] 1b; Harrison ss; Thomas c; Holmes 3b; and Parago lf.

26. "Outdoor Pastimes," *Buffalo Courier*, April 18, 1887: 4.

27. "Diamond Dust," *Glens Falls* (New York) *Times*, May 23, 1887: 5.

28. "The National Game," *Boston Herald*, April

23, 1887: 5; "Boston Beats Buffalo," *Boston Daily Globe*, April 23, 1887: 5. In contrast to the vast majority of Buffalo's box scores in April, this pair included columns for at-bats and stolen bases. They showed Boston with 12 and 13 steals, respectively. As for Buffalo's steals, the former showed Grant and a third baseman named "Comee" each with one, but the latter instead showed Remsen as the only Bison with a steal (while showing Buffalo's third baseman as "Connell."). A line score in an outlying paper listed all three Bisons as having stolen a base. See "Base Ball," *Fall River* (Massachusetts) *Daily Herald*, April 23, 1887: 1.

29. "Terrific Batting," *Boston Daily Globe*, April 24, 1887: 4. Of the three games against major league pitchers in which Grant drew a walk, this box score provides the strongest internal evidence that walks were counted as base hits, as under the new rule in effect for 1887 only. In particular, it shows Boston's King Kelly as walking twice. If those *weren't* counted as at-bats, he'd have had at least eight plate appearances, yet almost all of his teammates also had six at-bats, including Radbourn in the ninth spot. There were no sacrifices listed, and the only two Boston hitters with just five at-bats each reached base after being hit by a pitch. Therefore, instead of being 4-for-6 plus two walks in eight plate appearances, under the past century's scoring rules Kelly was really 2-for-4 plus two walks in six plate appearances, and instead of being 1-for-6 plus a walk in seven plate appearances, Grant was really 0- for-5 plus a walk in six plate appearances.

30. "Diamond Sparkles," *Rochester Democrat and Chronicle*, April 24, 1887: 7.

31. "Buffalos, 16; Lynns, 7," *Boston Daily Globe*, April 28, 1887: 3. One hometown daily confirmed that it was Buffalo's first win of the month. See "'Judge' Waters Wins," *Buffalo Commercial Advertiser*, April 28, 1887: 3.

32. *Sporting Life* was quoted in "Out-Door Sports," *Sunday Truth*, May 1, 1887: 8.

33. "Lost the First Game," *Buffalo Sunday Morning News*, May 1, 1887: 1; "Alas for Jersey City," *Rochester Democrat and Chronicle*, May 3, 1887: 7. As was true for much of 1886, Buffalo's dailies often didn't print box scores for road games, but Rochester's paper could be counted on for printing several International League box scores most days.

34. "Sporting Notes," *Jersey Journal* (Jersey City, New Jersey), May 5, 1887: 3. No Buffalo players drew a walk in the game. This paper's account provided detailed pitch counts for both team's hurlers.

35. The *Utica Herald* was quoted in "Eight to Seven," *Buffalo Courier*, May 8, 1887: 3. See also "Rochester Stock Way Up," *Rochester Democrat and Chronicle*, May 7, 1887: 6. Grant played an errorless game at second base, with eight chances, but he really sparkled on offense by leading all Buffalo players with three runs scored and four hits (though two of the latter might actually have been walks). He also reached base after being hit by a pitch.

36. "The Pennant Battles," *Rochester Democrat and Chronicle*, May 8, 1887: 2.

37. "Around the Bases," *Syracuse Daily Standard*, May 10, 1887: 1.

38. "By Just One Little Run," *Rochester Democrat and Chronicle*, May 12, 1887: 7.

39. "Bad Buffalos," *Buffalo Express*, May 15, 1887: 8; "Base Ball Briefs," *Buffalo Courier*, May 15, 1887: 3; "Toronto in Tears," *Sunday Truth*, May 15, 1887: 1. The latter's box score listed all players who received a base on balls and noted that those were all scored as hits.

40. "Invincible Bisons," *Buffalo Daily Times*, May 18, 1887: 1.

41. "President Gilbert, Attention," *Buffalo Express*, May 22, 1887: 8. For a very similar account, see "Mean Work at Hamilton," *Buffalo Courier*, May 22, 1887: 5. Much of the latter's wording is identical, but two differences are substituting "pantaloons" for "breeches" and omitting the umpire's name. Also, Grant's "pantaloons were ripped above the knee" instead of being ripped "to pieces." More importantly, the *Courier* attributed the report to an anonymous "eye witness" rather than Chapman. The following week, the *Rochester Post-Express* said McDonald's umpiring was "manifestly unjust" to Buffalo in a game against Rochester, as quoted in "Kicking on the Umpire," *Buffalo Times*, May 31, 1887: 3.

42. "The Home Team Second," *Rochester Democrat and Chronicle*, May 20, 1887: 6. This was an edition of the *Buffalo Times* published the next day that incorrectly had Friday, May 20, 1887, on its front page only, and thus online researchers might go by that page's box score showing an extra-inning win by Buffalo, 6–5.

43. "Spring Sporting," *Buffalo Times*, May 21, 1887: 1.

44. "Base Ball Notes," *Oswego* (New York) *Palladium*, May 16, 1887: 4; "Out on a Fly," *Rochester Democrat and Chronicle*, May 19, 1887: 6.

45. The *Rochester Herald* was quoted in "Notes," *Buffalo Sunday Morning News*, May 29, 1887: 1.

46. "Two Games Won," *Buffalo Express*, May 31, 1887: 5. In the first game, Grant also stole a base, fielded nine chances without an error, and helped turn a double play. The box score for the second game showed Grant with no hits yet listed him with two walks, indicating a decision to ignore that year's new rule to score walks as hits. However, contrast the box score in "Both Games Won," *Buffalo Courier*, May 31, 1887: 4. It showed Grant with one hit, and the description of the game said he singled during his team's five-run eighth inning.

47. For standings just before Buffalo's doubleheader sweep of Toronto, see "The World of Sport," *Buffalo Express*, May 29, 1887: 14.

48. "Newarks Done Up," *Buffalo Times*, June 2, 1887: 3. See also "Rainy Day Sports," *Buffalo Commercial Advertiser*, June 2, 1887: 3. In addition to his perfectly-timed homer, Grant also doubled.

49. "Two Little Errors," *Buffalo Express*, June 3, 1887: 5.
50. "Buffalo to the Front," *Buffalo Sunday Morning News*, June 5, 1887: 4.
51. "A Tight Squeeze," *Buffalo Express*, June 7, 1887: 6.
52. "Sporting Notes," *Buffalo Express*, June 7, 1887: 6; "Sporting Briefs," *Buffalo Times*, June 7, 1887: 3.
53. "Forfeited their Franchise," *Buffalo Courier*, June 4, 1887: 4; "Sporting Notes," *Buffalo Express*, June 7, 1887: 6.
54. "Climbing to the Top," *Buffalo Times*, June 9, 1887: 3; "Notes of the International League," *The Sun* (New York City), June 19, 1887: 12.
55. "The Buffalos Ahead," *Buffalo Times*, June 11, 1887: 3.
56. "General Chat," *Buffalo Express*, June 12, 1887: 8.
57. "Wednesday Sporting," *Buffalo Commercial Advertiser*, June 15, 1887: 3; "Great Guns!" *Buffalo Express*, June 15, 1887: 5; "Notes of the International League," *The Sun* (New York City), June 19, 1887: 12. For two photos of the second Parade House on the same site, see the bottom of https://buffaloah.com/a/archs/vaux/parade/index.html.
58. "Briefs," *Catholic Union and Times* (Buffalo, New York), June 16, 1887: 1; "Rough on Rochester," *Sunday Truth*, June 19, 1887: 8.
59. *Sporting Life* was cited in "Sporting Sayings," *Sunday Truth*, June 19, 1887: 8.
60. "Baseball Chat," *Buffalo Express*, June 26, 1887: 8; "Caught on the Fly," *The Sporting News*, April 23, 1887: 7. A few days into July, Fowler's announcement changed somewhat: It would start rather than end in the South, and, if that leg succeeded, a trip to California would follow. See "Diamond Dust," *Saint Louis Globe-Democrat*, July 5, 1887: 6.
61. "Tally Another," *Buffalo Express*, July 1, 1887: 8.
62. "Averages of Players," *Syracuse Standard*, July 3, 1887: 4.
63. James E. Overmyer, "Frank Grant," *Baseball History 4* (Westport, CT: Meckler, 1991), 31.
64. "Miners Downed," *Buffalo Times*, July 23, 1887: 4; "Thirteen to Nine," *Buffalo Courier*, July 24, 1887: 3; "A Regular Picnic," *Buffalo Commercial Advertiser*, July 28, 1887: 3; "Buffalo's [sic] Win Again," *Buffalo Times*, July 29, 1887: 4; "They Were Shut Out," *Buffalo Courier*, August 2, 1887: 4.
65. "Notes," *Buffalo Express*, July 5, 1887: 2.
66. "Two Dropped," *Buffalo Express*, July 2, 1887: 2.
67. "The Fourth's Sports," *Buffalo Times*, July 5, 1887: 3.
68. "Caught on the Fly," *Rochester Democrat and Chronicle*, July 15, 1887: 5.
69. "Sporting Notes," *Jersey Journal* (Jersey City), July 15, 1887: 3; "The Color Line Drawn in Baseball," *Evening Leader* (Wilkes-Barre, Pennsylvania), July 15, 1887: 4. Newark's *Daily Journal* also printed a similar account on July 15, as noted by John Thorn, the Official Historian of Major League Baseball, at https://ourgame.mlblogs.com/out-at-home-part-3-47bd2527f113. He said there was a 6–4 vote by the League's franchises in favor of the directive to Secretary White, but two of the six he listed, namely Jersey City and Toronto, had no representatives at the meeting, according to "The International League Meeting," *Buffalo Express*, July 15, 1887: 8. Thorn also listed Oswego as voting against, but that franchise dissolved at the end of May and had been replaced by Scranton.
70. "Caught on the Fly," *Rochester Democrat and Chronicle*, July 15, 1887: 5.
71. "Utica Stays In," *Buffalo Times*, July 14, 1887: 1; "Base Ball League," *Buffalo Commercial Advertiser*, July 14, 1887: 3; "The International League Meeting," *Buffalo Express*, July 15, 1887: 8; "The International League," *Buffalo Courier*, July 15, 1887: 4.
72. "Baseball Chat," *Buffalo Express*, July 17, 1887: 8.
73. "Baseball Notes," *Norfolk Virginian*, July 22, 1887: 1; "Diamond Dust," *Saint Louis Globe-Democrat*, July 22, 1887: 8. See also the National Baseball Hall of Fame's news release, "Ulysses Franklin 'Frank' Grant," January 19, 2006.
74. "Base Ball Gossip," *Evening Telegram* (Camden, New Jersey), July 23, 1887: 4; "Around the Bases," *Rochester Democrat and Chronicle*, July 26, 1887: 7.
75. "Base Ball Brieflets," *Sunday Telegram* (Providence, Rhode Island), July 31, 1887: 2.
76. "Baseball Chat," *Buffalo Express*, July 10, 1887: 8. See also Brian McKenna, "Bud Fowler," at https://sabr.org/bioproj/person/bud-fowler/. Binghamton's franchise folded on August 20.
77. Peter Mancuso, "July 14, 1887: The color line is drawn in baseball," https://sabr.org/gamesproj/game/july-14-1887-the-color-line-is-drawn/; see also "African American players banned," https://www.mlb.com/phillies/community/educational-programs/uya-negro-league/African American-players-banned.
78. "The World of Sport," *Buffalo Commercial Advertiser*, July 19, 1887: 3; "Sports of All Sorts," *Buffalo Commercial Advertiser*, July 20, 1887: 3; "Zell's Muff," *Buffalo Express*, July 20, 1887: 2.
79. "The Sporting World," *Buffalo Commercial Advertiser*, July 21, 1887: 3.
80. "General Sporting Notes," *Buffalo Courier*, July 24, 1887: 3.
81. "The Syracuse Stars," *Buffalo Commercial Advertiser*, July 26, 1887: 3. The second of Buffalo's two games against Syracuse in late July was a 5–4 win against Robert Higgins. In addition to errorless fielding, Grant took part in a double play and on offense contributed a single and a stolen base.
82. "They Were Shut Out," *Buffalo Courier*, August 2, 1887: 4.
83. "Sports of the Season," *The Critic* (Washington, D.C.), August 3, 1887: 4.

84. "Diamond Points," *Boston Globe*, August 5, 1887: 3. This detailed report was also used in "Base-Ball Notes," *Indianapolis Journal*, August 8, 1887: 5, and "Clips and Chips," *Saint Louis Post-Dispatch*, August 8, 1887: 5.

85. "Yesterday's Defeat," *Evening Leader* (Wilkes-Barre), August 9, 1887: 4.

86. "Syracuse Fails to Win," *Rochester Democrat and Chronicle*, August 20, 1887: 7. This account noted that no Bison reached second base until Hamburg got all the way to third in the ninth inning. The accompanying box score didn't include stolen bases, but see "A Fine Game," *Buffalo Daily Times*, August 20, 1887: 1. Robert Higgins played in this game, but only as a sub in center field.

87. "Sporting Matters," *Watertown* (New York) *Daily Times*, August 20, 1887: 8.

88. "Buffalo Leads Again," *Buffalo Evening News*, August 23, 1887: 1.

89. "The World of Sport," *Buffalo Express*, August 28, 1887: 8. The standings were reported a little differently in "Buffalo Laid Out," *Buffalo Sunday Morning News*, August 28, 1887: 1.

90. "The Color Line," *Sporting Life*, April 11, 1891: 6. This lengthy anecdote was printed without commentary as "Color Line in Baseball," *Buffalo Enquirer*, April 15, 1891: 3. See also "Drawing the Color Line," *Pittsburgh Press*, April 12, 1891: 6, though this earlier printing didn't credit *Sporting Life*. The African American second baseman rumored to be of interest to Cushman was identified as "Bruce Gordon" but there is no player by that name anywhere in the encyclopedic work of James E. Brunson III (Note 78), nor did any African American team in Milwaukee around then have a player with a similar name. A likely candidate was Bud Fowler, who had been wintering in Milwaukee, according to Harry T. Smith, "Two New Leagues," *Sporting Life*, January 3, 1891: 1.

91. "Buffalo Badly Beaten," *Rochester Democrat and Chronicle*, August 30, 1887: 7; "Racing and Ball Playing," *Buffalo Times*, August 31, 1887: 1; "The Opening Day," *Buffalo Times*, September 1, 1887: 1.

92. See Note 61.

93. "Notes and Comments," *Sporting Life*, June 20, 1888: 7.

94. "Sporting Gossip," *Evening Telegram* (Camden, New Jersey), August 31, 1887: 4; "Sporting Notes," *Buffalo Evening News*, September 3, 1887: 1. It was the latter newspaper that attributed the statement to the *Cincinnati Times-Star*.

95. "A Sleepy Game," *Buffalo Commercial Advertiser*, August 31, 1887: 3.

96. "They Turn the Tables," *Rochester Democrat and Chronicle*, September 2, 1887: 6.

97. "Baseball Chat," *Buffalo Express*, September 4, 1887: 8; "The National Game," *Morning Journal and Courier* (New Haven, Connecticut), September 9, 1887: 4; "In Fourth Place," *Sunday Truth*, September 4, 1887: 1. The *Truth* quoted Toronto's *News*.

98. *Sporting Times* was quoted in "Diamond Points," *Boston Daily Globe*, September 6, 1887: 3. Likewise, see "Clips and Chips," *Saint Louis Post-Dispatch*, September 9, 1887: 8.

99. "Dropping 'Em," *Buffalo Express*, September 3, 1887: 5; "The Same Old Story," *Rochester Democrat and Chronicle*, September 4, 1887: 2.

100. "The Bisons in Luck," *Buffalo Commercial Advertiser*, September 7, 1887: 3.

101. "Interesting Baseball Feats," *Lincoln* (Nebraska) *Evening Call*, May 5, 1888: 3. See also "Wonderful Base Ball Feats," *Buffalo Sunday Morning News*, May 6, 1888: 6. Several sources state that Grant stole home *twice* in some game during 1887, but without specifying the date. For example, see https://baseballhall.org/Hall of Famers/grant-frank.

102. "From First to Third," *Boston Herald*, September 8, 1887: 5; "Base-Ball Notes," *Indianapolis Journal*, September 11, 1887: 4; "Notes," *Public Ledger* (Memphis, Tennessee), September 15, 1887: 2.

103. "The Browns Refuse to Play," *Saint Louis Globe-Democrat*, September 12, 1887: 8; "A Color Line in Baseball," *New York Times*, September 12, 1887: 1; See also "Color Line in Base Ball," *Boston Daily Globe*, September 12, 1887: 2.

104. "Soundly Whipped," *Buffalo Express*, September 15, 1887: 8.

105. "Lost the Game," *Buffalo Courier*, September 18, 1887: 3.

106. "Won and Lost Again," *Buffalo Sunday Morning News*," September 18, 1887: 5. See also "The League Schedule" on the same page. This paper's winning percentages didn't quite match the Won-Lost totals it reported. However, its Won-Lost totals jibe with those in the next day's *Rochester Democrat and Chronicle*.

107. "Bisons Retaliate," *Buffalo Times*, September 20, 1887: 1; "Getting Even," *Buffalo Express*, September 20, 1887: 8; "The Agony Continues," *Rochester Democrat and Chronicle*, September 20, 1887: 7. The two Buffalo papers disagreed on whether the inside-the-park homer was hit into the left field corner or the left-center power alley, and the box scores in the latter two papers disagreed on who Buffalo's left and center fielders were.

108. "Beaten Again," *Buffalo Times*, September 21, 1887: 3; "Notes," *Buffalo Express*, September 21, 1887: 2; "Syracuse Stars," *Buffalo Commercial Advertiser*, September 21, 1887: 3.

109. "Sporting Briefs," *Buffalo Times*, September 21, 1887: 1.

110. "Rain, No Game," *Buffalo Times*, September 22, 1887: 1; "Alas, What Wrecks!" *Buffalo Express*, September 23, 1887: 5.

111. "Sporting Briefs," *Buffalo Times*, September 21, 1887: 1; "Much in Little," *Buffalo Commercial Advertiser*, September 20, 1887: 3; "Notes," *Buffalo Express*, September 23, 1887: 5.

112. "Base Ball," *Sporting Life*, November 3, 1887: 3.

113. "The Great Batting Feats of 1887," *The Sun* (New York City), April 8, 1888: 10. However, baseball-reference.com credits Holliday with only 16 home runs in 1887.

114. "The World of Sports," *Waterbury* (Connecticut) *Evening Democrat*, January 9, 1888: 4; "The World of Sport," *Buffalo Express*, January 15, 1888: 8.

115. David F. Chrisman, "Early RBI Leaders in the International League," *Baseball Research Journal*, 2003: 40.

116. *Sporting Life* was quoted in the *Sunday Truth*, October 2, 1887: 7, and that Buffalo weekly replied, "He'll play in Buffalo."

117. "To Stay in the League," *Buffalo Evening News*, September 29, 1887: 1.

118. "Doings on the Diamond," *Sunday Morning Leader* (Wilkes-Barre, Pennsylvania), October 2, 1887: 6. Among Frank Grant's African American opponents during his time with Buffalo, Stovey was the only one he would see regularly after 1888. In fact, when Grant was a fixture on the Cuban Giants, Stovey pitched for the club periodically through 1896.

119. "Ball and Bat," *Buffalo Commercial Advertiser*, September 29, 1887: 3; "Buffalo Expressions," *Buffalo Express*, September 29, 1887: 5.

120. "Briefs," *Catholic Union and Times* (Buffalo, New York), October 6, 1887: 1.

121. "Notes," *Sunday Truth*, October 9, 1887: 8; James Napora, "Houses of Worship: A Guide to the Religious Architecture of Buffalo, New York," 1995 Master of Architecture Thesis, reprinted in part at https://buffaloah.com/h/eastside/lower.html. Frank Grant wasn't listed in Buffalo's city directories during his years with the Bisons.

122. The *Buffalo Courier* was quoted in "Sporting Gossip of the Week," *Springfield* (Massachusetts) *Republican*, August 7, 1887: 3.

123. "Saturday Sporting," *Buffalo Commercial Advertiser*, October 22, 1887: 3.

124. "Barnie Is Happy," *The Times* (Philadelphia), October 16, 1887: 14. In mentioning Kappel, this article said he had played for Cincinnati's American Association team, but that was his brother, "Heinie" (Henry).

125. "Sporting News," *Buffalo Commercial Advertiser*, October 26, 1887: 3.

126. "Turf, Field and Ring," *Buffalo Commercial Advertiser*, November 21, 1887: 3.

127. "Grant Has Signed," *Buffalo Evening News*, November 23, 1887: 1.

Chapter 6

1. "Saturday Sporting," *Buffalo Commercial Advertiser*, October 8, 1887: 3.

2. "Sports of the Season," *Buffalo Commercial Advertiser*, October 7, 1887: 3; "Tonawanda," *Buffalo Times*, October 14, 1887: 2.

3. "Sporting News," *Buffalo Times*, October 21, 1887: 1; "Sporting Notes," *Buffalo Times*, October 24, 1887: 4; "The World of Sport," *Buffalo Express*, October 30, 1887: 5; "Monday Sporting," *Buffalo Commercial Advertiser*, October 31, 1887: 3.

4. "Base Ball Notes," *Plain Dealer* (Cleveland), December 14, 1887; "Winter Sporting," *Buffalo Commercial Advertiser*, December 15, 1887: 3; "Base Ball Notes," *Wheeling* (West Virginia) *Register*, December 18, 1887: 2. Even the Buffalo paper prefaced Grant's name with an incorrect initial, "J." See also "Sports of All Sorts," *Sunday Truth*, December 25, 1887: 8. "Chambers" may have been Ed Chamberlain.

5. "Sporting Record," *Buffalo Commercial Advertiser*, January 4, 1888: 3; "The Bonds of Matrimony," *Meriden Journal*, January 9, 1888: 2.

6. "Games and Pastimes," *Buffalo Commercial Advertiser*, March 26, 1888: 3.

7. "Sporting Record," *Buffalo Commercial Advertiser*, January 4, 1888: 3; "Sprightly Sports," *International Gazette* (Black Rock, Buffalo), May 26, 1888: 8. The Queen Citys roster announced in early 1888 was "John J. Lang, George E. Herle, Hank Kammeyer and Nick Briesaeb, batteries; W. Winterfinger, 1st base; F. Savage, 2d base; Geo. Helfrich, 3d base; J. Heinzenberger, s. s.; E. Hitzel, r.f.; G. Norwick, c. f.; J. Wallenhorst, l.f.; Frank Grant, manager." On the same day, the *Buffalo Evening News* printed this exact list except for any manager, but at least one other local paper did include him: see "Sporting Sayings," *Sunday Truth*, January 8, 1888: 8.

8. "Springtime Sports," *Sunday Truth*, March 25, 1888: 8. Several items throughout this column and the next shed light on the Queen Citys and Buffalo's amateur baseball scene broadly. The Queen Citys were to be one of four teams in the West Side league, while the Clippers and Travelers were "rumored" to form half of the East Side league.

9. "The Schedules," *Buffalo Express*, February 12, 1888: 19.

10. "Sports in Season," *Sunday Truth*, March 18, 1888: 8; "Springtime Sports," *Sunday Truth*, March 25, 1888: 8. The latter item added that other professionals in town were working out elsewhere: "At the armory, Chamberlain, of the Louisvilles, Rowe, of the Detroits, Myers, of Indianapolis, and Carroll, of St. Paul, together with several local players, are daily practicing." For insights about the city's historic arsenal, see a blog entry by Buffalo radio journalist Steve Cichon at http://blog.buffalostories.com/the-broadway-arsenal-aka-the-broadway-auditorium-aka-the-broadway-barns/.

11. "Races and Base Ball," *Buffalo Times*, July 12, 1886: 5. The box score includes a "J. Dee," and beneath it is a paragraph about Edward Allen. Based on this, these two web pages are for the same player: https://www.baseball-reference.com/register/player.fcgi?id=allen-004edw and https://www.baseball-reference.com/register/player.fcgi?id=allen-004. Dee had played 12 games in the majors in 1884.

12. "Monday Sporting," *Buffalo Commercial Advertiser*, April 2, 1888: 3; "Athletic Affairs," *Sunday Truth*, February 5, 1888: 8.

13. "A Victory for Washington," *Washington Post*, April 3, 1888: 1.

14. "The First Tie of the Season," *Washington Post*, April 4, 1888: 1.
15. "Shoch's Splendid Batting," *Washington Post*, April 5, 1888: 1.
16. "The First Home Victory," *Pittsburgh Daily Post*, April 9, 1888: 6; "Sporting," *Pittsburgh Press*, April 9, 1888: 3.
17. "Games and Pastimes, *Buffalo Commercial Advertiser*, April 10, 1888: 3; "Sports of All Sorts," *Buffalo Commercial Advertiser*, April 11, 1888: 3.
18. "Buffalo Sporting," *Buffalo Commercial Advertiser*, April 12, 1888: 3; "Walsh Hammered," *Buffalo Express*, April 13, 1888: 6. The latter headline seems unfair, given that the final score was only 2–0. It's possible that Sol White first watched Grant play in one or both games. White had played with Wheeling the prior year, and his Pittsburgh Keystones opened their 1888 season in Wheeling a week after Buffalo's visit, according to "Diamond Dust," *Wheeling* (West Virginia) *Daily Intelligencer*, April 19, 1888: 4. Wheeling was where White first saw Grant, according to "Sol White Recalls," *New York Age*, January 17, 1931: 6.
19. *Pittsfield Sun*, April 12, 1888: 4. This long paragraph didn't have a headline per se.
20. "Chapman's Chippies," *Cincinnati Enquirer*, April 14, 1888: 2.
21. "Very Fine," *Cincinnati Enquirer*, April 15, 1888: 10.
22. "Very Easy," *Cincinnati Enquirer*, April 16, 1888: 2.
23. "Beaten by Buffalo," *Courier-Journal* (Louisville, Kentucky), April 17, 1888: 6.
24. "Stratton's Strong Arm," *Courier-Journal*, April 18, 1888: 6; "Games and Pastimes," *Buffalo Commercial Advertiser*, April 18, 1888: 3.
25. "The Buffalo Team," *Indianapolis Journal*, April 18, 1888: 5.
26. "Played Without an Error," *Indianapolis Journal*, April 19, 1888: 5; "Sporting News," *Buffalo Evening News*, April 20, 1888: 9.
27. "Buffalo's Negro Ball Player, Grant," *Meriden Daily Journal*, April 23, 1888: 1. See also "Sprays of Sport," *Rocky Mountain News* (Denver), April 29, 1888: 5. This was also printed in full in "Buffalo's Negro Ball Player," *Solomon Valley Democrat* (Minneapolis, Kansas), May 11, 1888: 7.
28. "Sporting Briefs," *Buffalo Times*, April 25, 1888: 3; "The Buffalos Back," *Buffalo Evening News*, April 26, 1888: 7.
29. "Six and Six," *Buffalo Sunday Morning News*, April 29, 1888: 1.
30. "'Rah for Buffalo," *Buffalo Times*, April 30, 1888: 3.
31. "Base Ball Briefs," *Buffalo Sunday Morning News*, May 6, 1888: 8.
32. "The First Home Game," *Buffalo Times*, May 11, 1888: 3; "Victorious Bisons," *Buffalo Express*, May 12, 1888: 6.
33. "Great Base Ball," *Buffalo Sunday Morning News*, May 20, 1888: 5. This article indicated that Grant's homer drove in one teammate, but at least two other papers reported it as a three-run blast.

See "Poor Rochester!" *Sunday Truth*, May 20, 1888: 1, and "Sound the Cymbals," *Buffalo Express*, May 20, 1888: 8.
34. "Sporting News," *Buffalo Evening News*, May 22, 1888: 9.
35. "They Awake at Last," *Buffalo Times*, May 22, 1888: 3.
36. "Albany Paralyzed," *Buffalo Express*, May 23, 1888: 6; "The Buffalos Play Great Ball," *Buffalo Evening News*, May 23, 1888: 1.
37. "Albany Gets Even," *Buffalo Express*, May 24, 1888: 6; "Buffalos Lose a Close Game," *Buffalo Evening News*, May 24, 1888: 1 (Fifth Edition).
38. "Even Up," *Buffalo Express*, May 25, 1888: 6; "The Honors Were Easy," *Rochester Democrat and Chronicle*, May 25, 1888: 7. The first game's line score in the Rochester paper was obviously erroneous because it didn't show the two teams tied after nine innings, and it showed the wrong total for Buffalo. A bigger mistake was that Grant was listed atop the box score printed under "Today's Base Ball Games," *Buffalo Evening News*, May 24, 1888: 1 (Fifth Edition).
39. "Walloped Again!" *Buffalo Commercial Advertiser*, May 25, 1888: 3.
40. "General Chat," *Buffalo Express*, May 27, 1888: 8.
41. "Trounced Trojans," *Buffalo Express*, May 26, 1888: 5; "Notes," *Buffalo Evening News*, May 28, 1888: 2.
42. "Troy Terror-ized," *Sunday Truth*, May 27, 1888: 1.
43. "Pictures of the Buffalo Club," *Buffalo Express*, May 27, 1888: 8. On that page is where the *Express* explained the drawings. The drawings themselves were printed on page 12. The photographer mentioned was presumably John R. Potter, who had a studio at several locations in Buffalo for about 30 years; see http://cabinetcardphotographers.blogspot.com/2017/09/john-r-potter.html.
44. "Said to Be a Steal," *Buffalo Express*, May 30, 1888: 6.
45. "A Great Day for Ball," *Rochester Democrat and Chronicle*, May 31, 1888: 6; "Buffalos First Lose Then Win," *Buffalo Evening News*, May 31, 1888: 1.
46. "Games and Pastimes," *Buffalo Commercial Advertiser*, May 31, 1888: 3; "Buffalos First Lose Then Win," *Buffalo Evening News*, May 31, 1888: 1. Regarding that crucial inning, the two papers disagreed on such details as whether Grant reached on an error or on a hit, whether Hamburg followed with a single toward third base or reached himself on an error when the pitcher mishandled his line drive, and which batter drove in Grant to tie the game.
47. "Holiday Sports," *Buffalo Times*, May 31, 1888: 3.
48. "Beaten in Canada," *Buffalo Courier*, June 2, 1888: 4.
49. The *Toronto Mail* was quoted in "Sporting News," *Buffalo Evening News*, June 4, 1888: 1. Reasons why that Canadian newspaper said Grant

always received a warm welcome there could include being sarcastic, being oblivious, or being embarrassed to the point of trying to erase or rewrite history.

50. "A Long Struggle," *Buffalo Express*, June 5, 1888: 6; "Knocked Out," *Buffalo Times*, June 6, 1888: 3.

51. "They Braced Up," *Buffalo Express*, June 8, 1888: 6; "A Close Game," *Buffalo Times*, June 8, 1888: 3; "Just Our Luck," *Buffalo Commercial Advertiser*, June 8, 1888: 3; "Sporting Notes," *Buffalo Evening News*, June 8, 1888: 5. The first two accounts made it clear he didn't leave the game after that injury, which occurred before the second out of the inning.

52. "The Twinklers Win," *Buffalo Times*, June 9, 1888: 3; "Buffalos Beaten 9 to 0," *Buffalo Sunday Morning News*, June 10, 1888: 5. Fleet Walker caught in the first game, but Robert Higgins didn't pitch in either of them. The *Syracuse Standard* was quoted in "Sporting News," *Buffalo Evening News*, June 11, 1888: 14.

53. The *Syracuse Standard* was quoted in "Notes," *Buffalo Evening News*, June 13, 1888: 1.

54. "Summer Sporting," *Buffalo Commercial Advertiser*, June 14, 1888: 3.

55. "London Got Left," *Buffalo Express*, June 17, 1888: 8.

56. "Sporting Notes," *Buffalo Times*, March 21, 1888: 3.

57. "Done Up," *Buffalo Express*, June 19, 1888: 6. The box score in the *Buffalo Times* that day had a few significant inaccuracies, particularly in its line score.

58. "A Great Surprise," *Buffalo Courier*, June 20, 1888: 4.

59. "Defeated in Canada," *Buffalo Times*, June 21, 1888: 3.

60. "The Buffalos Win," *Buffalo Sunday Morning News*, June 24, 1888: 1; "General Chat," *Buffalo Express*, June 24, 1888: 10.

61. *Rochester Democrat and Chronicle*, June 22, 1888: 7. This item had no headline per se. The Rochester correspondent for *Sporting Life* was quoted and rebutted in "Talk of the Nines," *Buffalo Sunday Morning News*, June 24, 1888: 5.

62. "Only One Run," *Buffalo Times*, June 26, 1888: 3; "A Loose Game," *Buffalo Times*, June 28, 1888: 3; "Sports of July," *Sunday Truth*, July 1, 1888: 8. The box score in the *Times* on June 28 showed him as 2-for-2 plus the three walks, but he was shown as 2-for-5 with three walks in the box score that accompanied "Troy in Tears," *Buffalo Express*, June 28, 1888: 6. The latter's account, however, seemed to document all of his plate appearances, which numbered five including the walks. That discrepancy might have been explained by an item in the next column, under the headline "Notes": "The joint committee on baseball rules, according to a dispatch from Philadelphia last night, unanimously voted to take bases on balls from the error column. The base on balls will remain as a factor in earned runs."

63. "A Sorry Record," *Buffalo Courier*, July 5, 1888: 3.

64. "Where Will It End?" *Buffalo Courier*, July 6, 1888: 3; "General Chat," *Buffalo Express*, July 8, 1888: 8.

65. The World of Sport," *Buffalo Express*, July 8, 1888: 8.

66. "Strange, Very!" *Buffalo Express*, July 10, 1888: 6; "Sporting News," *Buffalo Evening News*, July 10, 1888: 5.

67. Notes of the Game," *Buffalo Courier*, July 11, 1888: 3.

68. "Barr Bothers Buffalo," *Rochester Democrat and Chronicle*, July 11, 1888: 7. See also "Pop Ups," two columns to the right on that page. "General Ball Chat," *Buffalo Express*, July 15, 1888: 5. Remsen's release was mentioned in "Base Ball Briefs," *Buffalo Commercial Advertiser*, July 13, 1888: 3.

69. "'Mickey' Walsh Released," *Buffalo Evening News*, July 30, 1888: 1 (Fifth Edition).

70. "Tied with Troy," *Buffalo Express*, July 14, 1888: 5; "A Chapter of Sports," *Buffalo Courier*, July 15, 1888: 3.

71. "The Old Story," *Buffalo Express*, July 17, 1888: 6. The prediction about him being idled for two weeks was in the next column, under "Notes."

72. "The Sporting Chapter," *Buffalo Courier*, July 17, 1888: 3. See also "Sporting Notes" on that same page; "Notes," *Buffalo Express*, July 17, 1888: 6.

73. "The Old, Old Story," *Buffalo Times*, July 18, 1888: 3; "Base Ball News," *Sunday Truth*, July 22, 1888: 8.

74. "Fresh from the Diamond," *Buffalo Sunday Morning News*, July 29, 1888: 6. That same paper later seemed to imply that Bittman was supposed to use Grant's cap in the field but that Bittman needed to use a pin to make it smaller. See "Ball Notes," *Buffalo Sunday Morning News*, August 19, 1888: 1.

75. "Buffalo Sporting," *Buffalo Commercial Advertiser*, July 17, 1888: 3; "Sporting Notes," *Buffalo Courier*, July 18, 1888: 3.

76. "Notes," *Buffalo Express*, July 24, 1888: 6; "Notes," *Buffalo Express*, July 25, 1888: 6; "Sporting Notes," *Buffalo Express*, July 30, 1888: 6. Grant was also called "Patsy" in "The World of Sport," *Buffalo Express*, November 18, 1888: 3; "Dust from the Green Diamond," *Buffalo Commercial Advertiser*, July 28, 1888: 3. Two examples of him being called "Paddy" were in "Budget of Sports," *Sunday Truth*, February 26, 1888: 8 and "Catching Up," *Buffalo Express*, August 31, 1888: 6.

77. "Dust from the Green Diamond," *Buffalo Commercial Advertiser*, July 28, 1888: 3

78. "He Brings Luck," *Buffalo Evening News*, May 28, 1888: 1; "Sports in Season," *Sunday Truth*, April 22, 1888: 8. See also "The Newsboys' Nine," *Buffalo Sunday Morning News*, May 20, 1888: 5. A short while later, another paper in town asked tersely, "Is Dallas Grant's mascot?" This was probably referring to young Walter. See "Baseball Chat," *Buffalo Express*, June 10, 1888: 8.

79. The *Pittsburg* [sic] *Chronicle* was quoted in full in "Politics Versus Base-Ball," *Portland (Maine) Daily Press*, June 9, 1888: 1. This was printed under the same headline in the *Hoxie Sentinel* (Kenneth, Kansas), June 28, 1888: 2.
80. "Groves Is a Mascot," *Buffalo Courier*, July 1, 1888: 12. The ad was also printed the next day, at a minimum.
81. "Base-Ball Notes," *Cincinnati Enquirer*, August 5, 1888: 11; "International League Notes," *The Sun* (New York City), August 5, 1888: 6; "Base Ball Notes," *Pittsburgh Daily Post*, August 10, 1888: 6. Oddly, as Grant's layoff started its third week, a different Pittsburgh paper proved that it was out of touch, apparently dusting off a very old one-liner. "Grant, the colored player in the Buffalo club, is playing a remarkably brilliant game at present," according to "Base Ball Briefs," *Pittsburgh Press*, August 8, 1888: 5. At least it was upbeat. See also "Notes," *Buffalo Express*, August 15, 1888: 6.
82. "Caught on the Fly," *The Sporting News*, August 11, 1888: 6. See also "The National Game," *Press Herald* (Pine Grove, Pennsylvania), August 10, 1888: 1; "Base Ball Briefs," *Daily Commonwealth* (Topeka, Kansas), August 12, 1888: 5.
83. The *Syracuse Courier*'s top 20 was reprinted in the *Buffalo Commercial Advertiser*, July 27, 1888: 2. In 52 games, Grant scored 62 runs and had 87 hits. Simple math produces an at-bats total of 213 for a .408 average. In second place was Ollie Beard of Syracuse, with an average of .380 in 11 more games (64 runs, 108 hits). Beard hit .270 in his three major league seasons, from 1889 through 1891.
84. "Walloped Again," *Buffalo Commercial Advertiser*, August 10, 1888: 3.
85. "A Chapter of Sports," *Buffalo Courier*, August 12, 1888: 3.
86. "Base Ball News," *Sunday Truth*, August 12, 1888: 8.
87. "The Sporting Chapter," *Buffalo Courier*, August 14, 1888: 3.
88. "All Broke Up," *Buffalo Express*, August 15, 1888: 6.
89. "Sporting Chapter, "*Buffalo Courier*, August 19, 1888: 3; "One More Game," *Buffalo Times*, August 21, 1888: 4; "Shut-Out No. 1," *Buffalo Express*, August 22, 1888: 6. The latter confirmed that the 15–0 win over Troy was the Bisons' seventh consecutive victory.
90. "A Chapter of Sports," *Buffalo Courier*, August 26, 1888: 6.
91. "A Chapter of Sports," *Buffalo Courier*, August 28, 1888: 3.
92. Grant's statistics were calculated by the author from box scores during the streak, with at-bats being included in at least one box score for every game. The National League statistics for 1888 are from https://www.baseball-reference.com/leagues/NL/1888-standard-batting.shtml, where statistical columns can be sorted from highest to lowest.
93. "Notes of the Diamond," *Buffalo Courier*, August 31, 1888: 3.
94. "A Base Runner," *Buffalo Express*, September 4, 1888: 6.
95. "Notes and Comments," *Sporting Life*, June 20, 1888: 7; "Sporting Gossip," *Evening Telegram* (Camden, New Jersey), August 31, 1887: 4; "Sporting Notes," *Buffalo Evening News*, September 3, 1887: 1. The latter newspaper attributed the statement to the *Cincinnati Times-Star*.
96. These statistics are from baseball-reference.com. One reason they could change over time is that there were several minor league players named O'Brien in the 1890s whose first names have yet to be identified, and one or more of them could have been this Billy O'Brien.
97. "The Sporting Chapter," *Buffalo Courier*, September 7, 1888: 3. For another box score of the game that didn't credit Grant with an assist, see "Yesterday's Ball Games," *Lightning Express* (Buffalo), September 7, 1888: 7.
98. "Sporting Generalities," *Buffalo Courier*, September 7, 1888: 3.
99. "The Sporting Chapter," *Buffalo Courier*, September 11, 1888: 3.
100. "The Lucky Seventh," *Buffalo Express*, September 14, 1888: 6; "The Sporting Chapter," *Buffalo Courier*, September 14, 1888: 3.
101. "Notes of the Game," *Buffalo Courier*, September 18, 1888: 3. Curry had a major league career consisting of two losses as a pitcher for Richmond of the American Association in 1884, and he managed Oswego in the International League for part of the 1887 season.
102. "The Sporting Chapter," *Buffalo Courier*, September 18, 1888: 3; "The First Time," *Buffalo Express*, September 18, 1888: 6.
103. "The Sporting Chapter," *Buffalo Courier*, September 19, 1888: 3; "Ten Innings, Tied," *Buffalo Express*, September 19, 1888: 6. The latter daily said in one spot that Grant switched to short for the fourth inning but later said that was for the fifth; its details about those innings indicate that the latter was correct.
104. Olympic, "Bits from Buffalo," *Sporting Life*, January 23, 1889: 3.
105. "Downed Again," *Buffalo Times*, September 22, 1888: 4; "Their Last Game Lost," *Buffalo Sunday Morning News*, September 22, 1888: 1.
106. "Lost the Last," *Buffalo Times*, September 26, 1888: 4; "The Reserved Bisons," *Buffalo Times*, September 28, 1888: 4.
107. "International Association," *Sporting Life*, October 3, 1888: 5.
108. "The Sporting Chapter," *Buffalo Courier*, September 29, 1888: 3. The batting order for the Cuban Giants was: G. Williams 2b; C. Williams c; Thomas 1b; Harrison ss; Boyd cf; Whyte p; Malone rf; Holmes 3b; Johnson lf.
109. "The Sporting Chapter," *Buffalo Courier*, October 2, 1888: 3. "October Sports," *Buffalo Sunday Morning News*, October 21, 1888: 8. Slugging percentages were taken from baseball-reference.com, where one can rank that column for all eight teams to identify the league's leaders.

110. James E. Overmyer, "The Unhappy Odyssey of a Great Ballplayer," *Berkshire Eagle*, February 5, 1990: A1, B6.

111. "The Sporting Chapter," *Buffalo Courier*, October 4, 1888: 3; "Chips from the Diamond," *The Sun* (New York City), October 6, 1888: 3.

112. "Sporting Notes" and "Chips from the Diamond," *The Sun* (New York City), October 8, 1888: 3; "Other Games" and "Chips from the Diamond," *The Sun*, October 9, 1888: 3.

113. "The Great Fair," *Daily Republican* (Wilmington, Delaware), October 10, 1888: 1. The batting order for the Cuban Giants was: G. Williams, 3b; C. Williams, c; Harrison, ss; Grant, 2b; Boyd, cf; "Sullivan," [Selden?] rf; Malone, p; Parago, lf; Johnson, 1b.

114. "Sporting News," *Buffalo Evening News*, October 15, 1888: 1.

115. "Sporting Notes," *Buffalo Courier*, October 27, 1888: 3; "A Chapter of Sports," *Buffalo Courier*, October 28, 1888: 3.

116. "Baseball Notes," *New York Herald*, November 6, 1888: 5; "Baseball Notes," *The Sun* (New York City), November 6, 1888: 3; "News of the Ball Players," *The Sun* (New York City), November 7, 1888: 3. The *Sun*'s line score showed the Cuban Giants with single runs in the first two innings and New York with single runs in the first and last innings, but one of those runs for the Cuban Giants was presumably a typo. The 2–1 final score was confirmed in "Base Ball," *The Inter-Ocean* (Chicago), November 18, 1888: 12.

117. "Von Der Ahe after Ball-Players," *The World* (New York City), November 11, 1888: 7; "Gossip of the Ball Field," *The Sun* (New York City), November 11, 1888: 6; "The Last Game of the Season," *Brooklyn Daily Eagle*, November 12, 1888: 2.

118. "Base Ball Notes," *The Sun* (New York City), November 12, 1888: 3.

119. "A New Base Ball League," *Trenton* (New Jersey) *Evening Times*, November 25, 1888: 9; "The World of Sport," *Buffalo Express*, November 25, 1888: 13. See also "Gossip of the Diamond," *Buffalo Courier*, November 25, 1888: 3.

120. "The Sporting World," *Buffalo Courier*, December 19, 1888: 3.

Chapter 7

1. "The Sporting World," *Buffalo Courier*, January 6, 1889: 3.

2. "International League News," *The Sun*, January 8, 1889: 3

3. Olympic, "Bits from Buffalo," *Sporting Life*, January 23, 1889: 3.

4. "Sporting News," *Buffalo Express*, January 30, 1889: 6.

5. "Cuban Giants in Florida," *Trenton Evening Times*, February 11, 1889: 2; "Base Hits," *Buffalo Express*, February 12, 1889: 6.

6. "Baseball Matters," *Buffalo Express*, February 10, 1889: 8.

7. "The Sporting World," *Buffalo Courier*, February 22, 1889: 3.

8. "The World of Sport," *Buffalo Express*, February 24, 1889: 8.

9. "Sporting News," *Buffalo Evening News*, February 26, 1889: 1.

10. "The Sporting World," *Buffalo Courier*, February 28, 1889: 3.

11. "The Sporting World," *Buffalo Courier*, March 28, 1889: 3.

12. "Sporting News," *Buffalo Express*, April 3, 1888: 6.

13. "Around the Bases," *Buffalo Evening News*, April 14, 1889: 2; "Sporting Matters," *Buffalo Commercial Advertiser*, March 5, 1889: 3.

14. "Sporting News," *Buffalo Express*, April 1, 1889: 6; "For the Pennant," *Buffalo Express*, April 7, 1889: 1.

15. "Basehits," *Buffalo Express*, April 11, 1889: 6; "The World of Sport," *Buffalo Express*, April 14, 1889: 7.

16. "Base Hits, *Buffalo Express*, April 18, 1889: 6; "Basehits," *Buffalo Express*, May 2, 1889: 6.

17. "The Sporting World," *Buffalo Courier*, April 14, 1889: 3. See also "Sporting Notes, *Detroit Free Press*, April 18, 1889: 3. The *Free Press* printed the *Courier*'s account in its entirety, and attributed it to that Buffalo daily, though it replaced both of the racial slurs with "Grant."

18. Hamilton, "Grant's Terms," *Buffalo Sunday Morning News*, April 14, 1889: 1.

19. "Base Ball Notes," *Cleveland Plain Dealer*, April 15, 1889: 2. This was reprinted, without attribution, in "Sullivan and Kilrain," *Buffalo Commercial Advertiser*, April 16, 1889: 3.

20. "Sporting Notes," *Chicago Tribune*, April 17, 1889: 3. For an example of the shared article on which the *Tribune*'s statement was likely based, see "All on Account of His Color," *Boston Herald*, April 15, 1889: 5. See also "The Color Line in Baseball," The *Daily Examiner* (San Francisco), April 16, 1889: 1.

21. "Base Hits," *Buffalo Express*, April 18, 1889: 6.

22. "Plenty of Sport," *Buffalo Sunday Morning News*, April 21, 1889: 3.

23. Joseph Overfield, "James 'Deacon' White," http://research.sabr.org/journals/james-deacon-white.

24. "Colored Ball Players," *The Sporting News*, March 23, 1889: 2.

25. "Discovery of the Slide," *Sporting Life*, October 24, 1891: 3.

26. "The National Game," *Buffalo Courier*, March 2, 1889: 3; "Base Hits," *Buffalo Express*, March 3, 1889: 8; "Sporting Matters," *Buffalo Commercial Advertiser*, March 5, 1889: 3.

27. "The Sporting Chapter," *Buffalo Courier*, October 4, 1888: 3.

28. "Base Ball Notes," *Pittsburgh Post*, October 16, 1888: 6; "To-Day's Game," *Pittsburgh Post*, April 19, 1889: 6. Possibly ranking second as a suspect is Ed Swartwood, who was a major leaguer for

Pittsburgh from 1882 through 1884 and who played for Hamilton in 1888. As he was preparing to manage Hamilton in 1889, he was quoted in Pittsburgh newspapers often, including around the time of the anonymous claim. Other candidates include Marr Phillips, Hamilton's shortstop, who was born in the Pittsburgh area and was buried there. In 1885 he played briefly for Pittsburgh's American Association team. A fourth is Tom Quinn, an Albany player who was buried in Pittsburgh. He played briefly with Pittsburgh in 1886 and caught for Pittsburgh's 1890 team in the Players' League. In early 1889, he was apparently living in Braddock, less than 10 miles from Pittsburgh. A fifth is Pete Weckbecker, another Albany player, who spent the winter of 1888–1889 in Harmony, 30 miles north of Pittsburgh. A sixth is Jim Toy, a Rochester player, who was born in Beaver Falls, about 30 miles northwest of Pittsburgh, and who was buried in nearby Beaver. Both Weckbecker and Toy may have lived just a little too far from Pittsburgh to have been considered "Pittsburgh boys" in that pre-automobile era. Lastly, Steve Toole, another Rochester player, was buried in Pittsburgh. His first recorded minor league team was based in New Brighton, about 30 miles northwest of Pittsburgh. However, he only played in 15 games for Rochester in 1888 and thus may have known almost nothing about Grant. Of course, there could have been IL players who were neither born nor buried in Pittsburgh but who nonetheless lived there that offseason. Also, the birthplaces and burial sites for a few players in the league weren't known as of this writing.

29. "The Race's Doings," *Cleveland Gazette*, April 13, 1889: 1. See also "Mr. Cleveland's Trip," *New York Times*, March 21, 1889: 1. The latter didn't mention any ballgame but otherwise documented Cleveland's stop in St. Augustine.

30. John M. Bright, a white man, had a very long association with the Cuban Giants. For an overview of his history with that team, plus a paragraph about his personal life, see "The Cuban Giants Playing 100th Game of the Season," *Berkshire Evening Eagle* (Pittsfield, Massachusetts), August 14, 1908: 14.

31. "The Middle States League," *Philadelphia Inquirer*, April 5, 1889: 6. The initial preseason schedule of the Cuban Giants included games in Jacksonville on April 5, in Savannah on April 6, and in Charleston on April 7; see "The Colored Champions," *Sporting Life*, February 27, 1889: 6. An African American paper's later overview of the Cubans' preseason put those first two games on April 8 and 9, respectively, but omitted any game in Charleston. See "The Race's Doings," *Cleveland Gazette*, April 13, 1889: 1. This newspaper presumably went to press before knowing the outcome of the first game. The Cuban Giants didn't arrive in time (if ever) to play the game on April 9, according to an item without a headline in the *Savannah* (Georgia) *Tribune*, April 13, 1889: 3.

32. "Amusements," *Washington Bee*, April 6, 1889: 3.

33. "Honors to the Cuban Giants," *Washington Post*, April 12, 1889: 6.

34. "Cuban Giants Beaten," *Washington Post*, April 13, 1889: 2; "Base Ball Gossip," *Evening Star* (Washington, D.C.), April 13, 1889: 6.

35. "No Game at Washington," *The Times* (Philadelphia), April 14, 1889: 2; "Baseball," *New York Times*, April 15, 1889: 5; "Cuban Giants' Arrival," *New York Age*, April 20, 1889: 1.

36. "Cuban Giant [sic], 7; Syracuse, 3," *Trenton Times*, April 16, 1889: 3; "Base Hits, *Buffalo Express*, April 18, 1889: 6; "Star Spring Record," *Sunday Herald* (Syracuse, New York), April 28, 1889: 5.

37. "Local Brevities," *Trenton Times*, April 18, 1889: 3; "No Game at Trenton," *Detroit Free Press*, April 19, 1889: 8.

38. "Giants at the Bat," *New York Herald*, April 22, 1889: 8. "To-Day's Game," *Hartford* (Connecticut) *Courant*, April 26, 1889: 1.

39. For example, see "The Color Line in Baseball," *Daily Wamegan* (Wamego, Kansas), April 22, 1889: 2. An African American newspaper later printed this as well (with a dateline of Buffalo, April 14): see "Race Doings, *Leavenworth* (Kansas) *Advocate*, May 4, 1889: 2.

40. For examples, see "The National Game," *Salisbury* (North Carolina) *Truth*, April 25, 1889: 1; "The National Game," *Hollis* (New Hampshire) *Times*, April 26, 1889: 4; "The National Game," *The Standard Gauge* (Brewton, Alabama), May 2, 1889: 1; "The National Game," *Abbeville* (South Carolina) *Press and Banner*, May 8, 1889: 2.

41. "Sporting Notes," *Buffalo Express*, May 16, 1889: 6. See also the league standings a little higher in that same column.

42. "Notes," *Sunday Truth*, May 26, 1889: 8.

43. "Victory for Lancaster," *Lancaster* (Pennsylvania) *Intelligencer*, May 2, 1889: 1.

44. "Lancaster Failed to Score," *Daily New Era* (Lancaster, Pennsylvania), May 3, 1889: 1; "Second Championship Game," *Lancaster Intelligencer*, May 3, 1889: 1. Both box scores specified that he had two stolen bases, but one in another newspaper only listed him with one. See "The Middle States League," *The Sun* (New York City), May 3, 1889: 6. "Umpire [William] Dean fined Capt. Thomas $10 for back talk," *The Sun* noted. The changes in the Cubans' lineup were that Williams batted leadoff and played right field, Thomas batted second and caught, Selden pitched, and Whyte batted last, playing left field instead of right.

45. "Hits from the Diamond," *Daily Patriot* (Harrisburg, Pennsylvania), May 3, 1889: 1;. "What Will the Harvest Be?" *Harrisburg Telegraph*, May 4, 1889: 1. In the city's 1888 and 1889 directories, the Washington Hotel was at 517 Walnut and associated with an A.H. Landis, who was presumably the proprietor.

46. "No Flies on the Colts," *Harrisburg Telegraph*, May 6, 1889: 1; "Another Victory," *Daily*

Patriot, May 6, 1889: 1; "Dreisockers," *Harrisburg Telegraph*, May 13, 1889: 1.

47. A single sentence about this game versus the Gorhams was in the *Brooklyn Daily Eagle*, May 6, 1889: 1. There wasn't a headline as such, but this mention was just above the headline, "The Game of Lacrosse."

48. "Bostons, 5; Cuban Giants, 2," *Boston Herald*, May 8, 1889: 4; T.H. Murnane, "Bostons Take It Easy," *Boston Daily Globe*, May 8, 1889: 3; "A Good Game of Ball," *Trenton Times*, May 8, 1889: 3. The latter's box score didn't list at-bats, but the *Herald*'s did. Grant was shown in it as 0-for-4, seemingly indicating that his sacrifice fly was scored as an at-bat. Murnane's detailed account indicated that Harrison was picked off after stealing second. Regarding Harrison's suspension and quick reinstatement by Govern, see "Local Brevities," *Trenton Times*, May 9, 1889: 3. For a profile of Trenton's manager, see Rory Costello, "S.K. Govern," https://sabr.org/bioproj/person/s-k-govern/.

49. "Stopped by the Storm," *Reading* (Pennsylvania) *Times*, May 11, 1889: 1; "Yesterday's Amateur Games," *Trenton Times*, May 12, 1889: 5.

50. "The Cubans Claim the Game," *Daily True American* (Trenton, New Jersey), May 14, 1889: 5; "All the Games Lost," *Trenton Times*, May 16, 1889: 3. The MSL also decided that the forfeit charged to Reading should be replayed, though the forfeit itself may never have been stricken from the standings. A very large ad for the "Chas. E. Mason" company was printed in *Sporting Life*, May 30, 1888: 11. See also Paul Browne, *The Coal Barons Played Cuban Giants: A History of Early Professional Baseball in Pennsylvania, 1889-1896* (Jefferson, NC: McFarland, 2013), 77–78.

51. "Middle States League Bulletin," *Harrisburg Telegraph*, May 29, 1889: 1. Regarding the MSL and the National Agreement, see "Base Ball News," *The Times* (Philadelphia), December 9, 1888: 14; "Middle States League to Begin Suit Against St. Louis and Athletics," *York* (Pennsylvania) *Dispatch*, July 1, 1889: 1.

52. "Ball and Bat," *Buffalo Commercial Advertiser*, June 4, 1889: 3.

53. "Sporting Notes," *Reading Times*, May 24, 1889: 1. See also the box score two columns to the left of that comment.

54. "Baseball at Weehawken," *New York Age*, May 25, 1889: 1.

55. "On the Fly," *Harrisburg Telegraph*, May 29, 1889: 1. Box scores for all four games were printed in Harrisburg's *Daily Patriot*. For example, see "Cubans 5, Ponies 4," *Daily Patriot*, May 30, 1889: 1. Beneath the line score, it specified, "Double play—Grant, unassisted."

56. "Five innings at Trenton," *Philadelphia Inquirer*, June 1, 1889: 6. The *Trenton Times* soon advertised a game for June 12 with Louisville's American Association team, but on that date the upper left corner of its third page stated that rain was expected for 24 hours starting at 3:00 that afternoon.

57. "Base Ball News," *Trenton Times*, June 8, 1889: 3; "From All Parts of the Union," *New York Tribune*, June 8, 1889: 7. For a staggering statistical account of the flood, see https://www.jaha.org/attractions/johnstown-flood-museum/flood-history/facts-about-the-1889-flood/.

58. "Trouble in the Middle States League," *The Sun* (New York City), June 9, 1889: 13; "Dreisockers," *Harrisburg Telegraph*, June 11, 1889: 1; "Base Ball News," *Cleveland Gazette*, July 20, 1889: 1. Through July 17, the Cuban Giants had a record of 63–16–2 in 81 games, according to "Hits and Misses," *Boston Herald*, July 21, 1889: 4. Their record in the Middle States League at the time was 30–8, meaning more than half of the games they played up to that date were exhibitions.

59. "The Giants are Safe," *Trenton Times*, June 13, 1889: 3.

60. "Base Ball," *Harrisburg Independent*, June 26, 1889: 1; "The League Managers Meet," *Daily Patriot*, June 26, 1889: 1.

61. "The Cuban Giants Monday," *Meriden Daily Journal*, May 20, 1889; "Base Ball Matters," *Meriden Daily Journal*, May 20, 1889: 8.

62. "The Cubans To-Morrow," *Meriden Daily Journal*, June 26, 1889: 4; "Brevities, *Meriden Daily Republican*, June 27, 1889: 3; "A Fine Ball Game," *Meriden Daily Republican*, June 28, 1889: 4.

63. "Great Base Ball Playing," *Meriden Daily Journal*, June 28, 1889: 1.

64. "Local Brevities," *Trenton Times*, June 7, 1889: 3; "Indians Against the Cubans," *Trenton Times*, June 27, 1889: 3; "The Middle States League," *Trenton Times*, June 30, 1889: 5; "A Race Conflict," *Daily True American*, June 29, 1889: 5. For an earlier game played by these visitors, see "Won by the Indians," *The Times* (Philadelphia), April 14, 1889: 2. See also Robert Tholkes, "Chief Bender—The Early Years," http://research.sabr.org/journals/chief-bender-the-early-years.

65. "The Cubans Too Much for Them," *Trenton Times*, July 7, 1889: 5; "A Ten-Innings Game," *Trenton Times*, July 8, 1889: 3.

66. "The Colored Ball Tossers Today," *Argus* (Albany, New York), July 13, 1889: 7; "They Were Easy Victims," *Albany Sunday Express*, July 14, 1889: 8; "Diamond-Field Notes," *Albany Evening Journal*, July 15, 1890: 1; "Can't Play Ball on Sunday," *Argus*, July 15, 1889: 8. The latter didn't include a box score or many details; "Grant, of last year's Buffalos," was the only visiting player named. The All-Americans' lineup for their first game was: Thomas, c; Boyd, ss; Schenk, rf; Brown, lf; Stovey, p; Collins, cf; Evans, 2b; Peterson, 3b; Davis, 1b. (Both teams had a player named Davis.) The *Argus*' preview of the game said two other Gorhams, "Vactor and Bell," were also on the team, and alluded to two players each "from the Resolutes of Boston and the Keystones of Philadelphia" but didn't name them. See also Nicole DiCicco's biography of George Davis at https://sabr.org/bioproj/person/george-davis/.

67. "Chips from the Diamond," *The Sun* (New

York City), July 22, 1889: 3. William Malone also broke into the lineup in the second game. At this point, the roster reported was: Collins, c; Stovey, p; Holmes, 1b; Grant, 2b; Harrison, ss; Malone, 3b, plus outfielders "Fagan, Shenck, Peterson and Fisher." It so happened that when the Cuban Giants beat the MSL's new Shenandoah club on July 18, Malone played for the latter club, and thus its lineup wasn't all-white for at least one game. These future game dates were listed for this new team: July 27 at Hoboken; July 28 "either at Monitor Park or Albany"; July 29 at Hudson, NY; July 30 at Amsterdam; July 31 at Canajoharie; "Aug. 1 open," August 2 at Kingston; and August 3 at Saugerties, NY.

68. "Base Ball," *York Dispatch*, July 16, 1889: 1; "Base Ball," *Hazleton* (Pennsylvania) *Sentinel*, July 17, 1889: 4.

69. "The League Managers Meet," *Daily Patriot*, July 22, 1889: 1; "The Cuban Giants Shut Out," *Daily Patriot*, July 23, 1889: 1; "Base Ball News," *Trenton Times*, July 25, 1889: 3.

70. "Resolutes Down the Cubans," *Meriden Daily Republican*, July 30, 1889: 1; *Meriden Daily Journal*, July 30, 1889: 1.

71. "Base Ball Matters," *Hudson* (New York) *Daily Evening Register*, July 30, 1889: 4; "Home Department," *Canajoharie* (New York) *Wide-Awake Courier*, August 6, 1889: 6.

72. "Gloversville Wins," *Gloversville* (New York) *Daily Leader*, July 31, 1889: 6; "The 'Blacks' Play Ball," *Gloversville Daily Leader*, August 2, 1889: 6. In the latter account, J. Johnson of the All-Americans was mentioned as one of the two umpires, but none of his teammates were named. See also "For Lovers of Baseball," *Gloversville Daily Leader*, July 26, 1889: 6. In that preview, the *Leader* called the visitors "the All Americans of New York city, a league nine chosen from the four best colored clubs in the United States.'"

73. "Local Sporting Matters," *Kingston* (New York) *Daily Freeman*, August 3, 1889: 4; "To Cross Bats To-day," *Argus*, August 3, 1889: 8; "A Small Crowd Sees a Good Game," *Argus*, August 4, 1889: 12. The *Argus'* preview made it seem like "Seldon" was Holmes's first name, and it incorrectly labeled all five of the players it named as members of the Cuban Giants. Collins, at least, certainly wasn't from that roster.

74. "With Hands Down," *Albany Sunday Express*, August 4, 1889: 8. Davis was again in Albany's lineup. The All-Americans' lineup was: Collins, cf and c; Fisher, c and cf; Grant, ss; Stovey, rf; Schenk, p and 3b; Patterson, 1b; Selden, 3b and p; Evans, 2b; Brown, lf.

75. See http://www.cnlbr.org/Portals/0/RL/Colored%20Championship%20Series%20(1867-1899)%202018-04.pdf.

76. "Easton Hotels Draw the Color Line," *York* (Pennsylvania) *Gazette*, August 3, 1889: 1; "Can't Bet Board," *Hazleton Sentinel*, August 3, 1889: 4. See also "Easton Hotels Draw the Colored Line," *Evening Capital* (Annapolis, Maryland), August 3, 1889: 4. The same exact article, including the headline, was also published the same day in the *Bridgeton* (New Jersey) *Evening News*, as another out-of-state example of coverage.

77. "Gentlemen of Color," *Southington* (Connecticut) *Weekly Phoenix*, August 9, 1889: 2.

78. "Harrisburg Loses a Game," *Daily Patriot*, August 9, 1889: 1; "They Redeem Themselves," *Daily Patriot*, August 10, 1889: 1; "Base Ball," *York Dispatch*, August 12, 1889: 1. Stecher had a major league career that lasted little more than a month, in late 1890, when he suffered the indignity of going 0–10 for the American Association's Philadelphia Athletics.

79. "A Game at Gloucester," *Philadelphia Inquirer*, August 12, 1889: 6. The All-Americans' game was summarized in a short item sans headline in the *New York Tribune*, August 12, 1889: 8.

80. "Jottings," *Courier-News* (Bridgewater, New Jersey), August 13, 1889: 1; "York, 6; Cuban Giants, 3," *Philadelphia Inquirer*, August 13, 1889: 6. Stovey may have been leading the All-Americans at this time. In Asbury Park, New Jersey, on August 14, he pitched in a game between "the waiters of the West End Hotel of Long Branch and the Ocean Hotel of Asbury Park." The opposing battery consisted of Vactor and Conover. See "An Exciting Game of Base Ball," *Asbury Park* (New Jersey) *Press*, August 15, 1889: 1.

81. "A Struggle for Honors," *Lebanon* (Pennsylvania) *Daily News*, August 16, 1889: 1. Stephen V. Rice, https://sabr.org/gamesproj/game/august-16-1889-integrated-baseball-in-pennsylvania-cuban-giants-defeat-lebanon-grays/.

82. Stars vs. All Americans," *Times Union* (Brooklyn), August 19, 1889: 4; "Too Much for the Domestics," *Times Union*, August 8, 1889: 4.

83. "Won by One," *Daily True American*, August 20, 1889: 5.

84. "The Last of the Season," *The Times* (Philadelphia), September 1, 1889: 9. Anderson was identified in "Behind the Bat," *Washington Post*, August 28, 1889: 6.

85. "The Giants Did Much Kicking," *Trenton Times*, August 29, 1889: 3; "Burlington Downed," *Philadelphia Inquirer*, August 28, 1889: 6.

86. "Wilmington Defeated," *Evening Journal* (Wilmington, Delaware) August 30, 1889: 4; "Cuban Giants Won," *Evening Journal*, September 2, 1889: 4; "Baseball at Wilmington," *New York Age*, September 9, 1889: 4.

87. "Lost by One Run," *Lebanon Daily News*, September 10, 1889: 1; "The Old Story," *Lebanon Daily News*, September 11, 1889: 1.

88. Henry Chadwick, editor, *Spalding's Base Ball Guide and Official League Book for 1890* (Chicago: A.G. Spalding & Bros., 1890), 89.

89. Paul Browne, *The Coal Barons Played Cuban Giants: A History of Early Professional Baseball in Pennsylvania, 1889–1896* (Jefferson, NC: McFarland, 2013), 91–92, 96–98. In between those pages, Browne profiled the Cubans' regular players during 1889.

90. "They Claim the Pennant," *Philadelphia Inquirer*, October 7, 1889: 6.

91. See Note 85.

92. "Foul and Out," *Daily Patriot*, November 8, 1889: 1. That paper had promised the MSL statistics on its front page at least twice, on October 21 and 31. For very detailed statistics compiled for just the Harrisburg club "by a careful base ball enthusiast," see "Middle States Champions," *Harrisburg Telegraph*, November 14, 1889: 1.

93. The *Harrisburg Telegram*—distinct from the *Harrisburg Telegraph*—was quoted in full in "Second Baseman Grant," *Cleveland Gazette*, September 21, 1889: 1.

94. "An Uninteresting Game," *Albany Morning Express*, September 15, 1889: 1; "A Bird's Eye View," *Gloversville Daily Leader*, September 24, 1889: 7. The Albany nine again included Davis in left field, batting cleanup, which likely means that Frank Grant and George Davis met at least three times that summer. For a full itinerary, though with "probably" noted for two of the games, see "Pickups," *Rochester Democrat and Chronicle*, September 15, 1889: 6. Bad weather cancelled some games, according to "Baseball Notes," *Gloversville Daily Leader*, September 20, 1889: 3.

95. "Rainy Day Sports," *Buffalo Commercial Advertiser*, September 16, 1889: 3; "Season Sports," *Sunday Truth*, September 22, 1889: 8; "The Giants Are Stranded," *Buffalo Evening News*, September 25, 1889: 1.

96. "Colored Nine Knocked Out," *Albany Morning Express*, September 28, 1889: 1; "A Cold Day for Albany," *Argus*, September 29, 1889: 12; "Albany's Downed Again," *Argus*, September 30, 1889: 8. The hometown nines only had a Davis in their lineup on September 29. In the Capital Citys' game, seven local players had the privilege of teaming with the four Cuban Giants. Six were listed by Brunson (Note 78) at page 341, and he provided three first names. The seven were Bishop, Charles Lett, Charles Teabout ("Tebout" in the box score), George Van Valkenburgh, E. Teabout, Chester, and "L'rence," the only one not in Dr. Brunson's list.

97. "Mets, 5; Cuban Giants, 4," *New York Times*, October 2, 1889: 8; "Notes of the Game," *Middletown (New York) Daily Argus*, October 5, 1889: 3; "Cuban Giants, 11; Hackett, Carhart & Co., 2," *New York Times*, October 6, 1889: 6. See also "Mets, 6; Cuban Giants, 1," *New York Times*, October 1, 1889: 3.

98. "Base Ball Notes," *Lebanon Daily News*, October 19, 1889: 1; "The Cuban Giants are All Right," *The Sun* (New York City), November 30, 1889: 4.

Chapter 8

1. "Genteel Sports," *Buffalo Commercial Advertiser*, January 21, 1890: 3.

2. The letter sent by Bright to Trenton's *Sunday Advertiser* was reported on at length in "Out-Door Sports," *Trenton Times*, December 29, 1889: 5. He also announced the appointment of Trenton resident M.E. Fitzgerald as his representative there.

3. "The Gorham Base Ball Club," *New York Age*, March 15, 1890: 3.

4. "Another Club for Harrisburg," *Philadelphia Inquirer*, March 5, 1890: 6; "Sporting Scintillations," *Harrisburg Telegraph*, March 6, 1890: 1. As mentioned previously, Clarence Williams was born and raised in Harrisburg. See his Negro Leagues Baseball Museum profile at https://nlbemuseum.com/history/players/williamscl.html.

5. "Sporting Small Shot," *Harrisburg Telegraph*, March 10, 1890: 4; "Base Ball," *Harrisburg Daily Independent*, March 10, 1890: 1. See also "Ball and Ball Players," *Daily Patriot*, March 10, 1890: 1. Under the same headline, the latter reported that Walker, Grant, and Stovey would play with the Gorhams but at the end of that article put Grant in Kreiter's lineup as well.

6. "Manager Kreiter's Statement," *Daily Patriot*, March 13, 1890: 1; "Sporting Splinters," *Harrisburg Telegraph*, March 13, 1890: 1.

7. "Sporting Splinters," *Harrisburg Telegraph*, March 20, 1890: 1. See also "Harrisburg Will Have the Cuban Giants," *Trenton Times*, March 24, 1890: 3.

8. J.M. Bright, "A Strong Team for Trenton," *Trenton Times*, March 28, 1890: 3.

9. "Base Ball Yesterday," *The Sun* (New York City), March 27, 1890: 6. The full lineup for the "colored team" was: Jackson, c; Stovey, lf; Grant, 2b; Nelson, ss and p; Collins, 1b; Holland, 3b; Fagen, p and ss; Taylor, cf; and Dean, rf.

10. "Here and There a Pointer," *Daily Patriot*, March 31, 1890: 1.

11. "Sporting Splinters," *Harrisburg Telegraph*, April 1, 1890: 1; "The Deal Arranged," *Daily Patriot*, April 1, 1890: 1.

12. "Coming Ball Players," *The Sun* (New York City), March 29, 1890: 5; "Games To-day," *The Sun*, March 30, 1890: 5.

13. "Sport of All Varieties," *Brooklyn Daily Eagle*, March 30, 1890: 9; "Stars, 16; Cuban Giants, 10," *The Sun*, April 6, 1890: 5.

14. "Sunday Ball Games," *New York Tribune*, April 7, 1890: 12.

15. "Worcesters, 16; Cuban Giants, 3," *Boston Herald*, April 9, 1890: 10; "The Giants Outbatted," *Washington Post*, April 12, 1890: 6; "Cuban Giants, 13; Houston, 9," *Philadelphia Inquirer*, April 13, 1890: 6; "Base-Ball," *Hartford Courant*, April 15, 1890: 2; "Base-Ball," *Hartford Courant*, April 16, 1890: 1. Nat Collins' release by the Cuban Giants was mentioned in "Base Ball Notes," *The Sun* (New York City), April 24, 1890: 4. The familial relationship between Andy and Robert Jackson was mentioned in Jerry Malloy's introduction to *Sol White's History of Colored Base Ball with Other Documents on the Early Black Game, 1886–1936* (Lincoln: University of Nebraska Press, 1995), xxiv.

16. "Behind the Bat," *Buffalo Commercial*

Advertiser, April 18, 1890: 10. Sol White also homered in that game.

17. "Our Giant Killers," *Evening Star* (Washington, D.C.), April 12, 1890: 11.

18. "The Giants Outbatted," *Washington Post*, April 12, 1890: 6.

19. "In the World of Sports," *Harrisburg Telegraph*, April 7, 1890: 1; "Sporting Sayings," *Harrisburg Telegraph*, April 8, 1890: 1. On April 7, the *Telegraph* brought up Grant twice, a few paragraphs apart. The second instance quoted from an item in the *New York Sun* about Grant and Holmes being the only two players from 1889 on Bright's payroll that preseason. Actually, Stovey was also on the Cuban Giants in 1889, for short stints early and late in the season. Conversely, if Holmes was on the payroll at all during 1889, it was likely for shorter than Stovey (in contrast to prior seasons, when Holmes *was* a regular). The *Sun's* comment was widely reprinted.

20. "Base Ball Notes," *The Sun* (New York City), April 12, 1890: 5; "Base Ball Notes," *Daily Independent* (Harrisburg), April 11, 1890: 1; "Diamond Dots," *Lebanon Daily News*, April 14, 1890: 1. Sol White made his debut with York on April 18.

21. "Bates has a Slow Drop," *Boston Daily Globe*, April 12, 1890: 1.

22. "Base Ball Notes," *Lebanon Daily News*, April 18, 1890: 1. Around this time, the York team was occasionally also called the Cuban Giants in newspapers, and adding to the potential for confusion was the fact that Kreiter's team played Washington shortly after Grant's nine did (faring no better, in a 15–1 loss). However, on the front page of the *Daily News* on April 16, the game on April 17 was specified as against the "Cuban Giants (Trenton)" and a game two days later was against "York (Cuban Giants)."

23. "Base Ball," *Harrisburg Telegraph*, April 17, 1890: 1.

24. "Grand Stand Chat," *Harrisburg Telegraph*, April 18, 1890: 1; "Grand Stand Chat," *Harrisburg Telegraph*, April 19, 1890: 6; "Which Club has Grant," *Harrisburg Daily Independent*, April 19, 1890: 1.

25. "Easton Bats Hard," *Free Press* (Easton, Pennsylvania), April 22, 1890: 3; "Notes of the Diamond Field," *Philadelphia Inquirer*, April 25, 1890: 6.

26. "Diamond Dust," *York Gazette*, April 23, 1890: 1; "Notes," *York Dispatch*, April 21, 1890: 1. Neither of these daily papers in York covered this controversy much. One distinct possibility is that they appreciated the talent Kreiter had already assembled and didn't think adding Grant would make that much difference.

27. "Diamond Dust," *Harrisburg Telegraph*, April 23, 1890: 1.

28. "Manager Kreiter's Statement," *Harrisburg Telegraph*, April 24, 1890: 1.

29. "Will the 'Mets' Move?" *Daily Patriot*, April 25, 1890: 1; "Scattering Hits," *Harrisburg Telegraph*, April 25, 1890: 1.

30. "Bleaching Board Briefs," *Harrisburg Telegraph*, April 30, 1890: 1; "No Game at Altoona," *Harrisburg Telegraph*, May 1, 1890: 1; "Base Ball Notes," *Harrisburg Daily Independent*, May 2, 1890: 1.

31. "Base Ball Notes," *The Sun* (New York City), April 23, 1890: 4; "The College Town," *North Adams* (Massachusetts) *Transcript*, May 8, 1890: 4. At least two Buffalo dailies eventually reported Clarence's signing. See "Little Pick-ups," *Buffalo Commercial Advertiser*, May 3, 1890: 12; "Base Ball Gossip," *Buffalo Evening News*, May 8, 1890: 3 (Second Edition).

32. "Ball Player at a Ball," *Boston Daily Globe*, August 8, 1889: 1; "Williamstown," *Albany Sunday Express*, August 11, 1889: 7.

33. "Williamstown," *Albany Sunday Express*, August 25, 1889: 7. Clarence Grant's attorney was named P.J. Ashe. See "Atty. P.J. Ashe, 86, Dies in Maryland," *North Adams Transcript*, January 26, 1946: 3.

34. "Berkshire County. Pittsfield," *Springfield* (Massachusetts) *Republican*, January 29, 1890: 6.

35. "Score Us One More," *Albany Morning Express*, April 29, 1890: 1; "The Giants Downed Again," *Argus*, April 29, 1890: 8; "The Giants Were Thrashed," *Albany Evening Journal*, April 29, 1890: 6. The batting order for the Cuban Giants was: Jackson, 3b, 2b; Stovey rf and lf; Grant, 2b and c; Garrison, ss; Holmes, 1b; Nelson, cf; Jackson, c and rf; Grant, lf and 3b; Jupiter, p.

36. "Albany's to the Fore," *Argus*, April 27, 1890: 12; "We Walloped 'Em," *Albany Morning Express*, April 28, 1890: 6; "The National Game," *Albany Evening Journal*, April 28, 1890: 6.

37. "Troy Again Defeated," *Troy* (New York) *Daily Times*, April 30, 1890: 3; "Troy Wins a Game," *Troy Daily Times*, May 1, 1890: 2.

38. "Diamond Tips," *Chattanooga* (Tennessee) *Daily Times*, August 11, 1890: 8.

39. "Base Ball Matters," *Hudson* (New York) *Evening Register*, May 3, 1890: 4; "The Base Ball Season Opened," *Columbia Republican* (Hudson, New York), May 8, 1890: 2; The *Register* printed a box score, and the Cubans' lineup was: A. Jackson, 3b; Stovey, lf; F. Grant, 2b; Garrison, ss; Holmes, 1b; Nelson, p; E. Grant, c; B. Jackson, rf; Jupiter, cf.

40. "Williams, 8; Cuban Giants, 2," *Boston Sunday Globe*, May 4, 1890: 3. The *Globe's* batting order for the Cuban Giants was (typos and all): J. Jackson, 3b; Stovey, lf; F. Grant, 3b; Garrison, ss; Holmes, 1b; Terrel, cf; B. Jackson, rf and c; P. Grant, c and rf; Jupiter, p; and Nelson, p. It's probably no coincidence that the other Grant's initial, P, rhymes with C and may thus have resulted from a mishearing, if not sloppy penmanship. Their lineup as printed presumably contained at least one other typo, because the leadoff hitter "J. Jackson" was almost certainly Andy Jackson, and it may similarly be no coincidence that the initial J rhymes with A.

41. "Williamstown," *Pittsfield Sun*, May 8, 1890: 4.

42. Bliss Perry, *And Gladly Teach* (Boston: Houghton Mifflin Company, 1935), 22. For a concise biography of Perry, see https://special collections.williams.edu/williams-history/biographies/bliss-perry-1860-1954/.

43. "Playing Ball in the Water," *Utica* (New York) *Daily Press*, May 6, 1890: 1. Stovey was called the team's captain in this article. It's possible that the "Grant" who played against Utica was instead Henry *Gant*, whose surname was often misspelled as Grant. In late April, "Manager Bright" of the Cuban Giants was expecting to sign "Henry Grant, the great coacher of the Keystones, of Pittsburg," but he and a second newcomer, "big Trusty," weren't projected to join the team until May 10, according to "Notes of the Diamond Field," *Philadelphia Inquirer*, April 30, 1890: 6. However, there was no Gant, Grant, or Trusty in the box score of the Cubans' game on May 10, nor in box scores for five games in the second half of May. Citations for those six: "Results of College Games," *The Times* (Philadelphia), May 11, 1890: 2; "Cuban Giants vs. Port Jervis," *Port Jervis* (New York) *Union*, May 17, 1890: 3; a box score for their game of May 19 was reported (in an article with no headline) in the *Bucks County Gazette* (Bristol, Pennsylvania), May 22, 1890: 3; "Burlington's First Defeat," *Philadelphia Inquirer*, May 22, 1890: 3; "Houston, 6; Cuban Giants, 5," *Philadelphia Inquirer*, May 25, 1890: 6; "Pottstown Defeats the Giants," *The Times* (Philadelphia), May 30, 1890: 2.

44. "Notes of the Game," *Harrisburg Daily Independent*, May 3, 1890: 1.

45. "The Base Ball World," *Harrisburg Daily Independent*, May 2, 1890: 1.

46. "A Waterloo for Altoona," *Daily Patriot*, May 6, 1890: 1. This article's second of three subheadlines was "Grant on Third Base" and was almost as large as the headline.

47. "A One-sided Game at Harrisburg," *Philadelphia Inquirer*, May 6, 1890: 6.

48. "Gossip of the Game," *Harrisburg Telegraph*, May 6, 1890: 1. See also https://www.nps.gov/cebe/learn/historyculture/sheridan-s-ride.htm.

49. "Notes on the Game," *Daily Patriot*, May 6, 1890: 1.

50. "Grant to be Enjoined," *The Times* (Philadelphia), May 6, 1890: 2.

51. "Harrisburg Wins," *Harrisburg Telegraph*, May 7, 1890: 1. See also "Sporting Spray" beneath the box score (for the first game only).

52. "Gunning for Grant," *Harrisburg Telegraph*, May 7, 1890: 1; "An Injunction Asked For," *Harrisburg Daily Independent*, May 7, 1890: 1; "Benjamin M. Nead, Lawyer and Historian, Dies Today in Chambersburg Homestead," *Evening News* (Harrisburg), March 31, 1923: 1–2.

53. "Playing for the Pennant," *Daily Patriot*, May 8, 1890: 1.

54. "Still After Grant," *Harrisburg Telegraph*, May 8, 1890: 1.

55. "In the Base Ball World," *Harrisburg Daily Independent*, May 12, 1890: 1;"The Base Ball World," *Lancaster Daily Intelligencer*, May 12, 1890: 1. The latter box score showed Grant with three hits and a final score of 21–2. The former showed him with only two hits and a final score of 22–2.

56. "Manager Farrington's Letter," *Daily Patriot*, May 9, 1890: 1; "Pooh-Bah Must Go," *Harrisburg Telegraph*, May 9, 1890: 1; "Jim Farrington Is Mad," *Philadelphia Inquirer*, May 9, 1890: 6.

57. "President Voltz Makes Answer," *Harrisburg Telegraph*, May 12, 1890: 2.

58. "The Grant Case," *Harrisburg Daily Independent*, May 12, 1890: 1; "Grant Will Play," *Harrisburg Telegraph*, May 12, 1890: 1 (Last Edition).

59. "In the Base Ball World," *Harrisburg Daily Independent*, May 13, 1890: 1.

60. "A Game of Pretty Hitting," *Daily Patriot*, May 13, 1890: 1; "The Ponies Lose Once More," *Daily Patriot*, May 14, 1890: 1.

61. "The Grant Case," *Daily Patriot*, May 15, 1890: 1; "Meeting of the Directors of the Interstate League," *Lebanon Daily News*, May 15, 1890: 1. Farrington accused Philadelphia's *Press* of mischaracterizing the meeting as including a vote of confidence for Voltz, according to "Base Ball Gossip," *Daily Patriot*, May 16, 1890: 1.

62. "Good Playing and a Victory," *Daily Patriot*, May 16, 1890: 1.

63. For McCarrell's biography, see https://www.legis.state.pa.us/cfdocs/legis/BiosHistory/MemBio.cfm?ID=5005&body=S.

64. "Will Grant Be Restrained," *Harrisburg Telegraph*, May 16, 1890: 1.

65. For examples, see "Base-Ball Notes," *The Sun* (Baltimore), May 9, 1890: 4;"Games on Many Diamonds," *New York Tribune*, May 9, 1890: 5; "Telegraph Brevities," *Yonkers* (New York) *Gazette*, May 10, 1890: 2.

66. "New Baseball Thunderbolt," *The World* (New York City), May 17, 1890: 1 (5 O'Clock Special); "Are Contracts Binding?" *Boston Daily Globe*, May 17, 1890: 1 (5:00 P.M. Edition).

67. "Notes," *Altoona* (Pennsylvania) *Times*, May 17, 1890: 4. See also "Baseball. Too Much Law," *Sporting Life*, May 24, 1890: 6.

68. "Grant Will Stay," *Harrisburg Telegraph*, May 19, 1890: 1.

69. "A Defeat without Mercy," *Daily Patriot*, May 24, 1890: 1; "Harrisburg Wins Another," *The Times* (Philadelphia), May 25, 1890: 2. Lancaster folded its franchise after this second loss to the Ponies and was replaced in June by a team in Allentown.

70. "The Great Game," *Daily Patriot*, May 26, 1890: 1. As of this writing, his baseball-reference stats for 1890 do not show him having played at shortstop in an EISL game. Also, several box scores for the first of two games on May 30 show him at second base (and in the leadoff spot), but his baseball-reference stats for 1890 don't show him at that position at all during 1890.

71. "Victory for the Farmers," *Daily Patriot*,

May 28, 1890: 1. The *Patriot* printed a dispatch from a York reporter, who decided to dub the Ponies "Farrington's farmers."

72. "A Second Time this Week," *Daily Patriot*, May 30, 1890: 1. For the EISL standings, see "The Championship Records" on the same page.

73. "Batting Averages," *Daily Patriot*, June 2, 1890: 1.

74. "In the Base Ball World," *Harrisburg Daily Independent*, June 6, 1890: 1; "Our National Game," *York Gazette*, June 9, 1890: 1.

75. "Grant Stays with Harrisburg," *Harrisburg Daily Independent*, June 7, 1890: 1; "Grant Can Play," *Harrisburg Telegraph*, June 7, 1890: 1. The editorial paragraph on the *Telegraph*'s second page didn't have a headline; it was in that page's first column.

76. "Grant Can Play," *Harrisburg Telegraph*, June 7, 1890: 1. For the full decision, see *Harrisburg Base-Ball Club v. Athletic Ass'n*, 8 Pa.C.C. 337. At the end, Simonton mentioned two baseball cases, in passing: *Philadelphia Base-Ball Club v. Hallman*, and *American Association Base-Ball Club of Kansas City v. Players' National League Base-Ball Club of Phila*. Special thanks to the Hon. Eugene G. Doherty, then Chief Judge of Illinois' 17th Judicial Circuit Court, for providing this decision.

77. "York Loses the Services of Grant," *Washington Post*, June 8, 1890: 6; "Injunction Refused," *Boston Herald*, June 8, 1890: 4; "The Injunction Denied," *Buffalo Evening News*, June 9, 1890: 1 (First Edition). For another example of interest outside of Pennsylvania, see "Local and General Notes," *Evansville* (Indiana) *Journal*, June 9, 1890: 1.

78. "Four Times in Succession," *Daily Patriot*, June 10, 1890: 1; "They Made It Five Straight," *Daily Patriot*, June 11, 1890: 1. Tragically, while at the ballpark on June 10, William Whyte received a telegram from New York that his wife had passed away, according to "Between the Innings," *Harrisburg Daily Independent*, June 11, 1890: 1.

79. "Harrisburg on Top," *Harrisburg Telegraph*, June 14, 1890: 1.

80. "Lebanon Fails To Get A Hit," *Daily Patriot*, June 21, 1890: 1. See also "The Championship Records" one column over.

81. "Another Victory," *Harrisburg Telegraph*, June 23, 1890: 1; "Base Ball News," *Daily Patriot*, June 23, 1890: 1.

82. "Another Victory," *Harrisburg Telegraph*, June 30, 1890: 1.

83. "Another Close Contests," *Daily Patriot*, June 30, 1890: 4.

84. "In the Base Ball World," *Harrisburg Daily Independent*, July 7, 1890: 1. See also "Base Ball Notes" at the bottom of the same column. "The Ponies' Hard Batting," *Daily Patriot*, July 9, 1890: 1.

85. "Selden Was Hit Hard," *Daily Patriot*, July 10, 1890: 1. Though that day's *Daily Independent* likewise showed Grant with five hits, box scores in four other papers showed him with four: The *Telegraph*, the *York Dispatch*, the *York Gazette*, and the *Philadelphia Inquirer*. Frustratingly, none of these newspapers' box scores had a column for at-bats.

86. "York Wins a Game," *Daily Patriot*, July 11, 1890: 4. "Grant knocked the ball out into the lot and made a home run while the fielders were hunting the ball in the high grass," according to "In the Base Ball World," *Harrisburg Daily Independent*, July 11, 1890: 1.

87. "Base Ball Gossip," *Lebanon Daily News*, July 8, 1890: 1.

88. "Lost by Errors," *The Times* (Altoona, Pennsylvania), July 17, 1890: 4; "Altoona Easily Defeated," *Daily Patriot*, July 17, 1890: 1. See also "The Championship Records" and "Inside the Foul Flags" one column to the right. *The Times* said the only homer at that ballpark longer than Grant's was "one by Matthews, of the Brooklyn's [sic]," but various searches of baseball-reference.com didn't identify a Brooklyn pro by that name prior to mid-1890.

89. "Grand Stand Chat," *Harrisburg Telegraph*, July 15, 1890: 1. The *Telegraph* quoted "a dispatch from Washington to the Philadelphia *Press*."

90. "From Inter-State to Atlantic," *Harrisburg Telegraph*, July 19, 1890: 1;"A Vital Question of Color," *Washington Post*, July 20, 1890: 6.

91. "To Shake the Inter-State," *Harrisburg Telegraph*, July 21, 1890: 1; "Harrisburg Is Admitted," *Daily Patriot*, July 22, 1890: 1. The lengthiest description of the conflict about Frank Grant may have been "Going into Fast Company," *Daily Patriot*, July 21, 1890: 1. He was named seven times in this article.

92. "Grant Will Play," *Harrisburg Telegraph*, July 22, 1890: 1.

93. "Heard About Town," *Washington Post*, July 22, 1890: 1. See also "We Get In," *Harrisburg Telegraph*, July 22, 1890: 1. The franchises objecting most strongly were instead Baltimore, Wilmington, and Jersey City, according to "Base Ball Trouble," *Cleveland Gazette*, August 2, 1890: 1. However, Jersey City's withdrawal was what had opened the door to Harrisburg's admission. Still, the *Gazette* quoted Harrisburg's *Telegram* (not *Telegraph*) in its effort to rebut the view of the Baltimore and Wilmington franchises.

94. "Admitted Into the Atlantic Association," *Lebanon Daily News*, July 31, 1890: 1.

95. "Downed Them Again," *Daily Patriot*, July 22, 1890: 4. See also "The Championship Record" one column to the right.

96. "Notes and Comments," *Harrisburg Telegraph*, July 22, 1890: 1. Interestingly, in that same compilation of tidbits, it was reported that the Hartford club was scheduled to "play a game by electric light" that week. Above this item were league standings, which showed the Ponies with one less win (38–24 instead of 39–24) than in the *Patriot* that same day.

97. The 1890 roster of the Washington Senators on baseball-reference.com shows this pitcher as career minor-leaguer Charles Daniels, albeit with

a question mark after his surname. The mix-up was likely due to the fact that Charles Daniels became an Atlantic Association umpire not long after Pete joined the Senators. See "Sparring for Wind," *Evening Star* (Washington, D.C.), May 30, 1890: 6; "Notes," *Hartford Courant*, June 16, 1890: 1.

98. "They Won the Initial Game," *Daily Patriot*, July 23, 1890, 1; "Won in the Tenth," *Harrisburg Telegraph*, July 23, 1890: 1. Both accounts indicate that Eagan was the first batter in the ninth and McCormick the last, but that would only account for two outs, not three. If McCormick really did make the third out, Eagan must have batted after one out. In fact, the hits by Grant and Koons did come after two outs, according to "In the Base Ball World," *Harrisburg Daily Independent*, July 23, 1890: 1. See also "Notes and Comments," *Harrisburg Telegraph*, July 23, 1890: 1.

99. "Victory a Second Time," *Daily Patriot*, July 24, 1890: 1; "No Game Yesterday," *Harrisburg Telegraph*, July 25, 1890: 1.

100. "Salaries of Ball Players," *Washington Post*, July 27, 1890: 14.

101. "Barnie Is Happy," *The Times* (Philadelphia), October 16, 1887: 14; "Base-Ball Notes," *The Sun* (Baltimore), July 25, 1890: 1 (of Supplement); "Notes and Comments," *Harrisburg Telegraph*, July 23, 1890: 1; "Around the Bases," *Harrisburg Telegraph*, July 25, 1890: 1. In the first of these two rebuttals, the *Telegraph* quoted a report about Barnie by the *Baltimore American*. Around the first of August, Barnie reportedly said he didn't object to Grant, according to "Grand Stand Chat," *Harrisburg Telegraph*, August 2, 1890: 1.

102. "Atlantic Association Record," *Brooklyn Daily Eagle*, July 22, 1890: 2; "A Game of Eleven Innings," *Daily Patriot*, July 26, 1890: 1; "The Second Game Lost," *Daily Patriot*, July 27, 1890: 1.

103. Henry Chadwick, "Chadwick's Chat," *Sporting Life*, July 26, 1890: 8. This paragraph by "the father of base ball" was quoted in "Inside the Foul Flags," *Daily Patriot*, July 28, 1890: 1.

104. "Lost by a Hair's Breadth," *Evening Journal* (Wilmington, Delaware), July 29, 1890: 2. Though this paper's box score didn't have a column for at-bats, it provided inning-by-inning details. In "Base Ball Notes" beneath the box score, the *Journal* announced that the rematch scheduled for that afternoon "had to be postponed on account of the heavy condition of the grounds."

105. "Base Ball Notes," *The Times* (Philadelphia), July 31, 1890: 2.

106. "Base Ball," *Harrisburg Daily Independent*, August 1, 1890: 1.

107. "First Game," *Harrisburg Telegraph*, August 2, 1890: 1.

108. "Hotel Keepers Object to Grant," *Harrisburg Telegraph*, August 7, 1890: 1.

109. "Costly Errors Did It," *Evening Journal* (Wilmington), August 7, 1890: 3.

110. "In the Base Ball World," *Harrisburg Daily Independent*, August 8, 1890: 1. In "Base Ball Notes" beneath the box score, the *Independent* reported briefly on the Clayton House's denial of lodging to Grant and editorialized that "the club rightly put up at another hotel."

111. "A Victory and a Defeat," *Sunday Herald* (Washington, D.C.), August 3, 1890: 5; "Once More to the Front," *Evening Star*, August 4, 1890: 8; "Base Ball Games," *Evening Star*, August 9, 1890: 16.

112. Harrisburg's *Telegram* was quoted at the conclusion of "Base Ball Trouble," *Cleveland Gazette*, August 2, 1890: 1.

113. "Some Race Doings," *Cleveland Gazette*, August 9, 1890: 1; "About Persons and Things," *Plaindealer* (Detroit), August 15, 1890: 4; "The Field of Sport," *Freeman* (Indianapolis), August 23, 1890: 7. See also "The Cuban Giants," *Cleveland Gazette*, August 23, 1890: 2; "Doings of the Race," *Cleveland Gazette*, September 6, 1890: 1.

114. "In the Base Ball World," *Harrisburg Daily Independent*, August 11, 1890: 1.

115. "Defeated by the 'Monarchs,'" *Harrisburg Daily Independent*, August 12, 1890: 4.

116. "Some Flashes from the Green Diamond," *Franklin Repository* (Chambersburg, Pennsylvania), August 9, 1890: 3; "Grand Stand Chat," *Harrisburg Telegraph*, August 12, 1890: 1.

117. The *Baltimore American* was quoted in "Grand Stand Chat," *Harrisburg Telegraph*, August 14, 1890: 1.

118. "Grand Stand Chat," *Harrisburg Telegraph*, August 15, 1890: 1; *The Sun* (Baltimore), August 15, 1890: 1. The *Baltimore American* was quoted in "Baltimore's Opinion of Our Club," *Harrisburg Telegraph*, August 16, 1890: 1.

119. "An Earnest Struggle," *The Sun* (Baltimore), August 16, 1890: 1 (of Supplement); "Base Ball Notes," *Harrisburg Daily Independent*, August 16, 1890: 1. The *Baltimore American* was quoted in "Baltimore's Opinion of Our Club," *Harrisburg Telegraph*, August 16, 1890: 1.

120. "Harrisburg Done Up," *Morning Herald* (Baltimore), August 16, 1890: 4; "An Earnest Struggle," *The Sun* (Baltimore), August 16, 1890: 1 (of Supplement).

121. "No Trouble at All," *Morning Herald* (Baltimore), August 17, 1890: 2.

122. "Base-Ball Notes," *The Sun* (Baltimore), August 16, 1890: 1 (of Supplement).

123. "Washington and Hartford Out," *The Sun* (Baltimore), August 16, 1890: 1 (of Supplement).

124. "The Bridegrooms Ahead," *New York Tribune*, August 19, 1890: 3; ""Grant's Fine Playing Won the Game," *Philadelphia Inquirer*, August 19, 1890: 3. For a box score, see "Atlantic Association," *New York Herald*, August 19, 1890: 9.

125. "Baltimore is out," *Harrisburg Telegraph*, August 19, 1890: 1 (Last Edition). This article was printed in the second column. In the first column, just a little lower, was an editorial sans headline that declared, "It was a sad day for base ball in Harrisburg when the home club joined the Atlantic Association."

126. "Shut Out at New Haven," *Harrisburg Daily Independent*, August 21, 1890: 1; "Base Ball," *Daily*

Patriot, August 22, 1890: 4. Grant wasn't listed as having stolen a base in "Base Ball Yesterday," *New Haven Register*, August 21, 1890: 3. On the other hand, this local account did note that "Grant's catch of a terrific liner from Schoeneck's bat elicited loud applause from the spectators." In the next day's edition, on the same page and under the same headline, the box score showed him with three hits, as did the *Patriot*, but the box score in New Haven's *Morning Journal and Courier* showed Grant with only two hits. The latter box score was at least a little sloppy, because its total hits and errors for the Ponies didn't sum the individual numbers correctly.

127. "At Home and Victory," *Daily Patriot*, August 26, 1890: 4; "Wilmington Defeated," *Daily Patriot*, August 27, 1890: 4; The *Daily Independent*'s box score for the first game credited Grant with only one double, but the *Telegraph*'s box score showed him with two, as did the *Patriot*'s.

128. "Wilmington Expelled," *Harrisburg Daily Independent*, August 26, 1890: 4.

129. "Luck Changing," *Daily Patriot*, August 30, 1890: 4. Grant's hits came off the "famous Serad," whom he first faced in early 1888 when Billy was a major leaguer.

130. "A Correction!" *Buffalo Enquirer*, June 25, 1924: 6.

131. "Vallee Wins a Game," *Daily Patriot*, September 2, 1890: 1.

132. "Newark's Victory," *Daily Patriot*, September 9, 1890: 4. See also the biography by C. Paul Rogers III at https://sabr.org/bioproj/person/hughie-jennings/.

133. See Ted Knorr, "Happy Birthday to the Negro Leagues!" *Patriot-News* (Harrisburg), February 14, 2020, at https://www.pennlive.com/opinion/2020/02/happy-birthday-to-the-negro-leagues-opinion.html. See also https://local21news.com/sports/content/ted-knorr-receives-recognition-for-work-with-negro-league.

134. "Victory at Last," *Daily Patriot*, September 11, 1890: 4.

135. "Keep It Up Now," *Daily Patriot*, September 18, 1890: 4.

136. "Another Victory Ours," *Daily Patriot*, September 20, 1890: 4.

137. "Harrisburg Vs. New Haven," *Reading* (Pennsylvania) *Times*, September 25, 1890: 1. The accompanying box score was astonishingly detailed, with 10 columns, yet somehow there wasn't a column for at-bats.

138. "From Behind the Bat," *Reading Times*, September 25, 1890: 1. The box score above this compilation of comments was as detailed as the previous day's.

139. "Base Ball Notes," *Harrisburg Daily Independent*, September 25, 1890: 1.

140. "Base Ball," *Harrisburg Telegraph*, September 30, 1890: 1; "A Pretty Game," *Daily Patriot*, October 1, 1890: 1; "Harrisburg Loses the Last Game," *Harrisburg Daily Independent*, October 1, 1890: 1. See also "Close of the Season," *Harrisburg Telegraph*, October 1, 1890. The latter's box score showed Lebanon with only two hits, but the other two credited them with three hits. The *Telegraph* said the Ponies' pitcher, John Cox, retired the first 23 batters in a row, and because the Ponies batted first, Lebanon didn't bat in the ninth inning. However, that would mean a perfect game was on the line when Grant made his error, and it would have occurred with two outs in the eighth inning. That's impossible, because the *Telegraph*'s own box score would then indicate that a minimum of six more Lebanon players batted after that crucial error (at least two of whom got hits), and yet somehow they scored no additional runs. Also, Frank Grant began a double play at some point in the game, which he couldn't have done if there had already been two outs in an inning.

141. "Base Ball," *Sporting Life*, November 1, 1890: 8. The chart showed him with an average .328 but 62/187 = .332, and thus he hit a little better than Reddy Mack, who was listed above him at .329.

142. "In the Base Ball World," *Harrisburg Daily Independent*, May 24, 1890: 1. The article specified that the contest was a "championship" game and thus not an exhibition. "In the Base Ball World," *Harrisburg Daily Independent*, May 26, 1890: 1; "In the Base Ball World," *Harrisburg Daily Independent*, July 3, 1890: 1; "In the Base Ball World," *Harrisburg Daily Independent*, July 10, 1890: 1; "In the Base Ball World," *Harrisburg Daily Independent*, July 11, 1890: 1; "Base Ball," "In the Base Ball World," *Harrisburg Daily Independent*, July 17, 1890: 1.

143. "A Game Easily Won," *Harrisburg Daily Independent*, October 2, 1890: 1. Back on September 22, the *Daily Independent* had said that the Ponies hadn't scheduled any postseason exhibition games. On the day of this game versus York, the *Telegraph* said the Ponies would indeed put on "a few" exhibitions, but that daily didn't provide any details. See "Base Ball Notes," *Harrisburg Daily Independent*, September 22, 1890: 1; "Grand Stand Chat," *Harrisburg Telegraph*, October 1, 1890: 1.

144. "Base Ball Briefs," *Harrisburg Telegraph*, October 11, 1890: 6.

145. ""Base Ball Briefs," *Harrisburg Daily Independent*, October 3, 1890: 1. This compilation of short news items also mentioned that the Ponies and Monarchs were supposed to play a game on October 4, but it was postponed.

146. "Dancing 'Monarchs,'" *Harrisburg Daily Independent*, October 10, 1890: 4; "Base Ball Briefs," *Harrisburg Telegraph*, October 10, 1890: 4. Max Vogt, a white man, was a local director of some significance, according to "State Capital Band Officers," *Harrisburg Telegraph*, January 16, 1889: 4.

147. "Personal Notes," *Daily Patriot*, November 21, 1890: 1; "Personal Paragraphs," *Harrisburg Telegraph*, December 4, 1890: 1; "Personal News and Gossip," *Sporting Life*, January 24, 1891, 3.

Chapter 9

1. "What's This? What's This?" *Harrisburg Telegraph*, February 20, 1891: 4; "Quiet in Base Ball," *Daily Patriot*, February 20, 1891: 1.
2. "The League Meets," *Daily Patriot*, March 17, 1891: 1; "It Will Be a Go," *Harrisburg Telegraph*, March 17, 1891: 4; "The Atlantic Base Ball League," *Lancaster* (Pennsylvania) *New Era*, March 17, 1891: 1; "The New Atlantic Association Likely to be a Go," *York Dispatch*, March 17, 1891: 1. The first of these articles included details about the differences between class C and D minor leagues. The new Atlantic Association would be the latter, and thus its franchises would "not have the privilege of reservation, but the contracts made by such clubs with players will be protected for the playing season at the rate of $300 for the release of any player." The *Patriot* also mentioned that Trenton's representative was named Fitzgerald; that may have been the gentleman working for Bright there about a year earlier.
3. "Base Ball," *Harrisburg Daily Independent*, March 19, 1891: 5; "May Yet Be a Success," *Harrisburg Daily Independent*, March 23, 1891: 1.
4. "Our National Game," *Harrisburg Telegraph*, March 24, 1891: 4.
5. "The 'Monarchs' in Altoona," *York Gazette*, March 31, 1891: 1; "The Atlantic Association," *Harrisburg Telegraph*, March 30, 1891: 1.
6. "World of Sports," *Waterbury* (Connecticut) *Evening Democrat*, April 3, 1891: 5.
7. "Base Ball Men," *Daily Patriot*, April 7, 1890: 1.
8. "The World of Sport," *Buffalo Express*, August 28, 1887: 8. Cushman's lies were not reprinted in the *Harrisburg Daily Independent*, the *Harrisburg Telegraph*, or the *Daily Patriot*.
9. "Requiescat in Pace," *Harrisburg Telegraph*, April 14, 1891: 1; "Our National Game," *Harrisburg Telegraph*, April 13, 1891: 1; "The Prospects for Base Ball," *Daily Patriot*, April 15, 1891: 1.
10. "Sports of All Kinds," *Daily Patriot*, April 18, 1891: 5; "The Colored Monarchs," *Harrisburg Daily Independent*, April 18, 1891: 1.
11. When "Miss Mary E. Wilson" was preparing to remarry in late 1892, an announcement in a local paper called her "an adopted daughter of William Adore, of this city," and noted that the ceremony would "take place at Mr. Adore's residence, 602 South street, and Rev. William Howard Day will officiate." See "Personal Paragraphs," *Harrisburg Telegraph*, December 5, 1892: 1.
12. Rod Leith, "Frank Grant: The baseball great who remained in obscurity," *South Bergenite* (Rutherford, New Jersey), September 26, 2013: B3.
13. A second couple and three other individuals were also listed at the same address, but "lodger" Delores Brown, who was not quite two years old, was actually their granddaughter.
14. "Bat and Ball," *Harrisburg Telegraph*, April 17, 1891: 4. Shortstop Eddie Sales was named as one of Grant's teammates. He played with Pittsburgh in the NL during 1890. From subsequent box scores, the other new recruits in Grant's final games with this genuinely integrated team were a first baseman named Drauby/Drawby (likely future major leaguer Jake), a third baseman named Sweitzer, an outfielder named Hoverter (surely his EISL teammate George or his brother, Sam), a shortstop named Graham (possibly James, who was with Lebanon in 1890), and a pitcher named Keffer (probably 1890 major leaguer Frank).
15. "Base Ball Season Opened," *Daily Patriot*, April 21, 1891: 5; "Shut out by Lebanon," *Harrisburg Daily Independent*, April 21, 1891: 8.
16. "Lebanon Gets a Blow," *Harrisburg Daily Independent*, April 22, 1891: 8.
17. "Home Club Again Victorious," *Daily Patriot*, April 23, 1891: 8; "Lebanon Again Defeated," *Harrisburg Daily Independent*, April 23, 1891: 8; "The Base Ball Arena," *Harrisburg Daily Independent*, April 24, 1891: 8; "Lebanon Victorious," *Daily Patriot*, April 24, 1891: 5.
18. "Our National Game," *Harrisburg Daily Independent*, April 25, 1891: 8; "Harrisburg Again Victorious," *Harrisburg Daily Independent*, April 27, 1891: 8; See also "Things Briefly Told" one column to the left and "Base Ball Notes" beneath the box score.
19. "World of Sports," *Waterbury Evening Democrat*, April 30, 1891: 4.
20. "World of Sports," *Waterbury Evening Democrat*, May 4, 1891: 4. This paper later reported the attendance as 567, but it was the highest total at their ballpark during the abbreviated CSL season, according to "World of Sports," *Waterbury Evening Democrat*, June 23, 1891: 4.
21. "Manhattans, Though Defeated, Play Well," *New York Herald*, May 5, 1891: 11.
22. "World of Sports," *Waterbury Evening Democrat*, May 6, 1891: 4.
23. "Cuban Giants 15, 'Mets' 3," *New York Herald*, May 11, 1891: 8; "It Is a Great Field," *Buffalo Enquirer*, May 11, 1891: 1; "Bat and Ball," *Harrisburg Telegraph*, May 12, 1891: 1.
24. "World of Sports," *Waterbury Evening Democrat*, May 15, 1891: 4.
25. "Malloy Will Play Again," *Meriden Journal*, June 2, 1891: 1.
26. "The Cubans Enjoy a 'Snap,'" *New York Herald*, May 18, 1891: 8.
27. "Cubans Defeat the Gorhams," *New York Tribune*, May 19, 1891: 4; "The Gorhams' Third Defeat," *New York Herald*, May 20, 1891: 8. Gant didn't play for the Gorhams in the third game.
28. "Princeton 1, Cuban Giants 0," *The Princetonian* (Princeton, New Jersey), May 22, 1891: 1; "They Can't Be Downed," *Reading Times*, May 21, 1891: 1.
29. "Colored Ball Tossers Want Big Money," *The Sun* (New York City), May 20, 1891: 5. This analysis said a key figure was John Bright's former associate, "McGovern," but that presumably referred to S.K. Govern, even though "McGovern" continued to be used in newspaper reports about the team in the following weeks.

30. "Base Ball," *Southington* (Connecticut) *Weekly Phoenix*, May 29, 1891: 2. Grant batted second. The rest of Ansonia's lineup was: Boyd cf; Bell, lf; Frye, 1b; Woods, 3b; Terrill, ss; Douglass, rf; W Jac'n, c; Whyte, p.

31. "From over the Mountain," *Meriden Journal*, May 25, 1891: 2. The game's attendance was reported in "Other State League Games," *Hartford Courant*, May 25, 1891: 1.

32. "Work Of The Ball Clubs," *New York Tribune*, May 25, 1891: 2. There was also a Gorhams box score at the bottom of the same column, but their lineup bore almost no resemblance to the one five days earlier. It was: Barton, c; Dickinson, rf; Leon, lf; Miller p; Williams, 1b; Freeman, ss; Gant (not Grant), cf; Holmes, 3b; Evans, 2b. Barton, Miller, and possibly Williams were the only ones who overlapped.

33. See John Thorn's blog at https://mlblogsourgame.wordpress.com/category/uncategorized/page/17/?iframe=true&preview=true%2Ffeed%2F. See also Christian Trudeau's research published in 2020 at https://sabr.org/journal/article/24-years-before-jackie-robinson-charlie-culver-broke-barriers-in-montreal/.

34. "The First Death," *Sporting Life*, June 20, 1891: 1.

Chapter 10

1. "Bat and Ball," *Harrisburg Telegraph*, May 4, 1891: 1; "Will We Have a New Team?" *Harrisburg Daily Independent*, May 11, 1891: 1.

2. The *Harrisburg Call* was quoted in "Base Ball," *Lebanon* (Pennsylvania) *Daily News*, May 18, 1891: 1. See also "Good News for Base Ball Enthusiasts," *Daily Patriot*, May 18, 1891: 5.

3. "Talk of a Pennsylvania State League," *Daily New Era* (Lancaster, Pennsylvania), May 18, 1891: 4.

4. "They Can't Be Downed," *Reading* (Pennsylvania) *Times*, May 21, 1891: 1.

5. "The Cranks Will Be Satisfied," *Daily Patriot*, May 21, 1891: 5.

6. "Ball Notes," *Courier-Journal* (Louisville, Kentucky), May 28, 1891: 6. For later examples, see "The National Game," *Cranbury* (New Jersey) *Press*, June 12, 1891: 4; "The National Game," *The North Carolinian* (Elizabeth City), June 17, 1891: 1.

7. "Bat and Ball," *Harrisburg Telegraph*, May 28, 1891: 1.

8. "Base Ball Yesterday," *Sun-Gazette* (Williamsport, Pennsylvania), May 29, 1891: 1; "Play Ball!" *Reading Times*, June 2, 1891: 1.

9. "World of Sports," *Waterbury* (Connecticut) *Evening Democrat*, June 4, 1891: 4.

10. "Sporting Notes," *Daily Patriot*, June 12, 1891: 3; "Sporting Notes," *Daily Patriot*, June 13, 1891: 3; "Sporting Notes," *Daily Patriot*, June 15, 1891: 3. About the third game, the *Telegraph* said that the Gorhams deserved "better patronage" after devoting just one sentence to that game, in "Bat and Ball," *Harrisburg Telegraph*, June 15, 1891: 1. That paper hadn't so much as printed a box score after Grant's return.

11. "Cuban Giants vs. Gorhams," *Lebanon Daily News*, June 16, 1891: 4; "Cuban Giants vs. Gorhams," *Lebanon Daily News*, June 17, 1891: 4. About two inches below the box score for the first game in Lebanon was a batter-by-batter account of the entire game. Unfortunately, Gant of the Cuban Giants was called "Grant" throughout. According to https://abvmlebpa.org/about/, Father Christ was 10 years into a 49-year tenure at his parish. See also "Bat and Ball," *Harrisburg Telegraph*, June 17, 1891: 1.

12. "Gorhams, 7; Norristown, 0," *The Times* (Philadelphia) June 18, 1891: 2; "Base Ball Gossip," *Harrisburg Daily Independent*, June 19, 1891: 5. Above this gossip was a paragraph and line score for the Gorhams' second win in Norristown, 10–2, at the expense of John Cox, the former Pony.

13. "Work Of The Ball Clubs," *New York Tribune*, May 25, 1891: 2; "'Mets,' 10; Gorhams, 1," *New York Herald*, June 1, 1891: 8.

14. "Semi-Professionals May Change Their Circuit," *New York Herald*, June 20, 1891: 8; "Who Represented Mr. Wallace?" *New York Herald*, June 26, 1891: 9. For the final standings of the Semi-Professional League in which the Gorhams were included, see "Among the Baseball Men," *New York Herald*, June 22, 1891: 9.

15. "Notes of the Diamond," *New York Herald*, July 20, 1891: 9.

16. "A Great Ball Game," *Reading Times*, June 26, 1891: 1. The teams met again the next day, but only 500 fans braved the threatening weather, and the game was rained out after four innings.

17. "Gorhams Win," *Wilkes-Barre* (Pennsylvania) *News*, June 30, 1891: 1; "Wilkes-Barre Downed," *Wilkes-Barre News*, July 1, 1891: 1.

18. "We Had Them by the Wool," *Scranton* (Pennsylvania) *Republican*, July 2, 1891: 5. The teams were scheduled to meet again the next day, but the game was rained out.

19. Art Ahrens, "Crowds of Days Gone By," *1972 Baseball Research Journal*, accessible at https://sabr.org/journal/article/crowds-of-days-gone-by/.

20. "The Lebanon Club," *Lebanon Daily News*, July 6, 1891: 1; "Bat and Ball," *Harrisburg Telegraph*, July 6, 1891: 1; "Jim Farrington's Luck," *Daily Patriot*, July 8, 1891: 3.

21. "The 'Mets' on Their Dignity," *New York Herald*, July 9, 1891: 8; "The Gorhams Get the Money," *New York Herald*, July 11, 1891: 8. Oddly, the box score showed both White and Grant at second base and no shortstop for the Gorhams.

22. "Cuban Giants Overwhelmed," *New York Tribune*, July 14, 1891: 3; "Gorhams in a Walk," *New York Herald*, July 27, 1891: 8.

23. "Field of Sports," *Harrisburg Daily Independent*, August 6, 1891: 5. Box scores for Gorhams games can be found on at least five days from July 13 to 20 in the *New York Herald* or the *New York Tribune*, and Cape May box scores on

July 26 and 28 in the *Philadelphia Inquirer* and *Times*.

24. "Gorhams Enjoy a Snap," *New York Herald*, August 10, 1891: 8. The identities of Nelson and Howe were confirmed in "The 'Mets' on Their Dignity," *New York Herald*, July 9, 1891: 8.

25. "Field of Sports," *Harrisburg Daily Independent*, August 15, 1891: 2. This compilation of news items led with the news about the Eastern Association, and then reported the Gorhams' 7–2 win in Cape May.

26. "The President Likes Base Ball," *Philadelphia Inquirer*, August 16, 1891: 3; "The President at Cape May," *Brooklyn Daily Eagle*, August 16, 1891: 1; "Harrison's Busy Day," *Boston Sunday Globe*, August 16, 1891: 2; "Amateur Baseball," *Sunday Herald* (Washington, D.C.), August 16, 1891: 9; "Harrison and Base Ball," *Morning News* (Savannah, Georgia), August 16, 1891: 2. Connecting the dots about Leiper was "A Great Victory," *The Post* (Camden, New Jersey), May 6, 1892: 1. See also Gary Ashwill, "Benjamin Harrison Sees the Big Gorhams" at https://agatetype.typepad.com/agate_type/2014/05/benjamin-harrison-sees-the-big-gorhams.html.

27. "An Easy Victory for the Gorhams," *New York Herald*, August 17, 1891: 8.

28. "A Bad Defeat for the U.V.M.," *Burlington* (Vermont) *Free Press and Times*, August 20, 1891: 5. The box score provided eight columns of data, including at-bats. Thomas had a double and stolen base for the Gorhams, but the box score showed his team's first baseman as "Cornish."

29. Though O'Connor graduated from Dartmouth, his baseball-reference.com entry indicates that he also attended the University of Vermont. See "Personal Mention," *Burlington Free Press and Times*, May 18, 1891: 5.

30. "Fight on a Ball Field," *The Times* (Philadelphia), August 29, 1891: 2. This account said Randow's first name was Edward. City directories around then show no Edward Randow, though there was a Frederick. Regardless, if the *Trenton Times* ever mentioned the first name of a ballplayer named Randow around then, it was always Charles.

31. "A Good Game," *Trenton Times*, August 29, 1891: 1; "Some Sporting Gossip," *Trenton Times*, February 7, 1892: 3; "Trade League Averages," *Trenton Times*, October 25, 1891: 3. City directories identified Randow's job as potter. His age at the time of the riot was based on the 1900 census.

32. "The Crowd Given a Surprise," *Daily True American*, August 29, 1891: 5.

33. "Many Struck Out," *Jersey City* (New Jersey) *News*, August 29, 1891: 5; "A Baseball Game Leads to a Fight," *New York Tribune*, August 29, 1891: 12; "Fight on a Ball Field," *The Times* (Philadelphia), August 29, 1891: 2.

34. "A Row at the Ball Grounds," *Trenton Times*, August 29, 1891: 1.

35. "Almost a Riot," *Daily True American*, August 29, 1891: 5.

36. "Trenton Tips," *New York Age*, July 25, 1891: 1. For a concise profile of Herbert, see Jennifer B. Leynes, "Three Centuries of African American History in Trenton: Significant People and Places," pages 14 and 9, at http://trentonhistory.org/wp-content/uploads/Trentons-African American-History-Manual-2015.pdf. See also "R. Henri Herbert Wins Position," *New York Age*, May 27, 1909: 3. This lengthy profile happened to be published shortly before his death. For a brief biography of the Justice of the Peace who was involved, see "Stroke Fatal to Captain Matheson," *Trenton Times*, October 18, 1918: 1.

37. "Captain Seaman Better," *Trenton Times*, August 29, 1891: 1; "Capt. C.H. Seaman Dead at 84 Years," *Trenton Times*, April 28, 1914: 2.

38. "Field of Sports," *Harrisburg Daily Independent*, September 1, 1891: 2; "Allertons on a Leather Hunt," *New York Herald*, September 14, 1891: 8. Keeler was not in the Allertons' lineup when the Gorhams played them on August 16 and 23. He had also played with the Allertons in 1890, according to Burt Solomon, *Where They Ain't: The Fabled Life and Untimely Death of the Original Baltimore Orioles, the Team that Gave Birth to Modern Baseball* (New York: Main Street Books, 2000), 136.

39. "The Trenton Boys Almost Swamped under by the Gorhams," *Daily True American*, September 19, 1891: 5.

40. "Base Ball Notes," *Daily Patriot*, September 21, 1891: 5.

41. "Semi-Professional Players Hard at Work," *New York Herald*, September 28, 1891: 8.

42. "Great Game for the Gorhams," *Plainfield* (New Jersey) *Daily Press*, September 28, 1891: 4. This coverage spanned a column and a half, and the box score included eight columns of data.

43. "Base Ball Gossip," *Elmira* (New York) *Gazette*, September 29, 1891: 6.

44. "Camden Takes the Gorhams Into Camp," *Philadelphia Inquirer*, October 3, 1891: 3.

45. "Gorhams Hit the Ball Hard," *New York Herald*, October 5, 1891: 8; "Of Course the Gorhams Won," *New York Herald*, October 12, 1891: 8. Abe Harrison also wasn't listed in any of the lineups, nor was Henry Gant. By October 14, Sol White was in Bellaire, West Virginia to spend the winter, according to "Bellaire," *Wheeling* (West Virginia) *Daily Intelligencer*, October 14, 1891: 3.

46. *Sol White's History of Colored Base Ball with Other Documents on the Early Black Game, 1886–1936* (Lincoln: University of Nebraska Press, 1995), 85.

47. "Cuban Giants and Gorham Clubs Claim the Same Five Players," *The Sun* (New York City), January 19, 1892: 4; "Amateurs with Bat and Ball," *New York Herald*, January 24, 1892: 28; "The Gorhams," *Lebanon Daily News*, February 15, 1892: 3.

48. *Sol White's History of Colored Base Ball*, 5.

49. "The Keystones Strengthening," *Pittsburgh Daily Post*, March 25, 1892: 6; "Morris-Madden," *Cleveland Gazette*, April 16, 1892: 1.

50. "Grant Likes Harrisburg," *Daily Patriot*, April 6, 1892: 6.

51. "Notes of the Diamond," *New York Herald*, April 6, 1892: 11; "Giants' Good Exercise," *The World* (New York City), April 7, 1892: 6; "Manager Ward's Judicious Work in the South," *Brooklyn Daily Eagle*, April 7, 1892: 1.

52. The *New York Press* was quoted in "Around the Bases," *Buffalo Courier*, April 13, 1892: 8.

53. "Out at First Base," *Boston Herald*, May 5, 1892: 10. For an early example of Kelly's remark, see "Sporting Notes," *Pittsburgh Post-Gazette*, May 12, 1892: 6. This comment was credited to the *New York World* in "World of Sports," *Waterbury Evening Democrat*, May 13, 1892: 5. It also appeared in at least two Chicago papers, the *Philadelphia Inquirer*, Washington's *Evening Star*, and the *Brooklyn Daily Eagle*. Kelly made a similar wisecrack in late June, according to "A One-Sided Affair," *Boston Journal*, June 28, 1892: 3.

54. "Keystones and Standards To-Day," *Pittsburgh Daily Post*, April 15, 1892: 6; "Sporting," *Pittsburgh Press*, April 15, 1892: 5. In the latter paper, see also "Late Sporting News" on page 6.

55. "Base Ball on Deck," *Argus* (Albany, New York), April 17, 1892: 9; "New Haven Victorious," *New Haven* (Connecticut) *Register*, April 20, 1892: 3; "A Very One-Sided Contest," *Morning Journal and Courier* (New Haven, Connecticut), April 21, 1892: 5. The Gorhams' lineup on April 16 was: O. Jackson, 1b; C. Williams, c; Grant, ss; Selden, p and cf; A. Jackson, 3b; Stovey, lf; Malone, cf and p; Terrill, 2b; and Davis, rf.

56. *Sol White's History of Colored Base Ball*, 20, 24.

57. "Cuban Giants on Top," *New York Herald*, April 25, 1892: 8. The price of admission was noted in a two-line ad in *The Sun* on the day of the game, on page 5. The attraction was "Comical Harrison," suggesting that Grant's former housemate had become known around New York City for animated coaching. Regarding Bowes, see "Amateur Gossip," *New York Herald*, May 1, 1890: 32.

58. "Great Big Loss," *Star-Gazette*, April 26, 1892: 8; "Nineteen to One," *Star-Gazette*, April 27, 1892: 8.

59. "Cuban Giants at Ithaca," *The World* (New York City), May 12, 1892: 7. This page's box scores displayed 11 columns of data. This game made an impressive $208 for Cornell's Base Ball Association, according to detailed budget information printed in "Graduate Treasurer Treman's Report," *Cornell Daily Sun* (Ithaca, New York), November 3, 1892: 1.

60. "Cuban Giants, 11; Flushings, 5," *The Sun* (New York City), May 2, 1892: 5; "With the Players," *Star-Gazette*, May 3, 1892: 7.

61. "Nearly But Not Quite," *Passaic* (New Jersey) *Daily News*, May 9, 1892: 6; "Leontines Badly Defeated," *The World* (New York City), May 9, 1892: 3. Clarence Williams had agreed to "finish the season with the Keystones and efforts are being made to secure Second Baseman Grant," according to "Late Sporting Notes," *Pittsburgh Press*, May 11, 1892: 7.

62. "Senators Fail to Score," *New York Herald*, May 16, 1892: 5

63. "Baseball in the Rain," *New York Herald*, May 23, 1892: 8. Less than a month later, Roseman was "thinking of organizing a colored team in opposition to the Cuban Giants and the Gorhams," according to "Baseball Notes," *Chicago Tribune*, June 20, 1892: 6.

64. "Cuban Giants Win Again," *New York Herald*, May 30, 1892: 5.

65. "Sunday Games of Baseball," *New York Herald*, June 6, 1892: 8; "Errors Won for Binghamton," *Buffalo Courier*, June 7, 1892: 3. Keeler's baseball-reference.com entry shows June 6 as his debut with Binghamton, though his professional/minor league debut was earlier that season with Plainfield of the Central New Jersey League.

66. "Walden," *Middletown* (New York) *Daily Press*, June 7, 1892: 2; "Won in the Eleventh," *Burlington Free Press and Times*, June 9, 1892: 4; "U.V.M., 4; Cuban Giants, 3," *Boston Daily Globe*, June 10, 1892: 2.

67. Pond's baseball-reference.com entry indicates that he attended Norwich University in Northfield, Vermont, in addition to the University of Vermont. See "Schedule of Base Ball Games," *Burlington Free Press and Times*, February 27, 1892: 1.

68. "The Giants Win," *Rutland* (Vermont) *Daily Herald*, June 11, 1892: 4, 3. Douglass' first name is from James E. Brunson III, *Black Baseball, 1858–1900: A Comprehensive Record of the Teams, Players, Managers, Owners and Umpires* (Jefferson, NC: McFarland, 2019), 666. First baseman John H. Frye of the Cuban Giants was the son of G.W. Frye, 403 Spruce Street, Harrisburg, according to "Personal," *Harrisburg Daily Independent*, August 24, 1892: 1.

69. "Amateur Baseball Stars," *New York Herald*, June 12, 1892: 29; "Sunday Games on the Diamond," *New York Herald*, June 13, 1892: 8; "Allertons Badly Defeated," *The World* (New York City), June 13, 1892: 6.

70. "Cuban Giants Coming," *Trenton Times*, June 12, 1892: 3; "The Trentons Beaten," *Daily True American*, June 15, 1892: 5. Uplander's time with Hazleton was noted in "Base Ball News," *Trenton Times*, August 20, 1889: 3. His time with Hartford was mentioned in "Base Ball Topics," *Trenton Times*, August 2, 1891: 3

71. "Amateurs Have Their Inning," *New York Herald*, June 20, 1892: 11.

72. "Great Barrington," *Berkshire County Eagle*, June 22, 1892: 5. The score was only 12–5 according to "Great Barrington," *Connecticut Western News* (Canaan, Connecticut), June 23, 1892: 2. The latter, however, devoted a single sentence to the game, whereas the former described it in a full paragraph.

73. "Northampton, 10; Cuban Giants, 2," *Boston*

Daily Globe, June 25, 1892: 5; "Northampton, 7; Cuban Giants, 2," *Boston Sunday Globe*, June 26, 1892: 4. One of the two umpires was "A. Douglas," probably the Cubans' extra player, Albert Douglass. For examples of the ads mentioning Frank Grant, see the front pages of the *Springfield Republican* on June 22 and 24, 1892.

74. "Manager Chapman," *Buffalo Courier*, June 25, 1892: 8.

75. "The Story of the Games," *Meriden Daily Republican*, July 5, 1892: 6; "An Old-Time Fourth," *Daily Times* (New Brunswick, New Jersey), July 5, 1892: 1; "Manhattans Lose at Home," *The World* (New York City), July 5, 1892: 9.

76. "World of Sports," *Waterbury Evening Democrat*, July 19, 1892: 5. Klobedanz and LaChance had recently quit Portland's team in the New England League, according to "Baseball Items," *Daily Journal* (Logansport, Indiana), July 16, 1892: 6.

77. "Cuban Giants Easy Winners," *New York Herald*, July 25, 1892: 8.

78. "Cuban Giants Victorious," *New York Herald*, August 1, 1892: 8. See also "Timely and Terrific," *Meriden Journal*, June 28, 1886: 2. On August 1, at least two Cleveland newspapers printed a box score showing "Grant, 2b" batting third for the Pittsburgh Keystones on July 31, around the same time Frank Grant was playing on Long Island. Those box scores also showed the Keystones with a third baseman named "Gant." However, based on a preview of that Keystones game, their third baseman was named "Gaul," in which case "Grant" was very likely Henry Gant, even though he wasn't listed in the same preview. See "Among the Amateurs," *Cleveland Leader*, July 31, 1892: 3.

79. "Jeanesville Won," *Daily Standard* (Hazleton, Pennsylvania) August 6, 1892: 1.

80. Nearly 2,000 "Cuban Giants Defeat Senators," *New York Herald*, August 8, 1892: 8. For a box score, see "Made the Cubans Hustle," *The World* (New York City), August 8, 1892: 2.

81. "Matters and Things," *Plattsburgh* (New York) *Republican*, August 20, 1892: 1; "Cuban Giants Win," *Elizabethtown* (New York) *Post*, August 25, 1892: 2. On the latter page, see also the next article about the game on August 19 in Rouses Point, New York, "Cuban Giants Defeated by Hotel Champlains."

82. "The Cuban Giants Saturday," *Berkshire Eagle*, August 23, 1892: 3; "Berkshire County," *Springfield Republican*, August 24, 1892: 6; "Berkshire County," *Springfield Republican*, August 26, 1892: 6. The Cuban Giants were also hoping to play in Pittsfield around September 21, but shortly before that date the nine "sent word that they could not afford to come for one game," according to "Base Ball Matters," *Berkshire Eagle*, September 20, 1892: 3.

83. "Won by the Cuban Giants," *Washington Post*, September 1, 1892: 6. See also "Cuban Giants and All Washington," *Washington Post*, August 28, 1892: 6. Carrington was profiled in "Campbell Carrington, Veteran Lawyer, Dead," *Evening Star*, July 19, 1917: 7.

84. "Won by the Cuban Giants," *Washington Post*, September 2, 1892: 6; "Made It Three Straight," *Washington Post*, September 3, 1892: 6; "The Blaine Invincible Club," *Evening Star*, August 30, 1892: 5; *Official Programme of Exercises and Illustrated Inaugural History Commemorating the Inauguration of Theodore Roosevelt as President of the United States, Charles W. Fairbanks as Vice-President of the United States* (Washington, D.C.: Otto A. Sontag, Publisher, 1905), 104. See also "The Colored Republicans," *Evening Star*, November 7, 1888: 8.

85. "Three Straight Games," *Scranton Republican*, September 22, 1892: 5; "Baseball Notes," *The Sun* (New York City), September 21, 1892: 5. For an overview of Charlie Gelbert's athletic career, see https://footballfoundation.org/hof_search.aspx?hof=2101.

86. "A Baseball Muddle," *Scranton Times*, September 23, 1892: 5.

87. "Cuban Giants' Walkover," *New York Herald*, September 26, 1892: 8.

88. "Baseball Notes," *The Sun* (New York City), October 10, 1892: 4; "Sunday Baseball All Over," *New York Herald*, October 17, 1892. Rounding out the Cubans' batting order were Chamberlain, 1b; "Parago, lf; Freem'n, cf; and Dick'son, rf. The final score was incorrectly reported as 15–12 in "With the New York Nine," *Brooklyn Daily Eagle*, October 17, 1892: 8.

Chapter 11

1. "Middle States League," *The Sun* (New York City), December 20, 1892: 4; "Baseball Notes," *The Sun*, February 18, 1893: 4.

2. "Base Ball Notes," *Middletown Daily Press*, January 30, 1893: 7; "Base Ball Briefs," *Pittsburgh Press*, February 5, 1893: 6.

3. "Cuban Giants on Deck Again," *The World* (New York City), March 22, 1893: 6; "Baseball Notes," *The Sun*, March 22, 1893: 5. Malone wasn't named by either of those papers, but he and Clarence Williams were both "notified to report on April 22d to Manager Bright at the Long Island grounds," according to "Base Ball News," *Harrisburg Telegraph*, March 24, 1893: 1. This would seem to imply that the two had wintered in Harrisburg but that Frank Grant hadn't.

4. "Senators Win a Close Game," *The World*, April 17, 1893: 6; "Senators Win on Wild Pitching," *New York Herald*, April 17, 1893: 11.

5. "Baseball Beginning," *Newark* (New Jersey) *Sunday Call*, April 23, 1893: 6; "Of Race Interest," *Cleveland Gazette*, April 29, 1893: 1; "Sunday Baseball Games," *The World*, April 24, 1893: 6.

6. "Cuban Giants Win," *The Press* (New York City), May 1, 1893: 6. The Cuban Giants were scheduled to play the Paterson nine on April 29, but that game was rained out.

7. "Williams, 9; Cuban Giants, 4," *Boston Daily Globe*, May 3, 1893: 7. The box score included a TB column, presumably for Total Bases, but those numbers generally didn't match the lists of players with doubles and triples.

8. "Stopping Sunday Games," *New York Tribune*, May 8, 1893: 3.

9. "The Season Opened," *Burlington Free Press and Times*, May 11, 1893: 4; "Cuban Giants Win a Game," *Burlington Free Press and Times*, May 13, 1893: 5.

10. "Cuban Giants, 9; Blackinton, 8," *Boston Sunday Globe*, May 14, 1893: 4.

11. "No Trouble to Pile Up Runs," *Reading Times*, May 16, 1893: 4.

12. "Cuban Giants Down Royersford," *Philadelphia Inquirer*, May 18, 1893: 3; "Cubans Again Victorious," *Camden Daily Telegram*, May 20, 1893: 1.

13. "A Big Crowd at Van Nest," *The World*, May 22, 1893: 6.

14. "Cuban Giants' Schedule Here," *Washington Post*, May 14, 1893: 6; "Cuban Giants Defeat the Y.M.C.A.," *Evening Star* (Washington, D.C.), May 23, 1893: 8; "Base Ball Notes," *Evening Star*, May 24, 1893: 7; "Amateur Base Ball," *Evening Star*, May 25, 1893: 10. See also "The Monarchs of Boston," *Evening Star*, June 21, 1893: 9.

15. "Bodily Development," *Paterson* (New Jersey) *Daily Press*, May 29, 1893: 1.

16. "The Cuban Giants Arrive," *Meriden Daily Journal*, June 1, 1893: 1; "Now Play Ball," *Meriden Weekly Republican*, June 1, 1893: 1; "Some Gilt-Edged Baseball," *Meriden Daily Journal*, June 2, 1893: 1; "Live Sporting News," *Morning Record* (Meriden, Connecticut), June 2, 1893: 1.

17. "Sunday on the Diamond," *The Sun* (New York City), June 5, 1893: 2; "Giants Get Another Game," *Reading Times*, June 6, 1893: 1; "Pottsville and the Giants," *Pottsville* (Pennsylvania) *Daily Republican*, June 7, 1893: 4; "A Benefit for Salmon," *Daily Miners' Journal* (Pottsville, Pennsylvania), June 7, 1893: 1.

18. "A Brilliant Game!" *Evening Herald* (Shenandoah, Pennsylvania), June 9, 1893: 1; "The Giants Down Us," *Daily Miners' Journal*, June 10, 1893: 1; "Base Ball," *Evening Herald*, June 20, 1894: 1. By coincidence, that compilation of news items also mentioned an upcoming Cubans game. See also "Are Making a Record," *Pottsville Daily Republican*, June 8, 1893: 1. This player, first name unknown as of this writing, is probably M.J. Salmon: https://www.baseball-reference.com/register/player.fcgi?id=salmon003.

19. "Not a Base Hit off Bowers," *Boston Herald*, June 13, 1893: 8; "Talk About Town," *Bellows Falls* (Vermont) *Times*, June 15, 1893: 6. Bowers' brief 1895 stint is documented at https://www.baseball-reference.com/register/player.fcgi?id=bowers001her.

20. "Base Ball Matters," *Freeman's Journal* (Cooperstown, New York), June 22, 1893: 5; Tom Heitz, "Sol White & Frank Grant Played for the Cuban Giants," *The Oil Can* (Cooperstown Rotary Club, Vol. 83, No. 47), June 6, 2006: 1–3. The Cuban Giants played again in Cooperstown on August 1 and 2, and it was presumably Sol White who batted second and played first base in both games.

21. "Defeated at Last," *Middletown* (New York) *Daily Argus*, June 20, 1893: 8.

22. "Emeralds Badly Beaten," *The World*, June 26, 1893: 3; "Baseball," *Jersey Journal* (Jersey City, New Jersey), July 1, 1893: 3; "The Arena of Sport," *Paterson Daily Press*, July 3, 1893: 1. For an introduction to Patterson's career, see Gregory Bond, "Too Much Dirty Work: Race, Manliness, and Baseball in Gilded Age Nebraska," *Nebraska History* 85 (2004): 172–185, available at https://history.nebraska.gov/sites/history.nebraska.gov/files/doc/publications/2004-Dirty_Work.pdf. Miller's first name was provided in "General Sporting Notes," *Pittsburgh Press*, January 9, 1894: 5. See also Mark E. Eberle, "George William Castone: An Integrated Baseball Life at the Close of the Nineteenth Century," available at https://scholars.fhsu.edu/all_monographs/6/.

23. "Cuban Giants Leave Hoboken," *Jersey City* (New Jersey) *News*, July 7, 1893: 8.

24. "The Asylums Were Defeated," *Middletown Daily Times*, July 8, 1893: 7. "Whyte" batted second and played first base. "Sol White, second base" was listed among the Cuban Giants in "Baseball Notes," *The Sun* (New York City), April 29, 1893: 8. The Cubans had indeed "secured" him, according to "Of Race Interest," *Cleveland Gazette*, May 6, 1893: 1. However, he was regularly reported with the Boston Colored Monarchs during May and at least into early June; e.g., see "Base Ball Notes," *Boston Daily Globe*, June 3, 1893: 6. He returned to the Cuban Giants from that Boston team no earlier than June, according to Floyd J. Calvin, "Sol White Recalls Baseball's Greatest Days," *Pittsburgh Courier*, March 12, 1927: 16. William Whyte, whose last game in 1893 with the Cubans might have been on June 29, tended to bat last that season, whether he pitched or played right field. See "Pottstown and Cuban Giants," *The Times* (Philadelphia), June 30, 1893: 2.

25. "The Entertaining Cubans," *Watertown* (New York) *Daily Times*, July 12, 1893: 5; "The Cuban Giants 'Rattle' the Boys," *Cleveland Gazette*, July 22, 1893: 2; "The Arena of Sports," *Paterson Daily Press*, July 17, 1893: 1; "The Arena of Sports," *Paterson Evening News*, July 17, 1893: 1.

26. "Asylums, 8; Cuban Giants, 6," *The Sun* (New York City), August 1, 1893: 4; "Splendid Ball Playing," *Middletown Daily Press*, August 1, 1893: 7. Both of these papers noted the Cubans' streak.

27. "Notes of Sport," *Paterson Evening News*, April 24, 1893: 1; "Hot Grounders," *Harrisburg Telegraph*, May 27, 1893: 1; "Base Ball Notes," *Harrisburg Daily Independent*, August 18, 1893: 5; "Jessup," *Scranton Republican*, August 1, 1893: 5.

28. In fact, the Cuban Giants supposedly lost just four days before their loss on July 31, by a score of 6–5 in Lansford, Pennsylvania, according

to "The Cubans Lose," *Daily Standard* (Hazleton, Pennsylvania), July 28, 1893: 1. However, this paper expressed uncertainty about the report it received. Conversely, the Cubans actually won that game, 4–1, according to "Base Ball," *Freeland* (Pennsylvania) *Tribune*, July 31, 1893: 1. On the other hand, the Cubans reportedly lost to Lansford on July 31—the same day as their streak-ending loss in Middletown, New York—according to "Base Ball," *Evening Herald* (Shenandoah, Pennsylvania,) August 2, 1893: 5. One might wonder if there were some lies emanating from Lansford.

29. "Game Won by Meriden," *Morning Record* (Meriden, Connecticut) July 22, 1893: 1; "The Cuban Giants Whipped," *Meriden Daily Journal*, July 22, 1893: 1; "Fine Ball Playing," *Meriden Daily Republican*, July 22, 1893: 2; "Base Ball Yesterday," *New Haven Register*, July 22, 1893: 3. Grant also didn't play in the Cubans' game two days earlier, against the Acmes in Waterbury.

30. "Newsy Notes of Interest" and "The Tour of the Town," *Pokeepsie Evening Enterprise* (Poughkeepsie, New York), July 18, 1893: 4, 8; "Cuban Giants Defeated," *Poughkeepsie* (New York) *Daily Eagle*, July 18, 1893: 8; "Base Ball," *Poughkeepsie Daily Eagle*, July 19, 1893: 8.

31. "Trenton Vs. Cuban Giants," *Daily True American*, July 25, 1893: 5.

32. "Both Home Teams Lose," *Paterson Evening News*, August 7, 1893: 1. The box score listed only one double play (unless it was supposed to indicate that the same players turned multiple twin killings).

33. "Base Ball," *Poughkeepsie Daily Eagle*, October 2, 1893: 6.

34. "Shenandoah Screenings," *Pottsville Daily Republican*, July 31, 1893: 3.

35. Reading's home opener in the Pennsylvania State League was on July 24, according to "Reading's First Home Game," *Philadelphia Inquirer*, July 25, 1893: 6.

36. "The New Ball Park," *Reading Times*, September 26, 1893: 1; "Billy Witman, Outlaw Leader Had Many Years In Baseball," *Reading Times*, April 14, 1913: 9. See also Clement J. Cassidy, "Political Career of William A. Witman, Sr.," https://www.berkshistory.org/multimedia/articles/political-career-of-william-a-witman-sr/.

37. "Sporting," *Reading Eagle*, July 29, 1893: 2; "Sporting Editor's Lament," *Reading Times*, July 29, 1893: 1; "Notes," *Easton* (Pennsylvania) *Free Press*, July 29, 1893: 5.

38. For examples, see the *Easton Free Press* quoted in "Notes of the Game," *Scranton Daily Republican*, July 31, 1893: 3; "Diamond Sparklings," *Harrisburg Telegraph*, July 31, 1893: 1.

39. "Sporting," *Reading Eagle*, July 30, 1893: 2. The *Reading World* was quoted in "Base Ball," *Evening Herald* (Shenandoah) August 2, 1893: 5. On July 29, a team called the Cuban Giants also played 30 miles from Shenandoah, in Williamstown, Pennsylvania, and drew 1,700 fans, according to "Williamstown Waifs," *Lykens* (Pennsylvania) *Register*, August 4, 1893: 4. A different Cuban Giants team—possibly Harrisburg's—playing in that region had a battery of Devinney and Davis, according to "Games Elsewhere," *The York* (Pennsylvania) *Daily*, August 3, 1893: 1. Meanwhile, on August 3, "the celebrated Cuban Giants of New York" won a game in Corning, New York (about 10 miles from Pennsylvania), according to "From Corning," *Elmira Gazette*, August 4, 1893: 8. This victory netted an African American restaurateur $100 and earned the Cuban Giants box seats at the opera house that evening.

40. Creating the potential for confusion around this time is the fact that a Reading man named James F. Grant had just become a State League umpire, according to "General Sporting Notes," *Philadelphia Inquirer*, July 22, 1893: 3. See also "Won on Its Merits," *Daily Patriot* (Harrisburg), July 25, 1893: 5.

41. "Baseball Notes," *Brooklyn Daily Times*, August 12, 1893: 2. "Baseball Notes," *The Sun* (New York City), August 14, 1893: 6.

42. August 6 presents a bit of a mystery relating to the Cuban Giants' other Hall of Famer, Sol White. "White, 1st b" batted second for the Cubans in Paterson that day, according to "Cuban Giants, 14; Paterson, 6," *The Sun* (New York City), August 7, 1893: 6. However, on that same day, "White, 1b" batted sixth for an African American club called the Clippers in Chicago, according to "Edgars, 18; Clippers, 8," *Inter-Ocean* (Chicago), August 7, 1893: 3. According to James Brunson—see Note 10 in Chapter 5, except on page 1267—the Clippers' player was Sol White, in his only game with that club (which had merged temporarily with another Illinois club, called the Eclipse).

43. "Success of the Colored Men," *Evening Journal* (Wilmington, Delaware), September 6, 1893: 4. The Cuban Giants also won a morning game in Plainfield, New Jersey on September 4, according to "The Crescents Win and Lose," *Plainfield* (New Jersey) *Courier*, September 5, 1893: 3.

44. "Bunted Balls," *Harrisburg Telegraph*, September 1, 1893: 1; "A Great Game," *Harrisburg Daily Independent*, August 31, 1893: 8; "In the Grand Stand," *Daily Patriot*, September 4, 1893: 5. The *Telegraph*'s preview referred to Grant's team as the "Cuban Giants of St. George's Island, New York." The Cubans' guarantee for the game was $124, according to "Base Ball Bits," *Daily Miners' Journal* (Pottsville, Pennsylvania), September 12, 1893: 1.

45. "In the Line of Sport," *Paterson Daily News*, September 11, 1893: 1. "Jimmy" Meakim had pitched that season for Buffalo's Eastern League team, according to "What Athletes Are Doing," *Passaic Daily News*, September 7, 1893: 1. Buffalo's Meakim was actually named George, and he pitched one major league game after 1892, his third major league season. The Cuban Giants beat Meakim and Paterson again a week later, but

Grant wasn't in the lineup. The Cuban Giants lost to Paterson at the Polo Grounds on September 20 by a score of 18–10, but it's possible that no New York City paper printed a box score.

46. "In the Line of Sport," *Paterson Daily News*, September 25, 1893: 1. "Handsome Dan" Murphy, who had an eight-game major league career with the New York Giants in 1892, was also supposed to join Paterson, according to "In the Line of Sport," *Paterson Daily News*, September 23, 1893: 1. Grant had robbed Murphy and Leo Smith of hits quite remarkably as a Harrisburg Pony in 1890.

47. "Sloppy Weather Ball," *Paterson Daily News*, October 9, 1893: 6. The Cubans' final game was a win in Newark on October 15 against that city's Ironsides, according to "Baseball Notes," *The Sun* (New York City), October 16, 1893: 7.

48. O.P. Caylor, "The Color Line Again," *Erie* (Pennsylvania) *Daily Times*, September 21, 1893: 2; "The S.O. Manual," *Harrisburg Telegraph*, October 11, 1893: 1. For more about Caylor, see Dave Nemec's biography at https://sabr.org/bioproj/person/o-p-caylor/.

49. "Base Ball Gossip," *Boston Herald*, October 30, 1893: 8. It may assist other researchers to know the team's record at earlier points. It was an "astonishing" 81-12-1, according to "Caught on the Fly," *Daily Patriot*, August 11, 1893: 5. Their record of 99-12-1 included 22 consecutive wins, according to "Sporting Notes," *Elmira Gazette*, September 2, 1893: 6. Their record was 106-13-1 through September 6, according to "G.A.R. Here Next Year," *Cleveland Gazette*, September 16, 1893: 1.

50. See "Sporting in General," *Pittsburgh Press*, December 4, 1893: 5.

51. "Base Ball Matters," *Findlay* (Ohio) *Courier*, December 26, 1893: 4. Gary Ashwill has compiled considerable information about Grant Johnson at https://agatetype.typepad.com/agate_type/home-run-johnson/.

52. "Noted Colored Ball Players," *Pittsburg Daily Post*, January 9, 1894: 6. This article noted that Grant had been nicknamed the "Colored Dunlap." This paragraph implied that both Miller and Grant were wintering in Pittsburgh.

53. "North Adams," *Springfield Republican*, March 24, 1894: 7.

54. Brunson (see Note 10 in Chapter 5), 585.

55. Williams College did get mentioned shortly thereafter in the context of integration, though because an African prince named Beselow, from Liberia, had been enrolled there. See "Called to His Native Haunts," *Berkshire Eagle*, March 26, 1894: 1.

56. "The Cuban Giants Ready to Play Ball," *The Sun* (New York City), April 21, 1894: 9. The Cuban Giants were supposed to play a game against a picked nine on March 24, according to "About the Baseball Players," *New York Tribune*, March 23, 1894: 6. However, it's unknown whether the game was actually played.

57. "Bits of Sport," *Harrisburg Telegraph*, April 24, 1894: 1.

58. "Easton Defeats Cuban Giants," *The Times* (Philadelphia), April 24, 1894: 6.

59. "Cuban Giants Downed," *Daily Patriot*, April 25, 1894: 2; "Giants Take Their Turn," *Daily Patriot*, April 26, 1894: 5.

60. "Easy Prey for Giants," *Rochester* (New York) *Democrat and Chronicle*, May 3, 1894: 10. This article called Andy Jackson the Cuban Giants' captain.

61. "Other Games," *Washington Post*, May 6, 1894: 15; "Base Ball Season Open," *Berkshire Eagle*, May 8, 1894: 5. See also "Notes" beneath the box score. As of this writing, https://www.baseball-reference.com/register/team.cgi?id=09a73468 incorrectly identifies this team as representing Pittsfield, New York instead of Pittsfield, Massachusetts, an understandable error given its membership in the New York State League.

62. "It Was Not a Shut-Out," *Evening Express* (Lock Haven, Pennsylvania), May 19, 1894: 1.

63. "Cuban Giants 25, New Bedfords 3," *Boston Daily Globe*, May 24, 1894: 4.

64. See a paragraph without a headline in the *Findlay Courier*, May 24, 1894: 4, at the bottom of the third column. See also Phil Williams' biography of Johnson at https://sabr.org/bioproj/person/grant-johnson/.

65. "Cuban Giants Win," *Daily Patriot*, June 1, 1894: 5.

66. "Baseball Notes," *Washington Post*, June 10, 1894: 15.

67. "Cuban Giants Win," *New Haven Register*, June 21, 1894: 3.

68. "Camden Beaten by the Giants," *Philadelphia Inquirer*, July 5, 1894: 3.

69. "A Very Close Game," *Middletown Daily Argus*, August 7, 1894: 5.

70. "Cuban Giants, 19; Salem, 6," *Philadelphia Inquirer*, August 11, 1894: 3.

71. "Cuban Giants the Winners," *New York Tribune*, August 20, 1894: 10.

72. "Another for Cuban Giants," *Philadelphia Inquirer*, August 31, 1894: 3.

73. Tony Kissel, "Leading Off: The Cuban Giants" in *The Negro Leagues Were Major Leagues: Historians Reappraise Black Baseball* (Jefferson, NC: McFarland, 2019), 144; "At Newark," *The Sun* (New York City), September 3, 1894: 6; "Base-Ball Notes," *Saint Louis Globe-Democrat*, September 9, 1894: 9.

74. "Where Was Fall River?" *Boston Post*, September 12, 1894: 3; "Play Ball," *Fall River* (Massachusetts) *Evening News*, September 13, 1894: 4.

75. See the column-long ad in the *Mansfield* (Pennsylvania) *Advertiser*, September 5, 1894: 3. On the second day, the Cubans beat the Demorests of Williamsport there, 18–10, according to "Sporting Notes," *Harrisburg Daily Independent*, September 27, 1894: 5. See also "The Fair!" *Mansfield Advertiser*, October 3, 1894: 3.

76. "Buffalo and Cuban Giants Will Play," *Buffalo Commercial Advertiser*, September 28,

1894: 10; "Frank Boyd's Bisons," *Buffalo Courier*, September 30, 1894: 20; "Buffalo Disgraced," *Buffalo Express*, October 1, 1894: 9.

77. "The Giants Won," *Findlay Courier*, October 2, 1894: 4; "Other Games," *Cleveland Leader*, October 3, 1894: 3.

78. "Brunette Ball Team Wins," *Inter Ocean*, October 7, 1894: 11; "Cuban Giants Are Lucky," *Inter Ocean*, October 8, 1894: 6. For details about the first game, see https://www.seamheads.com/NegroLgs/year.php?yearID=1894&lgID=IND.

79. "Duck Hollow Screams," *The News* (Paterson, New Jersey), October 15, 1894: 1; "Base Ball Notes," *Brooklyn Daily Eagle*, October 14, 1894: 3.

80. "Gossip of the National Game," *Boston Herald*, December 3, 1894: 2.

81. Kissel, 145.

82. "Personal Paragraphs," *Harrisburg Telegraph*, November 10, 1894: 1; "Diddlebock's League to Meet," *Harrisburg Telegraph*, January 7, 1895: 1.

83. "Personal Paragraphs," *Harrisburg Telegraph*, December 5, 1892: 1. It was in this announcement, shortly before the ceremony, that she was identified as "Miss Mary E. Wilson, an adopted daughter of William Adore." Ricketts was from Dover, Delaware. "The wedding will take place at Mr. Adore's residence, 602 South street, and Rev. William Howard Day will officiate."

84. "Mary's In Trouble," *Harrisburg Telegraph*, November 1, 1893: 1; "Wind-up of Court," *Harrisburg Telegraph*, January 13, 1894: 1.

Chapter 12

1. "Base Ball Gala Days," *Fall River Evening News*, April 20, 1895: 5; "Ten to Six," *Fall River Daily Globe*, April 22, 1895: 1. On the latter page, see also "From the Coop" beneath the box score.

2. "Reading and Cuban Giants," *Philadelphia Inquirer*, April 24, 1895: 4; "Cuban Giants Win Hands Down," *The Times* (Philadelphia), April 25, 1895: 8; "Cuban Giants Outplayed by Pottsville," *The Times*, April 26, 1895: 8.

3. "A Yellow Game," *Pottsville* (Pennsylvania) *Daily Republican*, April 25, 1895: 2; "The Base Ball Field," *Evening Herald* (Pottsville, Pennsylvania), April 25, 1895: 1.

4. "Authors and Publishers," *Buffalo Commercial*, May 10, 1895: 6; "Literature," *The Weekly Wisconsin* (Milwaukee), September 7, 1895: 4.

5. "A Poor Game," *Worcester* (Massachusetts) *Sunday Spy*, May 19, 1895: 1; "Tables Turned," *Worcester Daily Spy*, May 29, 1895: 3. See also this blog post by SABR member Ryan Whirty: https://homeplatedontmove.wordpress.com/2019/09/16/the-cuban-giants-meet-louis-sockalexis/.

6. "The Cuban Giants Win," *New York Tribune*, May 20, 1895: 3;"Cuban Giants, 10; Recreation, 9," *The Sun* (New York City), June 10, 1895: 8. Selden won the latter game by swatting a three-run homer with one out in the bottom of the ninth inning.

7. "The Coons Won," *Hazleton* (Pennsylvania) *Plain Speaker*, June 6, 1895: 8; "Cuban Giants and Bridgeton," *Philadelphia Inquirer*, June 25, 1895: 5; "Cuban Giants and Salem," *Philadelphia Inquirer*, July 3, 1895: 5. In contrast to the first article's racist headline, the reporter mentioned "Williams, the old-time catcher, who but for his color would be one of the stars in the National League," but used that same slur before ending his sentence. Grant wasn't in the Giants' lineups on June 24 or 25, the latter in Hagerstown, Maryland. Nelson played second base, and apparently Chamberlain ("Ch'ain" and "C'lain" in the box scores) was Grant's replacement, though he batted last and played first base.

8. "Notes of the Amateur Teams," *Detroit Free Press*, July 25, 1895: 2; "Fowler's Funny Fancies," *Daily Telegram* (Adrian, Michigan), August 9, 1895: 2.

9. "A Short-Stop for the Phillies," *Philadelphia Inquirer*, August 23, 1895: 5; "Baseball Notes," *Washington Post*, August 25, 1895: 4.

10. "Hartfords Lose Again," *Hartford Courant*, August 8, 1895: 5. This article referred to Oscar Jackson as the Cubans' captain.

11. "A Great Game of Ball," *Hartford Courant*, September 11, 1895: 6. Jupiter played center field for the Cubans and batted last. Jack Chesbro was supposed to pitch against the Cuban Giants but missed his train, according to "Make-up of Meridens," *Meriden Daily Journal*, September 12, 1895: 5.

12. "Lost in One Inning," *Berkshire Evening Eagle*, September 12, 1895: 1. The two teams had met once previously that season. See "But One Run Scored," *Berkshire County Eagle*, August 14, 1895: 1.

13. The series was announced at least six days prior to the start of play. For example, see "A Series of Base Ball Games," *Newport* (Rhode Island) *Daily News*, September 3, 1895: 5.

14. "Base Ball," *Newport* (Rhode Island) *Mercury* September 7, 1895: 1; "Base Ball," *Fall River Evening News*, September 10, 1895: 7; "Other Games," *Evening Bulletin* (Providence, Rhode Island), September 12, 1895: 2; "The Sporting World," *Windham County Reformer* (Brattleboro, Vermont), September 13, 1895: 1. The latter misspelled "quadrangular" but was also the only paper of the four to capitalize the Q and the L.

15. "Too Easy for Fun," *Fall River* (Massachusetts) *Daily Herald*, September 23, 1895: 7.

16. "Cuban Giants' First Win," *Boston Daily Globe*, September 17, 1895: 3; "By a Small Margin," *Newport Daily News*, September 18, 1895: 8.

17. Kissel (see Note 73 in Chapter 12), 145.

18. "Cuban Giants Beat Orange," *New York Times*, September 29, 1895: 15.

19. "Local Facts and Comments," *Wellsboro* (Pennsylvania) *Agitator*, September 11, 1895: 3.

20. "Williamstown," *North Adams* (Massachusetts) *Transcript*, November 5, 1895: 3.

21. "Cuban Giants," *Buffalo Enquirer*, February 17, 1896: 8.

22. "Baseball Notes," *Buffalo Evening News*, March 14, 1896: 6.
23. "Baseball Notes," *Evening Times* (Washington, D.C.), February 26, 1896: 4. Trusty's first name was rarely mentioned in newspapers, but see "A Game Full of Runs," *The Times* (Philadelphia), June 6, 1896: 10. This article said he used to play for the Giants' opponent that day, Lambertville. Shep Trusty, a pitcher for the Cuban Giants in their earliest seasons, when they defeated two major league teams, had passed away in 1890.
24. Letter to the editor, *The Sun* (New York City), March 15, 1896: 8.
25. "Sporting Gossip," *Daily Patriot*, March 19, 1896: 2.
26. "Baseball Notes," *The Sun* (New York City), March 28, 1896: 5.
27. "Their First Game," *The Gazette* (York, Pennsylvania), April 15, 1896: 1; "Under New Management," *The York Daily*, April 16, 1896: 1. The first article implied that "Grant and Sol White" turned a nifty double play, but the box score only listed a double play by Trusty and White.
28. "First Blood," *Carbondale* (Pennsylvania) *Leader*, April 17, 1896: 5; "We Win Again," *Carbondale Leader*, April 18, 1896: 6.
29. "Brownies Beat the Cuban Giants," *Rochester Democrat and Chronicle*, April 19, 1896: 15; "Cuban Giants Were Too Easy," *Rochester Democrat and Chronicle*, April 20, 1896: 11.
30. "Hartford Played Ball," *Hartford Courant*, April 21, 1896: 4.
31. "Scrumptious," *Lewiston* (Maine) *Evening Journal*, April 24, 1896: 5; "Lewiston 9, Cuban Giants 1," *Boston Daily Globe*, April 24, 1896: 12.
32. "A Great Finish," *Portland* (Maine) *Daily Press*, April 25, 1896: 2; "Giants Not in It," *Portland Daily Press*, April 27, 1896: 2.
33. "Scranton Lost the Game," *Scranton* (Pennsylvania) *Tribune*, April 28, 1896: 6; "Scranton Won the Game," *Scranton Tribune*, April 29, 1896: 8.
34. "Their First Defeat," *Wilkes-Barre* (Pennsylvania) *Record*, April 30, 1896: 7.
35. "Easton Batted Hard and Timely," *The Times* (Philadelphia), May 1, 1896: 4.
36. "The Giants Won," *Worcester Daily Spy*, May 6, 1896: 8.
37. "Genuine Cuban Giants," *Evening Times* (Washington), May 23, 1896: 3.
38. "Cubans Bunched Hits," *Boston Daily Globe*, May 28, 1896: 3.
39. "Memorial Day Games," *Meriden Daily Journal*, May 30, 1896: 1
40. "Cuban Giants 6; Bridgeton, 2," *Bridgeton* (New Jersey) *Evening News*, June 2, 1896: 1; "Twelve Innings," *Morning Herald* (Hagerstown, Maryland), June 3, 1896: 4; "Drew Their Teeth," *Morning Herald*, June 4, 1896: 4. On August 21, a Cuban Giants team—not necessarily Bright's—lost to the South Jersey League champs, Salem, by a score of 7 to 4, as reported briefly in "Salem to Disband, *Philadelphia Inquirer*, August 22, 1896: 3.
41. "Hanover 1; Cuban Giants 8," *The Gazette* (York), June 5, 1896: 1.
42. "Lost to Cuban Giants," *Rochester Democrat and Chronicle*, June 26, 1896: 15.
43. "Games at Other Places," *The World* (New York City), June 28, 1896: 5; "Passed Balls," *Philadelphia Inquirer*, June 29, 1896: 5. The visiting team was advertised as "John M. Bright's famous genuine Cuban Giants" in "The Orange Athletic Club," *Montclair* (New Jersey) *Times*, June 27, 1896: 5.
44. "Cuban Giants Win," *Asbury Park* (New Jersey) *Daily Press*, June 30, 1896: 1; "Cuban Giants Win Twice," *Asbury Park Daily Press*, July 1, 1896: 1. An ad for the first game, on page of the edition published June 29, said the Genuine Cuban Giants would face a team "composed of all Collegians."
45. "Cuban Giants and Le National," *The Gazette* (Montreal), July 7, 1896: 5; "Other Games," *The Sun* (New York City), July 12, 1896: 8.
46. "Orange, 8; Cuban Giants, 6," *New York Times*, July 26, 1896: 6. Understandably, at least one of the Giants may have remained bitter toward Westervelt after he joined the Orange club, based on a somewhat vague report in "Amateur Notes," *The Times* (Philadelphia), January 23, 1898: 12. That read, "Mark McGrillis will in all probability play at Orange. Since Mark attempted to square accounts with one of the Cuban Giants who endeavored to render Huyler Westerveldt [sic] hors du combat, he has been persona non grata with some of the Orange rooters, but, after his brilliant work last season, these fans have taken him to their hearts, forgiving his past offenses."
47. See two articles without headlines: *Freeman's Journal* (Cooperstown), August 20, 1896: 3; *Freeman's Journal*, August 27, 1896: 3.
48. "Wednesday's Ball Game," *Evening Eagle* (Pittsfield, Massachusetts), September 11, 1896: 1. The headline is assumed, because there is a large chunk of this page missing online, but this daily's article appears to be identical to the one in the weekly *Berkshire County Eagle*, printed under that headline on September 16.
49. "Baseball," *North Adams Transcript*, September 25, 1896: 5.
50. "Orange, 9; Cuban Giants, 2," *New York Times*, September 27, 1896: 7. Sol White's departure by then, to join the Cuban X-Giants against the Page Fence Giants, was confirmed in "Bellaire," *Wheeling* (West Virginia) *Register*, September 25, 1896: 5.
51. "Williamstown," *North Adams Transcript*, October 2, 1896: 3.
52. "Base Ball Gossip," *Boston Herald*, February 18, 1897: 2.
53. "Good Ball Game," *North Adams Transcript*, October 9, 1896: 1; "Autumn Ball Game," *Evening Eagle*, October 10, 1896: 8; "The Blackintons Win," *North Adams Transcript*, October 12, 1896: 1.
54. "Late Base Ball," *Evening Eagle*, October 31, 1896: 5.
55. "The Game Was a Tie," *North Adams Transcript*, January 18, 1897: 3; "A Challenge," *North*

Adams Transcript, February 8, 1897: 4; "Polo Game Postponed," *North Adams Transcript,* February 8, 1897: 3. Other team members were Patrick Keefe, Homer White, Harry Beebe, Norman Dale, and George Bryant.

56. "Baseball Notes," *The Sun* (New York City), February 5, 1897: 4; "Base Ball Gossip," *Boston Herald*, February 18, 1897: 2; "The Cuban Giants," *The Sporting News*, February 13, 1897: 7.

57. See "'Colored Championship' Series" by the Center for Negro Leagues Baseball Research, pages 5–7, at http://www.cnlbr.org/Portals/0/RL/Colored%20Championship%20Series%20(1867-1899)%202018-04.pdf.

58. "Diamond Glimmers," *Boston Herald*, March 3, 1897: 2; "To Join His Team," *North Adams Transcript*, April 10, 1897: 3.

59. "The Black Wonders," *The Sporting News*, March 27, 1897: 6. Bright said he offered two dates to Chicago at the end of July and would play in Chicago on August 28 and 29. He also argued that the only genuine "colored championship" occurred at Hoboken in 1890, for a silver ball trophy, between the Keystones, the Norfolk Red Sox, the Gorhams, and his Cuban Giants, who were undefeated in that tournament. As of this writing, that tourney isn't included in "Colored Championship' Series" by the Center for Negro Leagues Baseball Research, at http://www.cnlbr.org/Portals/0/RL/Colored%20Championship%20Series%20(1867-1899)%202018-04.pdf.

60. "Sport about Everything from Everywhere," *Buffalo Times*, April 5, 1897: 6.

61. "Among the Ball Players," *Lancaster* (Pennsylvania) *Daily Intelligencer*, April 12, 1897: 4; "The First Game," *Daily New Era* (Lancaster, Pennsylvania), April 13, 1897: 1; "Opened with Victory," *Lancaster Daily Intelligencer*, April 13, 1897: 1. A third local paper, the *Morning News*, incorrectly reported the score as 11–4 on its front page, though its line score showed 13 runs for the home team.

62. "Lancaster Wins Again," *Morning News* (Lancaster, Pennsylvania), April 14, 1897: 1; "Three-Time Winners," *Lancaster Daily Intelligencer*, April 15, 1897: 1. The first lineup for the X-Giants was: W. Jackson, cf; A. Jackson, 3b; Williams, c; O. Jackson, lf; Wilson, 3b; Selden, p; Smith, 2b; B. Jackson, rf; and Kelly, ss. Clarence Williams, Selden, and all four Jacksons were much more familiar names in original/genuine Cuban Giants' lineups than most of those in Grant's batting order the previous day.

63. "The Other Giants Downed," *Reading Times*, April 14, 1897: 1; "Reading Browns in Good Shape," *Reading Times*, April 15, 1897: 1.

64. "Nice Luscious Peaches," *Scranton Republican*, April 17, 1897: 4.

65. "Cubans Defeated," *Passaic* (New Jersey) *City Herald*, April 19, 1897: 1.

66. "Base-Ball," *The Dickensonian* (Carlisle, Pennsylvania), April 24, 1897: 1.

67. "Cuban Giants Nicely Beaten," *Rochester Democrat and Chronicle*, April 22, 1897: 10.

68. "Cubans Downed," *Syracuse* (New York) *Standard*, April 23, 1897: 2. The umpire was Henry Lampe of the home team, who pitched briefly in the National League during 1894 and 1895.

69. "Vickery's Great Work," *Hartford Courant*, April 24, 1897: 7; "League Opens Today," *Hartford Courant*, April 26: 1897: 5.

70. "Local Briefs," *Newport* (Rhode Island) *Daily News*, April 26, 1897: 5; "Beaten by a Run," *Newport Daily News*, April 27, 1897: 7.

71. "Reversed the Score," *Newport Daily News*, April 28, 1897: 8.

72. "Cuban Giants 7, Wesleyan, 0," *Boston Daily Globe*, April 29, 1897: 3.

73. "Bristol Loses First Game," *Bristol* (Connecticut) *Herald*, May 6, 1897: 1; "Carter with Cubans," *Meriden Daily Journal*, April 30, 1897: 1. As of this writing, it may not have been reported by any baseball historian in recent decades that Carter soon took a step across the color line, so to speak. In mid-June, he left the Cuban Giants to pitch for Bristol's team, which he had defeated so easily, and thus pitched in a white minor league. See "Gardner's Great Batting," *Meriden Daily Journal*, June 19, 1897: 8.

74. "Cuban Giants 8, Williams 7," *Springfield Republican*, May 9, 1897: 2.

75. "Local Base Ball," *Johnstown* (New York) *Daily Republican*, May 14, 1897: 3; "Base Ball," *Johnstown Daily Republican*, May 17, 1897: 3.

76. "Were Marks for Auburn," *Rochester Democrat and Chronicle*, May 21, 1897: 14.

77. "Saturday's Game," *Johnstown Daily Republican*, May 24, 1897: 5; "Base Ball Bullheadness," *Johnstown Daily Republican*, May 26, 1897: 7.

78. "Three Victories," *North Adams Transcript*, June 1, 1897: 1; "North Adams 8, Cuban Giants 7," *Boston Daily Globe*, June 20, 1897: 2; "North Adams 11, Cuban Giants, 8," *Boston Daily Globe*, June 27, 1897: 2; "Stanleys at Their Best," *Berkshire Evening Eagle*, July 1, 1897: 1, 8.

79. "Games of Baseball," *Jersey City News*, June 7, 1897: 5. See also the *Evening Journal* (Jersey City, New Jersey) on the same date, page 3, column 4.

80. "Carsey's Team Defeated," *New York Evening Journal*, June 21, 1897: 8. This article did indeed call Cleveland's NL team the Indians, twice, and the subheadline referred to "Sockalexis and His Tribe."

81. "The World of Sports," *Jersey Journal*, June 28, 1897: 2. This article said the teams also played to a tie at some point, but there's a distinct possibility that it was referring to the Cuban X-Giants.

82. For example, see "Brevities," *Cortland* (New York) *Semi-Weekly Standard*, June 18, 1897: 5.

83. "Unions Even with Cuban Giants," *Chicago Tribune*, June 15, 1897: 4.

84. "Plattsburghs the Victors," *Burlington* (Vermont) *Daily Free Press*, July 16, 1897: 2; "The Darkies Hit Dowd," *Burlington Daily Free Press*, July 17, 1897: 2; "Victory for Cubans," *Burlington Daily Free Press*, July 19, 1897: 1.

85. "A Good Game," *The Gazette* (Montreal), July 19, 1897: 5.
86. "Cuban Giants 11, Dalton 2," *Berkshire Evening Eagle*, July 26, 1897: 1, 5.
87. "Sunday Ball Games," *Jersey City News*, August 2, 1897: 4.
88. "Cuban Giants 6, Plattsburg[sic] 3," *Boston Daily Globe*, August 10, 1897: 7; "Cuban Giants Laid Low," *Burlington Daily Free Press*, August 11, 1897: 1.
89. "With the Local Players," *Chicago Tribune*, August 28, 1897: 4; "Unions, 21; Cuban Giants, 12," *Chicago Tribune*, August 29, 1897: 12; "With the Amateurs," *Daily Inter Ocean* (Chicago), August 30, 1897: 4.
90. "Home Run Exhibition," *Morning Record* (Traverse City, Michigan), September 3, 1897: 1; "They Took 'Em All," *Muskegon* (Michigan) *Daily Chronicle*, September 7, 1897: 7.
91. "Base Ball Notes," *Knoxville* (Tennessee) *Tribune*, September 5, 1897: 10. The same item appeared (without a headline) in the *Tuscaloosa* (Alabama) *Gazette*, September 9, 1897: 4.
92. "Base Ball," *Hazleton* (Pennsylvania) *Sentinel*, September 25, 1897: 3; "Turned the Tables," *Jersey Journal*, September 27, 1897: 6; "Hot Ball Game for Sunday," *The World* (New York City), September 29, 1897: 8.
93. "Games of Baseball," *Jersey Journal*, September 30, 1897: 6. The winner was only to receive 67 percent, not 75 percent, according to "Colored Giants in Battle," *Jersey City News*, October 6, 1897: 5.
94. "At Weehawken," *The Sun* (New York City), October 4, 1897: 8; "Cubans to Meet Again," *New York Evening Journal* October 6, 1897: 9.
95. "Colored Nines Still Playing," *Boston Herald*, October 7, 1897: 2; "Failed to Materialize," *Morning Journal and Courier* (New Haven, Connecticut), October 8, 1897: 5.
96. "Games of Baseball," *Jersey Journal*, October 11, 1897: 2; "At Weehawken," *The Sun* (New York City), 1897: 8. Oddly, a preview of what was probably the final game for Bright's team said they had defeated the Cuban X-Giants in the series. See "Nationals vs. Cuban Giants," *Brooklyn Citizen*, October 14, 1897: 6. This raises the possibility that the line score of the Stamford game had the teams reversed. On the other hand, Sol White (see Note 46, except on page 37) recalled the X-Giants winning two out of three, though he said the series was "played three successive Sundays," which clearly doesn't seem to be the case.
97. "Nationals, 15; Genuine Cuban Giants, 13," *Brooklyn Daily Eagle*, October 18, 1897: 3.
98. "Will Probably Form a Club," *North Adams Transcript*, December 9, 1897: 3. "The club last winter was composed of Patrick Keefe, Frank Grant, the well known baseball player; George Bryant, Homer White, Arthur Hunt, William Davis, Harry Beebe and Peter McMahon." However, it was James McMahon, not Peter, who was the club's organizer in February. Otherwise, Keefe, White, Beebe, and Bryant were listed with Grant both times. See also "Williamstown," *Albany* (New York) *Morning Express*, March 7, 1892: 7.

Chapter 13

1. "Preliminary Baseball Talk," *North Adams Transcript*, January 6, 1898: 8.
2. "Base Ball," *Trenton Times*, January 21, 1898: 6.
3. "Local Intelligence," *North Adams Transcript*, January 26, 1898: 5; "Base Ball," *Trenton Times*, February 23, 1898: 6.
4. "Cuban X Giants," *Times-Union* (Albany, New York), March 19, 1899: 8.
5. "Cuban X Giants Win First Game," *North Adams Transcript*, April 2, 1898: 16.
6. "Baseball Is Here," *Sunday Call* (Newark, New Jersey), 1898: 9. Nelson entered the game at some point to pitch, and Jordan moved from right field to pitch at some point as well. Oddly, the box score shows "C. Williams, c" as the tenth batter despite already having "Williams, c" batting third.
7. "Local Intelligence," *North Adams Transcript*, April 5, 1898: 5. This series had been arranged many weeks earlier, as reported in "Baseball at Old Point," *Norfolk Virginian*, February 12, 1898: 3. The latter article named the manager of the Chamberlin Baseball Club as R.L. White—see also Brunson (Note 68), page 1268.
8. "Giants, 12; Hygeia, 4," *Daily Press* (Newport News, Virginia), April 7, 1898: 4; "Cuban X-Giants Win Again," *North Adams Transcript*, April 8, 1898: 8; "Surprised the Cuban Giants," *Washington Post*, April 9, 1898: 8. The *Daily Press* reported the score of the second win over the Chamberlan team as 13–8, but the *North Adams Transcript* printed a line score showing the totals as 17–7. For more information about the Hygeia Hotel's team, see Brunson (Note 68), page 263.
9. E.B. Lamar, Jr., "Lamar's Figures," *Sporting Life*, November 5, 1898: 6. Lamar listed the results for 18 games throughout the year against African American teams. It's possible the X-Giants played white teams on April 5, 10, and 11, but there is no known record of any such games.
10. "Local Intelligence," *North Adams Transcript*, April 11, 1898: 5; "Cuban X Giants Win Easily," *North Adams Transcript*, April 13, 1898: 8; "Local Intelligence," *North Adams Transcript*, April 14, 1898: 5; "Cuban X Giants Again," *North Adams Transcript*, April 15, 1898: 8. The latter incorrectly claimed the X-Giants were undefeated to that point in the month. On April 11, the *New York Sun* showed the X-Giants scheduled to play Norfolk that day, but it's unknown whether that game occurred. It could have been against that city's Atlantic League team. The X-Giants' original schedule (see Note 2) listed games in Washington and Baltimore on April 13 and 14, but those were apparently replaced by additional games in Virginia.

11. "Allentown Still Winning," *The Times* (Philadelphia), April 17, 1898: 10. The X-Giants' original schedule (see Note 2) included a game in Reading the day before, but because the team stayed longer in Virginia than originally planned, April 15 was presumably a travel date.

12. "The First Home Game Won," *Springfield Republican*, April 19, 1898: 3.

13. "N. Bedford, 19; Cuban Giants, 8," *Pawtucket* (Rhode Island) *Times*, April 20, 1898: 2; "Cubans Can Hit Hard," *Boston Daily Globe*, April 21, 1898: 12.

14. "Getting into Form," *Fall River Daily Herald*, April 22, 1898: 6. Walker was reportedly born on August 1, 1881, and thus was exactly 16 years younger than Grant.

15. "Our Other Team Wins," *North Adams Transcript*, April 23, 1898: 16. If "Hatcher" was really Grant Thatcher, then Brockton had a pitcher who later went 4-1 for Brooklyn early the next century.

16. "Other Games," *The Sun* (New York City), April 24, 1898: 10.

17. "Fall Rivers Won," *Fall River Daily Globe*, April 26, 1898: 26; "Baseball Gossip," *Fall River Daily Herald*, April 27, 1898: 6; "Bad Baseball Weather," *Fall River Daily Globe*, April 28, 1898: 6.

18. "News of the Diamond," *North Adams Transcript*, April 27, 1898: 8. This paper also announced that Lamar had hired an Arthur M. Nichols as his "advertising agent." The X-Giants' original schedule (see Note 2) included games on April 28 and 29 in Newport, Rhode Island, presumably against that city's team in the New England League, but there's no sign either game actually occurred.

19. "Cuban Giants 3, Holy Cross 2," *Boston Daily Globe*, May 5, 1898: 2.

20. "Cubans Win at the Finish," *North Adams Transcript*, May 6, 1898: 5; "Cubans Win an Easy Game," *North Adams Transcript*, May 7, 1898: 8; "Williams Team 'Deweyed,'" *North Adams Transcript*, May 8, 1898: 5.

21. "Lost by the Outfielders," *Oswego* (New York) *Daily Palladium*, May 10, 1898: 6. This article called the X-Giants "a stronger team than the Cuban Giants that played Friday and Saturday last."

22. "Holy Cross 12, Cuban X Giants 5," *Boston Sunday Globe*, May 15, 1898: 2; "College Boys Defeat Cubans," *North Adams Transcript*, May 16, 1898: 8. The latter had the larger of the two attendance estimates.

23. "Cuban X-Giants 14, Worcester Lyceum 7," *Springfield Republican*, May 22, 1898: 4. In contrast to the *North Adams Transcript*'s coverage, this paper included a box score.

24. "Poughkeepsie's Downed," *Poughkeepsie Daily Eagle*, May 28, 1898: 8.

25. "Memorial Day Baseball," *North Adams Transcript*, May 31, 1898: 5. In contrast to that local paper, the *Springfield Republican* printed box scores for the game on May 28 and the first game of the doubleheader.

26. "No More Cubans," *North Adams Transcript*, June 1, 1898: 8.

27. "Bristol," *Hartford Courant*, June 14, 1898: 12.

28. "Baseball Notes," *Morning Record* (Meriden), June 4, 1898: 5; "Meriden Leads Again," *Meriden Daily Republican*, June 21, 1898: 2; "Slow, Listless Game," *Morning Record*, June 21, 1898: 5. Grant presumably drew one of the three walks issued to his team.

29. *Pittsburg Press*, July 5, 1898: 5. There was no headline per se. The preface to McGuire's remarks called Grant "Hughey" instead of Frank. "Grant's almost perfect action with his hands remind me of the great skill of Heinie Reitz," McGuire also said.

30. "Great Record of Atlantic City Nine," *Philadelphia Inquirer*, September 17, 1898: 5. The dates of the Cuban X-Giants' games were July 11–15, 23, 27–29; August 24–26, 31; and September 2–3 (doubleheader on the latter date).

31. "Games on the Diamond," *Jersey Journal*, July 28, 1898: 6; "Cuban X Giants 8; Hoboken, 0," *New York Tribune*, August 1, 1898: 5; "Chips from the Diamond," *Jersey City News*, July 21, 1898: 4.

32. "Base Ball Notes," *Lancaster* (Pennsylvania) *Morning News*, August 13, 1898: 4.

33. "Oak Park, 17; Cuban Giants, 11," *Chicago Tribune*, September 11, 1898: 14. This article included a box score.

34. "Cubans Win and Tie," *Chicago Tribune*, September 12, 1898: 4.

35. "At Sharon, Wis.," *The Sun* (New York City), September 15, 1898: 6. The pitcher they faced, Bubser, was probably George Bubser, a pitcher for nearby Rockford, Illinois' Western Association team around then.

36. "Other Games," *The Sun* (New York City), September 17, 1898: 6. See also "Personal Matters," *Harvard* (Illinois) *Herald*, September 23, 1898: 9. The latter confirms that the game in Elkhorn was on a Friday.

37. "Local Games Are Arranged," *Daily Inter Ocean*, September 14, 1898: 4; "Unions, 5; Cuban Giants, 3," *Chicago Tribune*, September 18, 1898: 6..

38. "Giants Defeat the Unions," *Chicago Tribune*, September 19, 1898: 4; "Cuban Giants, 11; Chicago Unions, 10," *Daily Inter Ocean*, September 19, 1898: 4; E.B. Lamar, Jr., "Lamar's Figures," *Sporting Life*, November 5, 1898: 6.

39. "Dust from the Diamond," *South Bend* (Indiana) *Tribune*, September 19, 1898: 3; "Other Games," *The Sun* (New York City), September 20, 1898: 5; "Cuban Giants, 6; Unions, 2," *Chicago Tribune*, September 21, 1898: 4. The *Tribune* referred to "a series of seven games" but 4-1-1 is only six. That might not be an error, because the *Tribune* may have meant a best-of-seven, which ended early when one team won four games. Regardless, much more likely to be erroneous was *The Sun*'s coverage on September 20. *The Sun*

printed line scores for a doubleheader, with the second game won by the X-Giants, 11–10. For one, a weekday doubleheader in a neutral city was probably rare in that era. Also, 11–10 was the score of the second game of the doubleheader *in Chicago* a day earlier, and *The Sun*'s numbers for all nine innings are identical to the *Inter Ocean*'s (see previous Note—the *Tribune*'s differed slightly). *The Sun* apparently had a stray second game lying around from the previous day and attached it to the line score of a single game in Michigan City. Lastly, it's clear that the Unions had five runs in that Michigan City game, but the total for the X-Giants is a little iffy. The X-Giants did all their scoring in the eighth inning, and *The Sun*'s line score seems to show a "3" there, and for their final total. But the print was a bit blurry, so if the X-Giants actually exploded for an 8-run eighth, however unlikely when they'd been shut out to that point, then they won that game.

40. "Newark vs. Cuban X Giants," *Jersey City News*, September 24, 1898: 16; "The World of Sports," *Jersey Journal*, September 26, 1898: 7. The preview said it would be "their first appearance in two months in the Metropolitan district."

41. "Sports and Sportsmen," *Jersey City News*, October 3, 1898: 4; "Cuban X Giants Champion," *Jersey City News*, October 10, 1898: 5; E.B. Lamar, Jr., "Lamar's Figures," *Sporting Life*, November 5, 1898: 6. For statistics from the championship series games for which box scores survived, see https://www.seamheads.com/NegroLgs/team.php?yearID=1898&teamID=CXG&LGOrd=1.

42. "Next Monday," *East Liverpool* (Ohio) *Evening News Review*, October 12, 1898: 9.

43. E.B. Lamar, Jr., "Lamar's Figures," *Sporting Life*, November 5, 1898: 6.

44. "Cuban X Giants, 12; Fordham College, 11," *Brooklyn Daily Eagle*, March 30, 1899: 6; "Baseball Season Opened," *Passaic* (New Jersey) *Daily News*, April 10, 1899: 2. A game scheduled for April 2 at Weehawken was cancelled due to coldness, according to "Too Wintry for Baseball," *Jersey Journal*, April 3, 1899: 8. The "Cuban Giants" skipped a third game against the Atlantic League foes, according to "Baseball Skirmishing," *Paterson Evening News*, April 11, 1899: 6.

45. "At Jasper Field," *The Sun* (New York City), April 16, 1899: 9.

46. "Cuban X-Giants Defeat Hoboken," *Jersey City News*, April 24, 1899: 5; "Cuban X Giants Lost," *The World* (New York City), April 27, 1899: 7; "Base Ball Notes," *Brooklyn Daily Eagle*, April 28, 1899: 14.

47. "Baseball Game Today," *Meriden Morning Journal*, May 13, 1899: 2; "Sporting News," *Meriden Morning Record*, May 15, 1899: 2.

48. "Sporting News," *Meriden Morning Record*, May 23, 1899: 2. Jack Chapman did manage at Meriden again at some point during 1899, but apparently not at the time of these two games.

49. "Cuban X Giants 6; Dartmouth 5," *Meriden Morning Record*, May 24, 1899: 1; "Dartmouth Has Its Turn," *Boston Daily Globe*, May 25, 1899: 4; "Vermonters Were Easy," *Burlington* (Vermont) *Free Press*, May 26, 1899: 7; "Another Victory for the Giants," *Burlington Free Press*, May 27, 1899: 6.

50. The original plan was for 20 games, according to an article without a headline in the *Albion* (Indiana) *Democrat*, June 15, 1899: 9.

51. "Unions Defeat Cuban Giants," *Chicago Tribune*, June 12, 1899: 4.

52. "Cuban Giants, 9; Chicago Unions, 0," *St. Louis Daily Globe-Democrat*, June 13, 1899: 11; "That Ball Game," *Dixon* (Illinois) *Evening Telegraph*, June 16, 1899: 4. The St. Louis paper identified the site as Sycamore, Illinois, but a paper in northern Illinois that had a dateline of Sycamore made it clear the game was actually in the nearby city of DeKalb—and it reported an extra run for the victors: "Cuban Giants, 10; Chicago Unions, 0," *Freeport* (Illinois) *Daily Journal*, June 13, 1899: 1. "An immense crowd," as one area daily described it, resulted in seats collapsing, "and several ladies were injured," according to "DeKalb," *Rockford* (Illinois) *Daily Register-Gazette*, July 17, 1899: 4.

53. "Chicago Unions, 12; Cuban Giants, 11," *Chicago Record*, June 17, 1899: 6; "Unions Defeat the Giants," *Chicago Tribune*, June 19, 1899: 4; "Chicago Unions, 8; Cuban Giants, 7," *Chicago Record*, June 20, 1899: 6. Besides Chicago itself, Sharon, Wisconsin may have been the only community to host more than one game. See "Chicago Unions, 13; Cuban Giants, 5," *South Bend* (Indiana) *Tribune*, June 27, 1899: 6.

54. "Evansville Is Enthusiastic," *Janesville* (Wisconsin) *Daily Gazette*, June 21, 1899: 5; "Miscellaneous Games," *Chicago Tribune*, June 23, 1899: 4; *Fort Wayne* (Indiana) *News*, June 22, 1899: 3. The latter one-sentence item had no headline.

55. "Unions Are Defeated Again," *Chicago Tribune*, June 26, 1899: 4; "In Baseball Circles," *Sturgeon Bay* (Wisconsin) *Advocate*, July 1, 1899: 5; "Base Ball Notes," *Janesville Daily Gazette*, July 3, 1899: 1.

56. "Miscellaneous Games Yesterday," *Chicago Record*, July 3, 1899: 6; "Atlantic City Wins," *Philadelphia Inquirer*, July 5, 1899: 6; "X-Giants Beat Mount Holly," *Philadelphia Inquirer* July 20, 1899: 4.

57. "Cuban X Giants Defeat All Cubans," *New York Tribune*, August 14, 1899: 3; "The World of Sports," *Jersey Journal*, August 21, 1899: 6. See also "The World of Sports," *Jersey Journal*, August 2, 1899: 8. This article provides a little background information about the All-Cuban team, beneath which is a line score for an X-Giants game.

58. "Cuban Giants, 7; Columbias, 4," *Chicago Tribune*, September 11, 1899: 10.

59. "'All Coons Look Alike,'" *Detroit Free Press*, September 18, 189: 8. That startling headline, which the newspaper itself put in quotes, might have been mocking any Detroit players who had an unenlightened view of race relations.

60. "Dust from the Diamond," *South Bend Tribune*, September 21, 1899: 3; "Sporting News,"

Saginaw (Michigan) *News*, September 22, 1899: 6; "Giants Are the Champions," *Chicago Tribune*, September 25, 1899: 4. The headline refers to the fact that the morning game of the doubleheader didn't get rained out, and the Columbia Giants thus won their series with the Unions. The X-Giants' total wins in the series is from page 9 of "Colored Championship' Series" by the Center for Negro Leagues Baseball Research, at http://www.cnlbr.org/Portals/0/RL/Colored%20Championship%20Series%20(1867-1899)%202018-04.pdf.

61. "Cuban Giants Shut Out," *The Times* (Philadelphia), September 29, 1899; "Cuban X-Giants Win," *Philadelphia Inquirer*, October 1, 1899: 14.

62. "George Carey Will Play First Base," *East Liverpool Evening News Review*, September 22, 1899: 6; "Diamond Dust," *Meriden Daily Journal*, October 16, 1899: 9.

63. "Hughey Grant," *Buffalo Commercial*, February 8, 1900: 5. The original source for this tribute may have been the *Washington Post* two days earlier, but it's nice to know that at least one Buffalo daily printed it.

64. "Cuban Giants Going to Cuba," *Pittsburgh Press*, February 9, 1900: 5; "Cuban X Giants Go to Cuba," *The World* (New York City), February 10, 1900: 8. Some sources in recent years state that Sol White also went on this trip, and while that might have been Lamar's hope or expectation, there doesn't seem to be evidence that White actually did.

65. "Base Ball in Cuba," *Harrisburg Telegraph*, February 28, 1900: 1; "Havana Nine Plays a Good Game," *Chicago Tribune*, March 4, 1900: 18.

66. "Cuban Giants, 7; San Francisco, 3," *Chicago Tribune*, March 6, 1900: 9; "Cuban X Giants in Cuba," *The World* (New York City), March 14, 1900: 10. The dateline of the latter is March 9, but the game was on a Wednesday, according to "Base Ball Notes," *Waterbury Evening Democrat*, March 14, 1900: 8.

67. "Grant to Captain Cuban Giants," *Jersey Journal*, March 26, 1900: 8; "The Cuban Giants," *Sporting Life*, March 31, 1900: 8.

68. "Baseball Notes," *The Sun* (New York City), April 7, 1900: 5.

69. "Cuban Giants' Successful Trip," *New York Tribune*, April 16, 1900: 9. Right above this brief article is "Cuban X Giants Victorious," complete with a box score.

70. "Jerseys, 5; Cuban Giants, 3" *Jersey City News*, May 14, 1900: 5.

71. "Bons Were Beaten," *Paterson Evening News*, May 21, 1900: 1; "Gossip of the Game," *St. Louis Post-Dispatch*, May 23, 1900: 5.

72. "Against Jeffries," *Evening Citizen* (Ottawa, Ontario), May 25, 1900: 1; "Jeffries Ruled Off," *Los Angeles Times*, May 26, 1900: 4; "Cuban Giants Beat Princeton Giants," *Daily True American* (Trenton), May 29, 1900: 9; "Dust from the Diamond," *Trenton Times*, May 29, 1900: 6.

73. "Niagara's Triumph," *Buffalo Courier*, June 11, 1900: 9; "Ashtabula 6—Cuban Giants 0," *Cleveland Plain Dealer*, June 17, 1900: 16; "Cuban Giants Won," *St. Louis Republic*, June 17, 1900: 10. See also "Other Games," *Cleveland Leader*, June 13, 1900: 6, which describes William Bell preventing a grand slam with a "sensational catch" at the top of the left field fence (though the visitors lost anyway).

74. For example, see "Amateur Baseball," *Daily Inter Ocean*, June 14, 1900: 8.

75. "Columbia Giants, 3; Cuban Giants, 1," *Chicago Tribune*, June 18, 1900: 8; "Columbia Giants, 3; Cuban Giants, 1," *Daily Inter Ocean*, June 18, 1900: 8. The previews said the teams were supposed to play at 10:30 and 3:30, but those dailies only reported on one game and didn't even allude to a second.

76. "Will be a Fast Game," *Belvidere* (Illinois) *Daily Republican*, June 13, 1900: 2. Robinson and Williams were identified as the Giants' battery for that game in "Chicago Unions, 11; Cuban Giants, 8," *Chicago Tribune*, June 20, 1900: 7.

77. "Notes," *Saginaw News*, June 23, 1900: 6.

78. "Columbia Giants, 10; Cuban Giants, 9," *Chicago Tribune*, June 25, 1900: 8. Like previews of the prior Sunday's game, a preview of this game said the two teams "will play the last two games of the Chicago series at the Giant's [sic] park, Thirty-ninth street and Wentworth avenue, today. The first game will be played at 10:30 in the morning and the other at 3:30 in the afternoon." See "Among the Amateurs," *Chicago Tribune*, June 24, 1900: 18.

79. "Cuban Giants Won," *Erie* (Pennsylvania) *Daily Times*, July 2, 1900: 5.

80. "The World of Sports," *Jersey Journal*, July 19, 1900: 8. Bright also announced the release of William Bell.

81. "The World of Sports," *Jersey Journal*, August 27, 1900: 8; "Great Game at Rutherford," *Passaic Daily News*, September 10, 1900: 5.

82. "Amateur Baseball," *Detroit Free Press*, September 15, 1900: 6.

83. "Giants Tie Milwaukee," *South Bend Tribune*, September 25, 1900: 3. Their paragraph probably came from the *Milwaukee Daily News*. The *Milwaukee Journal* apparently didn't even report the score.

84. "Mack's Men Win Good Game," *Milwaukee Journal*, September 26, 1900: 10.

85. "Who Are the Champions," *Racine* (Wisconsin) *Daily Journal*, October 1, 1900: 8.

86. "Columbia Giants, 5; White Stockings, 3," *Daily Inter Ocean*, October 1, 1900: 8.

87. "Nine Innings Without a Run," *Chicago Tribune*, October 8, 1900: 8; "White Stockings, 8; Columbia Giants, 4," *Daily Inter Ocean*, October 8, 1900: 8.

88. "Championship at Stake," *Chicago Daily News*, October 10, 1900: 2; "Today's Union-Columbia Game," *Chicago Tribune*, October 13, 1900: 6.

89. "Unions Beat Columbia Giants," *Chicago*

Tribune, October 14, 1900: 18; "Sporting Notes," *Jackson* (Michigan) *Citizen Patriot*, October 17, 1900: 8; "For the Colored Championship," *Chicago Tribune*, October 21, 1900: 19; "Baseball Briefs," *Detroit Free Press*, October 23, 1900: 6.

90. "Another Last Ball Game," *Daily Inter Ocean*, November 2, 1900: 8; "Sporting Notes," *Chicago Daily News*, November 5, 1900: 2.

91. Here is an example of mixing up Charlie and Frank in this context: "It is openly asserted that 'Tokie' is none other than Grant, a negro second baseman known as the 'colored Dunlap,' who played with the Cuban Giants,"—"Base Ball News," *Waterbury Democrat*, March 21, 1901: 7. For a very detailed account of McGraw's ploy, see Brian McKenna's biography of Charlie Grant at https://sabr.org/bioproj/person/charlie-grant/.

92. "Among Local Ball Tossers," *New York Press*, March 28, 1901: 4.

93. "Field Club Wins from Genuine Cuban Giants," *Daily Standard Union* (Brooklyn), April 15, 1901: 9.

94. "Cuban Giants Outplayed," *Yonkers* (New York) *Statesman*, June 3, 1901: 3; "Berry Won Game by Fine Pitching," *Philadelphia Inquirer*, July 7, 1901: 30.

95. "Diamond Dust," *Potsdam* (New York) *Courier Freeman*, July 10, 1901: 3.

96. "Two Baseball Games," *Watertown* (New York) *Daily Times*, July 13, 1901: 8; "Plattsburgh Going Up," *Ogdensburg* (New York) *Journal*, July 15, 1901: 4; "Base Ball," *Potsdam* (New York) *Courier Freeman*, July 17, 1901: 5; "Normal Notes," *Potsdam Courier Freeman*, May 1, 1901: 6. In 1900, brothers named John and Francis Finnegan, ages 21 and 18, respectively, lived in Potsdam with their parents. The occupation for both was "at school."

97. "Cuban Giants Win," *Rochester Democrat and Chronicle*, August 14, 1901: 13; "Skellys vs. Cuban Giants," *Daily Standard Union*, September 9, 1901: 9; "Skellys vs. Cuban Giants," *Daily Standard Union*, September 23, 1901: 9. On September 21, a team called the Foresters, in Grant's native Berkshire County, included a third baseman named Grant and pitcher named Brown "of the colored Lebanon club," but it seems unlikely that was Frank Grant. See "Foresters Win Final," *Berkshire Evening Eagle*, September 23, 1901: 7.

98. "Sporting Snapshots," *Philadelphia Inquirer*, February 25, 1902: 10; "Sports and Sportsmen," *Jersey City News*, March 31, 1902: 4. For a box score of the game on March 30, see "Cuban X Giants to Play Hoboken," *Jersey Journal*, April 1, 1902: 6. The latter article noted that the Genuine Cuban Giants borrowed three players from the X-Giants; Charlie Grant was on the Cuban X-Giants at that point, but he wasn't among the X-Giants named.

99. "With the Amateurs," *Daily Standard Union*, April 12, 1902: 9; "Future Events," *Daily Standard Union*, April 20, 1902: 9.

100. "Amateur Baseball," *Daily Standard Union* (Brooklyn), April 30, 1902: 9. The latter coverage was unusual for a daily paper, because it was reporting on a game three days earlier (and no weekend intervened).

101. "Other Games," *Jersey City News*, May 8, 1902: 4.

102. "Philadelphia Giants Win First Game!" *Philadelphia Evening Item*, April 24, 1902: 9; "Sport," *The Freeman* (Indianapolis), May 10, 1902: 2. In addition to reporting on the Giants' first game, the *Item* previewed the two games against the All-Virginia team. Their lineup included a shortstop named Stewart Grant.

103. "Reading Wins Easily," *Reading* (Pennsylvania) *Daily Times and Dispatch*, April 29, 1902: 5; "First Home Run," *Reading Daily Times and Dispatch*, May 2, 1902: 5; "Last Exhibition," *Reading Daily Times and Dispatch*, May 3, 1902: 3. In the middle game, Grant was shown as having only one hit instead of two but with seven putouts instead of six in "Base Ball," *Reading* (Pennsylvania) *Eagle*, May 2, 1902: 7. The Pennsylvania State League's season lasted only from May 2 to 26 because Organized Baseball dissolved it when it failed to pay a required fee. Therefore, when the Philadelphia Giants played Williamsport on May 28, its lineup bore little resemblance to its Pennsylvania State League roster. The same was true when the Giants played Lancaster on July 29.

104. "West Jersey Giants Lose," *Philadelphia Inquirer*, May 4, 1902: 25; "Battle of Giants," *Philadelphia Inquirer*, May 5, 1902: 6; "Philadelphia Giants Win," *Philadelphia Inquirer*, May 9, 1902: 10. These *Inquirer* articles didn't mention that the West Jersey Giants were also an African American team, but that was noted in "New Stand on the Cricket Ground," *Evening Journal* (Jersey City, New Jersey), May 15, 1902: 10.

105. "A Very Close Call," *Morning Tribune* (Altoona, Pennsylvania), May 24, 1902: 7.

106. "The Future Greats," *Philadelphia Inquirer*, June 2, 1902: 6; Dr. Layton Revel and Luis Munoz, "Early Pioneers of the Negro Leagues: Walter 'Slick' Schlichter," Center for Negro League Baseball Research, 2016: 5; this article is accessible online at http://www.cnlbr.org/Portals/0/EP/Walter%20Schlichter%202018-04-.pdf.

107. "Colored Teams Play Ball," *Philadelphia Inquirer*, June 7, 1902: 10.

108. "Base-Ball Extraordinary," *Wellsboro* (Pennsylvania) *Agitator*, June 11, 1902: 1; "Giants Win Double Header," *Philadelphia Inquirer*, May 28, 1902: 10; "Philadelphia Giants Lose," *Philadelphia Inquirer*, June 24, 1902: 10; "Giants Win 12-Inning Game," *Philadelphia Inquirer*, June 25, 1902: 10. The information about Williams was provided in a paragraph without a headline in *The Columbian* (Bloomsburg, Pennsylvania), June 26, 1902: 5.

109. "Giants Won Another," *Evening Journal* (Jamestown, New York), August 12, 1902: 5; "On Amateur Diamonds," *Daily Standard Union* (Brooklyn), September 23, 1902: 9. In these examples of games in New York, Grant happened to get two hits in each (2-for-4 in the August game).

110. "Sports," *Harrisburg Daily Independent*, July 31, 1902: 7; "Giants 2-H.A.C. 1," *Daily Patriot*, August 5, 1902: 7; "At Last a Victory—H.A.C. Played Ball," *Harrisburg Telegraph*, September 5, 1902: 2; "Giants Lose in Eleventh," *Daily Patriot*, September 6, 1902: 7.

111. "Haverlings Defeated," *Rochester Democrat and Chronicle*, August 19, 1902: 13; "Philadelphia Giants Win," *Philadelphia Inquirer*, August 26, 1902: 11.

112. "Ingersoll Dropped Two," *Free Press* (Easton, Pennsylvania), September 2, 1902: 3; "Ingersoll Twice Beaten," *Philadelphia Inquirer*, September 2, 1903: 11.

113. "Athletics Down Giants," *Philadelphia Inquirer*, October 3, 1902: 10.

114. "Athletics and Giants," *Philadelphia Inquirer*, October 7, 1902: 10.

115. "Independent Clubs Organize," *Daily Patriot*, January 30, 1903: 7; "Where Baseball Players Will Perform this Year," *Evening Journal* (Wilmington, Delaware), March 31, 1903: 8.

116. Floyd J. Calvin, "Sol White Recalls Baseball's Greatest Days," *Pittsburgh Courier*, March 12, 1927: 16. White also said the Giants and the Cuban X-Giants were in the "Independent League" along with white clubs in Harrisburg, Williamsport, Altoona, and Lancaster.

117. "Wants and Doings of the Ball Tossers," *Daily Standard Union* (Brooklyn), April 20, 1903: 9. At the National League grounds that same day, the Pastime A.C. beat a *white* club called the Philadelphia Giants, 4–2, according to "Amateur Baseball," *Daily Standard Union*, April 26, 1903: 7.

118. See Calvin's interview with Sol White, at Note 116, and "Easy for Philadelphia Giants," *Philadelphia Inquirer*, May 27, 1903: 10.

119. "Philadelphia Giants Defeat Chester," *Philadelphia Inquirer*, July 10, 1903: 10; "Sports," *Harrisburg Daily Independent*, July 17, 1903: 2.

120. "Double Header Was Played," *Morning News* (Wilmington, Delaware), August 18, 1903: 7. Those were the final games of this Wilmington club, which wasn't the Wilmington A.A. team but had just been purchased by them, for the purpose of combining them. That was explained in "News of a Day Down in Delaware," *Philadelphia Inquirer*, August 18, 1903: 9.

121. "The Future Greats," *Philadelphia Inquirer*, August 30, 1903: 12.

122. "Highly Colored Affair," *Philadelphia Inquirer*, September 6, 1903: 12.

123. For detailed statistics for both teams, see https://www.seamheads.com/NegroLgs/year.php?yearID=1903.

124. "Cuban X-Giants Win First Game," *Philadelphia Inquirer*, September 13, 1903: 14.

125. "Colored Championship Game as Seen by Artist Thomas," *Daily Standard Union*, September 15, 1903: 8.

126. "Cuban X-Giants Won Miserable Game," *Trenton Times*, September 15, 1903: 9; "M'Clellan Lost Pitcher's Battle," *Morning Post* (Camden, New Jersey), September 16, 1903: 3.

127. "Cuban X-Giants Are Champions," *Daily Patriot*, September 19, 1903: 7; "X-Giants Beat the Phillies," *Camden* (New Jersey) *Daily Courier*, September 26, 1903: 1.

128. "Won the Final Game," *Harrisburg Telegraph*, October 8, 1903: 6.

Chapter 14

1. "Pittsburg's [sic] Crack Colored Ball Team," *Pittsburgh Daily Post*, February 22, 1904: 6; "Base Ball Chat," *Altoona* (Pennsylvania) *Tribune*, March 18, 1904: 3; "Smoky City Giants Are Strong," *Pittsburgh Daily Post*, April 12, 1904: 8; "Base Ball Chat," *Altoona Tribune*, April 20: 1904, 3; "Giants Are Stronger," *Pittsburgh Daily Post*, June 14, 1904: 8.

2. "Marquettes vs. Royal Giants," *Daily Standard Union* (Brooklyn), April 2, 1904: 8; "Marquette Team Won," *Brooklyn Daily Eagle*, April 6, 1904: 12. For Marquettes manager J.A. Roach's letter to the editor, see "Baseball," *Jersey Journal* (Jersey City, New Jersey), April 25, 1904: 10.

3. "Little Grinds for Rooters," *Altoona* (Pennsylvania) *Morning Times*, April 4, 1904: 5; "Phila. Giants, 3, Murray Hill, 0," *New York Times*, April 4, 1904: 6.

4. "Baseball Items of Interest," *New York Times*, April 14, 1904: 7; "Baseball at Olympic Park," *Morning Call* (Paterson, New Jersey), April 18, 1904: 3; "Baseball at Olympic Park," *Morning Call* (Paterson, New Jersey), April 21, 1904: 3.

5. "Baseball at Olympic Park," *Passaic* (New Jersey) *Daily Herald*, April 25, 1904: 5.

6. "All-Oneida Nine Beaten by the Cuban Giants," *Post Standard* (Syracuse, New York), May 2, 1904: 3.

7. "Nothing But the Cubans," *Berkshire Evening Eagle* (Pittsfield, Massachusetts), May 31, 1904: 8. On Saturday, May 14, the Philadelphia Giants' second baseman named Grant was taken out of a ballpark by two policemen after trying to hit the umpire, but that was presumably Charlie. See "Fight at Camden," *Harrisburg Telegraph*, May 16, 1904: 6.

8. "On the Diamond," *Daily Home News* (New Brunswick, New Jersey), June 21, 1904: 2; *Asbury Park* (New Jersey) *Morning Press*, June 29, 1903: 1, 3; "Giants Won an Exciting Game," *Camden* (New Jersey) *Post-Telegram*, June 29, 1903: 3. The crowd for the latter game was 3,000, The roster of the Princeton X-Giants once included a W. Williams at second base and a T. Williams at shortstop, according to "Baseball," *Trenton Sunday Advertiser*, April 19, 1903: 7.

9. "On the Amateur Diamond," *Brooklyn Daily Times*, May 28, 1904: 4;"Two Good Games at Brighton Grounds," *Daily Standard Union*, June 11, 1904: 4.

Notes—Chapter 14

10. "Baseball Chat," *The Chat* (Brooklyn), June 18, 1904: 7. The "Orpheum Giants" lost by almost the same score on June 11 to the same team, according to "Other Games Today," *Brooklyn Citizen*, June 12, 1904. The battery for the Giants in that game was Abbott and Williams. See also "Amateur Baseball," *Daily Standard Union*, June 23, 1904: 8.

11. "Sunday Games," *Daily Standard Union*, June 24, 1904: 8. There was no overlap with the lineup of the "Orpheum Giants" in the box score printed on June 23.

12. "Baseball and Sporting News," *Plainfield* (New Jersey) *Courier-News*, June 24, 1904: 4; "Old Battery Will Be at the Points," *Perth Amboy* (New Jersey) *Evening News*, July 9, 1904: 3. Other Colored Giants named were Kelly, 3b; Nelson, p; Smith, 1b; Butler, 2b; Devoe, c; Mathews, lf; Valentine, cf; and Penno, rf.

13. "In the Field of Sports," *Plainfield Courier-News*, July 18, 1904: 5; "Old Trick Decided Game," *Stamford* (Connecticut) *Daily Advocate*, August 15, 1904: 3; "Colored Giants Win from Oreos," *Asbury Park* (New Jersey) *Evening Press*, September 9, 1904: 1. Grant was captain of the New York Colored Giants by mid-July, if not earlier, according to "Baseball Notes," *Plainfield Courier-News*, July 14, 1904: 5.

14. "Last Baseball for the Season," *Evening Record* (Hackensack, New Jersey), October 17, 1904: 1; "Saturday's Game," *Morning Call* (Paterson, New Jersey), October 17, 1904: 9. The first of these box scores, which showed Grant batting second, credited him with two runs scored, 16 putouts at first base, and no assists (or errors). The other box score showed him batting third, with only one run scored and only 10 putouts but also one assist. The first box score listed ten Giants, including Bolden, rf and Matthews, lf, but the other box score listed only nine, and instead of those two it included a second player named Jackson, rf.

15. "Cogan's Team Put Giants Down and Out," *Paterson Evening News*, April 3, 1905: 9; "Amateur Baseball," *Daily Standard Union*, May 1, 1905: 3. By this point, if not months earlier, the contact person for the New York Colored Giants was Moses Corbin, 52 West 135th Street. That was according to "Members of Baseball Managers' Protective Association of G.N.Y.," *Daily Standard Union*, March 18, 1905: 4.

16. "Waller Had Game Arm; Westfield Beaten," *Plainfield Courier-News*, May 15, 1905: 5.

17. "Baseball," *Yonkers* (New York) *Herald*, June 26, 1905: 5.

18. "Twelve-Inning Tie Game," *Brooklyn Citizen*, August 24, 1905: 6; "New York Colored Giants," *Daily Standard Union*, August 25, 1905: 9.

19. "Amateur Baseball," *Daily Standard Union*, August 28, 1905: 3.

20. "Amateur Baseball," *Daily Standard Union*, September 4, 1905: 3; "Cuban Giants Beat Berwick," *Philadelphia Inquirer*, September 26, 1905: 15.

21. "Sporting Notes," *Berkshire Evening Eagle* (Pittsfield, Massachusetts), September 14, 1905: 10.

22. Bob Mayer, "The Asylum Base Ball Club: The Great Reunion Game, September 29, 1905," *The National Pastime: Baseball in the Big Apple* (Society for American Baseball Research), 2017, available at https://sabr.org/journal/article/the-asylum-base-ball-club-the-great-reunion-game-september-29-1905/.

23. "Deciding Game Won by the Ridgewoods," *Daily Standard Union*, October 2, 1905: 3; "Marquette Loses a Game," *Brooklyn Citizen*, October 2, 1905: 3. Charlie Grant played in two games for the Philadelphia Giants nearby, including one in the morning at the Brighton Oval, according to "Philadelphia Giants Beat the Brightons," *Daily Standard Union*, October 2, 1905: 3.

24. "Brightons Defeat the All-Professionals," *Daily Standard Union*, October 9, 1905: 5. The afternoon box score was printed two columns to the right, under the headline, "Paramounts Lose Again to Loughlin Lyceum." In the morning game's box score, F. Grant led off for the Philadelphia Giants and C. Grant batted third for the Genuine Cuban Giants, but those first initials were presumably reversed.

25. "Cuban Giants Were Easy for the Paramounts," *Daily Standard Union*, October 23, 1905: 3.

26. Carl W. Chester, "Ball Talk at the Barber Shop," *Buffalo Evening News*, January 31, 1906: 10.

27. "Wilmington Giants," *Philadelphia Inquirer*, April 1, 1906: 15.

28. "Royal Giants Strong," *Brooklyn Citizen*, April 6, 1906: 5; "Royal Giants Defeat Brightons in Close Game," *Daily Standard Union*, April 9, 1906: 8. There also wasn't a Grant in the Royal Giants' box score printed on April 2.

29. "Genuine Cuban Giants to Meet Marquettes," *Daily Standard Union*, May 19, 1906: 8.

30. Big Crowd Sees the Colored Men Win," *Yonkers Herald*, May 21, 1906: 7. Evidence that it was Frank Grant was printed elsewhere a few days later, in a preview of another New York Colored Giants game. "Grant, the star second baseman of the Cuban Giants, will play with the New Yorkers Sunday," according to "Great Game for Utica Fans at Utica Oval," *Daily Standard Union*, May 26, 1906: 8.

31. "Home Teams Will Have to Hustle in Order to Down Visiting Nines," *Daily Standard Union*, Jun 22, 1906: 8.

32. "Royal Giants Still on the Winning Path," *Daily Standard Union*, July 20, 1906: 9; "Royal Giants Found Dawson to Their Liking," *Daily Standard Union*, July 21, 1906: 5.

33. "Brooklyn Giants 7, New York Giants 3," *Springfield* (Massachusetts) *Daily Republican*, July 28, 1906: 3. As of this writing, this game is the only one of Frank Grant's 1906 season that is recorded at Seamheads.com.

34. "Sports," *Daily Home News* (New

Brunswick, New Jersey), August 13, 1906: 3; "Amateur and Semi-Pro. Baseball News," *Daily Standard Union*, September 5, 1906: 9.

35. "Loughlins Will Try to Trim Baltimore Giants," *Daily Standard Union*, August 23, 1906: 8.

36. "Fitchburg 9, B.G. 1," *Boston Herald*, September 7, 1906: 7; "Ends with Victory," *Fitchburg* (Massachusetts) *Daily Sentinel*, September 10, 1906: 1.

37. "Pittsfield One Run Behind at the Close," *Berkshire Evening Eagle*, July 26, 1907: 12.

38. "How the Colored Teams Line up this Season," *Daily Standard Union*, March 1, 1907: 10.

39. "Big Game To-morrow," *Brooklyn Citizen*, March 29, 1907: 5; "With the Amateurs and the Semi-Pros," *Brooklyn Daily Eagle*, June 27, 1907: 24.

40. "Fast Game Is Due Sunday," *Perth Amboy* (New Jersey) *Evening News*, April 19, 1907: section 2, page 1; "Sports," *Daily Home News* (New Brunswick, New Jersey), May 15, 1907: 3; "3,500 People Saw Giants Wallop Shine's Team," *Daily Home News*, May 20, 1907: 1–2. In the preview on May 15, the other New York Colored Giants mentioned were Nelson, Pitcher Dawson, Lavelle, and "Ha Ha" Robinson. All of these surnames appeared often in Grant's box scores in those years, especially Nelson and Dawson.

41. "Lively Sport for Greenville Fans," *Jersey Journal*, July 13, 1907: 7.

42. "On Amateur Diamonds," *Brooklyn Daily Eagle*, August 12, 1907: 17. Watkins didn't play, but that wasn't necessarily unusual for him that year. In any event, Grant wasn't listed among the nine Colored Stars just two days earlier, in "Pop Watkins' Team in Two Games with Howards," *Daily Standard Union*, August 9, 1907: 6.

43. "Uticas Lose First Game," *Brooklyn Citizen*, August 19, 1907: 3. Frank Grant was confirmed as a member of Watkins' team in "Games at Meyerrose Park," *Brooklyn Citizen*, August 23, 1907: 3. On that occasion, Watkins' team was called the Cuban Stars.

44. "Cuban Giants Beat Ex-Giants Twice," *Brooklyn Daily Eagle*, August 25, 1907: section 5, page 4. The newness of the Brooklyn X-Giants was made clear in "Hussey Will Back New Colored Team," *Daily Standard Union*, August 21, 1907: 6.

45. "Games at Meyerrose Park," *Brooklyn Citizen*, August 23, 1907: 3. This was repeated almost word for word in "Play for Colored Title," *Brooklyn Citizen*, August 27, 1907: 3.

46. "Stars Get Back at Giants," *Philadelphia Record*, September 5, 1907: 9. As of this writing, this is Grant's lone game of 1907 in his Seamheads.com entry. Besides Bradley, James, and Holland, his teammates in that game were Bill Monroe, John Patterson, Grant "Home Run" Johnson, Bob Jordan, and Bill Merritt. The box score listed a "Buegner, cf" but that was presumably Harry Buckner.

47. As an example of coverage of this league early in its season, see "Philadelphia Giants Won," *Brooklyn Daily Eagle*, July 28, 1907: 8. More information about the league is available from SABR historian Gary Ashwill at https://agatetype.typepad.com/agate_type/2014/02/the-negro-league-youve-never-heard-of.html.

48. Frank Grant was reportedly a member of the Royal Giants on at least two other occasions, so he might have played non-league games with them. He was mentioned as a team member in these previews of Royal Giants games: "National League," *Every Evening* (Wilmington, Delaware) July 11, 1907: 6; "Minor Baseball," *Brooklyn Times*, September 13, 1907: 5.

49. "Giants Still Champions," *Philadelphia Record*, September 6, 1907: 8; "Chatham Too Fast for Colored Giants," *Daily Standard Union*, September 15, 1907: 7.

50. "What Is Going On in the World of Baseball," *Morning Call* (Paterson, New Jersey), September 23, 1907: 3. A few days later, Watkins' Cuban Giants were scheduled to play St. John's Catholic Club, with guest star Hal Chase from New York's American League club. However, coverage of the game—if it was played—may not have occurred. See "Hal Chase on This Team," *Brooklyn Citizen*, September 28, 1907: 3.

51. "Wall's All-Leaguers Beat Colored Stars," *Daily Standard Union*, October 20, 1907: 6.

52. "Joe Wall's Team Beat Colored Stars," *Brooklyn Daily Eagle*, November 6, 1907: 15.

53. "Union Leaguers Beat Pop Watkins' Giants," *Brooklyn Daily Eagle*, April 19, 1908: section 5, page 7; "Ridgewood Too Fast for the Colored Stars," *Daily Standard Union*, April 19, 1908: 7; "Ridgewoods Win Easily," *Brooklyn Citizen*, April 19, 1908: 6. The first paper's box score included Grant, but the other two, which seem to draw from a similar source, omitted him. There are numerous differences among all three, but the *Eagle*'s seems more complete. It credited three doubles, not two, and recorded three double plays (including one involving Grant) instead of just one. It also specified sacrifice hits and a hit batsman, both of which were omitted from the other two box scores.

54. "Royal Giants Taken into Camp by Brightons," *Daily Standard Union*, April 6, 1908: 4.

55. "Brooklyn X Giants Have a Fast Team," *Daily Standard Union*, May 13, 1908: 6.

56. See box scores without headlines in the same paper about five weeks apart: *Daily Standard Union*, May 26, 1908: 7; July 1, 1908: 7.

57. "With the Amateurs and Semi-Pros," *Brooklyn Daily Eagle*, August 17, 1908: section 2, page 4; "Woodhavens Register Deciding Run in Ninth," *Daily Standard Union*, August 24, 1908: 4; "With the Amateurs and Semi-Pros," *Brooklyn Daily Eagle*, August 31, 1908: section 2, page 5.

58. F.D. Ellis, "Appeal for Fowler," *Sporting Life*, December 19, 1908: 9. This letter was also printed in *The Freeman* (Indianapolis), February 5, 1909: 7.

59. Lester A. Walton, "In the Sporting World," *The New York Age*, March 25, 1909: 6; "Ridgewood Wins Opener," *Brooklyn Daily Eagle*, March 29, 1909: section 2, page 8; "Baseball Notes," *The New*

York Age, April 22, 1909: 6. A benefit game for Fowler was scheduled for October 24, between the Royal Giants and Joe Wall's All-Leaguers, but it's unclear whether that game was played. See "Royal Giants—All Leaguers," Brooklyn Daily Eagle, October 20, 1909: section 2, page 4.

60. "Baseball on Totowa Oval," *Morning Call* (Paterson, New Jersey), August 18, 1909: 3; "At Totowa Oval," *Morning Call*, August 25, 1909: 3. "Three Games for Totowas," *Morning Call*, August 31, 1909: 6. Booker was a member of the historically significant African American team in Celeron, New York that played in an all-white minor league in 1898. See Greg Peterson, "The Celeron Acme Colored Giants," https://www.chautauquasportshalloffame.org/2019/wp-content/uploads/2019/06/celoronacme.pdf.

61. "With the Amateurs and Semi-Pros," *Brooklyn Daily Eagle*, September 27, 1909: section 2, page 5.

62. "With the Amateurs and Semi-Pros," *Brooklyn Daily Eagle*, September 30, 1909: section 2, page 5; "Colored Stars Easy for Joe Wall's Team," *Daily Standard Union*, October 1, 1909: 8.

63. "With the Amateurs," *Brooklyn Daily Eagle*, October 4, 1909: section 2, page 4; "Colored Stars Lose to the All-Leaguers," *Daily Standard Union*, October 4, 1909: 7.

64. "Watkins' Giants Beat Jamaica Woodhulls," *Brooklyn Daily Eagle*, October 10, 1909: sports section, page 8.

65. "Among Local Ball Tossers," *New York Press*, February 27, 1910: 3.

66. Mrs. Grant's first name is interpreted by Ancestry.com as "Celia," but the "C" has a big loop at the top and diagonal line in front of it, making it resemble the occasional capital "R" lower on the page.

67. For Gary Ashwill's analysis of which Grant(s) played on the Black Sox, see https://agatetype.typepad.com/agate_type/2015/10/new-york-black-sox-1910.html. In New Brunswick on September 11, 1910, the same Grant played for the Black Sox against the Pittsburgh Giants and then with the Giants against a local team, according to an item without a headline in the *New Brunswick (New Jersey) Daily Times*, September 13, 1910: 7.

68. "With the Amateurs and the Semi-Pros," *Brooklyn Daily Eagle*, August 15, 1910: section 2, page 3; "N.Y. Colored Giants Lose to Patersons," *Daily Standard Union*, August 15, 1910: 10; "Pitchers' Duel at Bronx Oval," *The New York Age*, September 8, 1910: 6. The first baseman for Paterson was probably Joe Wall. Toward the end of Grant's playing career, Wall was in opposing lineups with unusual frequency. Possible explanations include that Wall had the ability to coax Grant out of semi-retirement, or would urge opposing teams to put Grant in their lineups. Another possibility is that Wall led or at least played on teams that had better success getting their box scores into various newspapers.

69. "Professionals by One Run," *Brooklyn Daily Eagle*, August 21, 1910: sports section, page 6. Olympic Field was at 136th Street and Fifth Avenue in Manhattan, according to "Wall's All-Leaguers Defeat Colored Giants," *Daily Standard Union*, September 11, 1910: 5. There was no Grant in the Colored Giants' lineup, nor with the Colored Stars the next day.

70. "Amateur Baseball," *Daily Standard Union*, March 13, 1911: 11. The Savannah Colored Giants were members of the "Interstate B.B.A." and their contact for games was named Charles Williams. Besides "Grant" in right field, their roster included Mitchell, p; Jones, p; Ray, p; Fuller, c; Goode, 1b; Redding, 2b; Lockery, 3b; Hargrove, ss; Martin, lf; and Wormsley, cf.

71. "Tottenville Is Ready to Play," *Perth Amboy (New Jersey) Evening News*, August 11, 1911: 9.

72. *Daily Standard Union*, June 20, 1911: 11. There was no headline per se. "Red Bank Team Won," *Daily Record* (Long Branch, New Jersey), July 5, 1911: 7.

73. In Ancestry.com's New York Marriage License Indexes, her name was entered as Arelia Hasel, and her husband was Frank U. Grant.

74. "Oritani Will Meet the Colored Giants," *The Record* (Hackensack, New Jersey), September 29, 1911: 1; "Final Game for Indians," *The Record*, October 2, 1911: 1.

Chapter 15

1. "Bellaire Wins from Negroes," *Wheeling (West Virginia) Intelligencer*, June 16, 1913: 7; "Attorney Stanton to Toss out First Ball," *Pittsburgh Press*, May 20, 1913: 19. By mid-May, a team called Daddy Clay's Pittsburgh Giants changed its name to Daddy Clay's Pitt Giants, according to "Colored Teams Meet Tomorrow," *Pittsburgh Press*, May 9, 1913: 29. A second baseman named Clay played for the Pittsburgh Giants reportedly managed by Charlie Grant in 1914.

2. "Phoenix Book Opening Game," *Altoona (Pennsylvania) Tribune*, April 21, 1914: 10; "Pittsburgh Giants Here Want Game Saturday," *Daily Patriot* (Harrisburg, Pennsylvania), May 14, 1914: 10; ""Giants Will Play," *Harrisburg (Pennsylvania) Telegraph*, May 18, 1914: 8; "Championship Series at Island Park," *Harrisburg Telegraph*, May 20, 1914: 6.

3. "Live Baseball News from the Semipros," *Commercial Tribune* (Cincinnati), March 29, 1914: section 5 (Sporting Section), page 3; "Colored Teams to Play," *Courier-Journal* (Louisville, Kentucky) April 26, 1914: section 3, page 3; "The Cincinnati Stars," *The Freeman* (Indianapolis), August 15, 1914: 7. Box scores confirming that Charlie actually played for the Stars are rare, but see "Stars 14—Uricho 7," *Commercial Tribune*, August 24, 1914: 7.

4. "Spinney Teams in Good Form," *Commercial Tribune*, May 24, 1914: section 5 (Sporting Section), page 3; "The Amateur Money Question Is

Baffling Many Managers," *Commercial Tribune*, June 28, 1914: 16.

5. "Local Sporting," *News-Herald* (Franklin, Pennsylvania), June 2, 1914: 3. To add to the complexity of the situation, in May a Pittsburgh Colored Giants team with a lineup totally different than Grant's team of the same name played at New York City's Dexter Park, as documented in "Many Runs Gathered in as Cypress Hills Take Game," *Brooklyn Daily Eagle*, May 4, 1914: 14.

6. "Manhattan A.A.," *Philadelphia Tribune*, April 15, 1916: 7; "Blue Ribbon Notes," *Philadelphia Tribune*, May 20, 1916: 7.

7. "Sporting Notes," *Berkshire Evening Eagle* (Pittsfield, Massachusetts), September 14, 1905: 10.

8. "Notice," *North Adams Transcript*, February 27, 1909: 3. This was reprinted at least twice, on March 6 and 13.

9. Willis Grant and Hattie H. Grant, "Card of Thanks," *North Adams Transcript*, March 29, 1916: 7; "Death of Amelia C. Grant," *North Adams Transcript*, March 25, 1916: 7. The siblings' address was stated as 89 Spring Street.

10. "Miss Hattie H. Grant Dies at Home Today," *North Adams Transcript*, June 15, 1920: 9; "Obituary," *North Adams Transcript*, July 23, 1926: 2; "Willis W. Grant Dies at House of Mercy Hospital," *North Adams Transcript*, February 18, 1929: 9.

11. "Minetta Street, Tough, Crooked and Dilapidated, to Be Wiped out under Civic Betterment Plan," *The Sun* (New York City), December 10, 1916: 14.

12. "Social Events," *Pittsburgh Courier*, November 22, 1930: section 2, page 2. Frank Miller and his son were scheduled to leave for their visit to the McTurners on October 25, according to "Pitt Lyceum," *Pittsburgh Courier*, October 25, 1930: 6.

13. "Diamond Men in Reunion," *New York Amsterdam News*, January 27, 1932: 13. See also Romeo L. Dougherty, "Sportopics," *New York Amsterdam News*, December 30, 1931: 12.

14. W. Rollo Wilson, "Sport Shots," *Pittsburgh Courier*, February 6, 1932: section 2, page 4.

15. "Greenlee Represents Crawfords at Fete," *Pittsburgh Courier*, February 13, 1932: section 2, page 5.

16. "Frank Grant, Noted Baseball Star of Generation Ago, Dies," *The New York Age*, June 5, 1937: 8; Cum Posey, "Posey's Points," *Pittsburgh Courier*, July 3, 1937: 18.

17. *Bisons 2019 Media Guide*: 92.

18. Bob Stedler, "Sport Comment," *Buffalo Evening News*, October 30, 1945: 23. Stedler happened to note that Reidy "was probably the first left-handed catcher in organized baseball."

19. Jessica Willis, "Game, Fame Catch the Spotlight" *Berkshire Eagle*, August 11, 2006: B1. It was mentioned that the "gray clapboard house that is currently standing at 54 Spring St." might have housed the Grant family.

20. Dom Amore, "For Baseball Pioneer, Meriden a Key Stop," *Hartford* (Connecticut) *Courant*, July 30, 2006: A1, A11.

Bibliography

Periodicals

Abbeville Press and Banner, Abbeville, South Carolina, 1886–1887, 1889
Adams Freeman, Adams, Massachusetts, 1886
The Afro-American, Baltimore, 1932
Albany Evening Journal, 1889–1890
Albany Morning Express, 1889–1890, 1892
Albion Democrat, Albion, Indiana, 1899
Altoona (Morning) Times, Altoona, Pennsylvania, 1890, 1904
The Argus, Albany, 1885, 1889–1890, 1892
Asbury Park (Evening) Press, Asbury Park, New Jersey, 1889, 1896, 1903–1904
Atchison Blade, Atchison, Kansas, 1892
Baltimore American, 1887, 1890
Bellows Falls Times, Bellows Falls, Vermont, 1893
Belvidere Daily Republican, Belvidere, Illinois, 1900
Berkshire County Eagle, Pittsfield, Massachusetts, 1865–1898
Berkshire (Evening) Eagle, Pittsfield, Massachusetts, 1865–1898, 1901, 1904–1905, 1907, 2006
Boston Globe, 1884–1895, 1897–1899
Boston Herald, 1886–1890, 1892–1894, 1897, 1906
Boston Journal, 1886, 1892
Boston Post, 1886, 1894
Bridgeton Evening News, Bridgeton, New Jersey, 1889, 1896
Bristol Herald, Bristol, Connecticut, 1897
Brooklyn (Daily) Times, 1893, 1904, 1907
Brooklyn Citizen, 1897, 1904–1907
Brooklyn Daily Eagle, 1888, 1890, 1892, 1894, 1897, 1899, 1904–1910, 1914
Bucks County Gazette, Bristol, Pennsylvania, 1890
Buffalo Commercial (Advertiser), 1886–1888, 1894–1995, 1900
Buffalo Courier, 1886–1888, 1892, 1894, 1900
Buffalo Enquirer, 1886–1888, 1896
Buffalo Evening News, 1886–1888, 1890, 1896, 1906, 1945
Buffalo Express, 1886–1888, 1894
Buffalo Sunday Morning News, 1886–1888
Buffalo Times, 1886–1888, 1897
Burlington Clipper, Burlington, Vermont, 1886
Burlington Free Press and Times, Burlington, Vermont, 1886, 1891–1893, 1897, 1899
Camden Daily Courier, Camden, New Jersey, 1903
Camden Daily (Post-)Telegram, Camden, New Jersey, 1887–1888, 1893, 1903
Canajoharie Wide-Awake Courier, Canajoharie, New York, 1889
Carbondale Leader, Carbondale, Pennsylvania, 1896
Catholic Union and Times, Buffalo, New York, 1887
The Chat, Brooklyn, 1904
Chattanooga Daily Times, 1890
Chicago Daily News, 1900
Chicago Record, 1899
Chicago Tribune, 1889, 1892, 1897–1900
Cincinnati Enquirer, 1888
Cincinnati Times-Star, 1887
Cleveland Gazette, 1886–1890, 1892–1893
Cleveland Leader, 1887, 1892, 1894, 1900
Columbia Republican, Hudson, New York, 1890
The Columbian, Bloomsburg, Pennsylvania, 1902
Commercial Tribune, Cincinnati, 1914
Connecticut Western News, Canaan, Connecticut, 1892
Cornell Daily Sun, Ithaca, New York, 1892
Cortland Semi-Weekly Standard, Cortland, New York, 1897
Courier-Journal, Louisville, Kentucky, 1888, 1891. 1914
Courier-News, Bridgewater, New Jersey, 1889
Cranbury Press, Cranbury, New Jersey, 1891
The Critic, Washington, D.C., 1887
Daily Commonwealth, Topeka, Kansas, 1886, 1888
Daily Evening Bulletin, Philadelphia, 1867
Daily Examiner, San Francisco, 1889
Daily Home News, New Brunswick, New Jersey, 1904, 1906–1907
Daily Inter Ocean, Chicago, 1888, 1893–1894, 1897–1898, 1900
Daily Journal, Logansport, Indiana, 1892
Daily Miners' Journal, Pottsville, Pennsylvania, 1893
Daily New Era, Lancaster, Pennsylvania, 1889, 1891, 1897
The (Daily) Post, Pittsburgh, 1886–1889, 1892, 1894, 1904
Daily Press, Newport News, Virginia, 1898
Daily Record, Long Branch, New Jersey, 1911
Daily Republican, Wilmington, Delaware, 1888
Daily Standard, Hazleton, Pennsylvania, 1892–1893
Daily Standard Union, Brooklyn, 1901–1911
Daily Star, Long Island City, New York, 1886
Daily Telegram, Adrian, Michigan, 1895

Daily Times, New Brunswick, New Jersey, 1892, 1910
Daily True American, Trenton, New Jersey, 1889, 1891–1893, 1900
Daily Wamegan, Wamego, Kansas, 1889
Democrat and Chronicle, Rochester, New York, 1886–1888, 1894, 1896–1897, 1901–1902
Detroit Free Press, 1886, 1889, 1895, 1899–1900
The Dickensonian, Carlisle, Pennsylvania, 1897
Dixon Evening Telegraph, Dixon, Illinois, 1899
East Liverpool Evening News Review, East Liverpool, Ohio, 1898–1899
Elizabethtown Post, Elizabethtown, New York, 1892
Elmira (Star-)Gazette, Elmira, New York, 1891–1893
Erie Daily Times, Erie, Pennsylvania, 1893, 1900
Evansville Journal, Evansville, Indiana, 1890
Evening Bulletin, Providence, Rhode Island, 1895
Evening Capital, Annapolis, Maryland, 1889
Evening Citizen, Ottawa, Ontario, 1900
Evening Express, Lock Haven, Pennsylvania, 1894
Evening Herald, Pottsville, Pennsylvania, 1895
Evening Herald, Shenandoah, Pennsylvania, 1893
Evening Journal, Jamestown, New York, 1902
Evening Journal, Wilmington, Delaware, 1889–1890, 1893, 1903
Evening Leader, Wilkes-Barre, Pennsylvania, 1886–1887
Evening News, Harrisburg, Pennsylvania, 1923
Evening Record, Hackensack, New Jersey, 1904, 1911
Evening Star, Washington, D.C., 1888–1890, 1892–1893
Evening Telegram, Providence, Rhode Island, 1886–1887
Evening Times, Washington, D.C., 1896
Every Evening, Wilmington, Delaware, 1907
Fall River Daily Globe, Fall River, Massachusetts, 1895, 1898
Fall River Daily Herald, Fall River, Massachusetts, 1887, 1895, 1898
Fall River Evening News, Fall River, Massachusetts, 1894–1895
Findlay Courier, Findlay, Ohio, 1893–1894
Fitchburg Daily Sentinel, Fitchburg, Massachusetts, 1906
Fort Wayne News, Fort Wayne, Indiana, 1899
Franklin Repository, Chambersburg, Pennsylvania, 1890
Free Press, Easton, Pennsylvania, 1890, 1893, 1902
Freeland Tribune, Freeland, Pennsylvania, 1893
The Freeman, Indianapolis, 1890, 1902, 1909, 1914
Freeman's Journal, Cooperstown, New York, 1893, 1896
Freeport Daily Journal, Freeport, Illinois, 1899
Frostburg Mining Journal, Frostburg, Maryland, 1886
The Gazette, Montreal, Quebec, 1896–1897
Glens Falls Times, Glens Falls, New York, 1887
Gloversville Daily Leader, Gloversville, New York, 1889
Gloversville Morning Herald, Gloversville, New York, 1913
Greenpoint Daily Star, Brooklyn, New York, 1905
Harrisburg Daily Independent, 1889–1894, 1902–1903
Harrisburg Telegram, 1889
Harrisburg Telegraph, 1889–1894, 1900, 1902–1904, 1914
Hartford Courant, 1886, 1889–1891, 1895–1898, 2006
Hartford Journal, 1886
Hazleton Plain Speaker, Hazleton, Pennsylvania, 1895
Hazleton Sentinel, Hazleton, Pennsylvania, 1889, 1897
Hollis Times, Hollis, New Hampshire, 1889
Hoxie Sentinel, Kenneth, Kansas, 1888
Hudson Daily Evening Register, Hudson, New York, 1889–1890
Indianapolis Journal, 1887–1888
Intelligencer Journal, Lancaster, Pennsylvania, 1867, 1889–1890, 1897
International Gazette, Black Rock, Buffalo, New York, 1888
Jackson Citizen Patriot, Jackson, Michigan, 1900
Janesville Daily Gazette, Janesville, Wisconsin, 1899
Jersey City News, Jersey City, New Jersey, 1891, 1893, 1897–1898, 1900, 1902
Jersey (Evening) Journal, Jersey City, New Jersey, 1867, 1886–1887, 1893, 1897–1900, 1902, 1904, 1907
Johnstown Daily Republican, Johnstown, New York, 1897
Kingston Daily Freeman, Kingston, New York, 1889
Knoxville Tribune, Knoxville, Tennessee, 1897
Leavenworth Advocate, Leavenworth, Kansas, 1889
Lebanon Daily News, Lebanon, Pennsylvania, 1889–1892
Lewiston Evening Journal, Lewiston, Maine, 1896
Lightning Express (Buffalo, New York, 1888
Lincoln Evening Call, Lincoln, Nebraska, 1888
Los Angeles Times, 1900
Lykens Register, Lykens, Pennsylvania, 1983
Mansfield Advertiser, Mansfield, Pennsylvania, 1894
The Mercury, Sandersville, Georgia, 1886
Meriden Daily Journal, 1886–1899
Meriden Daily Republican, 1883–1898
Meriden Morning Record, 1893, 1899
Middletown Daily Argus, Middletown, New York, 1889, 1893–1894
Middletown Daily Press, Middletown, New York, 1892–1893
Middletown Daily Times, Middletown, New York, 1893
Milwaukee Journal, 1900
Montclair Times, Montclair, New Jersey, 1896
Morning Call, Paterson, New Jersey, 1904, 1907, 1909
Morning Herald, Baltimore, 1890
Morning Herald, Hagerstown, Maryland, 1896
Morning Journal and Courier, New Haven, Connecticut, 1887, 1892
Morning News, Lancaster, Pennsylvania, 1897–1898
Morning News, Savannah, Georgia, 1891
Morning News, Wilmington, Delaware, 1903

The (Morning) Post, Camden, New Jersey, 1892, 1903
Morning Record, Traverse City, Michigan, 1897
Morning Tribune, Altoona, Pennsylvania, 1902, 1904, 1914
Muskegon Daily Chronicle, Muskegon Michigan, 1897
Nashville Banner, 1887
National Republican, Washington, D.C., 1887
New Haven Register, New Haven, Connecticut, 1886, 1890, 1892–1894
The New York Age, 1889–1890, 1909–1910, 1931, 1937
New York Amsterdam News, 1929, 1931–1932, 1962
New York Evening Journal, 1897
New York Herald, 1886, 1888, 1891–1893
New York Times, 1887, 1889, 1895–1896, 1904
New York Tribune, 1867, 1889–1891, 1893–1895, 1899–1900
Newark Daily Journal, Newark, New Jersey, 1887
Newark Sunday Call, Newark, New Jersey, 1893, 1898
Newport Daily News, Newport, Rhode Island, 1895, 1897
Newport Mercury, Newport, Rhode Island, 1895
News-Herald, Franklin, Pennsylvania, 1914
Norfolk Virginian, 1887, 1898
North Adams Transcript, North Adams, Massachusetts, 1884–1898, 1909, 1916, 1920, 1926, 1929
The North Carolinian, Elizabeth City, North Carolina, 1891
Ogdensburg Advance and St. Lawrence Weekly Democrat, Ogdensburg, New York, 1886
Ogdensburg Journal, Ogdensburg, New York, 1901
Oswego Daily Palladium, Oswego, New York, 1887, 1898
Passaic City Herald, Passaic, New Jersey, 1897, 1904
Passaic Daily News, Passaic, New Jersey, 1892–1893, 1899
Paterson Daily Press, Paterson, New Jersey, 1893
Paterson (Evening) News, Paterson, New Jersey, 1893–1894, 1899–1900, 1905
The Patriot, Harrisburg, Pennsylvania, 1889–1894, 1896, 1902–1903, 1914
Pawtucket Times, Pawtucket, Rhode Island, 1898
Perth Amboy Evening News, Perth Amboy, New Jersey, 1904, 1907, 1911
Philadelphia Evening Item, 1902
Philadelphia Inquirer, 1886, 1889–1903, 1905–1906
Philadelphia Press, 1890
Philadelphia Record, 1907
Philadelphia Tribune, 1916
Pittsburgh Courier, 1927, 1930, 1932, 1937
Pittsburg(h) Press, 1888, 1891–1894, 1898, 1900, 1913
Pittsfield Sun, Pittsfield, Massachusetts, 1864–1898
Plain Dealer, Cleveland, 1887, 1889, 1900
Plaindealer, Detroit, 1890
Plainfield Courier(-News), Plainfield, New Jersey, 1893, 1904–1905
Plainfield Daily Press, Plainfield, New Jersey, 1891
Plattsburgh Republican, Plattsburgh, New York, 1885–1886, 1892
Plattsburgh Sentinel, Plattsburgh, New York, 1885
Plattsburgh Telegram, Plattsburgh, New York, 1886
Pokeepsie Evening Enterprise, Poughkeepsie, New York, 1893
Port Jervis Union, Port Jervis, New York, 1890
Portland Daily Press, Portland, Maine, 1888, 1896
Post-Gazette, Pittsburgh, 1892
Potsdam Courier Freeman, Potsdam, New York, 1901
Pottsville Daily Republican, Pottsville, Pennsylvania, 1893, 1895
Poughkeepsie Daily Eagle, Poughkeepsie, New York, 1893, 1898
The Press, New York City, 1893, 1901, 1910
Press Herald, Pine Grove, Pennsylvania, 1888
The Princetonian, Princeton, New Jersey, 1891
Public Ledger, Memphis, Tennessee, 1887
Racine Daily Journal, Racine, Wisconsin, 1900
Reading Eagle, Reading, Pennsylvania, 1893, 1902
Reading Times (and Dispatch), Reading, Pennsylvania, 1889–1891, 1893, 1896, 1902
Reading World, Reading, Pennsylvania, 1893
Richmond Daily Dispatch, 1867
Rochester Post-Express, Rochester, New York, 1887
Rockford Daily Register-Gazette, Rockford, Illinois, 1899
Rocky Mountain News, Denver, 1888
Rogersville Herald, Rogersville, Tennessee, 1886
Rutland Daily Herald, Rutland, Vermont, 1892
Saginaw News, Saginaw, Michigan, 1899–1900
Saint Louis Globe-Democrat, 1887, 1894, 1899
Saint Louis Post-Dispatch, 1887, 1900
Saint Louis Republic, 1900
Salisbury Truth, Salisbury, North Carolina, 1889
San Francisco Call, 1893
Savannah Tribune, Savannah, Georgia, 1889
Scranton Republican, Scranton, Pennsylvania, 1891–1893, 1896
Scranton Times, Scranton, Pennsylvania, 1892
Scranton Tribune, Scranton, Pennsylvania, 1896
Solomon Valley Democrat, Minneapolis, Kansas, 1888
South Bend Tribune, South Bend, Indiana, 1898–1900
South Bergenite, Rutherford, New Jersey, 2013
Southington Weekly Phoenix, Southington, Connecticut, 1889, 1891
Spokesman-Review, Spokane, Washington, 1949
Sporting Life, 1886–1898, 1900, 1908
The Sporting News, 1887–1889, 1897
Sporting Times, 1887
Sportsman's Referee, 1887
Springfield Republican, Springfield, Massachusetts, 1882–1887, 1890, 1892, 1894, 1897–1898, 1906
Stamford Daily Advocate, Stamford, Connecticut, 1904
The Standard Gauge, Brewton, Alabama, 1889
Sturgeon Bay Advocate, Sturgeon Bay, Wisconsin, 1899
The Sun, Baltimore, 1887, 1890
The Sun, New York City, 1886–1900, 1916
Sun-Gazette, Williamsport, Pennsylvania, 1891
Sunday Herald, Syracuse, New York, 1889
Sunday Herald, Washington, D.C., 1890–1891

Sunday Truth, Buffalo, New York, 1886–1888
Syracuse (Post) Standard, Syracuse, New York, 1886–1887, 1897, 1904
Syracuse Courier, Syracuse, New York, 1888
The Times, Philadelphia, 1887–1903
Times-Union, Albany, 1899
Times Union, Brooklyn, 1889
Trenton Sunday Advertiser, Trenton, New Jersey, 1889, 1903
Trenton Times, Trenton, New Jersey, 1886–1898, 1900, 1903
Troy (Daily) Times, Troy, New York, 1878, 1885, 1890
Tuscaloosa Gazette, Tuscaloosa, Alabama, 1897
Utica Daily Press, Utica, New York, 1890
Utica Herald, Utica, New York, 1887
Valley Gleaner, Lee, Massachusetts, 1885
Washington Bee, 1889
Washington Post, 1887–1890, 1892–1895, 1898
Waterbury Evening Democrat, Waterbury, Connecticut, 1888, 1891–1892, 1900–1901
Watertown Daily Times, Watertown, New York, 1887, 1893, 1901
The Weekly Wisconsin, Milwaukee, 1895
Wellsboro Agitator, Wellsboro, Pennsylvania, 1895, 1902
Wheeling Daily Intelligencer, Wheeling, West Virginia, 1888, 1913
Wheeling Register, Wheeling, West Virginia, 1887, 1896
Wilkes-Barre News, Wilkes-Barre, Pennsylvania, 1891
Wilkes-Barre Record, Wilkes-Barre, Pennsylvania, 1896
Windham County Reformer, Brattleboro, Vermont, 1895
Worcester Spy, Worcester, Massachusetts, 1895–1896
The World, New York City, 1888, 1890, 1892–1893, 1896–1897, 1899–1900
Yale News, New Haven, Connecticut, 1886
Yonkers Gazette, Yonkers, New York, 1890
Yonkers Herald, Yonkers, New York, 1905–1906
Yonkers Statesman, Yonkers, New York, 1901
The York Daily, York, Pennsylvania, 1893, 1896
York Dispatch, York, Pennsylvania, 1889–1891
York Gazette, York, Pennsylvania, 1889–1891, 1896

Selected Articles

Ahrens, Art. "Crowds of Days Gone By," 1972 Baseball Research Journal. https://sabr.org/journal/article/crowds-of-days-gone-by/.
Amore, Dom. "For Baseball Pioneer, Meriden a Key Stop," *Hartford* (Connecticut) *Courant,* July 30, 2006: A1, A11.
Ashwill, Gary. "Benjamin Harrison Sees the Big Gorhams." https://agatetype.typepad.com/agate_type/2014/05/benjamin-harrison-sees-the-big-gorhams.html.
Caylor, O.P. "The Color Line Again," *Erie* (Pennsylvania) *Daily Times,* September 21, 1893: 2.
Chrisman, David F. "Early RBI Leaders in the International League," *Baseball Research Journal,* 2003: 40.
Clark, Robert A. "Communication," *North Adams Transcript,* March 22, 1944: 9.
Coyden, T.M. "The Binghamton Club," *The Sporting News,* April 23, 1887: 5.
Dupont, Kevin Paul. "Finally Touching Home: Pittsfield-born African-American Grant to be Inducted into Hall of Fame Today," *Boston Globe,* July 30, 2006: C1.
Gentile, Derek. "A Place in Baseball History," *Berkshire Eagle,* July 31, 2006: 1.
Heitz, Tom. "Sol White & Frank Grant Played for the Cuban Giants," *The Oil Can* (Cooperstown Rotary Club, Vol. 83, No. 47), June 6, 2006: 1–3.
Lamar, E.B., Jr. "Lamar's Figures," *Sporting Life,* November 5, 1898: 6.
Leith, Rod. "Frank Grant: The Baseball Great Who Remained in Obscurity," *South Bergenite* (Rutherford, New Jersey), September 26, 2013: B3.
Malloy, Jerry. "Out at Home: Baseball Draws the Color Line, 1887," *The National Pastime,* Society for American Baseball Research, Fall 1983: 14–28.
Mancuso, Peter. "July 14, 1887: The color line is drawn in baseball." https://sabr.org/gamesproj/game/july-14-1887-the-color-line-is-drawn/.
Mayer, Bob. "The Asylum Base Ball Club: The Great Reunion Game, September 29, 1905," *The National Pastime: Baseball in the Big Apple,* Society for American Baseball Research, 2017. https://sabr.org/journal/article/the-asylum-baseball-club-the-great-reunion-game-september-29-1905/.
McKenna, Brian. "Charlie Grant." https://sabr.org/bioproj/person/charlie-grant/.
_____. "Frank Grant." https://sabr.org/bioproj/person/frank-grant/.
Moses, Alvin, and Sol White, "Fleet Walker Was Catcher on Toledo Mudhen's Nine," *The Afro-American* (Baltimore), February 6, 1932: 15.
O'Gara, Roger. "Fair or Foul," *Berkshire Eagle* (Pittsfield, Massachusetts), August 11, 1970: 16.
Overmyer, James E. "The Unhappy Odyssey of a Great Ballplayer," *Berkshire Eagle* (Pittsfield, Massachusetts), February 5, 1990: 1.
Pollard, Fritz. "The Story of Negro Baseball," *New York Amsterdam News,* May 26, 1962: 35.
Rowell, Jeffrey Clarke. "Moses Fleetwood Walker and the Establishment of a Color Line in Major League Baseball, 1884–1887," *The Atlanta Review of Journalism History* (Volume 12), Spring 2015: 97–121.
Thiessen, Dennis. "Radical Changes to the Playing Rules: The 1886 Winter Meetings," *Base Ball's 19th Century "Winter" Meetings* (Phoenix: Society for American Baseball Research, 2018), 247–259.
Thorn, John. "A Brief History of the Pitching Distance," February 27, 2015. https://ourgame.mlblogs.com/a-brief-history-of-the-pitching-distance-3210e7874d5c.
_____. "The Pittsfield 'Baseball' Bylaw of 1791:

What It Means," August 3, 2011. https://ourgame.mlblogs.com/the-pittsfield-baseball-bylaw-of-1791-what-it-means-940a3ccf08db.

_____. "Safe at Home," June 18, 2011. https://ourgame.mlblogs.com/safe-at-home-97756ecc6861.

Turner, Steve. "Berkshire Blacks: The Struggle for Equality Began Two Centuries Ago," *Berkshire Eagle*, August 28, 1976: 18.

White, Sol. "Our Baseball Leagues," *New York Amsterdam News*, February 20, 1929: 6.

_____. "Sol White Recalls," *The New York Age*, January 17, 1931: 6.

Willis, Jessica. "Game, Fame Catch the Spotlight," *Berkshire Eagle*, August 11, 2006: B1.

Wilson, W. Rollo. "Eastern Snapshot," *Pittsburgh Courier*, January 16, 1926: 12.

_____. "Sport Shots," *Pittsburgh Courier*, February 6, 1932: section 2, page 4.

Books

Brown, Irene Quenzler, and Richard D. Brown. *The Hanging of Ephraim Wheeler: A Story of Rape, Incest, and Justice in Early America*. Cambridge: The Belknap Press of Harvard University Press, 2003.

Browne, Paul. *The Coal Barons Played Cuban Giants: A History of Early Professional Baseball in Pennsylvania, 1889–1896*. Jefferson, NC: McFarland, 2013.

Brunson, James E., III. *Black Baseball, 1858–1900: A Comprehensive Record of the Teams, Players, Managers, Owners and Umpires*. Jefferson, NC: McFarland, 2019.

Chadwick, Henry, editor. *Spalding's Base Ball Guide and Official League Book for 1890*. Chicago: A.G. Spalding & Bros., 1890.

Child, Hamilton. *Gazetteer of Berkshire County, Mass., 1725–1885*. Syracuse: Syracuse Journal, 1885.

Clark, Dick, and Larry Lester, eds., *The Negro Leagues Book*. Cleveland: Society for American Baseball Research, 1994.

Heaphy, Leslie A. *The Negro Leagues, 1869–1960*. Jefferson, NC: McFarland, 2003.

Hogan, Lawrence D. *Shades of Glory: The Negro Leagues and the Story of African-American Baseball*. Washington, D.C.: National Geographic Society, 2006.

James, Bill. *The Politics of Glory*. New York: Macmillan, 1994.

Kissel, Tony, "Leading Off: The Cuban Giants." *The Negro Leagues Were Major Leagues: Historians Reappraise Black Baseball*. Jefferson, NC: McFarland, 2019, 140–146.

Litwack, Leon F. *North of Slavery: The Negro in the Free States, 1790–1860*. Chicago: University of Chicago Press, 1960.

McCormack, Shaun. *Willie Mays*. New York: Rosen, 2003.

Official Programme of Exercises and Illustrated Inaugural History Commemorating the Inauguration of Theodore Roosevelt as President of the United States, Charles W. Fairbanks as Vice-President of the United States. Washington, D.C.: Otto A. Sontag, Publisher, 1905.

Overmyer, James E. "Frank Grant," *Baseball History No. 4: An Annual of Original Baseball Research*. Westport, CT: Meckler, 1991, 24–38.

_____, Kevin Larkin, Larry Moore, and Tom Daly. *Baseball in the Berkshires*. Stockbridge, MA: Melville Press, 2016.

Perry, Bliss. *And Gladly Teach*. Boston: Houghton Mifflin, 1935.

_____. *The Plated City*. New York: Charles Scribner & Sons, 1895.

Peterson, Robert. *Only the Ball Was White: A History of Legendary Black Players and All-Black Professional Teams*. New York: Oxford University Press, 1992.

Smith, J.E.A. *The History of Pittsfield, Massachusetts, from the Year 1800 to the Year 1876*. Springfield, MA: C.W. Bryan & Co., 1876.

Solomon, Burt. *Where They Ain't: The Fabled Life and Untimely Death of the Original Baltimore Orioles, the Team That Gave Birth to Modern Baseball*. New York: Main Street Books, 2000.

Twenty-Ninth Report to the Legislature of Massachusetts Relating to the Registry and Return of Births, Marriages and Deaths in the Commonwealth, for the Year ending December 31, 1870. Boston: Wright & Potter, 1872.

Vital Records of Hinsdale, Massachusetts: To the Year 1850. Boston: New-England Historic Genealogical Society, 1902.

White, Sol. *Sol White's History of Colored Base Ball with Other Documents on the Early Game*. Ed. Jerry Malloy. Lincoln: University of Nebraska Press, 1995.

Index

Numbers in *bold italics* indicate pages with illustrations

Abbey, Bert 140
Abbott (1904 Cuban Giants teammate) 190–191, 194, 253n10
Adams, Massachusetts 18, 22
Adams Renfrews 22–23, 39, 163
Addison (1909 Watkins' Giants teammate, 1910 New York Colored Giants) 198, 199
Adore, Elizabeth (son's maternal grandmother) 156
Adore, Mary Elizabeth *see* Wilson, Mary Adore
Adore, William J. (son's maternal grandfather or stepgrandfather) 125, 137, 156, 196, 236n11, 244n83
Adrian, Michigan 128, 158, 164; *see also* Page Fence Giants
Albany Capital Citys (Black team) 97–98, 230n96
Albany, New York 23, 24, 65, 68, 69, 74, 76, 91–92, 96, 97, 98, 103, 104, 138, 172, 227n28, 229n67
Alberts, Gus 53–55, 60
All-Virginia (Black) team 184
All-Washingtons (Black team) 143
Allen, Edward 61, 222n11
Allentown, Pennsylvania 112, 113, 120, 171, 232n69
Allertons (New Jersey semi-pro team) 101, 132, 133, 135, 139–140, 141, 143, 238n38
Altoona, Pennsylvania 99, 104, 105, 106, 108, 110, 113, 123, 124, 184, 252n116
American Association 4, 22, 31, 34, 35, 41, 42, 49, 59, 62–64, 71, 82, 88, 94, 116, 117, 123, 131, 132, 139, 152, 229n78
American League 164, 177, 181, 183, 184, 185, 192
Amole, Doc 165
Amsterdam, New York 92, 229n67

Anderson, Dave 94
Anderson, Pete 160
Andrews (1907 Watkins' Colored Stars teammate) 195
Andrus, Wyman 79, 86
Anson, Cap 52, 194
Ansonia (Connecticut) Cuban Giants 124, 126–128, 237n30
Asbury Park, New Jersey 162, 190, 191, 229n80
Ashe, P.J. 231n33
Ashtabula, Ohio 179
Ashwill, Gary 153, 199, 243n51, 254n47, 255n67
Asylums *see* Middletown Asylum Base Ball Club
Atchison Blade (Black newspaper in Kansas) 4
Atkinson, Al 67
Atlantic Association (1890) 4, 100, 102, 113–114, 115–116, 117, 118, 119, 120, 121–122, 123, 124, 126, 236n2
Atlantic City, New Jersey 125, 155, 173, 176, 184, 185, 196, 202
Atlantic City Collegians 173, 185
Atlantic League 160, 164, 165, 166, 170, 171, 174, 175, 247n10, 249n44
Atwood, Theresa (great-greatgranddaughter of Frank Grant) x
Auburn, New York 166
Auster (1904 Opequon Giants/Orpheum Giants teammate) 190
Australia trips (proposed) 99, 158, 159

Bachmann, Louis 203
Bachmann, Norbert 203
Bagley, Eugene 26, 46, 94, 101, 214n9, 214n10
Bailey (1900 Cuban Giants teammate) 178
Bainbridge, New York 166

Baker (Plattsburgh Nameless teammate) 23
Baker, Norm 117
Baker, Samuel R. 18–19, 212n70
Baldwin, Mark 157
Baltic Avenue, Atlantic City, New Jersey 125, 196
Baltimore Colored Giants (1906) 195, 197
Baltimore Orioles (American Association team) 42, 59, 117, 119
Baltimore Orioles (1890 Atlantic Association team) 113, 114, 115, 117, 118, 119–120, 233n93, 234n101
Barber, Lizzie 137
Barnes, Ross 5, 177
Barnie, Billy 4, 59, 115, 118, 119, 234n101
Barnes Colored Americans (1901 Black team in Pittsburgh) 182
Barrett, Jimmy 172
Barton, George 93, 129, 130, 131, 136, 137, 146, 237n32
Barton, William 21, 212n4, 213n8
Basbra (possibly Barber, 1910 New York Colored Giants) 199
Bashra (possibly Barber, 1910 New York Colored Giants) 199
Basto (Greylocks teammate) 22
Bates, John 189
Bath, New York 185
Baxter, Frank 112
Beard family (British ancestors) 9
Beatin, Ed 68
Beaulieu, Tom (Frank Grant fictionalized) 15
Beebe, Harry (ice polo teammate) 246n55, 247n98
Belcourt (1897 Montreal Nationals) 167

263

Index

Bell (1890 Pacific Slope tour teammate) 99
Bell (1901 Cuban Giants teammate) 182
Bell (1906 Baltimore Colored Giants teammate) 195
Bell (1910 Gorhams teammate) 198
Bell, Frank 127, 139, 228n66, 237n30
Bell, P. (1900 Chicago Columbia Giants teammate) 181
Bell, William 178, 184, 185, 187, 195, 250n73, 250n80
Belvidere, Illinois 180
Bender, Chief 91
Berkshire County, Massachusetts 7, 8, 9, 12, 16, 18, 19, 20, 22, 23, 24, 164, 184, 190, 251n97
Berkshire Hotel 9, 10, 210n15
Best (1905 Cuban Giants teammate) 192
Beverly National Cemetery, Beverly, New Jersey (only known son's gravesite) 206
Binga, William 181, 185, 187
Binghamton, New York 36–37, 41, 43, 45, 47, 49, 51, 60, 139, 220n76
Bishop (Albany Capital Citys teammate) 230n96
Bishop, Bill 43, 83, 85
Bittman, Henry 71, 224n74
"Black Dunlap" (nickname) *see* "Colored Dunlap"
Blackintons (Berkshire County team) 20, 147, 163
Blaine Invincible Republican Club (Black political organization) 144
Bloomsburg, Pennsylvania 184, 192
Bloomsburg (Pennsylvania) Literary Institute and State Normal School 184
Boggs, Wade 6, 77
Bolen (1902 Philadelphia Giants teammate) 184
Booker, Billy 191, 192, 198, 255n60
Booker's Giants (1909 Black team) 198
Boone, James E. 197
Borton *see* Barton, George
Boston 26, 50, 60, 152
Boston (National League team) 44–45, 87, **87**, 100, 102, 142, 166
Boston Americans (Red Sox) 184
Boston Colored Monarchs 153, 241n24
Boston Resolutes (1887 National Colored Base Ball League team) 50, 228n66
Bowen, Cy 166
Bowen, Ed 156
Bowers, Herbert 149
Bowes, Frank 139, 143, 239n57
Boyd, Ben 86, 87, 100, 112, 127, 139, 140, 144, 218n25, 225n108, 226n113, 228n66, 237n30
Boyhood Reminiscences: Pictures of New England Life in the Olden Times in Williamstown (memoir) 13; *see also* Danforth, Keyes
Braden, James N. 113, 119, 122
Bradley, Phil 192, 196, 254n46
Bragg, Jesse 198
Brattleboro, Vermont 149
Bressette (Greylocks teammate) 22
Bridgeport, Connecticut 30, 33, 44
Bridgeton, New Jersey 158, 162
Bright, John M. 84, 90, 95–96, 98, 99, 100–103, 109, 126, 136–137, 138, 145, 146, 150, 153, 154, 159–160, 161, 163–164, 165, 167, 168, 169, 170, 178, 181, 182, 184, 189, 201, 227n30, 230n19, 236n2, 236n29, 245n40, 246n59, 247n96
Brightons (1904 white team) 191, 194, 253n23, 253n24, 253n28, 254n54
Bristol, Connecticut 127, 166, 173, 246n73
Brockton, Massachusetts 171
Brokaw (1906 Baltimore Colored Giants teammate) 195
Brooklyn, New York 160, 183, 185, 187, 194, 195, 196, 197, 198, 199
Brooklyn Colored Giants (1908) *see* Brooklyn X-Giants
Brooklyn Field Club (1901 opponent) 182
Brooklyn Giants (1907 Black team led by Watkins) 196
Brooklyn Royal Giants (1907 Black team) 194, 195, 196, 254n46; *see also* Royal Giants (1904 Black team in New York)
Brooklyn X-Giants (1907–1908 Black team) 196, 197
Brouthers, Dan 27, 58, 68
Brown (1890 Cuban Giants teammate) 101
Brown (1900 Cuban Giants teammate) 178
Brown, Delores (great granddaughter) *see* Watson, Delores Brown
Brown, Dorothy Grant (only known grandchild) 125, 202
Brown, John A. 189
Brown, Larry 204–205
Brown, Louisa (mother-in-law) 203; *see also* Grant, Malvania Holden Morris
Brown, Tom 5, 177
Browne, Paul 95
Bruley (Plattsburgh Nameless teammate) 23
Brunswicks (Berkshire County team) 22–23
Bryant, George (ice polo teammate) 246n55, 247n98
Bryant, Frank 204
Bryant, Geraldine 204
Bryant, Wayland 204
Bubser, George 248n35
Buck (1901, 1904 Cuban Giants teammate) 182, 191
Buckley, John 161
Buckner, Harry 181, 185, 187, 195, 254n46
Buegner *see* Buckner, Harry
Buffalo (National League team) 27, 35, 62, 74, 75
Buffalo, New York 35–78, 80, 81, 83, 85, 88, 97, 102, 111, 127, 137, 155, 193, 206, 216n11, 2156n12, 217n41, 219n33, 221n107, 222n121
Buffalo Baseball Hall of Fame (1988) 206
Buffalo Bisons (International League/Association) 1, 4, 5, 24, 27, 35–78, 79, 80, 81, 82, 83, 85, 88, 92, 97, 124, 137, 160, 166, 172, 177, 189, 190, 193, 197, 206, 220n81, 221n107
Buffalo Clippers (amateur or semi-pro team) 60, 61, 216n15
Buffalo Courier (newspaper) 75, 142
Buffalo Enquirer (newspaper) 6, 127, 217n42
Buffalo Evening News/Sunday Morning News 59, 72, 81, 193, 206, 231n31
Buffalo Express (newspaper) **66**, 75, 80–81, 85–86
Buffalo Queen Citys (amateur or semi-pro team) 61, 222n7, 222n8
Buffalo Travelers (amateur or semi-pro team) 37, 60, 61, 216n15, 222n8
Burdock, Jack 5, 177
Burlington, New Jersey 94
Burlington, Vermont 31, 132
Burnett, Tex 204–205

Index

Burnham, Walter 25, 26, 27, 30, 116, 172, 214n13
Butler (1904 Colored Giants teammate) 191, 192, 253n12
Butler (1911 New York Colored Giants) 199
Butts (teammate(s) in 1900s) 178, 191, 194

California trips (proposed) 50, 60, 153, 156, 158, 159, 175
Calihan, Tom 41, **48**
Callahan, William 21, 212n5, 213n8
Camden, New Jersey 136, 139, 141, 148, 154, 184, 188, 190
Camden Daily Telegram 4, 148
Canajoharie, New York 92, 229n67
Candee, Cassius C. 77
Cape May, New Jersey 94, 132, 135, 237n23
Capital Colored All-Americans (Lansing, Michigan) 158; *see also* Colored All-Americans
Carbondale, Pennsylvania 160
Carlisle, Pennsylvania 161, 165
Carlisle Indian Industrial School 161
Carrillo (1904 New York Colored Giants teammate) 191–192; *see also* Corrilo (1909 Booker's Giants teammate)
Carrington, Cambell 144, 240n83
Carroll, Cliff 78, 79, 80, 86
Carsey, Kid 167, 168
Carter, "Chesty" 177
Carter, Charles "Kid" 166, 184, 185, 198, 246n73
Caruthers, Bobby 181
Cary (1894 Cuban Giants teammate) 153
Cary, John 153
Cassopolis, Michigan 180
Castone, George William 149, 241n22
Catto, Harry 93, 146, 179
Caylor, O.P. 152
Chadbourne, Albert Hopkins 14
Chadwick, Henry 116
Chamberlain, Ed 222n4, 240n88, 244n7; *see also* Chambers
Chamberlins (1898 Black team in Virginia) 171, 247n7, 247n8
Chamberlins *see* Hampton (Virginia) Chamberlins
Chambers 60, 222n4
Chapman, Jack 4, 35, 36–37, 39–40, 41, 42, 43, 46, 47, **48**, 49, 51, 57, 58, 61, 68, 70, 71, 73, 75, 77, 78, 81, 85, 86, 97, 142, 161, 173, 219n41, 249n48
Charleston, Oscar 204–205
Chase (1911 New York Colored Giants) 199
Chase, Hal 254n50
Chesbro, Jack 154–155, 162–163, 192, 193, 244n11
Cheshire, Massachusetts 8, 210n7
Chester (Albany Capital Citys teammate) 230n96
Chester, Pennsylvania 141, 177, 186
Chicago 155, 175
Chicago (National League team) 131
Chicago Columbia Giants (Black team) 176–177, 178, 179–180, 181–182
Chicago Edgars (baseball team) 156
Chicago Unions/Union Giants (Black team) 156, 164, 168, 174, 175–176, 179, 180, 181–182
Chicago White Stockings (1900 American League) 181
Christ, Fr. Adam 130, 237n11
Cincinnati Red Stockings (American Association team) 62–63, 88
Cincinnati Stars (1914 Black team) 201, 255n3
Civil War 7, 8, 9, 10, 17, 106
Clancy (Trenton police detective) 135
Clark (1890 Cuban Giants) 100
Clark, Robert A. 14
Clarke, Nat 197
Clarkson, Dad 155
Cleveland (National League team) 167, 173
Cleveland Gazette (Black newspaper) 32, 89, **97**, 117, 137, 149, 217n33, 218n24, 227n31, 230n93, 233n93, 234n112, 241n24, 243n49
Cleveland, Pres. Grover 84, 227n29
Clifton, New Jersey (cemetery site) 205
Clippers (Berkshire County team) 21
Cogan, Dick 191
Cole, William 160
College Football Hall of Fame 144
College of the Holy Cross (Worcester, Massachusetts) 157–158, 161, 170, 172
Collins, Chub 46, 50, 77
Collins, Danny 15, 211n48
Collins, Jimmy 155
Collins, Nat Fred 92, 99, 102, 197, 228n66, 229n67, 229n73, 229n74, 230n9
color line (banning Black players) 5, 11, 38, 51–52, 56, 59, 69, 89–90, 113–114, 128, 152, 157, 172, 182, 190, 194, 209n3, 217n28, 217n42, 218n4, 220n69, 220n77, 221n90, 221n103, 226n20, 227n39, 229n76, 243n48, 246n73
Colored All-Americans (1889) 91–92, 93, 94, 101, 102, 228n66, 229n72, 229n74, 229n79, 229n80; *see also* Capital Colored All-Americans (Lansing, Michigan)
"colored championship" 93, 100, 162, 164, 168, 171, 174, 175, 181, 186, 246n56, 246n59, 250n60, 251n89; of Greater New York 196, 199
"Colored Dunlap" (nickname) 38, 42, 44, 58, 86, 88, 92, 103, 104, 122, 131, 137, 189, 217n31, 243n52, 251n91, 252n125
Colored Giants (1904 team, possibly New York Colored Giants) 191; *see also* New York Colored Giants
Colored Opequon Giants of Savannah, Georgia *see* Opequon Giants ("Colored") of Savannah, Georgia
Colored Stars (1910 team) 199
Comee (unknown 1887 Buffalo teammate) 219n28
Comstock, Marc 20
Connecticut State League 25, 124, 126, 128, 141, 142, 149, 154, 158, 166, 173, 236n20
Connell (unknown 1887 Buffalo teammate) 219n28
Coogan, John 33
Cooper, George (Pottsville, Pennsylvania police officer) 157
Cooperstown, New York 149, 162, 206, 241n20
Corbin, Moses 253n15
Cornell University 139, 239n59
Corning, New York 242n39
Cornish (1891 Gorhams teammate) 238n28
Corrilo (1909 Booker's Giants teammate) 198; *see also* Carrillo (1904 New York Colored Giants teammate)
Cortland, New York 167
Country Club of Pittsfield 10
Cox, John 126, 131, 235n140, 237n12

Crane, Ed 53–55
Crane, Sam 131
Crane, T. (Greylocks teammate) 22
Criollos (1900 baseball team in Cuba) 178
Crocker, Harriet "Hattie" *see* Grant, Harriet "Hattie" Crocker
Cronin, Jack 172
CSL *see* Connecticut State League
Cuba (1900) 177–178, 179
Cuban Giants (Genuine, Original) 4, 19, 30, 42, *44*, 50, 56, 76, 77, 78, 79, 80–82, 84–86, *86*–89, *89*–96, 97–98, 100–103, 104–105, 106, 108, 109, 110, 114, 123, 124, 126–128, 129, *130*, 131, 132, 133, 136–137, 138, 139–141, *141*–144, 145–*156*, 156–163, 164–*168*, 168–169, 170, 175, 178–180, *180*–181, 182, *182*–184, 189–190, 192–193, 194, 195, 196, 197, 201, 211n48, 211n54, 215n46, 217n31, 218n25, 225n108, 226n113, 226n116, 226n30, 226n31, 228n58, 228n67, 229n73, 230n96, 231n19, 231n22, 231n22, 231n35, 231n40, 232n43, 237n11, 239n63, 240n82, 240n6, 241n20, 241n24, 241n28, 242n39, 242n42–242n45, 243n56, 244n11, 245n23, 245n40, 245n43, 245n44, 245n46, 246n59, 246n62, 246n73, 248n21, 249n44, 251n98, 253n24
Cuban Giants Juniors (Harrisburg, Pennsylvania) 19; *see also* Young Cuban Giants (Trenton, New Jersey)
Cuban National League 177
Cuban Stars (1907 team, players actually from Cuba) 196
Cuban X-Giants 159, 161, 163, 164, 165, 167, *168*–169, 170–178, *178*–*179*, 179, 180, 186–188, 192, *193*
Cumberland Valley League (1896) 162
Curry, Wesley 76, 225n101
Curtiss, Irving (aka Jim) 20, 22–23
Cushman, Charles H. (Toronto manager) 39, 53–55, 124, 221n90, 236n8
Cushman, Charles W. (Buffalo Baseball Company) 39, 51, 77
Cypress Hill Cemetery, Long Island, New York 199

Daily, Ed 44, 62
Dale, Norman (ice polo teammate) 246n55
Dallas, Walter 72, 224n78
Dalton, Massachusetts 9, 10, 12, 18, 21–22, 168, 210n14
Dalton Lone Stars (Berkshire County team) 21–22
Danforth, Keyes 13–14, 104, 211n40
Daniels, Charles 233n97
Daniels, Pete 114–115, 233n97
Dartmouth College (New Hampshire) 175
Davis, Ambrose 60, 91, 99, 129, 137, 138, 139, 228n66, 239n55
Davis, George 91, 229n74, 230n94, 230n96
Davis, John "Daisy" 35–36
Davis, William (ice polo teammate) 247n98
Dawson (1905–1906 New York Colored Giants teammate) 192, 194, 198, 199, 253n32, 254n40
Day (1901 Cuban Giants teammate) 182
Day (1902 Philadelphia Giants teammate) 185
Day, Bill 160
Day, Eddie 164, 165
Day, the Rev. William Howard 236n11, 244n83
Dean (1890 teammate) 230n9
Dean, William 108, 227n44
Dee, Jim 61, 65, 222n11
Delaney (1907 Watkins' Colored Stars, 1908 Brooklyn X-Giants teammate) 195, 197
Delavan, Wisconsin 181
Dell/Dill, Susan 18
De Mond (1897 Cuban Giants teammate) 168
Demont (1904 Cuban Giants teammate) 191
Denny, Jerry 28
Detroit, Michigan 85, 170, 181, 249n59
Detroit Plaindealer (Black newspaper) 117
Detroit Tigers (Western League) 177
Detroit Wolverines (National League team) 27, 68–69, 78, 82, 222n10
Devinney (1893 Cuban Giants player) 242n39
Devoe, Josh 204–205
Devoe, Wallace 191, 192, 194, 198–199, 253n12
DeWitt, Edward 18–19
Dickinson College (Carlisle, Pennsylvania) 165

Dick'son (likely Dickinson; 1892 Cuban Giants teammate) 240n88
Dixon, George (boxer) 4, 151–152
Dixon, Illinois 176
Dorow (1909 New York Colored Giants teammate) 198
Douglass, Albert 140, 237n30, 240n73
Douglass, Frederick 4, 143, *144*
Dowd, Tommy 155
Dowling, Pete 181
Doyle, Jack 6
Doyle, Patrick 93
Drauby/Drawby (Jake?) 236n14
Dudley (1904 Opequon Giants/Orpheum Giants teammate) 190
Dugdale, Dan 57
Dumont (1901 Cuban Giants teammate) 182
Dun Building (Buffalo, New York landmark) 217n41
Duncan, Evelina (cousin) *see* Lansing, Evelina Duncan
Duncan, John Perry (uncle) 12, 14
Duncan, Lucy Hoose (aunt) 12, 14
Dunkle, Davey 154
Dunlap, Fred 38–39, 62, 217n34; *see also* "Colored Dunlap" (nickname)
Dunn, Steve 35, 39, 61
Dwyer, Edward 21, 212n5
Dwyer, Frank 21

Eagan, Bill 107, 112, 115, 116, 123, 131, 234n98
Eason, Mal 196
East, Hattie 61
East Ridgelawn Cemetery (Clifton, New Jersey) 205, *205*
Easterday, Henry 47, *48*
Eastern Association (previously 1890 International League) 123, 124, 126, 129, 131
Eastern Inter-State League 99, 103, 104, 105–106, 107–108, 109, 111–112, 113, 114, 116, 120, 121–122, 123, 126, 232n70, 233n72, 236n14
Eastern League 25–27, 29–31, 33–34, 41, 44, 82, 140, 155, 160, 161, 164, 165, 166, 167, 170, 171, 215n46, 215n47, 216n66
Easton, Pennsylvania 92–93, 95, 99, 103, 108, 110, 147, 151, 153, 161, 185
Educational Home

(Philadelphia institution for Native Americans0 91
Egan, C. 205
Eggler, Dave 216n5
EISL *see* Eastern Inter-State League
Elkhorn, Wisconsin 174, 248n36
Ellis, F.D. 197
Elmira, New York 26, 139, 214n9
Emory (1908 Brooklyn X-Giants teammate) 197
Enfield, Connecticut 207
England trip (proposed) 158, 159
Erie, Pennsylvania 180
Evans (1889 Colored All-Americans teammate) 92, 228n66, 229n74, 237n32
Evansville, Wisconsin 176

Fagan/Fagen (1889 Colored All-Americans teammate) 229n67, 230n9
Fall River, Massachusetts 155, 157, 159, 171, 172
Fanning, Jack **48**, 53, 60, 68–69, 75, 77
Farrell, Jack 141
Farrell, William Edgar 185; *see also* Ferrell (1909 Frank Grant's Colored Stars)
Farrington, James 99–100, 101, 103–104, 105, 107–109, 110, 114, 117, 123, 124, 126, 129, 131, 144, 232n61
Farrington, Lottie 126
Farrow, John (umpire) 32, 214n28
Fay (Trenton police officer) 135
Feat, Harry (father-in-law) 191; *see also* Grant, Aurelia Moore
Fee, Jack 144
Fern, Joe 6, 16
Ferrell (1909 Frank Grant's Colored Stars) 198; *see also* Farrell, William Edgar
Ferson, Alex 84
Fiall (1911 New York Colored Giants) 199
Fields, Jocko 39
Fields, Lena *see* Grant, Lena Fields
54th Regiment Massachusetts Volunteer Infantry (all Black) 9
Findlay, Ohio 154, 155
Finke, George 151
Finlayson, Pembroke 196
Finnegan/Finnigan (1901 white teammate on Cuban Giants) 183, 251n96

Firle, Michael 37
Fisher (1889 Colored All-Americans teammate) 92, 94, 198, 229n67, 229n74
Fisher (1909 Watkins' Giants teammate) 198
Fisher, Chauncey 147, 181
Fitch-Hoose House 9
Fitchburg, Massachusetts 195
Fitzgerald, M.E. 100, 230n2, 236n2
Florida 79, 81, 84
Flushing, New York 139, 143
Flynn, James 69–70, 74, 75
Flynn, John 21, 22, 212n4, 212n5, 213n8
Foley, Edward 156
Fond du Lac, Wisconsin 174
Fonda, New York 97
Foote, Emily Grant (descendant of Clarence Grant) x, 9, 203, 207, 209ch1n3; *see also* Royston, Marion Grant
Foote-Minich, Carolyn (descendant of Clarence Grant) x
Footes, Robert 185, 187, 195, 197
Fordham College (New York City) 175
Foresters (1901 Berkshire County team) 251n97
Fort Edward Stars 24
Fort Wayne, Indiana 128, 176
Foster, Rube 186–187, 188
Foulkrod, Frank 115, 118
Fowler, Bud (real name John W. Jackson, Jr.) 38, 41, 45–46, 47, 49, 50, 51, 60, 64, 82, 83, 128, 155, 158, 182, 197, 220n60, 221n90, 255n59
Fox, Bill 142
Franas (1910 New York Colored Giants) 199
France *see* Paris, France
Frances (1910 New York Colored Giants) 199
Francis, Bill (1910 New York Colored Giants) 199
Frank Grant's Colored Stars (1909) 198
Franklin (1908 Brooklyn X-Giants teammate) 197
Freeman (Cuban Giants teammate) 101, 237n32, 240n88
The Freeman (Black newspaper in Indianapolis) 117, 258
French and Indian War 9
Frye, John H. 50, 86, 89, 93, 100, 127, 128, 140, 144, 160, 161, 218n25, 237n30, 239n68
Fuestya *see* Trusty
Fuller (1909 Booker's Giants

teammate, 1910 Colored Stars, 1911 Manhattan Colored Giants) 198, 199, 200
Fulmer, Chris 149

Gallaway (1905 Cuban Giants teammate) 192
Galley (1897 Cuban Giants teammate, aka Grelly/Galey/ Gailley?) 165, 168
Galligan, John **48**, 49
Galt House (earliest hotel by that name in Louisville, Kentucky) 64
Galvin, Pud 45, 62
Gannon, Bill 157
Gant (1910 Manhattan Colored Giants) 199–200
Gant, Henry 127, 130–131, 13, 138, 163–164, 189, 199– 200, 202, 232n43, 236n27, 237n32, 237n11. 238n45, 240n78
Garcia (1901, 1904 Cuban Giants teammate) 182, 183, 190
Gardner (1911 Manhattan Colored Giants) 200
Garfield, President James A. 17, 212n65
Garrison, Ross 101, 102, 103, 127, 164, 165, 168, 170, 171, 174, 231n35, 231n39, 231n40
Gaul (1892 Pittsburgh Keystones) 240n78
Gelbert, Charlie (College Football Hall of Fame) 144
Genesee Hotel (Buffalo, New York) 39, 217n43
Genuine Cuban Giants *see* Cuban Giants
Georgia Giants *see* Brooklyn X-Giants
Gettinger, Tom 118, 126
Getzein, Charles "Pretzels" 27
Gibbs, Charles "Lady" 75
Gibson, Whitey 116, 122
Gifford (1892 Cuban Giants teammate) 139
Gilbert, Frank T. 51
Gilman, Pit 46
Gilmore, Frank 62
Girard, Charlie 196
Gleason, Kid 55, 154
Glen Cove, Long Island, New York 197
Globe Clothing Company 49
Glory (1989 movie) 9
Gloucester, New Jersey 93
Gloversville New York 92, 97, 163–164, 174
Good(e) (1910 Colored Stars 1911 Manhattan Colored Giants) 199, 200

Goodson, M.E. 204
Gordon (1905 Cuban Giants teammate) 192, 199
Gordon, Bruce 221*n*90
Gordon, Robert *see* Jordan, Robert
Gorhams (Black team) 4, 60, 85, 87, 91, 92–93, 95, 99, 100, 101, 102, 103, 114, 124, 127–128, 129–130, **130**–138, 140, 146, 152, 161, 164, 198, 228*n*47, 228*n*66, 230*n*5, 236*n*27, 237*n*32, 237*n*10, 237*n*12, 237*n*14, 237*n*21, 237*n*23, 238*n*25, 238*n*28, 238*n*38, 239*n*55, 246*n*59; *see also* Harrisburg Gorhams (1891)
Gorman, Arthur Pue 11
Gormley, Joe 131
Goshen, Massachusetts 9, 211*n*35
Govern, Stanislaus Kostka 87, 90, 98, 99, 131, 228*n*48, 236*n*29
Graham, James 236*n*14
Graham, Vasco 158
Grant, Amelia Catherine (sister) 10, 13, 16, 202–203, 256*n*9
Grant, Aurelia Moore (wife, 1905–1911) 191, 198, 199–200, 255*n*66, 255*n*73
Grant, Catherine (great-grandmother) *see* Grant, Katy
Grant, Charlie/Charley (Black baseball player but not close relative) 176, 179, 181, 182, 184, 187, 188, 189, 190, 194, 195, 199, 200, 201–202, 251*n*91, 251*n*98, 252*n*7, 253*n*23, 255*n*1, 255*n*3
Grant, Charlotte (sister) 10, 13, 17
Grant, Clarence (brother) 10, 13, 14, 16, 17–19, 21–22, 31, 39, 104, 105, 133, 163, 203, 206, 207, 211*n*48, 231*n*31, 231*n*33; descendants of x, 13, 17, 203, 206, 207, 209*ch*1*n*3, 231*n*31, 231*n*33
Grant, Cornelia *see* Hamilton, Cornelia Grant
Grant, Dorothy (granddaughter) *see* Brown, Dorothy Grant
Grant, Emily *see* Foote, Emily Grant
Grant, Fannie (niece) 18
Grant, Frances Hoose "Fannie" (mother) 7, 8, 9, 10, 11, 12, 13, 14, 17
Grant, Frank W. (only known offspring) 125–126, 156, 185–186, 196, 202, 205–206
Grant, Frank: barehanded/one-handed fielding of 24, 28, 29, 33, 43, 55, 90, 91, 102, 112, 119, 120, 177; coaching by 91, 102, 105, 130, **187**, 188, 198; descendants of x, 125–126, 156, 185–186, 196, 202, 205–206, 236*n*13; funeral of 205; ice hockey/ice polo 104, 163, 169; hit by pitch 42, 53, 82, 113, 165, 177, 179, 196, 219*n*35; hitting for cycle 47; lodging and meals of 64, 86 90–91, 93, 107, 116, 117, 119, 153, 164, 176, 234*n*110; night game 184, 233*n*96; pennant races 53–58, 90, 95–96, 114, 142; possibly undiscovered photographs of 66, 80, 96, 147, 170, 223,*n*43; quotations of 91, 94, 102, 107, 137, 160; salary/earnings of 22, 24, 35, 38, 49, 64, 71, 77, 79, 81, 85, 89, 92, 103, 104, 107, 118, 121, 123, 128, 129, 131, 154, 158, 168, 176, 180, 185, 217*n*34; statistics of 3, 6, 33–34, 39, 50, 58, 77, 83, 96, 98, 115, 121–122, 178, 216*n*62, 217*n*38, 218*n*16, 218*n*23, 219*n*28, 219*n*46, 224*n*62, 225*n*83, 225*n*92, 225*n*109, 228*n*48, 230*n*92, 232*n*70, 235*n*141, 242*n*44, 249*n*41, 252*n*123; steal of home 56, 221*n*101; triple plays 29, 70, 94, 112, 128, 184; winning streak (Buffalo, 1888) 74
Grant, Franklin (father) 7, 8, 9, 10, 13
Grant, Frederick Dent 72
Grant, George Danforth (nephew) 13; *see also* Danforth, Keyes
Grant, Harriet "Hattie" (sister) 10, 13, 203
Grant, Harriet "Hattie" Crocker (daughter-in-law) 125, 202
Grant, Henrietta H. "Nettie" Porter (sister-in-law) 17, 19
Grant, Jacob (grandfather) 7, 8, 9, 210*n*5
Grant, James F. (umpire, presumably no relation) 242*n*40
Grant, Katy (great-grandmother, aka Catherine) 210*n*5
Grant, Lena Fields (grandmother) 7, 8, 210*n*6
Grant, Leroy (Black baseball player but not close relative) 199
Grant, Lewis/Louis (nephew) 17
Grant, Lucy (sister) 10, 13, 16
Grant, Malvania Holden Morris (wife, 1918–1921) 203
Grant, P. (1890 Cuban Giants teammate, possibly brother Clarence) 231*n*40
Grant, Rensselaer 7
Grant, Stewart (no known relation) 251*n*102
Grant, Sylvanus (first cousin) 7, 9, 209*ch*1*n*2, 211*n*33
Grant, Titus (great-grandfather) 209*ch*1*n*3
Grant, Pres./Gen. Ulysses 7, 29, 41, 72, 160, 210*n*18, 217*n*36
Grant, Ulysses F. *see* Grant, Frank
Grant, Walter (brother) 10
Grant, Willis (brother) 10, 12, 13, 19, 169, 203, 211*n*32
Grant's Colored Stars (1909) *see* Frank Grant's Colored Stars (1909)
Great Barrington, Massachusetts 18, 141
Great Britain (ancestry to 1400s) 9
Green (1901 Cuban Giants teammate) 182, 183
Green, Barney 197
Green(e), Pop 200
Greenfield, Massachusetts 173, 194, 195
Greenlee, Gus 204
Greenwood, Bill 34
Greylock Hall (resort) 12
Greylock Institute (school) 15, 22
Greylocks (Berkshire County team) 20, 22–23, 39, 62, 143, 214*n*23
Griffin, Emerson 185
Griffin, Sandy 45
Griswold, Lorenzo 18
Gross (1911 Manhattan Colored Giants) 200
Groves, George W. (shoemaker) 72
Gruber, Henry 68

Hackensack, New Jersey 191, 200
Hagerstown, Maryland 162, 224*n*7
Hall-of-Fame *see* National Baseball Hall of Fame
Hamburg, Charlie 43, 47, **48**, 71, 74, 76, 78, 153, 221*n*86, 223*n*46

Index

Hamilton, Charles (first cousin) 10
Hamilton, Cornelia Grant (aunt) 10, 12, 211*n*33
Hamilton, Lucretia Hoose (aunt) 10
Hamilton, Ontario 38, 46–47, 49, 50, 55, 56, 60, 66, 67, 69, 70, 71, 76, 79, 216*n*6, 227*n*28
Hamilton, William (uncle) 10
Hampshire County, Massachusetts 9
Hampton, Virginia 171
Hampton (Virginia) Chamberlins (1898 Black team) 171, 247*n*7, 247*n*8
Handiboe, Jim 45
Hanlon, Ned 68
Hanover, Maryland 162
Hanover, New Hampshire 175
Hardenbergh, Henry Janeway 203
Hardiman, John 21, 213*n*8
Hargrove (1911 New York Colored Giants) 199
Harris, Irene (adopted daughter) 191, 198
Harrisburg (1889 Middle States League) 84, 86, 88, 90, 91 92, 93, 95–96, 99–100, 106; *see also* York Monarchs
Harrisburg, Pennsylvania 19, 84, 86, 88, 90, 91, 92, 93, 95–96, 99–101, 102–126, 127, 128, 129–130, 131, 132, 136, 137, 138, 139, 144, 148, 150, 152, 153, 156, 182, 185, 186, 188, 201, 233*n*76, 233*n*93, 234*n*125, 235*n*126, 235*n*140, 235*n*143, 235*n*145, 239*n*68, 240*n*3, 243*n*46, 252*n*116
Harrisburg Base-Ball Club v. Athletic Ass'n (court case) 106–111, 124, 233*n*76
Harrisburg Gorhams (1891) 129–131
Harrisburg Ponies (1890) 4, 19, 99–101, 102–104, 105–124, 125–126, 153, 230*n*92, 233*n*76, 233*n*93, 233*n*96, 234*n*125, 235*n*126, 235*n*140, 235*n*143, 235*n*145, 243*n*46
Harrisburg Telegraph (newspaper) 4, 86, 114, 127, 152–153, 201, 237*n*10
Harrison, Abe 86, 87, 91, 100, 101, 124–125, 132, 136, 137, 139, 140, 144, 146, 148, 157, 164, 168, 218*n*25, 225*n*108, 226*n*113, 228*n*48, 229*n*67, 238*n*45, 239*n*57
Harrison, Pres. Benjamin **132**, 133

Hart, Billy 63, 67, 70
Hart, Jim 50, 181
Hartford, Connecticut 26, 29, 30, 32, 102–103, 114, 116, 119, 127, 158, 160, 166, 233*n*96
Harvey (1911 Manhattan Colored Giants) 200
Hasel, Mary (mother-in-law) 191; *see also* Grant, Aurelia Moore
Havana, Cuba 176, 177–178
Havana All Cubans 176
Hawk(e) (1907 Watkins' Colored Stars, 1908 Brooklyn X-Giants teammate) 195, 197
Hawley, Marvin 166
Hayes (1906 Baltimore Colored Giants teammate) 195
Hazleton, Pennsylvania 92, 94, 95, 143, 158
Hecker, Guy 63
Heitz, Tom 149
Hempstead, Long Island 152
Henerey (1909 Booker's Giants teammate) 198; *see also* Henry (1907 Watkins' Colored Stars teammate)
Henry (1907 Watkins' Colored Stars teammate) 195; *see also* Henerey (1909 Booker's Giants teammate)
Henry, John 158
Herbert, R. Henri 125, 238*n*36
Higgins (reported 1896 Cuban Giants teammate) 160
Higgins, Robert 41, 49, 51, 55, 59, 64, 69, 193, 218*n*4, 220*n*81, 221*n*86, 224*n*52
Hill (1902 Philadelphia Giants teammate) 184
Hill, J. (1900 Cuban Giants teammate) 178
Hill, John (1910 Gorhams teammate) 198
Hill, Pete? (1900 Cuban Giants teammate) 178
Hinson, Frank 160
Hobart, Indiana 176
Hoboken, New Jersey 78, 95, 136, 146, 148, 149, 174, 175, 176, 181, 229*n*67, 246*n*59
Hogan, Lawrence 12
Holden, Joseph (father-in-law) 203; *see also* Grant, Malvania Holden Morris
Holland (1889 Colored All-Americans teammate) 93, 230*n*9
Holland, Billy 196, 197, 198, 204, 254*n*46
Holliday, Bug 58, 221*n*113
Holmes, Ben 92, 101, 197, 218*n*25, 225*n*108, 229*n*67,

229*n*73, 231*n*19, 231*n*35, 231*n*39, 231*n*40, 237*n*32
Holy Cross *see* College of the Holy Cross
Hoose, Amos (uncle) 9
Hoose, Edward (first cousin) 9
Hoose, Frances *see* Grant, Frances Hoose
Hoose, Hannah Persip/Percip (grandmother) 8
Hoose, Louisa *see* McDonald, Louisa Hoose
Hoose, Lucretia *see* Hamilton, Lucretia Hoose
Hoose, Lucy *see* Duncan, Lucy Hoose
Hoose, Phillip/Philip (grandfather) 8
Hoose House *see* Fitch-Hoose House
Hoover, Billy 47
Hopkins (umpire in 1893) 150, 151
Hotel Champlain (Black team in Plattsburgh, New York) 143, 145, 240*n*81
Hotel Ponce de Leon (St. Augustine, Florida) 84
Hoverter (1891 Harrisburg teammate) 236*n*14
Howard, Doc 161, 168, 170, 171, 173, 174, 175
Howe, Shorty 132
Hubbell (Plattsburgh Nameless teammate) 23–24; *see also* Hubbell, J.C.
Hubbell, Julius Caesar 23–24, 213*n*19, 213*n*20
Hudson (1908 Brooklyn X-Giants teammate) 197
Hudson, New York 92, 105, 229*n*67
Hudson River League 191
Hudspeth, Robert 204
Humphries, John 51
Hunt family (neighbors) 17, 169, 247*n*98
Hurley, Jerry 87
Husting, Bert 185
Hygeia Hotel (Black baseball team in Hampton, Virginia) 171

Independent League 252*n*116
Indianapolis (National League team) 63, 64
injunction *see Harrisburg Base-Ball Club v. Athletic Ass'n*
International Association 55, 61, 64, 65, 68, 69, 76, 77, 78, 82, 115, 218*n*3
International League (aka

"Association") 5, 6, 24, 27, 35, 37, 38, 39, 41, 42, 43, 45, 47, 49, 50, 51–52, 54, 55, 56, 57, 58, 59, 77, 82, 83, 85, 123, 124, 172, 216n6, 216n12, 218n3, 219n33, 225n101; see also Eastern Association
Interstate B.B.A. (1911) 255n70
Iona Colored Giants (1907) 195

Jackson (1906 Baltimore Colored Giants teammate) 195
Jackson (1911 Manhattan Colored Giants) 200
Jackson (no first name, Cuban Giants et al,) 102, 144, 150, 162, 169, 200, 253n14
Jackson (two Ansonia Cuban Giants teammates) 126
Jackson, Andy 99, 101, 105, 127, 129, 132, 145, 146, 148, 150, 151, 153, 154, 157, 160, 170, 171, 174, 175, 177, 178, 230n15, 231n35, 231n39, 231n40, 239n55, 243n60, 246n62
Jackson, B. 102, 127, 160, 231n39, 246n62; see also Jackson, Robert
Jackson, Dave 60
Jackson, George Washington Randolph "Rans" 41
Jackson, Oscar 99, 127, 129, 132, 146, 148, 153, 157, 158, 160, 161, 175, 197, 231n35, 239n55, 244n10, 246n62
Jackson, Robert 60, 102, 197, 204, 230n15, 231n40; see also Jackson, B.
Jackson, William 140, 146, 148, 153, 157, 160, 168, 170, 175, 191, 237n30, 246n62
James, Bill 3
James, Gus 196
James, Willie "Knucks"/"Nux" 204, 205
Jamison, Jacob 163
Jeffries, James J. (boxer) 178–179, 180
Jenkins, "Fats" 204–205
Jennings, Hughie 120, 122
Jersey City, New Jersey 11, 27, 30, 32, 43, 45, 113, 115, 169, 178, 220n69, 233n93
Jersey City News 133–134
Jessup, Pennsylvania 150
Johnson (1888 Cuban Giants teammate) 225n108, 226n113
Johnson (1889 Colored All-Americans teammate) 93; see also Johnson, J.
Johnson (1890 Cuban Giants teammate) 101

Johnson (1907 Watkins' Colored Stars teammate) 195
Johnson (1909 Frank Grant's Colored Stars) 198
Johnson (1909 New York Colored Giants teammate) 198
Johnson (1910 Colored Stars) 199
Johnson, George "Chappie" 181; see also "Crappy" 162
Johnson, Grant "Home Run" 153, 154, 155, 158, 179, 194, 243n51, 243n64, 254n46
Johnson, H. 100
Johnson, Harry 101, 217n31
Johnson, J. 229n72; see also Johnson (1889 Colored All-Americans teammate)
Johnstown, New York 163–164, 166–167, 174
Johnstown (Pennsylvania) Flood 89, **89**, 228n57
Jolie (umpire) 160
Joliet, Illinois 176, 181
Jones (1901 Cuban Giants teammate) 182, 198, 255n70
Jones (1909 Frank Grant's Colored Stars) 198
Jones, George 164
Jones, John 19
Jones, Joseph 116
Jordan, Robert 160, 161, 163–164, 165, 168, 170, 171, 174, 175, 178, 197, 198, 247n6, 254n46
Joss, Addie 181
Jupiter (1897 Cuban Giants teammate) 168, 231n35, 231n39, 231n40, 244n11

Kansas 4, 72, 73, 85
Kappel, Joe 59, 76, 162, 2128n21, 222n124
Katoll, Jack 172, 177
Keating, Bob 26, 214n16
Keefe, George 74, 84–85
Keefe, Patrick (ice polo teammate) 246n55, 247n98
Keefe, Tim 212n2
Keeler, "Wee" Willie 4, 135, 139–140, 141, 238n38, 239n65
Keener, Harry 147
Keffer, Frank 236n14
Kelly (1897 Cuban X-Giants teammate) 246n62
Kelly (1904 Colored Giants teammate) 191
Kelly (1905 Cuban Giants teammate) 192
Kelly (1907 Watkins' Colored Stars teammate) 195
Kelly (1909 Frank Grant's Colored Stars) 198

Kelly (1909 New York Colored Giants teammate) 198
Kelly (1910 Gorhams teammate) 198
Kelly, M. (1904 Cuban Giants teammate) 191
Kelly, Mike "King" 51, 138. 158
Kelly, William "King" 182, 190–191, 192, 195. 198, 253n12
Keltner, Ken 3
Kennedy, Eddie 131
Ketrick, Larry 145
Keystones see Pittsburgh Keystones
Kilroy, Matt 42
Kilroy, Mike 86
Kinderhook, New York 9, 210n5, 211n35
King (possibly King Kelly; 1910 Gorhams teammate) 198
Kingston, New York 92, 229n67
Kissel, Tony 155, 156, 159
Klobedanz, Fred 142, 157
Knorr, Ted 120
Knouff, Ed 42
Knowlton, George 33
Koons, Harry 112, 115, 234n98
Kreiter, J. Monroe 99–100, 101, 102–104, 106, 107, 111, 120, 124, 230n5, 231n22, 231n26
Krock, Jeremy 206
Kunkel, District Attorney George 106, 108, 109

L. Bachmann & Co. 203
LaChance, Candy 142
Lamar, Edward B. 159–160, 170, 173, 174, 175, 177, 241n9, 248n18
Lampe, Henry 166, 246n68
Lancaster, Pennsylvania 84, 86, 99, 107, 108, 110, 123, 124, 164, 165
Lancey (1906 Baltimore Colored Giants teammate) 195
Land, Bill 194
Landis, A.H. 227n45
Landis, Doc 28
Lane (Trenton police detective) 135
Lansford, Pennsylvania 241n28
Lansing, Evelina Duncan 211n37
Lansing, Richard H. (cousin's husband) 211n37
Lansing, Michigan 158
Lavelle (1904 Cuban Giants teammate) 190, 254n40
Leach, Tommy 162
Leary (Plattsburgh Nameless teammate) 23
Lebanon, Pennsylvania 94,

Index

95, 99, 103, 108, 112, 113, 114, 117, 118, 120, 121, 122, 123, 126, 129, 130, 131, 235n140, 236n14, 237n11, 251n97
Lehane, Mike 43, **48**, 53, 57, 58, 59, 68, 74, 79
Leiper, Jack 132, 238n26
Leith, Rod 125
Lenox, Massachusetts 8, 10, 210n5, 210n6
Lett, Charles 230n96
Lewiston, Maine 160
Lincoln, Ezra 155
Lock Haven, Pennsylvania 154
Loft Building (New York City landmark) 203, **204**
London, Ontario 65, 66, 68, 69, 74, 75, 76, 83
Long Island, New York 26, 29, 77, 78, 85, 87, 94, 101, 127, 128, 136, 138, 139–140, 141, 142, 143, 145, 146–147, 148, 149, 151, 152, 158, 183, 197, 240n78, 240n3
Long Island Athletics 29, 215n46
Long Island Grounds (ballpark) 77, 78, 85, 87, 94, 127, 128, 138, 139–140, 141, 142, 143, 145, 146–147, 149, 240n3
Long Island Stars 26, 94, 101, 158
Loughlin Lyceum (baseball team) 192, 193, 195
Louisville (American Association team) 63
L'rence (presumably Lawrence, Albany Capital Citys teammate) 230n96
Ludington, Michigan 167
Lykens, Pennsylvania 152
Lynch (brothers on Williams College team) 147
Lynn, Massachusetts 45
Lyons (1904 Cuban Giants teammate) 190

Mack, Connie 32, 43, 181, 216n59
Mack, Reddy 115, 117, 235n141
Mackey, John 164; see also Mickey (1897 Cuban Giants teammate)
Madison, Art 163, 192
Mahaney (Greylocks teammate) 22
Mahanoy City, Pennsylvania 185
Maher, Richard 21, 212n5
Mallete (1911 Manhattan Colored Giants) 200
Malloy, Jerry 3, 230n15, 261
Malone, William 50, 86, 93, 100, 108, 124, 126, 127, 129, 132, 145, 164, 165, 168, 225n108, 226n113, 229n67, 239n55, 240n3
Malone, New York 24, 31
Manhattan A. A. baseball team (Philadelphia, 1916) 202
Manhattan Athletic Club 127
Manhattan College (New York City) 171, 175
Manhattan Colored Giants (1911) 200
Manning (1906 Baltimore Colored Giants teammate) 195
Mansell, Mike 32
Mansfield, Pennsylvania 155, 156
Maranville, Walter "Rabbit" 16
Marley (1904 Colored Giants teammate) 191
Marquettes (white team) 190, 192, 197
Maryland Club of Baltimore 126
Mason, Charles E. 88, 228n50
Matanzas, Cuba 177
Matheson, John 135, 238n36
Mathews/Matthews (1904 Colored Giants, 1909 Booker's Giants teammate) 191, 198, 253n12, 253n14
Matthews (unknown Brooklyn player) 233n88
Mattingly, Don 6, 77
Mayer, Bob 192
Mayfield, Fred 50
Mays, Willie 11
McCarrell, Samuel John Milton 109, 111
McCarthy, Tommy 29
McClennan, Nat 177–178
McConnell (1910 New York Colored Giants) 199
McCormick, Jerry 106, 112, 121, 144, 234n98
McDonald (1910 New York Colored Giants) 199; see also McDonald, Gifford
McDonald (International League umpire) 46–47, 49, 219n41
McDonald, Duncan (uncle) 12
McDonald, Gifford 204; see also McDonald (1910 New York Colored Giants)
McDonald, Louisa Hoose (aunt) 10, 12
McDougal, Sandy 161
McFarlan, Dan 160, 165
McGlone, John 43
McGovern, Manager 131, 236n29; see also Govern, Stanislaus Kostka

McGraw, John 182
McGrillis, Mark 245n46
McGuire, Deacon 5, 173, 177, 248n29
McGurk, Charles 133–134
McKeever, Jimmy 189
McLean, William 53
McMahon, James 104, 163, 247n98
McMahon, Peter (ice polo teammate) 247n98
McPartlin, Frank 174
McQuery, Mox 57
McTurner, Ida 204
McTurner, Louis 204
Meakim, George 152, 242n45
Meanor (1906 Baltimore Colored Giants teammate) 195
Melvill House 9–10
Melville, Herman 9, 210n16
Melville, Robert 9, 210n16
Meriden, Connecticut 20, 25–34, 35, 61, 64, 90, 126, 127, 128, 142, 148, 150, 161, 173, 175, 214n27
Meriden Resolutes 90, 92, 214n5, 216n66
Meridens (Eastern League team) 25–34, 35, 62, 68, 78, 82, 96, 106, 116, 143, 144, 173
Merritt, Bill 254n46
Merritt, George 190
Meyers, E.K. 106, 153
Michael, Caroline E. (aunt) 210n6
Michigan (1897, 1899 tours) 168, 177
Michigan City, Indiana 174, 248n39
Michigan State League 128
Mickey (1897 Cuban Giants teammate) 168, 169; see also Mackey, John
Middle States League (1889) 78, 84, 86, 87–88, 89–90, 91–92, 93–94, 95, 96, 99, 112, 133, 228n50, 229n58, 229n67, 230n92
Middle States League (1893) 146
Middlebury College (Vermont) 147
Middletown, Connecticut 166
Middletown, New York 149, 150, 154, 192, 241n28
Middletown (New York) Asylum Base Ball Club 149, 150, 154, 192
Millar, Albert 106, 108, 109
Miller (1901 Cuban Giants teammate) 182
Miller, Charles 60

Index

Miller, Frank 100, 101, 129, 130, 131, 149, 150, 153, 159, 160, 161, 164, 165, 189, 204, 237*n*32, 243*n*52, 256*n*12
Miller, Frank, Jr. 204
Miller, George Frederick 143
Miller, Geraldine (Frank Miller's daughter) *see* Bryant
Miller, Ida (Frank Miller's daughter) *see* McTurner
Minetta Street, Manhattan 191, 199, 203, 256*n*11
Mitchell, Fred 185
Mongin, Sam 204
Monroe, Bill 185, 187, 254*n*46
Monroes (white team) 128, 138
Montiverde, Judge 152
Montreal, Quebec 162, 167
Mooney, John 21, 22, 212*n*4, 212*n*5, 213*n*8
Mooney, Michael 21, 22
Moore, Aurelia *see* Grant, Aurelia Moore
Moore, Frank (adopted son/stepson) 191, 198
Morris, Ed 42
Morris, Malvania Holden *see* Grant, Malvania Holden Morris
Morris, Nelles (housemate) 198, 203
Morrisey (Greylocks teammate) 22
Moulton (1897 Cuban Giants teammate) 165
Mount Holly, New Jersey 176
Mowke (1909 Frank Grant's Colored Stars) 198
Moynihan, Timothy 172
MSL *see* Middle States League
Mullane, Tony 179, 180
Murphy (Brooklyn X-Giants teammate) 197
Murphy (1906 Baltimore Colored Giants teammate) 195
Murphy, Con 85
Murphy, Dan 120
Murphy, Ed 166
Murphy, Pat 78
Murphy, Willie 32, 143
Murray Hills (amateur New York team) 145, 148
Murry, F. 213*n*8
Muskegon, Michigan 167
Myers, E. (1908 Brooklyn X-Giants teammate) 197
Myers, L. (1908 Brooklyn X-Giants teammate) 197

National Agreement (pact governing professional leagues) 88, 109, 122, 228*n*51, 236*n*2
National Association of Base Ball Players (NABBP) 11, 217*n*28
National Association of Colored Baseball Clubs of the United States and Cuba (1907–1910) 196
National Association of Independent Base Ball Clubs (1903–1904) 185
National Baseball Hall of Fame 3, 5, 6, 7, 10, 24, 66, 125, 149, 206, 220*n*73
National Colored Base Ball League (1887) 137, 216*n*9
National League 15, 22, 27, 35, 39, 41, 42, 43, 44–45, 58, 61–62, 63–64, 68–69, 74, 75, 78, 82, 84, 87, 88, 94, 100, 102, 104, 107, 114, 131, 132, 133, 137, 139, 140, 142, 143, 144, 147, 152, 154, 155, 157–158, 160, 161, 164, 165, 166, 172, 173, 174, 181–182, 191, 192, 196–197, 198
National Register of Historic Places 8, 9
Nationals (1897 Brooklyn-area team) 169
Nead, Benjamin M 106–107, 108, 109
Nealson (1909 New York Colored Giants teammate) 198
Nebraska State League 128, 146
Negro Leagues Grave Marker Project 125, 206
Nelson (1906 Baltimore Colored Giants teammate) 195
Nelson (1910 Colored Stars) 199
Nelson, Candy 131, 132
Nelson, John 60, 99, 101, 105, 127, 136, 139, 140, 142, 144, 146, 148, 153, 155, 157, 160, 164, 168, 170, 174, 175, 177–178, 185, 187, 190, 191, 192, 194, 195, 198–199, 230*n*9, 231*n*35, 231*n*39, 231*n*40, 238*n*24, 244*n*7, 247*n*6, 253*n*12, 254*n*40
New Bedford, Massachusetts 154, 159, 171
New Britain, Connecticut 27, 33
New Brunswick, New Jersey 142, 190, 195
New England League 27, 45, 124, 155, 157, 159, 160, 161, 164, 166, 170, 171, 172, 248*n*18
New Haven, Connecticut 28, 90, 114, 116, 119, 120–121, 132, 138, 154, 168–169
New Jersey 77, 135, 162

New Orleans Pinchbacks (Black team around 1897) 164
New York Age (Black newspaper) 85, 88, 95, 99, 197, 205
New York Amsterdam News (Black newspaper) 209*n*20, 212*n*73, 256*n*13
New York Black Sox (1910) 199, 255*n*67
New York Black Yankees (1932) 204
New York Catholic Protectory Emeralds (baseball team) 148, 149
New York City 4, 7, 26, 27, 73, 87, 90, 100, 102, 123, 126, 127, 131–132, 137, 139, 143, 147, 148, 153, 155, 159, 170, 174, 176, 178, 184, 190, 191, 192, 194, 196, 199, 204, 205
New York Colored Giants 191–192, 194, 195, 197, 198, 199
New York Giants (National League team) 78, 137, 138, 140, 158, 159
New York Herald (newspaper) 4
New York Metropolitans (American Association team) 131–132
New York Metropolitans (semi-pro team) 85, 94, 127
New York Semi-Professional League (1891) 127, 128, 130, 132, 136, 138, 237*n*14
New York State 7, 8, 9, 17, 24, 26, 31, 92, 96, 135, 184
New York State League 104–105, 154, 166, 167, 172, 243*n*61
New York Tribune (newspaper) 11
Newark, New Jersey 27, 30, 32–33, 45, 47–48, 49, 50, 52, 53, 56–57, 58, 77, 114, 116, 119, 120–121, 141, 148, 155, 171, 174, 175, 182, 243*n*47
Newark, New York 162
Newburyport, Massachusetts 27
Newport, Rhode Island 159, 164, 166, 248*n*18
Niagara University (Lewiston, New York) 179
night game 184, 233*n*96
Norfolk Rex Sox (Black team in Virginia) 164, 246*n*59, 247*n*10
Norristown, Pennsylvania 90, 91, 94, 130, 139, 237*n*12
North Adams, Massachusetts 22, 147, 153, 159, 167, 170–171, 172–173, 192, 203
North Hudson, New Jersey 167

Index

Northampton, Massachusetts 142
Northern New York League 182
Norwalk, Connecticut 77, 90, 124
Norwich, Connecticut 127
Nott (1910 Colored Stars) 199
Nyack, New York 197

Oak Park, Illinois 174
O'Brien, Billy 75, 225n96
O'Connor, Frank 133, 238n29
O'Day, Hank 42, 61
Odel, Elizabeth (great great-grandmother) 8–9
Odel, Ichabod (great great-grandfather) 8–9
Odel, Isaac 9
Odel, Molley *see* Persip, Molly Odel
Ogdensburg, New York 24, 153
Ohio State League 62
Old-Timers Association 204
O'Loughlin (umpire) 165
Olympic Field (New York City) 199, 255n69
Olympic Park (Buffalo, New York) 35, 53, 61, 67, 86
Olympic Park/Field (Paterson, New Jersey) 148
Oneonta Normal School (New York) 149
O'Neill, Norris **48**
Opequon Giants ("Colored") of Savannah, Georgia 190–191
Orange, New Jersey 146, 159, 162, 163, 195
Orient Giants (1902 Black team) 184
Original Cuban Giants *see* Cuban Giants
O'Rourke, Mike 115, 117
Orpheum Giants (Black team from Savannah, Georgia) 190
Oswego, New York 37, 41, 47, 49, 172, 218n4, 220n69
Oswego Daily Palladium (New York newspaper) 5, 47, 172
Overmyer, James x, 6, 10, 24, 33, 50, 55, 77, 206, 213n14, 261
Oxford, Michigan 177

Page Fence Giants (Black team in Adrian, Michigan) 158, 163, 164
Panic of 1873 (economic depression) 16
Pappalau, John 172
Parade House (Buffalo, New York) 49, 220n57
Parago (Cuban Giants teammate) 218n25, 226n113, 240n88
Paramount Field Club (white team) 192, 193
Paris, France (proposed trip) 178
Parker, Bob 177–178
Parks (1909 Watkins' Giants teammate) 198
Passaic, New Jersey 139
Paterson, New Jersey 146, 148, 149, 150–151, 152, 156, 165, 175, 178, 190, 191, 196, 198, 199
Patterson, John W. "Pat" 146, 149, 153, 157, 159–160, 161, 181, 185, 187, 229n74, 241n22, 254n46
Payne, Andrew 184, 185
Penn Yan, New York 183
Penno, Dan 139, 140, 144, 146, 148, 182, 191, 192, 194, 253n12
Pennsylvania 93, 109, 111, 129, 135
Pennsylvania Railroad 137–138
Pennsylvania State League 129, 144, 147, 151, 153, 154, 158, 160, 161, 184, 201
Perrin (1897 Cuban Giants teammate) 168
Perry, Arthur Latham 13, 14, 17
Perry, Bliss 13–17, 22, 105, 157, 182, 211n43, 211n49, 232n42
Persip, Estella 209ch1n2
Persip, John (great-grandfather) 8, 9
Persip, John (relative still alive in 1970) 209ch1n2
Persip, Molly Odel (great-grandmother, aka Mary) 8–9, 210n11
Persip/Percip, Hannah *see* Hoose, Hannah Persip/Percip
Petersburgh, Virginia 171
Peterson (1889 Colored All-Americans teammate) 93, 228n66, 229n67
Pettit, Bob 15, 20, 22, 25, 26, 28, 34, 52, 58, 160
Pfeffer, Fred 5, 177
Philadelphia (National League team) 44, 94, 131, 133, 158
Philadelphia Athletics (1890 American Association team) 116
Philadelphia Athletics (1902 American League champions) 185
Philadelphia Giants (Black team) 19, 183–**186**, 186, **187**, 187, 188, 189, 190, 193, 194, 195, 196, 197, 199, 200, 251n103, 252n7, 253n24
Philadelphia Giants (white team in 1889 Middle States League) 84, 88, 91, 95, 96
Philadelphia Giants (white team in 1903) 252n117
Philadelphia Quaker Giants (Black team) 189, 195
Philadelphia Tribune (Black newspaper) 202
photographs, possibly undiscovered 66, 80, 96, 147, 170, 223,n43
Pioneers (San Francisco baseball team) 50
Pittsburgh (National League team) 42, 43–44, 62
Pittsburgh, Pennsylvania 153, 182, 189; *see also* Smoky City Colored Giants, Pittsburgh Giants
Pittsburgh Barnes Colored Americans *see* Barnes Colored Americans
Pittsburgh Courier (Black newspaper) 204, 205, 241n24, 252n116
Pittsburgh Giants (1914 Black team, Bright's) 201–202
Pittsburgh Keystones 50, 73, 137, 138, 164, 223n18, 232n43, 239n61, 240n78, 246n59
Pittsfield, Massachusetts 7, 8, 9–10, 12, 14, 18, 22, 62, 96, 105, 143, 154, 158, 163, 192, 211n33, 218n2
Pitz, Herman 143
Plainfield, New Jersey 136, 191, 242n43
Plainfield Daily Press (New Jersey newspaper) 4, 136
Plainville, Connecticut 127
The Plated City (novel with fictionalized Frank Grant) 15, 157, 182
Plattsburgh, New York 23–24, 31, 44, 143, 167, 168, 213n19, 213n24
Plattsburgh Nameless 23–24, 31, 44, 62, 213n27, 215n50
Pointer, William 41, 218n4
Pokeepsie Evening Enterprise 150; *see also* Poughkeepsie, New York
Pole (1910 New York Colored Giants teammate) 199
Poles, Spottswood 199 204
Pollard, Fritz 6
Polo Grounds (New York City ballpark) 98, 100, 127, 131–132, 243n45
Pond, Arlie 140, 147
Poole (1910 New York Colored Giants teammate) 199
Poole, Ed 196

Port Henry Witherbees 23, 24
Port Jervis, New York 98, 139
Porter, Henrietta H. "Nettie" see Grant, Henrietta H. "Nettie" Porter
Porter, Dr. Henry 17, 212n66
Porter, Merdellon D. 21, 212n4, 212n5, 213n8
Portland, Maine 27, 124, 160–161
Portugal (possible ancestry) 8
Posey, Cum 205
Potsdam, New York 182, *182*-183, 251n96
Potter, John R. (photographer) 66, 223,n43
Pottstown, Pennsylvania 139
Pottsville, Pennsylvania 148, 157
Poughkeepsie, New York 132, 150–151, 173
Powell (1911 Manhattan Colored Giants) 200
Pownal, Vermont 163
Pratt, Mamie Anderson (undertaker) 205
Princeton College 85, 127
Princeton (New Jersey) Giants/X-Giants (Black team) 179, *180*, 190, 252n8
Providence, Rhode Island 28–29, 30, 51
Purvis, James *48*, 49

Quadrangular League (1895 tournament) 159, 244n14
Quinn, Jack 213n22, 214n27, 215n43, 215n52

Racine, Wisconsin 181
Radbourn, Charles "Old Hoss" 45
Railway Car Association 39, 217n41
Ramsley (1906 Baltimore Colored Giants teammate) 195
Randow, Charles 133–136, 141, 151, 238n30, 238n31
Reading, Pennsylvania 84, 87, 88, 91, 121, 123, 124, 127, 129, 131, 132, 133, 147, 148, 151, 157, 165, 184, 228n50, 242n40, 248n11
Rector, Connie 204
Reese (1909 Frank Grant's Colored Stars) 198; see also Reeves (1908 Brooklyn X-Giants teammate)
Reeves (1908 Brooklyn X-Giants teammate) 197; see also Reese (1909 Frank Grant's Colored Stars)

Reidy, Bill 155
Reidy, James 216n15
Reidy, John J. "Sandy" 46, *48*, 49, 50, 53, 59, 60, 61, 66, 68, 70, 75, 77, 206, 216n15, 256n18
Reipschlager, Charlie 131
Reitz, Heinie 5, 177, 248n29
Remsen, Jack 30–31, 35, 37, 41, 45, *48*, 50, 69–70, 105
Renfrews (Berkshire County team) see Adams Renfrews
Renfroe, William James 41, 51, 218n4
Resolutes (Berkshire County team) 21; see also Boston Resolutes; Meriden Resolutes
Retel, Dr. M. 61
Revolutionary War 9
Rhode Island 7
Richardson (Colored Giants teammate) 191
Richardson (1904 Colored Giants teammate) 191
Richardson, Hardy 68
Ricketts, Mary see Wilson, Mary Adore
Ricketts, Milton 156, 244n83
Ridgewoods (New York semi-pro team) 143, 185, 192
Rigler (1910 New York Colored Giants) 199
Roat, Deputy Sheriff Harry 107; see also Sheesley, Sheriff William
Robinson (1909 Pop Watkins' Giants teammate) 198, 254n40
Robinson (1910 Colored Stars) 199, 254n40
Robinson, Jackie 24, 217n28, 237n33
Robinson, James 153, 157, 158, 159, 160, 161, 163, 164, 165, 169, 170, 174, 175, 177, 178, 189, 250n76, 254n40
Robinson, William "Yank" 5, 56, 177
Rochester, Indiana 176
Rochester, New York 45, 47, 51, 54, 61, 65, 66, 67, 69, 70, 74, 154, 160, 165, 219n33
Rochester Democrat and Chronicle 45, 50, 219n33, 223n38
Rockwood, B.C. 213n8
Rogers, John I. 109
Roschi(e), John E. *48*
Roseman, Chief 131, 139, 239n63
Rothermel, Bobby 147
Rothwell (1890 Cuban Giants teammate) 102
Rough and Readys

(Williamstown team) 15, 20, 22, 105
Rouses Point, New York 240n81
Rowe, Jack 68, 78, 79–80, 81, 82, 83
Royal Giants (1904 Black team in New York) 190; see also Brooklyn Royal Giants
Royersford, Pennsylvania 148
Royston, Marion Grant (descendant of Clarence Grant) 206; see also Foote, Emily Grant
Russ, Jim 106
Rutland, Vermont 140, 141
Ryan, Red 204–205

SABR see Society for American Baseball Research
Safford (Greylocks, Plattsburgh Nameless teammate) 22, 23; see also Safford, J.H., Safford, W.B.
Safford, John Henry 23–24, 213n18, 213n19, 213n20
Safford, Walter Bradbury 23–24, 213n18–213n20
St. Augustine, Florida 79, 81, 84, 227n29
St. John's Catholic Club baseball team 254n50
St. Louis Browns (American Association team) 42, 56, 116, 123
St. Louis Browns (National League team) 155
St. Louis College (New York City) 155
St. Louis Globe-Democrat (newspaper) 51
St. Louis Republican (newspaper) 38
Salem, New Jersey 155, 158, 245n40
Sales, Eddie 236n14
Salmon, M.J. 148–149, 241n18
Sampson / Samson (1901 Cuban Giants teammate) 183
San Francisco (1900 baseball team in Cuba) 178
San Francisco, California 50
Sanders, Georgia (female first name, not the state) 122
Santop, Louis 204
Satterfield (1905 Cuban Giants, 1909 New York Colored Giants teammate) 192, 198
Saugerties, New York 229n67
Savannah, Georgia 190, 199, 227n31, 255n70; see also Opequon Giants ("Colored"); Orpheum Giants
Savannah Colored Giants (1910,

Index

probably a Gant and not Grant) 199, 255*n*70
Sax. Steve 6, 77
Say, Jimmy 126
Say, Lou 126
Scales, George 204–205
Scheffler, Ted 152
Schenectady, New York 166
Schenk (1904 Opequon Giants/Orpheum Giants teammate) 190
Schenk/Schruck/Shenck (1889 Colored All-Americans teammate) 93, 228*n*66, 229*n*74
Schlichter, Walter 183, 184
Schruck (1889 Colored All-Americans teammate) *see* Schenk
Scranton, Pennsylvania 49, 53, 56, 131, 144–145, 161, 165, 214*n*9, 220*n*69
Seaman, Captain Charles H. 135
Seamheads.com Negro Leagues Database 6, 178, 186
Seay, Dick 204
Sebron (slaveowner in New York) 8
Selden, William 50, 86, 89, 92, 100, 108, 110, 111–112, 113, 122, 125, 127, 129, 132, 134, 135, 137, 153, 157, 158, 160, 168, 170, 171, 175, 226*n*113, 227*n*44, 229*n*73, 229*n*74, 233*n*85, 239*n*55, 244*n*6, 246*n*62
Senators (New York semi-pro team) 136, 139, 141, 143, 146; *see also* Washington Senators
Serad, Billy 62, 74, 235*n*129
Seybold, Socks 164, 185
Sharon, Wisconsin 174, 176, 249*n*53
Shaw, Dupee 43
Sheckard, Jimmy 160
Sheesley, Sheriff William 106; *see also* Roat, Deputy Sheriff Harry
Sheldon, Illinois 174
Shenandoah, Pennsylvania 96, 148, 151, 157, 229*n*67
Shenck (1889 Colored All-Americans teammate) *see* Schenk
shin guards 82–83
Shire, Moses 48
Shoch, George 75
Shreve, Lev 63
Sidney, New York 166
Siege of Boston (1775–1776) 9
Simmons (1904 Opequon Giants/Orpheum Giants teammate) 190

Simon, Hank 77
Simonds (1911 New York Colored Giants) 199
Simonton, Judge John 106, 107, 108, 109, 110, 111, 233*n*76
slavery 7, 8, 9, 10, 210*n*8
Smith (1899 Cuban X-Giants teammate) 175, 246*n*62
Smith (New York Colored Giants teammate(s)) 191, 192, 198, 253*n*12
Smith (1904 Colored Giants teammate) 191
Smith (1906 Baltimore Colored Giants teammate) 195
Smith (1909 Booker's Giants teammate) 198
Smith, C. (1897 Cuban Giants teammate) 168
Smith, Judge Clarence 14
Smith, Harry 184, 185, 195
Smith, Leo 119, 152, 243*n*46
Smith, Mike 89
Smoky City (Pittsburgh) Colored Giants 189
Society for American Baseball Research (SABR) 1, 94, 192. 199, 244*n*5
Sockalexis, Louis 157–158, 161, 167, 244*n*5, 246*n*80
Somerville, New Jersey 94
Sontag (umpire) 160
South Jersey League 155, 158, 162
South Street, Harrisburg 125, 137, 236*n*11, 244*n*83
South Williamstown, Massachusetts 15, 16, 22
Southington, Connecticut 93, 127–128
Sowders, Bill 87
Sowders, Len 77, 87
Sporting Life (weekly publication) 4, 25, 30, 34, 38, 39, 45, 54, 55, 58, 69, 76, 82, 116, 121, 122, 124, 197, 217*n*26, 217*n*42, 221*n*90, 224*n*61, 259
The Sporting News 38, 43, 50, 73, 82, 83, 164
Spring Street, Williamstown, Massachusetts 13, 14, 16, 17, 19, 159, 169, 202, 206, 211*n*34, 211*n*37, 256*n*9, 256*n*19
Springfield, Massachusetts 26, 141 (image caption), 142, 171
Squires (Plattsburgh Nameless teammate) 23
Stagg, Amos Alonzo 28
Stamford, Connecticut 85, 168–169, 191, 247*n*96
Standards (Florida team) 79

Stanleys (1980s Berkshire County team) 159, 163, 167, 173
Stecher, William 93, 229*n*78
Stedler, Bob 206
Steen, Dr. Alexander M. 87
Stemmyer, Bill 44
Sterling, Illinois 180
Stewart, Ace 147
Stewart, "Delahanty" 177
Stimmel, Archie 161
Stivetts, Jack 88
Stockbridge, Matt 213*n*8
Stovey, George 32, 41, 45, 47–48, 49, 50, 51, 52, 56, 58, 78, 84, 86, 92, 94, 99, 100, 101, 102, 105, 127, 129, 132, 135–136, 139, 140, 143, 146, 153, 157, 193, 216*n*60, 222*n*118, 228*n*66, 229*n*67, 229*n*74, 229*n*80, 230*n*5, 230*n*9, 230*n*19, 231*n*35, 231*n*39, 231*n*40, 232*n*43, 239*n*55
Stovey, Harry 154
Stratton, Scott 63
Strunz (Greylocks teammate) 22
Sturgeon Bay, Wisconisn 176
Sullivan (Cuban Giants teammate) 226*n*113
Sullivan, John L. (boxer) 46, 186
Sullivan, Ted 51, 117
Sunday Telegram (Providence, Rhode Island) 51
Sutton, Massachusetts 9
Sweitzer (1891 Harrisburg teammate) 236*n*14
Syracuse, New York 37, 38, 41, 46, 49, 52–53, 55, 57, 58, 59, 64, 67, 69, 73, 74, 78, 83, 85, 86, 97, 165, 220*n*81
Syracuse Standard (newspaper) 5, 37, 166

Tate, Pop 115, 117
Taunton, Massachusetts 172
Taylor (1890 teammate) 230*n*9
Taylor, Jim 160; *see also* Taylor (1890 teammate)
Teabout, Charles 230*n*96
Teabout, E. 230*n*96
Tenney, Judge Sanborn 14, 211*n*45
Terrell (1911 New York Colored Giants) 199
Terrill, Winslow 113, 128, 132, 136, 145, 153, 160, 231*n*40, 237*n*30, 239*n*55
Thatcher, Grant 172, 174, 248*n*15
"There's a New Coon in Town" (song) 36, 44, 216*n*9

Index

Thomas, A.F. (cartoonist) **187**-188
Thomas, Arthur 60, 78, 79, 87, 88, 92, 94, 97, 100, 112, 122, 124, 126, 127, 129, 131, 132, 134, 135, 218n25, 225n108, 227n44, 228n66, 238n28, 252n125
Thomas, Jules 204
Thompson (1909 New York Colored Giants teammate) 198
Thompson, Sam 68, 80
Thorn, John 3–4, 8, 128, 220n69
Tighe, Jack 157
Tilley, Nanita (great-great-greatgranddaughter of Frank Grant) x
Titcomb, Ledell 78
Toronto, Ontario 35, 36, 37, 39, 46, 47, 50, 53–55, 56, 57, 58, 60, 66–67, 69, 74, 75, 85, 124, 220n69, 223n49
Tranter, Edward 6
Traverse City, Michigan 168
Tremblay (Plattsburgh Nameless teammate) 23
Trenton, New Jersey 78, 80, 84–96, 99, 100, 102, 123, 124, 133, 134–135, 136, 141, 151, 179, 188
Trinity College (Hartford, Connecticut) 26, 27, 28
triple plays 29 (two), 70, 94, 112, 128, 184
Troy, Dasher 131
Troy, New York 64, 66, 69, 73–74, 76, 105
Trusty, Job 159, 160, 161, 184, 245n27
Trusty, Shep 44, 60, 232n43, 245n23
Tucker (1904 Cuban Giants teammate) 191
Twineham, Art 155

Underground Railroad 9, 210n14
Union College (Schenectady, New York) 166
University of Rochester (New York) 154
University of Vermont (U.V.M.) 31, 132–133, 140, 147, 154, 175
Uplander, Barney 141
Utica, New York 27, 37–38, 45, 48, 51, 105, 124, 196, 232n43

Vactor (1889 Colored All-Americans teammate) 228n66, 229n80
Valentine (1904 Colored Giants teammate) 191, 253n12
Vallee, Howard 118
Van Valkenburgh, George 230n96
Varney, Dike 183
Vermont (1898 tour) 172
Viau, Lee 63
Vickery, Tom 155
Vincent, Major League Baseball Commissioner Fay 206–207
Vine Street, Buffalo, New York 59
Virginia (1898 tour) 170, 171; see also All-Virginia (Black) team
Vogt, Max 122, 235n146
Voltz, W.H. 103, 108, 109–110, 232n61
Voorhees, George D. 135

Walden, New York 140
Walker, Moses Fleetwood "Fleet" 1, 31, 32, 41, 45, 47, 49, 50, 51, 54, 55, 56, 58, 64, 69, 74, 78, 83, 85, 97, 99, 100, 193, 215n52, 215n533, 215n56, 224n52, 230n5
Walker, Tom 171
Walker, Welday 1
Wall, Joe 196–197, 198, 199, 255n59, 255n68
Wallace (1904 Cuban Giants teammate) 190, 198
Waller, Red 192
Walsh, Mickey 41, 46, **48**, 49, 59, 60, 70
Ward, P. (1900 Chicago Columbia Giants teammate) 181
Ward, Piggy 161, 164
Washington (National League team) 42–43, 61–62, 75, 84, 140
Washington, Tom 195
Washington, D.C. 80, 81, 99, 100, 143, 148, 161
Washington Bee (Black newspaper) 84
Washington Post (newspaper) 43, 115, 154, 158, 209n15
Washington Senators (Atlantic Association team) 102, 113–115, 117, 118, 119
Waterbury, Connecticut 28, 29, 31, 32, 127, 142, 215n56
Waters, Jock 204
Watertown, New York 149
Watkins, John M. "Pop" 178, 182, 190, 192, 195–197, 198, 254n42, 254n43, 254n50
Watkins' Colored Giants (1907–1908) 196, 197
Watkins' Colored Professionals (1907) 196

Watkins' Colored Stars (1907) 195
Watkins' Giants (1909) 198
Watson, Delores/Dolores Brown (great-granddaughter of Frank Grant) 236n13
Weed (Plattsburgh Nameless teammate) 23
Weehawken, New Jersey 85, 88, 100, 132, 135, 168, 169, 178, 249n44
Werner, Maria 137
Wesleyan University (Connecticut) 166
West, Hattie 61
West Jersey Giants (Black team) 184, 251n104
West New York, New Jersey 167, 174
West 17th Street, New York City 203
Western League 177
Westervelt, Huyler 159, 162, 245n46
Wheeler, Betsy 8
Wheeler, Ephraim 8
Wheeling, West Virginia 62
White, C.D. 51
White, Deacon 27, 68, 78, 97
White, Homer (ice polo teammate) 246n55, 247n98
White, R.L. 247n7
White, Sol 6, 15, 19, 24, 93, 99, 101, 102, 108, 121–122, 127–128, 129, 132, 136, 137, 138, 145, 149, 153, 154, 155, 156, 158, 159–160, 161, 162–163, 164, 168, 170, 171, 172, 174, 175, 176, 179, 181, 183, 184, 185, 187, 188, 197, 201, 204–205, 207, 209n22, 211n52, 212n73, 223n18, 231n16, 237n21, 238n45, 241n20, 241n24, 242n42, 245n27, 247n96, 250n64, 252n116, 252n118, 260, 261
White, William (official scorer) 99; possibly White, William F.
White, William Henry 97
Whitman, William see Wittman, William Abbott
Whitney, Jim 42
Whyte (aka White), William F. 77, 86, 88, 97, 99, 100, 110, 113, 114, 139, 140, 144, 146, 225n108, 227n44, 233n78, 237n30, 241n24
Wiggs, Jimmy 181
Wilkes-Barre, Pennsylvania 51, 52, 57, 131, 161
Williams (1902 Philadelphia Giants teammate) 184
Williams (1904–1905 Cuban Giants teammate(s)) 190, 192

Williams, Blanch 104
Williams, Charles 255n70
Williams, Clarence 85, 86, 87, 89, 97, 100, 107, 108, 110, 113, 114, 117, 118, 124, 125, 127, 129, 132, 134–135, 137, 138, 139, 140, 146, 152, 155, 156, 157, 158, 160, 168, 171, 177, 190, 192, 195, 197, 200, 218n25, 225n108, 226n113, 230n4, 239n55, 239n61, 240n3, 246n62, 247n6
Williams, Dave 184
Williams, E. (1907 Watkins' Colored Stars teammate) 195
Williams, Elijah 104
Williams, George 85, 89, 93, 97, 99, 100, 112, 121, 122, 124, 127, 129, 132, 134, 136, 137, 139, 194, 197, 218n25, 225n108, 226n113
Williams, Joe ("Smokey" or "Cyclone") 204, 205
Williams, Willia 204
Williams College 12, 13, 14, 15, 20, 23, 27, 105, 133, 147, 153, 154, 161, 163, 166, 172, 212n2, 213n18, 213n19, 243n55
Williamson, Ned 82–83
Williamsport, Pennsylvania 129, 243n75, 251n103, 252n116
Williamstown, Massachusetts 12–14, 16, 17, 18, 19, 20, 25, 27, 96, 99, 105, 147, 161, 163, 164, 169, 192, 202–203, 206–207, *207*, 211n35, 211n37, 212n61

Williamstown, Pennsylvania 242n39
Williamstown House of Local History 16
Willis, Vic 166
Wilmington, Delaware 77, 94–95, 114, 115–117, 120, 123, 124, 184, 186, 188, 194, 233n93
Wilmington Giants (1906 Black team) 194
Wilson (1899 Cuban X-Giants teammate) 175–176
Wilson (1901 Cuban Giants teammate) 182
Wilson (1909 Frank Grant's Colored Stars) 198
Wilson, George 158
Wilson, Howard "Highball" 185
Wilson, James 125
Wilson, Mary Elizabeth Adore (son's mother) 125–126, 137, 156, 236n11, 244n83
Wilson, Ray 170, 171, 177–178
Wilson, W. Rollo 204
Wilson, Zeke 152
Winham, Lafayette "Lave" 198
winning streak (Buffalo, 1888) 74
Wittman, William Abbott 151
Womsley (1911 New York Colored Giants) 199
Wood, Fred 216n5
Wood, Pete 35, 216n5
Woods (Ansonia teammate) 237n30

Woods, Walt 161
Worcester, Massachusetts 102, 114, 157, 172, 173
Wright (1908 Brooklyn X-Giants teammate) 197
Wright, Joe 147
Wright, Rasty 46–47

Xavier Athletic Club (New York amateur team) 147

Yale College/University 28, 44, 149
Yastrzemski, Carl 6, 77
Yeager, Joe 164
Yonkers, New York 182, 192, 194
York, Pennsylvania 84, 88, 90, 92, 93–94, 95, 99–100, 102, 108, 109–113, 114, 118, 120, 121–122, 160
York Monarchs (black Eastern Inter-State League team) 100, 102, 103–104, 106. 108, 112, 114, 118, 120, 121–122, 123, 124, 126, 235n145
Young, Bill 120
Young, Nick 104, 107
Young Cuban Giants (Trenton, New Jersey) 87; *see also* Cuban Giants Juniors (Harrisburg, Pennsylvania

Zecher, William 123, 126
Zell, Harry **48**, 220n78

www.ingramcontent.com/pod-product-compliance
Lightning Source LLC
Chambersburg PA
CBHW060337010526
44117CB00017B/2865